James R. Moran   4 —
                  12/17

THE SCIENCE OF PREVENTION

THE SCIENCE OF PREVENTION

METHODOLOGICAL ADVANCES FROM ALCOHOL AND SUBSTANCE ABUSE RESEARCH

EDITED BY

KENDALL J. BRYANT,

MICHAEL WINDLE, AND

STEPHEN G. WEST

AMERICAN PSYCHOLOGICAL ASSOCIATION
WASHINGTON, DC

Published by
American Psychological Association
750 First Street, NE
Washington, DC 20002

Copies may be ordered from
APA Order Department
P.O. Box 92984
Washington, DC 20090-2984

In the UK and Europe, copies may be ordered from
American Psychological Association
3 Henrietta Street
Covent Garden, London
WC2E 8LU England

Typeset in Goudy by EPS Group Inc., Easton, MD

Printer: Port City Press, Baltimore, MD
Jacket Designer: Minker Design, Bethesda, MD
Technical / Production Editor: Tanya Y. Alexander

Library of Congress Cataloging-in-Publication Data
The science of prevention : methodological advances from alcohol and substance
  abuse research / [edited by] Kendall J. Bryant, Michael Windle, Stephen G. West.
      p. cm.
    ISBN 1-55798-439-5 (casebound)
    1. Alcoholism—Research—Methodology. 2. Alcoholism—Prevention—
Research.   3. Substance abuse—Research—Methodology.   4. Substance
abuse—Prevention—Research.   I. Bryant, Kendall J.   II. Windle, Michael T.
III. West, Stephen G.
    HV5035.S37   1997   97-14910
    362.29'17—dc21   CIP

British Library Cataloguing-in-Publication Data
A CIP record is available from the British Library

Printed in the United States of America
First edition

CONTENTS

CONTRIBUTORS

Leona S. Aiken, Arizona State University

Robert L. Bangert-Drowns, University at Albany, State University of New York

Kendall J. Bryant, National Institute on Alcohol Abuse and Alcoholism, Rockville, MD

Kathleen K. Bucholz, Washington University School of Medicine

Isabel Chevillard, University at Albany, State University of New York

Suzanne M. Colby, Brown University

Linda M. Collins, Pennsylvania State University

Michael L. Dennis, Chestnut Health Systems, Bloomington, IL

Stewart I. Donaldson, Claremont Graduate School

Mark A. Foss, Chestnut Health Systems, Bloomington, IL

John W. Graham, Pennsylvania State University

William B. Hansen, Wake Forest University

Andrew C. Heath, Washington University School of Medicine

Scott M. Hofer, University of Manchester, England

Ita G. G. Kreft, California State University, Los Angeles

Richard D. Lennox, Chestnut Health Systems, Bloomington, IL

David P. MacKinnon, Arizona State University

Pamela A. F. Madden, Washington University School of Medicine

W. G. Manning, University of Minnesota

Nicholas G. Martin, Queensland Institute of Medical Research, Australia

Steven P. Reise, University of California, Riverside

Susannah Scarborough Rousculp, University of Southern California

Joseph L. Schafer, Pennsylvania State University

Kenneth J. Sher, University of Missouri

Wendy S. Slutske, Washington University School of Medicine

Wayne F. Velicer, University of Rhode Island
Elisabeth Wells-Parker, Mississippi State University
Stephen G. West, Arizona State University
Keith F. Widaman, University of California, Riverside
Michael Windle, Research Institute on Addictions, Buffalo, NY
Phillip K. Wood, University of Missouri

PREFACE

The primary objective of this book is to describe a variety of new methods for addressing many of the problems that arise in the design and analysis of prevention research. These methods are general; most can be applied to the full range of areas of prevention research, including alcohol use and abuse, smoking, unsafe sex, health problems, poor school performance, criminal behavior, mental health problems, and illicit drug use, as well as to a variety of other areas in which research is conducted in field settings. These methods have evolved or have been adapted from other disciplines as prevention research has become increasingly sophisticated over the past 15 years. Prevention researchers now conduct basic psychosocial research studying risk factors varying in level from genes to communities; efficacy research designed to develop and test new interventions for individuals, families, schools, or communities to reduce the risk of the development of problem behaviors; and even effectiveness research designed to evaluate programs as they are disseminated and implemented in communities across the country. The backbone of each of these types of research is solid methodology that both answers the specific questions posed by the investigators and ensures that valid conclusions can be drawn from the findings.

Several recent publications call for the development of a broad conceptual framework for a science of prevention. The report by the Institute of Medicine, "Reducing Risks for Mental Disorders: Frontiers in Preventive Intervention Research," and recent articles such as "The Science of Prevention: A Conceptual Framework and Some Directions for a National Research Program" challenge prevention researchers across many fields to develop general principles that integrate an understanding of risk and protective factors with the delivery of preventive interventions. Each of these reports emphasizes the need for greater methodological rigor in prevention science. For example, the Institute of Medicine report concludes its introductory remarks by stating that "there could be no wiser investment in our country than a commitment to foster the prevention of mental disorders and the promotion of mental health through rigorous research with the highest of methodological standards. Such a commitment would yield the potential for healthier lives for countless individuals and the general advancement of the nation's well-being" (Mrazek & Haggerty, 1994, p. xvii).

In this spirit, we seek to explore and promote through this book the highest methodological standards by focusing on several promising new methodological advances in the area of prevention research. The goal of this book is to promote critical thinking among new and established investigators about how to design research and analyze research findings. Although the substantive focus of many chapters is on applications to the prevention of alcohol and substance use, nearly all of the methodological principles and statistical models are general and have potential application to the full range of areas in which prevention research takes place.

The contributors to this book share their knowledge from an informed, applied perspective. Most are active researchers in the field of substance abuse prevention who are also methodological experts. They have a firsthand knowledge of not only the methodological, statistical, and measurement issues but, equally important, the substantive issues of their field. Several authors attempt to integrate substantive and methodological issues, addressing concerns that are rarely discussed in depth in either textbooks or research reports. The extensive examples and discussion of issues in this book will introduce young investigators to both the complex methodological challenges that can arise in prevention research and promising new methods of meeting those challenges. Even highly experienced, sophisticated investigators are likely to find new ideas and methods that can be added to their methodological arsenal for future use in their own program of research.

The idea for this book originated at a meeting of methodologists and researchers in February 1994 that was sponsored by the National Institute on Alcohol Abuse and Alcoholism (NIAAA). The goal of that meeting was to identify recent advances in research design and analysis in alcohol studies and other fields of prevention research. Researchers with strong methodological interests from the alcohol prevention community and from related fields of prevention research were brought together to present and discuss a variety of promising new research methods. Participants and other selected authors then were requested to write papers that applied their thinking about thorny methodological issues to prevention problems in the alcohol and substance abuse fields and to illustrate these problems with examples from their research. Some contributors discussed a range of new methodologies and recent advances that could enhance the design and analysis of prospective alcohol-related research; other contributors focused on design, measurement, and analysis strategies to provide better estimates of the efficacy of preventive interventions.

Many of the recent advances involve the application of new analytical techniques that can be used to tease apart the subtle, complex effects of alcohol use on the individual, the family, and the broader social environment. Many of these analytic techniques are made possible by the development and increased availability of sophisticated computer hardware and software. Whereas only 30–40 years ago researchers spent hours doing single t tests or analyses of variance by hand or on calculators, they can now solve multigroup structural equation models or run customized statistical simulation programs in a few minutes on their home computers. This increased statistical computing power afforded by technological advances must be harnessed and guided by critical thought and prudent decision making: For statistical models to provide good answers, they must be matched appropriately to both the research question and research design. This book seeks to contribute to this endeavor by presenting the lessons learned by experienced substantive and methodological investigators from the field.

REFERENCE

Mrazek, P. J., & Haggerty, R. J. (Eds.). (1994). *Reducing the risks for mental disorders: Frontiers for preventive intervention research.* Washington, DC: National Academy Press.

ACKNOWLEDGMENTS

We would like to express our appreciation to the chapter contributors to this book for sharing their insights as experienced researchers and often performing additional analyses to illustrate key methodological points. We also would like to express our gratitude to the reviewers, whose perceptive comments were formative in the development of the manuscripts. In addition, we would like to recognize the NIAAA for its support of the initial meeting on assessing new methods in alcohol prevention research. Furthermore, we would like to acknowledge those individuals who supported us in the development and publication of this book, at both the NIAAA and the American Psychological Association. In the end, this book truly was a group effort.

INTRODUCTION

OVERVIEW OF NEW METHODOLOGICAL DEVELOPMENTS IN PREVENTION RESEARCH: ALCOHOL AND SUBSTANCE ABUSE

KENDALL J. BRYANT, STEPHEN G. WEST, AND MICHAEL WINDLE

PREVENTION SCIENCE

A new science of prevention is evolving rapidly (Coie et al., 1993; Mrazek & Haggerty, 1994). Prevention researchers are posing a range of basic and applied scientific questions that are answered with a range of methodological approaches. At one end of this research continuum, prevention researchers conduct basic psychosocial research to study the development of disorders such as alcohol abuse, drug abuse, mental illness, and adult criminal behavior. They also focus on understanding the precursors of maladaptive behaviors (e.g., unsafe sexual activity, dropping out of school) whose consequences can alter achieving one's potential to become a healthy adult. In each case, a central focus has been on the identification of early signs of difficulties and the emergence of developmental sequences, or stages, of disorders and maladaptive behaviors. This basic psychosocial research provides a formative basis for the design of early preventive interventions. It helps identify risk factors associated with the individual, the family, the peer group, the school, and the neighborhood that may contribute to the development of disordered behaviors. It helps identify protective factors associated with each of these influences that may prevent the development of disordered behaviors or promote the development of healthy behaviors. Interventions guided by a base of careful psychosocial theory and research provide a systematic, coherent approach for the application of prevention science. The evaluation of these interventions in careful trials provides strong evidence for or against the efficacy of intervention. Successful interventions then can be disseminated and tested in multiple sites, enhancing the understanding of the intervention in different populations and settings. On the agenda for prevention research is the development of a strong knowledge base for identification of risk and protective factors as well as the design, evaluation, and dissemination of interventions. These include interventions that enhance the impact of protective factors or, more traditionally, attempt to mitigate the impact of risk factors (Price, 1983). Each type of prevention research underlying this agenda involves complex methodological, measurement, and statistical problems. Many of these problems are not fully addressed in the traditional areas of research methodology, such as laboratory experimentation, survey research, and clinical trials research, in which many investigators have received their training (see Aiken, West, Sechrest, & Reno, 1990). Consequently, the evolution of prevention science has raised a clear need to develop and disseminate new and more powerful methodologies that are well suited to the needs of this complex enterprise.

RISK AND PROTECTIVE FACTORS

Researchers have identified the concepts of risk and protective factors as key constructs necessary for developing a science of prevention research. Risk factors are identified as attributes of individuals or environments that increase the chances of developing a disorder such as alcoholism, heart attack, depression, or a host of other diagnosable disorders or maladaptive behaviors. They also may lead to greater severity or longer duration of the disorder. Risk factors may be genetic, biological, psychological, social, or environmental in origin. Protective factors decrease the risk of disorders or maladaptive behaviors in several ways. They may reduce exposure to risk factors, disrupt important processes involved in the development of the disorder, interact with the risk factor to reduce its effects, or directly decrease dysfunction (Wheaton, 1985). Prevention begins with the careful description of the interplay between individual risk and protective factors, often over the life course of an individual. The nature of the relationship between the risk and protective factors may be described and their relationships elaborated through the use of statistical models. Often, special statistical models will be needed, such as in the study of genetic influences on the risk of alcoholism or other disorders (see chap. 5). Interventions may be designed to change relationships among risk and protective factors and both proximal (e.g., better school performance, better parent–child relations) and longer term outcomes (e.g., likelihood of adult maladaptive behavior).

LINKS BETWEEN BASIC PSYCHOSOCIAL AND APPLIED INTERVENTION RESEARCH

Ideally, as noted earlier, basic psychosocial research precedes the development of focused interventions. The psychosocial research identifies risk factors associated with the development of the disorder and protective factors associated with the prevention of the disorder. Of particular importance are the critical factors that are potentially modifiable and that could serve as the target of an intervention (Wolchik et al., 1993). However, even the best basic psychosocial research typically does not explain how these risk and protective factors may be changed. Change techniques that target these potentially modifiable factors can often be identified from previous interventions; other behavior-change literature; clinical practice; or the creative insights of researchers, clinicians, or community workers. Other important risk factors (e.g., genetics, family poverty) may not be easily modifiable, but they may be useful in selecting individuals who would be likely to receive the maximum benefit from the intervention. Still other individual and contextual characteristics identified in basic psychosocial research may affect the acceptance or the effectiveness of the intervention as it is implemented in new sites.

Basic psychosocial research also can provide a strong basis for the design of the intervention trial. The quality of design, measurement, and analysis decisions is closely related to the clarity with which the basic theoretical model has been specified (Lipsey, 1993). Decisions about what variables to measure, how they should be measured, the timing of these measurements, and the statistical models that best capture the development of the disorder or problem behavior all depend on a strong foundation of psychosocial research.

Finally, the results of well-designed intervention trials can help inform basic psychosocial research (Coie et al., 1993). In particular, randomized trials of interventions provide especially strong tests of developmental theory. To the extent that the risk and protective factors targeted by the intervention are changed, the maladaptive behavior is changed, and the risk and protective factors can be shown to mediate the change in the maladaptive behavior, the developmental theory is supported. Other less supportive outcomes may suggest a potential need for revision of the theory, the use of an alternative or better implemented intervention, or possible limits in generalizing the developmental theory to new populations or contexts. The combination of randomization and the manipulation of targeted variables permits stronger causal inferences than other forms of research. When the intervention targets the important risk and protective factors identified by psychosocial theory, the results of the randomized trial yield results that can add strongly to the original theory.

METHODOLOGICAL AND STATISTICAL ISSUES IN LONGITUDINAL DESIGNS

There is a common focus across many of the chapters of this book on developing appropriate designs and statistical models for analyzing longitudinal data, whether those data arise from basic psychosocial or applied intervention studies. Prospective longitudinal designs in psychosocial studies create a host of issues that need to be addressed to interpret the findings of studies appropriately. For example, measurement issues arise, such as the selection of the optimal number and spacing (i.e., the time between) of measurement occasions (see chaps. 1 and 2). Inappropriate timing of measurement occasions can lead to failures to detect important influences of risk factors or interventions. For example, antisocial behavior is reliably predicted by a child's association with deviant peers at age 12 but not at age 10 (Dishion, Patterson, Stoolmiller, & Skinner, 1991). Interventions may have important short- or long-term effects that may not be detected without careful attention to the measurement framework.

Longitudinal data also are typically not statistically independent; observations that are collected at adjacent points in time often are more similar than observations that are collected at more separated points in time (serial dependency). Similarly, data collected in school classrooms and other group settings also are not statistically independent; students in the same classroom tend to be more similar than students in different classrooms (clustering). Such dependency structures must be analyzed using special statistical models so as not to bias model fit statistics and tests of parameters (see chaps. 7 and 8). These statistical models often have an additional heuristic benefit: They permit researchers to address important new questions about their data. For example, in school-based prevention studies, variability in outcome (e.g., reduction in alcohol use) may be influenced not only by individual-level characteristics of students but also by classroom-level influences (e.g., the amount of intervention training for each teacher or size of the class) and school-level influences (e.g., the level of administrative support and money allocated for substance abuse prevention). The models presented in this book provide methods to assess the impact of such multiple-level influences appropriately.

Another issue that is considered in several chapters in this book is the role of measurement error. Measurement error in independent variables leads to bias in the estimates of regression coefficients. Latent variable models (e.g., structural equation models, latent class analysis) produce theoretically error-free estimates of regression coefficients (see chaps. 2 and 3). In addition, models have been developed to account for correlations among errors across time. For example, social desirability bias may be characterized as an individual difference variable: Because the same individuals are being measured repeatedly, a systematic (reliable) pattern of covariation is introduced that is not accounted for by the repeatedly measured primary trait, nor is it random error. Examples of addressing the issues of measurement error and correlated errors over time are provided in subsequent chapters (see chaps. 2, 3, and 7).

Other problems in estimating regression coefficients arise from serious violations of the assumptions of statistical models. These may be reflected in the distribution of the original variables or in the distribution of disturbances (e.g., residuals, errors in prediction) associated with regression models. Several chapters consider alternative statistical models and estimators that address problems resulting from dichotomous dependent variables or nonnormally distributed measured variables (see chaps. 2–4). As is illustrated in the subsequent chapters of this book, a failure to address such violations of assumptions often results in biased estimates and fit statistics that lead to incorrect statistical inferences.

Longitudinal designs open up a wide variety of statistical modeling options depending on the type of data that have been collected and the questions that are of interest. For categorical variables, this book includes recent contributions in latent transition analysis and latent Markov modeling for the longitudinal analyses of categorical data (see chaps. 2 and 3). For continuous variables, approaches such as autoregressive structural equation modeling, growth curve modeling, and concomitant and pooled time series analyses are presented for longitudinal data (see chaps. 2 and 7). Longitudinal research also typically involves the loss of participants over time, which may be substantial in studies of highly mobile populations (e.g., homeless families) that are conducted over a number of years. Missing value estimation procedures are reviewed, with available software identified for missing value estimation of both continuous and categorical variables (see chap. 10).

These are only a few issues presented in this book that stem from the use of longitudinal research designs. A range of other issues that arise in measurement, intervention research, and literature reviews also are considered. Among these issues are the comparison of measures across different groups (e.g., gender, ethnic, language; see chap. 9), understanding the individual effects and mediators of multicomponent prevention programs (see chap. 6), designing investigations that optimize the statistical power analysis of the tests of hypotheses (see chap. 11), and assessing the methodological quality of individual studies that contribute to meta-analytic findings based on entire research literatures (see chap. 12).

ALCOHOL USE PREVENTION: AN ILLUSTRATION

Many of the methodological issues raised in prevention research are generic. Issues associated with problems such as measurement error, missing data, and appropriate timing of measurements arise in all areas of prevention research. However, in this book we focus primarily on the prevention of alcohol use and abuse. There are three reasons for this: First, this focus helps ground our presentation of complex methodologies in a single familiar area of prevention research and provides a coherent framework for understanding the interplay of many factors. Second, alcohol use also raises unique issues because it is a legal drug whose use in moderation in appropriate contexts leads to few consequences. Third, alcohol abuse involves clear costs to the individual and to society. Individuals who drink too much may suffer both the physical (e.g., increased risk of injury and early death) and social (e.g., increased risk of divorce, job loss) consequences of alcohol use and dependence. For society, the estimated cost for alcohol abuse in 1990 was about $100 billion (Rice, 1993). This includes the cost of treatment settings such as hospital emergency rooms, inpatient and outpatient alcohol and drug treatment programs, and costs associated with the consequences of alcohol misuse, such as crime, motor vehicle crashes, and special diseases such as fetal alcohol syndrome. Among the costs that are less easily quantifiable are the suffering of individuals in families with alcohol problems, increased risks of transmission of other diseases such as HIV and AIDS, and the reduced quality of life attributable to alcohol-impaired work performance.

As noted earlier, although many methodological issues are generic, special concerns arise in the study of alcohol. Alcohol is a legal drug, available in many forms, and readily accessible to adults. Many individuals choose to drink no alcohol, and most who do drink actively limit their use. Often, specific occasions (e.g., dinner with a friend) or physical settings (e.g., a local bar) provide the context for use. Some contexts may promote responsible drinking; others promote abuse. Individuals may select to be in contexts that promote or discourage alcohol use.

Investigators may study the development of regular patterns of drinking. For some individuals, these patterns may be relatively stable, whereas for others they may change substantially over the life course. Alternatively, investigators may study the quantity of drinking on a specific occasion in terms of number of standard drinks. These pattern and quantity-of-consumption measures may only be weakly related: Regular alcohol intake and occasional heavy drinking may be the result of largely distinct developmental and social influences. Such special characteristics of alcohol use are framed as methodological issues throughout this book, and illustrations of research are provided that demonstrate the fit between both knowledge of alcohol use characteristics and design and analysis issues.

MEASURING INTERACTIONS AND CONTEXT EFFECTS

Situations, physical settings, and social norms exert a strong influence on increasing or decreasing alcohol use and on changing the associated consequences in the environment. For example, a domestic argument might become violent because the participants are drinking; in a bar setting, servers and patrons might interact to limit the number of drinks; social groups may set norms that encourage responsible or potentially harmful drinking behavior. Interactions of individual attributes with physical and social contexts pose complex analytic issues for the researcher. Furthermore, naturally changing variables measured at the community or even the societal level (e.g., geographical distribution of alcohol outlets or the cost of alcohol) may greatly modify individual behavior and moderate the individual predisposition to harmful or hazardous drinking. Of special concern to prevention researchers is the study of co-occurring behaviors, such as drinking and driving, that greatly increase the risk of consequences to the individual and society. Either behavior alone may involve relatively low risk; however, the co-occurrence of these behaviors leads to a high risk for injury.

ORGANIZATION OF THIS BOOK

This book is divided into three parts to help illustrate different issues facing the prevention researcher working in the alcohol area. The first part, Expanding the Knowledge Base: Alternative Models, focuses on issues in basic psychosocial research. Our focus here is on prospective longitudinal research and the measurement of risk and protective factors for alcohol misuse over time. Illustrated here are the definition, measurement, and modeling of temporal effects such as developmental trajectories and sequence of substance use. The second part, Design and Analysis of Intervention Models, focuses on the design and analysis of interventions that seek to change alcohol and other substance misuse and the physical and social consequences of that misuse. Particular emphasis is placed on the identification of effective components of interventions and the investigation of how these may interact with multiple levels of individual and environmental factors. The third part, Improving Methodological Quality, targets specific methodological issues that have a significant impact on the quality of research projects. These include a focus on the comparability of measurement across groups, options for the handling of missing values, statistical power analysis, and quality criteria in meta-analytic studies.

Part I: Expanding the Knowledge Base: Alternative Models

The first part focuses on issues in designing basic psychosocial research on the development of alcohol use. In chapter 1, Sher and Wood describe the full range of research decisions facing the alcohol researcher conducting prospective research. They draw from their own research to illustrate choices in the selection of measures and the design and analysis of their own prospective studies. Although the authors identify the complexity of the research undertaking, they also describe how an appropriate match between research question and design and analysis can be accomplished. Among the many topics that are briefly addressed and revisited in subsequent chapters is the need to make distinctions among alcohol-related phenomena (e.g., alcohol use, alcohol disorders) and to measure the validity of alcohol-related behavior. A key decision facing the researcher is how to establish temporal references for reported alcohol use behaviors and the selection of appropriate item response formats. The authors discuss the critical implications for temporal spacing of measurement occasions and the need to consider alternative models of stability and growth for characterizing patterns of alcohol use disorders. Many technical issues also must be considered in model identification and specification, robustness and generalizability of models, and the comparative testing of alternative models.

In chapter 2, Windle discusses the types of latent-variable models of change that are available and illustrates their comparison within a single study. Four general modeling approaches to change are explored. The first modeling approach focuses on continuous-variable covariance structure models, specifically autoregressive latent-variable models that evaluate (rank-order) stability of alcohol use across time. The second modeling approach focuses on latent growth curve models that are useful in evaluating (latent) mean-level changes across time and the shape (e.g., linear, quadratic) of the temporal pattern of mean levels. Time-invariant and time-covarying predictors are introduced in these statistical models to account for variability in initial differences in alcohol use (at Time 1) and variability in intraindividual growth trajectories. The third modeling approach focuses on a latent trait–state model that decomposes cross-temporal patterns of alcohol use into general trait, state, method, and random error components. The fourth modeling approach focuses on latent Markov models to accommodate the prospective study of categorical variables and discrete latent classes. This chapter provides an appreciation of the multiple available models for studying change with alcohol data and the need to explore the temporal patterning and dynamic organization of alcohol behaviors offered through new analytic techniques.

In chapter 3, Collins, Graham, Rousculp, and Hansen introduce a new statistical model, latent transition analysis, that permits researchers with panel data to test stage-sequential models of development. The development of substance use is modeled so that individuals progress in stages along multiple pathways (e.g., never using to having tried alcohol, never using to having tried tobacco) and individuals may be in multiple stages at the same time (e.g., the status of having tried both alcohol and tobacco). Two important features of the model are that (a) researchers may place restrictions, so that certain theoretically specified transitions may not take place over time (e.g., the rapid transition from no use to being a regular smoker is not theoretically permitted) and (b) multiple indicators may be used to provide theoretically error-free estimates of each latent status. Collins et al. illustrate the application of latent transition analysis to the early development of substance use in junior high school students. Of interest, children who were heavy users of caffeine started to use other substances earlier and progressed more rapidly through the sequence of stages of early development of substance use than did children who used no caffeine or a moderate amount of caffeine.

In chapter 4, Manning focuses on issues involved in fitting alternative statistical models to a specific alcohol-related variable: the average daily consumption of alcohol. Studying daily alcohol consumption necessitates a variety of considerations on the researcher's part to appropriately specify statistical models that correspond with the processes generating the data. Alcohol consumption data typically are nonnormally distributed; these data also include nondrinkers who can be expected to be unaffected by any influences that increase or decrease consumption in drinkers. Thus, models that take into account the discontinuity in the distribution of this important variable may be important in describing or predicting alcohol consumption. Further complexities arise because there does not appear to be a simple linear function that adequately captures the relationship between potential influences and consumption in light, moderate, and heavy drinkers. This chapter identifies salient issues involved in the statistical analysis of daily alcohol consumption and provides alternative models to evaluate their adequacy and impact on recovering model parameters. Although the illustrations provided are relative to alcohol demand functions, the generalizability to other (noneconomic) domains of study is evident.

In chapter 5, Heath, Slutske, Bucholz, Madden, and Martin relate genetic risk factors to clinical disorders. Although there is a range of measurement issues in determining both the biological aspects of gene contributions and diagnostic reliability for a disorder such as alcoholism, there are rapid improvements in both assaying gene loci and diagnostic reliability. Prevention researchers seek to understand and moderate the relationship between genetic risk factors and disorders. Progress in genetics research has begun to delineate the complex pathways for genetic influences and to illustrate how these unfold over time. The importance of environmental determinants and the interdependence of causal factors are being revealed. The contribution of genetic and environmental factors changes throughout the life span, thus requiring an understanding of the relationship between individuals and their physical and social environments. Genetic as well as environmental factors that increase exposure to risk situations may determine trajectories for development over time that culminate in a disorder such as alcoholism. Protective factors at both the genetic and environmental levels also may come into play to alter the emergence or expression of a disorder. Twin, adoptee, and family studies provide the basis for naturalistic experiments on the relative contributions of both genetic and environmental components and their interaction.

Part II: Design and Analysis of Intervention Models

In Part II, the focus is shifted to research designed to delineate the nature of the action of the preventive intervention and evaluate its efficacy. In chapter 6, West and Aiken note that preventive interventions are often composed of multiple components. They focus on design and statistical modeling methods for understanding the unique effects of each component in such multicomponent interventions. They consider the underlying assumptions and strengths and weaknesses of several research designs that permit researchers to at least partially untangle the effects of at least some of the individual components. They also consider the strengths and limitations of mediational analysis, a statistical modeling strategy that tests whether the data are consistent with the underlying psychosocial theory and the theory of the intervention. This strategy is illustrated in an analysis of the unique influence of each of four components of an intervention to promote early screening for breast cancer. West and Aiken conclude that combining mediational analysis with enhancements in research design holds great promise of maximizing both the basic science and applied science contributions of preventive trials.

In chapter 7, Velicer and Colby provide a detailed presentation of time series analysis, a statistical procedure appropriate for repeated, equally spaced observations on a single individual or unit (e.g., monthly reports of a state's alcohol-related highway fatalities). Time series analysis can be used to study intervention effects, providing a model of the pattern of change over time. It also can be used to study the influence of one (or more) series on another (e.g., daily drinking and depressed mood) and can be extended to the study of the series of several individuals, as in daily diary studies. Time series may produce several technical problems in statistical modeling, the most serious of which is that repeated observations on the same unit are unlikely to be independent (serial dependency). Velicer and Colby provide methods for identifying and addressing these problems and illustrate these methods by selecting models of nicotine regulation that best represent different types of smokers. They also illustrate intervention analysis with an example that examines the effect of relaxation therapy on blood pressure. The chapter concludes with a consideration of both the specific issues related to applying time series analysis to alcohol treatment and prevention data and many of the general practical issues involved in conducting time series analyses.

In chapter 8, Kreft considers statistical modeling issues that arise when interventions are delivered in group contexts. For example, school-based alcohol prevention programs are typically implemented at the level of classrooms or even entire schools. Under these conditions, the responses of students in the same classroom are unlikely to be statistically independent. Early studies used classes as the basis for evaluating program impact; however, this approach discards important sources of information at the individual level. The use of hierarchical linear models permits the examination of program effects and their variability at the class and individual levels. In addition, the influence of other classroom-level influences (e.g., teacher experience) and individual-level influences (e.g., parental drinking patterns) can be examined. Finally, the pattern of interactions between the class and individual levels of analysis can be explored. These analyses may be extended to data structures having three levels in the hierarchy (i.e., individuals, classes, schools).

Part III: Improving Methodological Quality

Part III focuses on several important general methodological issues related to improving the quality of prevention research. In chapter 9, Widaman and Reise focus on the key issue of ensuring that the same construct is being measured in different groups (or over time). Although other areas, such as ability testing, have developed methods to calibrate test items in various groups, this has not been the case in prevention research. Widaman and Reise provide an extensive discussion of the measurement characteristics for key variables and constructs in prevention research. The authors distinguish among the different types of invariance that are critical to scale and construct measurement. Using structural equation modeling techniques, they develop a series of models and provide examples for researchers that illustrate how to understand, test, and interpret invariance analyses used for psychological instruments. They suggest methods of instrument and scale development necessary for producing reliable and valid results among multiple groups (e.g., gender, ethnic groups) and over multiple measurement occasions.

In chapter 10, Graham, Hofer, Donaldson, MacKinnon, and Shafer address a key issue in longitudinal psychosocial and intervention research: missing data. They focus on understanding the patterns and the sources of missing data in prevention studies. For example, some of the missing data may be purely random, whereas other data may be systematically lost, such as when heavy teenage drinkers drop out of school. Researchers using longitudinal study designs have difficulty finding all of the original participants at follow-up, or incomplete waves of data are collected because of research demands. Research questions often are best answered by hard-to-reach populations such as substance abusers or the homeless, whose transient nature makes it difficult to keep track of them. Graham et al. study the nature of missing data in several data sets and discuss several techniques for addressing various structures and types of missing data. They suggest methods for designing measures and using analytic techniques that remain robust even in the case of substantial data loss.

In chapter 11, Dennis, Lennox, and Foss provide several practical techniques for designing research with adequate statistical power. Statistical power is the probability that the research will detect an effect of a specified size, if the effect indeed exists in the population. Although increasing the sample size will increase statistical power, large samples often are not easily obtained or are costly. Key ideas in estimating the power of a study at the design stage are presented, with some of the complexities that inevitably arise in longitudinal research (e.g., participant attrition). Dennis et al. present simple steps the investigator may take to increase the power of a study. These steps focus on increasing effect sizes and decreasing error variance. The authors provide a detailed practical guide for understanding issues concerning statistical power and how to increase the power of prevention and treatment interventions.

In chapter 12, Bangert-Drowns, Wells-Parker, and Chevillard consider an important issue in research synthesis. The fundamental purpose of research synthesis is to draw valid conclusions from collections of studies using narrative review or meta-analytic methods. However, variation in methodological quality is a chief complication in developing such generalizations. Bangert-Drowns et al. clarify the issues concerning the use of narrative reviews and meta-analyses as useful tools. They discuss the pros and cons of these summary approaches and provide an illustration of a specific approach to identifying the quality of research for drunk driving interventions using expert-generated anchored ratings. The development of a general measure of quality has been lacking in the selection and inclusion of studies in meta-analytic approaches; the authors demonstrate that there are consequences in the variability of effect sizes related to the overall quality of the studies included in any meta-analysis. They point out the different options for developing and applying quality criteria. Among the issues that may be important in determining the quality of research syntheses are the degree of random assignment of individuals to conditions, representativeness of the sample, use of unpublished results, ability to identify causal relationships between variables, control group characteristics, and interrater reliability for core constructs and observed outcome variables.

LIMITATIONS OF THIS BOOK: SOME FUTURE METHODOLOGICAL ISSUES

Despite the many important contributions contained in this book, we would be remiss if we did not note that we were unable to represent all the potentially useful methodological techniques for fully understanding alcohol and other substance use problems or the effects of interventions designed to prevent those problems. What follows is a list of five areas that we believe will be especially important.

1. *Integration of multiple types of measures.* Self-reports, reports of knowledgeable informants, cognitive measures, behavioral measures, and physiological measures may provide different perspectives on a construct (Funder & West, 1993). What can be learned from what is common among the measures? What can be learned from what is unique? Do some measures or informants provide better assessments than others for specific constructs or specific populations? As a wider range of data is collected from multiple sources, it becomes increasingly important to understand how to integrate these data optimally. Although the multitrait–multimethod approach has provided a cornerstone of the behavioral sciences disciplines (see Campbell & Fiske, 1959; Marsh & Grayson, 1995), this approach has been used in alcohol prevention studies infrequently and may be limited by the low levels of convergence obtained across some sets of measures.

2. *New statistical models.* Many new statistical models are emerging that have not been discussed here. We were unable to include a chapter on survival models (Willett & Singer, 1993), which can identify risk and protective factors that predict the length of time before an outcome occurs (e.g., age at first diagnosis of alcoholism, length of time to relapse after treatment). Likewise, we did not consider a variety of other computer-intensive methods (Efron & Tibshirani, 1993) and Bayesian methods for analyzing complex psychosocial and intervention studies (Gelman, Carlin, Stern, & Rubin, 1995) that may be particularly valuable with nonnormally distributed data. We also did not consider exploratory and modern graphical analyses that help researchers discern patterns in data (Cleveland, 1994; Tukey, 1977). These analyses help researchers detect problems with their statistical models and identify promising data-based hypotheses for testing in future research. Of course, this is a partial list: Promising new techniques will continue to be identified as researchers try out new statistical models and models from other disciplines in prevention data sets.

3. *Alternative research designs.* We did not consider the full range

of alternative designs that are available for testing interventions when randomization is not possible. A variety of quasi-experimental designs (Cook & Campbell, 1979), some of which can provide inferences of causal effects approaching those of the randomized experiment, offer one set of alternatives. Alternative designs such as the case control methods and enhanced versions thereof also may provide additional insights into intervention effectiveness (Armenian, 1994; Schlesselman, 1982).

4. *Qualitative research.* This book focuses exclusively on quantitative research methods, yet qualitative methods also can offer insight into the development of alcohol-related problems and the sources of effectiveness of interventions. Qualitative research is a subtle and complex area that should be recognized for its own methods and approaches to theory building. It can be particularly useful in providing information about the lives of hard-to-study populations. However, it has been the hope and wish of many researchers that the strengths of qualitative methodology could be combined with the strengths of quantitative research (Cook & Reichardt, 1979). Many quantitative researchers already rely on focus groups and elicitation procedures to gain insight into the development of quantitative instruments in specialized populations. How these two heuristically different forms of research may be integrated should be examined more fully (Reichardt & Rallis, 1994).

5. *Selection.* Prevention researchers are interested in making statements about the effects of risk and protective factors and the effects of interventions in populations. Although some populations, such as communities and school districts, are relatively easy to define, other populations are very difficult to enumerate. For example, there is no defined population of parents with alcohol problems, which could be the focus of a study of children of alcoholics. Depending on the method of recruitment (e.g., history of alcohol-related work problems, health maintenance organization referrals, driving under the influence violators, community samples, alcohol treatment centers), it is possible to obtain samples that differ greatly in the history and severity of alcohol-related problems. Even in cases in which a target population can be defined (e.g., people living in a specific metropolitan area), great differences may exist in the ability to locate and recruit different types of participants into studies. For example, homeless individuals may be particularly difficult to locate; the children of substance-addicted parents who do not attend school may be particularly difficult to recruit into many studies. Researchers may inadvertently select particularly well-functioning or poorly functioning individuals into their studies, precluding generalization of the results to larger populations or particular subgroups of interest (e.g., ethnic minorities, homeless populations).

CONCLUSION

The contributions in this book present a sample of a number of the more important recent advances in prevention research methodology. We believe that the chapters in this book help identify several key issues, offer solutions, and help serve to stimulate careful thinking about methodological issues in prevention research. We provide an introduction to many of the issues of research design, statistical analysis, and measurement that are becoming increasingly prominent in the field of prevention science. The chapters provide illustrations of techniques designed to address those issues as well as avenues to pursue those areas of interest further. We hope that new researchers will be given an understanding and that experienced researchers will be given new insights into how many of the difficult methodological issues of prevention research can be addressed successfully.

REFERENCES

Aiken, L. S., West, S. G., Sechrest, L., & Reno, R. R. (1990). Graduate training in statistics, methodology, and measurement in psychology: a survey of PhD programs in North America. *American Psychologist, 45*, 721–734.

Armenian, H. K. (1994). Applications of the case control method [Special issue]. *Epidemiologic Reviews, 16*(1).

Campbell, D. T., & Fiske, D. W. (1959). Convergent and discriminant validation by multitrait–multimethod matrix. *Psychological Bulletin, 56*, 81–105.

Cleveland, W. S. (1994). *Visualizing data.* Summit, NJ: Hobart Press.

Coie, J. D., Watt, N. F., West, S. G., Hawkins, J. D., Asarnow, J. R., Markman, H. J., Ramey, S. L., Shure, M. B., & Long, B. (1993). The science of prevention: A conceptual framework and some directions for a national research program. *American Psychologist, 48*, 1013–1022.

Cook, T. D., & Campbell, D. T. (1979). *Quasi-experimentation: Design and analysis issues for field settings.* Boston: Houghton Mifflin.

Cook, T. D., & Reichardt, C. S. (Eds.). (1979). *Qualitative and quantitative methods in evaluation research.* Beverly Hills, CA: Sage.

Dishion, T. J., Patterson, G. R., Stoolmiller, M., & Skinner, M S. (1991). Family, school, and behavioral antecedents to early adolescent involvement with antisocial peers. *Developmental Psychology, 27*, 172–180.

Efron, B., & Tibshirani, R. J. (1993). *An introduction to the bootstrap.* New York: Chapman & Hall.

Funder, D. C., & West, S. G. (Eds.). (1993). Viewpoints on personality: Consensus, self–other agreement and accuracy personality judgments [Special issue]. *Journal of Personality, 61*(4).

Gelman, A., Carlin, J., Stern, H., & Rubin, D. (1995). *Bayesian data analysis.* New York: Chapman & Hall.

Lipsey, M W. (1993). Theory as method: Small theories of treatments. In L. B. Sechrest & A. G. Scott (Eds.), *Understanding causes and generalizing about them* (pp. 5–38). San Francisco: Jossey-Bass.

Marsh, H. W., & Grayson, D. (1995). Latent variable models of multitrait–multimethod data. In R. H. Hoyle (Ed.), *Structural equation modeling: Concepts, issues and applications* (pp. 177–198). Newbury Park, CA: Sage.

Mrazek, P. J., & Haggerty, R. J. (Eds.). (1994). *Reducing the risks for mental disorders: Frontiers for preventive intervention research.* Washington, DC: National Academy Press.

Price, R. H. (1983). The education of a prevention psychologist. In R. D. Felner, L. A. Jason, J. J. Moritsugu, & S. S. Farber (Eds.), *Preventive psychology: Theory, research and practice* (pp. 290–296). Elmsford, NY: Pergamon Press.

Reichardt, C. S., & Rallis, S. F. (Eds.). (1994). *The qualitative–quantitative debate: New perspectives.* San Francisco: Jossey-Bass.

Schlesselman, J. J. (1982). *Case control studies: Design, conduct, analysis.* New York: Oxford University Press.

Tukey, J. W. (1977). *Exploratory data analysis.* Reading, MA: Addison-Wesley.

Wheaton, B. (1985). Models for the stress-buffering functions of coping resources. *Journal of Health and Social Behavior, 26,* 352–365.

Willett, J. B., & Singer, J. D. (1993). Investigating onset, cessation, relapse, and recovery: Why you should, and how you can, use discrete-time survival analysis to examine event occurrence. *Journal of Consulting and Clinical Psychology, 61,* 952–965.

Wolchik, S. A., West, S. G., Westover, S., Sandler, I. N., Martin, A., Lustig, J., & Tein, J.-Y. (1993). The children of divorce parenting intervention: Outcome evaluation of an empirically based program. *Journal of Community Psychology, 21,* 293–331.

I

EXPANDING THE
KNOWLEDGE BASE:
ALTERNATIVE MODELS

1

METHODOLOGICAL ISSUES IN CONDUCTING PROSPECTIVE RESEARCH ON ALCOHOL-RELATED BEHAVIOR: A REPORT FROM THE FIELD

KENNETH J. SHER AND PHILLIP K. WOOD

When planning and conducting a prospective study on alcohol use or other dimensions of alcohol-related behavior, researchers are faced with numerous questions. What aspects of alcohol-related behavior are to be studied? What are the most appropriate ways to measure study constructs? On how many occasions should alcohol-related behavior be assessed and over what period of time? How are longitudinal data to be analyzed statistically? Resolution of these and related questions involve numerous considerations that are rarely addressed systematically. In this chapter, we discuss selected issues and problems that we have encountered in our own ongoing prospective study of young adults who are at low and high risk for

Preparation of this chapter was supported partly by Research Grant R01 AA7231. We thank Michael Windle, who provided extremely helpful comments on drafts of this chapter. Both authors contributed equally to the preparation of this chapter.

the development of alcohol problems. A number of important aspects of conducting prospective research, such as sampling, staff supervision, data management, and participant retention, are not addressed (see Stouthamer-Loeber & van Kammen, 1995, for a useful overview of these issues). Moreover, specialized treatment of other design and data-analytic issues—such as data imputation (as addressed in chap. 10 of this volume), alternatives for handling the censoring of alcohol consumption data (see chap. 4, this volume), designs for preventive intervention studies (see chap. 6, this volume), and multilevel data (see chap. 8, this volume)—is addressed elsewhere and is not considered here.

In discussing selected methodological issues in prospective studies of alcohol-related behavior, we try to avoid making explicit pronouncements about the appropriateness of specific design features, measurement strategies, and statistical analyses. Instead, our stance is that the myriad of alternatives that researchers must consider at each stage of the research enterprise must be evaluated in the context of the specific scientific questions being addressed. Consequently, rather than generating prescriptive solutions to commonly encountered dilemmas, we attempt to highlight some critical issues and their implications with a goal of conveying the range and types of decisions that researchers must confront.

The chapter focuses on three general issues confronting researchers who are interested in studying alcohol use and misuse in a prospective context: (a) conceptual distinctions among different aspects of alcohol-related behavior and their operationalization; (b) issues in the design and analysis of longitudinal latent-variable models and the implications of different measurement intervals; and (c) the classification of participants on the basis of the longitudinal patterning of diagnosis. Specific issues raised by our own research are highlighted throughout.

MEASUREMENT OF ALCOHOL-RELATED BEHAVIOR

Distinctions Among Alcohol-Related Phenomena

The broad term *alcohol-related behavior*, or *alcohol involvement*, subsumes a number of related yet conceptually distinct concepts, such as alcohol use, heavy alcohol use, problem drinking, alcohol abuse, and alcohol dependence. Before discussing these distinctions further, we note that the consumption of alcoholic beverages, by itself, is not necessarily a problem behavior or even an unwanted behavior. Indeed, there are credible data that suggest that moderate consumption of alcoholic beverages is health promoting (e.g., Marmot & Brummer, 1991). Thus, in contrast to thinking about the use of illicit drugs and tobacco, researchers should remember that when they think about alcohol consumption, they need to be careful about assuming that any use at all is problematic. Indeed, some degree of alcohol use is normative in many populations (including among minors, for whom such use is legally proscribed), and abstinence from alcohol may represent a form of social deviance in some groups.

At its simplest, the term *alcohol use* refers to the consumption of alcoholic beverages. Researchers traditionally distinguish between the quantity of beverages consumed on an occasion (expressed in units of absolute alcohol or standard drink equivalents), the number of drinking occasions in a specified period of time (e.g., week, month, and year), and a total estimate of the volume (sometimes expressed as quantity–frequency or Q–F) of alcohol consumed in a given period of time. Because of within-subjects variability in the amount of alcohol consumed across occasions, researchers also often attempt to assess this type of variability. Although some investigators, such as Cahalan, Cisin, and Crossley (1969), have obtained detailed drinking histories to calculate an index of volume variability, this approach is used less frequently now in population-based epidemiological surveys (although detailed time line follow-back interviews are frequently used in treatment research; see L. C. Sobell & Sobell, 1992; M. B. Sobell et al., 1980). Instead, many researchers calculate a frequency of *heavy consumption* (defined either "objectively" by reference to drinking that exceeds some threshold such as "five or more drinks per occasion" or "subjectively" by references to drinking that results in intoxication or drunkenness).

In contrast to alcohol-related behaviors that are defined in quantitative terms on the basis of consumption, the concepts of alcohol-related consequences or problems and alcohol dependence (e.g., Edwards, 1986) are defined on the basis of the effects of consumption on the person. Alcohol-related consequences include a variety of negative psychological, social, and medical consequences that result directly from alcohol consumption. Alcohol dependence is a syndrome incorporating a range of signs and symptoms indicative of the importance that alcohol consumption plays in the life of the drinker, including both psychological components (e.g., preoccupation with drinking) and physiological components (e.g., tolerance and withdrawal phenomena). Both alcohol-related consequences and the alcohol dependence syndrome can be viewed as dimensional constructs that can be graded in intensity from *absent* to *severe*. (Indeed, it is possible that these dimensional constructs are themselves multidimensional; see, e.g., Babor et al., 1992; White & Labouvie, 1989.)

Although several approaches to diagnosis and classification of pathological alcohol use have been proposed (e.g., Jellinek, 1960; National Council on Alcoholism, 1972; World Health Organization [WHO], 1992), the most widely adopted criteria in North America are those established by the American Psychiatric Association (1994) in the fourth edition of the *Diagnostic and Statistical Manual of Mental Disorders* (DSM–IV). The

DSM–IV proposes two major classifications of alcohol use disorders: alcohol abuse and alcohol dependence. The criteria for alcohol dependence incorporate several of the characteristics described by Edwards (1986) and roughly correspond to what many would call *alcoholism*. The criteria for alcohol abuse focus more on alcohol-related consequences and approximate the more general terms *problem*, *harmful*, or *hazardous* drinking (see also WHO, 1992).

Although measures of alcohol use typically correlate in the moderate-to-high range with measures of alcohol consequences and dependence symptoms, the correlates of these two broad domains often can be different (e.g., Sadava, 1985). In a study of young adults who were children of alcoholics (COAs), Sher, Wood, Crews, and Vandiver (1995) found that certain presumed etiological variables (e.g., novelty seeking) were associated equally with measures of consumption, alcohol-related problems, and dependence symptoms. Other variables (e.g., those related to negative affectivity), however, were virtually unrelated to consumption measures but moderately related to alcohol-related problems and dependence symptoms (Sher et al., 1995). Thus, in modeling etiological processes, it probably is hazardous to assume that measures of consumption are adequate proxies for more pathological aspects of drinking.

Although the distinction between alcohol dependence and alcohol abuse is important both clinically and theoretically, most of the published research on the epidemiology and prevention of alcohol-related behavior in nonclinical samples, especially in young populations, fails to distinguish between these constructs. In our own research on college students, we thought that we would find the concept of alcohol dependence to have little relevance, especially at baseline, when the overwhelming majority of participants were 18–19 years of age. However, when the participants' neurocognitive performance was examined as a function of (past-year) alcohol abuse and dependence (as assessed with criteria from the third edition of the DSM [DSM–III]; American Psychiatric Association, 1980), we found, as shown in Table 1, that those who met criteria for alcohol dependence

TABLE 1
Relation Between Alcohol-Use Disorder Diagnosis and Selected
Cognitive Measures in First-Time College Freshmen

Measure	No diagnosis ($n = 370$)	Alcohol abuse ($n = 88$)	Alcohol dependence ($n = 31$)
Block Design (WAIS–R)	36.0$_a$	35.0$_a$	29.7$_b$
Trails–A (HRNB)	20.1$_a$	19.5$_a$	23.1$_b$
Trails–B (HRNB)	45.8$_a$	42.7$_a$	52.3$_b$

Note. Means with different subscripts differ from each other at the .05 level. WAIS–R = Wechsler Adult Intelligence Scale—Revised; HRNB = Halstead–Reitan Neuropsychological Test Battery.

(n = 31) showed deficits on cognitive measures sensitive to alcoholism relative to those who met criteria for alcohol abuse (n = 88) and to those who failed to meet criteria for an alcohol use disorder (n = 370). Abusers (without alcohol dependence) did not differ from those who failed to diagnose with an alcohol use disorder. (Note that the *DSM–III* operationalization of alcohol dependence, unlike that of the *DSM–IV*, requires the presence of physical dependence symptoms. Thus, it is unclear whether similar findings would have resulted from *DSM–IV* categorizations.)

Although these findings are of interest in their own right, they again illustrate the lack of equivalence of different definitions of pathological alcohol involvement. If dependence symptoms had not been assessed, it is possible that a relation between an aspect of alcohol-related behavior (i.e., dependence) and cognitive deficit would have gone undetected. Historically, school- and community-based studies of adolescents and young adults have not given much attention to dependence symptoms, but the reasons for this are unclear. We suspect that it stems largely from research traditions on adolescent health behavior that typically have ignored dependence symptomatology, rather than any empirical studies indicating a lack of utility for this construct in this population.

In summary, *alcohol-related behavior* is a broad term that refers to a range of phenomena encompassing alcohol use (e.g., frequency of consumption, typical quantity consumed, frequency of heavy consumption), negative alcohol consequences, and dependence symptomatology. Although all of these variables correlate positively with each other, they are empirically and conceptually distinct. Even though some predictor variables appear to be (approximately equally) associated with multiple domains of alcohol-related behavior, other variables appear to be differentially associated with specific domains (e.g., the presence of alcohol problems). Consequently, researchers always need to consider the specific aspects of alcohol-related behavior that they wish to investigate and to be careful when specifying the nature of their findings and drawing generalizations. Nevertheless, we believe that for a number of purposes, it is often useful to consider more complex constructs that include elements from these various domains to characterize alcohol involvement in broad terms. However, when this is done, it should be done deliberately and with the goals of a specific study question in mind.

Issues in the Assessment of Alcohol-Related Behaviors

Although deciding what aspects of alcohol-related behavior is to be targeted is an important initial step in planning a research study, several measurement issues also require further consideration. Specifically, researchers need to consider how they are going to measure the constructs of interest.

Temporal References for Reporting Behavior

The issue of reporting intervals for measures of consumption, problems, and dependence symptoms has not received much attention in the literature. (A possible exception to this is the work on the time line followback interview technique; L. C. Sobell & Sobell, 1992; M. B. Sobell et al., 1980). It is certainly true that the choice of reporting intervals depends partly on the specific aspects of alcohol-related behavior that are being assessed and the hypotheses under investigation. For example, a study on "hangover" effects or acute trauma might focus on a relatively short time period before the assessment, investigations of chronic alcohol effects or prediction of drinking patterns would quite likely focus assessment on relatively long periods of prior use, and prevention and treatment studies typically focus on a discrete time interval after an intervention.

However, the research question often is not as clear-cut as to implicate a specific time interval for assessment, and other considerations arise. For example, longer reporting intervals (e.g., the past 90 days, the past year) may capture more typical consumption patterns and are less likely to be subject to transient variations induced by situational variables (e.g., vacations, holidays, illness) that can affect drinking patterns. Additionally, many adverse consequences of consumption (e.g., alcohol-related arrests, loss of employment, breakup of a relationship) occur sporadically and are more likely to be missed as reporting intervals decrease. Unfortunately, retrospection across longer reporting intervals places greater cognitive demands on individuals, and accuracy is likely to deteriorate. Individuals with extremely variable or light drinking patterns may have particular difficulty recalling their alcohol use over the long term relative to individuals whose consumption is highly patterned. One obvious way to balance the strengths and weaknesses of shorter versus longer rating intervals is to assess short-term alcohol consumption frequently. However, in addition to the obvious logistical complexities, frequent assessments probably increase the possibility that participants will provide stereotypical responses, place a greater burden on participants, and are likely to increase missing data.

In many respects, the dilemma of whether to ask participants to report alcohol use over a longer or shorter interval is similar to the "bandwidth–fidelity" dilemma discussed in the test construction literature (Cronbach, 1970; Cronbach & Gleser, 1965; taken from Shannon & Weaver's, 1949, information theory). The bandwidth–fidelity dilemma describes good test construction as a trade-off between the choice to measure a relatively prescribed topic extremely well versus measuring a broad range of performance but with an accompanying loss of resolution of the specific facets of interest. The bandwidth–fidelity analogy is drawn from the way that high tape speeds in a recording result in higher fidelity but at the price of reduced duration.

In our ongoing study, we find the correlation between past-year and past-month estimates of quantity–frequency (Q–F) to be relatively large ($r = .64$). However, even in cross-sectional analyses, the relation between key independent variables and Q–F was found to differ as a function of the specific reporting interval used to measure Q–F. As noted earlier, in many cases there are good a priori reasons to select a given reporting interval. However, in other cases, there are no clear guidelines, and it may be useful to assess multiple time frames. In our own research, we have sometimes taken the mean of both shorter term (i.e., past 30 days) and longer term (i.e., past year) measures in the hope that the trade-off between precision and typicality (or, alternatively, fidelity and bandwidth) would best be captured in a composite, but this remains an unvalidated assumption on our part.

Item Response Formats

The fixed format of standardized questionnaires often imposes a pattern of drinking on a participant who does not adequately reflect the structure of his or her typical drinking. For example, some existing questionnaire items combine Q–F in several plausible combinations but logically exclude certain combinations that are not implausible and present problems for the participant whose drinking behavior does not fit one of the response alternatives. Even if Q–F is not confounded, response alternatives to simple frequency items often can create similar problems for the participant when *regularity* is assumed in the wording of response alternatives. For example, the phrase "number of times per week" implies that there is some generalizability of typical drinking across weeks.

In the example shown in Exhibit 1 from Mayer and Filstead's (1979) Adolescent Alcohol Involvement Scale, a participant who drinks on Friday and Saturday night on two weekends a month would be presented with a dilemma on how to respond to the item. A number of other plausible patterns of drinking would present similar problems for participants. The sample item from Engs's (1990) Student Alcohol Questionnaire potentially has the same problem.

Many measurement approaches to substance use (especially in the drug use area) assess the number of use occasions, say, in the last month, and do not appear to be prone to this type of criticism. However, simple frequency counts do not provide information about the regularity of drinking (especially for relatively infrequent drinkers) and sacrifice information about patterning.

Additional issues arise when assessing the frequency of various alcohol-related problems or dependence symptoms, as shown in Table 1. Reflecting researchers' desire to have fixed-response formats across items, it is not uncommon to see a single response format applied to a set of items

EXHIBIT 1
Selected Items From Two Alcohol Involvement Scales

Item 1 from Mayer and Filstead's (1979) Adolescent Alcohol Involvement Scale

How often do you drink?
- a) never
- b) once or twice a week
- c) once or twice a month
- d) every weekend
- e) several times a week
- f) every day

Item 9 from Engs's (1990) Student Alcohol Questionnaire

Let's take beer first. How often, on the average, do you *usually* have a beer?
1. every day
2. at least once a week but not every day
3. at least once a month but less than once a week
4. more than once a year but less than once a month
5. once a year or less

Note. Item 1 from "The Adolescent Involvement Scale: An Instrument for Measuring Adolescents' Use and Misuse of Alcohol," by J. Mayer and W. Filstead, 1979, *Journal of Studies on Alcohol, 40.* Copyright 1979 by Rutgers Center of Alcohol Studies. Reprinted with permission. Item 9 from *Student Alcohol Questionnaire* (unpublished manuscript), by R. Engs, 1990. Copyright 1990 by R. Engs. Reprinted with permission from the author.

that are heterogeneous with respect to likely frequency of occurrence. For example, White and Labouvie (1989), in their Rutgers Alcohol Problem Index (sample items presented in Exhibit 2 with additional research items), suggested that a single-response format ranging from *never* to *more than 10 times* (in five steps) can be applied to the set of consequence items contained in their inventory. However, as can be seen in Exhibit 2, the fit between item content and the response alternatives appears to vary considerably across items. For example, it is unlikely that some consequences are experienced as a finite number of discrete occurrences. Additionally, some consequences are unlikely to occur many times for an individual within a relatively short time frame. We do not wish to argue that the approach of a common response format is not useful, only that researchers need to be aware of what they are asking of their participants when participants complete the surveys. Obviously, approaches that weight each consequence by the number of occurrences need to be particularly concerned with the meaning of total scores on these instruments.

Although some data (e.g., Hays et al., 1994; Hays & Huba, 1988) suggest that survey researchers' quest for optimal wording and response alternatives might not make much of a practical difference, it seems desirable to design instruments that capture the fundamental nature of the variables of interest accurately. To some extent, this consideration must be balanced against the possibility of confusing participants and the increased

EXHIBIT 2
Sample Items From White and Labouvie's (1989) Rutgers Alcohol
Problem Index and Other Alcohol-Related Problems Not Included in
the Scale

Items that are hard to quantify with respect to distinct occurrences

12. Felt that you had a problem with alcohol
22. Felt physically or psychologically dependent on alcohol

Items that are (presumably) easy to quantify with respect to distinct occurrences

13. Missed a day (or part of a day) of school or work
16. Passed out or fainted suddenly

Items that are very important clinically but are unlikely to occur on a frequent basis (e.g., "more than 10 times") for adolescents

*A21. Been in trouble with the police for having or drinking alcohol
*A26. Been in an alcohol treatment program

Note. Index items from "Towards the Assessment of Adolescent Problem Drinking," by H. White
and E. Labouvie, 1989, *Journal of Studies on Alcohol*, 50. Copyright 1989 by Alcohol Research
Documentation, Inc., Rutgers Center of Alcohol Studies. Reprinted with permission.
*Item not included in final version of the scale.

time required for participants to complete items with different response formats. Careful, guided piloting of instruments always seems indicated.

Other Issues

There are numerous additional issues concerning the assessment of alcohol-related behavior not discussed here that are probably equally as important as those mentioned earlier. For example, there are issues of mode of survey administration, such as paper-and-pencil versus interview versus computer administered (e.g., Marshall, Hays, & Nicholas, 1994; Skinner & Allen, 1983), lay versus clinical diagnostic interviews (e.g., Sher & Trull, 1996), use of collaterals (e.g., Sher & Trull, 1996), use of biological markers (e.g., Allen & Litten, 1993), and inconsistent responding (e.g., Turner, Lessler, & Gfroerer, 1992).

In summary, the assessment of alcohol-related behavior is a complex undertaking. Although the various domains of alcohol-related behavior are interrelated, there is sufficient unique variance associated with each of these domains that researchers need to be careful to distinguish conceptually among these different constructs. Furthermore, relatively little is known about the more severe forms of alcohol-related behavior in youthful, nonclinical samples because researchers usually do not ask the relevant questions. Attention to the more morbid aspects of alcohol involvement may be indicated in a number of nonclinical populations, even those involving youth.

Assessment of alcohol-related behavior often involves asking participants to report histories of their alcohol use and its consequences over time. Shorter reporting intervals may elicit more reliable and accurate reports but at the expense of a more representative assessment of typical alcohol-related behaviors. Longer term assessment is particularly valuable in resolving the alcohol-use patterns of light or sporadic drinkers and in detecting alcohol consequences that occur infrequently. Regardless of the domains of alcohol-related behaviors being assessed and the reporting intervals used to assess them, attention to the structure and format of the items used to assess aspects of alcohol-related behavior is always indicated. An item's response options can pose challenges for the participant whose drinking behavior does not fit well with the choices permitted. A standard response format for assessing alcohol-related behavior might be well suited for some behaviors (e.g., those that occur at an intermediate rate) but be less than optimal for others (e.g., those that occur at high or low rates). However, varying response options can be confusing to participants, potentially leading to unreliable reporting, and the practical effects of different response formats may be relatively inconsequential.

ISSUES IN THE DESIGN AND ANALYSIS OF PROSPECTIVE STUDIES

There are many methodological decisions to be made when designing and analyzing studies that examine stability and change in alcohol-related behavior. In this section, we focus on several issues that have been salient to us in our own research and have arisen in others' research as well. We focus first on several related topics relevant to an understanding of the stability of drinking and its consequences: (a) general considerations in the construction of autoregressive latent-variable models (especially the specification of a "base" model) and the testing of prospective effects; (b) the implication of the temporal spacing between measurement occasions; (c) state–trait and other alternative models of stability and growth; and (d) categorizing patterns of alcohol use disorder diagnoses over time.

These issues are discussed and illustrated using data drawn from our ongoing, prospective study of substance use, abuse, and dependence in a young-adult cohort of men and women at high and low risk for the development of alcohol problems (described in more detail by Sher, Walitzer, Wood, & Brent, 1991). In one series of analyses, we were interested in the extent to which so-called escape or escapist reasons for drinking, which have been found to be strong correlates of alcohol use and abuse in cross-sectional studies, would predict alcohol use prospectively. Although stated reasons for drinking usually are thought to represent alcohol use motivations, it also is possible that these reasons represent "after-the-fact" interpretations of the effects experienced when drinking or the choice of a socially acceptable attribution for drinking. The main purpose of these analyses was to determine the direction of influence between these constructs as operationalized as factors over time; that is, are Escape Reasons for Drinking predictive of later Alcohol Use, a consequence of prior Alcohol Use, or both? Before describing and discussing these analyses, it is useful to discuss the data on which these analyses are based and the considerations that went into the estimation of these models.

The Study

At baseline, participants for this study represented 489 freshmen at a large midwestern university chosen from an initial screening sample of 3,156 entering, first-time freshmen (representing approximately 80% of all entering, first-time freshmen). Participants who reported a family history of paternal alcoholism were considered COAs. A comparably sized sample who reported an absence of substance use disorders in all first- and second-degree relatives and an absence of antisocial personality disorder in first-degree relatives were recruited as controls (non-COAs). More details of baseline ascertainment and recruitment can be found in Sher et al. (1991). Of the 465 participants assessed at all four annual waves of data collection, 23 were missing data on at least one indicator variable at one wave and could not be included in our four-wave models without relying on imputed data. The following analyses focused on the 442 participants with complete data on all indicators.

Escape Reasons for Drinking were assessed with seven items adapted from those used by Cahalan et al. (1969), and Alcohol Use was assessed using several measures of quantity, frequency, and heavy use. These are presented in Exhibit 3.

To provide a rough characterization of mean levels of alcohol use and escape reasons for drinking over the course of the study, we first computed $2 \times 2 \times 4$ (Family History $\times$ Gender $\times$ Year) repeated measures analyses of variance (with Greenhouse–Geisser correction). For purposes of these analyses, our escape reasons for drinking measure was an unweighted sum of the individual items making up the scale; the alcohol use measure was an unweighted sum of the five drinking measures after they had been "standardized" on the basis of Year 1 means and standard deviations. Children of alcoholics reported higher levels of consumption than did non-COAs ($p < .05$), and men reported higher levels of consumption than did women ($p < .0001$). No effects concerning the time variable were significant, except for a Time $\times$ Family History interaction. Men reported more Escape Reasons for Drinking than did women ($p < .01$), and COAs reported more escape reasons than did non-COAs ($p < .05$). No other effects were significant.

EXHIBIT 3
Items Used to Assess Escape Reasons for Drinking and Alcohol Use

Escape Reasons for Drinking indicators
  1. I drink because it helps me to relax. (RFDAR1)
  2. I drink when I want to forget my problems. (RFDAR2)
  3. I drink to forget my worries. (RFDAR3)
  4. I drink to cheer me up when I am in a bad mood. (RFDAR4)
  5. I drink because I need it when I am tense or nervous. (RFDAR5)
  6. I drink when there is nothing better to do. (RFDAR6)
  7. I drink to get high, buzzed, etc. (RFDAR7)

Alcohol Use indicators
  1. Alcohol quantity/frequency per week based on past month. (TOTQF)
  2. Frequency of alcohol consumption per week, based on past year. (ALCF)
  3. Quantity of alcohol consumption per week, based on past year. (ALCQ)
  4. Number of times drunk in the past 30 days. (DNK30)
  5. Heavy drinking occasions in the past 30 days. (HVY30)

Note. Escape Reasons for Drinking indicators adapted from "American Drinking Practices: A National Study of Drinking Behavior and Attitudes," by D. Cahalan, I. Cisin, and H. Crossley (Monograph No. 6). Copyright 1969 by the *Journal of Studies on Alcohol*, Inc., Rutgers Center of Alcohol Studies. Adapted with permission.

General Considerations in Model Construction

In the reporting of structural models (either with or without latent variables), researchers often fail to describe the considerations underlying the model or models that are being tested, almost as if there were only a single plausible model for evaluating the data and the analysis merely involved estimating that single model. However, it often is the case that several (or many) possible models can be specified. In our work, choices in specification of alternative models were made with two considerations in mind. First, models used to demonstrate a possible prospective effect should include those paths or covariances that could produce a spurious prospective effect if omitted. For example, a longitudinal model that did not allow indicator variables to correlate over time could produce overestimates of construct stability because true stability is conflated with method variance (associated with specific indicators) over time. Second, attempts should be made to select the most defensible, parsimonious model for the data. Examination of model parsimony forces one to examine some of the relative contributions of aspects of the measurement and structural components of the model. We now discuss the specific ways these two principles affected our specification, evaluation, and interpretation of competing models.

Specification of the Base Model

Many authors (e.g., Anderson & Gerbing, 1988) have discussed the need for a separate consideration of the measurement and structural components of a model. Briefly, the measurement component in a model concerns whether the manifest variables under study constitute "good" indicators of the latent variables of interest. The structural component of a model, by contrast, represents relations among the constructs of a study.

In multiwave studies, three additional concerns arise in the specification and evaluation of a longitudinal measurement model: (a) the extent and nature of autocorrelation of measurement error associated with the manifest variables; (b) the extent of factorial invariance over time; and (c) whether contemporaneous (i.e., within a measurement occasion) disturbance terms are correlated or independent.

In longitudinal latent-variable models, it is necessary to estimate not only the measurement errors associated with manifest variables but also the correlation of measurement errors over time because a given indicator variable may possess a certain amount of "method variance" unrelated to the latent variable of interest but correlated with subsequent administrations of the measure (Rindskopf & Rose, 1988). In general, two models for correlated measurement error have been used: an autoregressive model of measurement error and a factorial model. Autoregressive models of measurement error assume that measurement error at one time of testing affects the next measurement occasion. Although it is possible to specify autoregressive models of correlated error of length greater than a lag of 1, most often autoregression is estimated only between adjacent measurement occasions. Autoregressive models generally assume that serial correlation between measurement occasions represents a transient phenomenon that "wears itself out" over time (i.e., correlations between measurement occasions are the greatest between adjacent measurement occasions and decrease as the number of intervening measurement occasions increases). By contrast, researchers sometimes note general patterns of correlation among the same indicators across multiple occasions and have interpreted this as a general "method factor" relating to the format, response sets, and assessment technique of a particular observed variable (i.e., that measurement errors are correlated, but not as a simple function of the number of intervening measurement occasions). It would seem reasonable to believe that the true state of affairs is probably some combination of these two processes. With four measurement occasions it would be possible to model both first-order autoregressive effects and the magnitude of the method variance associated with each variable simultaneously in a manner analogous to the state–trait models described later. We decided, however, simply to specify covariances among the errors associated with each manifest variable across all measurement occasions. In this way, a critic of the proposed prospective effects could not raise the counterargument that the prospective effect is merely an artifact of a misspecification of other change processes unrelated to the latent variables of interest.

Factorial invariance, briefly defined, is the degree to which the latent variables represent the same construct over time or over different populations. In a study of a single population with multiple measurement occasions, the factorial invariance question addresses whether the latent variable of interest represents the same construct over time or whether the nature of the latent variables changes over time, as evidenced by different patterns of factor loadings or, more dramatically, a change in the number of factors required to represent the data.

In our analyses, we estimated a variety of structural models, to make a judgment about the invariance of the latent variables of interest. Specifically, following Bentler (1989), Horn, McArdle, and Mason (1983), and Horn and McArdle (1992), we explored whether it would be reasonable to impose equality constraints over time on factor loadings, factor disturbances, error variances, and covariances between contemporaneous disturbances and covariances of lag length of 1, 2, and 3 years between errors. On the basis of an examination of fit indexes and conceptual grounds, it seemed most reasonable to adopt a model in which factor loadings for the indicator variables are constrained to be equal over time, whereas all other estimated parameters are allowed to vary across occasions. We did not explore the possibility of factor splitting across measurement occasions (Cattell, 1988), but we do note that exploratory factor analyses of these constructs across occasions failed to find any evidence for a two-factor solution. In one respect, it is probably a conservative strategy to allow all but the most essential features of the measurement model (i.e., the factor loadings) to be free across occasions. On the other hand, it is probably a good idea to investigate whether some type of factorial invariance beyond the factor loadings can be found in the data, as equality of variances may sharpen the precision of estimated effects and may make the model more parsimonious by requiring estimates of fewer parameters. In addition, it is a substantively relevant hypothesis to test whether the latent variable has the same variability across measurement occasions.

In a study in which constructs are measured on multiple occasions, the decision of whether to correlate endogenous disturbances over time is important and sometimes overlooked. Researchers often will assume that the unique variation on subsequent testings of a construct is uncorrelated with the unique variation on other constructs. In most situations, it would seem advisable to specify covariances between disturbances because these covariances model third-variable explanations for a relationship between the two constructs at any given time (such as common time-specific environmental effects that disrupt both of the autoregressive processes). Failure to include these parameters means that any such third-variable relationships are expressed via compound paths of the structural parameters of the model (i.e., autoregressive paths, cross-lagged paths, or both can be spuriously inflated). Although not applicable in our case, in some cases it might be defensible to model the relationships between disturbances at any given time by means of a causal arrow (path) rather than a sling (covariance; see Spirtes, Glymour, & Scheines, 1993).

Model Identification and Specification

Because participants in our study were sampled on the basis of family history and this variable is viewed as being ontogenetically prior to other variables in the model, we included family history as an exogenous variable. We decided to estimate the effects of family history after correcting for attenuation attributable to unreliability of the variable. This was accomplished by specifying that the latent variable of Family History had unit variance, and the path from the error variance associated with the manifest family history variable was fixed to .2861, the square root of the estimated error variance associated with the manifest variable. (Estimated error variance was calculated by multiplying the observed variance of the variable by one and subtracting the internal consistency of the measure; Crews & Sher, 1992.) In standardized solutions, this value was .57. To secure an identified model for the Escape Reasons for Drinking and Alcohol Use factors, one factor loading for Alcohol Use on all occasions was set to 1, and one factor loading for Escape Reasons for Drinking on all occasions was set to −1. (Setting these loadings to −1 rather than 1 merely means that the scale of the factors was reversed from the direction indicated in the items, so that a high score on this factor indicated that the individual gave more reasons to drink. Equivalently, this model could have been fit by reversing these items before the analysis.) As explained earlier, all models in this section assumed that all possible covariances exist among the errors of each manifest variable and itself over subsequent administrations.

Initially, maximum likelihood estimates were computed for a variety of plausible invariance hypotheses. Because these invariance hypotheses are hierarchically nested, it was possible to compare their performance via inclemental fit measures (Marsh, Balla, & McDonald, 1988). On the basis of these fits and conceptual grounds, a measurement model for the factors was chosen that constrained factor loadings to be the same over time but that allowed error variances and covariances in the model to vary over time.

Additional Base Model Specifications

After this procedure, we chose a base model for the autoregressive structure of the constructs. On the basis of the relative fit of these models and the magnitude of the estimated autoregressive coefficients, we decided to allow subsequent measurement occasions to be affected only by the immediately preceding occasion for both the Escape Reasons for Drinking and Alcohol Use variables. The fit of this base model was as follows: $\chi^2(1074, N = 442) = 2,988.44$, $p < .05$, Bentler–Bonett normed fit index (NFI) = .81, Bentler–Bonett nonnormed fit index (NNFI) = .86. Using this model as a base, the primary focus of subsequent analyses was to examine the increment in fit associated with the addition of cross-lagged paths between Escape Reasons for Drinking and Alcohol Use (and the sign and magnitude of these paths when their addition resulted in an increment in model fit).

Prospective Effects for the Four-Wave Model

The fully crossed model showed a significant improvement in fit over the "skeptical" autoregressive base model, $\chi^2(6, N = 442) = 16.43$, $p < .05$, although the overall NFI (.81) and NNFI (.86) were unchanged. This increment in fit is indicative of a prospective relation between Alcohol Use and Escape Reasons for Drinking. It is possible to calculate separately the relative increments of the cross-paths from Alcohol Use to Escape Reasons for Drinking and cross-paths from Escape Reasons for Drinking to Alcohol Use by means of nested chi-square difference tests. Given that eight potential cross-paths were being tested, such an approach helped control for experimentwise error.

When this was done, we found that the model with Alcohol Use to Escape Reasons for Drinking cross-paths produced a significant chi-square change compared with the base model, $\chi^2(3, N = 442) = 9.77$, $p = .02$. Furthermore, addition of cross-paths from Escape Reasons for Drinking to Alcohol Use to the model already containing cross-paths from Alcohol Use to Escape Reasons for Drinking did not result in further improvement of fit, $\chi^2(3, N = 442) = 6.66$, $p > .05$. By contrast, the model involving Escape Reasons for Drinking to Alcohol Use cross-paths did not result in a significant improvement in model fit over the base model, $\chi^2(3, N = 442) = 7.19$, $p > .05$, and the addition of the Alcohol Use to Escape Reasons for Drinking cross-paths (to the model already containing cross-paths from Escape Reasons for Drinking to Alcohol Use) resulted in a significant improvement in model fit, $\chi^2(3, N = 442) = 9.24$, $p = 03$. Although the pattern of statistical significance associated with individual paths may yield slightly different paths of significance, the general interpretation from the four-wave model appears to be that Alcohol Use affects subsequent Escape Reasons for Drinking, with no evidence for an Escape Reasons for Drinking effect on Alcohol Use or reciprocal relations. Standardized cross-paths associated with Alcohol Use to Escape Reasons for Drinking ranged from .06 to .09.

Temporal Spacing Between Measurement Occasions: Analysis of a Two-Wave Model

The issue of the temporal spacing between measurement occasions often is addressed in the context of conducting intervention studies, and there are at least general principles of follow-up in both treatment and prevention studies. The issue is probably most clear-cut in treatment studies, in which there is interest in assessing both short-term efficacy and the durability of treatment effects (e.g., Kazdin & Wilson, 1978). In the area of addiction treatment, where relapse rates in the period immediately following treatment are known to be high, multiple follow-up assessments during the first-year posttreatment are common and are designed to track patients through the period of highest risk for relapse (usually the first 3 months following initial abstinence; Hunt, Barnett, & Branch, 1971). Compared with treatment studies, the issue of follow-up in preventive intervention studies is more complex for at least two reasons: The period of risk for the onset of targeted problems (a) can vary across problems and (b) can be lengthy. Nevertheless, consideration of the nature of the intervention and the epidemiology of the problem targeted for prevention should provide a reasonable basis for making decisions about planning postintervention follow-ups.

By contrast, in prospective research focused on etiological processes such as the current study, choosing the length between measurement occasions can be a perplexing task. Investigators are often well informed with respect to optimal sampling, measurement strategies, and analytical techniques. However, they often lack sufficient knowledge of the extent and nature of the time-bound functional relationships that exist for a given set of variables. Consequently, they have to rely on their own (usually arbitrary) judgment in deciding how often to assess a sample over time.

Additionally, the choice of the length of a follow-up interval is tied closely to the types of change expected in the data. For example, if the researcher is interested in assessing differential, roughly linear trajectories of performance over time, the choice of a follow-up interval may be relatively unimportant, provided that it is of sufficient length to capture meaningful change. However, if the researcher is interested solely in hypotheses concerning covariation, timing may be critical for capturing the functional relation between a predictor and criterion. Temporal intervals between measurement occasions that are too long may cause contingent relationships between constructs to be obscured by other sources of random variation; however, lengths that are too short may not be informative because a postulated relationship has not yet occurred. In the current data set with multiple waves of assessment, we could simulate the effect of varying intervals between measurement occasions on the detection and the direction of prospective cross-paths.

First, note that the data presented in Figure 1 indicate high stabilities in both constructs over time, which led us to wonder whether this relatively high stability precluded finding the hypothesized effects. We therefore considered a two-wave model (Wave 1 to Wave 4) with a 3-year interval between assessment occasions (shown in Figure 2). The specification of a base model for the two-wave model proceeded in a way similar to that described for the four-wave model but was less complex because the model involved only two measurements. The correction for attenuation attributable to the unreliability of the family history variable was the same as described earlier, and factor loadings fixed to 1 and -1 also were the same. The fit of this base model was as follows: $\chi^2(268, N = 442) = 898.32$, $p < .001$, NFI = .86, NNFI = .86.

The addition of the cross-paths resulted in significant improvements in fit relative to the base model, $\chi^2(2, N = 442) = 9.56$, $p < .01$, NFI = .86, and NNFI = .88. In the same fashion as outlined for the four-wave model, chi-square difference tests were conducted to determine whether it would be more reasonable to conclude that Escape Reasons for Drinking affects subsequent Alcohol Use, that Alcohol Use affects subsequent Escape Reasons for Drinking, or that both constructs affect each other. Results indicate that a model with only the cross-path from Escape Reasons for Drinking to Alcohol Use appears the most reasonable because it significantly improved fit over the base model, $\chi^2(1, N = 442) = 9.55$, $p = .002$, and the subsequent addition of a cross-path from Alcohol Use to Escape Reasons for Drinking did not, $\chi^2(1, N = 442) = 0.01$; $p > .05$. By contrast, no support was found for a significant Alcohol Use to Escape Reasons for Drinking cross-path. Addition of the cross-path from Alcohol Use to Escape Reasons for Drinking did not significantly improve model fit over the base model, $\chi^2(1, N = 442) = 0.39$, $p > .05$. Furthermore, a model including both cross-paths fit the data significantly better than did a model with only an Alcohol Use to Escape Reasons for Drinking cross-path, $\chi^2(1, N = 442) = 9.17$, $p < .01$. Thus, in contrast to the findings from the four-wave model, in which a prospective effect was found from Alcohol Use to Escape Reasons for Drinking, the two-wave model indicated a prospective effect from Escape Reasons for Drinking to Alcohol Use.

Another way of examining how the proposed prospective associations vary as a function of length of interval involves comparing the results of two-wave analyses using only Years 1 and 4, Years 2 and 4, and Years 3 and 4. These models have the same numbers of parameters across analyses and allow examination of whether the apparent time-bound differences characterizing the two- and four-wave models would appear more as a function of the length of the interval, not the different numbers of parameters in the model or some idiosyncratic characteristics of the Year 4 assessments. Examination of these additional models revealed standard-

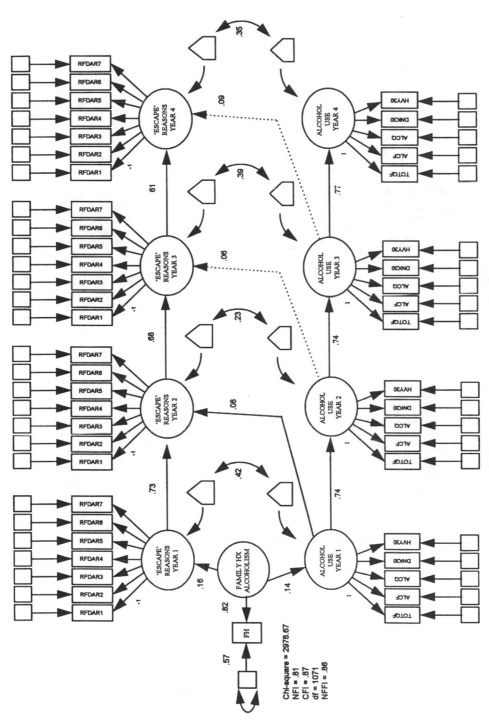

Figure 1. Four-wave autoregressive model of the relation between Escape Reasons for Drinking and Alcohol Use over 3 years. (See Exhibit 3 for explanation of abbreviations associated with manifest variables in the figure.) Family Hx = Family History.

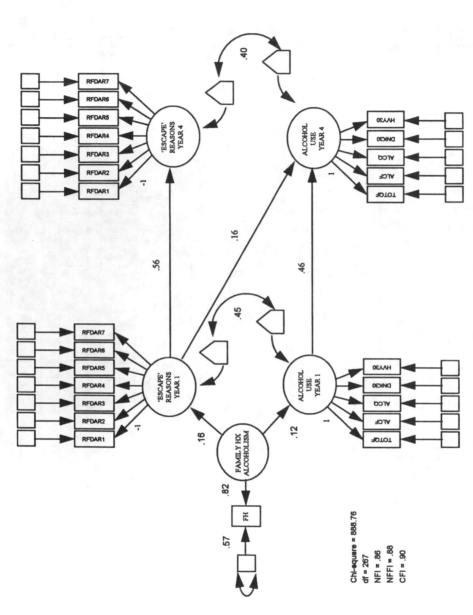

Figure 2. Two-wave autoregressive model of the relation between Escape Reasons for Drinking and Alcohol Use over 3 years.

ized cross-paths that were intermediate between the two- and four-wave models, even though measures of model fit were highly similar (e.g., the NFI values for the models for Years 1–4, 2–4, and 3–4 were .86, .86, and .84, respectively). Thus, this examination of the other two-wave models involving Year 4 supports the view that it is the length of the follow-up interval, not artifacts associated with a differing number of parameters in the two- and four-wave models or peculiarities of Year 4 measurement, that leads to the different patterns of findings across two- and four-wave models.

Robustness and Generalizability of the Obtained Models

There are several threats to the accuracy of the parameter estimates derived from any multivariate model. For example, gender-related differences in Alcohol Use and Escape Reasons for Drinking could artifactually inflate the estimation of the association between these two constructs, especially at earlier times of measurement. In addition, inclusion of participants who abstain from alcohol could inflate estimates of autocorrelation and thus affect the estimate of other model parameters. Partialing gender did not have any appreciable effects on the findings. Eliminating abstainers weakened (but did not eliminate) the prospective effect of Alcohol Use on Escape Reasons for Drinking in the four-wave analysis and slightly strengthened the findings in the two-wave analysis. Evaluation of the robustness of a statistical technique generally centers on other violations of model assumptions (particularly distributional assumptions, as is evident in the development of "distribution-free" loss functions, corrections to the chi-square goodness-of-fit statistic, as well as "robust" and bootstrap estimates of standard errors; see, e.g., Boomsma, 1986; Browne, 1984; Satorra & Bentler, 1994). However, it is important to consider threats to a proposed functional relationship that are an artifact of the agglomeration of distinct subsets of individuals.

Although it is far from conclusive, there is literature suggesting that men and women might differ in the etiology and consequences of their alcohol use (Sher, 1994). Consequently, it is important to evaluate the generalizability of our models across gender. We therefore conducted a series of both two- and four-wave models involving multigroup analysis with cross-group constraints following the outline of Bentler (1989). The models for both groups were not found to be different, except for the error variances associated with the observed variables, $\chi^2(49, N = 442) = 674.18$, $p < .01$, relative to the strict invariant model. For the two-wave model, the same pattern of results was found, except the disturbance terms for men and women also were different (relative to the strictly invariant model), $\chi^2(33, N = 442) = 298.65$, $p < .01$. Both models meet the general criteria for structural invariance for men and women.

Summary of Findings From Traditional Autoregressive Models

These analyses replicate and extend the cross-sectional literature on the relation between Escape Reasons for Drinking and Alcohol Use by not only demonstrating cross-sectional associations but also showing prospective effects above and beyond autocorrelation and contemporaneous "third variables." However, the nature of the prospective effects appears to be determined by the interval between measurement occasions. At relatively short (i.e., 1-year) intervals, there is prospective evidence for alcohol consumption to affect subsequent reasons for drinking. Additionally, no evidence was found of an effect leading from reasons for drinking to consumption at the shorter intervals. At longer intervals, however, the reverse appears to be true, with Escape Reasons for Drinking prospectively influencing Alcohol Use, but not vice versa. Although the substantive findings of these analyses are important and both suggest an etiological role for escape reasons for drinking and document that alcohol use can affect subsequent stated reasons for drinking, the methodological implications of our pattern of results appear to be particularly relevant for prospective research more generally. In attempting to resolve the direction of effect between alcohol use and putative etiological variables, the timing of follow-up assessments appears to be critical.

Superficially, it might seem that frequent assessments of alcohol use and presumed causal factors would provide the most useful data for discovering meaningful associations simply because of increased temporal precision. However, in our case, larger prospective effects were detected only over longer intervals. This is probably attributable to several factors related to the stability of alcohol use. First, most behavior patterns, if assessed over a sufficiently long interval to capture the regularity of behavior, are likely to be more stable simply as a function of both temporal proximity and the likelihood that important environmental variables and transient states persist across measurement occasions. If one wanted to make predictions from relatively enduring traits, there needs to be sufficient variability in outcome variables that are not accounted for by earlier behavior (i.e., autoregression) to permit prediction from the variables of interest. The same argument probably does not hold when attempting to predict from more transient phenomena such as mood states associated with discrete life events. Alternatively, if one is interested in discovering the consequences of alcohol consumption, shorter time intervals could be more sensitive because the effects of variability in drinking might be relatively transient. These temporal issues need to be considered when evaluating findings from prospective investigations.

Alternative Approaches to Autoregressive Models

The proposed two- and four-wave models assume that the latent variables of Alcohol Use and Escape Reasons for Drinking represent variables that possess a time-dependent stability, and it is assumed that no patterns of increasing heteroscedasticity indicate some pattern of differential growth or change over time. If these assumptions do not hold, alternative structural models can be used to describe the phenomena under study. If it is the case that measurement error is not specifically time bound, some types of longitudinal studies can be analyzed using a longitudinal trait–state model (Steyer, 1987; Steyer & Schmitt, 1990a, 1990b; Steyer, Schwenkmezger, & Auer, 1990). If it is the case that the variability in performance differs as a function of mean level, a variety of growth curve models can be used on the data (e.g., McArdle & Epstein, 1987; Meredith & Tisak, 1990; Muthen, 1991).

Toward a More Critical Examination of Autoregressive Effects

Consider the upper left-hand corner of Figure 3, which shows the structural model in Figure 1. In this model, the construct of Escape Reasons for Drinking at any occasion from Years 2–4, for example, is considered to be a function of five things: (a) Escape Reasons for Drinking at the immediately preceding occasion (as modeled by the autoregressive path from the previous measurement occasion); (b) Alcohol Use at the immediately preceding occasion (as modeled by the cross-path from the previous occasion); (c) any third-variable or structural effects associated with the Al-

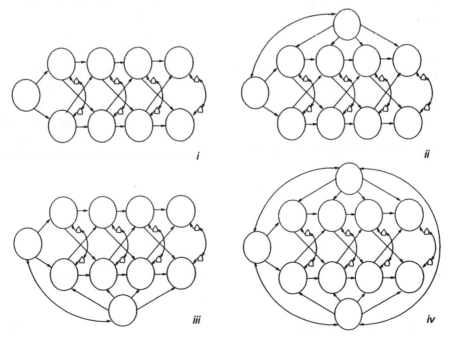

Figure 3. Alternative approaches to covariance modeling of Alcohol Use and Escape Reasons for Drinking over four waves of data collection.

cohol Use construct and the Escape Reasons for Drinking construct at that measurement occasion (as modeled by the covariance between the disturbance terms associated with the two constructs at that occasion); (d) joint effects of both previous Escape Reasons for Drinking and Alcohol Use on the previous occasion (as modeled by compound paths involving constructs such as Family History, or covariances, such as the covariance between the disturbances associated with Alcohol Use and Escape Reasons for Drinking on the preceding occasion); and (e) some unique variability in the Escape Reasons for Drinking constructs associated with that occasion (as modeled by the disturbance variance). Year 1 Escape Reasons for Drinking, for example, is assumed to have no relationship to Year 3 or Year 4 Escape Reasons for Drinking except as an indirect effect via Year 2. As such, the patterns of correlation of these latent constructs should demonstrate the familiar "simplex" pattern; stability of the construct (as measured by the test–retest correlation) should decrease as a function of a greater duration between occasions. Furthermore, in autoregressive models of Lag Length 1, the stability of longer lengths should be a product of all stabilities that connect two time points. For example, if we ignore the role of Alcohol Use for the moment, the stability of Escape Reasons for Drinking from Year 1 to Year 3 should be .73, the stability from Year 1 to Year 2 should be .68, and the stability of Year 2 to Year 3 should be .50. To the extent that the reliability from Year 1 to Year 3 is greater than this, there is some evidence that an autoregressive model of Lag Length 1 does not fit the data well.

One way to remediate this problem within the autoregressive model is to consider the addition of lag lengths greater than one. Indeed, the addition of such lag lengths greater than one does significantly increment the fit of the model. Such analyses are not presented here because of the interpretational problems presented by these longer length lags. Specifically, several of the longer lag lengths in the model were significant and negative. When longer lag lengths are significant and negative, it is often taken as evidence for cyclicity in the data or as evidence that the process under study is a dissipative one, in which the system cannot sustain a high level of activity for a long time. For these data, however, such an interpretation seemed unlikely, given that additional analyses revealed no significant polynomial trends over time and that models of "bounce back" or "short-term bursts" across years have not been described in the literature. It seemed more reasonable to consider alternatives to a strict autoregressive model, which still permitted the estimation of some components of Alcohol Use or Escape Reasons for Drinking that "wear themselves out" over time.

In contrast to autoregressive models, under state–trait models, the constructs under study do not undergo only state-to-state changes strictly as a function of time. Instead, the construct of Escape Reasons for Drinking, for example, describes to some extent an abiding interindividual difference, although some unique variation (not attributable to measurement error) in this construct may be present on any particular occasion. In studies that incorporate three or more measurement occasions, it is possible to examine whether the data are better modeled by a strictly autoregressive model, by a general stable trait model, or, as described shortly, by some combination of the two.

The fact that longitudinal data may be modeled either by general trait factors that span measurement occasions or by autoregressive components between adjacent measurement occasions was noted by Dwyer (1983) for path models involving manifest variables. Steyer (1987; also see Kenny & Zautra, 1995, for an example of state–trait decomposition involving a manifest-, as opposed to latent-variable model) observed that data with three or more occasions of measurement can be fit by latent-variable models with both general trait components and occasion-specific components. (We note that although these models sometimes refer to the occasion as the *state*, we believe that occasion is best thought of as a mixture of state and trait components. The state component is probably best represented by the disturbance associated with a measurement occasion.)

In our study, examples of some of the possible latent trait–state models are shown in Panels ii, iii, and iv of Figure 3. In Panel iv, the relative components of trait Escape Reasons for Drinking and trait Alcohol Use are indicated by trait superfactors at the top and bottom of the figure. In addition to these effects, the autoregressive effects from occasion to occasion are modeled. Although it is possible to allow the loadings on these superfactors to be different values (i.e., to assume that the measurement of the trait at any particular time is essentially congeneric with other measurement occasions), we found that doing so provided no significant advantage in fit over the "tau-equivalent" assumption of equal loadings. Furthermore, the tau-equivalent assumption of equal loadings on trait factors resulted in a more interpretable pattern of autoregressive and cross-loadings.

Although a model that contains both state and trait components still retains autoregressive paths between occasions and crossed effects across constructs, the magnitude and interpretation of such paths under such a state–trait model are different from the traditional crossed autoregressive model such as the one presented in Figure 1. In a state–trait model, variability in a construct is thought to be a function of the overall trait (as measured by paths from the superfactor to any given measurement occasion); variability unique to a given measurement occasion (as measured by the disturbance associated with a measurement occasion); possible "carryover" effects from the immediately preceding measurement occasion (for postbaseline measurement occasions); and variability attributable to other constructs in the model.

Given that variability on any given measurement occasion is decomposable into these components, what conceptual interpretation should be given to the proposed carryover effects specified in the model? Such carryover effects are not, for example, attributable to "method variance" at the item level because such variability is modeled by the correlated errors at the manifest-variable level across all measurement occasions. Likewise, "method variance" common to all of the items across occasions is confounded with estimates of general trait variability and would not contribute to the proposed carryover effect between two measurement occasions. In the example of the latent construct of Alcohol Use on any given measurement occasion, carryover effects may represent a form of "inertia" from the immediately preceding occasion. Practically speaking, a significant autoregressive carryover effect means that knowledge of an individual's alcohol use at the previous measurement occasion provides information about current alcohol use above and beyond knowledge of the individual's general level of alcohol use over the course of the study. Determination of a significant carryover effect, however, does not conclusively prove the existence of such an inertial component. It also may be that such carryover effects reflect the effects of unmeasured third variables that operate across contiguous measurement occasions. For example, in college populations it may be that some degree of alcohol consumption is determined by students' residence hall environment. Because migration from one residence hall to another occurs for some but not all students (although it is rare for students to remain in the same residence hall for all 4 years), the carryover autoregressive path in alcohol use might be explained by the effects of the residence hall environment.

Although functional relationships within a state–trait decomposition of longitudinal data are open to alternative third-variable explanations, the approach can be used to address often-unconsidered third-variable explanations for crossed and autoregressive effects found under the more traditional model. The state–trait model allows the estimation of a persistent traitlike global association between trait Escape Reasons for Drinking and trait Alcohol Use in addition to prospective associations from occasion to occasion with and between the constructs. In our research example, then, it is reasonable to explore three questions: (a) Does the addition of traitlike superfactors increment the fit of the structural model? (b) If so, what is the interpretation of the patterns of cross-lagged relationships and factors? (c) What is the nature of the family history effect under such a model?

To answer the first question, notice that the autoregressive and crossed effects models of Figure 1 are nested within the trait–state models of Figure 3. As such, it is possible to estimate whether the addition of the trait superfactors represents a significant increment in the variability beyond that accounted for in the model shown in Figure 1. The chi-square difference associated with the inclusion of both trait superfactors was statistically significant when the two-superfactors model was compared against the base model of Figure 1, $\chi^2(5, N = 442) = 73.71$, $p < .001$. Additional chi-square difference tests showed that the addition of each superfactor uniquely incremented model fit and that this was true regardless of the pattern of cross-paths associated with the four-wave model.

Assuming, then, that the two-superfactors model is appropriate for these data, whether prospective cross-paths of lag length equal to one exist for these data can be reexamined. Under such a state–trait model, none of the chi-square difference tests associated with the cross-paths were significant (all $ps > .15$), although the general magnitude of the chi-square differences again favored a model of prospective paths from Alcohol Use to Escape Reasons for Drinking.

Given the conflicting pattern of results from the autoregressive and state–trait models, some comment seems appropriate as to which model is most likely, given the data at hand. On one hand, the state–trait model has some intellectually appealing aspects. First, it seems reasonable to believe that stable interindividual differences in both Alcohol Use and Escape Reasons for Drinking exist in study populations and it is unlikely that the influence of early measurements has an effect only via intermediate measurement occasions. Indeed, if autoregressive effects of lag lengths greater than 1 are considered in the four-wave model of Figure 1, such longer length intervals significantly increment model fit, but the magnitude of estimated lag effects does not conform to the traditional notions of stochastic error, in that longer lagged effects often are larger in magnitude than shorter lagged effects and sometimes are negative. This is not to say, however, that it is manifestly evident that a traditional cross-lagged effect is inappropriate. It may well be that alcohol use over time does represent a stochastic process, and estimation of a trait–state model unfairly penalizes the parameters of interest. The state–trait model, although relatively parsimonious in terms of the additional degrees of freedom required to estimate effects, disaggregates, to some extent, covariation between constructs and over time by specifying two sets of compound paths. It is possible that this dilution of effects unfairly hobbles the statistical tests used (an example of this process is presented in our discussion of Family History effects). Nevertheless, it seems reasonable to use state–trait models because they represent an alternative class of explanations for any proposed prospective etiological relationship.

It is instructive to compare and contrast the significance and magnitude of the Family History effects in the original autoregressive and cross-path model shown in Figure 1 and the trait–state model shown in Figure 4. Note that in both the two- and four-wave autoregressive models, the statistical significance associated with paths from Family History indicate significant relationships (the paths from Family History to Year 1 Escape Reasons for Drinking and Alcohol Use constructs were .16 and .14, respectively). In Figure 4, however, only the standardized path to Escape Reasons for Drinking was statistically significant (standardized path = .09). None of the correlations of Family History with trait Escape Reasons for Drinking or trait Alcohol Use were statistically significant. Although both models yielded roughly similar estimates of the correlation of Family History with Year 1 Escape Reasons for Drinking and Alcohol Use, it appears that this relationship may be roughly equally partitioned between the state and trait components of these constructs. Dropping either the covariances associated with Family History from the model or dropping the Family History paths to Year 1 did not result in the other Family History path becoming significant. Dropping both the covariances associated with Family History and the direct paths to Year 1 resulted in a significant decrease in model fit, however. Determination of whether Family History exerts a general effect on Alcohol Use and Escape Reasons for Drinking, a Year 1 effect, or some combination does not appear to be resolvable, given these

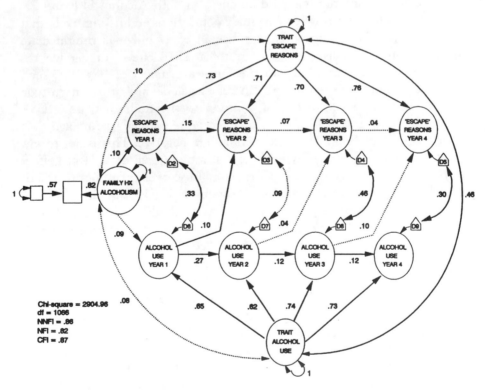

Figure 4. State–trait model of Alcohol Use and Escape Reasons for Drinking over 3 years.

data. The methodological point to be drawn from findings such as these is that researchers need to consider the implications of alternative longitudinal modeling approaches on detecting and quantifying the effects of interest.

Simultaneous Modeling of Means and Variability

In situations in which differential change and growth are present in the data, covariance structure models may fail to capture the true change processes that underlie the data. In these situations, a variety of growth curve models are available to researchers (e.g., McArdle & Epstein, 1987; Meredith & Tisak, 1990). Some of these models assume that individual performance over time is a linear composite of reference curves, but they otherwise make no assumptions about the nature of the underlying growth patterns (such as Tucker's, 1966, growth curve model). Other models decompose individual growth patterns into linear and quadratic and higher order components (e.g., Muthen, 1991) or some generalized linear model such as a logistic regression or a Markovian transition model (e.g., Diggle, Liang, & Zeger, 1994).

A related innovation in the analysis of longitudinal data is the development of a class of techniques referred to as *hierarchical linear models* or *random regression models* (e.g., Bryk & Raudenbush, 1987; Gibbons et al., 1993). Although these techniques can be shown to be applicable in a number of research contexts, they are well suited to longitudinal designs because they (a) are useful for decomposing state and trait influences; (b) allow for the inclusion of participants who fail to provide data at all measurement occasions (and thus minimize attrition bias); (c) permit the inclusion of both temporally static (e.g., gender) and time-dependent covariates; (d) model individual growth parameters as well as the general group pattern of means; and (e) accommodate designs with variable timing of observations (see Gibbons et al., 1993, for an overview of these issues).

Growth curve models can be used to characterize the heterogeneity of individual differences in the course of alcohol use and its sequelae. Therefore, they might be particularly useful for investigating the predictors of the course of alcohol-related behavior. Thus, although autoregressive models with prospective cross-lags can be used for examining patterns of reciprocal influences among multiple autoregressive processes, there are several alternatives to modeling alcohol-related behavior over time, and the choice of the specific strategy depends largely on the nature of the hypothesis under investigation. However, whatever approach is used, there are multiple decisions to be made at each stage of the model-building process, and these decisions can have critical effects on the results obtained.

TABLE 2
Percentage of Participants Receiving a *DSM–III* Lifetime Diagnosis at
Baseline Who Continue to Receive the Same Lifetime Diagnosis
1 Year Later

Diagnosis	Our sample	Helzer, Spitznagel, and McEvoy (1987)
Alcohol abuse, dependence, or both	75	66
Drug abuse, dependence, or both	63	66
Antisocial personality disorder	63	68
Major depression	38	43

Note. *DSM–III* = third edition of the *Diagnostic and Statistical Manual of Mental Disorders.*

Patterns of Stability of Diagnosis Over Time

Related to the problem of heterogeneity, of course, is the issue of subtyping individuals on the pattern of their drinking problems over time. For example, Zucker (1987) proposed two subtypes of "alcoholism" with early ages of onset: a developmentally limited form and a more chronic, antisocial form. This and other taxonomies have focused interest on the stability and course of alcohol-related diagnoses over time.

Before presenting some data on stability that are based on "past year" diagnoses, it is worthwhile to mention that it is probably a bit hazardous to assume that changes in diagnostic criteria over time accurately reflect changes in diagnostic status. To illustrate this point, we describe data on the unreliability of lifetime diagnosis from our project (see Vandiver & Sher, 1991, for an extended evaluation of this issue). One way of looking at the reliability of symptom reporting is to look at the proportion of individuals who meet lifetime diagnostic criteria for a given disorder at one point in time who continue to meet lifetime diagnostic criteria at a later point in time. If participants are completely reliable in reporting, the percentage of individuals who meet lifetime diagnostic criteria at baseline who "rediagnose" on follow-up should be 100%. However, as can be seen in Table 2, in our sample (using the Diagnostic Interview Schedule–Third Edition referenced to *DSM–III* criteria), the percentage rediagnosing was considerably less; 75% for alcohol use disorders, 63% for drug use disorders, 63% for antisocial personality disorder, and only 38% for major depression.

We were genuinely concerned about our methods when we became aware of these results and recomputed analogous statistics from Helzer, Spitznagel, and McEvoy's (1987) report of stability of the Diagnostic Interview Schedule over a 1-year interval. As can be seen in Table 2, our data are not much different from theirs in this regard. There are probably several reasons for this instability (Goodwin & Sher, 1993; Vandiver & Sher, 1991), but the key issue here is that changes in diagnostic status can reflect both true changes in alcohol-related behavior as well as inconsistency in reporting over time. Although diagnoses based on shorter time intervals (e.g., past month, past 6 months, past year) presumably are less likely to evidence the degree of unreliability noted for lifetime diagnoses, it is undoubtedly still present. Thus, the following data should be viewed with this in mind.

In Figure 5, we present data on the stability of both a "broad-band" diagnosis—alcohol abuse, dependence, or both—and a "narrow-band" diagnosis—alcohol dependence. As can be seen by examination of the top left of Figure 5, the majority of individuals diagnosing with DSM–III (12-month) alcohol abuse and dependence at later waves of the study first diagnosed at Wave 1. Moreover, this general pattern is evident in subgroups defined on the basis of family history and sex (left middle), with the possible exception of the women with a negative family history. There is a similar but less striking pattern when we examine alcohol dependence diagnoses (top and middle right). Measures of diagnostic stability, kappa, and Yule's Y indicate moderate-to-good stability over intervals of 1 year, 2 years, and 3 years (bottom). Furthermore, and surprisingly, the stabilities do not appear to decrease much over increasingly long intervals.

As can be seen in Figure 6, we can logically create 16 different patterns of diagnosis over the four waves of assessment. We were interested in determining the extent to which any of these patterns occurred at frequencies that significantly exceeded the expectation based on the marginal proportions. Any such pattern suggests that individuals can be distinguished empirically on the patterning or chronicity of diagnosis. We used a Bayesian approach to configural frequency analysis to assess the extent that each of these patterns occurred at rates that exceeded chance (Wood, Sher, & von Eye, 1994). Only four patterns were found to occur at rates exceeding base-rate expectations: (a) consistent nondiagnosers (the "0000" type); (b) consistent diagnosers (the "1111" type); (c) freshman abusers (the "1000" type); and (d) freshman–sophomore abusers (the "1100" type). Interestingly, these four types were those that were found to be most strongly related to a family history of alcoholism in our sample. Although we find the application of configural frequency analysis to our data promising, and it is roughly consistent with Zucker's (1987) theory, it is unsatisfying in certain respects. First, a large proportion of our participants were not classified into significant "types," and thus it was difficult to know what to make of this information. For example, were they sporadic cases or misclassifications of one of the identified types? Second, the use of this technique requires increasingly large sample sizes as the number of measurement occasions increases. Nevertheless, it is useful in helping us to identify temporal patterns of diagnosis for classification purpose.

Multiple answers to the question of how to resolve these issues are possible. A successful resolution of this issue involves a consideration of

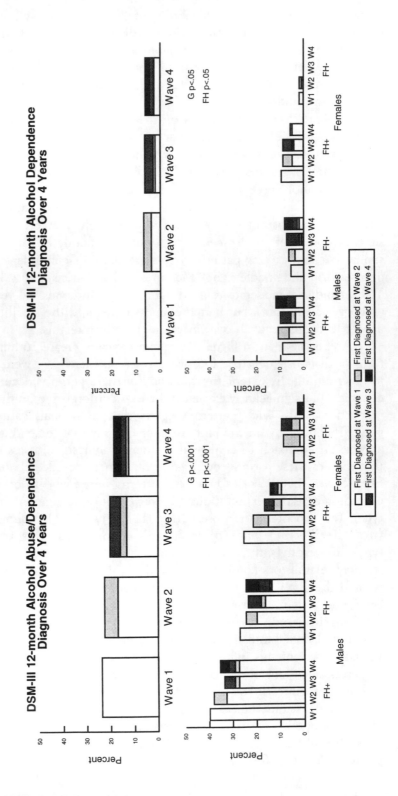

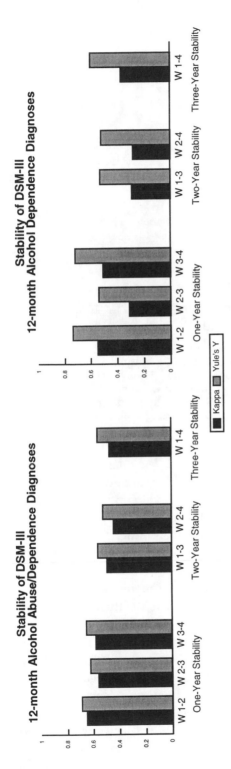

Figure 5. Stability of *DSM–III* (12-month) alcohol use disorder diagnoses over 3 years. *DSM–III* = third edition of the *Diagnostic and Statistical Manual of Mental Disorders*. FH+ = family history positive; FH– = family history negative.

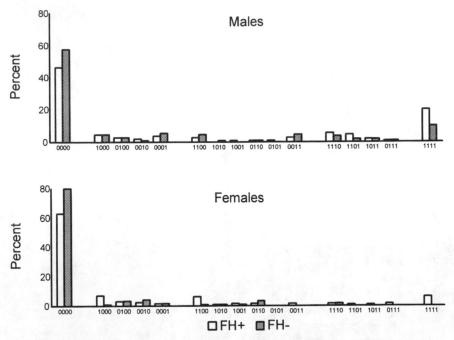

Figure 6. Temporal patterns of diagnosis over the four waves. Note that 0s represent no *DSM–III* (12-month) alcohol use disorder diagnosis and 1s represent a *DSM–III* (12-month) alcohol use disorder. Thus, a "1000" pattern represents individuals who diagnosed during the first wave and failed to diagnose at all during subsequent waves. *DSM–III* = third edition of the *Diagnostic and Statistical Manual of Mental Disorders.*

what a diagnosis of 12-month alcohol abuse and dependence means conceptually. It seems clear that the observed variable represents a categorical variable. Following Bartholomew (1987), if the underlying latent variable represents a categorical continuum, then a latent class analysis of mixtures could be used to divide the data into likely categorizations, with a probability assigned to each observed configuration in terms of which underlying group such individuals actually belonged to. On the other hand, it also would be that the diagnosis patterns in this study represent gradations of a continuum that is expressed as a function of time in this study. In this case, for example, 0000 and 1111 diagnoses merely represent the end points in the severity of diagnosis, with 1000 and 1100 merely being mild, developmentally limited versions of alcohol abuse. If this were the case, the underlying latent variable would be continuous and not categorical in nature, and the methods of latent trait analysis (Dayton & Macready, 1983) would be more appropriate. Extensions of these techniques to longitudinal designs have already been developed (Formann, 1994; Macready & Dayton, 1994; Spiel, 1994). At this stage of our research program, we have not yet thoroughly probed the implications of differing approaches to modeling the course of alcohol use disorder, but we believe that this general approach is potentially important but underused.

CONCLUSION

Taken together, the considerations discussed here highlight a number of issues facing the researcher conducting prospective investigations of alcohol-related behavior. Our intent has not been to prescribe how such studies should be conducted or analyzed but to share our knowledge of relevant literature and our experiences as practitioners and reviewers of research in the area. Certainly, our sampling of issues to be highlighted is somewhat selective, as are our discussions of various facets of these issues. Nevertheless, we believe that many of the issues that we have addressed in this chapter are of considerable importance and of general relevance to research in this area but are rarely discussed in either textbooks or research reports. For individuals embarking on research programs involving alcohol-related behavior, prospective research, or both, we believe that considerations of the issues discussed earlier will prove to be a helpful starting point in their endeavors.

REFERENCES

Allen, J. P., & Litten, R. Z. (1993). Psychometric and laboratory measures to assist in the treatment of alcoholism. *Clinical Psychology Review, 13,* 223–239.

American Psychiatric Association. (1980). *Diagnostic and statistical manual of mental disorders* (3rd ed.). Washington, DC: Author.

American Psychiatric Association. (1994). *Diagnostic and statistical manual of mental disorders* (4th ed.). Washington, DC: Author.

Anderson, J. C., & Gerbing, D. W. (1988). Structure equation modeling in practice: A review and recommended two-step approach. *Psychological Bulletin, 103,* 411–423.

Babor, T. F., Hoffman, M., DelBoca, F. K., Hesselbrock, V., Meyer, R. E., Dolinsky, Z. S., & Rounsaville, B. (1992). Types of alcoholics: I. Evidence for an empirically derived typology based on indicators of vulnerability and severity. *Archives of General Psychiatry, 49,* 599–608.

Bartholomew, D. J. (1987). *Latent variable models and factor analysis.* London: Griffin.

Bentler, P. (1989). *EQS structural equations program manual.* Los Angeles: BMDP Statistical Software.

Boomsma, A. (1986). On the use of bootstrap and jackknife in covariance structure analysis. *COMPSTAT, 7,* 205–210.

Browne, M. W. (1984). Asymptotically distribution-free methods for the analysis of covariance structures. *British Journal of Mathematical and Statistical Psychology, 37*, 62–83.

Bryk, A. S., & Raudenbush, S. W. (1987). Application of hierarchical linear models to assessing change. *Psychological Bulletin, 101*, 147–158.

Cahalan, D., Cisin, I. H., & Crossley, H. M. (1969). *American drinking practices: A national study of drinking behavior and attitudes* (Monograph No. 6). New Brunswick, NJ: Rutgers Center of Alcohol Studies.

Cattell, R. B. (1988). The meaning and strategic use of factor analysis. In J. R. Nesselroade & R. B. Cattell (Eds.), *Handbook of multivariate experimental psychology* (2nd ed., pp. 131–203). New York: Plenum.

Crews, T., & Sher, K. J. (1992). Using adapted Short MASTs for assessing parental alcoholism: Reliability and validity. *Alcoholism: Clinical and Experimental Research, 16*, 576–584.

Cronbach, L. J. (1970). *Essentials of psychological testing.* (3rd ed.). New York: Harper & Row.

Cronbach, L. J., & Gleser, G. C. (1965). The signal/noise ratio in the comparison of reliability coefficients. *Educational and Psychological Measurement, 24*, 467–480.

Dayton, C. M., & Macready, G. B. (1983). Latent structure of repeated classifications with dichotomous data. *British Journal of Mathematical and Statistical Psychology, 36*, 189–201.

Diggle, P. J., Liang, K.-Y., & Zeger, S. L. (1994). *Analysis of longitudinal data.* Oxford, England: Clarendon Press.

Dwyer, J. H. (1983). *Statistical models for the social and behavioral sciences.* New York: Oxford University Press.

Edwards, G. (1986). The alcohol dependence syndrome: A concept as stimulus to enquiry. *British Journal of Addiction, 81*, 171–183.

Engs, R. C. (1990). *Student Alcohol Questionnaire.* Unpublished manuscript, Indiana University, Bloomington, IN.

Formann, A. K. (1994). Measuring change using latent class analysis. In A. von Eye & C. Clogg (Eds.), *Latent variables analysis: Applications for developmental research* (pp. 294–312). Thousand Oaks, CA: Sage.

Gibbons, R. D., Hedeker, D., Elkin, I., Waternaux, C., Kraemer, H. C., Greenhouse, J. B., Shea, T., Imber, S. D., Sotsky, S. M., & Watkins, J. T. (1993). Some conceptual and statistical issues in analysis of longitudinal psychiatric data: Application to the NIMH Treatment of Depression Collaborative Research Program dataset. *Archives of General Psychiatry, 50*, 739–750.

Goodwin, A. H., & Sher, K. J. (1993). Effects of induced mood on diagnostic interviewing: Evidence for a mood and memory effect. *Psychological Assessment, 5*, 197–202.

Hays, R. D., Bell, R. M., Damush, T., Hill, L., DiMatteo, M. R., & Marshall, G. N. (1994). Do response options influence self-reports of alcohol use? *International Journal of the Addictions, 29*, 1909–1920.

Hays, R. D., & Huba, G. J. (1988). Reliability and validity of drug use items differing in the nature of their response options. *Journal of Consulting and Clinical Psychology, 56,* 470–472.

Helzer, J. E., Spitznagel, E. L., & McEvoy, L. (1987). The predictive validity of lay Diagnostic Interview Schedule diagnoses in the general population: A comparison with physician examiners. *Archives of General Psychiatry, 42,* 657–666.

Horn, J. L., & McArdle, J. J. (1992). A practical and theoretical guide to measurement invariance in aging research. *Experimental Aging Research, 18,* 117–144.

Horn, J. L., McArdle, J. J., & Mason, R. (1983). When is invariance not invariant: A practical scientist's look at the ethereal concept of factor invariance. *The Southern Psychologist, 1,* 179–188.

Hunt, W. A., Barnett, L. W., & Branch, L. G. (1971). Relapse rates in addiction programs. *Journal of Clinical Psychology, 27,* 455–456.

Jellinek, E. M. (1960). *The disease concept of alcoholism.* New Haven, CT: Hillhouse.

Kazdin, A. E., & Wilson, G. T. (1978). Criteria for evaluating psychotherapy. *Archives of General Psychiatry, 35,* 407–411.

Kenny, D. A., & Zautra, A. (1995). The trait–state model for multiwave data. *Journal of Consulting and Clinical Psychology, 63,* 52–59.

Macready, G. B., & Dayton, C. M. (1994). Latent class models for longitudinal assessment of trait acquisition. In A. von Eye & C. Clogg (Eds.), *Latent variables analysis: Applications for developmental research* (pp. 245–273). Thousand Oaks, CA: Sage.

Marmot, M., & Brummer, E. (1991). Alcohol and cardiovascular disease: The status of the U-shaped curve. *British Medical Journal, 303,* 565–568.

Marsh, H. W., Balla, J. R., & McDonald, R. P. (1988). Goodness-of-fit indexes in confirmatory factor analysis: The effect of sample size. *Psychological Bulletin, 103,* 391–410.

Marshall, G. N., Hays, R. D., & Nicholas, R. (1994). Evaluating agreement between clinical assessment methods. *International Journal of Methods in Psychiatric Research, 4,* 249–257.

Mayer, J., & Filstead, W. J. (1979). The Adolescent Alcohol Involvement Scale: An instrument for measuring adolescents' use and misuse of alcohol. *Journal of Studies on Alcohol, 40,* 291–300.

McArdle, J. J., & Epstein, D. (1987). Latent growth curves with developmental structural equation models. *Child Development, 58,* 110–133.

Meredith, W., & Tisak, J. (1990). Latent curve analysis. *Psychometrika, 55,* 107–122.

Muthen, B. (1991). Analysis of longitudinal data using latent variable models with varying parameters. In L. Collins & J. Horn (Eds.), *Best methods for the analysis of change: Recent advances, unanswered questions, future directions* (pp. 1–17). Washington, DC: American Psychological Association.

National Council on Alcoholism. (1972). Criteria for the diagnosis of alcoholism. *American Journal of Psychiatry, 129,* 127–135.

Rindskopf, D., & Rose, T. (1988). Some theory and application of confirmatory second-order factor analysis. *Multivariate Behavioral Research, 23,* 51–67.

Sadava, S. W. (1985). Problem behavior theory and consumption and consequences of alcohol use. *Journal of Studies on Alcohol, 46,* 392–397.

Satorra, A., & Bentler, P. M. (1994). Corrections to test statistics and standard errors in covariance structure analysis. In A. von Eye & C. C. Clogg (Eds.), *Latent variables analysis: Applications for developmental research* (pp. 399–419). Thousand Oaks, CA: Sage.

Shannon, C., & Weaver, W. (1949). *The mathematical theory of communication.* Urbana: University of Illinois Press.

Sher, K. J. (1994). Studies of risk at individual levels. In R. Zucker, G. Boyd, & J. Howard (Eds.), *The development of alcohol problems: Exploring the biopsychosocial matrix of risk* (NIAAA Research Monograph No. 26, pp. 77–108). Rockville, MD: U.S. Department of Health and Human Services.

Sher, K. J., & Trull, T. J. (1996). Methodological issues in psychopathology research. *Annual Review of Psychology, 47,* 371–400.

Sher, K. J., Walitzer, K. S., Wood, P., & Brent, E. E. (1991). Characteristics of children of alcoholics: Putative risk factors, substance use and abuse, and psychopathology. *Journal of Abnormal Psychology, 100,* 427–448.

Sher, K. J., Wood, M., Crews, T., & Vandiver, T. A. (1995). The Tridimensional Personality Questionnaire: Reliability and validity studies and derivation of a short form. *Psychological Assessment, 7,* 195–208.

Skinner, H. A., & Allen, B. A. (1983). Does the computer make a difference? Computerized versus face-to-face self-report assessments of alcohol, drug, and tobacco use. *Journal of Consulting and Clinical Psychology, 51,* 267–275.

Sobell, L. C., & Sobell, M. B. (1992). Timeline follow-back: A technique for assessing self-reported alcohol consumption. In R. Z. Litten & J. P. Allen (Eds.), *Measuring alcohol consumption: Psychosocial and biochemical methods* (pp. 41–72). Totowa, NJ: Humana Press.

Sobell, M. B., Maisto, S. A., Sobell, L. C., Cooper, A. M., Cooper, T. C., & Sanders, B. (1980). Developing a prototype for evaluating alcohol treatment effectiveness. In L. C. Sobell, M. B. Sobell, & E. Wood (Eds.), *Evaluating alcohol and drug abuse treatment effectiveness: Recent advances* (pp. 129–150). Elmsford, NY: Pergamon Press.

Spiel, C. (1994). Latent trait models for measuring change. In A. von Eye & C. Clogg (Eds.), *Latent variables analysis: Applications for developmental research* (pp. 274–293). Thousand Oaks, CA: Sage.

Spirtes, P., Glymour, C., & Scheines, R. (1993). Causation, prediction, and search. *Springer-Verlag lecture notes in statistics* (Vol. 81). New York: Springer-Verlag.

Steyer, R. (1987). Konsistenz und Spezifität: Definition zweier zentraler Begriffe der Differentiellen Psychologie und ein einfaches Modell zu ihrer Identifikation [Consistency and specificity: The definition of two central concepts of differential psychology and a simple model for their identification]. *Zeitschrift für Differentielle und Diagnostishe Psychologie, 8,* 245–258.

Steyer, R., & Schmitt, M. J. (1990a). The effects of aggregation across and within occasions on consistency, specificity and reliability. *Methodika, 4,* 58–94.

Steyer, R., & Schmitt, M. J. (1990b). Latent state–trait models in attitude research. *Quality and Quantity, 24,* 427–445.

Steyer, R., Schwenkmezger, P., & Auer, A. (1990). The emotional and cognitive components of trait anxiety: A latent state–trait anxiety model. *Personality and Individual Differences, 11,* 125–134.

Stouthamer-Loeber, M., & van Kammen, W. B. (1995). *Data collection and management: A practical guide.* Thousand Oaks, CA: Sage.

Tucker, L. (1966). Learning theory and multivariate experiment: Illustration of generalized learning curves. In R. B. Cattell (Ed.), *Handbook of multivariate experimental psychology* (pp. 476–501). New York: Rand McNally.

Turner, C. F., Lessler, J. T., & Gfroerer, J. C. (Eds.). (1992). *Survey measurement of drug use: Methodological studies.* Rockville, MD: National Institute on Drug Abuse.

Vandiver, T., & Sher, K. J. (1991). Temporal stability of the Diagnostic Interview Schedule. *Psychological Assessment, 3,* 277–281.

White, H. R., & Labouvie, E. W. (1989). Towards the assessment of adolescent problem drinking. *Journal of Studies on Alcohol, 50,* 30–37.

Wood, P. K., Sher, K. J., & von Eye, A. (1994). Conjugate and other distributional methods in configural frequency analysis. *Biometrical Journal, 36,* 387–410.

World Health Organization. (1992). *The ICD-10 classification of mental and behavioral disorders: Clinical descriptions and diagnostic guidelines.* Geneva, Switzerland: Author.

Zucker, R. A. (1987). The four alcoholisms: A developmental account of the etiologic process. In P. C. Rivers (Ed.), *Nebraska Symposium on Motivation: Vol. 34. Alcohol and addictive behavior* (pp. 27–83). Lincoln: University of Nebraska Press.

2

ALTERNATIVE LATENT-VARIABLE APPROACHES TO MODELING CHANGE IN ADOLESCENT ALCOHOL INVOLVEMENT

MICHAEL WINDLE

The study of change is relevant for many prominent research questions posed in alcohol studies. Life course, or natural history, studies have focused on changes in drinking behaviors across the life span and on the identification of salient risk factors that influence individual trajectories (e.g., Fillmore, 1987; Vaillant, 1983; Zucker, 1992). Alcohol and substance use prevention studies have focused on how interventions at various levels (e.g., individual, peer, school, community) change the onset, frequency, or intensity of alcohol and other substance use behaviors (e.g., Ellickson & Bell, 1990; Holder & Howard, 1992; Pentz et al., 1989). Alcohol treatment outcome studies have focused on how various treatment conditions influence a plethora of parameters related to changes in drinking behaviors (e.g., total abstinence, duration of controlled drinking, time to relapse; Marlatt & Gordon, 1985; Prochaska, DiClemente, & Norcross, 1992).

This research was supported in part by National Institute on Alcohol Abuse and Alcoholism Grant A37-07861.

It is fortuitous that interest in many of these prominent research questions pertinent to change in alcohol studies is paralleled by a heightened interest in statistical models of change in the broader literature of quantitative methods (e.g., Collins & Horn, 1991; Tuma & Hannan, 1984; von Eye, 1990; Willett, 1988). There has been a considerable history of the study of the measurement of change (e.g., Harris, 1963), but recent advances, facilitated by computer technology (e.g., rapid convergence for estimators), have spawned an accelerating number of quantitative methods to model change (e.g., for a "sampling" of models, see Collins & Horn, 1991, and von Eye & Clogg, 1994). The purpose of this chapter is to discuss some points of intersection between issues pertinent to modeling change in alcohol studies and the application of several relatively recent latent-variable (LV) modeling approaches to evaluate change. The LV modeling approaches include both *continuous variable* mean- and covariance-structure models and *categorical variable* latent Markov models. The application of these two broad LV modeling approaches is illustrated by using the same observed data that were obtained from a four-wave panel design of adolescent drinking behavior (for details of the panel design, see Windle, 1994). Before presenting data on the specification and evaluation of the alternative LV modeling approaches, I provide some background material to facilitate an appreciation of the history and relevance of the approaches and applications. First, I briefly describe some alternative ways of conceptualizing and measuring change for continuous variable statistical models. Second, I discuss issues related to the continuous versus discrete measurement of alcohol behaviors.

ALTERNATIVE WAYS OF CONCEPTUALIZING AND MEASURING CHANGE WITH CONTINUOUS VARIABLES

There are numerous ways of conceptualizing and measuring change with continuous variables, from the use of simple difference scores and residual change scores to polynomial functions and multivariate growth parameters (e.g., Dwyer, Feinleib, Lippert, & Huffmeister, 1992; Willett, 1988). For continuous variable longitudinal panel data, an initial distinction in measuring change is whether the change to be measured is in reference to the maintenance (or change) of the relative ordering of individuals across time or to changes in average (mean) levels across time. The definition of change according to the stability of the individual-differences approach centers on the relative ordering of individuals across time; thus, perfect stability (i.e., no change) would be indicated if every participant in a sample at Time 2 increased his or her performance over that at Time 1 by a given constant.[1] For example, assume that the Time 1 level of alcohol consumption indicated that participants drank an average of 1 drink a day. Assume at Time 2 that each participant increased his or her drinking levels by an additional 10 drinks a day (i.e., Time 1 drinking level + 10). The computation of a test–retest correlation, corresponding to the stability of individual differences, would indicate perfect stability (i.e., a Pearson product–moment correlation of 1.0) or no change in the relative ordering of participants across time. However, for this example, assuming a reasonable sample size and approximate normality of the distribution of variates, statistical models (e.g., repeated measures multivariate analysis of variance [MANOVA]) focused on mean-level differences are highly likely to indicate substantial change in drinking levels across time. That is, an average increase of 10 drinks at Time 2 from 1 drink at Time 1 would indicate substantial discontinuity in drinking behavior across this two-wave interval. The point of this simple illustration is to indicate that (a) conceptualizations and measurement of change are variable and (b) much different conclusions about change may be drawn depending on the approach to change that is adopted.

For continuous variable longitudinal panel data, traditional methods of analyses for investigating changes in mean levels have included repeated measures analysis of variance (ANOVA) or MANOVA statistical models. The use of the repeated measures MANOVA model often is more consistent with assumptions about the data (i.e., sphericity assumptions are relaxed) than the repeated measures ANOVA model (although if sphericity and other assumptions are met, the repeated measures ANOVA model may provide greater statistical power; see Stevens, 1986). Variations and extensions of the general repeated measures MANOVA approach have included recent advances that facilitate alternative specifications of the covariance structure for unbalanced data, the estimation of missing data using the EM algorithm, and flexibility in modeling linear and nonlinear growth functions (e.g., Jennrich & Schluchter, 1986; Ware, 1985).

Other recent advances in the modeling of continuous variable longitudinal panel data include the use of random regression, mixed, and hierarchical linear models (HLMs; e.g., Bryk & Raudenbush, 1987; Gibbons, Hedeker, Waternaux, & Davis, 1988) to address salient issues in the measurement of change. The HLM approach provides increased flexibility in the measurement of change relative to the standard repeated measures MANOVA model. For example, the HLM approach may accommodate irregularly spaced measurement occasions and the inclusion of time-varying as well as time-invariant covariates. It also permits the estimation of person-specific deviations (or individual growth curves) from the aggregate

---

[1] Similarly, perfect stability (i.e., $r = 1.0$) would be indicated if every participant in a sample at Time 2 decreased his or her performance relative to Time 1 by a given constant or if the same scores were obtained by every participant at Time 1 and Time 2.

average (or mean-level) response trend across time (for more detail on HLM models, see chap. 8 of this volume; also see Bryk & Raudenbush, 1987).

Other relatively recent approaches to the statistical modeling of continuous variable longitudinal data have included covariance and moment structure models with LVs (e.g., Duncan, Duncan, & Hops, 1994; McArdle, Hamagami, & Hulick, 1994; Windle & Miller, 1990). The advantages and limitations of covariance and moment structure modeling have been well documented in numerous books (e.g., Bollen, 1989; Dwyer, 1983), review articles (e.g., Bentler, 1980; Rogosa, 1988), and special review issues (e.g., *Child Development*, 1989, Vol. 58; *Journal of Educational Statistics*, 1987, Vol. 12). Although a critique of this literature is beyond the scope of this chapter, I illustrate several potential advantages of covariance and moment structure modeling using four-wave panel data on adolescent drinking.

CONTINUOUS VERSUS DISCRETE MEASUREMENT OF ALCOHOL BEHAVIOR WITH LONGITUDINAL PANEL DATA

For many applications in alcohol studies, variables are measured, or are created, in which the repeatedly measured dependent variable of interest is categorical (e.g., having or not having an alcohol disorder, light vs. moderate or heavy drinker). Although there is considerable controversy about the value of deriving categorical variables when continuous variable alternatives exist, strong arguments have been voiced for the advantages of latent categorical variables in some research applications (e.g., Meehl, 1992; Stern, Arcus, Kagan, Rubin, & Snidman, 1995). For example, Stern et al. cited a series of studies conducted by Kagan and colleagues (e.g., Kagan, Reznick, & Snidman, 1988) that support two temperament types (or qualitative categories) among children: the inhibited and the uninhibited to the unfamiliar. They argued that these two types of children differ systematically on a range of behavioral variables (e.g., latency to approach an unfamiliar person or object) and other characteristics (e.g., body build, eye color, reactivity of the sympathetic nervous system) that are internally homogeneous *within* types but different *between* types.

Similar issues over the conceptualization and measurement of alcohol behaviors as continuous versus categorical exist in the alcohol studies literature. Three examples are provided: First, there has been considerable interest in identifying drinking types (e.g., steady vs. episodic) in which the pattern of alcohol use may have implications for alcohol-related social, legal, and medical problems, as well as for possible differential prevention and intervention. Various quantity- and frequency-based typologies (e.g., Hilton, 1987) have the similar objective of identifying distinct, internally homogeneous types that will provide more useful discriminating information than either treating alcohol use as a continuous variable or treating alcohol behaviors as a dichotomously scored psychiatric disorder. A second example is that there is increasing interest in substance use studies to identify unique factors that differentially predict *substance use* from *substance abuse* and to multiple distinctive (internally homogeneous) developmental pathways that may characterize substance abuse patterns (see, e.g., Glantz & Pickens, 1992). Elliott, Huizinga, and Menard (1989) have suggested that contrary to the homogeneity of adolescent problem behaviors hypothesized by Jessor's (1989) problem behavior syndrome, adolescent delinquency, substance use, and poor mental health each has unique precursors. To the extent that these problem behaviors have distinct and internally homogeneous precursors, they may be characterized as qualitatively different.

A third example that has supported the usefulness of qualitatively distinct types has emerged from the study of pattern-based versus variable-based approaches to data analyses and interpretation (e.g., Hinde & Dennis, 1986; Magnusson & Bergman, 1988). The pattern-based approach has been proposed to complement the more standard variable-based approach to facilitate inquiry into different patterns of intraindividual change across time. That is, in prospective research designs, the individual rate of change, and the precursors and correlates of variable rates of change, may differ systematically among subgroups of individuals. Aggregating across participants, which is frequently done using the variable-based approach, may obscure significant changes that are occurring across time among subgroups. Thus, if one subgroup is decreasing its alcohol use across time and a second subgroup is increasing its alcohol use across time, the aggregate (mean-level) change score may reflect no significant differences for cross-time change; however, data analyses by appropriately identified subgroups would have yielded two significant patterns of change for alcohol use, one increasing and the other decreasing. Furthermore, the precursors and correlates associated with these change patterns may differ (e.g., more alcohol-using friends may contribute to increases in alcohol use, whereas greater involvement in church activities may predict decreases in alcohol use).

Schulenberg, Wadsworth, O'Malley, Bachman, and Johnston (1996) used the pattern-based approach to study initial differences that accounted for variability in subgroups who differed in patterns of binge drinking from adolescence to young adulthood. In a comparison of chronic versus decreased binge-drinking subgroups, Schulenberg et al. identified several variables (e.g., being female, having higher self-efficacy and work readiness, drinking less to get drunk), measured in the senior year of high school, that differentiated the adolescents who decreased their binge drinking from adolescence to young adulthood from those who persisted in binge drinking into young adulthood (the chronic pattern). Note that these two groups had highly similar levels of binge drinking in their senior year and did not differ with regard to several other potentially confounding variables (e.g., antisociality and rebelliousness, grade point average) that might have contributed to different binge-drinking trajectories into young adulthood. The unique pattern of precursors distinguishing these two trajectories of growth (as well as other less continuous patterns of binge drinking) might have been obscured in more traditional, variable-based approaches that often rely on linear regression models. Nonlinear patterns not necessarily evident in linear-oriented, variable-based approaches may, in some instances, be identified using a pattern-based approach.

There are alternative analytical approaches to measuring qualitatively distinct categories or types. In alcohol studies, a frequently used approach has been to make arbitrary, but not whimsical, splits for variables (e.g., quantity and frequency of use) and to proceed with construct validity issues by examining subtype differences on variables in which the groups are expected to differ (e.g., with regard to alcohol-related problems at home, with friends, at work, or with legal authorities). This approach does not use a formal statistical model to substantiate the proposed internal structure of the distinct types. Perhaps the most commonly used formal statistical model to identify subtypes in alcohol studies has been the use of cluster analytic methods (e.g., Morey & Skinner, 1986). Cluster analytic methods typically use continuous observed (or manifest) variables to identify discrete, unobserved (or latent) subtypes. By contrast, traditional factor analysis is used with continuous manifest variables to identify underlying continuous latent variables. The latent Markov modeling framework that is presented later in this chapter is used to identify discrete latent variables and latent classes, or subtypes, with categorical manifest variables (Langeheine & Van de Pol, 1990).

In this chapter I do not suggest that one LV model or statistical modeling approach (e.g., latent Markov modeling) is superior to others. Rather, I discuss some alternative ways of measuring change with alcohol data and, more important, emphasize the need to pursue the temporal patterning and dynamic organization of alcohol behaviors to facilitate answers to research questions of interest in alcohol studies.

DATA SET USED IN APPLICATIONS

The data used in these applications were derived from a four-wave panel study of approximately 1,150 adolescents. The sample was principally White and middle class, and the initial assessment included 10th and 11th graders, with 6-month intervals between occasions of measurement (see Windle, 1994, for a further description). Active informed-consent procedures were used (parent and adolescent consent), and approximately 74% of the eligible adolescent sample participated in the study. The retention rate across any contiguous measurement occasion exceeded 90%, and 84% of the sample participated at all four waves of measurement.

Three alcohol behavior variables were used in the applications in this study. They were (a) average alcohol use in the past 30 days (using standard conversion formulas; e.g., Armor & Polich, 1982); (b) heavy, or binge, drinking, defined as the number of days during the past month that the adolescent reported consuming six or more drinks during a drinking episode; and (c) the number of alcohol problems (e.g., with friends, family, teachers, or legal authorities due to drinking, passing out, missing school) in the past 6 months. Because all three of these variables were nonnormally distributed, I used a log transformation (natural logarithm of [Y + 10]) to stabilize the variance for each of the variables.

COVARIANCE STRUCTURE MODELING WITH LVs: AN AUTOREGRESSIVE MODEL APPLICATION

Covariance structure modeling encompasses a broad range of statistical model specifications, including path analysis, confirmatory factor analysis, and structural equations with latent variables. In describing covariance structure modeling, it is common to distinguish between the *measurement model*, which is used to specify item–factor (or manifest indicator–latent variable) relations, and the *structural model*, which is used to specify predictive or presumed causal relations among variables. The measurement model may be represented as

$$y = \Lambda_y \eta + \varepsilon,$$

where y corresponds to observed Y variables; Λ_y corresponds to a factor loading matrix linked with the latent η variables; and ε corresponds to errors of measurement associated with y. The general form of the structural model may be represented as

$$\eta = B\eta + \Gamma\xi + \zeta,$$

where η corresponds to an $(r \times 1)$ vector of endogenous (or dependent) variables, B is an $(r \times r)$ matrix of parameters (coefficients) relating endogenous variables to each other, Γ is an $(r \times s)$ matrix of parameters (coefficients) relating the endogenous variables to the exogenous (independent) variables, ξ is an $(s \times 1)$ vector of exogenous variables, and ζ is an $(r \times 1)$ vector of errors in equations (or disturbance terms).

In this illustration, covariance structure modeling was used with four-wave panel data to evaluate alternative autoregressive covariance structure models. Autoregressive covariance structure models provide a frequently used approach to evaluate the (rank-order) stability of individual differences for an LV across time. By the term *autoregressive*, I mean modeling change by regressing a variable X at time $t + 1$ on the same variable X at time t. When LVs are used in such autoregressive models, errors of measurement may be modeled statistically, and thus the resulting autoregressive coefficients of the LVs are estimated while correcting for measurement error. The failure to model statistically such measurement error may bias parameter estimates, including those for the autoregressive coefficients.

In covariance structure modeling, alternative models may be specified and compared to evaluate their adequacy in reproducing the observed data, which, in this application, was a 12×12 variance–covariance matrix of the three alcohol behaviors—alcohol use, heavy (or binge) drinking, and alcohol problems—measured at each of the four waves of measurement. The three alcohol behaviors were specified as manifest indicators (i.e., observed variables measured with some level of error of measurement) of the LV, alcohol involvement, at each wave. The specified models were selected to demonstrate salient points regarding error-free measurement; the estimation of correlated errors; and comparative, nested model fit comparisons.

For this application, there were 12 manifest variables (three measured at each of the four waves of measurement) and four LVs. The 12 linear equations associated with the measurement model were as follows:

$$Y_{11} = \lambda_1 F1 + e_1$$

$$Y_{21} = \lambda_2 F1 + e_2$$

$$Y_{31} = \lambda_3 F1 + e_3$$

$$Y_{12} = \lambda_4 F2 + e_4$$

$$Y_{22} = \lambda_5 F2 + e_5$$

$$Y_{32} = \lambda_6 F2 + e_6$$

$$Y_{13} = \lambda_7 F3 + e_7$$

$$Y_{23} = \lambda_8 F3 + e_8$$

$$Y_{33} = \lambda_9 F3 + e_9$$

$$Y_{14} = \lambda_{10} F4 + e_{10}$$

$$Y_{24} = \lambda_{11} F4 + e_{11}$$

$$Y_{34} = \lambda_{12} F4 + e_{12},$$

where Y_{ij} is the observed score of each variable $_i$ at wave $_j$, λ_k is the factor loading of each manifest variable on the respective four factors (Factors

1–4 [F1–F4]), and e_l is the measurement error associated with the imperfect measurement (or unreliability) of the observed score for each variable. More concretely, this measurement model specifies that alcohol use, heavy drinking, and alcohol problems, measured at each of four waves of assessment, may be used as manifest indicators of the four LVs of alcohol involvement (measured at Time 1, Time 2, Time 3, and Time 4). Note that unlike exploratory factor analysis, each manifest indicator "loads" on only one factor; hence, for example, alcohol use at Time 1 is freely estimated to load on Factor 1 (alcohol involvement − Time 1) but is fixed to zero with regard to loading on F2–F4.

Although the measurement model consists of the specification of the manifest indicator–LV relations, the following three linear equations are associated with the structural model:

alcohol involvement (Time 2) = β_1 (alcohol involvement at Time 1) + u

alcohol involvement (Time 3) = β_2 (alcohol involvement at Time 2) + v

alcohol involvement (Time 4) = β_3 (alcohol involvement at Time 3) + w,

where each endogenous (dependent) variable (e.g., alcohol involvement) is predicted by alcohol involvement at the immediately preceding measurement occasion and an error in equations component (e.g., u, v, w) to represent unaccounted-for variation. The β_n corresponds to parameter estimates (regression coefficients) of the independent (LVs) on the respective (latent) dependent variables. The structural model specifies that the scores of the LV at $t + 1$ are adequately accounted for by the score variation at t. For example, this model suggests that score variation in alcohol involvement at Time 3 is adequate to account for variation in alcohol involvement at Time 4; variation in alcohol involvement at Times 1 and 2 are thus proposed to be statistically trivial with regard to their direct influences on alcohol involvement at Time 4 (i.e., direct-path coefficients may be fixed to zero).

Table 1 shows the goodness-of-fit indexes for the alternative models specified to account for the observed variance–covariance matrix. The independence, or null, model is not a true "substantive" model; rather, it serves as a baseline model that is used for comparative purposes. The independence model is specified so that it implies that all covariances (or correlations) among the manifest indicators may be fixed to zero. Not surprisingly, the hypothesis tested by the independence model specification was rejected for these data. A more substantively meaningful hypothesis was tested with reference to the second model specified, referred to as a first-order autoregressive model without correlated errors. For this model, the measurement model was specified so that the three variables of alcohol use, heavy drinking, and alcohol problems at each wave were manifest

TABLE 1
Goodness-of-Fit Information for Alternative Models of the Stability of
Alcohol Involvement for Adolescents ($n = 761$)

Model specification	χ^2	df	Normed fit index	Comparative fit index
Independence (or null) model	6,611.61	66	—	—
First-order autoregressive structure without correlated errors	995.68	57	.85	.86
First-order autoregressive structure with correlated errors	537.18	48	.92	.93
Model comparison				
Models 2 and 3	458.50	9	—	—

Note. Nested model comparisons indicate that the hypothesis of no difference in fit between the two models must be rejected ($p < .001$).

indicators of the LV of alcohol involvement at the respective waves; thus, the 12 manifest variables were used as indicators of four LVs. To establish a common metric for the four LVs, I specified equality constraints for the respective factor loadings for respective manifest indicators at each wave of measurement[2] (e.g., the factor loadings of alcohol use on alcohol involvement were constrained to equivalence for each of the four waves; see Byrne, Shavelson, & Muthén, 1989, for a useful discussion of equality constraints and their substantive significance).

The first-order autoregressive model included three structural regression coefficients corresponding to Time 4 alcohol involvement being regressed on Time 3 alcohol involvement, Time 3 alcohol involvement being regressed on Time 2 alcohol involvement, and Time 2 alcohol involvement being regressed on Time 1 alcohol involvement. Errors of measurement were freely estimated for each of the 12 manifest indicators, thus providing latent variables corrected for measurement to enhance the precision of parameter estimates corresponding to the autoregressive (i.e., rank-order, stability) structure of the specified model. Note that this model did not specify that errors of measurement were correlated across time. The exclusion of freely estimated correlated errors for the same manifest variables across time (e.g., errors for alcohol use at Time 1 and Time 2) may yield a more parsimonious model (i.e., fewer parameters estimated) but also may not be plausible for the observed data and may indeed contribute to bias in the parameters estimated. The failure to freely estimate correlated errors for the same measures across time may confound the stability of constructs

[2]Specific statistical tests for each equality constraint using a probability level of .01 indicated that the hypothesis of equivalence (or invariance) was rejected for one constraint; sensitivity analysis (see Byrne, Shavelson, & Muthén, 1989) indicated that retaining this equality constraint did not significantly alter other parameter estimates or model fit statistics.

across time with the stability of systematic components of measurement error (e.g., method variance associated with response sets).

The goodness-of-fit indexes for Model 2 indicate that (a) this model demonstrates a substantial improvement in fit relative to the independence model and (b) there appears to be some misfit for the model in that the fit indexes are below the preferred .90 level or higher. A plausible source of misfit might have been the failure to freely estimate parameters corresponding to correlated errors for the same manifest variables across time. Model 3 included the first-order autoregressive structure of Model 2, plus the estimation of nine parameters corresponding to correlated errors for the same manifest variables across time. The goodness-of-fit statistics (see Table 1) indicated that Model 3 provided a plausible representation of the alcohol involvement change process via the first-order autoregressive structure model specification (i.e., fit indexes exceeded .90). Furthermore, because Model 2 was nested within Model 3, chi-square difference tests could be conducted to evaluate the relative efficacy of the two models (see Hu & Bentler, 1995, for a further discussion of model comparisons and model fit statistics). This was accomplished by subtracting the chi-square values from the two models (995.68 − 537.18 = 458.50), subtracting the degrees of freedom for the two models (57 − 48 = 9), and examining for statistical significance the difference chi-square statistic and degrees of freedom using a chi-square probability distribution. A chi-square value of 458.50 with 9 degrees of freedom yielded a probability level less than .001. Thus, the hypothesis that Model 2 would account for the data as well as Model 3 had to be rejected; Model 3 was a more plausible model.

The findings for the first-order autoregressive model with correlated errors are shown in Figure 1. This figure indicates that seven of the nine correlated errors were statistically significant and that the first-order (i.e., $t - 1$) representation yielded stability coefficients that were statistically significant ($p < .001$), of high magnitude, and nearly uniform for contiguous waves. A comparison of these (measurement error) corrected LVs with the Pearson product−moment correlations associated with the test−retest correlations of the manifest indicators indicated a substantial increase (the Pearson correlations averaged about .6). Hence, using the autoregressive structure model with LVs increased the precision of measurement for the rank-order stability of alcohol involvement. An estimate of the proportion of variance accounted for in the structural equations was obtained by squaring the designated regression residuals (the Ds) and subtracting this quantity from 1.0 (e.g., $D4 = .60^2 = .36$; $1 - .36 = .74$); therefore, 74% of the variance of alcohol involvement at Time 4 was accounted for in this specified model. Therefore, on the basis of these model comparisons, it may be concluded that a first-order autoregressive structure model with correlated errors adequately reproduces the observed variance−covariance matrix.

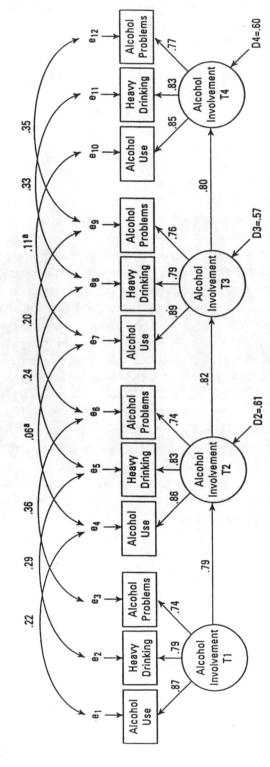

Figure 1. First-order autoregressive model with correlated errors for same manifest indicators at each successive measurement occasion. Standardized solution, $\chi^2(48, N = 761) = 537.18$, normed fit index = .92. T1 = Time 1; T2 = Time 2; T3 = Time 3; T4 = Time 4. [a]Parameters not statistically significant at the .05 level; all other parameters statistically significant at the .001 level.

The substantive findings indicate high levels of rank-order stability across the four waves of assessment for alcohol involvement.

LATENT GROWTH CURVE MODEL

The autoregressive model presented previously focused on the stability of individual differences (or rank ordering) for adolescent alcohol involvement across time using data from the variance–covariance matrix. Such models do not directly incorporate information pertinent to mean levels or intercepts and thus do not address research questions such as the following: Does the (latent) mean level of adolescent alcohol involvement change (e.g., increase or decrease) across time? If so, what shape or functional form (e.g., straight line or quadratic) is indicated? Latent growth models (LGMs) provide a useful approach to address such research questions (e.g., Browne & Arminger, 1995; McArdle, 1988; Meredith & Tisak, 1990; Willett & Sayer, 1994). LGMs are particularly useful when the variable or behavior under investigation manifests a reasonably systematic trend across time for each participant but in which there may be individual variability in initial level, rate of change, or final level. This suggests that LGMs may be useful in a number of applications in alcohol studies that focus on the developmental course of intraindividual differences. Such applications could include phenomena such as changes in drinking behaviors across time or the evaluation of intraindividual change trajectories in drinking behaviors for children and adolescents exposed to different preventive interventions. Note, however, that if the behavior under investigation is not related systematically across time or, more specifically, to the time intervals assessed in a given study, LGMs will not necessarily provide an optimal methodology for assessing a range of research questions.

LGMs are appropriate for use with repeated measures data that are time structured or "balanced on time" (Ware, 1985), such as when the number and spacing of intervals of assessment are equal across participants (see Bryk & Raudenbush, 1987, for methods of addressing longitudinal data when these restrictive criteria are relaxed). Furthermore, LGMs are most usefully applied when data are collected on at least three waves of measurement, preferably more waves. Two-wave LGMs may be specified and estimated, but constraints are imposed on tests of the shape of growth (e.g., a quadratic parameter may not be estimated in the standard linear, polynomial model specification), and often unrealistic assumptions need to be imposed on the model (e.g., fixing error variances to zero) to achieve model identification.[3] Importantly, LGMs assume that the variable or behavior

---

[3]It is beyond the scope of this chapter to discuss inherently nonlinear growth models (i.e., models that are nonlinear with regard to parameters).

under investigation changes systematically with time; the rate and shape of this change (growth) may be estimated via the specification and estimation of LGMs.

The basic LGM may be represented by the following notation:

$$y = \Lambda z + u,$$

where y is the $p \times 1$ vector of repeated measures at equal intervals, Λ is the $p \times m$ parameter matrix of sequential values of the proposed growth curve, z is the unobserved weights of the curve, and u is the measurement error. If one allows $E(z) = \zeta$, $\text{cov}(z, z') = \phi$, $\text{cov}(u, u') = \Psi$, and $\text{cov}(z, u') = 0$, then the mean and covariance structures for y are

$$\mu = E(y) = \Lambda \zeta$$

$$\text{cov}(y, y') = \Lambda \Phi \Lambda' + \psi.$$

Although this model appears to be similar to that derived previously for the measurement (factor-analytic) model, it differs in that for the LGM, μ is generated for the mean vector, and the elements of Λ are viewed as values characterizing a smooth (linear or nonlinear) trend (for a more detailed discussion, see Browne & Arminger, 1995).

In the subsequent illustration, the emphasis is on the mean structure, and the covariance structure is largely ignored (see Aiken, Stein, & Bentler, 1994, for a treatment outcome application of a mean and covariance structure model, and Willett & Sayer, 1996, for a more general discussion). Also, the focus is on the repeated assessment of one variable—alcohol use—rather than the multiple indicator approach used in the autoregressive covariance structure model. This was done to simplify the presentation; there are several ways of modeling latent growth curves for multiple variables and multiple indicator–latent variables simultaneously (see, e.g., McArdle, 1988; Willett & Sayer, 1996).

Four-wave data for male adolescent alcohol use were used to demonstrate an application of the LGM. Figure 2 shows a two-factor LGM for the four-wave alcohol use data. The first factor (F1) refers to the estimated intercept factor for alcohol use, corresponding to sample information about the mean (M) and variance (D) of the collection of individual intercepts that are estimated to describe each person's growth curve.[4] The second factor (F2) refers to the estimated slope factor for alcohol use, representing the sample information about the average slope parameter (M) and its

---

[4]The symbols M and D are used to refer to mean and variance terms, respectively, consistent with the terminology used in the EQS program that was used for these analyses. Other symbols could have been used for this purpose.

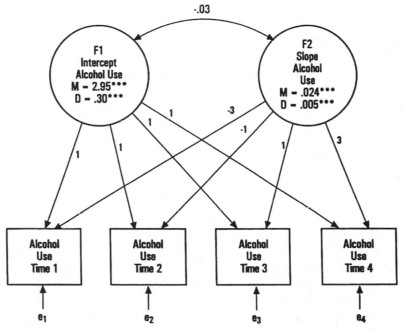

Figure 2. Two-factor latent growth model for boys' alcohol use for four waves of measurement. F1 = Factor 1; F2 = Factor 2; M = mean; D = variance; e_i = measurement error associated with the imperfect measurement of the observed score for each variable.

variance (D) that are estimated from the data. The model was specified so that the intercept served as the starting point (i.e., initial status) for any change (growth) in alcohol use across time; therefore, factor loadings were fixed to 1.0 for F1. Orthogonal polynomial coefficients were used to fix the factor loadings for the slope parameters (F2). The factor loadings for F2 (the slope factor) establish the time metric for the function to be evaluated and may be fixed, as in the current application, or freely estimated (with only one or more parameters fixed to identify the shape factor).[5]

The goodness-of-fit indexes supported the adequacy of the hypothesized model, $\chi^2(5, N = 387) = 11.54$, $p > .05$, normed fit index [NFI] = .98, comparative fit index [CFI] = .99. The findings for the specified model indicated that there were significant initial differences in alcohol use and significant individual differences in the rate of change (growth) for alcohol use across the four waves of measurement. If the parameters estimated for F1 (i.e., M and D) were nonsignificant, this would have indicated that the sample did not differ significantly with regard to their estimated initial levels of alcohol use (i.e., all boys drank approximately the same amount);

[5]Although in some applications it may be preferable to freely estimate the factor loadings for the shape factor, the fixed coefficient approach simplifies the presentation, and the polynomial model used often provides a reasonable approximation to the data (e.g., Burchinal & Appelbaum, 1991).

this hypothesis was rejected. If the parameters estimated for F2 (M and D) were nonsignificant, this would have indicated that the sample did not change systematically via a linear functional form across the four waves of measurement; this hypothesis also was rejected because there was a significant general trend toward an increase in alcohol use across time. An additional parameter, corresponding to the correlation between F1 and F2, also was estimated. This parameter is often of substantive significance in LGMs because it assesses whether initial status (F1) is correlated with the rate of change (F2). For example, the rate of change of adolescents just beginning to use alcohol at Wave 1 may actually be greater than the rate of change of adolescents who are already at high levels of alcohol use at Wave 1 (this would produce a significant negative correlation between F1 and F2). Alternatively, if the adolescents already drinking at high levels at Wave 1 increased their rate of drinking across time more rapidly than adolescents drinking at low levels at Wave 1, a positive correlation between F1 and F2 would be indicated. In this application, the F1–F2 correlation was not statistically significant. Thus, initial differences in alcohol use among these male adolescents was not significantly related to their rate of change in alcohol use across four waves of measurement spanning the 2-year interval.

In addition to evaluating hypotheses about differences in initial levels of an attribute (e.g., alcohol use) and intraindividual variability in the rate of growth, predictors also may be specified in LGMs to account for the variation in these growth parameters. Figure 3 shows three exogenous (i.e., independent) variables (i.e., childhood conduct disorder symptoms, percentage of drinking friends at Time 2, and the difference in the percentage of drinking friends between Time 2 and Time 4) as predictors of F1 and F2. Childhood conduct disorder symptoms were measured using the summation of seven items (e.g., often involved in fist fights, had problems with stealing) characterizing the adolescents' behavior before the age of 12 (see Windle, 1993, for a more in-depth description of this measure). The percentage of friends drinking was obtained by initially requesting adolescents to indicate how many close friends they had and then asking them to indicate how many of these close friends drank alcohol. The number of close friends drinking then was divided by the total number of close friends, and the resulting dividend was multiplied by 100 (scores therefore ranged from 0% to 100%). The percentage of friends drinking was assessed only at Time 2 and Time 4.

It would have been preferable in this application to have measured the percentage of friends drinking at Time 1, but for purposes of this illustration, I proceed with the initial assessment point at Time 2. A time-varying covariate (predictor) was created by subtracting the percentage of drinking friends at Time 2 from the percentage of drinking friends at Time 4. In essence, this allowed me to test the hypothesis that increases in the

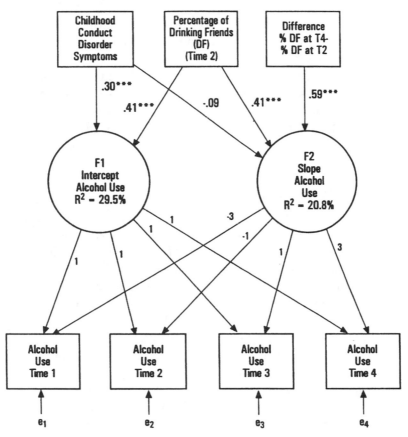

Figure 3. Two-factor latent growth model for boys' alcohol use with three predictors. F1 = Factor 1; F2 = Factor 2; T2 = Time 2; T4 = Time 4; e_i = measurement error associated with the imperfect measurement of the observed score for each variable.

percentage of drinking friends across time would significantly predict a greater increase (or acceleration) in alcohol use across time. The use of time-varying predictors, relative to more frequently used time-invariant predictors (e.g., childhood conduct disorder symptoms), facilitated the evaluation of more dynamic processes unfolding over time.

The findings for this model indicated an adequate global model fit, $\chi^2(12, N = 387) = 57.01$, NFI = .95, CFI = .96. Statistically significant predictors of individual variation in initial levels of alcohol use were higher levels of childhood conduct disorder symptoms and a higher percentage of drinking friends (the difference variable was not used as a predictor of F1).[6] These predictors accounted for 29.5% of the variance in the initial levels of alcohol use among the boys in this sample. Statistically significant pre-

---

[6]Note that in practice, one would not use a Time 2 predictor to predict a Time 1 variable; its purpose here is simply to illustrate how one specifies predictors in a latent growth model.

dictors of variation in intraindividual growth trajectories were the percentage of drinking friends at Time 2 and increases in the percentage of drinking friends across the 1-year interval from Time 2 to Time 4. Hence, the percentage of drinking friends at Time 2 functioned as a distal predictor of accelerated rates of alcohol use among boys, and the difference score functioned as a more dynamic predictor suggesting that increases in the percentage of drinking friends across time predicts a greater acceleration in the growth of alcohol use across time. The impact of childhood conduct disorder symptoms was limited to individual variation in initial levels of alcohol use, but it was not a significant predictor of a more accelerated pattern of growth. It is plausible that the impact of these childhood conduct disorder symptoms influenced an earlier onset of alcohol use and higher initial levels, but it did not influence accelerated growth across the interval measured in this study. The predictors accounted for 20.8% of the variation in the intraindividual growth trajectories.

This relatively straightforward example of adolescent alcohol use illustrates the potential usefulness of LGMs to address a range of issues associated with the study of change (growth). In this example, I evaluated an LGM; however, it is possible within LGMs to model higher order polynomial models (e.g., quadratic, cubic) within the constraints of the number of time points in the research design. Furthermore, additional time-invariant and time-covarying predictors could be specified, and such exogenous variables may include multiple indicator–latent variables. It also is possible to conduct simultaneous group LGMs to evaluate, for instance, differences in the growth of alcohol use for different preventive intervention samples. Although the development of the statistical basis for latent growth curve models is not new (for reviews, see Burchinal & Appelbaum, 1991; McArdle & Epstein, 1987; Stoolmiller, 1995), the somewhat more widespread application in the behavioral sciences has been a recent phenomenon (e.g., Duncan et al., 1994; Stoolmiller, Duncan, Bank, & Patterson, 1993), precipitated in part by the ease of application via standard covariance structure modeling programs such as EQS (Bentler, 1989) and LISREL (Jöreskog & Sörbom, 1993). LGMs are likely to be of increasing usefulness in future research as investigators further pursue questions about the complex, dynamic (time-patterned) relations that characterize behaviors such as alcohol and substance use and abuse.

LATENT TRAIT–STATE MODEL

A relatively recent development in covariance structure modeling has been the development of longitudinal models referred to as *latent trait–state models* (LTSMs; e.g., Dumenci & Windle, 1996; Kenny & Zautra, 1995; Steyer & Schmitt, 1994). LTSMs provide an alternative method of using longitudinal covariance structure data to evaluate issues of relevance to the dynamics of human behavior. Similar to autoregressive covariance structure models, a covariance matrix of items or manifest indicators is used in the specification and evaluation of an LTSM. However, whereas an autoregressive covariance structure model is used to investigate the (rank-order) stability of a repeatedly measured LV (correcting for measurement error and including correlated residuals), LTSMs are designed to decompose the covariance relations of a repeatedly measured latent (or manifest) variable into four components: general trait, state, specific trait, and random error.

General trait components refer to enduring characteristics that presumably manifest a relatively high degree of coherence, or stability, across a given interval of assessment, whereas *state* components refer to changing (dynamic) characteristics that may manifest systematic (reliable) relations at any single time point (e.g., at Time 1 or at Time 2) but are not stable across time points. *Specific trait* (or method) components refer to manifest-indicator-specific sources of covariation across occasions of measurement that are not captured either by the general trait or the state components, yet they are reliably measured and distinct from the *random-error* component. The subsequent example in this section is used to clarify the components and their measurement in the LTSM. The measurement and evaluation of trait and state components have long been of interest to researchers who have identified a range of mood variables (e.g., depression, anxiety), physiological variables (e.g., blood pressure, electrical brain activity), personality constructs, and personal values (e.g., Nesselroade, 1987; Zevon & Tellegen, 1982) characterized by trait and state components.

Steyer and his colleagues (e.g., Steyer, Majcen, Schwenkmerzger, & Buchner, 1989; Steyer & Schmitt, 1994) used covariance structure modeling to simultaneously estimate and obtain reliable estimates of trait, state, and method (or trait-specific) components for the repeated measurement of continuous variables. The basic equation for the decomposition of effects in this LTSM model is

$$\text{var}(Y_{ij}) = \lambda_{ij}^2\gamma_j^2 \text{ var}(\xi) + \lambda_{ij}^2\text{var}(\zeta_j) + \kappa_{ij}^2\text{var}(\xi_i) + \text{var}(\varepsilon_{ij}),$$

where the first term (i.e., $\lambda_{ij}^2\gamma_j^2$ var[ξ]) refers to stable (traitlike) individual differences in the measured variable across time; the second term refers to unstable (statelike) features of the measured variable over time and the Person × (Testing) Situation interaction; the third term refers to stable individual differences specific to the method of assessment (e.g., systematic response biases); and the fourth term refers to unsystematic variation in var(ε_{ij}), or the random-error component.

Figure 4 illustrates the parameterization of the LTSM model for the level of alcohol involvement measured at four waves. As in previous mod-

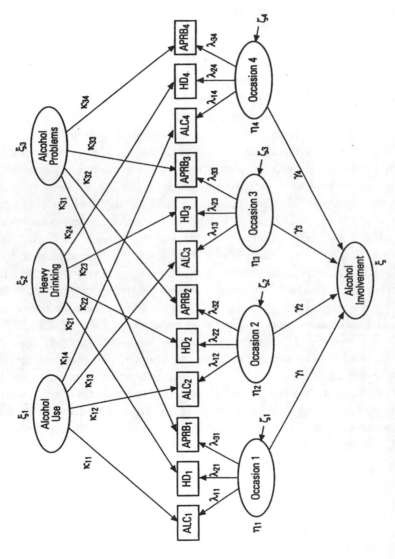

Figure 4. Latent trait–state method model of adolescent alcohol involvement for four waves of measurement. ALC = alcohol use; HD = heavy drinking; APRB = alcohol problems.

els, the 12 × 12 variance–covariance matrix (alcohol use, heavy drinking, and alcohol problems at each of four waves) was used as the input matrix. The LTSM model was parameterized as follows: the lambdas (λ_{ij}^2), kappas (κ_{ij}^2), and gammas (γ_j^2) refer to factor loadings associated with zetas (ζ_i; the occasion factors), ksis (ξ_i; the method factors), and ksi (ξ; the second-order "trait" alcohol involvement factor), respectively. The zetas (ζ_j) refer to the occasion factor disturbances, and the epsilons (ε_{ij}) are the error variances associated with the ith observed variables measured at the jth occasions.

A broad range of alternative, nested models may be evaluated using the LTSM approach (e.g., a latent state model, a general method model) to assess the adequacy of more parsimonious (i.e., simplified) models to account for the observed data (for details, see Dumenci & Windle, 1996). It also is possible to impose various equality constraints on parameters estimated (e.g., the equivalence of factor loadings $\lambda_{ij} = \lambda_{i.}$) to assess hypotheses about factor invariance and assumptions underlying measurement models (e.g., parallel measures). Finally, it is possible to obtain an overall estimate of the multivariate reliability of the measure and the decomposition of effects into the components of common trait (consistency), occasion specificity (state), method (or specific trait) specificity, and random error. For the variance–covariance data modeled in this application (see Figure 4), the multivariate reliability was .73, with the percentages of variance accounted for by general trait, state, and specific trait being 41%, 18%, and 14%, respectively (random error accounted for the remaining 27% of the variance), $\chi^2(48, N = 761) = 146.27$, CFI = .985.

Substantively, this model indicated that alcohol involvement was reliably measured by the 12 indicators used. The decomposition of effects indicated that the largest portion of systematic covariation was accounted for by a stable, general trait component of alcohol involvement. However, similar to previous research that has investigated trait and state components (e.g., Nesselroade, 1987), there also was a substantial, reliable state component of alcohol involvement that reflected systematic covariation within (but not across) occasions of measurement. The idea that alcohol involvement across adolescence involves both a relatively stable general component and a fluctuating state component provides an alternative perspective to "either–or" orientations that have often been proffered. From the latent trait–state perspective, in the aggregate, these data suggest that alcohol involvement manifests some degree of stability across the four waves of measurement but that systematic (reliable) variation in alcohol involvement occurs at each wave of measurement. The presumed causes of such state (occasion) fluctuations may be multiple (e.g., family conflict during one time period but not another, involvement with more deviant peers at one time period but not another).

The generalizability of these substantive findings regarding general trait and state components of alcohol involvement across other adolescent populations (e.g., other ethnic groups, treatment samples) or other portions of the life span remains to be investigated. On the basis of previous research (e.g., Fillmore, 1987), one might hypothesize high but nearly comparable levels of general trait and state components for alcohol involvement throughout young adulthood, but a shift toward relatively higher levels of general trait (vs. state) components during later adulthood, when drinking behavior presumably stabilizes. Similarly, if one were to study the stability and change of daily mood states (e.g., depression, anxiety) across the initial 2 weeks of alcoholic treatment (subsequent to detoxification), there may be nearly comparable levels of trait and state components of negative affect; however (assuming abstinence), the subsequent 2 weeks may reveal a higher ratio of trait-to-state components. The development of the LTSM is in its early stages and has yet to be systematically applied in substance use studies. Nevertheless, for many research questions concerned with distinguishing between reliable trait and state components (e.g., fluctuations in daily mood states associated with pharmacological treatments among alcoholic patients), the LTSM may prove useful.

Summary

Three alternative LV approaches to modeling stability and change in alcohol and substance use with continuous variables were described and illustrated in terms of adolescent alcohol use. The first-order autoregressive covariance structure model provided an evaluation of the rank-order, test–retest stability of a latent construct over time. By using a multiple-indicator approach to assess the repeatedly measured LV alcohol involvement, the resulting (test–retest) stability coefficients were corrected for measurement error. Furthermore, by the estimation of correlated errors among repeatedly measured manifest indicators, parameter bias for the stability coefficients was reduced, and overall model fit was significantly improved. The latent growth curve model focused on the evaluation of (latent) mean-level changes across time and on time-invariant and time-covarying predictors of such changes. Analytically, a primary difference between the autoregressive covariance structure approach and the latent growth curve approach is that the former uses data from the variance–covariance matrix (largely ignoring data on mean levels and intercepts), and the latter uses data from the mean levels (largely ignoring the variance–covariance data in some applications, although this is not intrinsic to the approach).

Substantively, the autoregressive covariance structure approach provides a method to assess the relative rank ordering of individuals across occasions of measurement, whereas the latent growth curve modeling approach provides a method of evaluating and characterizing variability in intraindividual growth (change) trajectories in mean levels across time.

The latent trait–state model provided yet a third approach to evaluating issues relevant to the stability and change of behavior. This approach seeks to decompose the repeatedly measured variance–covariance data into constituents representing general trait, state, specific trait (or method), and random-error components. The statistical modeling of these three approaches to evaluate issues of stability and change may be implemented with commercially available structural equations modeling programs such as LISREL, EQS, AMOS, and SEPATH (for reviews of these programs, see Byrne, 1995, and Hox, 1995).

DISCRETE TIME LATENT MARKOV MODELS

In many research applications, the repeatedly measured variable investigated consists of discrete categories (e.g., a participant does or does not have an alcohol disorder). The analysis of such repeated measures categorical data is spawning a new generation of statistical models designed to accommodate the longitudinal modeling and estimation of multiway contingency tables (e.g., Andersen, 1980; Hagenaars, 1990). In this chapter, the focus is on one particular categorical modeling approach: Markov chain modeling (e.g., Langeheine & Van de Pol, 1990; Meiser & Ohrt, 1996).[7] A Markov process suggests that the dependence between an outcome at trial $t + 1$ may be modeled directly as a function only of trial t. That is, only the previous state occupied by the generating process is relevant in determining its future behavior (Howard, 1971). As such, an outcome at trial $t + 4$ may be modeled directly as a function of trial $t + 3$ only (hence, trials $t + 2$, $t + 1$, and t are not necessary to predict the behavior at $t + 4$). In Markov chain modeling, the repeatedly measured categorical manifest variables are specified as indicators of a categorical LV. Thus, similar to LV modeling using covariance structure analysis, there are manifest indicators and a presumed LV. However, whereas continuous variables are used in covariance structure modeling to measure a unitary, underlying continuous LV, categorical variables are used in the Markov chain models (presented in this chapter) to measure discrete underlying classes or types. That is, Markov chain models partition (or classify) the total population into a set of mutually exclusive and jointly exhaustive latent subpopulations.

Recent advances in Markov chain modeling have included attempts to provide a more encompassing framework for testing a range of alternative models, incorporating more computationally tractable estimation procedures, and delineating an error of measurement conceptualization for

---

[7]In this chapter the focus is on Markov chains with discrete state space defined as (X_n, $n = 0$, 1, 2, . . .). Markov chains with continuous state spaced defined as (X_n, $n = -\infty$, ∞) also may be used in some applications (for more information, see Guttorp, 1995, and Medhi, 1994).

the assessment of the proposed measurement model more clearly (e.g., Langeheine, 1988, 1994; Langeheine & Van de Pol, 1990). Furthermore, advances in the statistical modeling of Markov chain models have paralleled some advances in covariance structure models with regard to specifying constrained, or restricted, models (e.g., by using equality constraints and fixing parameters), evaluating alternative nested models via statistical criteria (e.g., chi-square differences test), and conducting simultaneous group analyses (e.g., testing the invariance of parameters across gender groups).

For the applications presented in this chapter, I used a 16-fold table that reflected the binary categorization of adolescents as either lighter or heavier drinkers at each of the four waves of measurement. For the Markov chain models, a two-category manifest variable of lighter drinker (less than 30 drinks in the past month) and heavier drinker (30 or more drinks in the past month) was created for each of the four occasions of measurement, thus yielding 16 response patterns (i.e., $2^4 = 16$). Adolescents who reported abstaining at all four time periods (i.e., no drinks during the past 6 months at all four measurement occasions) were excluded from the analyses. Abstainers were excluded for both substantive and practical purposes. Substantively, Heath, Meyer, Jardin, and Martin (1991) reported that the inheritance of abstinence differs from the inheritance of frequency and quantity dimensions of drinking (i.e., different genes are associated with abstinence versus drinking frequency and quantity), and thus a single liability dimension for the inheritance of alcohol consumption is inadequate. Practically, their inclusion would have greatly increased the number of response patterns (i.e., to $3^4 = 81$) and would have contributed to a number of zero or sparse cells. Given that the latent Markov models were principally designed to be illustrative, I thought it would be more prudent to use the two-category manifest variable.[8]

For the four-wave panel design used in this application, the latent Markov model may be represented by

$$\rho_{ijkl} = \sum_{abcd} \delta_a^1 \rho_{i|a}^1 \lambda_{b|a}^2 \,^1\rho_{j|b}^2 \lambda_{c|b}^3 \,^2\rho_{k|c}^3 \lambda_{d|c}^4 \,^3\rho_{l|d}^4,$$

where ρ_{ijkl} corresponds to the model expected proportion of cell $ijkl$ (i, j, k, and l are the categories of the discrete LV at the four waves of measurement). δ_a is the proportion for class a of the latent (marginal) distribution

---

[8]Approximately 15% of the adolescents reported being abstainers at all four waves. At any single wave, the percentage of abstainers ranged from 33.0% to 39.7%. Adolescents who reported alcohol use on at least one occasion of measurement were assigned to the lighter (or nonheavier) drinking group even if they abstained at one, two, or three occasions of measurement. A total of 667 adolescents (347 girls and 320 boys) with complete response data for variables used in these analyses comprised the effective sample.

at the first wave of measurement. The distribution represents the conditional probabilities $\rho_{i|a}^1$ for responding category i of the LV, given membership in latent class a; $\lambda_{b|a}^{2\,1}$ reflects latent transition probabilities denoting change (including no change) in group membership from Wave 1 to Wave 2. At Wave 2, the latent distribution is characterized by conditional response probabilities $\rho_{j|b}^2$, and $\lambda_{c|b}^{3\,2}$ reflects the latent transition probabilities denoting change in group membership from Wave 2 to Wave 3. The remaining parameters in the model may be similarly interpreted with regard to the latent distribution and the latent transition probabilities (see Langeheine, 1994, for elaborations to the multiple-indicator model and to "pathlike" diagrams for these categorical LVs).

Four separate models were specified and evaluated statistically for adequacy of fit. The adequacy of the specified models was evaluated in relation to how well the observed response patterns (or counts for response patterns) were accounted for by the implied model; thus, the objective was to minimize the discrepancies between observed and expected counts. The models varied in terms of alternative specifications regarding expectations for change across time and with regard to assumptions about errors of measurement. Findings for the four models (Models A–D) are summarized in Table 2.

TABLE 2
Observed and Expected Counts, Likelihood Ratio Test Statistics, and
Degrees of Freedom for Several Models

Time[a]				Observed counts	Expected counts for model[b]			
1	2	3	4		A	B	C	D
0	0	0	0	315	310.83	332.80	324.41	302.37
0	0	0	1	137	46.55	65.14	52.63	150.13
0	0	1	0	9	46.55	31.97	18.94	17.69
0	0	1	1	31	11.91	46.07	50.14	27.69
0	1	0	0	13	46.55	21.25	18.94	12.94
0	1	0	1	20	11.91	16.93	13.77	9.81
0	1	1	0	3	11.91	15.27	11.30	4.60
0	1	1	1	13	15.28	39.43	50.89	15.77
1	0	0	0	18	46.55	17.78	19.46	24.12
1	0	0	1	22	11.91	7.51	14.14	14.53
1	0	1	0	3	11.91	5.84	15.99	4.30
1	0	1	1	18	15.28	13.83	8.44	13.18
1	1	0	0	2	11.91	5.30	11.61	3.93
1	1	0	1	17	15.28	12.36	8.44	11.80
1	1	1	0	5	15.28	12.28	6.92	11.40
1	1	1	1	41	37.36	33.25	41.00	42.74
Likelihood ratio					292.30	164.58	209.52	31.46
*df*s					12	10	8	6

[a]Categories refer to lighter drinking (0) and heavier drinking (1).
[b]These models are A, two-class latent class model; B, two-class latent Markov model; C, two-chain mixed Markov model; and D, nonstationary two-class latent Markov model.

The Model A specification corresponded to a classical two-class latent class model in which all response probabilities were constrained equal within classes. The model thus assumes that (a) change is independent of the category a person belonged to at a previous time point and (b) the probability of classification (e.g., as a lighter drinker) is constant across time within classes. In essence, no latent change is posited for this model; thus it may serve as somewhat of a baseline model. That is, if this (no-change) model adequately accounts for the data, then alternative models estimating parameters corresponding to change would not appear to be necessary. The baseline model (Model A) did not provide an adequate fit for the data, $\chi^2(12, N = 667) = 292.30$, and the hypothesis of no latent change must be rejected.

The Model B specification was a latent Markov chain model, in which restrictions imposed on the classic two-class latent class model (i.e., in which the transition matrix is fixed to an identity matrix) were relaxed. The latent Markov chain model relaxes the assumption of no latent change across time and attempts to capture heterogeneity (change) via conditional response probabilities; however, homogeneity, or time stationarity, is assumed with regard to latent transitions (i.e., all transition rates must change over time in the same way). The findings for Model B suggest an improvement in fit over Model A, $\chi^2(2, N = 667) = 127.72$, $p < .001$. This suggests that parameters corresponding to change need to be incorporated into a model designed to account for the observed response patterns. Although Model B provided an improvement in fit relative to Model A, it did not provide an adequate statistical fit to the data, $\chi^2(10, N = 667) = 164.58$, $p < .001$.

Similar results were indicated for Model C, which was a two-chain mixed Markov model that assumed stationarity and tested the hypothesis that the observed response patterns were generated by a mixture of two Markov chains, each of which could be characterized by specific dynamics (Langeheine, 1994). However, unlike the latent Markov chain model, the mixed Markov model assumes that the data are free of measurement error. The model provided a significant improvement in fit relative to Model A, $\chi^2(4, N = 667) = 82.78$, $p < .001$, but did not provide an adequate fit to the data, $\chi^2(8, N = 667) = 209.52$, $p < .001$. The absence of modeling measurement error is likely to have contributed to the misfit.

The Model D specification was a two-class latent Markov model, but stationarity constraints were relaxed. Time-stationarity assumptions are met if all transition rates change over time in the same way. For example, for drinking behavior, stationarity implies that the probability that individuals who are in Class 1 (e.g., light drinkers) at Time 1 and change to Class 2 (e.g., heavier drinkers) at Time 2 will be equivalent to the probability of Time 2 light drinkers changing to Time 3 heavy drinkers and the probability of Time 3 light drinkers changing to Time 4 heavy drinkers. If any transition rates increase over time and others decrease, or if the rates of increase or decrease vary for different time segments, the stationarity assumption may be violated. Model D, which relaxed the stationarity assumption, provided a much improved fit to the data relative to Models A, B, or C, as evaluated by chi-square difference tests. Furthermore, an inspection of the observed and expected counts for Model D in Table 3 indicate only a few minor discrepancies of concern, and these occurred principally with more irregularly observed response patterns for a limited number of participants.

Parameter estimates for Model D are provided in Table 3. According to the model, 79.9% of the participants at Time 1 were in Class 1, which consisted primarily of lighter drinkers (96.2%). Class 2 consisted of 20.1% of the participants at Time 1 and had a mixture of lighter and heavier drinkers, although the latter group (heavier drinkers) was dominant (79.0%). The latent transition probabilities for the two classes for each contiguous wave of measurement provide information relevant to the stability and change of class membership across time. For example, in reference to the Time 1–Time 2 transition matrix, for Class 1 98.6% of the adolescents were stable (i.e., they were still members of Class 1 lighter drinkers), and only 1.4% were estimated to have made a transition to Class 2 (heavier drinkers). For Class 2, 81.5% of the adolescents were stable, and 18.5% were estimated to have made a transition to Class 1 lighter drinkers. Class 1 also demonstrated relatively high stability for the Time 2–Time 3 transition; however, there was considerably more change for Class 1 associated with the Time 3–Time 4 transition. For the Time 3–Time 4 transition, 61.9% of the adolescents were stable, but 38.1% were estimated to have made the transition to Class 2 (heavier drinkers). These findings illustrate why the stationary latent Markov model (Model B) that had been specified was rejected; transition rates were not time homogeneous but reflected a different transition rate between Time 3 and Time 4 relative to Time 1 and Time 2 or Time 2 and Time 3.

Table 4 shows the estimated proportions of stability and change for Models A, B, and D. An error of measurement interpretation was used by conceptualizing the modal response probabilities for each class as reliabilities and nonmodal response probabilities as error rates (e.g., Langeheine, 1988; Langeheine & Van de Pol, 1990).[9] The general findings across the three models were similar, indicating that although the stability of adolescent alcohol use was common among many users, change also characterized a substantial subgroup. Furthermore, the change was more strongly in the direction of increases in drinking, especially between Waves 3 and 4. This could be attributed to seasonal influences (e.g., testing was completed in late April) or to seniors beginning to celebrate before graduation.

---

[9]Note that Model C assumed that there was no error of measurement; therefore, the error of measurement approach used for Models A, B, and D was not used for this model.

TABLE 3

Estimated Parameter Values and Standard Errors for Nonstationary Two-Class Latent Markov Model D

	Class proportion		Response probabilities				Latent transition probabilities									
			Lighter		Heavier		Time 1–Time 2				Time 2–Time 3				Time 3–Time 4			
							Class 1		Class 2		Class 1		Class 2		Class 1		Class 2	
Class	PE	SE	PE	SE	PE	SE	PE	SE	PE	SE	PE	SE	PE	SE	PE	SE	PE	SE
1	.799	.025	.962	.009	.038	.009	.986	.016	.014	.016	.941	.017	.059	.017	.619	.032	.381	.032
2	.201	.025	.210	.031	.790	.031	.185	.071	.815	.071	.000	—	1.000	—	.000	—	1.000	—

Note. A parameter value of .000 or 1.000 indicates convergence to a boundary value. PE = parameter estimate.

TABLE 4
Estimated Proportions of Stability and Change in Models A, B, and D

	Model		
	A[a]	B[b]	D[b]
Stability		.723	.623
True stability	.521	.504	.457
Error	.479	.219	.166
Change		.277	.377

[a]Two-class, latent class model assumes no change.
[b]Results refer to an error of measurement interpretation of the classical latent class model.

Summary

Four alternative Markov chain models were specified and evaluated in terms of their adequacy to reproduce the 16-fold response pattern table corresponding to the four-wave, dichotomous indicator drinking variable (lighter vs. heavier drinkers). The "no-change" classical latent class model was rejected, indicating that change was indeed occurring. The stationary, two-class latent Markov model provided a better statistical fit than did the classical latent class model, but it still did not fit the data well; similar results were indicated for the two-chain mixed Markov model that assumed no measurement error. The nonstationary, two-class latent Markov model provided a substantial improvement in statistical fit relative to the other models (but not an ideal fit). Relaxing the stationarity assumption enhanced the fit of the model by not constraining transition rates to equivalence for each contiguous wave of measurement. The nonstationary, two-class latent Markov model indicated substantial stability of adolescent alcohol use across time as well as significant change, especially between Waves 3 and 4.

Markov chain models have been used frequently in a variety of fields (e.g., engineering, physics, biology), but they have been used much less in the behavioral sciences generally and alcohol and substance use studies specifically. Yet, as exemplified in the example on adolescent alcohol use, such models may be useful in analyzing issues relevant to the stability and change in drinking behavior with repeatedly measured categorical variables. The findings of the adolescent alcohol use example suggest that nonstationarity (or nonhomogeneous chains) characterizes the Markov chain process. Such nonhomogeneous chains have not been thoroughly studied in the Markov chain literature (e.g., Medhi, 1994), although such chains may characterize many dynamic, alcohol-related variables. There also have been some advances in the modeling of exogenous (independent) variables to predict key parameters (e.g., transition probabilities) of Markov chain models (e.g., Hamerle & Ronning, 1995). It thus appears that Markov chain models may provide an exciting and useful technology for addressing primary issues of stability and change with repeatedly measured categorical variables.

For the Markov chain model applications in this chapter, the PAN-MARK (PANel analysis using MARKov chains) program (Van de Pol, Langeheine, & De Jong, 1991) was used to evaluate alternative models of the stability and change of alcohol use for adolescents across the four waves of measurement. PANMARK is a menu-driven program that accommodates the specification and estimation of a wide range of mixed Markov latent class models. Maximum-likelihood estimates are provided using the EM algorithm, randomly selected alternative start values may be requested to avoid local maxima, and first-order derivatives of the log-likelihood toward each independent parameter may be requested, along with an identification test.

CONCLUSION

Several alternative LV approaches to the statistical modeling of longitudinal stability and change of adolescent alcohol involvement have been presented in this chapter. The first-order autoregressive covariance structure modeling approach with LVs was used to illustrate the "error-free" measurement of rank-order (test–retest) stability for the LV alcohol involvement. The first-order autoregressive model with correlated errors provided a plausible statistical fit for the observed data, and a high stability of individual differences in alcohol use behaviors was found across time. The latent growth curve model was used to estimate the linear growth for mean levels of boys' alcohol use across the four waves of measurement. The LGM indicated that there was significant individual variation in alcohol use regarding initial (Time 1) levels of use and significant variation in the linear intraindividual growth trajectories. The time-invariant predictors of childhood conduct disorder symptoms and the percentage of drinking friends significantly predicted variation in initial levels of use. The time-invariant predictor of percentage of drinking friends at Time 2 and the time-covarying predictor of increases in the percentage of drinking friends across Time 2 and Time 4 predicted variation in the linear growth (slope) of alcohol use across time. The LTSM indicated that adolescent alcohol involvement consisted of both reliable trait components and reliable state components; thus, alcohol use among adolescents could not be categorically described as either highly stable or unstable but as reflecting a more dynamic process characterized by both stable and changing components.

Four alternative models were specified and evaluated using Markov chain modeling. A no-change classical two-latent-class model was rejected, as were two other models: one that specified time stationarity and one that attempted to account for response pattern heterogeneity via additional Markov chains. A nonstationary, two-class latent Markov model provided the most adequate fit for the data. Transition rates were not estimated to be constant across time; rather, they were freely estimated for contiguous measurement occasions. The latent transition probabilities indicated substantially greater rates of change for Class 1 (lighter drinkers) to Class 2 (heavier drinkers) during the Time 3–Time 4 transition than the Time 1–Time 2 or Time 2–Time 3 transitions. Overall, this model indicated substantial stability of adolescent alcohol use across time for the two subpopulations as well as considerable change, most often in the direction of movement toward heavier drinking.

From the perspective of alternative LV approaches to the stability and change of alcohol and substance use behaviors, it is evident that each of these approaches is relevant for addressing specific research hypotheses. If the principal research question is focused on the rank-order stability of individual differences across time (independent of the dynamics of mean-level changes), an autoregressive covariance structure model with LVs (and correlated error terms) may be suitable and certainly would be preferable to standard test–retest Pearson correlations. If the principal research question is focused on changes in mean levels across time and on predictors of such changes, then latent growth curve models may be more suitable. If the principal research question is focused on the partitioning, or decomposition, of covariance relations into constituent elements of general trait, state, specific trait (or method), and random-error components, then the latent trait–state model may be more suitable. Finally, with repeatedly measured categorical variables, latent Markov models provide a useful approach to assess stability and change via transition probabilities across contiguous waves of assessment. As noted at the beginning of this chapter, these four alternative LV approaches are not exhaustive of the current armamentarium of statistical models to evaluate changes in behavior, but they do represent a few promising approaches that may be of value to alcohol and substance use researchers.

Although the applications in this chapter pertained to adolescent alcohol involvement, mean- and covariance-structure and Markov chain modeling may be used in cognate fields of prevention studies (e.g., substance use, mental health, education) to study change phenomena and predictors of such changes. Statistical models such as those presented in this chapter may be used to address more adequately many pertinent research questions in prevention studies relevant to change associated with natural history development, prevention, and treatment outcome. As was illustrated in this chapter, longitudinal statistical models exist for continuous and categorical variables. Future research may benefit by using more than one of the approaches described in this chapter to characterize different aspects of the dynamic change processes that appear to be endemic to much of the behavioral phenomena under investigtion.

REFERENCES

Aiken, L. S., Stein, J. A., & Bentler, P. M. (1994). Structural equation analyses of clinical subpopulation differences and comparative treatment outcomes: Characterizing the daily lives of drug addicts. *Journal of Consulting and Clinical Psychology, 62,* 488–499.

Andersen, E. B. (1980). *Discrete statistical models with social science applications.* Amsterdam: North-Holland.

Armor, D. J., & Polich, J. M. (1982). Measurement of alcohol consumption. In E. M. Pattison & E. Kaufman (Eds.), *Encyclopedic handbook of alcoholism* (pp. 72–81). New York: Gardner Press.

Bentler, P. M. (1980). Multivariate analysis with latent variables: Causal modeling. *Annual Review of Psychology, 31,* 419–456.

Bentler, P. M. (1989). *Theory and implementation of EQS, a structural equations program.* Los Angeles: BMDP Statistical Software.

Bollen, K. A. (1989). *Structural equations with latent variables.* New York: Wiley.

Browne, M. W., & Arminger, G. (1995). Specification and estimation of mean- and covariance-structure models. In G. Arminger, C. C. Clogg, & M. E. Sobel (Eds.), *Handbook of statistical modeling for the social and behavioral sciences* (pp. 185–249). New York: Plenum.

Bryk, A. S., & Raudenbush, S. W. (1987). Application of hierarchical linear models to assessing change. *Psychological Bulletin, 10,* 147–158.

Burchinal, M., & Appelbaum, M. I. (1991). Estimating individual developmental functions: Methods and their assumptions. *Child Development, 62,* 23–43.

Byrne, B. M. (1995). One application of structural equation modeling from two perspectives: Exploring the EQS and LISREL strategies. In R. H. Hoyle (Ed.), *Structural equation modeling: Concepts, issues, and applications* (pp. 138–157). Thousand Oaks, CA: Sage.

Byrne, B. M., Shavelson, R. J., & Muthén, B. (1989). Testing for the equivalence of factor covariance and mean structures: The issue of partial measurement invariance. *Psychological Bulletin, 105,* 456–466.

Collins, L. M., & Horn, J. L. (Eds.). (1991). *Best methods for the analysis of change: Recent advances, unanswered questions, future directions.* Washington, DC: American Psychological Association.

Dumenci, L., & Windle, M. (1996). A latent trait–state model of adolescent depression using the Center for Epidemiologic Studies—Depression Scale. *Multivariate Behavioral Research, 31,* 313–330.

Duncan, T. E., Duncan, S. C., & Hops, H. (1994). The effects of family cohesiveness and peer encouragement on the development of adolescent alcohol use: A cohort-sequential approach to the analysis of longitudinal data. *Journal of Studies on Alcohol, 55,* 588–599.

Dwyer, J. H. (1983). *Statistical models for the social and behavioral sciences.* New York: Oxford University Press.

Dwyer, J. H., Feinleib, M., Lippert, P., & Huffmeister, H. (Eds.). (1992). *Statistical models for longitudinal studies of health.* New York: Oxford University Press.

Ellickson, P. L., & Bell, R. M. (1990). Drug prevention in junior high: A multisite longitudinal test. *Science, 247,* 1299–1305.

Elliott, D. S., Huizinga, D., & Menard, S. (1989). *Multiple problem youth: Delinquency, substance use, and mental health problems.* New York: Springer-Verlag.

Fillmore, K. M. (1987). Women's drinking across the adult life course as compared to men's. *British Journal of the Addictions, 82,* 801–810.

Gibbons, R. D., Hedeker, D., Waternaux, C. M., & Davis, J. M. (1988). Random regression models: A comprehensive approach to the analysis of longitudinal psychiatric data. *Psychopharmacology Bulletin, 24,* 438–443.

Glantz, M., & Pickens, R. (Eds.). (1992). *Vulnerability to drug abuse.* Washington, DC: American Psychological Association.

Guttorp, P. (1995). *Stochastic modeling of scientific data.* London: Chapman & Hall.

Hagenaars, J. A. (1990). *Categorical longitudinal data: Log-linear panel, trend, and cohort analysis.* Newbury Park, CA: Sage.

Hamerle, A., & Ronning, G. (1995). Panel analysis for qualitative variables. In G. Arminger, C. C. Clogg, & M. E. Sobel (Eds.), *Handbook of statistical modeling for the social and behavioral sciences* (pp. 401–451). New York: Plenum.

Harris, C. W. (Ed.). (1963). *Problems in measuring change.* Madison: University of Wisconsin Press.

Heath, A. C., Meyer, J., Jardin, R., & Martin, N. G. (1991). The inheritance of alcohol consumption patterns in a general population twin sample: II. Determinants of consumption frequency and quantity consumed. *Journal of Studies on Alcohol, 52,* 425–433.

Hilton, M. E. (1987). Changes in American drinking patterns and problems, 1967–1984. *Journal of Studies on Alcohol, 48,* 515–522.

Hinde, R. A., & Dennis, A. (1986). Categorizing individuals. *International Journal of Behavioral Development, 99,* 105–119.

Holder, H. D., & Howard, J. M. (Eds.). (1992). *Community prevention trials for alcohol problems.* Westport, CT: Praeger.

Howard, R. A. (1971). *Dynamic probabilistic systems: Vol. 1. Markov models.* New York: Wiley.

Hox, J. (1995). AMOS, EQS, and LISREL for Windows: A comparative review. *Structural Equation Modeling, 2,* 79–91.

Hu, L. T., & Bentler, P. M. (1995). Evaluating model fit. In R. H. Hoyle (Ed.), *Structural equation modeling: Concepts, issues, and applications* (pp. 76–99). Thousand Oaks, CA: Sage.

Jennrich, R. I., & Schluchter, M. D. (1986). Unbalanced repeated-measures models with structured covariance matrices. *Biometrics, 42,* 805–820.

Jessor, R. (1989). Problem-behavior theory, psychosocial development, and adolescent problem drinking. *British Journal of Addictions, 82,* 435–446.

Jöreskog, K. G., & Sörbom, D. (1993). *LISREL 8: User's reference guide.* Chicago: Scientific Software.

Kagan, J., Reznick, J. S., & Snidman, N. (1988). Biological bases of childhood shyness. *Science, 240,* 167–171.

Kenny, D. A., & Zautra, A. (1995). A trait–state error model for multiwave data. *Journal of Consulting and Clinical Psychology, 63,* 52–59.

Langeheine, R. (1988). Manifest and latent Markov chain models for categorical panel data. *Journal of Educational Statistics, 13,* 299–312.

Langeheine, R. (1994). Latent variable Markov models. In A. von Eye & C. C. Clogg (Eds.), *Latent variable analysis: Applications for developmental research* (pp. 373–395). Thousand Oaks, CA: Sage.

Langeheine, R., & Van de Pol, F. (1990). A unifying framework for Markov modeling in discrete space and discrete time. *Sociological Methods and Research, 18,* 416–441.

Magnusson, D., & Bergman, L. R. (1988). Individual and variable-based approaches to longitudinal research on early risk factors. In M. Rutter (Ed.), *Studies of psychosocial risk: The power of longitudinal data* (pp. 45–61). New York: Cambridge University Press.

Marlatt, G. A., & Gordon, J. R. (1985). *Relapse prevention.* New York: Guilford Press.

McArdle, J. J. (1988). Dynamic but structural equation modeling of repeated measures data. In R. B. Cattell & J. Nesselroade (Eds.), *Handbook of multivariate experimental psychology* (2nd ed., pp. 561–614). New York: Plenum.

McArdle, J. J., & Epstein, D. (1987). Latent growth curves within developmental structural equation models. *Child Development, 58,* 110–133.

McArdle, J. J., Hamagami, F., & Hulick, F. (1994). Structural equation models in alcohol research. In R. A. Zucker, G. M. Boyd, & J. Howard (Eds.), *The development of alcohol problems: Exploring the biopsychosocial matrix of risk* (NIAAA Monograph No. 24, pp. 341–385). Washington, DC: U.S. Department of Health and Human Services.

Medhi, J. (1994). *Stochastic processes* (2nd ed.). New York: Wiley.

Meehl, P. E. (1992). Factors and taxa, traits and types, differences of degree and differences in kind. *Journal of Personality, 60,* 117–174.

Meiser, T., & Ohrt, B. (1996). Modeling structure and chance in transitions: Mixed latent partial Markov-chain models. *Journal of Educational and Behavioral Statistics, 21,* 91–109.

Meredith, W., & Tisak, J. (1990). Latent curve analysis. *Psychometrika, 55,* 107–122.

Morey, L. C., & Skinner, H. A. (1986). Empirically derived classifications of alcohol-related problems. In M. Galanter (Ed.), *Recent developments in alcoholism* (Vol. 4, pp. 145–168). New York: Plenum.

Nesselroade, J. R. (1987). Some implications of the trait–state distinction for the study of development across the life-span: The case of personality research. In P. B. Baltes, D. L. Featherman, & R. M. Lerner (Eds.), *Lifespan development and behavior* (Vol. 8, pp. 163–189). Hillsdale, NJ: Erlbaum.

Pentz, M. A., Dwyer, J. H., MacKinnon, D., Flay, B., Hansen, W., Wang, E., & Johnson, C. A. (1989). A multi-community trial for primary prevention of adolescent drug abuse. *Journal of the American Medical Association, 26,* 3259–3266.

Prochaska, J. O., DiClemente, C. C., & Norcross, J. C. (1992). In search of how people change: Applications for addictive behaviors. *American Psychologist, 47,* 1102–1114.

Rogosa, D. (1988). Myths about longitudinal research. In K. W. Schaie, R. T. Campbell, W. Meredith, & S. C. Rawlings (Eds.), *Methodological issues in aging research* (pp. 171–209). New York: Springer.

Schulenberg, J., Wadsworth, K. N., O'Malley, P. M., Bachman, J. G., & Johnston, L. D. (1996). Adolescent risk factors for binge drinking during the transition to young adulthood: Variable- and pattern-centered approaches to change. *Developmental Psychology, 32,* 659–673.

Stern, H., Arcus, D., Kagan, J., Rubin, D. B., & Snidman, N. (1995). Statistical choices in temperament research. *International Journal of Behavior Development, 18,* 407–423.

Stevens, J. (1986). *Applied multivariate statistics for the social sciences.* Hillsdale, NJ: Erlbaum.

Steyer, R., Majcen, A. M., Schwenkmerzger, P., & Buchner, A. (1989). A latent state–trait anxiety model and its application to determine consistency and specificity coefficients. *Anxiety Research, 1,* 281–299.

Steyer, R., & Schmitt, T. (1994). The theory of confounding and its application in causal modeling with latent variables. In A. von Eye & C. C. Clogg (Eds.), *Latent variable analysis: Applications for developmental research* (pp. 36–67). Thousand Oaks, CA: Sage.

Stoolmiller, M. (1995). Using latent growth curve models to study developmental processes. In J. M. Gottman (Ed.), *The analysis of change* (pp. 103–138). Hillsdale, NJ: Erlbaum.

Stoolmiller, M., Duncan, T., Bank, L., & Patterson, G. R. (1993). Some problems and solutions in the study of change: Significant patterns in client resistance. *Journal of Consulting and Clinical Psychology, 61,* 920–928.

Tuma, N. B., & Hannan, M. T. (1984). *Social dynamics: Models and methods.* New York: Academic Press.

Vaillant, G. E. (1983). *The natural history of alcoholism.* Cambridge, MA: Harvard University Press.

Van de Pol, F., Langeheine, R., & DeJong, W. (1991). *PANMARK user manual:*

Panel analysis using Markov chains. Voorburg, The Netherlands: Central Bureau of Statistics.

von Eye, A. (1990). *Statistical methods in longitudinal research* (Vols. 1 & 2). San Diego, CA: Academic Press.

von Eye, A., & Clogg, C. C. (1994). *Latent variable analysis: Applications for developmental research*. Thousand Oaks, CA: Sage.

Ware, J. H. (1985). Linear models for the analysis of longitudinal studies. *American Statistician, 39*, 95–101.

Willett, J. B. (1988). Questions and answers in the measurement of change. *Review of Research in Education, 15*, 345–422.

Willett, J. B., & Sayer, A. G. (1994). Using covariance structure analysis to detect correlates and predictors of individual change over time. *Psychological Bulletin, 116*, 363–381.

Willett, J. B., & Sayer, A. G. (1996). Cross-domain analyses of change over time: Combining growth modeling and covariance structure analysis. In G. A. Marcoulides & R. E. Schumacker (Eds.), *Advanced structural equation modeling: Issues and techniques* (pp. 125–157). Mahwah, NJ: Erlbaum.

Windle, M. (1993). A retrospective measure of childhood behavior problems and its use in predicting adolescent problem behaviors. *Journal of Studies on Alcohol, 54*, 422–431.

Windle, M. (1994). A study of friendship characteristics and problem behaviors among middle adolescents. *Child Development, 65*, 1764–1777.

Windle, M., & Miller, B. A. (1990). Problem drinking and depression among DWI offenders: A three-wave longitudinal study. *Journal of Consulting and Clinical Psychology, 58*, 166–174.

Zevon, M. A., & Tellegen, A. (1982). The structure of mood change: An idiographic/nomothetic analysis. *Journal of Personality and Social Psychology, 43*, 111–122.

Zucker, R. A. (1992). Alcohol involvement over the lifespan: A developmental perspective on theory, course and method. In L. S. Gaines & P. H. Brooks (Eds.), *Alcohol studies: A lifespan perspective* (pp. 122–145). New York: Springer.

3

HEAVY CAFFEINE USE AND THE BEGINNING OF THE SUBSTANCE USE ONSET PROCESS: AN ILLUSTRATION OF LATENT TRANSITION ANALYSIS

LINDA M. COLLINS, JOHN W. GRAHAM,
SUSANNAH SCARBOROUGH ROUSCULP, AND WILLIAM B. HANSEN

This chapter has two objectives: to introduce a relatively new methodology, latent transition analysis (LTA; Collins, Graham, Long, & Hansen, 1994; Collins & Wugalter, 1992), and to demonstrate its usefulness in alcohol prevention research.

LTA is an extension of latent class theory (Goodman, 1974) that allows the user to estimate and test models of stage-sequential development. Researchers may be more accustomed to thinking in terms of strictly quantitative development, in which change can be characterized by increases and decreases in a particular variable, such as test scores, self-esteem, or amount of alcohol consumed per week. Stage-sequential development is distinguished from quantitative development by the involvement of qualitatively different stages. Individuals develop by passing through

This research was supported by Grant DA04111 from the National Institute on Drug Abuse.

these stages. A well-known example of a stage-sequential model is Piaget's (1928) theory of cognitive development. According to this theory, as a child's intellectual ability grows, the child progresses from the sensori-motor stage to the preoperational stage to concrete operations to formal operations. These stage transitions represent qualitative changes in the way the child organizes and interprets information. For example, a child who has mastered concrete operations understands that when matter is re-shaped, as when liquid is poured into a container of a different shape, the amount of matter is not changed. A child in the preoperational stage does not understand this. In many stage-sequential processes, there is accompanying quantitative development, as in this one, where the stage transitions are accompanied by an overall quantitative increase in intellectual ability.

LTA can be used to evaluate various aspects of a stage-sequential model. It can help the user to assess whether a hypothesized set of stages is a realistic representation of a data set. It can be used to compare different models of the stage transition process. For example, in Piaget's (1928) model, development takes place only in a forward direction. A researcher testing this model might compare its fit with a model in which bidirectional change is allowed. LTA also can be used to assess group differences in the incidence of stage transitions, which is the focus of this chapter.

LTA has been used to test stage-sequential models of the acquisition (and loss) of behaviors that mitigate HIV risk in intravenous drug users (Posner, Collins, Longshore, & Anglin, 1996), models of the development of gender roles in adolescence (McGroder, Collins, Barber, & Eccles, 1996), and the transtheoretical model (Prochaska & DiClemente, 1983) applied to smoking cessation (Velicer, Martin, & Collins, 1996). In this chapter we illustrate LTA by using it to estimate and test a stage-sequential model of the substance use onset process. In stage-sequential models, sub-stance use usually is treated as a discontinuous variable, with two or more levels, for example, never tried versus tried a substance or abstainer versus light user versus heavy user. Stages can be defined in any number of ways, involving a single substance or combinations of substances and use levels. A substantial body of work investigating stage sequences of substance use onset (Donovan & Jessor, 1983; Hamburg, Kraemer, & Jahnke, 1975; Huba, Wingard, & Bentler, 1981; Kandel, 1975; Kandel & Faust, 1975; Kandel & Logan, 1984; Mills & Noyes, 1984; Windle, Barnes, & Welte, 1989) has demonstrated that stage-sequential models are useful in numer-ous aspects of substance use research. In particular, these models can be an excellent way to illuminate the role that alcohol plays in the overall onset process.

Invariably, the results of stage-sequential investigations of the sub-stance use onset process indicate that for most individuals, alcohol plays a role at the beginning or near the beginning of the process. Collins and colleagues (Collins, Graham, Long, & Hansen, 1994; Collins, Graham, Rousculp, et al., 1994; Graham, Collins, Wugalter, Chung, & Hansen, 1991) have used LTA to investigate stage-sequential models of the early substance use onset process, primarily on the basis of prospective longitudinal data on children in the seventh grade at the outset of the study and then measured again a year later. Because their interest was in the beginning part of the process, the focus was on low levels of use, such as initial trying of a substance. Collins, Graham, Long, and Hansen defined stages of the onset process as follows: trying alcohol, trying tobacco, having experienced drunkenness, and advanced use (defined as more regular use of tobacco or alcohol or any use of marijuana). They used LTA to test whether any particular sequence or sequences of these activities described the data. They found that the beginning of the onset process was characterized by an initial experience with alcohol and that an experience with drunkenness also was a part of the process. Both alcohol and tobacco appeared to be part of the onset process for most study participants.

The finding that alcohol and tobacco play a role early in the onset process is not a surprising one. These substances are present in many homes, and although few parents condone their use by children, it is fairly easy for most children to obtain these substances. Thus, with one exception, these are the psychoactive drugs most readily available to children. The one exception, the drug that is even more readily available to children, is caffeine. Caffeine is present in many of the soft drinks that are advertised heavily to young people. Cola drinks such as Coke and Pepsi have caffeine, as do some noncola soft drinks, such as Mountain Dew, and some of the recently introduced mixtures of juice and tea, such as Snapple. Also, children can obtain coffee and tea in the home and elsewhere easily. Caffeine is generally considered to be a completely harmless drug in moderate doses. However, preliminary data suggest that heavy use of caffeine might be a risk factor for initiating the onset process. If it is, the probability of initiating the onset process will be higher for individuals using unusually large amounts of caffeine. We illustrate the use of LTA in this chapter by investigating this hypothesis.

LTA

We briefly discuss the LTA model here. For a more complete explanation, see Collins and Wugalter (1992) and Graham et al. (1991).

LTA is a latent variable model for longitudinal panel data. By the term *latent variable model*, we mean that we are measuring a theoretically error-free latent variable using fallible observed variables. In the LTA procedure, the latent variable has two important special features. First, it is *dynamic* (i.e., individuals exhibit growth or change on this latent variable over time). Second, it is conceptualized as a *sequence of stages*.

In this study, the latent variable was substance use onset. It was measured in seventh grade and again in eighth grade by four fallible observed variables: an alcohol item, a tobacco item, a drunkenness item, and an item indicating advanced use (the items are described in more detail in the next section). Figure 1 shows the substance use onset process found to fit well in these data by Collins, Graham, Long, and Hansen (1994). In LTA, stages are called "latent statuses." For example, an individual who has tried both tobacco and alcohol, but who has not gone on to drunkenness or advanced use, is in the "tried alcohol, tried tobacco" latent status. LTA models the prevalence of latent statuses and the incidence of transitions between latent statuses.

Only certain latent statuses are consistent with any given model. The eight latent statuses in Collins, Graham, Long, and Hansen's (1994) model are denoted in the circles in Figure 1. They are as follows: "no use"; "tried alcohol only"; "tried tobacco only"; "tried alcohol and tobacco"; "tried alcohol, been drunk"; "tried alcohol, been drunk, engaged in advanced use"; "tried alcohol and tobacco, engaged in advanced use"; and "tried alcohol and tobacco, been drunk, engaged in advanced use." The arrows between the circles depict where there is movement between the latent statuses and the possible direction of the movement. In some cases, movement is theoretically possible in only one direction, such as from "tried alcohol and tobacco" to "tried tobacco only"; in other cases, movement is

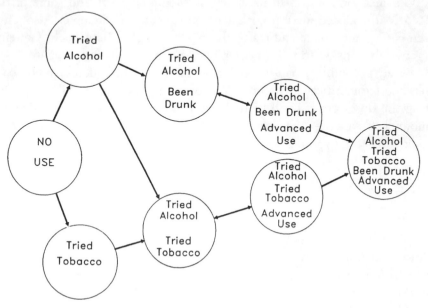

Figure 1. Stage-sequential model of substance use onset reported in Collins, Graham, Long, and Hansen (1994).

possible in both directions, such as between "tried alcohol and tobacco" and "tried alcohol and tobacco, engaged in advanced use." In this model, individuals begin their substance use experience with either alcohol or tobacco. Those who start with alcohol may go on either to tobacco or to a first experience with drunkenness. From these points there is a variety of possible paths through the remaining latent statuses, as depicted in the figure. It is expected that only a subset of individuals completes the entire process. Note that this is only a model of the beginning of the onset process; this is why the model does not contain harder substances such as cocaine.

The LTA Mathematical Model

(This section may be skipped without loss of continuity.) The substance use research that is described here involves a dynamic latent variable (substance use onset) and a static latent variable (caffeine risk). We used the following manifest indicators of the dynamic latent variable: an alcohol use item, a tobacco use item, an item asking about drunkenness, and an advanced use item that was a composite of several substance use items. Data on these items were collected in seventh grade and again in eighth grade. Caffeine risk was measured with a single caffeine use item at seventh grade only.

The following expresses this in more mathematical terms. Suppose there are two occasions of measurement with the first taken at time t and the second at time $t + 1$ and that at each time there are four manifest indicators of a dynamic latent variable: Item 1, with $i, i' = 1, \ldots I$ response categories; Item 2, with $j, j' = 1, \ldots J$ response categories; Item 3, with $k, k' = 1, \ldots K$ response categories; and Item 4, with $l, l' = 1, \ldots L$ response categories. These items correspond to the alcohol, tobacco, drunkenness, and advanced use items mentioned earlier. Suppose further that there is a single indicator of a static latent variable, Item 5, with $m = 1, \ldots M$ response categories. This corresponds to the caffeine risk indicator mentioned earlier. Note that i, j, k, l, and m refer to responses obtained at time t, and i', j', k', and l' refer to responses obtained at time $t + 1$. The extension to more than two occasions, fewer than four indicators or more than four indicators of the dynamic latent variable, or more than one indicator of the static latent variable is direct. There are $g = 1, \ldots G$ latent classes. There are $a, b = 1, \ldots S$ latent statuses, with a denoting a latent status at time t and b denoting a latent status at time $t + 1$.

Let $Y = (i, j, k, l, m, i', j', k', l')$ represent a "response pattern," a vector of possible responses made up of a single response to the manifest indicator of the exogenous variable and responses to the four items at times

t and $t + 1$. Then the estimated proportion of a particular response pattern, $P(Y)$, is expressed as follows:

$$P(Y) = \sum_{g=1}^{G} \sum_{a=1}^{S} \sum_{b=1}^{S} \gamma_g \rho_{m|g} \delta_{a|g} \rho_{i|a,g} \rho_{j|a,g} \rho_{k|a,g} \rho_{l|a,g} \tau_{b|a,g} \rho_{i'|b,g} \rho_{j'|b,g} \rho_{k'|b,g} \rho_{l'|b,g}.$$

Parameters Estimated in the LTA Model

In the LTA models discussed in this article, four different types of parameters are estimated:

γ_g represents the proportion in latent class g. In our example, there are two such parameters, one representing the proportion of individuals in the high-caffeine-risk category and the other representing the proportion of individuals in the low-caffeine-risk category.

$\delta_{a|g}$ represents the proportion in latent status a at Time 1 conditional on membership in latent class g; in other words, this parameter is the conditional proportion of participants in each latent status at the first occasion of measurement. Using the latent variable shown in Figure 1 as an example, examples of this parameter would be the proportion of individuals who at Time 1 have used only tobacco, given that they are in the low-caffeine-risk latent class; the proportion of individuals who at Time 1 have used only tobacco, given that they are in the high-caffeine-risk latent class; and the proportion of individuals who at Time 1 have used only alcohol, given that they are in the low-caffeine-risk latent class.

$\tau_{b|a,g}$ is a transition probability representing the probability of membership in latent status b at time $t + 1$ conditional on membership in latent status a at time t and membership in latent class g. These parameters represent the probability of moving to a particular latent status at the second occasion of measurement conditional on latent status membership at the first occasion and latent class membership. In our example, one transition probability is the probability of moving to the alcohol and tobacco latent status at the second occasion, given membership in the alcohol-only latent status at the first occasion and the low-caffeine-risk latent class.

The fourth type of parameter LTA estimates is measurement parameters. These parameters assess the degree of error in each observed item. There are measurement parameters associated with the static latent variable and the dynamic latent variable. $\rho_{m|g}$ is a parameter associated with an item measuring the static latent variable. It represents the probability of response m to an item, conditional on membership in latent class g. $\rho_{i|a,g}$ is a parameter associated with an item measuring the dynamic latent variable. It represents the probability of response i to Item 1 at time t, conditional on membership in latent status a at time t and latent class g; $\rho_{i'|b,g}$ represents the probability of response i' to Item 1 at time $t + 1$, conditional on membership in latent status b at time $t + 1$ and latent class g; and so on.

The rhos play two roles in LTA models: First, they map the manifest items onto the latent statuses and latent classes in much the same way that factor loadings map variables onto factors. For example, if the probability of responding no to each of the substance use items is high for a particular latent status, this would be interpreted as a "no substance use" latent status. If in another latent status the probability of responding yes is high for the alcohol item and the probability of responding no is high for the remaining items, this latent status would be interpreted as "tried alcohol only." The second role that the rhos play is reflecting measurement precision. If measurement is error free, each manifest response is determined completely by latent status membership, and all the rhos are zero or one. In general, the closer these parameters are to zero or one for a particular item, the closer the relationship between latent status membership and manifest responses.

LTA as a Measurement Model

There are many analogies between LTA (and also latent class models in general) on the one hand and other measurement models such as factor analysis (e.g., Comrey & Lee, 1992) or structural equation modeling (e.g., Jöreskog & Sörbom, 1989) on the other. Both LTA and factor analysis are latent variable models in which fallible observed variables serve as indicators of error-free unmeasured variables. Both procedures involve a measurement model that maps the observed variables onto the latent variables. In factor analysis, the latent variable is continuous and is usually measured by continuous indicators, whereas LTA involves discrete latent variables and indicators. In factor analysis, factor loadings provide the link between observed and unmeasured variables; in LTA, the measurement parameters serve this purpose. However, the LTA measurement parameters cannot be interpreted in exactly the same way as factor loadings. With factor loadings, a large absolute value is a strong loading, whereas a value close to zero indicates no relationship, or a weak relationship, between a variable and a factor. By contrast, LTA rho parameters are estimates of probabilities, so a value near zero or near unity indicates "sureness," or a strong relationship between a measured variable and a latent variable. A value close to $1/J$, where J is the number of response alternatives, indicates no relationship between a measured variable and an observed variable. Negative values are impossible.

The researcher setting out to conduct a study involving LTA has to think through some issues similar to those that arise in factor analytic and structural equation modeling studies. In factor analysis, the researcher must consider exactly which variables, and how many, will be measured and then ultimately expected to define each factor. In LTA studies, the researcher must make the same decision about the manifest variables that will define the dynamic latent variable and, when relevant, the exogenous static latent variable. Multiple indicators improve measurement in LTA and other latent class models, as they do in factor-analytic models. However, in LTA, as in all latent class models, there are costs as well as benefits associated with adding indicators. These models are essentially large multiway contingency tables, in which every variable adds a dimension. A table with many cells can require a large sample size for adequate parameter estimation. Collins, Fidler, and Wugalter (1996) and Collins and Tracy (in press) have demonstrated that under many conditions, satisfactory parameter estimation can be obtained with a ratio of sample size to number of cells as small as .07.

The manifest variables incorporated in an LTA analysis must be categorical. In general, we have found that LTA models are most straightforward conceptually when the variables are dichotomous or trichotomous. If chosen a priori, such variables have the advantage of being easy for study participants to answer. However, the variables can have more categories, and the number of categories can vary. Continuous variables or variables with too many categories can be dichotomized or collapsed. This procedure is sometimes accompanied by a loss of information, but if the variable is highly skewed or some categories are small, the loss of information is often minimal. The choice of variables depends, of course, on how the dynamic latent variable of interest is to be operationalized. In the example in this chapter, we relied primarily on items asking whether the individual had ever tried a substance. This meant that we were operationalizing many stages such that a reversal of development was not possible (the advanced use stage is an exception). Another model of drug use might focus on everyday habits and use variables such as typical use in a week. In this case, backward movement would be possible, and would occur whenever an individual reduced his or her weekly drug use.

METHOD

Participants

The participants in this study completed a drug use survey as seventh graders in either the fall of 1987 or fall of 1988 and again as eighth graders 1 year later, as part of the Adolescent Alcohol Prevention Trial (AAPT; Graham, Rohrbach, Hansen, Flay, & Johnson, 1989; Hansen & Graham, 1991; Hansen et al., 1988). The study participants were 4,325 students who had complete data for relevant measures at pretesting and posttesting and were taken from a sample of 5,242 seventh graders who completed the survey at pretesting. The subsample used in this study was ethnically mixed, containing primarily White, Latino, and Asian Americans.

Measures

The measures used in this study included lifetime alcohol use ("How many drinks of alcohol have you had in your whole life?"), lifetime cigarette use ("How many cigarettes have you smoked in your whole life?"), and lifetime drunkenness ("How many times have you ever been drunk?"). The alcohol item was coded 0 if the respondent reported no use or sips for religious services and was coded 1 for sips (not for religious services) or more in one's lifetime. The cigarette item was coded 0 for never tried and 1 for one puff or more in one's lifetime. The drunkenness item was coded 0 for never been drunk and 1 for been drunk once or more.

Several other measures were used in the analyses reported in this chapter, including alcohol use in the previous month and previous week, tobacco use in the previous month and previous week, and lifetime marijuana use. Models involving these items separately showed considerable instability. It appeared that much of the instability stemmed from the fact that these were young adolescents with low levels of use. Thus, these items tapping greater involvement with various substances were combined into a single composite item reflecting advanced use. The combined item was scored 0 if the respondent had engaged in no alcohol use and no tobacco use in the previous week and the previous month and had never used marijuana; otherwise, it was coded 1.

Definition of Caffeine Risk

In this exploratory study, *caffeine risk* was defined in five ways. In each definition, a single indicator of caffeine risk was used. Using the item "How many cups of coffee have you had in your lifetime?" we defined caffeine risk as (a) having had 6 or more cups of coffee during one's lifetime and (b) having had 20 or more cups of coffee in one's lifetime. Using the item "How many cups of coffee have you had in the last month?" we defined caffeine risk as (c) having had 6 or more cups of coffee in the past month. Using the item "How many cola drinks have you had in the last week?" we defined caffeine risk as (d) having had 6 or more cola drinks and (e) having had 20 or more cola drinks.

RESULTS

Cross-Validation

Before the analyses were performed, the sample was divided randomly into Subsamples A and B. All analyses were performed separately on each subsample and compared to assess the stability of the findings.

Detailed Examination of One Model

To illustrate the LTA approach, we examine the estimation and testing of one LTA model in detail. All analyses reported here were performed using a computer program called LTA (Collins, Wugalter, & Rousculp, 1992), which is available from Linda M. Collins. The model tested was the one illustrated in Figure 1, with the addition of a static latent variable. The static latent variable was the caffeine risk variable, with two latent classes: low risk (no more than 6 cups of coffee in the past month) and high risk (more than 6 cups of coffee in the past month). Thus, the following parameters were estimated: probability of membership in each of the two latent classes, low caffeine risk and high caffeine risk (gammas); the probability of membership in each of the latent statuses at the outset, conditional on latent class membership (deltas); the probability of transitioning from one latent class to another (taus); and measurement parameters (rhos).

Parameter Restrictions

The models tested in this study involved restrictions on certain parameters. The LTA program allows the user to impose restrictions involving fixing a parameter to a particular prespecified value or constraining two or more parameters to be equal to a single estimated value. There are two reasons for imposing constraints on parameter estimates. One reason is conceptual. Theory sometimes dictates that a parameter should be equal to a particular value or that several parameters are equal to each other. To test these fundamental aspects of a model, it is necessary to use parameter restrictions. For example, a theory might predict that learning takes place only in a forward direction, so that no unlearning or forgetting takes place. If there is no forgetting, then the probability of moving from a latent status involving advanced knowledge to a latent status involving less advanced knowledge is, in theory, zero. To test this model using LTA, a researcher might fix all transition probabilities corresponding to this type of movement to zero. Another example is the situation in which a model of no change is to be tested. In that case, all the tau parameters are set to zero, except the ones corresponding to membership in the same latent status across time. Finally, it is usually a good idea to set the rho parameters equal across times and latent classes. This ensures that the meaning of the latent statuses is consistent across time and groups. It is just as difficult to interpret changes in rho parameters across time and groups as it is to interpret changes in factor loadings.

The other reason for imposing constraints is to achieve identification. When a model is underidentified, this means that there is not enough information in the data to estimate all the parameters individually. This is

usually caused by trying to estimate too many parameters. In most cases
identification can be achieved by reducing the number of individual parameters to be estimated.

In this study, parameter restrictions were imposed for the following
reasons: (a) In order to simplify the interpretation of the results, the matrices of rho (measurement) parameters for items measuring the latent statuses were constrained equal across the two times and across the two latent
classes. (b) Further constraints were imposed to limit the number of rho
parameters that were estimated independently. For each item, a particular
response was expected conditional on latent status. For example, we expected that those in the no-use latent status would be more likely to respond no to each of the substance use items than they would be to respond
yes. This led to four possibilities: responses of yes when yes was expected,
no when no was expected, unexpected responses of yes when no was expected, and no when yes was expected. For each item, we constrained the
probabilities of expected yes responses to be equal to each other and the
probabilities of expected no responses to be equal to each other. (Because
the unexpected responses were the complements, we also effectively constrained them.) Thus, two rho parameters were estimated for each item,
resulting in a total of eight rho parameters estimated. (c) Because there
was a single item measuring caffeine risk status in each of the five definitions, it was necessary to impose a constraint on these rho parameters to
achieve identification. In this case, we specified that the probability of
responding yes to the caffeine item for the low-caffeine-risk group equaled
the probability of responding no to the caffeine item for the high-caffeine-
risk group; in other words, the probability of error responses was identical.
(d) Constraints also were imposed on the lower triangle of the tau matrix.
In theory, there should be no possibility of regressing from a more advanced
latent status to a less advanced latent status in this model because it is
impossible to have tried a substance at one time and then never to have
tried it at a later time. However, even though it is theoretically impossible,
much reported backsliding does occur, presumably because of erroneous or
careless responding. If lower triangular tau elements are not estimated, the
models fit less well, and the rho (measurement) parameters often are affected in ways that limit clear interpretation of the model. In these analyses, we constrained all the below-diagonal elements of the tau matrix to
be equal within a row, with a few exceptions in which backsliding was
possible theoretically. This resulted in estimating one backsliding parameter
per row.

Model Fit

The adequacy of the fit of latent transition models was tested using
the G^2 statistic, which is assumed to be distributed as a chi-square. The G^2

TABLE 1
Measurement Parameters (Rhos) for One Model

Latent status	Ever tried		Ever been drunk	Any advanced use
	Tobacco	Alcohol		
No use	.04	.02	.01	.02
Alcohol	.04	.97	.01	.02
Tobacco	.98	.02	.01	.02
Alcohol + tobacco	.98	.97	.01	.02
Alcohol + drunkenness	.04	.97	.75	.02
Alcohol, drunkenness, advanced	.04	.97	.75	.61
Alcohol, tobacco, advanced	.98	.97	.01	.61
Alcohol, tobacco, drunkenness, advanced	.98	.97	.75	.61

Note. Rho parameters are the probability of responding yes to these items conditional on latent status membership.

for this model was 412.68 with 423 *dfs* (where *df* = the number of response patterns − the number of parameters estimated − 1). Under the chi-square distribution, the expectation is equal to the degrees of freedom, so this looks like a reasonably well fitting model (however, there are problems with the assumption that the G^2 is distributed as a chi-square; see Collins, Fidler, Wugalter, & Long, 1993).

Rho Parameters

Table 1 shows some of the rho parameters for the items measuring the dynamic latent variable. (Table 1 includes only the probabilities of responding yes to each item conditional on latent status; the probabilities of responding no to each item conditional on latent status can be obtained by subtracting each of the probabilities in Table 1 from one.) Examination of this table shows that the estimates of the rho parameters were consistent with the model being tested. For example, the conditional probability of responding yes to any of the use items was low for the no-use group because these individuals had never tried a substance. Overall, the parameter estimates were closer to zero and one than they were to .5, indicating that the dynamic latent variable was being measured well (this is conceptually similar to having large factor loadings). There also was a rho parameter associated with the static latent variable, which was estimated to be 1.0.

Gamma and Delta Parameters

The gamma parameters, the probabilities of membership in each latent class, were .95 for the low-caffeine-risk latent class and .05 for the high-caffeine-risk latent class. Table 2 shows the delta parameters, or the probabilities of being in a particular latent status at the first observation,

TABLE 2
Delta Parameters for One Model

	Latent class	
Latent status	Low caffeine risk	High caffeine risk
No use	.37	.17
Alcohol	.27	.24
Tobacco	.03	.02
Alcohol + tobacco	.14	.05
Alcohol + drunkenness	.03	.01
Alcohol, drunkenness, advanced	.02	.09
Alcohol, tobacco, advanced	.03	.05
Alcohol, tobacco, drunkenness, advanced	.11	.37

Note. Delta parameters are the probability of latent status membership conditional on caffeine risk.

conditional on caffeine risk status. Table 2 shows that the probability of being in the no-use latent status at the outset was considerably higher for the low-caffeine-risk individuals than for the high-caffeine-risk individuals. It also shows that membership in the most advanced latent status, "tried alcohol and tobacco, been drunk, engaged in advanced use," was more likely for the high-risk group than for the low-risk group. Although the prevalence of membership in the "tried alcohol and tobacco" latent status was considerably higher for the low-risk group than for the high-risk group, this should not be interpreted as evidence of more progress along the substance use continuum for the low-risk group. Rather, this is consistent with the idea that the high-risk individuals were more likely to be members of the three latent statuses involving advanced use, leaving fewer to be members of the five less advanced latent statuses.

Tau Parameters

Table 3 contains the tau parameters. It is customary to arrange them in the matrix shown there. The rows of this matrix correspond to latent status at Time 1, and the columns correspond to latent status at Time 2, where, in this example, the times are seventh and eighth grades, respectively. Each element represents the probability of a transition into the column latent status, given that the individual was in the row latent status in seventh grade. Because the column elements are conditional on the row elements, each row of the matrix must sum to one. In this model, separate tau matrices were computed for the two caffeine risk groups. In Table 3, the tau matrix for the low-risk group and the tau matrix for the high-risk group are juxtaposed to make it easier to compare them.

The first element in the first row of the matrix in Table 3, .62, is the probability of being in the no-use latent status in eighth grade, conditional

TABLE 3
Transition Probability Matrix (Tau Parameters)

Seventh-grade latent status	Caffeine risk	Eighth-grade latent status							
No use	Low	.62	.23	.01	.06	.02	.01	.01	.04
	High	.33	.48	.15	.00	.00	.01	.03	.00
Alcohol	Low	.11	.68	.00	.10	.02	.00	.04	.06
	High	.02	.51	.00	.15	.10	.10	.04	.08
Tobacco	Low	.00	.00	.50	.17	.00	.00	.06	.28
	High	.00	.00	.00	.00	.00	.00	.00	1.00
Alcohol + tobacco	Low	.02	.02	.02	.65	.02	.02	.08	.19
	High	.00	.00	.00	.83	.00	.00	.17	.00
Alcohol + drunkenness	Low	.00	.00	.00	.00	.41	.12	.00	.46
	High	.00	.00	.00	.00	.00	.74	.00	.26
Alcohol, drunkenness, advanced	Low	.00	.00	.00	.00	.00	.64	.00	.36
	High	.00	.00	.00	.00	.26	.24	.00	.50
Alcohol, tobacco, advanced	Low	.01	.01	.01	.20	.01	.01	.64	.11
	High	.05	.05	.05	.17	.05	.05	.58	.00
Alcohol, tobacco, drunkenness, advanced	Low	.01	.01	.01	.01	.01	.01	.01	.93
	High	.01	.01	.01	.01	.01	.01	.01	.92

Note. Some rows do not sum exactly to one because of rounding.

on membership in the no-use latent status in seventh grade, for the low-risk group. The element just below it, .33, is the corresponding probability for the high-risk group. This indicates that the probability of being in the no-use latent status in eighth grade, given membership in this status in seventh grade, was greater for the low-caffeine-risk group than it was for the high-caffeine-risk group. The corresponding probabilities for the "tried alcohol only," "tried tobacco only," "tried alcohol, been drunk," and "tried alcohol, been drunk, engaged in advanced use" latent statuses also were larger for the low-caffeine-risk group than for the high-caffeine-risk group, indicating a tendency for the low-risk group to move more slowly through the onset process. However, this was not completely consistent across the entire matrix. The order of the probabilities across the caffeine risk groups was reversed for the "tried alcohol and tobacco" latent status, and the probabilities were roughly equal for the last two latent statuses.

Summary of Results on All Caffeine Risk Definitions

Table 4 shows the estimated proportion of participants in the high-caffeine-risk group according to each definition. These estimates vary depending on the extremity of the caffeine risk definition. Approximately 38% of the sample was at risk according to the least extreme definition (more than 6 cups of coffee in one's lifetime). No more than 5% were at

TABLE 4
Estimated Proportions in No-Use Latent Status in Seventh Grade Broken Down by Caffeine Risk

Caffeine risk definition	Subsample	Estimated proportion in high-risk group	Estimated proportion in no-use latent status (δ)	
			Low risk	High risk
Coffee (cups)				
>6 lifetime	A	.38	.48	.24
	B	.39	.47	.21
>20 lifetime	A	.18	.41	.19
	B	.16	.41	.16
>6 in past month	A	.05	.37	.17
	B	.05	.38	.15
Cola (drinks)				
>6 in past week	A	.22	.39	.22
	B	.24	.41	.22
>20 in past week	A	.03	.38	.25
	B	.04	.34	.20

risk according to the most extreme definitions (more than 6 cups of coffee in the past month and more than 20 cola drinks in the past week).

Because so many different definitions of caffeine risk were tested in the course of this investigation, it was impossible to present all the full models in detail in this chapter. We originally hypothesized that high caffeine use would be associated with the beginning of the onset process. For this reason, we summarize the results by presenting estimates of two parameters for comparison across the low- and high-caffeine-risk groups. Table 4 shows the prevalence of the no-use latent status, indicating that the onset process had not begun. Table 5 contains incidence of not transitioning out of the no-use latent status between seventh and eighth grade. Results are reported for both cross-validation subsamples.

Tables 4 and 5 show that the results are remarkably consistent across the two cross-validation subsamples and across the various definitions of caffeine risk. Across all samples and definitions of caffeine risk, participants in the low-caffeine-risk group were 1.5–2.5 times as likely to be in the no-use latent status in seventh grade as were those in the high-caffeine-risk group. The differences between the high-risk and low-risk groups were larger when caffeine risk was defined in terms of coffee intake than when it was defined in terms of cola intake, but the effect was there for cola intake. In addition, across the board, the low-caffeine-risk participants who were in the no-use latent status were more likely to be there in eighth grade than were their high-caffeine-risk counterparts, by a factor usually approximately 1.2 but ranging as high as 1.9. In other words, among the participants who had not initiated the substance use onset process by sev-

TABLE 5
Estimated Probabilities of Not Initiating the Substance Use Onset Process Broken Down by Caffeine Risk

Caffeine risk definition	Subsample	Estimated probability of not transitioning out of the no-use latent status (τ)	
		Low risk	High risk
Coffee (cups)			
>6 lifetime	A	.68	.58
	B	.74	.56
>20 lifetime	A	.64	.55
	B	.71	.60
>6 in past month	A	.62	.33
	B	.70	.54
Cola (drinks)			
>6 in past week	A	.63	.40
	B	.70	.57
>20 in past week	A	.64	.36
	B	.63	.52

enth grade, the high-caffeine-risk participants were more likely to initiate the process by eighth grade than were the low-caffeine-risk participants.

Although we were primarily interested in the early onset process, and in fact the results were more consistent for the early part of the model, it is interesting to examine the most advanced latent status in our model: "alcohol, tobacco, drunkenness, and advanced use." Table 6 shows the prevalence of membership in this latent status at seventh grade, broken

TABLE 6
Estimated Proportions in Advanced-Use Latent Status in Seventh Grade Broken Down by Caffeine Risk

Caffeine risk definition	Subsample	Estimated proportion in advanced-use latent status (δ)	
		Low risk	High risk
Coffee (cups)			
>6 lifetime	A	.07	.22
	B	.07	.21
>20 lifetime	A	.09	.30
	B	.10	.30
>6 in last month	A	.11	.37
	B	.11	.43
Cola (drinks)			
>6 in past week	A	.09	.26
	B	.08	.28
>20 in past week	A	.18	.43
	B	.12	.39

down by caffeine risk. In every case, those in the high-caffeine-risk latent class were more likely than those in the low-caffeine-risk latent class to be in this latent status, by a factor ranging from 2.4 to 3.9.

DISCUSSION

LTA is a methodology for estimating and testing stage-sequential models in longitudinal data. In this chapter, we have demonstrated how LTA can be used to fit models of early substance use onset and to arrive at estimates of prevalence of stage memberships and incidence of stage transitions that are adjusted for the effects of measurement error.

In this study, we used LTA to investigate whether heavy use of caffeine would be a predictor in the early part of the substance use onset process. We defined *heavy use of caffeine* in several different ways, in terms of both coffee and cola soft drinks. By all of our definitions of *heavy caffeine use*, those in the high-caffeine-risk latent class were more likely to have initiated the substance use onset process by seventh grade, and those who had not initiated by seventh grade were more likely to do so by eighth grade. The increased risk of onset related to caffeine use was greater for coffee than for cola. For coffee, the probability of onset was greater for the more extreme definitions of caffeine risk. The level of caffeine consumption required to elevate risk was surprisingly low. Increased risk was found for as little caffeine consumption as 6 cups of coffee in one's lifetime and 6 cola drinks in the past week. The results replicated well and consistently across the two cross-validation subsamples.

The results of this study suggest that high use of caffeine is associated with an increased probability that an individual will initiate the onset process. This implicates caffeine as a predictor in the early substance use onset process, but it does not tell us exactly what the role of caffeine is, if any. These analyses cannot be considered causal. In particular, the finding that those in the high-caffeine-risk latent class were more likely to have initiated the onset process by seventh grade presents a causal sequencing problem. It is possible that the high-caffeine-risk participants initiated the onset process earlier than the low-caffeine-risk participants, and that is the reason why they were more likely to be further along in the onset sequence when they were first measured in seventh grade. However, the possibility cannot be ruled out that the high caffeine use was adopted after or at the same time as the initiation of the onset process for these participants. Somewhat more compelling was the prospective finding that among those who had not initiated the onset process by seventh grade, individuals in the high-caffeine-risk group were more likely to begin the process by eighth grade. Because most of those who initiated the onset process did so with alcohol, these finding are likely to be of particular interest to alcohol use researchers.

Another question is the nature of the relationship between caffeine risk status and onset. Even if high caffeine use seems to precede substance use onset, it may not be that the caffeine use per se is causing the increased onset rates. One possible explanation for these findings is that children who are sensation seekers by nature begin their substance use experience with the most readily available substance there is: caffeine. Thus, high caffeine use is possibly the first outward sign of a sensation-seeking nature. Another possibility is that children who consume large amounts of caffeine are spending a lot of time consuming beverages with friends. If the beverage is sometimes coffee, this suggests that they are trying to act and appear adult by doing things that adults do. The logical next step for these children may be alcohol use, tobacco use, or both, which are also badges of adulthood in their eyes. A third possibility is that children who are consuming large amounts of caffeine have parents who are not supervising their diets and possibly not supervising them properly in other areas as well, leaving opportunities for experimentation with substances. In none of these explanations does caffeine use play a causal role. On the other hand, Shoaib, Swanner, Schindler, and Goldberg (1996) found that rats that were randomly assigned to a high-caffeine-intake condition later showed increased voluntary intake of nicotine than did a control group. This is consistent with the idea that heavy doses of caffeine are related causally to later use of nicotine.

Limitations of This Study

This study has several important limitations. First, the caffeine risk definitions were not all independent. Two of the caffeine risk definitions that were based on coffee were dichotomizations of a single coffee-use variable, and the two caffeine risk definitions that were based on cola were dichotomizations of a single cola-use variable. Second, it could be that relatively high consumption of *any* beverage would predict increased onset of alcohol use. With these data, we cannot rule out the possibility that having six cans of Seven-Up per week is also associated with increased onset of alcohol use between seventh and eighth grades. Because caffeine use was not a primary focus of the AAPT study, only limited data on caffeine use or consumption of other nonalcoholic beverages were collected. A third limitation is that coffee and cola intake were not measured precisely. Children were asked how many cups of coffee and how many drinks of cola, without any explicit definition or standardization of these terms. Usually, unreliability in measurement works against finding results as substantial and consistent as these, but it is possible that the subjective nature of these responses introduced some artifact. A more thorough investigation, focused on the role of caffeine in the onset process, is needed to improve understanding of the role caffeine plays, if any, in the early substance use onset process.

Limitations and Future Directions of LTA

LTA is a relatively new procedure and as such has some noteworthy limitations. One limitation is that currently, the exogenous variable must involve discrete categories, such as the risk categories used here: gender, experimental conditions, and so on. Furthermore, the number of such categories that can be used in a single analysis is limited because the number of parameters that must be estimated increases dramatically with each group that is added. We currently are working on adding the capability for involving continuous predictors to LTA models. This general framework will allow some expansion of the role of both continuous and discrete exogenous predictors. Another limitation is that currently, standard errors are not computed by the LTA program. Standard errors are not a straightforward result of the estimation procedure used by LTA, the EM algorithm. We are working on adding standard errors to the program. We also plan to expand the procedure considerably to allow prediction of one dynamic latent variable by another. This would allow, for example, the testing of models of whether changes in a child's drug use can be predicted by changes in peer drug use.

REFERENCES

Collins, L. M., Fidler, P. L., & Wugalter, S. E. (1996). Some practical issues related to estimation of latent class and latent transition parameters. In A. von Eye & C. C. Clogg (Eds.), *Analysis of categorical variables in developmental research* (pp. 133–146). San Diego, CA: Academic Press.

Collins, L. M., Fidler, P. L., Wugalter, S. E., & Long, J. L. (1993). Goodness-of-fit testing for latent class models. *Multivariate Behavioral Research, 28,* 375–389.

Collins, L. M., Graham, J. W., Long, J., & Hansen, W. B. (1994). Crossvalidation of latent class models of early substance use onset. *Multivariate Behavioral Research, 29,* 165–183.

Collins, L. M., Graham, J. W., Rousculp, S. S., Fidler, P. L., Pan, J., & Hansen, W. B. (1994). Latent transition analysis and how it can address prevention research questions. In L. M. Collins & L. Seitz (Eds.), *Advances in data analysis for prevention intervention research* (NIDA Research Monograph No. 142). Washington, DC: U.S. Government Printing Office.

Collins, L. M., & Tracy, A. J. (in press). Identifiability and stability of complex latent transition models involving multiple occasions of measurement and second-order processes. *Kwantitatieve Methoden*.

Collins, L. M., & Wugalter, S. E. (1992). Latent class models for stage-sequential dynamic latent variables. *Multivariate Behavioral Research, 27*, 131–157.

Collins, L. M., Wugalter, S. E., & Rousculp, S. S. (1992). *Latent transition analysis (LTA) program manual* (Version 1.0). Los Angeles: University of Southern California.

Comrey, A. L., & Lee, H. B. (1992). *A first course in factor analysis* (2nd ed.). Hillsdale, NJ: Erlbaum.

Donovan, J. E., & Jessor, R. (1983). Problem drinking and the dimension of involvement with drugs: A Guttman scalogram analysis of adolescent drug use. *American Journal of Public Health, 73*, 543–551.

Goodman, L. A. (1974). Exploratory latent structure analysis using both identifiable and unidentifiable models. *Biometrika, 61*, 215–231.

Graham, J. W., Collins, L. M., Wugalter, S. E., Chung, N. K., & Hansen, W. B. (1991). Modeling transitions in latent stage-sequential processes: A substance use prevention example. *Journal of Consulting and Clinical Psychology, 59*, 48–57.

Graham, J. W., Rohrbach, L., Hansen, W. B., Flay, B. R., & Johnson, C. A. (1989). Convergent and discriminant validity for assessment of skill in resisting a role play alcohol offer. *Behavioral Assessment, 11*, 353–379.

Hamburg, B. A., Kraemer, H. C., & Jahnke, W. (1975). A hierarchy of drug use in adolescence: Behavioral and attitudinal correlates of substantial drug use. *American Journal of Psychiatry, 132*, 1155–1163.

Hansen, W. B., & Graham, J. W. (1991). Preventing alcohol, marijuana, and cigarette use among adolescents: Peer pressure resistance training versus establishing conservative norms. *Preventive Medicine, 20*, 414–430.

Hansen, W. B, Graham, J. W., Wolkenstein, B. H., Lundy, B. Z., Pearson, J. L., Flay, B. R., & Johnson, C. A. (1988). Differential impact of three alcohol prevention curricula on hypothesized mediating variables. *Journal of Drug Education, 18*, 143–153.

Huba, G. J., Wingard, J. A., & Bentler, P. M. (1981). A comparison of two latent variable causal models for adolescent drug use. *Journal of Personality and Social Psychology, 40*, 180–193.

Jöreskog, K. G., & Sörbom, D. (1989). *LISREL 7 user's reference guide*. Chicago: Scientific Software.

Kandel, D. B. (1975). Stages in adolescent involvement in drug use. *Science, 190*, 912–914.

Kandel, D. B., & Faust, R. (1975). Sequence and stages in patterns of adolescent drug use. *Archives of General Psychiatry, 32*, 923–932.

Kandel, D. B., & Logan, J. A. (1984). Patterns of drug use from adolescence to young adulthood: I. Periods of risk for initiation, continued risk, and discontinuation. *American Journal of Public Health, 74*, 660–666.

McGroder, S. M., Collins, L. M., Barber, B. L., & Eccles, J. S. (1996). *Gender-role identity development among high school girls and boys: A latent transition analysis approach.* Unpublished manuscript.

Mills, C. J., & Noyes, H. L. (1984). Patterns and correlates of initial and subsequent drug use among adolescents. *Journal of Consulting and Clinical Psychology, 52,* 231–243.

Piaget, J. (1928). *Judgement and reasoning in the child.* New York: Harcourt Brace.

Posner, S. F., Collins, L. M., Longshore, D., & Anglin, D. (1996). The acquisition and maintenance of safer sexual behaviors among injection drug users. *Substance Use and Misuse, 31,* 1995–2015.

Prochaska, J. O., & DiClemente, C. C. (1983). Stages and processes of self-change of smoking: Toward an integrative model of change. *Journal of Consulting and Clinical Psychology, 51,* 390–395.

Shoaib, M., Swanner, L. S., Schindler, C. W., & Goldberg, S. R. (1996, March). *Genetic and environmental factors in nicotine self-administration.* Paper presented at the Second Annual Scientific Conference of the Society for Research on Nicotine and Tobacco, Washington, DC.

Velicer, W. F., Martin, R. A., & Collins, L. M. (1996). Latent transition analysis for longitudinal data. *Addiction, 91*(Supplement), S197–S209.

Windle, M., Barnes, G. M., & Welte, J. (1989). Causal models of adolescent substance use: An examination of gender differences using distribution-free estimators. *Journal of Personality and Social Psychology, 56,* 132–142.

4

ALTERNATIVE ECONOMETRIC MODELS OF ALCOHOL DEMAND

W. G. MANNING

In analyzing the demand for and consumption of alcohol, a number of statistical and econometric models have been used. Although a recent review of the alcohol demand literature by Leung and Phelps (1993) provides some comments on methodology, much of the work has focused on what factors affect behavior, with less attention paid to the statistical nature of the models being used to explain alcohol consumption (ALC). For studies of aggregate demand, one would expect relatively smooth responses to the variables of interest. In that case, standard variations on least squares regression modeling should provide consistent and robust estimates of the demand. However, for the analysis of individual consumer data, the consumption of alcohol has three characteristics that can cause severe estimation problems. First, a large proportion of the adult population does not consume alcohol during the year. Data from the 1983 National Health Interview Survey (NHIS) in the Appendix indicate that two of five adults are not current drinkers. Second, the distribution of ALC among drinkers is skewed. See Tables A1 and A2 for evidence of the extreme skewness (skewness greater than 16) for reported average daily consumption.[1] Be-

---

[1] If ethanol were normally distributed, skewness would equal 0, and kurtosis would equal 3. The departures from the values expected under normality in Table A1 are significant ($p < .001$).

cause of these first two characteristics, models estimated using some variant of ordinary least squares applied directly to ALC may yield imprecise and usually inconsistent estimates of the effects of price, income, and other factors on the demand for alcohol.[2] The third potential problem is that one might expect that heavier drinkers would have a different response to price and other factors than light or moderate drinkers. The more commonly used estimation strategies assume that these groups have the same underlying coefficients in their response. Thus, these models could yield biased estimates of demand responses for some important subgroups of clinical, economic, or policy interest.

In this chapter, I describe several alternative econometric models for average daily or total alcohol demand and examine their advantages and disadvantages.[3] These models include analysis of covariance (ANCOVA), Box–Cox (1964) transformed single-equation models, and two-part Tobit and Adjusted Tobit models.[4] I also discuss model estimation when the underlying coefficients shift systematically as one moves from nondrinkers to light to moderate-to-heavy drinkers. In what follows, the list of independent variables is assumed to be given by either the underlying conceptual model or the policy question of interest. Thus, the focus is on how ALC is modeled rather than on issues related to which variables should be included or how the variables are measured.

ANCOVA MODELS

If the analyst is concerned with the effect of some set of factors that are continuous, rather than discrete alternatives, he or she may rely on an ANCOVA approach, in which ALC is modeled as

$$ALC_i = x_i \gamma_1 + v_i, \qquad (1)$$

where x is a row vector of exogenous explanatory variables, γ_1 is a column vector of coefficients to be estimated, and v is often assumed to be an independently and identically distributed (i.i.d.) error term with zero mean.

---

[2]As Duan, Manning, Morris, and Newhouse (1983) and Manning et al. (1988, Appendix C) have shown for the case of medical care expenditures, models that exploit the similar characteristics of the distribution of health care expenditures yield estimates with less mean square error. Those studies also indicate that failure to model the distribution correctly can lead to misestimates of key parameters, such as the response to health insurance. This chapter addresses similar issues for the modeling of alcohol demand.
[3]The consumption of alcohol also can be modeled as the product of the frequency of consumption and the quantity at a sitting. For an economic example, see Kenkel (1996).
[4]These models are for continuous or limited dependent variables. If the data are discrete (e.g., the number of drinks), then an analyst should consider count models, such as Poisson or negative binomial regression models. See McCullagh and Nelder (1983) for additional details. Note that the Poisson assumption is probably invalid for drinking data because the variance greatly exceeds the mean (see Table A1).

The principal advantage of this model is its simplicity of estimation and interpretation.

This model has two principal disadvantages for demand applications: First, the assumption that the error term is i.i.d. is untenable in the presence of censoring unless the explanatory variables have no coefficients or are set up as mutually exclusive, discrete alternatives. In general, least squares applied to a limited dependent variable will provide inconsistent estimates of the response surface (Kennedy, 1992). For some part of the range of the independent variable x, the error term and x must be correlated. Figure 1 shows a plot of data points (*), the true S-shaped response of the probability to a single covariate x, and the ordinary least squares estimated regression line. At low or high values of x, it is possible to get predictions of probabilities that are either negative or exceed one. In those ranges of x, the average residual will be positive (for low x) or negative (for high x) because of the limited range of the dependent variable. The result is a bias in the estimated response; in this case, toward zero. This bias can be reduced by estimating a least squares model in some suitable polynomial in x. However, the polynomial approach may be unwieldly if there are several covariates in the model. Second, the estimates are sensitive to extreme values, especially if the dependent variable is badly skewed, as it is with ALC.

TRANSFORMED MODELS

The next model attempts to obtain more robust estimates by dealing with the skewness problem in the ALC dependent variable. The solution is to use a Box–Cox power transformation to make the dependent variable more normal in its distribution, in the hope that it will provide a more normally distributed error term. In a Box–Cox model, the dependent variable (ALC) is transformed to equal $[(\text{ALC}^\lambda - 1)/\lambda]$ if $\lambda \neq 0$ and $\log(\text{ALC})$ if $\lambda = 0$. The parameters (γ and λ) can be estimated by maximum likelihood if λ is not known and by ordinary least squares (OLS) if it is. Because ALC is approximately log normal in its distribution (Bruun et al., 1975; Lederman, 1956), the log transformation is the natural power transform to use. To avoid taking the log of zero, a constant c needs to be added to ALC before transformation; this addition of a constant before taking the power transformation forms the two-parameter version of the Box–Cox model. Formally, the model is

$$\log(\text{ALC}_i + c) = x_i\gamma_2 + \theta_i, \tag{2}$$

where x is a row vector of exogenous explanatory variables (e.g., price, income, age, or gender), γ_2 is a column vector of coefficients to be estimated,

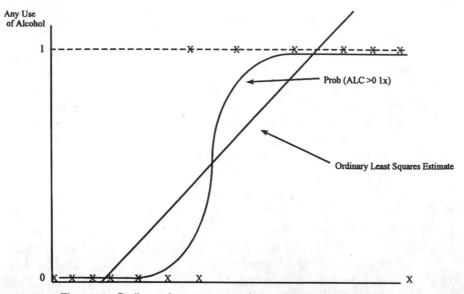

Figure 1. Ordinary least squares for a dichotomous variable.

and θ is assumed to be an i.i.d. error term with zero mean. If one ignores the censoring of ALC at zero, then the expected value of ALC is

$$E(ALC_i) = [\exp(x_i \gamma_2 + 0.5 var(\theta))] - c, \qquad (3)$$

where exp indicates the exponential if the error is log normally distributed with constant variance.

The principal advantages of this model are that (a) the estimates should be more robust because of the reduced skewness in the data and (b) the estimates should be more precise because the coefficient of variation is reduced if the distribution is approximately log normal.

This model has one principal disadvantage for demand applications. As in the ANCOVA model, the assumption of an i.i.d. error term is untenable in the presence of censoring unless the explanatory variables have zero coefficients or are set up as mutually exclusive, discrete alternatives. As noted earlier, least squares applied to a limited dependent variable will provide inconsistent estimates of the coefficients of interest (Kennedy, 1992).

TWO-PART MODELS

Rather than risk the bias from censoring, a more appropriate modeling approach is to deal with the censoring explicitly. In modeling medical use and alcohol demand, researchers have relied on two-part (or two-equation) multiple regression models (Duan & Manning, 1984; Duan et al., 1983; Manning, Blumberg, & Moulton, 1995; Manning, Duan, & Rogers, 1987; Manning & Morris, 1981; Manning, Newhouse, et al., 1987). The essence of the two-part model is to decompose one observed random variable, ALC, into two observed random variables. These two variables are whether a person drinks any alcohol (ALC > 0) and how much alcohol a person drinks if he or she drinks any at all (ALC|ALC > 0).

This model uses two equations to model these two aspects of the distribution of consumption. The first equation is a logit (or probit) equation for the probability that a person will have any ALC. This equation separates the nondrinkers from the drinkers and addresses the censoring problem. The second equation uses a regression for the logarithm of the amount consumed if any alcohol is consumed.[5] The log transformation of consumption for the group of drinkers reduces dramatically, but it does not completely eliminate the undesirable skewness in the distribution of consumption among current drinkers, which is the second problem mentioned earlier. As the data reported in Table A1 indicate, the logarithmic transformation to average daily consumption, if any, reduces the skewness to .18. This is much less than that observed for the raw, untransformed variable. However, it is still significantly greater than what one would expect from a normally distributed variate.[6] Nevertheless, one should expect the estimates from this model to be much more robust than those that might be obtained from ordinary least squares applied to untransformed ALC or transformed ALC without an explicit modeling of the censoring.

More formally, the first equation is either a logit or probit regression equation for the dichotomous event of zero versus any ALC. For the sake of comparisons with the class of Tobit models (discussed later), the probit version of the two-part model is described here:[7]

$$I_i = x_i\alpha + \varepsilon_i, \tag{4}$$

where x_i is a row vector of given individual characteristics, α is a column vector of parameters to be estimated, and ε_i is assumed to be a normally distributed i.i.d. error term with unit variance. If the index I_i is positive, then the ith individual will have positive ALC; otherwise, consumption will be zero. In the range of most ALC data, the logit and probit models have similar cumulative density functions (CDFs) and are virtually indistinguishable.

---

[5]If the focus in on the number of days with five or more drinks, the two equations are as follows: any 5+ days, and log of the number of 5+ days.

[6]Note that the kurtosis statistic indicates that log (ethanol) is shorter tailed than a normal variate. The absence of long tails also should make the results more robust.

[7]In Manning et al. (1995), and for the split-sample analysis reported later, we used the logistic regression variant of the two-part model because it has a simple, closed form for the price and income elasticities.

The second equation is a linear model on the log scale for positive ALC if person i is a current drinker:

$$\log(\text{ALC}_i | \text{ALC}_i > 0) = x_i \beta + \varepsilon_i, \tag{5}$$

where x_i is a row vector of given individual characteristics, β is a column vector of parameters to be estimated, and ε_i is the error, which is assumed to be conditionally independent. For the last equation, the error need not be normally distributed (Duan et al., 1983). Because the likelihood function for this model is separable between the two equations (because of the way conditional densities are calculated), the two equations can be estimated separately. There is no need to assume that the two error terms are uncorrelated; see Duan and Manning (1984) and Duan et al. (1983) for further discussion and an example with a correlated error term.

If the error term ε in the (log) conditional consumption equation is identically and normally distributed, then the expected consumption of alcohol for the ith person would be

$$E(\text{ALC}_i) = \Phi(x_i \alpha) \times \exp(x_i \beta + \sigma^2/2), \tag{6}$$

where Φ is the normal CDF. If a logistic regression were used, then the term $\Phi(\ )$ would be replaced by $p_i = \text{prob}(\text{ALC}_i > 0) = 1/(1 + \exp(-x_i a))$, where a would be the logit coefficient vector.

The factor $\exp(\sigma^2/2)$ is the adjustment $E[\exp(\varepsilon)]$ in the mean for the retransformation[8] of the error term in the second (or conditional) equation if ε is normally distributed with variance σ^2. The normal assumption for ε may not be satisfied for alcohol data. As a result of this nonnormality, the factor $[\exp(\sigma^2/2)]$ may not necessarily be the correct adjustment in the mean for the retransformation from the logarithmic scale to the untransformed scale and would lead to statistically inconsistent predictions of the total demand curve for alcohol.[9] Instead, I would suggest the smearing estimate developed by Duan (1983) unless the data exhibit a normally distributed residual.[10] The smearing estimate is a nonparametric estimate of the retransformation factor $\Psi = E[\exp(\varepsilon)]$, which equals the sample average of the exponentiated least squares residuals. The smearing estimate is statistically consistent for the retransformation factor if the error distribution does not depend on the characteristics x (e.g., price and income).

A consistent estimate of the expected alcohol consumption from the two-part model is therefore provided by

---

[8]If $\ln(y) = \mu + \varepsilon$, then the expected value of y is $E(y) = [\exp(\mu)] E[\exp(\varepsilon)]$. The last term is positive, even if $E(\varepsilon) = 0$.
[9]For the National Health Interview Survey data, the normal transformation is off by less than 2%.
[10]As Duan (1983) demonstrated, small departures from normality on the log scale can cause substantial inconsistency if the departure is in the right tail of the distribution.

$$E(ALC_i) = \Phi(x_i\hat{\alpha})[\exp(x_i\hat{\beta})]\Psi, \qquad (7)$$

where $\Psi = 1/n \sum [\exp(\ln(ALC_i) - x_i\hat{\beta})]/n$, $\Phi(x_{i\hat{\alpha}})$ is the predicted probability based on the probit regression estimate of α, and $\hat{\beta}$ is the least squares estimate of β.

COMPARISON OF THE ANCOVA, TRANSFORMED, AND TWO-PART MODELS

To assess the relative performance of these three alternative modeling approaches, I used a variant of the split-sample methodology used by Duan et al. (1983). One of the major concerns with ANCOVA models is that they may overfit data on ALC because of the skewness in ALC. If overfitting is an issue, one would expect the ANCOVA model to perform well on the data used for estimation but to poorly forecast the behavior of other data sets drawn randomly from the same population. To test this conjecture, as well as the performance of transformed and two-part models, a split-sample validation approach was used. The National Health Interview Survey (NHIS) 1983 data described in the Appendix was ordered from low to high on the basis of a randomly assigned variable, and each case then was assigned to 1 of 50 subpopulations based on that order. Then, for varying sample sizes, each model was estimated on one subsample and evaluated on the remaining subsample. For example, each of the models was estimated on the first 10% of the subpopulations ($n = 1,884$), and forecasts were made to the remaining 90% of the subpopulations. For each case of the forecast sample, the average forecast bias

$$\overline{\text{bias}} = \bar{y} - \bar{\hat{y}}_{\text{forecast}}$$

and the mean square forecast error (MSFE)

$$\text{MSFE} = \frac{1}{n} \sum (\text{bias}_i)^2$$

were calculated and averaged over the subpopulation. This process was repeated for the estimation sample consisting of the first 20% of the randomly ordered data, the first 30%, the first 40%, and then the first half of the data.

To test the forecast performance, I relied on sign tests for the subpopulations in the forecast sample. If the ANCOVA were performing poorly relative to a two-part model, the proportion of the forecast subpopu-

TABLE 1
Subpopulation Sign Tests for the Mean Square Forecast Error (MSFE)
on the Forecast Sample Fraction of Subpopulation in Which Model 1
Had a Higher MSFE

Model 1	Model 2	% of Full NHIS sample in estimation sample				
		10	20	30	40	50
OLS	Transformed					
	Normal	.00**	.00**	.00**	.00**	.00**
	Smearing	.00**	.00**	.00**	.00**	.00**
	Two part					
	Normal	.82**	.65*	.71**	.50	.48
	Smearing	.80**	.65*	.71**	.47	.48
Transformed: Normal	Transformed					
	Smearing	1.00**	1.00**	1.00**	1.00**	1.00**
	Two part					
	Normal	1.00**	1.00**	1.00**	1.00**	1.00**
	Smearing	1.00**	1.00**	1.00**	1.00**	1.00**
Transformed: Smearing	Two part					
	Normal	1.00**	1.00**	1.00**	1.00**	1.00**
	Smearing	1.00**	1.00**	1.00**	1.00**	1.00**
Two part: Normal	Two part					
	Smearing	.42	.40	.46	.37**	.44

Note. OLS = ordinary least squares; NHIS = National Health Interview Survey.
*$p < .10$. **$p < .05$.

lations with a greater MSFE would be well higher than .50 (50%). If it were performing better than the alternative, then the fraction would be well less than .50. The significance of the tests was based on a binomial assumption that the models were equally good (i.e., the fraction of cases with higher MSFE for any model would be .50). Table 1 shows the MSFE tests for the ANCOVA model, a log-transformed model with a normal theory retransformation, a log-transformed model with a smearing retransformation, a two-part model with a normal theory retransformation, and a two-part model with a smearing retransformation. The results indicate that both variants of the two-part model outperformed the ANCOVA model when the sample size was moderate (1,884–5,652 cases). As the sample size approached 8,000+ cases (40% or 50% of the NHIS 1983 sample), however, there were no statistically significant differences between the two-part and ANCOVA models. For the full range of sample sizes, the log-transformed models were significantly worse (i.e., had a higher MSFE) than either the ANCOVA or two-part models. For the two-part model, there were no significant differences between the normal theory retransformation and the smearing retransformation. The top of Table 2 shows the MSFE for each model, averaged over the forecast sample. Comparisons of estimators based on the absolute value of forecast bias across subpopulations exhibited a pattern similar to those for the MSFE.

TABLE 2
Test of Goodness of Fit on the Forecast Sample

Model	\% of full NHIS sample in estimation sample				
	10	20	30	40	50
	Mean square forecast error				
OLS	1.055	1.017	1.024	1.038	1.098
Transformed					
Normal	6.228	6.347	6.860	8.378	8.293
Smearing	2.531	2.201	2.294	2.916	2.754
Two part					
Normal	1.046	1.013	1.022	1.040	1.100
Smearing	1.047	1.014	1.022	1.040	1.101
	F on forecast bias				
OLS	12.92	9.33	6.05	3.46	3.39
Transformed					
Normal	719.69	680.80	593.54	495.73	400.35
Smearing	338.38	267.72	250.63	245.31	180.71
Two part					
Normal	7.23	6.02	4.94	4.29	4.69
Smearing	7.39	6.08	4.97	4.35	4.73

Note. All F tests for bias are significant at the .05 level. NHIS = National Health Interview Survey; OLS = ordinary least squares.

As a second test of the forecast sample performance of each model, I regressed the forecast bias from each model on the full set of covariates in the model. If there were no appreciable overfitting, the F ratio for this equation would be statistically insignificant. The bottom of Table 2 displays the Fs for each of the alternative models. All of the models tended to overfit the data to some extent. However, the worst one appeared to be the log-transformed model. For small and moderate-size data sets (1,884–5,652 cases), the ANCOVA model exhibited greater overfitting (higher F, corresponding to larger differences between the model estimated on the first $100x\%$ of the data and the $100[1-x]\%$ of the data from the forecast sample) than did the two-part models. For the larger data sets, the difference appeared to be negligible. When sets of coefficients for demographics, region, income and education, and price were examined, they exhibited the same pattern of overfitting as the full set of covariates.

These two sets of tests indicate that the two-part model was more robust and less prone to overfitting than the log-transformed model for ALC. For small and moderate-size samples, the two-part models performed better than the ANCOVA model and were similar for larger data sets.

TOBIT MODELS

The econometric literature provides an additional class of models for continuous but limited dependent variables, in which the limitation is attributable to either right or left censoring. These models are based on the univariate and bivariate normal distribution. They include the Tobit model (Tobin, 1958) and the Adjusted Tobit model (van de Ven & van Praag, 1981a, 1981b). The Tobit model has been more widely used by health economists. In the alcohol area, there is the work of Kenkel (1993), Moore and Cook (1995), and Sloan, Reilly, and Schenzler (1995).

Both models can be viewed as variants of the class of sample selection models (Maddala, 1983). Like the two-part model, these models are often two-equation models, with one equation (typically a probit) for whether there is any drinking and another equation for the amount of drinking. For simplicity's sake, I first describe the Adjusted Tobit model and then treat the traditional Tobit model as a special case. The underlying model uses two equations:

$$I_i = x\delta_1 + \eta_{1,i}, \tag{8}$$

$$w_i = x_i\delta_2 + \eta_{2,i}, \tag{9}$$

$$\log(ALC_i) = w_i \qquad \text{if } I_i > 0, \tag{10}$$

and

$$\log(ALC_i) = -\infty \qquad \text{if } I_i \leq 0, \tag{11}$$

where δ_1 and δ_2 are column vectors of coefficients to be estimated and $\eta_{1,i}$ and $\eta_{2,i}$ are the error terms for the two equations. Thus, if the index I_i is strictly positive, one observes that ALC is equal to the exponential of w_i. If the index is not positive, however, one observes zero consumption. The two error terms are drawn from a bivariate normal distribution:

$$(\eta_{1,i}, \eta_{2,i}) \sim N\left(0, \sum\right), \tag{12}$$

where

$$\sum = \begin{pmatrix} 1 & \rho\tau \\ \rho\tau & \tau^2 \end{pmatrix}. \tag{13}$$

Under the assumptions of the Adjusted Tobit model, the expectation of ALC is given by

$$E(ALC_i) = \Phi(x_i\delta_1 + \rho\tau)\exp(x_i\delta_2 + 0.5\tau^2), \tag{14}$$

where exp is the exponential and Φ is the normal CDF. This calculation depends critically on the error being multivariate normal and alcohol being transformed by the log in Equations 10 and 11.

The simple Tobit model is a limiting case of the Adjusted Tobit, in which $I_i = w_i/\tau$, $\tau\delta_1 = \delta_2$, $\tau\eta_{1,i} = \eta_{2,i}$, and $\rho = 1$. In this case, if the index I is not positive, ALC is zero. If the index is positive, then the level of alcohol consumed equals the exponential of the index I_i for the probit function (multiplied by τ). In most applications of the Tobit, the second equation would be for alcohol consumed, not the log of (or any other transformation of) the quantity of alcohol consumed. If the amount of alcohol consumed is not transformed, then the expected level of consumption under the Tobit model is

$$E(ALC_i) = [\Phi(x_i\delta_2/\tau)](x_i\delta_2 + \lambda\tau) \tag{15}$$

and

$$\lambda = \frac{\phi\left(\dfrac{x_i\delta_2}{\tau}\right)}{\Phi\left(\dfrac{x_i\delta_2}{\tau}\right)}, \tag{16}$$

where ϕ is the normal probability density function (PDF) and Φ is the normal CDF.

Both the Tobit and the Adjusted Tobit models can be estimated by either full information maximum likelihood or limited information maximum likelihood (see Maddala, 1983, for a description of each method for the Tobit, and van de Ven & van Praag, 1981a, for the Adjusted Tobit model). There is no requirement in the Adjusted Tobit model that the set of covariates included in the first equation of the model be identical with the set in the second equation. The model can be identified further by the nonlinearity of the full model's specification. However, identification by functional form is usually not recommended because the findings are not robust and the estimator is numerically poorly behaved; for an example of the latter, see the discussion of the results in Manning, Duan, and Rogers (1987).

Note that the first equation of the Adjusted Tobit model is identical to the first equation of the probit version of the two-part model. There is no corresponding relationship between the second equation in each model. Under the two-part model, the second equation is a conditional model that is linear and additive with a conditionally independent error term. Under the Adjusted Tobit model, the second equation is an unconditional linear model with an additive error term, which may or may not be independent of the error term in the equation for any use. The independence occurs if $\rho = 0$.

COMPARISON OF TWO-PART, TOBIT, AND ADJUSTED TOBIT MODELS

One concern about the two-part model in the econometrics literature flows from the seeming similarity of the two-part and Adjusted Tobit models. Some have argued that if the true model were a selection-model-based arrangement (e.g., the Adjusted Tobit in Equations 8–13), but the two-part model (as in Equations 4, 5, and 7) were estimated, then the beta estimates would be inconsistent (Hay & Olsen, 1984). Manning, Duan, and Rogers (1987) tested this conjecture by using a Monte Carlo study of the behavior of the two-part model when the true model was an Adjusted Tobit model. The evaluation considered two alternative situations in which (a) there was only one regressor that was the same in Equations 8 and 9 and (b) the two equations each had a single but different regressor. The first of these corresponds to the typical medical or alcohol demand case in which the same variables influence the likelihood of any consumption as the amount of consumption, although the magnitude of that influence can differ across the two equations. The second corresponds to the typical labor market application of the sample selection model (Heckman, 1974, 1976, 1979), in which some variables affect one but not the other equation.[11]

Manning, Duan, and Rogers (1987) evaluated the results of the two-part and Adjusted Tobit models on the basis of the bias and mean square error using Equations 7 and 15 for the predictions of total consumption from each model. When the covariates in each equation were the same, the limited information maximum likelihood (LIML) of the Adjusted Tobit model was more poorly behaved than was the two-part model, despite the fact that the two-part model was misspecified. When the rho was high, the LIML version of the Adjusted Tobit model was still poorly behaved. The full information maximum likelihood (FIML) version was negligibly worse than the two-part model in bias and negligibly better in the mean square error. Thus, the concern about the potential bias in the two-part model from ignoring the correlation seems to be misplaced for this case, even if the correlations between the two error terms are high. The real problem

[11]In the literature on women's labor force participation, it is often assumed that a woman's willingness to work for pay (technically, her reservation wage) depends on the number of children under six she has but is not a function of past work experience. The employer's wage offer depends on her years of experience but is not influenced by the ages of her children. A woman will enter the labor force if her reservation wage is less than or equal to the employer's wage offer. Under these circumstances, this selection model analog of Equations 8–13 can be considered a simultaneous equations model with quantifying, exclusion restrictions.

is the often poor performance of the Adjusted Tobit model, especially if estimated by LIML.[12]

The case with exclusion restrictions (i.e., different xs in Equations 8 and 9) tells a different story. In that case, the LIML estimates were well behaved, with a lower bias and mean square error than the two-part model. However, the magnitude of the difference was not large. Thus, if the application does have exclusion restrictions, the Adjusted Tobit appears to be a viable alternative. However, if there are no exclusion restrictions, it may be more poorly behaved than the alternative even if the Adjusted Tobit is the true model. In most applications, researchers do not have the luxury of knowing that a specific model is the true one.

If the true model is not of the Adjusted Tobit or selection model variety, the question is still unresolved as to which model is more robust. The econometric literature suggests that the estimates from the Tobit and selection models are hypersensitive to even minor departures from the underlying assumptions of the model (or of exclusion restrictions and i.i.d. errors); see comments by Goldberger (1980), Hurd (1979), and Olsen (1980) for results on related models. Specifically, minor departures from normality in the error term, homoscedasticity, and the restrictive assumptions on the index and error terms for the Tobit model are sufficient to generate badly biased estimates of the model parameters. For an overview of the issues with Tobit models, see Greene (1990).

In the case of alcohol, one special concern is that the distribution of consumption does not fully exhibit the pattern that is associated with the Adjusted Tobit model. The data reported in Table A1 have the positive skewness in the log of ALC (conditional on any drinking) that one would expect based on a positive rho correlation.[13] However, the conditional distribution also should be longer tailed than a normal distribution (kurtosis greater than 3); the estimates in Table A1 indicate a significantly shorter tailed distribution than a normal distribution.

In modeling, Tobit and Adjusted Tobit models should be avoided for several reasons. First, there is no conceptual reason why it is necessary to model the correlation between the likelihood of having any use and the level of use equations. In this case, the correlation coefficient is a nuisance parameter. Second, the two-part model is consistent in the presence of correlated errors across equations (Duan & Manning, 1984). Third, in the Monte Carlo comparison discussed earlier, we found that two-part models behaved as well and sometimes behaved better than Adjusted Tobit models (Manning, Duan, & Rogers, 1987). Finally, the Tobit and the Adjusted Tobit model estimates are not robust to minor departures from the under-

---

[12]The limited information maximum likelihood version is the more commonly found estimator for models like the selection and Adjusted Tobit models.
[13]A positive rho correlation implies that if a person is more likely to drink at all because of unmeasured characteristics, then he or she also is going to drink more heavily.

lying assumptions of the model. Minor problems of model specification, functional form, heteroscedasticity, or nonnormal error terms are sufficient to cause appreciable biases with either of these two approaches. By contrast, the two-part model can be easily modified to accommodate issues of heteroscedasticity and normality of the error term, as Duan et al. (1983) reported.

If the Tobit model is being considered, the analyst should verify that the model's restrictive assumptions are met in the data being used. Pagan and Vella (1989) surveyed tests that may be used. Three recent issues of the *Journal of Econometrics* (Vol. 32, Issue 1; Vol. 34, Issue 1; and Vol. 34, Issue 2) have been devoted to robust methods and specification tests for limited dependent variables.

QUANTILE REGRESSION

The preceding models provide estimates of the response of ALC if the true model is additive (on the scale of estimation) with constant coefficients across individuals. Both the two-part and the Adjusted Tobit models allow the response of drinkers to covariates to differ from those of nondrinkers, whereas the Tobit model assumes that the index function for the decision to drink is the same as that for the level of drinking. However, researchers are often concerned about more than the differences between drinkers and nondrinkers. For example, one policy and behavioral problem is to determine whether heavy drinkers have the same price elasticity (or response to income or other factors) as light and moderate drinkers. The answer to this question is an essential ingredient in estimating the second best optimal tax for alcohol if light and heavy drinkers impose different costs on others in society (Blumberg, 1992; Phelps, 1988; Pogue & Sgontz, 1989). Unfortunately for this issue, the two-part and Adjusted Tobit models assume that heavy drinkers differ from light drinkers by only a constant shift factor that depends on $E[\exp(\varepsilon_{light}/\varepsilon_{heavy})]$. Thus, the price response is driven by the deterministic part: the price terms in β in the case of the two-part model and δ_2 in the case of the Adjusted Tobit model. Equivalently, the models assume a world in which the demand curves for light, moderate, and heavy drinking are parallel.

One method that permits heavy and light drinkers to have different price elasticities is to allow the beta coefficients in the two-part model to vary by quantiles (q) of the data rather than to be a constant. Conditional on the covariates x, $100 \cdot q\%$ of the observations would have negative residuals. The remaining $100 \cdot (1 - q)\%$ would have positive residuals.[14]

---

[14]The regression plane passes through at least k of the N data points. As a result, $q(N - k - 1)$ will have negative residuals.

Koenker and Bassett (1978, 1982) and Bassett and Koenker (1982) proposed estimating such quantile regressions using a linear programming approach; to my knowledge, the first application of this method to ALC can be found in Manning et al. (1995). The technique minimizes a weighted sum of the absolute deviations of the error term:

$$\underset{b_q}{\text{Min}} \left[\sum_{y_i \geq x_i b_q} q|y_i - x_i b_q| + \sum_{y_i < x_i b_q} (1 - q)|y_i - x_i b_q| \right], \qquad (17)$$

where b_q is the estimate of β_q. Thus, the least (or minimum) absolute deviation regression model for estimating the median response is a special case of this approach.

Note that in this model, the qth quantile of drinking depends on two factors: the characteristics x of the individual and the quantile of the individual conditional on x. For many purposes, it is essential to know whether the price elasticity (or the response to some other covariate) varies significantly with consumption, the net of other covariates.[15] To test that hypothesis, one must focus on the response conditional on x.

Quantile regression also can be accomplished by iterative weighted least squares, with $y_i = \ln(\text{ALC}_i|\text{ALC}_i > 0)$. To estimate β_q for the qth quantile, the weights are $q/|r_i|$ if the residual for the ith observation is positive and $(1-q)/|r_i|$ if the ith residual is negative, where r_i is the residual for the ith observation. If the model is homoscedastic, then the covariance of the estimated coefficients $V(b_q)$ is

$$V(b_q) = \frac{q(1 - q)}{(f^2(q))} (X'X)^{-1}, \qquad (18)$$

where $f(q)$ is the PDF for the quantile.[16] Manning et al. (1995) estimated the model using iterative weighted least squares rather than linear programming methods.

Figure 2 shows the quantile regression estimates for the price elasticity from Manning et al. (1995). The price elasticity estimates vary significantly across quantiles, with the response not being appreciably or significantly different from zero among the heaviest users. Thus, assuming a constant price response in the demand for alcohol (among drinkers) is inappropriate. Assuming a constant price elasticity actually leads to a higher estimate of the price response than is in fact the case. However, the estimated income

---

[15]Because the welfare calculations depend on the level of consumption, those calculations require the simulation of the quantiles of the distribution of consumption (Blumberg, 1992).
[16]If there are two quantiles, i and j, then the covariance matrix is
$$\Omega \otimes (X'X)^{-1},$$
where the ith, jth $(i \leq j)$ element of Ω is
$$\omega_{ij} = \frac{q_i(1 - q_j)}{f(q_i)f(q_j)}.$$

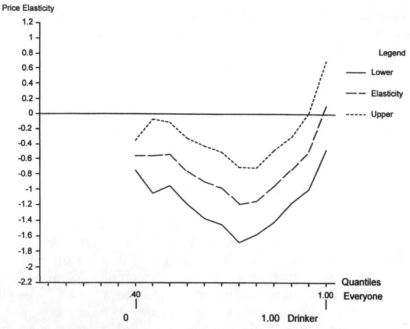

Figure 2. Estimated price elasticities with 95% confidence interval.

elasticities vary little across the quantiles.[17] Thus, in the case of alcohol, the assumption that betas are equal across quantiles appears to be reasonable for some variables (e.g., income), but it does not appear reasonable for other variables (e.g., price).

CONCLUSION

In this chapter, I have discussed alternative methods for estimating the demand for or consumption of alcohol. The choice of estimation approach is important because ALC data exhibit three characteristics that may cause estimation problems:

1. ALC is a limited dependent variable, with many observations stacked up or censored at zero consumption.
2. The consumption among drinkers is highly skewed.
3. The response to important covariates may vary with the level of their consumption in a manner not captured by covariates.

Some traditional models can deal with one or more of these problems. Transformed or Box–Cox models can deal with the skewness. Two-part and Tobit models can deal with both the censoring and the skewness. Of

---

[17]The estimates for the more extreme quantities are significantly different from the median response.

these, the two-part model is probably the most robust. The two-part model performs better than ANCOVA models for sample sizes of the order of 2,000–6,000 cases and is no worse in larger samples. The two-part model outperformed the transformed model in the split-sample validation. It also is more robust than the Adjusted Tobit model when the Adjusted Tobit is the true model.

The third problem requires the use of something like quantile regression methods. Preliminary estimates based on self-reported alcohol consumption indicate that obtaining different responses for different quantiles is a serious issue for price but that it may not be for other variables such as income. In any event, a constant beta across all ranges of consumption may be an untenable modeling assumption.

At this point, researchers know that the results for modeling alcohol demand by individuals can be sensitive to the approach selected. Further comparisons of alternative models should help us decide which models fit the demand for alcohol.

REFERENCES

Bassett, G., Jr., & Koenker, R. (1982). An empirical quantile function for linear models with iid errors. *Journal of the American Statistical Association, 77,* 407–415.

Blumberg, L. J. (1992). *Second best alcohol taxation: Balancing appropriate incentives with deadweight loss.* Unpublished doctoral dissertation, University of Michigan.

Box, G. E. P., & Cox, D. R. (1964). An analysis of transformation. *Journal of the Royal Statistics Society, Series B, 26,* 211–243.

Bruun, K., Edwards G., Lumio, M., Makela, K., Pan, L., Popham, R. E., Room, R., et al. (1975). *Alcohol control policies in public health perspective.* Helsinki, Finland: Finnish Foundation for Alcohol Studies.

Duan, N. (1983). Smearing estimate: A nonparametric retransformation method. *Journal of the American Statistical Association, 78,* 605–610.

Duan, N., & Manning, W. G. (1984). Choosing between the sample-selection model and the multi-part model. *Journal of Business and Economic Statistics, 2,* 283–289.

Duan, N., Manning, W. G., Morris, C. N., & Newhouse, J. P. (1983). A comparison of alternative models for the demand for medical care. *Journal of Economic and Business Statistics, 1,* 115–126.

Duan, N., Manning, W. G., Morris, C. N., & Newhouse, J. P. (1985). Comments on selectivity bias. In R. M. Scheffler & L. F. Rossiter (Eds.), *Advances in health economics and health services research: Vol. 6. Biased selection in health care markets* (pp. 19–24). Greenwich, CT: JAI Press.

Goldberger, A. S. (1980). *Abnormal selection bias* (Social Science Research Institute Rep. No. 8006). Madison: University of Wisconsin.

Greene, W. H. (1990). *Econometric analysis.* New York: Macmillan.

Hay, J. W., & Olsen, R. J. (1984). Let them eat cake: A note on comparing alternative models of the demand for health care. *Journal of Business and Economic Statistics, 2,* 279–282.

Heckman, J. (1974). Shadow prices, market wages, and labor supply. *Econometrics, 42,* 679–694.

Heckman, J. (1976). The common structure of statistical models of truncation, sample selection, and limited dependent variables, and a sample estimator for such models. *Annals of Economic and Social Measurement, 5,* 475–592.

Heckman, J. (1979). Sample bias as a specification error. *Econometrica, 47,* 153–167.

Hurd, M. (1979). Estimation in truncated samples when there is heteroscedasticity. *Journal of Econometrics, 11,* 247–258.

Kenkel, D. S. (1993). Drinking, driving, and deterrence: The effectiveness and social costs of alternative policies. *Journal of Law and Economics, 36,* 877–913.

Kenkel, D. S. (1996). New estimates of the optimal tax on alcohol. *Economic Inquiry, 34,* 296–319.

Kennedy, P. (1992). *A guide to econometrics.* Cambridge, MA: MIT Press.

Koenker, R. W., & Bassett, G. W. (1978). Regression quantiles. *Econometrica, 46,* 33–50.

Koenker, R. W., & Bassett, G. W. (1982). Robust tests for heteroscedasticity based on regression quantiles. *Econometrica, 50,* 43–61.

Lederman, S. (1956). *Alcool, alcoolisme, alcoolisation* (Vol. 1). Paris: Presses Universitaries de France.

Leung, S. F., & Phelps, C. E. (1993). "My kingdom for a drink . . . ": A review of estimates of the price sensitivity of demand for alcoholic beverages. In M. E. Hilton & G. Bloss (Eds.), *Economics and the prevention of alcohol-related problems* (NIAAA Research Monograph No. 25).

Maddala, G. S. (1983). *Limited-dependent and qualitative variables in econometrics.* Cambridge, England: Cambridge University Press.

Manning, W. G., Blumberg, L., & Moulton, L. H. (1995). The demand for alcohol: The differential effect of price. *Journal of Health Economics, 14,* 123–148.

Manning, W. G., Duan, N., & Rogers, W. H. (1987). Monte Carlo evidence on the choice between sample selection and two-part models. *Journal of Econometrics, 35,* 59–82.

Manning, W. G., Morris, C. N., Newhouse, J. P., Orr, L. L., Duan, N., Keeler, E. B., Leibowitz, A., Marquis, K. H., Marquis, M. S., & Phelps, C. E. (1981). A two-part model of the demand for medical care: Preliminary results from the health insurance experiment. In J. van der Gaag & M. Perlman (Eds.),

Health, economics, and health economics (pp. 103–124). Amsterdam: North-Holland.

Manning, W. G., Newhouse, J. P., Duan, N., Keeler, E. B., Leibowitz, A., & Marquis, M. S. (1987). Health insurance and the demand for medical care: Evidence from a randomized experiment. *American Economic Review, 77*, 251–277.

McCullagh, P., & Nelder, J. A. (1983). *Generalized linear models.* London: Chapman & Hall.

Moore, M. J., & Cook, P. J. (1995). *Habit and heterogeneity in the youthful demand for alcohol* (NBER Working Paper No. 152). Cambridge, MA: National Bureau of Economic Research.

Olsen, R. J. (1980). A least squares correlation for selectivity bias. *Econometrica, 48*, 1815–1920.

National Center for Health Statistics. (1985). *The National Health Interview Survey design, 1973–84, and procedures, 1975–83* (DHHS Pub. No. PHS 85-1320). Washington, DC: U.S. Government Printing Office.

Pagan, A. R., & Vella, F. (1989). Diagnostic checks for models based on individual data: A survey. *Journal of Applied Econometrics, 4*, S29–S59.

Phelps, C. E. (1988). Death and taxes: An opportunity for substitution. *Journal of Health Economics, 7*, 1–24.

Pogue, T. F., & Sgontz, L. G. (1989). Taxing to control social costs: The case of alcohol. *American Economic Review, 79*, 235–243.

Sloan, F., Reilly, B. A., & Schenzler, C. (1995). Effects of tort liability and insurance on heavy drinking and drinking and driving. *Journal of Law and Economics, 38*, 49–78.

Tobin, J. (1958). Estimation of relationships for limited dependent variables. *Econometrica, 26*, 24–36.

van de Ven, W. P., & van Praag, B. M. (1981a). Risk aversions of deductibles in private health insurance: Application of an adjusted tobit model to family health care expenditures. In J. van der Gaag & M. Perlman (Eds.), *Health, economics, and health economics* (pp. 125–148). Amsterdam: North-Holland.

van de Ven, W. P., & van Praag, B. M. (1981b). The demand for deductibles in private health insurance: A probit model with sample selection. *Journal of Econometrics, 17*, 229–252.

APPENDIX

The data source on alcohol consumption reported here (and in Manning, Blumberg, & Moulton, 1995) is the Alcohol and Health Practices supplement to the 1983 National Health Interview Survey (NHIS); the supplement was completed by 22,418 individuals aged 17+ years during calendar year 1983. The sample was a random sample of the civilian, noninstitutionalized population of the United States (see National Center for Health Statistics [NCHS], 1985, for the description of the methods and instruments used in the NHIS, and Manning et al., 1995, for the construction of the sample).

The actual sample size for this analysis was 18,844. Alcohol prices and the overall cost of living index have been linked by the NCHS to the 1983 NHIS by the respondents' probability sampling unit (PSU). Although the major PSUs are identified on the NHIS public use tape, smaller cities and rural areas are not. As a result, the NCHS had to link the price data directly to these PSUs. They performed such a match at the individual PSU level for all PSUs with 100,000 residents or at the state level for states with PSUs with a combined population of 100,000. Nearly 3,000 of the lost cases were because of missing information on drinking, price, or lack of an NCHS match.

An individual was considered a current drinker if he or she had more than 12 drinks in any year and had a drink in the past 12 months, according to responses to questions about the frequency of drinking and quantity consumed when they drank beer, wine, and spirits. For current drinkers, the average daily consumption of ethanol was based on an NCHS-constructed aggregate consumption. For each beverage (beer, wine, and spirits), the NHIS provides data on the number of days that an individual drank during the past 2 weeks, how much he or she drank on each of those days, the total number of drinks in the 2-week period, and the number of ounces per drink. Because intoxication is a risk factor for drunk driving, I included the number of days in the past year with 5 or more drinks as a proxy for bouts of heavy drinking. I have split this variable into an indicator for any days with five or more drinks and the natural log of any number of days with five or more, if any.

Summary statistics on average daily ethanol consumption are shown in Table A1. A frequency of ranges of average daily consumption and of the number of days with 5 or more drinks are shown in Tables A2 and A3.

TABLE A1
Summary Statistics in Alcohol Consumption 1983 NHIS

Name	Definition	M	SD	Skewness	Kurtosis
Ethanol	Ounces of ethanol	0.3590	1.0392	16.572	580.982
Drinks	Indicator for current drinker	0.6037	0.4891	—	—
lneth	Log of ounces of ethanol consumed if drinks = 1	−1.4309	1.3435	0.1837	2.4405
days5pls	Days with 5 or more drinks	8.0437	37.0026	7.1878	60.7861
any5pls	Indicator for any days with 5 or more drinks	0.2295	0.4205	—	—
ln5pls	Log of days with 5 or more drinks	2.2427	1.5911	0.4535	2.3735

Note. NHIS = National Health Interview Survey.

TABLE A2
Summary Statistics on Daily Ethanol Consumption

	Population	
Percentile	Everyone	Current drinkers
0	0.00	0.01
5	0.00	0.03
10	0.00	0.04
25	0.00	0.09
50	0.06	0.23
75	0.32	0.64
90	0.96	1.44
95	1.67	2.25
99	3.84	4.94
M	0.36	0.59
Variance	1.08	1.65

TABLE A3
Frequency of Days of Heavy Drinking

No.	%
0	77.05
1	2.88
2	2.63
3	1.70
4	1.33
5	1.39
6–10	3.28
11–15	1.96
16–20	1.04
21–30	1.68
31–40	0.47
41–50	0.67
51+	3.93

Note. Heavy drinking was the number of reported days with 5 or more drinks.

5

BEHAVIORAL GENETIC METHODS IN PREVENTION RESEARCH: AN OVERVIEW

ANDREW C. HEATH, WENDY S. SLUTSKE, KATHLEEN K. BUCHOLZ, PAMELA A. F. MADDEN, AND NICHOLAS G. MARTIN

In this chapter, we focus on the potential contributions of behavioral genetic methods to prevention research. We use illustrations drawn primarily from research on alcoholism. However, as reviewed in a recent book on behavioral genetic methods in behavioral medicine (J. R. Turner, Cardon, & Hewitt, 1994), these same methods apply to a broad range of other disorders, including diverse topics such as obesity and eating disorders, stress, cardiovascular reactivity, smoking, and illicit drug use. We begin by reviewing the evidence for an important genetic contribution to alcoholism risk. We then provide an overview of the types of research questions that may be addressed most powerfully in a behavioral genetic framework, ex-

This work was supported by National Institutes of Health Grants AA07535, AA07728, AA09022, and AA10249; by grants from the Australian National Health and Medical Research Council; and by Postdoctoral Training Grant MH17104. We acknowledge the contributions to the ideas discussed in this review of our colleagues on the Australian Twin Project and the Missouri Adolescent Twin Project, in particular Laura Bierut, Stephen Dinwiddie, Michael Dunne, and Dixie Statham.

panding on ideas originally summarized by Heath (1993). We examine some of the research challenges that arise in behavioral genetic research on alcoholism and other disorders. Finally, from these considerations, we draw conclusions about appropriate sampling strategies for prevention research in a behavioral genetic framework and examine their implications for other prevention and epidemiological research strategies.

THE GENETIC CONTRIBUTION TO ALCOHOLISM RISK

Adoption and twin studies using samples that have been ascertained systematically from birth or adoption records provide compelling evidence for an important genetic influence on alcoholism risk in both men and women (Heath, Slutske, & Madden, in press; McGue, 1994). (Later, we review some of the problems associated with studies using twins identified through treatment sources, which have yielded more inconsistent results; Caldwell & Gottesman, 1991; Gurling, Oppenheim, & Murray, 1984; McGue, Pickens, & Svikis, 1992; Pickens et al., 1991.) Studies of samples of male like-sex twin pairs identified from birth records, conducted in Sweden (Allgulander, Nowak, & Rice, 1991, 1992; Kaij, 1960), Finland (Koskenvuo, Langinvainio, Kaprio, Lonnqvist, & Tienari, 1984; Romanov, Kaprio, & Rose, 1991), and the United States (Hrubec & Omenn, 1981), consistently have shown a higher (albeit not always significantly higher) rate of alcoholism in monozygotic (MZ) than in dizygotic (DZ) cotwins of male alcoholics. With one exception, adoption studies conducted in Denmark (Goodwin, Schulsinger, Hermansen, Guze, & Winokur, 1973; Goodwin et al., 1974), Sweden (Bohman, Sigvardsson, & Cloninger 1981; Cloninger, Bohman, & Sigvardsson, 1981, 1985), and the United States (Cadoret, 1994; Cadoret, Cain, Troughton, & Heywood, 1985; Cadoret, Troughton, & O'Gorman, 1987) have shown higher rates of alcoholism in the adopted-away sons of alcoholic biological parents than in control adoptees; the one study that failed to indicate a difference showed abnormally high rates of alcoholism in its male control adoptees (Cadoret, 1994). This consistency of findings is especially remarkable given the diversity of assessments of alcoholism used in different studies, ranging from diagnostic interviews (Cadoret, 1994; Cadoret et al., 1985, 1987; Goodwin et al., 1973, 1974) to U.S. Veterans Administration treatment records (Hrubec & Omenn, 1981), hospital discharge codes (Allgulander et al., 1991, 1992; Koskenvuo et al., 1984; Romanov et al., 1991; True et al., 1996), annotations in adoption records (Cadoret, 1994; Cadoret et al., 1985, 1987), and registrations with the Swedish Temperance Board, a now-defunct organization that was charged with handling cases of public drunkenness and other alcohol-related problems (Cloninger et al., 1981, 1985; Kaij, 1960; Kendler, Prescott, Neale, & Pedersen, 1997).

Evidence for an important genetic influence on alcoholism in women, based on samples ascertained systematically from birth or adoption records, has been much weaker. The Danish adoption study of Goodwin, Schulsinger, Knop, and Mednick (1977) and Goodwin, Schulsinger, Knop, Mednick, and Guze (1977) showed rates of alcoholism that were no higher in adopted-away daughters of alcoholic parents than in control female adoptees, while the Swedish adoption study of Cloninger and colleagues (Bohman et al., 1981; Cloninger et al., 1985) showed a significant association between alcohol problems in female adoptees and their biological mothers, but not their biological fathers. In the United States, one study did indicate a significantly elevated risk of alcoholism in the adopted-away daughters of alcoholic parents (Cadoret et al., 1985), but a second study by the same group did not (Cutrona et al., 1994). Findings from twin studies have been similarly inconclusive. No concordant alcoholic female pairs were found in the Finnish twin study (Koskenvuo et al., 1984), whereas in the similar study of Swedish twins by Allgulander et al. (1991, 1992), although there was a trend for higher rates of alcoholism in the MZ than in the DZ twins of alcoholic parents, this was not significant (reanalyzed by Heath, Slutske, & Madden, in press). In a study of female like-sex twin pairs born in Virginia, Kendler, Heath, Neale, Kessler, and Eaves (1992) could not reject the hypothesis of no genetic influence for alcohol dependence (as defined by criteria from the revised third edition of the *Diagnostic and Statistical Manual of Mental Disorders [DSM–III–R]*, American Psychiatric Association, 1987), although significant evidence for genetic effects was found if either a broader problem-drinking measure or a more restrictive measure requiring physiological dependence (defined as *tolerance* or *withdrawal*) was used.

The weakness of this evidence for a genetic influence on alcoholism risk in women has led some to suggest that there may be a subtype of alcoholism that is predominant in women and shows only modest heritability, with strong moderation by environmental influences (Cloninger, 1987). In high-risk research on the offspring of alcoholic parents, it has also led to a much stronger focus on men than women (e.g., as reviewed by Sher, 1991). Failure to reject the null hypothesis of no genetic influence in women, however, is not convincing evidence that genetic effects are unimportant. Such a failure also may be a function of low statistical power: Given the lower base rate of alcoholism in women (Kessler et al., 1994; L. N. Robins & Regier, 1991), much larger numbers of female relatives of alcoholic individuals are needed to demonstrate a genetic effect. A more convincing demonstration would be to show that genetic factors are significantly more important in men than in women, that is, that they account for a significantly higher proportion of the total variance in alcoholism risk (i.e., have significantly higher heritability). If low statistical power is explaining the negative results in women, it should not be possible to demonstrate significantly lower heritability of alcoholism in women than

EXHIBIT 1
Nine Key Questions About the Causes of Alcoholism

1. How do genes act to increase alcoholism risk? What are the mediators—biological, sociodemographic, or behavioral—of genetic influences on alcoholism risk?
2. Are individuals at high genetic risk also more likely to be exposed to high-risk environments (gene–environment correlation)?
3. What environmental risk factors contribute to alcoholism risk?
4. Can researchers identify individual genetic loci that contribute to differences in alcoholism risk and understand their mode of action?
5. Can researchers identify alcoholic subtypes with distinct modes of inheritance or type-specific risk factors?
6. How do genetic and environmental influences vary as a function of gender, birth cohort, or culture?
7. How do genetic and environmental influences unfold through time to determine the natural history of drinking and of alcohol-related problems?
8. What vulnerability or protective factors exacerbate or reduce the risk of alcoholism in individuals at high genetic risk? How important is Genotype × Environment interaction?
9. At what levels of exposure to alcohol does genetic predisposition become important?

in men. This is indeed what we have found. When we reanalyzed data from the genetic studies that included both women and men, we found that it was not possible in any study to reject the hypothesis that there was no gender difference in the magnitude of the genetic influence on alcoholism risk (Heath, Slutske, & Madden, in press). In the absence of further contrary data, we consider it most appropriate to assume that genetic factors play no less a role in determining alcoholism risk in women than in men.

The demonstration of a significant genetic influence on alcoholism risk is often (but erroneously) viewed as an end point for behavioral genetic research; instead, it should be viewed as a beginning (Heath, 1993). In Exhibit 1, we summarize nine key questions about the causes of alcoholism. The questions focus on how genes and environment coact and interact, how their influences unfold through development, and the behavioral and biological pathways from genotype to alcoholism risk. It will become apparent that progress in answering these questions is only just beginning. Because the questions provide a framework in which the influences of genes and environment may be studied jointly, behavioral genetic methods have enormous potential for addressing such questions.

DEFINING WHO IS AT RISK

On the basis of an unpublished series of meta-analyses (summarized by Heath, 1995a), we have estimated that in individuals of European ancestry, genetic factors may account for as much as 60% of the total variance in alcoholism risk. (Insufficient numbers of other population groups, such as African Americans or Hispanics, have been studied using behavioral genetic methods.) Results from a telephone interview survey of approximately 6,000 adult Australian twins (Heath, Bucholz, et al., in press) yielded comparable estimates for the heritability of alcoholism, operationalized as *DSM–III–R* alcohol dependence, in both women and men. This information in itself is important for prevention efforts because it confirms that abstinence, or increased vigilance about drinking practices, is necessary for those with a family history of alcoholism.

Unfortunately, assuming that multiple genetic and environmental risk factors contribute to differences in alcoholism risk, many individuals at high genetic risk will have no affected immediate family members. For example, assuming 60% heritability of a broadly defined measure of alcohol dependence, with a lifetime prevalence of 24% in men and 6% in women, in both parental and offspring generations, and allowing for a modest degree of assortative mating (i.e., the tendency for alcoholic individuals to marry other alcoholic individuals) with a spousal correlation of .4, we can compute that slightly more than 50% of the men who become alcoholic and 38% of the women will have no parental history of alcoholism. Conversely, many of those from a high-risk genetic background would not be expected to become alcoholic. Under these same assumptions, 40% of men who have only an alcoholic father, 44% of men who have only an alcoholic mother, but 65% of men with both parents alcoholic would be expected to become alcoholic. Because of the much lower base rate assumed for women than men, corresponding proportions for women would be only 11.6%, 13.6%, and 28.4%, respectively. (These illustrative estimates were obtained under the assumption that alcoholism liability is approximately normally distributed in the general population, by integrating the quadrivariate normal distribution for a correlational structure defined by our heritability and assortative mating parameters, ignoring shared environmental causes of familial resemblance.) For women with both an alcoholic mother and maternal aunt, the risk increases to 36.5% if both parents are affected, implying that special sampling schemes may be necessary for high-risk research on women (cf. Hill, 1995).

In what ways can researchers improve identification of individuals at increased risk of alcoholism, for whom targeted prevention efforts may be appropriate? Behavioral genetic methods can play a crucial role in addressing six related questions: (a) What mediating variables can researchers identify that explain the behavioral or biological pathways by which genetic and environmental risk factors act to increase alcoholism risk; (b) are individuals at high genetic risk more likely to be exposed to high-risk environments (genotype–environment correlation); (c) what environmental factors contribute to differences in alcoholism risk; (d) what individual genetic loci can researchers identify that contribute to differences in alcoholism risk, and what can they discover about their mode of action; (e) can researchers identify subtypes of alcoholic individuals, who may differ in their mode of inheritance or associated risk factors; and (f) how do genetic and environmental influences unfold through time to determine the natural history of drinking and of alcohol-related problems?

Mediating Variables

The search for mediating variables—in our case, variables that may intervene in the causal pathways from genotype (or environment) to alcoholism risk—has a long history in alcoholism research. Much recent pertinent work has been carried out within the framework of high-risk studies on the offspring of alcoholic parents and in epidemiological research on psychiatric comorbidity with alcoholism (see Sher, 1991, for a review of recent research). Examples may be found in Schuckit's (1984, 1985; Schuckit & Gold, 1988) alcohol challenge research demonstrating differences in objective (e.g., body sway) and subjective (e.g., self-rated intoxication) responses to alcohol between the sons of alcoholic and control parents, differences that were predictive of alcoholism rates at longitudinal follow-up (Schuckit, 1994), or in the evoked potential research of Begleiter, Porjesz, Bihari, and Kissin (1984) demonstrating P300 differences between alcohol-naive sons of alcoholic and control parents (see Polich, Pollock, & Bloom, 1994, for a recent review). In both cases, there is at least some evidence for an important genetic contribution to individual differences in these variables (Heath, Neale, Kessler, Eaves, & Kendler, 1992; Rust, 1975). Cross-sectional epidemiological studies have demonstrated strong comorbidity between alcoholism and a history of conduct disorder (Helzer & Pryzbeck, 1988), a disorder that typically has early onset and, in Australian twin data, has been found to have high heritability in both women and men (Slutske et al., 1997). Prospective studies of high-risk populations likewise have identified measures of impulsivity or behavioral undercontrol, and perhaps also of anxiety or negative affectivity, as potential mediators of alcoholism risk (Sher, 1991). Here again, the evidence for a major contribution of genetic factors to personality differences, from adoption, twin, and separated-twin studies, is strong (Eaves, Eysenck, & Martin, 1989; Loehlin, 1992). Thus, many potential mediators of genetic or environmental influences on alcoholism risk have been identified.

How can behavioral genetic methods advance this research? The demonstration in separate studies that such potential mediating variables are associated with differences in alcoholism risk and are heritable tells researchers little about how important a role they play in accounting for genetic influences on alcoholism risk. By comparing the covariances of alcoholism and a postulated mediating variable (a) within individuals and (b) between biologically related individuals (e.g., biological parent and adopted-away offspring or MZ vs. DZ twin pairs), it becomes possible to partition the total genetic variance in alcoholism risk into variance that is associated with differences in the postulated mediating variable and a residual genetic variance. Although we cannot, except under rare conditions (Neale & Cardon, 1992), leap from such an estimate to inferences about direction of causation, we can at least obtain lower bound estimates of how much of the genetic variance in alcoholism risk remains unaccounted for. With multivariate data measured on relatives, factor models estimating separate genetic and environmental factors (Neale & Cardon, 1992) and more elaborate models for the covariance structure of genetic and environmental influences on alcoholism risk and associated variables can be tested using standard multiple-group structural equation modeling. (Intuitively, it can be seen that a comparison of covariance matrices between relatives, that is, giving the covariances of Relative A's variables with Relative B's variables, in MZ vs. DZ twin pairs or biological vs. adoptive relative pairs, permits resolution of genetic vs. shared environmental covariance structures, whereas the additional information provided by the within-persons covariance matrix, that is, giving the covariances of variables within individuals, permits estimation of the within-families environmental covariance structure of alcoholism and related variables.)

Additionally, in the case of the twin design, several issues that can be addressed only by longitudinal follow-up in conventional high-risk designs can be addressed cross-sectionally. In a conventional high-risk design, studying single offspring of alcoholic and control parents, an association between parental alcoholism and mediators measured in the offspring (e.g., cortisol and prolactin measures of response to alcohol challenge; Schuckit & Risch, 1987) may reflect a variety of nongenetic causes, including comorbidity in the offspring generation (e.g., depression induced by parental alcoholism) and cross-assortative mating (e.g., if depressed mothers marry alcoholic fathers and transmit an increased risk of depression to their offspring). Only costly long-term follow-up studies will confirm that the postulated mediators are primary predictors of differences in alcoholism risk rather than of other outcome variables. In the twin design, by contrast, nongenetic causes of such an association will produce equally elevated values of the mediating variable in MZ and in DZ cotwins of alcoholic twins, allowing such nongenetic effects to be distinguished from genetic associations.

To date, the potential of behavioral genetic methods for identifying important mediating variables remains underexploited. Most major studies of the genetics of alcoholism have not addressed the question of how genetic influences are acting. McGue (1994) reviewed some of the evidence for the role of personality variables as mediators. In our own work, although we have not found personality variables to be important mediators, we have found results suggesting that even in populations of European ancestry there are polymorphic loci that lead to differences in alcohol preference or self-exposure and ultimately lead to differences in alcoholism risk: Even if we exclude twin pairs concordant for alcoholism (to avoid the complication of the effect of alcoholism on drinking patterns), maximum reported 24-hr consumption of alcohol is predictive of the *cotwin's* alcoholism risk and is significantly more strongly associated in MZ than DZ pairs (Heath, Slutske, et al., 1994). A rapid growth in the number of behavioral genetic publications on mediating variables is to be anticipated.

Genotype–Environment Risk Factors

The analysis of genotype–environment correlation may be viewed as a special case of the analysis of mediating variables, in which our focus is on the role of family (and potentially also friends) as mediators of differences in alcoholism risk. There are a variety of mechanisms by which individuals at high genetic risk for developing alcoholism also may come to be at high environmental risk (Eaves, Last, Martin, & Jinks, 1977; Heath, 1993; Plomin, DeFries, & Loehlin, 1977). These include the following: (a) genotype–environment autocorrelation, in which individuals at high genetic risk expose themselves to high-risk environments; (b) parent–offspring environmental influences in intact nuclear families, in which alcoholic parents both transmit genetic risk factors and create a high-risk rearing environment; (c) environmental influences by other biological relatives, such as older sibling or cotwin environmental influences; or (d) environmental influences by a spouse, partner, or peers who have correlated genetic risk because of selective mating or selective friendship (i.e., the tendency for individuals at high risk to assort with others at high risk). A variety of behavioral genetic designs may be used to resolve these various genotype–environment correlation effects, including prospective twin studies (to resolve the genotype–environment autocorrelation; Eaves et al., 1977), studies of twins and their parents or offspring or of adoptees and controls and their biological and adoptive relatives (to resolve parent–offspring and sibling environmental influences; Eaves, 1977; Fulker, 1981; Heath, Kendler, Eaves, & Markell, 1985), and studies of the spouses (or peers) of twin pairs (Heath, 1987; Heath & Eaves, 1985). As in the case of mediating variables, addressing such questions compels researchers to focus on the mechanisms by which genetic and environmental influences are transmitted rather than to be satisfied with statements about the importance of genetic factors, or of individual genetic loci, in the etiology of alcoholism.

From consideration of the issues of genotype–environment correlation, we are led naturally to the view that environmental risk factors can be studied most convincingly in the context of a genetic design. An observed correlation between parental marital discord and offspring alcoholism risk, for example, may merely be a *genetic* correlation that we would have observed to be equally as strong when marital discord was studied in the biological parents and associated with alcoholism risk in their adopted-away offspring. This might occur if parental alcoholism, sociopathy, or other potentially unmeasured heritable variables are contributing to risk of parental marital discord and if genetic risk factors for these disorders are transmitted to the offspring generation, for whom they increase alcoholism risk.

In principle, one might expect adoption designs to provide the most convincing evidence for environmental influences on alcoholism risk. In practice, however, as in the case of the Stockholm Adoption Study (Cloninger et al., 1981, 1985), stringent screening criteria for adoptive parents have the consequence that most adoptees are reared in low-risk environments. As an alternative to the adoption paradigm, the study of adult MZ and DZ twin pairs and their spouses and offspring (e.g., Heath et al., 1985; Nance & Corey, 1976) offers the best prospect for studying the environmental sequelae of parental alcoholism, controlling for genetic effects. By studying parenting behaviors such as marital discord in MZ and DZ twin pairs, the extent to which such measures are genetic correlates of alcoholism (i.e., elevated in the cotwins of alcoholic twins) can be determined. Under random mating, the genetic correlation between parent and child is the same as that between parent's MZ cotwin and parent's child, so that any excess of the parent–offspring compared with the MZ cotwin–offspring correlation is indicative of an environmental influence. If these two correlations do not differ significantly, this may indicate either genetic transmission or an influence on the twins' own parenting behavior of early rearing experiences and similar family background factors shared equally by twin pairs reared in the same family; these two possibilities may be distinguished by also obtaining data on DZ twin pairs and their offspring because the hypothesis of genetic transmission, but not that of shared family background influences, predicts a significantly lower DZ cotwin–offspring correlation than the parent–offspring and MZ cotwin–offspring correlations.

Assortative mating, by creating a genetic correlation between the twin parents and their spouses, also leads to the prediction of a higher parent–offspring than MZ cotwin–offspring correlation (Eaves & Heath, 1981; Heath et al., 1985). However, by obtaining data on the spouses of MZ and DZ twin pairs, the contributions of assortative mating to the genetic correlation between spouses may be modeled and adjusted for statistically (Heath & Eaves, 1985), so that a test for parent–offspring environmental influences is still possible. In theory, such a design is much less powerful than the classical adoption design in which, in the absence of selective placement effects, estimates of genetic and environmental influences are orthogonal (Heath et al., 1985). However, because the screening for good parenting skills that occurs in the adoption process does not apply in the twin-family design, in practice, this latter approach offers the best prospect of studying the environmental impact of parental alcoholism.

In a similar fashion, the study of twin pairs and their spouses offers the best prospect in naturalistic studies of resolving the environmental impact of a partner's drinking and related behaviors on the course of alcoholism or other psychopathology. Matched-pairs case-control comparisons of MZ twin pairs who are discordant for marriage to an alcoholic spouse, particularly when used in a prospective design, provide a test for the environmental impact of being married to an alcoholic individual. More generally, case-control comparisons of risk factor discordant pairs may prove helpful in confirming or disconfirming the postulated etiological role of an environmental risk factor, controlling for family background and (in the case of MZ pairs) for genotype. Thus, demonstration of a significant association between early sexual abuse and later alcoholism does not address the extent to which the association may reflect the influences of variables with common effects on both outcomes, such as a disrupted family environment, parental sociopathy, and so on (Dinwiddie et al., 1997). Finding that in twin pairs discordant for sexual abuse, alcoholism rates were significantly elevated in the abused twins but that in the nonabused twins, the rates did not differ from general population rates in nonabused individuals would more strongly support the hypothesis that sexual abuse is an important environmental risk factor for alcoholism. Comparison of alcoholism-discordant pairs, and pairs concordant for alcoholism but discordant for treatment, likewise permits naturalistic studies of the long-term socioeconomic, health, services use, and other outcomes of alcoholism and the extent to which these are ameliorated by treatment (True et al., 1996).

Identifying Susceptibility Loci

The term *susceptibility locus* has come to be used in genetic research on complex disorders such as alcoholism or cardiovascular disease to identify genes that contribute to differences in the risk of developing a disorder, to emphasize that there is no single "alcoholism" gene. Continuing efforts to identify such susceptibility loci in individuals of European ancestry, as well as Hispanics and African Americans, using both linkage and genetic association studies, have not yet yielded consistently replicable findings. Initial reports of a significant genetic association between the A1 allele at the DRD2 locus and alcoholism (Noble & Blum, 1991) have yielded a series of replication studies with both positive (Blum et al., 1993; Comings et al., 1991) and negative (Gelernter et al., 1991; Suarez et al., 1994; E.

Turner et al., 1992) findings. Unfortunately, such association studies have used a standard case-control methodology in which allele frequencies were compared in a series of alcoholic and control participants. Because marked differences in allele frequency at this locus (as well as many others) have been observed as a function of ethnic background (Barr & Kidd, 1993; Goldman, 1993), differences in the alcoholism rates between different ethnic groups will easily generate false-positive findings. Given the highly mixed ancestry of the U.S. population, in particular, appropriate matching of cases and controls is unlikely to be achieved. Research methods that avoid this problem are available, notably by examining DNA markers in a series of parents of alcoholic offspring and comparing the frequency of candidate alleles transmitted by the two parents to their alcoholic offspring and of the nontransmitted alleles, providing a matched-pairs comparison that controls for ethnic background (Falk & Rubinstein, 1987; Spielman, McGinnis, & Ewens, 1993). Positive associations with alcoholism obtained using such methods, however, have not yet been reported, to our knowledge.

The fact that susceptibility loci have not yet been identified in individuals of European ancestry does not, of course, imply that none exist. In individuals of Asian (e.g., Japanese, Chinese, or Korean) ancestry, the contribution of a polymorphism at the ALDH2 locus to differences in alcoholism risk is already well established. In some individuals of Asian ancestry, an allele is found at the ADLDH2 locus that leads to a flushing response, reduced alcohol consumption (Higuchi et al., 1991), and reduced alcoholism risk (for a review, see Thomasson, Crabb, & Edenberg, 1993). Unfortunately, almost all those of European, Hispanic, and African American ancestry appear to carry the "high-risk" gene.

There are several reasons for optimism about the likelihood that more susceptibility loci for alcoholism will be identified in the near future. The existence of rodent models for various aspects of drinking behavior, ranging from alcohol preference (Li, 1990) to withdrawal sensitivity (Crabbe, Belknap, & Buck, 1994), offers the prospect that genetic polymorphisms associated with these behavioral differences will be identified. The high degree of synteny between mice and humans, in particular, means that it will be possible to identify candidate chromosomal regions in humans where equivalent polymorphisms may be sought. The success of such strategies has already been demonstrated in work with mice strains selected to model hypertension (Hilbert et al., 1991) or obesity (Zhang et al., 1994).

There are, of course, no guarantees that the existing rodent models will identify key polymorphisms in human populations. However, the mapping of so-called *quantitative trait loci* (e.g., Kruglyak & Lander, 1995; Risch & Zhang, 1995), genes that contribute to variations in continuously distributed variables, also is becoming feasible in human samples, at least in the case of moderately or highly heritable traits (cf. Cardon et al., 1995).

By studying the number of alleles at a given locus (0, 1, or 2) that pairs of relatives (e.g., siblings) have inherited from common ancestors (e.g., parents), it is possible to test for an association between the degree of allele sharing at that genetic locus with the within-pairs trait variance: Significantly higher sibling correlations would be predicted for the pairs who share two alleles inherited from their two parents, intermediate correlations for those who share only one allele, and lower correlations for those who share neither allele at this locus. Although large numbers (e.g., many thousands) of sibling pairs must typically be screened for these methods to give adequate statistical power, the selection of pairs that are highly concordant for scores on the quantitative trait (e.g., both scoring above the 10th percentile) and of pairs that are highly discordant (e.g., with one in the bottom 30th percentile and the second in the top 10th percentile) means that a much reduced proportion needs to be genotyped (Eaves & Meyer, 1994; Risch & Zhang, 1995). In our own twin family studies in Virginia and Australia, self-report questionnaire measures of such quantitative risk factors as alcohol consumption level (Heath, 1995b) were obtained from more than 10,000 DZ twin and sibling pairs and trios, providing a basis for such targeted follow-up efforts.

The identification of individual genetic loci that contribute to alcoholism risk offers the eventual prospect of a much more refined analysis of the ways in which individual genetic loci and specific environmental risk factors coact. It also may offer the prospect of prevention efforts targeted at individuals identified as being at high genetic risk, although if, as in the case of the ALDH2 polymorphism in Asian populations, many such polymorphisms are found to have protective effects, this latter benefit may be more limited.

Identifying Alcoholism Subtypes

To the extent that alcoholism is a heterogeneous disorder, as has often been suggested (e.g., Babor et al., 1992; Cloninger, 1987; Jellinek, 1960), one might expect that it would be possible to uncover stronger associations between genetic or environmental risk factors and alcoholic subtypes than would be the case if all alcoholic individuals were combined. Behavioral genetic approaches clearly can be informative for this purpose. If researchers are able to demonstrate distinct coaggregation of particular alcoholism subtypes in families and to establish different modes of inheritance for different subtypes, confidence in a subtyping scheme would be greatly advanced (E. Robins & Guze, 1970). Despite various attempts to define such subtypes (e.g., Cloninger, 1987; Cloninger et al., 1981), however, none have been consistently supported by empirical data.

One approach to subtyping, which ultimately may allow joint testing of a genetic model and a model defining alcoholic subtypes (Eaves et al.,

1993), is provided by latent class analysis (LCA). LCA may be viewed as a categorical variant of factor analysis (Bartholomew, 1987). Factor analysis seeks to explain the correlations observed between a set of variables in terms of the linear effects on those variables of a small number of underlying continuously distributed latent variables or factors, and it postulates that if a sufficiently large number of factors is estimated, the residual terms for the observed variables will be statistically independent. Structural equation modeling may be used to test hypotheses about the number of factors needed to account for the observed correlations between variables and about the loadings of individual items on individual factors (i.e., whether a particular latent factor has a direct influence on a particular item). Similarly, LCA seeks to explain the associations between a set of binary or polychotomous items by the existence of a small number of mutually exclusive subject categories, or "classes," that differ in their item-endorsement probabilities; it also permits tests of hypotheses about the number of classes needed to explain the observed associations between items and about item-endorsement probabilities of individual items conditional on membership in a given class. A critical assumption of LCA is that within a class, item-endorsement probabilities are homogeneous for all class members and are statistically independent (Goodman, 1974; McCutcheon, 1987).

It might be anticipated that LCA would be an ideal technique for identifying subtypes of alcoholic individuals having different symptom profiles (cf. Cloninger, 1987). In analyses using only alcoholic symptom data, however, we have found that the classes identified appear to fall along a continuum of severity of alcohol-related problems (e.g., Bucholz et al., 1996; Heath, Bucholz, et al., 1994) rather than representing distinct subtypes. Figure 1, for example, shows results from a reanalysis (using a smaller number of alcoholic symptoms) of lifetime symptom data from a general community sample of Australian adult male twins (1,846 men who had more than minimal alcohol exposure; Heath, Bucholz, et al., 1994) for a four-class model. In addition to item-endorsement probabilities for each class, 95% confidence limits for these conditional probabilities, estimated by bootstrapping (Efron & Tibshirani, 1986), also are shown. All analyses were run using a program written by us, using the standard EM algorithm for LCA (McCutcheon, 1987). The four classes may be identified as those with no alcohol-related problems, heavy drinkers, those with moderate problems, and those with more severe problems. Prevalence estimates for these classes (equivalent to class membership probabilities) in our reanalysis were 41.4%, 40.1%, 15.2%, and 3.3%, respectively. In those labeled *heavy drinkers*, only symptoms such as "getting drunk when didn't want to," "using alcohol more than intended," tolerance, hazardous alcohol use, and alcohol-related blackouts were endorsed with a moderately high (.35–.63) probability. Only in the most severe class were symptoms such as "unable to stop or cut down on drinking" (.64) and withdrawal symp-

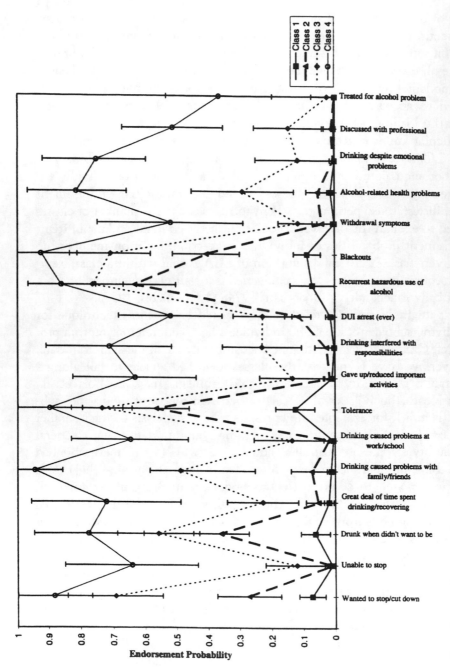

Figure 1. Symptom endorsement probabilities (and 95% confidence intervals) estimated by latent class analysis under a four-class model. Class membership probabilities are as follows: Class 1, ■, .41 (.31–.52); Class 2, ▲, .40 (.32–.49); Class 3, ◆, .15 (.07–.23); and Class 4, ○, .03 (.02–.05). Probabilities do not sum to 1 because of rounding error. DUI = driving under the influence.

toms (.52) endorsed with high probability. Endorsement probabilities for the moderate problems class were intermediate between those for the heavy drinking and severe problems classes. The analysis presented in Figure 1 ignores the fact that data were obtained on twin pairs. In principle, however, it should be possible to model jointly the causes of twin pair concordance and discordance for class membership and item-endorsement probabilities for each class (Eaves et al., 1993), although our own efforts in this regard suggest that such joint models are numerically ill-behaved, so that obtaining a global maximum-likelihood solution is a challenge.

Developmental Perspectives

Most psychiatric genetic researchers use as an outcome measure the presence or absence of a given disorder, assessed on a lifetime basis. On the basis of the results of our analyses of alcohol symptom data using LCA, however, we have come to believe that it is important to go beyond this simple lifetime approach. It is natural to question whether latent classes such as those illustrated in Figure 1 can be viewed as temporal stages in the course of alcoholism. Although this issue would be best addressed prospectively, it is possible to use retrospective reports of age of onset of individual symptoms to examine the accumulation of symptoms through time. Using an approach from event history analysis (Allison, 1984), a person−year file is created in which a separate vector of observations is created for each year of each respondent's drinking career (Nelson, Heath, & Kessler, 1997), indicating whether the respondent has reported experiencing any of the symptoms during or before that particular year of his or her life. Such data then may be used as input for an LCA, to obtain estimates of class membership and item-endorsement probabilities and to compute from these the most likely class membership for every symptom profile occurring in the data set. In this way, it becomes possible to search for risk factors that predict respondents' transitions between classes over time (Nelson et al., 1997). As others have noted (e.g., Collins et al., 1994), different risk factors may determine transitions from nonproblem use to experiencing first substance-related problems versus transitions from first to more severe problems; thus, identifying the stages in the natural history of alcohol use and abuse or dependence at which particular risk factors are operating would have important implications for prevention efforts (Nelson, Little, Heath, & Kessler, 1996).

Although these methods have not yet been applied in a genetic framework, to do so would be a necessary extension of this work. From a genetic perspective, it is natural to question whether genetic loci that influence the transition from moderate to excessive or problem drinking are the same as those that determine, for example, the probability of development of physiological dependence, as indicated by the presence of withdrawal symptoms. The twin design permits powerful tests of autoregressive (e.g., Eaves, Long, & Heath, 1986), growth curve, and similar developmental behavioral genetic models (e.g., Meyer & Neale, 1992). Of particular importance, with longitudinal data, or quasi-longitudinal data created from retrospective data, it allows researchers to test whether there would be stage-specific genetic or environmental influences on the course of alcohol-related problems and to test how these influences covary and interact. Thus, researchers can move away from the simple "lifetime" perspective that has dominated psychiatric genetic research.

AT RISK UNDER WHAT CONDITIONS?

Neither an individual's increased genetic risk of alcoholism nor increased environmental risk implies an alcoholic destiny. However great the risk factors, those who have never been exposed to alcohol will not become alcoholic. A second broad class of interrelated questions about the etiology of alcoholism that can be powerfully addressed using behavioral genetic methods and that have obvious relevance to prevention research, concerns the conditions under which genetic and environmental risk factors lead to alcoholism: (a) How do genetic and environmental influences vary as a function of gender, birth cohort, or culture? (b) What moderator variables—vulnerability or protective factors—interact with genetic risk of alcoholism or with environmental risk factors to determine outcome? (c) At what levels of exposure to alcohol does genetic predisposition become important?

Moderating Effects of Gender, Birth Cohort, and Culture

The extension of behavioral genetic methods to allow for interactions of genetic predisposition with gender, with birth cohort, and, in cross-cultural studies, with societal norms and associated social differences is straightforward. As in most multiple-group structural equation modeling analyses (Bollen, 1989), one can compare the fit of models that constrain genetic and environmental parameters to be the same across groups with models that allow parameters to differ between groups. In the case of unlike-sex relative pairs, it may be shown that the genetic covariance between relatives will be a function of the geometric mean of the male and female genetic variances (Bulmer, 1980). As more elaborate models incorporating mediating variables are developed, hypotheses about differences in the relative importance of different causal pathways from genotype to behavioral (or biological) differences to alcoholism risk can be similarly tested. In view of the important differences in drinking patterns that exist between societies and between genders, and the changes in drinking patterns that occur over time, one might anticipate that strong interaction effects would be found.

In the case of alcoholism, we commented earlier on the lack of evidence for male–female differences in the heritability of alcoholism from within-studies comparisons. The absence of a gender difference in the heritability of alcoholism does not, of course, imply equal rates of alcoholism in male and female relatives of alcoholic individuals. The gender difference in lifetime prevalence and the higher rates of alcoholism observed in male cotwins of alcoholic mothers compared with male DZ cotwins of alcoholic fathers (e.g., McGue et al., 1992) suggest that on average, women who become alcoholic are at higher genetic risk than men who become alcoholic. Results of a meta-analysis (Heath, 1995a) show a trend for reduced (rather than increased) heritability of alcoholism in Scandinavian men than in Scandinavian women and American men and women, but differences in methodology between studies, and the fact that several studies have excluded women, leave us uncertain about whether this reflects a Genotype × Culture (× Gender) interaction or is merely a consequence of methodological differences. Kendler et al. (1997) failed to find birth cohort differences in the heritability of alcoholism in an analysis of data on Swedish Temperance Board registrations in male twins; and in the same meta-analysis, we found remarkable consistency of heritability estimates across studies using different birth cohorts. To date, the evidence for interactions between genotype and gender, birth cohort, and culture is thus weak.

Genotype × Environment Interaction

Interactions of genotype with gender, birth cohort, or culture may be viewed as a special case of Genotype × Environment interaction, the moderating effect of environmental variables on genetic influences on alcoholism risk. Testing for such interactions is the most straightforward when the postulated moderating environmental variable is binary. Such a model can be tested in a multiple-group structural equation modeling (SEM) analysis, in which separate groups are created for relative pairs of a given type who are concordant nonexposed, discordant, or concordant for exposure to the moderating variable (Heath, Neale, Hewitt, Eaves, & Fulker, 1989). As in the previous examples, models are compared that constrain genetic and environmental parameters to be the same across groups and that estimate separate genetic or environmental parameters for nonexposed versus exposed conditions, with the geometric mean of the genetic or environmental variances under the two conditions being used for the covariance terms for discordant pairs. Comparison of the goodness of fit of the model constraining both genetic and environmental parameters across exposure conditions, with models that allow for differences in either genetic parameters (Genotype × Environment interaction) or environmental parameters (moderation of environmental risk factors), provides a likelihood ratio chi-square test for the significance of the postulated moderating effect (Heath, Neale, et al., 1989).

Reports of a significant Genotype × Environment interaction have emerged most often from the adoption study paradigm (Cadoret et al., 1985; Cloninger et al., 1981), although in a twin study of genetic influences on variation in alcohol consumption levels, we were able to demonstrate a significant interaction with marital status in women (Heath, Jardine, & Martin, 1989). Replicated examples of Genotype × Environment interaction are still wanting.

Exposure Effects on Alcoholism Vulnerability

In genetic research on substance use disorders, the task of resolving genetic influences on the level of self-exposure to alcohol, tobacco, or other drugs and genetic influences on the risk of becoming dependent for a given level of substance exposure is an important but neglected topic. Extensive twin data from both European, American, and Australian samples indicate an important genetic influence on alcohol consumption levels in general community (therefore predominantly nonalcoholic) samples (reviewed by Heath, 1995b); in addition, we noted earlier that in Asian samples, a polymorphism at the ALDH2 locus contributes to variability in drinking patterns. Researchers therefore must ask whether risk factors for substance dependence ultimately can be explained as risk factors for substance exposure or whether researchers can demonstrate genetic (or environmental) risk factors that specifically cause differences in risk of dependence among individuals with similar exposure histories. Related to this is the question of whether researchers can define "safe" drinking levels, short of complete abstinence, at which the risk to the biological relative of an alcoholic individual is not increased above general population rates, and "unsafe" levels, which, in presymptomatic individuals at high genetic risk, would indicate a need for early intervention efforts.

Behavioral genetic methods have the potential to make important contributions to such questions. To address the second question, an approach adapted from survival analysis (Lee, 1992) should be possible, in which researchers examine in biological relatives of alcoholic and random control participants the proportions of individuals who have experienced no alcohol-related problems at different levels of reported maximum alcohol consumption. One may wonder, for example, whether the difference in alcoholism rates between male and female siblings of an alcoholic male proband can be explained entirely by differences in the level of self-exposure to alcohol, implying that proportions of unaffected relatives will no longer be different when estimated conditional on level of alcohol exposure. To address the first question, we have begun to develop hierarchical models that allow joint estimation of genetic effects on substance exposure, and genetic effects on risk of dependence, given the level of substance exposure (e.g., Heath & Martin, 1993).

CHALLENGES FOR BEHAVIORAL GENETIC RESEARCH ON ALCOHOLISM

From a review of the potential of behavioral genetic methods for prevention research on alcoholism, we now move to a consideration of the practical limitations and their implications for research design. To understand the issues involved, it is helpful to consider the ways in which behavioral genetic data are used to quantify genetic and environmental contributions to alcoholism risk.

Quantifying Genetic and Environmental Influences

For purposes of illustration, Table 1 shows data from the twin studies of Hrubec and Omenn (1981), Kendler et al. (1992), and McGue et al. (1992). Hrubec and Omenn and Kendler et al. used birth-record-derived twin samples that were screened for history of alcoholism. Hrubec and Omenn's data are based on a register of American like-sex male twin pairs identified from birth records from 1917 through 1927; all of the participants had served in the military during World War II or the Korean War. For this study, the diagnosis of alcoholism was derived from a search of Veterans Administration records to identify reports of alcoholism or alcoholic psychosis. The data of Kendler et al. were based on a sample of twin pairs identified from birth records for the state of Virginia from 1915 through 1968 (although most of the pairs were born after 1945) and were based on interview assessments of lifetime history of *DSM–III–R* alcohol dependence. For these two samples, numbers of concordant unaffected, discordant, and concordant affected twin pairs are presented. The data of McGue et al., by contrast, were based on a mailed questionnaire survey of alcohol problems in a sample of twin pairs ascertained because at least one twin from the pair was identified from the records of an alcohol treatment facility. We therefore report the numbers of unaffected and affected cotwins of the alcoholic twin probands.

The Hrubec and Omenn (1981) and Kendler et al. (1992) studies permit direct estimates of the prevalence of alcoholism, as defined in those studies. In the Virginia data, 8.1% of the MZ female twins and 10.2% of the DZ female twins met broadly defined criteria for lifetime history of *DSM–III–R* alcohol dependence. In the Veterans Administration twin data, only 2.6% of the MZ male and 3.1% of the DZ male twins had a

TABLE 1
Twin Data on the Familial Aggregation of Risk From U.S. Twin Studies

Twin group	Hrubec and Omenn (1981)			McGue et al. (1992)		Kendler et al. (1992)		
	Concordant unaffected	Discordant	Concordant affected	Cotwin unaffected	Cotwin affected	Concordant unaffected	Discordant	Concordant affected
MZ males	5,661	230	41	20	65			
DZ males	7,110	416	28	44	52			
MZ females				9	8	510	65	15
DZ females				14	10	361	68	11
DZ cotwin female proband				5	18			
DZ cotwin male proband				45	20			

Note. Data are recomputed from the original publications by these authors. MZ = monozygotic; DZ = dizygotic.

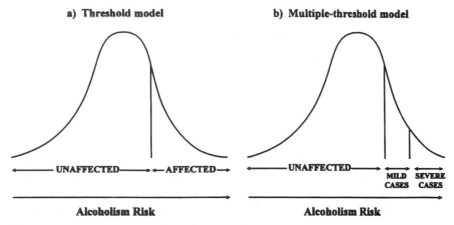

a) **Threshold model**

b) **Multiple-threshold model**

← UNAFFECTED → ← AFFECTED →

← UNAFFECTED → MILD SEVERE CASES CASES

Alcoholism Risk

Alcoholism Risk

Figure 2. Threshold and multiple-threshold models relating alcoholism liability to history of alcohol dependence. Individuals with liability scores below the threshold remain unaffected, whereas others become alcohol dependent (in the case of the multiple-threshold model, either mild or severe cases, depending on how deviant are their liability scores).

Veterans Administration alcoholism diagnosis. These latter data on average include much more seriously affected individuals, as is apparent from the high rates of alcoholic cirrhosis among alcoholics in the sample (22.7%). As might be expected from the base-rate differences, there are important differences in the estimates of the rates of alcoholism in the relatives of alcoholic individuals between these two studies. In the Virginia data, 31.6% of the cotwins of female MZ alcoholic individuals versus 24.4% of the cotwins of female DZ alcoholic individuals also met criteria for a life-time history of *DSM–III–R* alcohol dependence. Corresponding estimates of the risk ratio (i.e., the ratio of the rate of alcoholism in relatives of a given degree to the prevalence of alcoholism in the general population) were 3.9 for MZ pairs and 2.4 for DZ pairs. In Hrubec and Omenn's data, the rates of alcoholism were 26.3% for male MZ versus 11.9% for male DZ cotwins of alcoholic individuals, with risk ratios of 10.0 and 3.8, respectively. How can researchers find a metric that will allow them to pool such results from studies that have used widely different methodologies?

One approach that has long been used by geneticists (e.g., Pearson, 1900) is to work with tetrachoric or polychoric correlations (Olsson, 1979), assuming a "threshold" model (see Figure 2a). This assumes that (a) liability to alcoholism is determined by the additive effects of multiple risk factors, which may be genetic or environmental, and is (at least approximately) normally distributed in the general population and (b) the individuals who become alcoholic have liability scores that exceed some threshold value (scaled as a deviation from the mean—usually set to zero—of the liability distribution). Correlations between relatives for alcoholism liability may be estimated by maximum likelihood (Olsson,

1979). As shown in the multiple-threshold model in Figure 2b, narrower versus broader definitions of alcoholism may be represented using more versus less deviant threshold values. No direct test of these assumptions is possible in the case of binary data, although they certainly appear to be plausible for alcohol dependence. With three or more response categories, a chi-square test of the goodness of fit of the multiple-threshold model does become possible.

Table 2 shows, for a range of informative values, the proportions of concordant unaffected, discordant, and concordant affected relatives predicted for a given liability correlation between relatives and given population prevalence estimates (which may differ for first and second relatives because of gender, birth cohort, or other differences). Comparing first cases in which the prevalence is assumed to be the same in both relatives, it can be seen that the predicted rates of alcoholism in the relatives of alcoholic individuals increase as a function both of the magnitude of the liability correlation and of the prevalence of alcoholism, so that the same risk to relatives (e.g., 25%) may reflect a modest familial correlation for a highly prevalent trait ($r = .15$; 20% prevalence) or a much stronger correlation for a low prevalence trait ($r = .6$; 2.5% prevalence). The risk ratios for these two examples are much different (1.3 vs. 10.0), but the same risk ratio may likewise reflect much different degrees of familial correlation (e.g., correlations of .6, 10% prevalence vs. .3, 2.5% prevalence yield risk ratios of 3.9 and 3.8, respectively).

Table 2 also illustrates how, under the assumptions of a multiple-threshold model, the risk to relatives of more severe cases is increased relative to the risk to relatives of all alcoholic individuals (including milder cases). Suppose that a given operationalization of alcoholism identifies 30% of men but only 10% of women as having a lifetime history of alcohol dependence and the liability correlation between first-degree, unlike-sex relative pairs is .3. If this difference in prevalence reflects gender differences in thresholds for alcohol dependence, implying that compared with alcoholic men, alcoholic women must have accumulated more risk factors (i.e., they have more deviant liability scores) for alcoholism, then the predicted risk to a first-degree male relative of an alcoholic woman will be 50%, whereas the risk to a first-degree female relative of an alcoholic man will be only 16.7% (although the risk ratio is the same in each case, 1.67). Once again, even assuming the same prevalence for alcoholism (say, 30%), as defined for relatives of alcoholic individuals (e.g., assessed by a diagnostic interview), differences in the operationalization of alcoholism for alcoholic probands (identifying individuals in the top 30% vs. the top 2.5% of the liability distribution) may cause similar risk ratios to be associated with different liability correlations (e.g., correlations of .6 for the former case and .3 for the latter case both generate risk ratios of 1.9). We will see later

TABLE 2

Population Distribution of Pairs of Relatives With Both Alcoholic, Neither Alcoholic, or Only One Relative Alcoholic as a Function of Lifetime Prevalence of Alcoholism and Liability Correlation for Alcoholism of Relatives

Relative A prevalence (%)	Relative B prevalence (%)	Liability correlation	Both affected (%)	Discordant		Both unaffected (%)	Risk to relative of an alcoholic[a] (%)	Relatives' risk ratio[b] (%)
				A affected (%)	B affected (%)			
30	30	.6	17.3	12.7	12.7	57.3	57.6	1.9
		.3	12.8	17.2	17.2	52.8	42.7	1.4
		.15	10.9	19.1	19.1	50.9	36.2	1.2
30	10	.6	7.4	22.6	2.8	67.4	73.5	2.5
		.3	5.0	25.0	5.0	65.0	50.1	1.7
		.15	4.0	26.0	6.0	64.0	39.6	1.3
30	2.5	.6	2.1	27.9	0.4	69.6	85.6	2.9
		.3	1.4	28.6	1.1	68.9	57.3	1.9
		.15	1.1	28.9	1.4	68.6	43.0	1.4
20	20	.6	9.9	10.1	10.1	69.9	49.6	2.5
		.3	6.6	13.4	13.4	66.6	33.1	1.7
		.15	5.2	14.8	14.8	65.2	26.2	1.3
10	30	.6	7.4	2.7	25.0	65.0	24.5	2.5
		.3	5.0	5.0	25.1	65.0	16.7	1.7
		.15	4.0	6.0	26.0	64.0	13.2	1.3
10	10	.6	3.9	6.1	6.1	83.9	39.0	3.9
		.3	2.2	7.8	7.8	82.2	21.6	2.2
		.15	1.5	8.5	8.5	81.5	15.2	1.5
10	2.5	.6	1.4	8.6	1.1	89.9	55.7	5.6
		.3	0.7	9.3	1.8	88.2	27.3	2.7
		.15	0.4	9.6	2.1	87.9	17.4	1.7
2.5	2.5	.6	0.6	1.9	1.9	95.6	24.9	10.0
		.3	0.2	2.25	2.25	95.2	9.5	3.8
		.15	0.1	2.35	2.35	95.1	5.2	2.1

[a]Assumes that the prevalence of alcoholism as defined for an alcoholic proband is as for Relative B.
[b]Ratio of risk to the relative of a proband to prevalence in general population, assuming that prevalence of alcoholism as defined for relative is as for Relative A.

TABLE 3
Contributions of Genes and Environment to Alcoholism Liability
Correlations for Different Familial Relationships

Relationship	Genes	Environment shared by family members	Nonshared environment
MZ twin pairs	1	1	0
DZ twin pairs/biological parent and nonadopted child	.5	1	0
Biological parent/adopted-away child	.5	0	0
Adoptive parent/adopted child	0	1	0
Total population variance in alcoholism liability	1	1	1

Note. MZ = monozygotic; DZ = dizygotic.

that this issue becomes especially important when one tries to interpret data from clinically ascertained twin series.

On the basis of these considerations, if the assumptions of the multiple-threshold model are at least approximately valid, it clearly is not appropriate to attempt to pool estimates of alcoholism rates in relatives, or risk ratios, across studies, as has sometimes been attempted (e.g., Merikangas, 1990). One feasible strategy would be to estimate polychoric correlations between relatives separately for each study, with their asymptotic covariance matrix (e.g., using standard statistical packages such as PRELIS; Jöreskog & Sörbom, 1993b). Models would then be fitted to these data by means of packages for structural equation modeling such as LISREL (Jöreskog & Sörbom, 1993a) in a multiple-group analysis using an asymptotic weighted least squares fitting function. This approach has the advantage that it generalizes easily to multivariate problems, where one is interested in identifying potential mediators of genetic or environmental influences on alcoholism risk. Male like-sex twin pair correlations from the study of Hrubec and Omenn (1981) were as follows: MZ male pairs, .61 ± .04, and DZ male pairs, .33 ± .04. Female like-sex pair correlations from the Kendler et al. (1992) study were .53 ± .09 and .35 ± .11 for MZ and DZ pairs, respectively.

In Table 3, we summarize the contributions of genes, shared environment, and nonshared environment to the familial correlations for alcoholism of twins and adoptees and their biological parents. The expectations were derived under a highly simplified model used in the meta-analysis of Heath (1995a). We assume that all gene action is additive, ignoring complications such as genetic dominance or epistasis (gene–gene interactions). We ignore assortative mating (i.e., the tendency for alcoholic individuals to marry other alcoholic individuals), which, if present, might inflate estimates of the genetic contribution to alcoholism risk in adoption data and of the shared environmental contribution in twin data. (These differential effects will arise if matings of biological pairs who are both at increased genetic risk for alcoholism occur more often than would be expected by chance. In such a case, the correlation between the biological parent and the adopted-away child will reflect both genes transmitted from that parent to the child and, because of the genetic correlation between spouses induced by assortative mating, an indirect contribution via genes transmitted from the second parent. However, the genetic correlation between DZ twin pairs will be increased above the expected .5 under random mating, hence mimicking the effects of shared environmental effects in twin data.) We ignore selective placement (i.e., the tendency for individuals from a high-risk genetic background to be placed in a high-risk adoptive home) and other forms of genotype–environment correlation (as when, in intact families, a biological alcoholic parent both creates a high-risk rearing environment and passes on genes that increase alcoholism risk). We ignore Genotype × Environment interaction, which may arise if individuals differ in their vulnerability to environmental risk factors because of genetic differences or, conversely, if there are important environmental moderators of genetic risk. Thus, as a starting point, we are ignoring the complex interplay of genetic and environmental risk factors that is most relevant to prevention research on alcoholism.

When we fitted models to the Hrubec and Omenn (1981) and Kendler et al. (1992) data sets, we obtained estimates of the genetic contribution to variance in alcoholism risk (the "heritability" of alcoholism) of 63% for Hrubec and Omenn's data and 55% for the Kendler et al. data. In neither case did we find a significant shared environmental contribution to alcoholism risk. By contrast, in a reanalysis of the Stockholm Adoption Study data on temperance board registrations of Cloninger et al. (1985), we obtained a heritability estimate of only 37%, with no significant gender difference (Heath, Slutske, & Madden, in press). Reporting only these point estimates, however, could easily cause us to overestimate their precision. In epidemiology, it is accepted practice to report 95% confidence limits for odds ratios. For comparability, we have estimated the upper and lower bounds for the 95% confidence interval for these heritability estimates by finding those values of the genetic, shared environmental, and within-families environmental variances that produce a just-significant deterioration in fit of the model ($\chi_1^2 > 3.84$, $df = 1$). For the Swedish adoption data, the 95% confidence interval for the heritability estimate was 19%–56%; for the U.S. Veterans Administration twin data, it was 31%–69%; and for the Virginia twin data, it was 0–69%. Clearly, exclusive focus on point estimates of heritability can greatly mislead. From the Hrubec and Omenn (1981) and Kendler et al. (1992) twin studies, the 95% confidence intervals for the estimate of the shared environmental contribution to variance in alcoholism risk were 0–25% and 0–55%, respectively. In twin data (except when data on separated twins are available), there is a strong negative correlation between estimates of genetic and shared environmental variances. As a consequence, the 95% confidence limits are usually asymmetrical about the point estimates of these variances, as can be seen in our examples. This complication invalidates attempts to test for the significance of genetic and environmental parameters using the standard errors of those parameter estimates (e.g., Allgulander et al., 1991, 1992; Pickens et al., 1991; Romanov et al., 1991) because their sampling distribution is asymmetrical; likelihood ratio tests of the significance of dropping a genetic or shared environmental parameter from the model are more appropriate.

Clinically Ascertained Samples

The broad confidence intervals obtained for estimates of genetic and environmental parameters in the Kendler et al. (1992) and Hrubec and Omenn (1981) data sets, despite seemingly large sample sizes, reflect the low precision of these estimates for binary variables in random samples, particularly when the population prevalence is low. One noteworthy aspect of our simulations in Table 2 is the small differences in proportions of concordant unaffected relative pairs as a function of the relative pair liability correlation, particularly for low-prevalence traits. Most of the information about the magnitude of the familial correlation for alcoholism is derived from pairs with at least one alcoholic twin, as can be confirmed by statistical power calculations for genetic modeling (Neale, Eaves, & Kendler, 1996). This suggests that the research strategy of identifying alcoholic probands through treatment or other settings and conducting follow-up assessments with their relatives, as was used by McGue et al. (1992), would be an especially powerful one. Such a strategy also has been used in studies of twin series ascertained from treatment settings in London (Gurling et al., 1984), St. Louis (Caldwell & Gottesman, 1991), and, in a sample that overlapped with that used by McGue, Minnesota (Pickens et al., 1991). It also has been used with considerable success in family studies (e.g., Reich, Cloninger, Van Eerdewegh, Rice, & Mullaney, 1988) and in the adoption studies conducted by Cadoret (1994; Cadoret et al., 1985, 1987) and Goodwin et al. (1973, 1974). However, for behavioral genetic research, it is not without complications.

To estimate genetic and environmental contributions to alcoholism risk from clinically ascertained samples, researchers need to know not only the proportions of alcoholic and nonalcoholic relatives of the alcoholic probands but also two additional pieces of information: estimates of the population prevalence of alcoholism as defined for the alcoholic proband and alcoholism as defined for the relatives of the proband (as can be seen from Table 2). The researchers who have attempted to derive estimates of genetic and environmental parameters from such clinically ascertained samples (e.g., Caldwell & Gottesman, 1991; McGue et al., 1992; Pickens et al., 1991) have most commonly assumed that these two prevalence estimates will be the same and have used estimates derived from general population surveys such as the Epidemiological Catchment Area (ECA; e.g., L. N. Robins & Regier, 1991), adjusted for the age distribution of each twin group. Unfortunately, it is by no means clear that this is a reasonable assumption. In terms of the threshold models of Figure 2, this is equivalent to assuming that Figure 2A applies, so that individuals who get into treatment for alcoholism can be viewed as a random sample of alcoholism cases in the general population, at least with respect to alcoholism liability. An alternative and perhaps more plausible assumption is that Figure 2B applies, with alcoholic individuals in treatment disproportionately representing the severe cases, whereas those in community samples are predominantly mild cases (Heath, Bucholz, et al., 1994).

As we have shown elsewhere (Heath, Slutske, & Madden, in press), these different approaches lead to different estimates for correlations between relatives for alcoholism liability. For *DSM–III–R* alcohol abuse, for example, McGue et al. (1992) used prevalence estimates of 29.8% for MZ men, 28.1% for DZ men, 9.0% for MZ women, and 9.2% for DZ women, based on ECA data. Interpolating approximate values for the prevalence estimates for men and women from unlike-sex pairs (not given by McGue et al., 1992) and using the proportions of alcoholic and nonalcoholic co-twins from Table 1, we obtained the following estimates of the twin pair tetrachoric correlations: MZ male pairs, .87; DZ male pairs, .56; MZ female pairs, .61; DZ female pairs, .65; DZ unlike-sex pairs ascertained through female probands, .69; and DZ unlike-sex pairs ascertained through male probands, .99. Comparing the like-sex MZ and DZ correlations, McGue et al. concluded that genetic factors were an important determinant of alcoholism risk in men, but not in women. However, this conclusion was not supported by the high correlations estimated for unlike-sex pairs, which, indeed, will cause any simple genetic model to fail to fit these data: If genetic effects were the predominant cause of family resemblance in men and shared environmental effects in women, we would predict a zero or low correlation between unlike-sex pairs. As reviewed by Heath, Slutske, and Madden, only approximately 1 in 5 men in the ECA survey meeting criteria for *DSM–III* alcohol abuse or dependence and 1 in 4 women reported any alcohol-related treatment contacts. If we assume that it is the "severe" cases that are being represented in treatment settings, use prevalence estimates of 6.5% and 2.44% for male and female alcoholic probands, respectively, and retain the original McGue et al. estimates for their co-twins, we obtain estimated twin correlations of .58, .35, .46, .49, .55, and .57, respectively. The two estimates of the unlike-sex DZ correlation are still both moderately high, but at least they are also now comparable in magnitude to one another.

Not surprisingly, these different assumptions about how to adjust for nonrandom sample ascertainment also have an important effect on the estimates of the heritability of alcoholism. If we follow McGue et al. (1992) and assume that treated alcoholic individuals are a random sample of all alcoholic individuals and discard data from unlike-sex twin pairs, then we obtain heritability estimates (and 95% confidence intervals) of 0% (0–47%) for women and 62% (22%–94%) for men. Under the alternative severity model, assuming a much lower prevalence value for alcoholic probands than for relatives and using data from the unlike-sex pairs, we found no significant gender difference in the heritability of alcoholism (χ_2^2 = 3.62, df = 2, p > .05), obtaining a pooled heritability estimate of 18% that was nonsignificant (95% confidence limits = 0–40%). In practice, of course, neither model of the relationship between alcoholism liability and probability of getting into treatment is likely to be correct because factors such as comorbid drug abuse or other psychiatric disorders also may lead to the identification of individuals with mild alcohol problems in treatment series. For reasons such as these, our estimates of genetic and environmental parameters from treatment series will be clouded in uncertainty.

IMPLICATIONS FOR RESEARCH DESIGN

Two-Stage Sampling Schemes

In the analysis of twin and adoption data from clinically ascertained samples, researchers cannot avoid the difficulty that they do not know how to model the relationship between alcoholism liability and the probability of being represented in a treatment sample. This is not a problem if researchers are primarily interested in genetic linkage or association studies to identify individual genetic loci that contribute to alcoholism risk. However, it becomes more of a problem when researchers wish to use twins or adoptees to examine the joint action and interaction of genetic and environmental risk factors. Yet, as we have shown in Table 2, random sampling also is not an efficient strategy because it leads to inclusion of many concordant nonalcoholic relative pairs who provide minimal information about the causes of individual differences in alcoholism risk.

In response to this, we have pioneered the use of a two-stage sampling strategy in behavioral genetic research. In the first stage, brief diagnostic interviews are conducted with twin pairs and other family members. For twins, adoptees, and other rare population groups who may be spread over a large geographic area, we have found that conducting diagnostic interviews by telephone is a highly efficient strategy. For the second stage, a random sample of families and a high-risk sample selected from the remaining families on the basis of assessments made in the first stage are identified for more extensive follow-up. The use of random and high-risk samples permits case-base comparisons (cf. Wacholder, McLaughlin, Silverman, & Mandel, 1992), and in general facilitates data analysis, compared with the sampling scheme in which high- and low-risk samples are drawn and contrasted. Because families are selected on the basis of phenotypic data assessed on the entire sample in the first stage, estimates of population parameters in analyses of the selected sample as well as random-sample Stage 2 data can be obtained using maximum-likelihood methods (e.g., Eaves, Last, Young, & Martin, 1978; Lange, Westlake, & Spence, 1976) because Stage 2 data are missing at random, in the sense used by Little and Rubin (1987) and Little and Schenker (1995).

A critical decision in the implementation of two-stage sampling schemes is the choice of criteria used for inclusion in the high-risk sample. We noted earlier that oversampling on the basis of parental alcoholism is a much more efficient strategy for identifying men at high risk for alcoholism than for identifying women at high risk. A result well-known to quantitative geneticists (e.g., Falconer, 1981), but that applies equally under most plausible environmental models, is that selection on the basis of an individual's characteristics is a much more efficient strategy for identifying individuals at high risk than selecting on characteristics of the parents, although selecting on the phenotype of a MZ cotwin will be the second most efficient strategy. Thus, because our interest is in identifying risk factors for making transitions from heavy to problem drinking, or from problem drinking to alcohol dependence, selection of a high-risk sample of heavy or problem-drinking women will be much more efficient than selecting a sample of women with a history of parental alcoholism.

Cohort-Sequential Sampling

To the extent that we take a developmental rather than a cross-sectional, or lifetime, perspective on the etiology of alcohol dependence, we are forced to adopt longitudinal research designs. Early longitudinal studies in alcoholism and related fields (e.g., McCord & McCord, 1962; Vaillant, 1983) have used the traditional strategy of identifying a cohort of individuals of the same age and following them prospectively. Such an approach would work well in an era of stable research funding, stable assessment practices, and low geographic mobility. From the early 1950s (Bell, 1953), however, the value has been recognized of a cohort-sequential sampling scheme, in which, for example, cohorts of 11-, 13-, 15-, 17-, 19-, and 21-year-olds are identified at the beginning of a study and followed prospectively (e.g., every 2 years). Such a design permits, within a 5-year research project, the years from 11 to 26 to be spanned, and, because 11-year-olds have been followed at 13 and 15, 13-year-olds at 15 and 17, and so on, the design permits risk factors assessed in early adolescence to be related to outcomes in early adulthood.

Such designs have only recently begun to be used in behavioral genetic research (e.g., Hewitt, Eaves, Neale, & Meyer, 1988) and in alcoholism research (e.g., Duncan, Duncan, & Hops, 1994) but have enormous potential. In an era in which the continuity of research funds is uncertain and the updating of assessment approaches is as rapid (e.g., American Psychiatric Association, 1987, 1994) as might be expected under a "planned obsolescence" approach, these designs allow prospective data to be collected covering a broad range of ages while funding is still intact and assessments are still current. Because individual cohorts are followed over a relatively brief time span, problems of sample attrition are minimized. Finally, because multiple cohorts are assessed at the same age but in different years, the impact of sudden social changes (e.g., drug epidemics and declines) can be detected.

Combining a cohort-sequential design with a two-stage sampling approach, however, is not without problems. There is an implicit assumption that individuals from different cohorts can be viewed as being sampled from the same population, so that, for example, 21-year-olds sampled at the beginning of the study can be meaningfully compared with 21-year-olds taken into the study at age 17. Even if a high-risk sample is drawn on the basis of parental history of alcohol dependence, this would require that parental onset be before the age of initial assessment of the youngest cohort in the study; otherwise, cases with late parental onset would be disproportionately represented in cohorts entered into the study at older ages. Likewise, oversampling on the basis of offspring rather than parental characteristics would require that consideration be limited to behaviors with onset before the age of the youngest cohort taken into the study.

The Use of Twin Registers

Using a cohort-sequential sampling strategy raises additional challenges when researchers want to span the years from early adolescence into early adulthood, as is clearly necessary in alcoholism-related research. Researchers cannot simply recruit volunteers from schools—the most common research strategy with this age group—unless using a retrospective search of elementary school records from as many as 10 years earlier. Otherwise, researchers would miss school dropouts and would have great difficulty drawing an appropriate sample for cohorts aged 19+ at intake into a study. In research on twin pairs and other rare populations, meeting this challenge with adolescents has most usually required that individuals be identified from birth records (e.g., in the Minnesota Twin Study and our own Missouri Adolescent Twin Study) and tracked wherever they may be found.

BROADER IMPLICATIONS FOR EPIDEMIOLOGICAL AND PREVENTION RESEARCH

Although some of the research questions that we have discussed require working with special populations such as twins or adoptees, a behavioral genetic framework has more general implications for epidemiological and prevention research on alcoholism. First, a developmental perspective would appear to be important. In the recent U.S. National Comorbidity Survey (Kessler et al., 1994; Nelson et al., 1996), the median reported age of onset of most individual alcoholic symptoms was 20. Like smoking, alcoholism has increasingly become a disorder with pediatric onset, albeit with adverse sequelae occurring most frequently in later adulthood. Epidemiological surveys have most commonly focused on adult populations (L. N. Robins & Regier, 1991) or have included relatively small numbers of older adolescents because of the broad span of ages covered (Kessler et al., 1994). If our goal is to describe and understand early transitions into problem drinking and the predictors of transitions into more severe stages of alcohol-related problems, then a survey more narrowly focused on the years of adolescence and early adulthood would appear to be necessary. Researchers can start to refine hypotheses by making fuller use of retrospective data on ages of onset reported in adult surveys, but data reported by younger respondents are likely to have greater reliability and validity.

Second, alcoholism is a strongly familial disorder. In conventional survey research, in which the goal is to obtain highly precise estimates of the prevalence and incidence of a disorder, sampling is restricted to one individual per household to avoid the within-households correlations that would occur and the consequent increase in the sampling variance achievable with a given sample size if multiple individuals from the same household were sampled. If the goal is also to identify mediators and moderators of alcoholism risk, because many of these risk factors also are likely to be familial, direct interview assessment of all family members, including absentee individuals, would be preferable. The strategy of studying only one offspring per family, as in many high-risk research studies (Sher, 1991), seems indefensible because it loses the power of within-sibships comparisons. Although the statistical procedures for analyzing familial data are a little more complicated than in the case of samples of unrelated individuals, techniques such as bootstrapping (Efron & Tibshirani, 1986) greatly simplify the task of obtaining appropriately adjusted statistical tests.

Third, because alcoholism is strongly familial, there will be a relatively high proportion of uninformative low-risk families in any general community sample. A two-stage sampling strategy, in which a relatively low-cost screening interview is followed by more exhaustive follow-up of a random subsample and a subsample identified as being at high risk for alcoholism, would be the most efficient, as is the case with more conventional behavioral genetic designs. Of special concern, not only for epidemiological and prevention studies but also for high-risk research, is the fact that the standard technique of oversampling on the basis of a paternal history of alcohol dependence (assessed by personal interview), although highly productive for studying the causes of male alcoholism, is much less efficient for studies of alcoholism in women. Oversampling families with an alcoholic female relative, or preferably two female relatives (cf. Hill, 1995), would greatly increase the numbers of disorders of those who are expected to become alcohol dependent. Oversampling on the basis of an adolescent's own drinking problems will always be more efficient than oversampling because of problems in a first-degree relative, although it raises potential reporting bias problems, as in any retrospective research.

Fourth, researchers can obtain only limited data from a single cross-sectional survey of alcohol-related behaviors. For the purposes of prevention research, identifying predictors of transitions from alcohol use to early alcohol-related problems, and from early problems to more severe alcohol-related problems, can best be achieved in a prospective design. The cohort-sequential sampling strategy that we have discussed for behavioral genetic research is equally relevant here and brings the same advantages and challenges.

Finally, given the important role that genetic factors play in determining differences in alcoholism risk, there are strong arguments for wanting to include a genetic perspective in such epidemiological or prevention research. In the context of conducting in-person interviews with family members, the additional costs of obtaining and storing blood samples for genotyping are minimal. As individual genetic markers of alcoholism risk are identified, the potential for analyses of the coaction and interaction of genetic and environmental risk factors will be enhanced greatly. Ascertaining a parallel sample of genetically informative kinships such as twin pairs and their families, assessed using a protocol identical to that used in the broader community sample, will provide much additional information about questions such as those highlighted in Exhibit 1.

REFERENCES

Allgulander, C., Nowak, J., & Rice, J. P. (1991). Psychopathology and treatment of 30,344 twins in Sweden: II. Heritability estimates of psychiatric diagnosis and treatment in 12,884 twin pairs. *Acta Psychiatrica Scandinavica, 83,* 12–15.

Allgulander, C., Nowak, J., & Rice, J. P. (1992). Psychopathology and treatment of 30,344 twins in Sweden. *Acta Psychiatrica Scandinavica, 86,* 421–422.

Allison, P. D. (1984). *Event history analysis: Regression for longitudinal event data.* Newbury Park, CA: Sage.

American Psychiatric Association. (1987). *Diagnostic and statistical manual of mental disorders* (3rd ed., rev.). Washington, DC: Author.

American Psychiatric Association. (1994). *Diagnostic and statistical manual of mental disorders* (4th ed.). Washington, DC: Author.

Babor, T. F., Hofmann, M., DelBoca, F. K., Meyer, R. E., Dolinksy, Z. S., & Rounsaville, B. (1992). Types of alcoholics: I. Evidence for an empirically derived typology based on indicators of vulnerability and severity. *Archives of General Psychiatry, 49,* 599–608.

Barr, C. L., & Kidd, K. K. (1993). Population frequencies of the A1 allele at the dopamine D2 receptor locus. *Biological Psychiatry, 34,* 209.

Bartholomew, D. J. (1987). *Latent variable models and factor analysis.* London: Griffin.

Begleiter, H., Porjesz, B., Bihari, B., & Kissin, B. (1984). Event-related brain potentials in boys at risk for alcoholism. *Science, 225,* 1493–1496.

Bell, R. Q. (1953). Convergence: An accelerated longitudinal approach. *Child Development, 24,* 145–152.

Blum, K., Noble, E. P., Sheridan, P. J., Montgomery, A., Ritchie, T., Ozkaragoz, T., Fitch, R. J., Wood, R., Finley, O., & Sadlack, F. (1993). Genetic predisposition in alcoholism: Association of the D2 dopamine receptor TaqI B1 RFLP with severe alcoholics. *Alcohol, 10,* 59–67.

Bohman, M., Sigvardsson, S., & Cloninger, C. R. (1981). Maternal inheritance of alcohol abuse: Cross-fostering analysis of adopted women. *Archives of General Psychiatry, 38,* 965.

Bollen, K. A. (1989). *Structural equations with latent variables.* New York: Wiley.

Bucholz, K. K., Heath, A. C., Reich, T., Hesselbrock, V. M., Kramer, J. R., Nurnberger, J., & Schuckit, M. A. (1996). Can we subtype alcoholics? A latent class analysis of data from relatives of alcoholics in a multicenter family study of alcoholism. *Alcoholism: Clinical and Experimental Research, 20,* 1462–1471.

Bulmer, M. G. (1980). *The mathematical theory of quantitative genetics.* Oxford, England: Clarendon Press.

Cadoret, R. J. (1994). Genetic and environmental contributions to heterogeneity in alcoholism: Findings from the Iowa Adoption Studies. *Annals of the New York Academy of Sciences, 708,* 59–71.

Cadoret, R. J., Cain, C. A., Troughton, E., & Heywood, E. (1985). Alcoholism and antisocial personality: Interrelationships, genetic and environmental factors. *Archives of General Psychiatry, 42,* 161–167.

Cadoret, R. J., Troughton, E., & O'Gorman, T. W. (1987). Genetic and environmental factors in alcohol abuse and antisocial personality. *Journal of Studies on Alcohol, 48,* 1–8.

Caldwell, C. B., & Gottesman, I. I. (1991). Sex differences in the risk for alcoholism: A twin study. *Behavior Genetics, 21,* 563.

Cardon, L. R., Smith, S. D., Fulker, D. W., Kimberling, W. J., Pennington, B. F., & DeFries, J. C. (1995). Quantitative trait locus for reading disability on chromosome 6. *Science, 268,* 786–788.

Cloninger, C. R. (1987). Neurogenetic adaptive mechanisms in alcoholism. *Science, 236,* 410–416.

Cloninger, C. R., Bohman, M., & Sigvardsson, S. (1981). Inheritance of alcohol abuse: Cross-fostering analysis of adopted men. *Archives of General Psychiatry, 38,* 861–868.

Cloninger, C. R., Bohman, M., & Sigvardsson, S. (1985). Psychopathology in adopted-out children of alcoholics: The Stockholm Adoption Study. In M. Galanter (Ed.), *Recent developments in alcoholism* (Vol. 3, pp. 37–51). New York: Plenum.

Collins, L. M., Graham, J. W., Rousculp, S. S., Fidler, P. L., Pan, J., & Hansen, W. B. (1994). Latent transition analysis and how it can address prevention research questions. In L. M. Collins & L. A. Seitz (Eds.), *Advances in data analysis for prevention intervention research* (NIDA Research Monograph No. 142). Rockville, MD: U.S. Department of Health and Human Services.

Comings, D. E., Comings, B. G., Muhleman, D., Dietz, G., Shahbahrami, B., Tast, D., Knell, E., Kocsis, P., Baumgarten, R., Kovacs, B. W., Levy, D. L., Smith, M., Borison, R. L., Evans, D. D., Klein, D. N., MacMurray, J., Tosk, J. M., Sverd, J., Gysin, R., & Flanagan, S. D. (1991). The dopamine D2 receptor locus as a modifying gene in neuropsychiatric disorders. *Journal of the American Medical Association, 266,* 1793–1800.

Crabbe, J. C., Belknap, J. K., & Buck, K. J. (1994). Genetic animal models of alcohol and drug abuse. *Science, 264,* 1637–1816.

Cutrona, C. E., Cadoret, R. J., Suhr, J. A., Richards, C. C., Troughton, E., Schutte, K., & Woodworth, G. (1994). Interpersonal variables in the prediction of alcoholism among adoptees: Evidence for gene–environment interactions. *Comprehensive Psychiatry, 35,* 171–179.

Dinwiddie, S. H., Heath, A. C., Dunne, M. P., Bucholz, K. K., Madden, P. A. F., Slutske, W. S., Bierut, L., Statham, D. J., & Martin, N. G. (1997). *Early sexual abuse and psychopathology: A cotwin control study.* Manuscript in preparation.

Duncan, T. E, Duncan, S. C., & Hops, H. (1994). The effects of family cohesiveness and peer encouragement on the development of adolescent alcohol use: A cohort-sequential approach to the analysis of longitudinal data. *Journal of Studies on Alcohol, 55,* 588–599.

Eaves, L. J. (1977). Inferring the causes of human variation. *Journal of the Royal Statistical Society, Series B, 140,* 324–355.

Eaves, L. J., Eysenck, H. J., & Martin, N. G. (1989). *Genes, culture, and personality: An empirical approach.* London: Academic Press.

Eaves, L. J., & Heath, A. C. (1981). Detection of the effects of asymmetric assortative mating. *Nature, 289,* 205–206.

Eaves, L. J., Last, K. A., Martin, N. G., & Jinks, J. I. (1977). A progressive approach to non-additivity and genotype–environmental covariance in the analysis of human differences. *British Journal of Mathematical and Statistical Psychology, 30,* 1–42.

Eaves, L. J., Last, K., Young, P. A., & Martin, N. G. (1978). Model-fitting approaches to the analysis of human behavior. *Heredity, 41,* 249–320.

Eaves, L. J., Long, J., & Heath, A. C. (1986). A theory of developmental change in quantitative phenotypes applied to cognitive development. *Behavior Genetics, 16,* 143–162.

Eaves, L., & Meyer, J. (1994). Locating human quantitative trait loci: Guidelines for the selection of sibling pairs for genotyping. *Behavior Genetics, 24,* 443–455.

Eaves, L. J., Silberg, J. L., Hewitt, J. K., Rutter, M., Meyer, J. M., Neale, M. C., & Pickles, A. (1993). Analyzing twin resemblance in multisymptom data: Genetic applications of a latent class model for symptoms of conduct disorder in juvenile boys. *Behavior Genetics, 23,* 5–19.

Efron, B., & Tibshirani, R. (1986). Bootstrap methods for standard errors, confidence intervals, and other measures of statistical accuracy. *Statistical Science, 1,* 54–77.

Falconer, D. S. (1981). *Introduction to quantitative genetics.* London: Longman.

Falk, C. T., & Rubinstein, P. (1987). Haplotype relative risks: An easy reliable way to construct a proper control sample for risk calculations. *Annals of Human Genetics, 51,* 227–233.

Fulker, D. W. (1981). The genetic and environmental architecture of psychoticism, extraversion, and neuroticism. In H. J. Eysenck (Ed.), *A model for personality* (pp. 88–122). New York: Springer-Verlag.

Gelernter, J., O'Malley, S., Risch, N., Kramzler, H. R., Krystal, J., Merikangas, K., Kennedy, J. L., & Kidd, K. K. (1991). No association between an allele at the D2 dopamine receptor gene (DRD2) and alcoholism. *Journal of the American Medical Association, 266,* 1801–1807.

Goldman, D. (1993). The DRD2 dopamine receptor and the candidate gene approach in alcoholism. *Alcohol and Alcoholism* (Suppl. 2), 27–29.

Goodman, L. A. (1974). The analysis of systems of qualitative variables when some of the variables are unobservable: I. A modified latent structure approach. *American Journal of Sociology, 79,* 1179–1259.

Goodwin, D. W., Schulsinger, F., Hermansen, L., Guze, S. B., & Winokur, G. (1973). Alcohol problems in adoptees raised apart from alcoholic biological parents. *Archives of General Psychiatry, 28,* 238–243.

Goodwin, D. W., Schulsinger, F., Knop, J., & Mednick, S. (1977). Psychopathology in adopted and nonadopted daughters of alcoholics. *Archives of General Psychiatry, 34,* 1005.

Goodwin, D. W., Schulsinger, F., Knop, J., Mednick, S., & Guze, S. B. (1977). Alcoholism and depression in adopted-out daughters of alcoholics. *Archives of General Psychiatry, 34,* 751–755.

Goodwin, D. W., Schulsinger, F., Moller, N., Hermansen, L., Winokur, G., & Guze,

S. B. (1974). Drinking problems in adopted and nonadopted sons of alcoholics. *Archives of General Psychiatry, 31,* 164–169.

Gurling, H. M. D., Oppenheim, B. E., & Murray, R. M. (1984). Depression, criminality and psychopathology associated with alcoholism: Evidence from a twin study. *Acta Geneticae Medicae et Gemellologiae, 33,* 333–339.

Heath, A. C. (1987). The analysis of marital interaction in cross-sectional twin data. *Acta Geneticae Medicae et Gemelollogiae, 36,* 41–49.

Heath, A. C. (1993). What can we learn about the determinants of psychopathology and substance abuse from studies of normal twins? In T. J. Bouchard & P. Propping (Eds.), *Twins as a tool of behavioral genetics* (pp. 273–285). New York: Wiley.

Heath, A. C. (1995a). Genetic influences on alcoholism risk? A review of adoption and twin studies. *Alcohol Health and Research World, 3,* 166–171.

Heath, A. C. (1995b). Genetic influences on drinking behavior in humans. In H. Begleiter & B. Kissin (Eds.), *The genetics of alcoholism* (pp. 82–121). Oxford, England: Oxford University Press.

Heath, A. C., Bucholz, K. K., Madden, P. A. F., Dinwiddie, S. H., Slutske, W. S., Bierut, T. J., Statham, D. J., Dunne, M. P., Whitfield, J. B., & Martin, N. G. (in press). Genetic and environmental contributions to alcohol dependence risk in a national twin sample: Consistency of findings in men and women. *Psychological Medicine.*

Heath, A. C., Bucholz, K. K., Slutske, W. S., Madden, P. A. F., Dinwiddie, S. H., Dunne, M. P., Statham, D. J., Whitfield, J. B., Martin, N. G., & Eaves, L. J. (1994). The assessment of alcoholism in surveys of the general community: What are we measuring? Some insights from the Australian Twin Panel Interview Survey. *International Review of Psychiatry, 6,* 295–307.

Heath, A. C., & Eaves, L. J. (1985). Resolving the effects of phenotype and social background on mate selection. *Behavior Genetics, 15,* 15–30.

Heath, A. C., Jardine, R., & Martin, N. G. (1989). Interactive effects of genotype and social environment on alcohol consumption in female twins. *Journal of Studies on Alcohol, 50,* 38–48.

Heath, A. C., Kendler, K. S., Eaves, L. J., & Markell, D. (1985). The resolution of cultural and biological inheritance: Informativeness of different relationships. *Behavior Genetics, 15,* 439–465.

Heath, A. C., Madden, P. A. F., Cloninger, C. R., & Martin, N. G. (in press). Genetic and environmental structure of personality. In C. R. Cloninger (Ed.), *Personality and psychopathology.* Washington, DC: American Psychiatric Press.

Heath, A. C., & Martin, N. G. (1990). Psychoticism as a dimension of personality: A multivariate genetic test of Eysenck and Eysenck's psychoticism construct. *Journal of Personality and Social Psychology, 58,* 1–11.

Heath, A. C., & Martin, N. G. (1993). Genetic models for the natural history of smoking: Evidence for a genetic influence on smoking persistence. *Addictive Behaviors, 18,* 19–34.

Heath, A. C., Neale, M. C., Hewitt, J. K., Eaves, L. J., & Fulker, D. W. (1989).

Testing structural equation models for twin data using LISREL. *Behavior Genetics, 19,* 9–35.

Heath, A. C., Neale, M. C., Kessler, R. C., Eaves, L. J., & Kendler, K. S. (1992). Evidence for genetic influences on personality from self-reports and informant ratings. *Journal of Personality and Social Psychology, 63,* 85–96.

Heath, A. C., Slutske, W. S., & Madden, P. A. F. (in press). Gender differences in the genetic contribution to alcoholism risk and to alcohol consumption patterns. In R. W. Wilsnack & S. C. Wilsnack (Eds.), *Gender and alcohol.* New Brunswick, NJ: Rutgers University Press.

Heath, A. C., Slutske, W. S., Madden, P. A. F., Bucholz, K. K., Dinwiddie, S. H., Whitfield, J., Dunne, M. P., Statham, D. I., & Martin, N. G. (1994). Genetic effects on alcohol consumption patterns and problems in women. *Alcohol and Alcoholism* (Suppl. 2), 55–59.

Helzer, J. E., & Pryzbeck, T. R. (1988). The co-occurrence of alcoholism with other psychiatric disorders in the general population and its impact on treatment. *Journal of Studies on Alcohol, 49,* 219–224.

Hewitt, J. K., Eaves, L. J., Neale, M. C., & Meyer, J. M. (1988). Resolving causes of developmental continuity or "tracking": I. Longitudinal twin studies during growth. *Behavior Genetics, 18,* 133–151.

Higuchi, S., Muramatsu, T., Yamada, K., Muraoka, H., Kono, H., & Eboshida, A. (1991). Special treatment facilities for alcoholics in Japan. *Journal of Studies on Alcohol, 52,* 547–554.

Hilbert, P., Lindpaintner, K., Beckmann, J. S., Serikawa, T., Soubrier, F., Dubay, C., Cartwright, P., DeGouyon, B., Julier, C., Takahasi, S., Vincent, M., Ganten, D., Georges, M., & Lathrop, G. M. (1991). Chromosomal mapping of two genetic loci associated with blood pressure regulation in hereditary hypertensive rats. *Nature, 353,* 521–529.

Hill, S. Y. (1995). Vulnerability to alcoholism in women: Genetic and cultural factors. *Recent Developments in Alcoholism, 12,* 9–28.

Hrubec, Z., & Omenn, G. S. (1981). Evidence of genetic predisposition to alcoholic cirrhosis and psychosis: Twin concordances for alcoholism and its biological points by zygosity among male veterans. *Alcoholism: Clinical and Experimental Research, 5,* 207–215.

Jellinek, E. M. (1960). *The disease concept of alcoholism.* New Haven, CT: Hillhouse Press.

Jöreskog, K. G., & Sörbom, D. (1993a). *LISREL 8: Structural equation modeling with the SIMPLIS command language.* Chicago: Scientific Software.

Jöreskog, K. G., & Sörbom, D. (1993b). *PRELIS 2 user's reference guide.* Chicago: Scientific Software.

Kaij, L. (1960). *Alcoholism in twins: Studies on the etiology and sequels of abuse of alcohol.* Stockholm: Almqvist & Wiksell.

Kendler, K. S., Heath, A. C., Neale, M. C., Kessler, R. C., & Eaves, L. J. (1992). A population-based twin study of alcoholism in women. *Journal of the American Medical Association, 268,* 1877–1882.

Kendler, K. S., Prescott, C. A., Neale, M. C., & Pedersen, N. L. (1997). Temperance board registration for alcohol abuse in a national sample of Swedish male twins born 1902–1949. *Archives of General Psychiatry, 54,* 178–184.

Kessler, R. C., McGonalge, K. A., Zhao, S., Nelson, C. B., Hughes, M., Eshleman, S., Wittchen, H., & Kendler, K. S. (1994). Lifetime and 12-month prevalence of DSM-III-R psychiatric disorders among persons aged 15–54 in the United States: Results from the National Comorbidity Study. *Archives of General Psychiatry, 51,* 8–19.

Koskenvuo, M., Langinvainio, J., Kaprio, J., Lonnqvist, J., & Tienari, P. (1984). Psychiatric hospitalization in twins. *Acta Geneticae Medicae et Gemellologiae, 33,* 321–332.

Kruglyak, L., & Lander, E. S. (1995). Complete multipoint sib-pair analysis of qualitative and quantitative traits. *American Journal of Human Genetics, 57,* 439–454.

Lange, K., Westlake, J., & Spence, M. A. (1976). Extensions to pedigree analysis: III. Variance components by the scoring method. *Annals of Human Genetics, 39,* 485–491.

Lee, E. T. (1992). *Statistical methods for survival data analysis* (2nd ed.). New York: Wiley.

Li, T. K. (1990). Genetic animal models for the study of alcoholism. In C. R. Cloninger & H. Begleiter (Eds.), *Genetics and biology of alcoholism* (Banbury Rep. No. 33, pp. 217–223). Plainview, NY: Cold Spring Harbor Laboratory Press.

Little, R. J. A., & Rubin, D. B. (1987). *Statistical analysis with missing data.* New York: Wiley.

Little, R. J. A., & Schenker, N. (1995). Missing data. In G. Arminger, C. C. Clogg, & D. B. Sobel (Eds.), *Handbook of statistical modeling for the social and behavioral sciences* (pp. 39–76). New York: Plenum.

Loehlin, J. C. (1992). *Genes and environment in personality development: Individual differences and development series* (Vol. 2). Newbury Park, CA: Sage.

McCord, W., & McCord, J. (1962). A longitudinal study of the personality of alcoholics. In D. J. Pattman & C. R. Snyder (Eds.), *Society, culture and drinking patterns* (pp. 413–430). New York: Wiley.

McCutcheon, A. L. (1987). *Latent class analysis.* Newbury Park, CA: Sage.

McGue, M. (1994). Genes, environment and the etiology of alcoholism. In R. Zucker, G. Boyd, & J. Howard (Eds.), *The development of alcohol problems: Exploring the biopsychosocial matrix of risk* (NIAAA Research Monograph No. 26, NIH Publication No. 94-3495, pp. 1–40). Rockville, MD: U.S. Department of Health and Human Services.

McGue, M., Pickens, R. W., & Svikis, D. S. (1992). Sex and age effects on the inheritance of alcohol problems: A twin study. *Journal of Abnormal Psychology, 101,* 3–17.

Merikangas, K. R. (1990). The genetic epidemiology of alcoholism. *Psychological Medicine, 20,* 11–22.

Meyer, J. M., & Neale, M. C. (1992). The relationship between age at first drug use and teenage drug use liability. *Behavior Genetics, 22,* 197–213.

Nance, W. E., & Corey, L. A. (1976). Genetic models for the analysis of data from the families of identical twins. *Genetics, 83,* 811–826.

Neale, M. C., & Cardon, L. R. (1992). *Methodology for genetic studies of twins and families. NATO ASI series.* Dordrecht, The Netherlands: Kluwer Academic.

Neale, M. C., Eaves, L. J., & Kendler, K. S. (1996). The power of the classical twin study to resolve variation in threshold traits. *Behavior Genetics, 24,* 239–258.

Nelson, C. B., Heath, A. C., & Kessler, R. C. (1997). *Temporal progression of alcohol dependence symptoms in the U.S. household population: Results from the National Comorbidity Survey.* Manuscript submitted for publication.

Nelson, C. B., Little, R. J. A., Heath, A. C., & Kessler, R. C. (1996). Patterns of DSM–III–R alcohol dependence symptom progression in a general population survey. *Psychological Medicine, 26,* 449–460.

Noble, E. P., & Blum, K. (1991). The dopamine D2 receptor gene and alcoholism. *Journal of the American Medical Association, 265,* 2667.

Olsson, U. (1979). Maximum-likelihood estimation of the polychoric coefficient. *Psychometrika, 44,* 443–460.

Pearson, K. (1900). Mathematical contributions to the theory of evolution: VII. On the correlation of characters not quantitatively measurable. *Philosophical Transactions of the Royal Society of London, Series A, 195,* 1–47.

Pickens, R. W., Svikis, D. S., McGue, M., Lykken, D. T., Heston, L. L., & Clayton, P. J. (1991). Heterogeneity in the inheritance of alcoholism: A study of male and female twins. *Archives of General Psychiatry, 48,* 19–28.

Plomin, R., DeFries, J. C., & Loehlin, J. L. (1977). Genotype–environment interaction and correlation in the analysis of human variation. *Psychological Bulletin, 84,* 309–322.

Polich, J., Pollock, V. W., & Bloom, F. E. (1994). Meta-analysis of P300 amplitude from males at risk for alcoholism. *Psychological Bulletin, 115,* 55–73.

Reich, T., Cloninger, C. R., Van Eerdewegh, P., Rice, J. P., & Mullaney, J. (1988). Secular trends in the familial transmission of alcoholism. *Alcoholism: Clinical and Experimental Research, 12,* 458–464.

Risch, N., & Zhang, H. (1995). Extreme discordant sib pairs for mapping quantitative trait loci in humans. *Science, 268,* 1584–1589.

Robins, E., & Guze, S. B. (1970). Establishment of diagnostic validity in psychiatric illness: Its application to schizophrenia. *American Journal of Psychiatry, 126,* 983–987.

Robins, L. N., & Regier, D. A. (1991). *Psychiatric disorders in America.* New York: Free Press.

Romanov, K., Kaprio, J., & Rose, R. J. (1991). Genetics of alcoholism: Effects of migration on concordance rates among male twins. *Alcohol and Alcoholism* (Suppl. 1), 137–140.

Rust, J. (1975). Genetic effects in the cortical auditory evoked potential: A twin study. *Electroencephalography and Clinical Neurophysiology, 39*, 321–327.

Schuckit, M. A. (1984). Subjective responses to alcohol in sons of alcoholics and control subjects. *Archives of General Psychiatry, 41*, 879–884.

Schuckit, M. A. (1985). Ethanol-induced changes in body sway in men at high alcoholism risk. *Archives of General Psychiatry, 42*, 375–379.

Schuckit, M. A. (1994). Low level of response to alcohol as a predictor of future alcoholism. *American Journal of Psychiatry, 151*, 184–189.

Schuckit, M. A., & Gold, E. O. (1988). A simultaneous evaluation of multiple markers of ethanol/placebo challenges in sons of alcoholics and controls. *Archives of General Psychiatry, 45*, 211–216.

Schuckit, M. A., & Risch, S. C. (1987). Plasma cortisol levels following ethanol in sons of alcoholics and controls. *Archives of General Psychiatry, 44*, 942–945.

Sher, K. J. (1991). *Children of alcoholics: A critical appraisal of theory and research.* Chicago: University of Chicago Press.

Slutske, W. S., Heath, A. C., Dinwiddie, S. H., Madden, P. A. F., Bucholz, K. K., Dunne, M. P., Statham, D. J., & Martin, N. G. (1997). Genetic and environmental influences in the etiology of conduct disorder: A study of 2682 adult twin pairs. *Journal of Abnormal Psychology, 106*, 266–279.

Spielman, R. S., McGinnis, R. E., & Ewens, W. J. (1993). Transmission test for linkage disequilibrium: The insulin gene region and insulin-dependent diabetes mellitus (IDDM). *American Journal of Human Genetics, 52*, 506–516.

Suarez, B. K., Parsian, A., Hampe, C. L., Todd, R. D., Reich, T., & Cloninger, C. R. (1994). Linkage disequilibria at the D2 dopamine receptor locus in alcoholics and controls. *Genomics, 19*, 20.

Thomasson, H. R., Crabb, D. W., & Edenberg, H. J. (1993). Alcohol and aldehyde dehydrogenase polymorphisms and alcoholism. *Behavior Genetics, 23*, 131–136.

True, W. R., Heath, A. C., Romeis, J. C., Slutske, W. S., Bucholz, K., Scherres, F., Lin, N., Eisen, S. A., Goldberg, J., Lyons, M. S., & Tsuang, M. T. (1996, June). Models of treatment-seeking for alcoholism: The role of genes and environment. *Alcoholism: Clinical and Experimental Research, 20*, 1577–1581.

Turner, E., Ewing, J., Shilling, P., Smith, T. L., Irwin, M., Schuckit, M., & Kelsoe, J. R. (1992). Lack of association between an RFLP near the D2 dopamine receptor gene and severe alcoholism. *Biological Psychiatry, 31*, 285–290.

Turner, J. R., Cardon, L. R., & Hewitt, J. K. (1994). *Behavior genetic applications in behavioral medicine research.* New York: Plenum.

Vaillant, G. E. (1983). *The natural history of alcoholism.* Cambridge, MA: Harvard University Press.

Wacholder, S., McLaughlin, J. K., Silverman, D. T., & Mandel, J. S. (1992). Selection of controls in case-control studies. *American Journal of Epidemiology, 135,* 1019–1028.

Zhang, Y., Proenca, R., Maffei, M., Barone, M., Lepold, L., & Friedman, J. M. (1994). Positional cloning of the mouse obese gene and its human homologue. *Nature, 372,* 425–432.

II

DESIGN AND ANALYSIS OF INTERVENTION MODELS

6

TOWARD UNDERSTANDING INDIVIDUAL EFFECTS IN MULTICOMPONENT PREVENTION PROGRAMS: DESIGN AND ANALYSIS STRATEGIES

STEPHEN G. WEST AND LEONA S. AIKEN

Recent reviews agree in their conclusion that multiple early risk factors are associated with the later development of significant health, mental health, and substance abuse problems (Coie et al., 1993; Hawkins, Catalano, & Miller, 1992; Mrazek & Haggerty, 1994; Shaffer, Philips, & Enzer, 1989; Weissberg, Caplan, & Sivo, 1989). Consequently, programs aimed at preventing these problems typically will need to include multiple components that target the possible linkage between each risk factor and problem behavior. To cite two examples, Flay's (1985) review of school-based smoking prevention programs showed that successful programs were character-

This chapter was supported partially by National Institute of Mental Health Grant P50MH39246 and National Institute on Drug Abuse Grant DA 09757. The mammography research described in the section on mediational analysis was supported by National Cancer Institute Grant R03-CA46736. We thank Thomas D. Cook, William G. Graziano, David P. MacKinnon, and Jenn-Yun Tein for their comments on an earlier version of this chapter.

ized by six components: media material with similar-age peers, information on the immediate physiological effects of smoking, correction of misperceptions about the prevalence of smoking, discussion of family and media influences on smoking and methods of dealing with them, explicit learning of behavioral skills, and a public commitment procedure. Wolchik et al. (1993), in a program for divorced mothers, included components addressing the mother–child relationship, the noncustodial parent–child relationship, discipline strategies, and reduction of stressful events. Randomized trials comparing multicomponent prevention programs with a control group have provided evidence of successful outcomes in a variety of areas (e.g., Durlak & Wells, in press; Price, Cowen, Lorion, & Ramos-McKay, 1988). These successful demonstrations of the efficacy of prevention programs are beginning to give rise to new questions related to the multicomponent nature of these programs. These questions, in turn, focus prevention researchers on new designs and analyses in an attempt to understand how individual components of the program are producing their effects, questions of whether and how individual program components influence outcomes.

TENSIONS ASSOCIATED WITH DEVELOPMENT OF MULTICOMPONENT PROGRAMS

The development of multicomponent programs inevitably produces fundamental tensions between the applied science concerns of program development and the basic science concerns of research. Program developers have a central concern of maximizing the efficacy of the program. They attempt to develop an efficient intervention in which each component targets as many of the potential risk factors as possible, the components build on each other, and all parts of the program are well integrated. By contrast, basic researchers (who also may be involved in program development) are concerned with maximizing the informativeness of the results of the randomized trial for basic psychological theory. They hope to learn how the program affects each of the targeted risk factors and produces its effect on the final outcome of interest (e.g., substance abuse). This hope will be best realized to the degree that the components of the program are distinct; are each targeted at a unique risk factor; and can, in practice, be delivered separately or together.

During the period of initial program development and evaluation, the concerns of the program developers will often be given strong priority. Sechrest, West, Phillips, Redner, and Yeaton (1979) argued that interventions initially should be tested in what program developers believe is their strongest form. This approach maximizes the likelihood of a successful outcome for program participants, thereby helping to ensure continued program support and funding. Once a program has been demonstrated to be effective, however, further improvement of the program in terms of increased efficacy and decreased cost will often require a greater understanding of the basic processes through which each of the components of the intervention achieves its effects. At this point, the concerns of researchers may be given increased priority, requiring designs and analysis that permit probing of the role of each program component.

QUESTIONS FOR MULTICOMPONENT PROGRAMS

In this chapter, we consider designs and statistical analyses that address two intertwined questions that may be raised after the initial demonstration of the efficacy of a multicomponent program.

1. *Does each component of the program contribute to the outcome?* Basic researchers seek to show that each component of the program is producing the desired outcome in the service of establishing the construct validity of the independent variables (Cook & Campbell, 1979; Higginbotham, West, & Forsyth, 1988). Applied researchers may be interested in the efficacy of individual components for more pragmatic reasons. An individual component may reduce the efficacy of the overall intervention package or even lead to harmful effects for program participants. Or the program may include inert components that are neither harmful nor helpful but that are costly to include in the program package. Both basic and applied researchers would like to identify and delete such ineffective components from the overall program.

2. *Through what processes are the components of the program achieving their effectiveness on the ultimate outcome of interest?* Researchers are creating a new generation of prevention programs that are based on psychosocial theory and research on the development and maintenance of problematic behaviors (Bryan, Aiken, & West, 1996; Caplan, Vinokur, Price, & Van Ryn, 1989; Wolchik et al., 1993). Models of the precursors and determinants of problematic behaviors then are translated into interventions containing components specifically designed to modify these precursors. It is assumed that modifying precursors will lead to the prevention, delay of onset, or diminution of problematic behaviors. In a similar vein, researchers are developing models of the precursors or determinants of health- and mental-health-protective behaviors (e.g., cancer-screening tests, Aiken, West, Woodward, & Reno, 1994; safer sexual behavior, Fisher & Fisher, 1992) and are translating these models into interventions to encourage the protective behaviors. Through careful study of the processes through which these model-driven preventive interventions achieve their effects, intervention researchers can potentially provide some of the strongest information possible to inform basic researchers about the development of substance abuse, health, and mental health problems in children and

adults (Coie et al., 1993), as well as about the adoption and maintenance of salutary behaviors. Clear understanding of the processes through which the program operates also is important in making appropriate modifications that help make the program successful in new sites.

In this chapter, we consider the strengths, weaknesses, and areas of application of designs and statistical analyses that have been proposed to answer these two questions. First, we begin by examining practical and statistical considerations that limit the range of intervention designs that can be realistically considered. We then explore Question 1, considering currently used preventive intervention designs and other experimental designs suggested in the statistical literature. We then consider Question 2, examining strategies of studying mediation of treatment effects. Finally, we consider how design and statistical analysis might be brought together to provide a fuller understanding of the process through which each component contributes to the outcome.

SOME PRACTICAL AND STATISTICAL CONSIDERATIONS FOR PREVENTIVE TRIALS

Several practical and statistical considerations place important limits on the range of designs that may be considered by preventive trials.

Multiple Components

Most preventive programs have multiple, theoretically distinct components. For example, the earlier discussed social influences smoking prevention programs (Flay, 1985) include six components; the most recent revision of the program for divorced mothers (Wolchik et al., 1993) includes four components. Attempting to construct a full factorial design to investigate the main and interactive effects of the presence or absence of each component (two levels) leads to complex, infeasible designs. For example, construction of the $2 \times 2 \times 2 \times 2 \times 2 \times 2$ factorial design to investigate each of the possible combinations of the six components in the smoking prevention intervention requires 64 intervention conditions. The analysis of variance (ANOVA) of such a design produces 6 main effects, 15 two-way interactions, 20 three-way interactions, 15 four-way interactions, 6 five-way interactions, and 1 six-way interaction, most of which are not of any a priori theoretical interest to the researcher. These considerations suggest a focus on simpler designs that target the effects of interest.

Implementation Difficulties

In traditional laboratory experimentation, researchers are trained to create experimental settings in which each manipulation forms a module that can be swapped easily into or out of the experimental script. For example, whether the respondent is learning a difficult or easy list of words under stressful (Manipulation 1) or nonstressful (Manipulation 2) environmental conditions has little implication for any other part of the experiment. By contrast, prevention programs need to be integrated into a coherent unit, often extending over several sessions. Later components (e.g., better discipline strategies) may be designed to build on earlier components (e.g., improved parent–child relationships). These features often make it difficult to simply swap modules into and out of prevention programs without seriously affecting the overall coherence of the full program. Consequently, program variations in which components are added to or deleted from an existing program typically will be strictly limited in number because they may entail redesign of the entire program. Even under the ideal condition of having relatively independent modules corresponding to each component, it is unlikely logistically that more than four to six variations of a prevention program could be mounted.

Sample Size and Power

For a randomized trial to be worth doing, it must have adequate statistical power to detect differences among intervention conditions. Yet, many researchers continue to be unaware of the number of participants required to detect differences between treatment conditions with adequate power. Following Cohen's (1988), definitions, differences between intervention and control groups means (ds) of .20, .50, and .80 standard deviation units are considered to be small, moderate, and large effect sizes, respectively, and .80 is considered to be an adequate level of statistical power. In a randomized experiment in which there are an equal number of participants in the intervention and control groups, 52 total participants (26 per cell) would be needed to detect a large effect, 126 participants would be needed to detect a moderate effect, and 786 participants would be required to detect a small effect on the outcome measure with .80 power and an alpha of .05.[1] Durlak and Wells's (in press) review of 177 primary prevention programs in the mental health area suggests that the mean effect size is small to moderate (d = .34), suggesting that relatively large sample sizes typically will be needed to detect preventive effects reliably.

Although bigger samples will always be better statistically, larger samples often can be costly or impractical in obvious and nonobvious ways. If there is a fixed cost for program delivery and data collection for each participant, large sample sizes may be prohibitively expensive. Delivering

---

[1] These sample size requirements can be lowered by design improvements. The inclusion of a pretest measure that has a .5 correlation with the outcome measure in this example lowers the total number of participants required to 19, 61, and 584 to detect large, moderate, and small effect sizes, respectively, with .80 power.

programs to groups of participants often at several different sites (e.g., smoking prevention programs delivered in classrooms in different schools) may introduce variation in the nature and quality of implementation of the intervention over sites. Variation in the implementation of the intervention over instances or sites is a form of unreliability (i.e., irrelevant error variance in the intervention) that is equivalent to unreliability of predictor variables in multiple regression, which weakens tests of intervention effects. Such procedures also tend to produce clustering of outcome data (i.e., correlation of participants' responses within single administrations of the intervention). Clustering introduces biases into familiar statistical analyses (ANOVA, multivariate analysis of variance [MANOVA], multiple regression) because these analyses assume that all observations are completely independent. Standard significance tests applied to clustered data can lead to Type I error rates that far exceed the stated alpha value of .05 (e.g., $\alpha = .30$ for classrooms of 25 students) and an intraclass correlation of .05. Clustered data require special hierarchical statistical procedures (see Bryk & Raudenbush, 1992; Kreft, 1994; also see chap. 8 in this book) that produce unbiased tests of intervention effects; these unbiased tests typically yield less significance than the positively biased tests that ignore clustering. The economies of group administration of the program and group testing on the dependent variables also may be partially offset by the difficulties of delivering the program to and assessing the highest risk individuals. For example, children from low-income, disorganized families (e.g., homeless families) are less likely to be enrolled in school and, when enrolled, may be absent more frequently. Finally, interventions targeted at a specific risk group may be limited by the size of the population. For example, children who have a parent die during middle childhood or early adolescence appear to be at an extraordinarily high risk for the development of severe mental health problems (Gersten, Beals, & Kallgren, 1991). Yet, in a major metropolitan area, perhaps a few hundred parents who have a child in this age range can be expected to die in any given year.

Finally, as we consider in more detail later, researchers attempting to isolate the effects of a single component from an intervention package typically will be faced with a difficult task in the light of considerations of statistical power. Such effects are often smaller in magnitude than comparisons of overall intervention packages with control groups. Large sample sizes or special designs that increase statistical power may be needed to detect these effects.

TRADITIONAL RESEARCH DESIGNS: A REVIEW OF THE LITERATURE

To get a sense of current practice in the design of randomized preventive trials, we reviewed 3 years of past issues of the *Journal of Consulting* and *Clinical Psychology, Health Psychology,* and the *American Journal of Community Psychology,* which publish reports of such trials. Five types of designs were identified: (a) the treatment package strategy, (b) the comparative treatment strategy, (c) the dismantling strategy, (d) the constructive research strategy, and (e) factorial designs (see Kazdin, 1980, 1986). The first two designs are relatively common, whereas the latter three are used only infrequently in published prevention trials in these journals. An example of each approach is summarized from the larger prevention literature when possible and from the clinical treatment literature when no instances of the approach could be found.

1. *Treatment package strategy.* In this approach, the effectiveness of the total treatment package is contrasted with that of an appropriate comparison group. For example, Wolchik et al. (1993) randomly assigned custodial mothers sampled from county divorce records to receive either the full intervention program or a delayed intervention (control group) begun after posttest data were collected. The full intervention package consisted of 13 group and individual sessions containing components that addressed each of the four components identified earlier. Such designs are ideal for initial evaluations focusing on whether the program works and is worthy of further research (Sechrest et al., 1979). However, this design by itself provides little information about the effectiveness of individual treatment components or the processes through which they operate.

2. *Comparative treatment strategy.* In the comparative treatment strategy, two or more alternative interventions are compared directly. An additional no-treatment comparison group typically is included in the design to enhance the interpretability of the results (Kazdin, 1986). The goal of this strategy is to choose the most effective single intervention from the set of alternative interventions under consideration. For example, Hansen, Johnson, Flay, Graham, and Sobol (1988) randomly assigned 84 school classrooms to receive one of three intervention conditions: (a) the social influences drug abuse prevention program adapted from the school-based smoking prevention program described earlier; (b) an affective education program emphasizing stress management, values clarification, decision making, goal setting, and self-esteem building; or (c) no intervention (control). Such comparative designs can identify the most efficacious of a set of interventions as they were implemented in a particular randomized trial.[2] Although Hansen et al. (1988) compared entire programs, the comparative design also can be applied to compare the effectiveness of potential components of a larger intervention package. When the design is used in this

---

[2]More general interpretations about the relative efficacy of the interventions depend on meeting several important assumptions: The interventions should be of equal strength relative to the ideal treatment of that type, should be implemented with equal fidelity, and should be expected to affect the same outcome variables (Cooper & Richardson, 1986; Sechrest et al., 1979).

latter manner, it provides information about the effectiveness of each component in isolation from other components. Such information can be useful to program developers in the later design of a multicomponent intervention package.

3. *Dismantling strategy.* In the dismantling strategy, the full version of the program is compared with a reduced version in which one or more components have been eliminated. Criteria for selecting the components to be deleted from the treatment package vary; however, they often are based on theory, empirical research, or clinical impressions suggesting that the one or more deleted components may be inert or reduce the efficacy of the retained components. Components that are expensive or difficult to deliver also may become candidates for deletion. Dismantling designs often add a third no-treatment comparison group to enhance interpretability.

Pentz et al. (1989) used this design to study the effectiveness of combinations of entire intervention packages. They designed a comprehensive community drug abuse prevention program from four component programs: (a) a school-based social influences program (described earlier), (b) a component training parents in positive parent–child communication skills, (c) a component training community leaders in the organization of a community drug prevention task force, and (d) mass media coverage. The comprehensive program was compared with a reduced, lower cost version that included only the last two components. To the extent that the reduced version of the program produced outcomes that did not differ from the comprehensive program but did differ from a no-treatment comparison group, the researchers would be justified in concluding that the addition of the first two components did not appreciably add to the effectiveness of the comprehensive program over and above that of the reduced program comprising the last two components.[3]

4. *Constructive research strategy.* In the constructive research strategy, one or more components are added to a base intervention. The base intervention may be a single component or an entire program package. Added components that increase the efficacy of the base intervention are retained by program developers, whereas those that do not improve or that decrease efficacy relative to the base intervention are discarded.

To illustrate, Perri et al. (1988) examined the effects of several components designed to help maintain weight loss in obese adults. All participants received the base intervention, a 20-week behavior therapy program (B). Participants then were randomly assigned to receive one of four com-

---

[3]As we discuss in the section on factorial and fractional factorial designs, this comparison is not informative about the effectiveness of components A, B, or A + B considered alone. The effect of the full program reflects the main effect of each component taken separately plus all possible interactions among the components. The effect of the reduced version of the program reflects only the main effects and interactions among the components that are present in the reduced program.

binations of weight loss maintenance components or a fifth, control condition consisting of no additional maintenance components. The four maintenance interventions examined were (a) biweekly therapist contact (C), (b) biweekly therapist contact plus a social influence component (S) designed to enhance the participant's motivation, (c) biweekly therapist contact plus an aerobic exercise component (A), and (d) biweekly therapist contact plus a social influence component plus an aerobic exercise component. Thus, the five conditions of this constructive research study can be described as B, BC, BCS, BCA, BCAS.

Like the dismantling strategy, the constructive strategy can provide information about the efficacy of adding individual intervention components over and above a base intervention. Indeed, in most applications of these designs that are presently represented in the literature (i.e., comparing an intervention comprising Component A with one comprising Components A and B), the designs can be distinguished only by whether the researchers take A (constructive) or A + B (dismantling) as the base comparison group. The information about the efficacy of individual components provided by the constructive strategy depends on the theoretical rationale for the selection of components, the number of components that are added in each comparison, and the particular combinations of components that are selected relative to the full set of possible combinations.

5. *Factorial designs.* Complete factorial designs have long been among the most commonly used designs in laboratory experiments in psychology; they also have attracted modest attention in the psychotherapy research literature (Kazdin, 1980). In these designs, interventions representing all possible combinations of the levels of one component (Factor A) and the levels of a second component (Factor B) are created. For example, Webster-Stratton, Kolpacoff, and Hollinsworth (1988) randomly assigned parents of children with conduct problems to one of four conditions in a 2 × 2 factorial design: videotape modeling of parenting skills plus group discussion, videotape modeling only, group discussion only, and a waiting-list control group. This design permitted separate estimates of the effects of the videotape-modeling component (Factor A), the group discussion component (Factor B), and their interaction. Unfortunately, as we saw earlier, the extension of factorial designs to the investigation of more complex multicomponent interventions can lead to potential difficulties in interpretation, implementation, and statistical power.

INSIGHTS FROM THE STATISTICAL DESIGN LITERATURE

The experimental design literature in statistics and psychology (Box, Hunter, & Hunter, 1978; Mead, 1988; Steinberg & Hunter, 1984; Woodward, Bonett, & Brecht, 1990) offers a number of insights that are potentially useful in thinking about multicomponent programs. Here we discuss two. First, we reconsider the traditional research designs as partial implementations of factorial designs. Second, we briefly consider how other designs might be developed to test focused comparisons of interest. These considerations help refine and extend our understanding of designs to answer Question 1: Does the component contribute to the effect of the full program on the outcome?

Reconsidering Traditional Designs for Preventive Trials

Previously, we noted problems in the application of complete factorial designs to multicomponent preventive interventions. These designs quickly become impractical as more than two components need to be separately manipulated. Complete factorial designs may be simplified to fractional factorial designs in which only a systematically selected portion of all possible treatment combinations is implemented. Such simplification requires that the researcher identify the components and their main and interactive effects that are of greatest interest. It also requires that the researcher be willing to assume that certain other effects, typically higher order interactions, are negligible in magnitude. These are strong assumptions; they cannot be checked within a single preventive trial when fractional factorial designs are used. At the same time, these assumptions also apply to many of the traditional designs for preventive trials discussed earlier. Each of these can be considered to be a special case of fractional factorial or complete factorial designs.

Consider a simplified social influences smoking prevention program in which the three components are (a) correction of misperceptions about smoking prevalence (prevalence), (b) discussion of family and media influences on smoking (influences), and (c) a public commitment to not smoke (commitment). The three components may be combined into a 2 (prevalence) × 2 (influences) × 2 (commitment) factorial design in which each component is either present or not present. The eight possible intervention combinations (cells) of the full factorial design are numbered 1 through 8 and are illustrated in Part A of Exhibit 1. The ANOVA source table for the full factorial design would include 3 main effects, 3 two-way interactions, and 1 three-way interaction.

We now return to the traditional designs and show their relationship to the full factorial design. Design 1, the treatment package design, contrasts cell 1, in which none of the components are present (control condition), with cell 8, in which all of the three program components are present (see Part B in Exhibit 1). Design 2, the comparative treatment strategy, is shown in Part C in Exhibit 1. It contrasts the control condition, in which none of the compoments are present (cell 1), with cells in which only the prevalence component is present (cell 3), only the influences

EXHIBIT 1
Traditional Designs for Preventive Trials

A. Full factorial design (2 × 2 × 2 = 8 treatment conditions)

	No prevalence		Prevalence	
	No influence	Influence	No influence	Influence
No commitment	1	2	3	4
Commitment	5	6	7	8

B. Treatment package strategy (2 treatment conditions)

	No prevalence		Prevalence	
	No influence	Influence	No influence	Influence
No commitment	1	—	—	—
Commitment	—	—	—	8

C. Comparative Treatment Strategy (4 treatment conditions)

	No prevalence		Prevalence	
	No influence	Influence	No influence	Influence
No commitment	1	2	3	—
Commitment	5	—	—	—

D. Constructive/dismantling research strategy (4 treatment conditions)

	No prevalence		Prevalence	
	No influence	Influence	No influence	Influence
No commitment	1	—	3	4
Commitment	—	—	—	8

Note. A is the prevalence component, B is the influences component, and C is the commitment component. The cells of the full factorial design corresponding to each of the possible treatment combinations are numbered 1–8. Inclusion of the number in the fractional factorial design means that the treatment combination was included in the design. Dashes indicate that the treatment combination was not included in the design.

component is present (cell 2), and only the commitment component is present (cell 5). Design 3, the dismantling strategy, and Design 4, the constructive research strategy, can be considered together because they lead to identical designs when there is a full buildup (or teardown) of intervention components; an example design is illustrated in Part D of Exhibit 1. For example, one full buildup of intervention components would include four conditions: (a) a control condition in which none of the components are present (cell 1), (b) only the prevalence component is present (cell 3), (c) both the prevalence and influences components are present (cell 4), and (d) all three components are present (cell 8). These examples illustrate that each of the traditional intervention designs can be considered to be a subset of conditions from the full factorial design.

This analysis helps clarify some of the assumptions that are made in constructing each of the traditional designs. The comparative treatment design compares a set of intervention conditions, each of which is composed of a different single component, with a no-treatment comparison group. This design provides unbiased estimates of the effect of each component separately, but only in the absence of any of the other components. Predictions about the efficacy of combinations of the treatment components cannot be made without making assumptions that the effects of the components are strictly additive (i.e., all higher order interactions of the components are negligible).

The constructive research strategy adds each component sequentially to the treatment package in the following order: prevalence, influences, and commitment. In this design, each test reflects the contribution of the new component over and above the specific components that are already included. For example, the comparison of cell 8 (prevalence + influences + commitment) with cell 5 (prevalence + influences) tests the effectiveness of what the commitment component adds, given that prevalence and influences are already present in the treatment package. This design does not provide tests of the unique effect of each intervention component. Because the constructive and dismantling research strategies are equivalent when full buildup (or teardown) of all treatment combinations takes place, identical conclusions can be reached about the dismantling design.

These analyses help clarify the questions that are answered and the assumptions that are required by each design. The treatment package design alone tell us only the overall effect of the combination of components. It tells us nothing about the effects of the individual components or how they might combine to produce augmented or reduced effects. The comparative treatment strategy informs us about the unique effects of each component; however, it provides no information about the effectiveness of intervention packages comprising combinations of the components unless it is assumed that the components do not interact. The constructive treatment strategy informs us about one specific sequence of building up the intervention components; however, it does not provide information about the effects of individual components or about other nonexamined combinations of components (e.g., influences + commitment). We cannot be certain that the set of tested combinations of components will include the program representing the most efficacious combination of components.

This review indicates that the traditional designs are special cases of the full factorial design in which all possible combinations of the intervention components are represented. Each traditional design answers a different question and has different strengths and weaknesses. For maximum interpretability, all must make assumptions that certain interactions between components are negligible.

Possible New Designs for Focused Comparisons

If researchers are willing to assume that other effects are negligible, fractional factorial designs can be constructed to permit economical tests of a specific set of effects of interest. For example, suppose that researchers are interested in testing the main effects of prevalence, influence, and commitment and the Prevalence × Commitment interaction. They are willing to assume that all other interactions are negligible. Table 1 illustrates one five-condition design that provides unbiased tests of each of these effects. Box et al. (1978) described general methods for constructing fractional factorial designs that provide unconfounded estimates of main effects and two-way interactions if higher order interactions are assumed to be zero; Anderson and McLean (1984) provided a "cookbook" of these designs. These sources can be consulted to help develop customized designs that permit tests of the specific effects of interest to the investigator.

Many of the designs are highly economical relative to the full factorial designs. For example, consider the social influences smoking prevention programs described earlier, which have six components. Box et al. (1978) described a 16-cell design (quarter fraction) that provides unbiased estimates of all main effects and all two-way interactions for six factors, each having two levels, assuming that all three-way and above interactions are negligible. This design is distinctly more feasible than the full 2^6 factorial design, which requires 64 cells. At the same time, prevention researchers will rarely be able to mount large enough trials to permit even 16 intervention combinations to be investigated. Even these reduced designs can become impractical if several main effects and two-way interactions are of interest.

Comment

Fractional factorial designs adequately address Question 1. These designs focus on a few specific contrasts of interest and make strong assumptions that other effects are negligible to permit economical testing of hypotheses using a reduced number of intervention conditions. However, even these designs become too cumbersome given the severe restriction on the number of different intervention conditions that can be mounted in many preventive interventions. If assumptions about which effects are negligible are not reasonable, the estimates of the effects of interest will be biased because they will be confounded with higher order interactions. The effect of this problem will be the most profound on estimates of the efficacy of combinations of intervention components that are not included in the design. This issue of potential bias applies both to the first four traditional intervention designs reviewed in the previous section and to fractional factorial designs that are custom developed to test specific hypotheses. Re-

TABLE 1
Five-Condition Design: Estimates Main Effects of A, B, C, and A × B Interaction

Program Condition	A. Prevalence	B. Influence	C. Commitment
1	—	—	—
2	—	Yes	—
3	Yes	—	—
4	Yes	Yes	—
5	—	—	Yes

Note. Yes indicates component is included in program condition. Dash indicates component is not included in program condition. For example, in Condition 1 (control group), participants are not exposed to any program component; in Condition 4, participants are exposed to the prevalence and influence components, but not the commitment component.

searchers need to be attentive to the possibility that nonzero interactions among components have the potential to alter their conclusions.

Finally, researchers interested in comparing different single components, such as in the comparative treatment design, or combinations of components, such as in the dismantling and constructive research strategies, need to be attentive to issues of statistical power. Effect sizes are always computed relative to a comparison group. For example, if a full intervention package produces a moderate effect ($d = .5$) relative to a no-treatment control group, 126 total participants will be needed to have adequate statistical power to detect the effect. However, if one component accounts for 50% of the intervention effect, the effect size for the comparison of the full intervention package with this single component is reduced to .25. This means that 504 participants will now be required to detect the difference between the full treatment package and the single component.

These sample size requirements can be reduced by taking advantage of every feasible method of increasing the statistical power of the design and analysis. (Extensive discussion of these methods can be found in chap. 11 in this book, Hansen & Collins, 1994, and Higginbotham et al., 1988, chap. 2.) Design methods include a variety of strategies for sampling respondents, avoiding missing data, improving treatment implementation, and improving measurement. Statistical techniques include a variety of strategies for equating participants at pretesting (e.g., matching), models that reduce error variance (e.g., analysis of covariance), and methods for using all available data when data are missing (e.g., see chap. 10 in this book). Absent the use of these design and statistical methods to increase statistical power or the use of a large sample size, it will be difficult to detect differences between full and reduced versions of the intervention program. These considerations again underscore the importance of designs focused on detecting the theoretically most important effects rather than omnibus comparisons of several intervention conditions.

MEDIATIONAL ANALYSIS

Mediational analysis is a method to test the linkages from an intervention through intermediate *mediators* to ultimate program outcomes. The intermediate mediators are hypothesized determinants of the behavior in question, identified by theory and previous psychosocial research. It is assumed that an intervention has been designed to produce changes on these mediators, with the expectation that such change will produce the desired ultimate outcome. For example, to prevent smoking, an intervention might focus on increasing participants' resistance to peer pressure to smoke; resistance is the hypothesized mediator of the impact of the intervention on the delay of smoking onset. Mediational analysis provides an economical but less definitive approach to Question 1 than do factorial and fractional factorial designs. It also provides the best available method of addressing Question 2, the process through which each component of an intervention exerts its influence. Mediational analysis requires the existence of a model of the determinants of the behavior in question; these determinants serve as putative mediators in the mediational analysis.

Examining the Process of Behavior Change

In mediational analysis, one distinguishes between the putative mediators (i.e., the hypothesized determinants or constructs) in the model of behavior and the components (i.e., activities, materials) of an intervention designed to change levels on the mediators. In mediational analysis, the researcher articulates what Lipsey (1993; also see Wolchik et al., 1993) originally termed a "small theory." As we discuss in detail later in this chapter, the small theory needs to articulate (a) a program theory that specifies the links between each program component and the putative mediators and (b) a psychosocial theory that specifies the links among the putative mediators and between each putative mediating variable and the outcome variable.

Mediational analysis tests whether the intervention has produced change on the putative mediators (hypothesized constructs or determinants) and whether change in these mediators is, in turn, associated with changes in behavioral outcomes. Reliable measures of each of the putative mediators and each of the outcome variables are included in the design. Using statistical techniques such as multiple regression analysis and structural equation modeling, the researcher has some ability to probe the contribution of each of the putative mediators to the outcome. Unambiguous conclusions about the process by which individual program components have their effects (Question 2) require that individual components have distinctive linkages to specific mediators.

Bryan et al. (1996) provided an example of mediational analysis applied to condom use among newly sexually active young women. On the basis of psychosocial research (Bryan, Aiken, & West, in press), they hypothesized that newly sexually active young women fail to engage in safer sex practices partly because (a) they do not take responsibility for their sexual activity in a way that would lead them to be planful about sex and (b) they feel unable to control their partners' behavior in a sexual encounter. Responsibility for sexuality (responsibility) and control of the sexual encounter (control) served as constructs of a model of determinants of safer sexual behavior. Bryan et al. (1996) designed an intervention to increase condom use (the ultimate outcome) by creating distinct program components that targeted the responsibility and control mediators. Mediational analysis was used to test for linkages from the intervention to changes in level of responsibility and control and in turn from responsibility and control to condom use.[4]

To understand mediational analysis, it is useful to consider initially the case of a simple, one-component program that targets a single mediator. Imagine that a condom use program for young women was designed solely to increase young women's taking responsibility for their own sexual behavior; the increased sexual responsibility, in turn, is expected to lead to increased intentions to use condoms. Figure 1A depicts this simple, small theory of the single determinant of condom use intentions among young women. In a randomized trial, program participants are assigned to receive the sexual responsibility program or to serve as untreated controls. Each young woman's level of sexual responsibility and condom use intentions are assessed after completion of the program.

Following Judd and Kenny (1981a), three conditions must be met to demonstrate that responsibility for sexuality mediated the outcome. MacKinnon (1994) added a fourth condition (significance of tests of each mediated effect) that is particularly important when there are multiple mediators of program effects. We initially consider the three conditions of Judd and Kenny and then add MacKinnon's fourth condition in the context of multiple mediator models.

1. *Program to mediators.* The program must cause differences in the putative mediator; in our case, it is the measure of sexual responsibility. This can be tested with a simple two-group ANOVA or equivalently by regression analysis with a binary predictor (intervention or no intervention), which, if significant, would show that the program affected the mediator. The standardized regression coefficient from such an analysis is the path coefficient a in Figure 1A (1).

2. *Program to outcome.* The program must produce differences in the

---

[4]Actually, the model of Bryan et al. (1996) was somewhat more complex. It specified that acceptance and control were precursors of condom use self-efficacy, which in turn led to increased intentions to use condoms. Mediational analysis provided support for this longer mediational chain as well as a linkage from intentions to subsequent condom use.

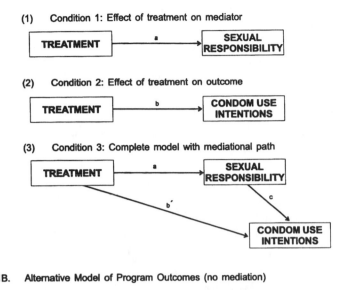

1A. Mediational analysis for a single component intervention

(1) Condition 1: Effect of treatment on mediator

TREATMENT —— a ——▶ SEXUAL RESPONSIBILITY

(2) Condition 2: Effect of treatment on outcome

TREATMENT —— b ——▶ CONDOM USE INTENTIONS

(3) Condition 3: Complete model with mediational path

TREATMENT —— a ——▶ SEXUAL RESPONSIBILITY

b′

c

CONDOM USE INTENTIONS

1B. Alternative Model of Program Outcomes (no mediation)

SEXUAL RESPONSIBILITY

TREATMENT .6 ↗   .3 ↘

CONDOM USE INTENTIONS

Figure 1. Mediational analysis of a single-construct theory of condom use intentions.

outcome; here it is condom use intentions. Again, this can be tested using an ANOVA or regression analysis, yielding the path coefficient b in Figure 1A (2).

3. *Demonstration of mediation.* The links from intervention to responsibility to intentions (paths a and c in Figure 1A [3]) represent mediation. When these paths are controlled, the magnitude of path b' must be significantly reduced relative to b in Condition 2. Operationally, path b' is measured in a regression equation or structural equation model predicting condom use intentions from the binary treatment variable and from sexual responsibility (see Baron & Kenny, 1986). If path b' does not differ from zero, sexual responsibility may be inferred to provide complete mediation of the effect of the program on condom use intentions. If the magnitude of path b' is significantly reduced relative to its value (b) in the test of Condition 2, sexual responsibility only partially mediates the effect of the program on condom use intentions. That the path b' from the program to condom use intentions is not reduced entirely to zero may indicate that there is at least one additional unmeasured mediator of con-

dom use intentions that is being affected by the program.[5] This additional mediator may represent other determinants of condom use inadvertently influenced by the program (e.g., peer group support for condom use engendered by having received the program with a group of same-age, newly sexually active young women who appear to approve of condom use). Many "nonspecific effects" of interventions may fall into this class of unmeasured mediators.

Conditions 1 and 2 are straightforward and have long been tested by researchers using mediational hypotheses. Rather than the regression analysis prescribed earlier (i.e., outcome predicted from treatment plus mediator), the mere demonstration of a correlation between the putative mediator and the outcome might appear to test Condition 3. In fact, this correlation must be nonzero if mediation is taking place. However, results in which mediation is not taking place also can result in a nonzero correlation. To illustrate, consider the result depicted in Figure 1B in which the intervention has two independent effects: an increase in sexual responsibility and an increase in condom use intentions. This result passes Conditions 1 and 2. Furthermore, because sexual responsibility and condom use intentions share the common third variable of program status, they will be correlated ($r = .18$ in this example; see Bryan et al., 1996). Only by imposing Condition 3 can we rule out this and some other possibilities that are not consistent with the small theory of the program.

Multiple Components and a Single Mediator

Our hypothetical example described a single program with a single component that was designed to change a single purported mediator. However, mediational analysis may be extended to investigate the influence of several program components on a single, common mediator of special theoretical interest. For example, Harackiewicz, Sansone, Blair, Epstein, and Manderlink (1987) conducted a mediational analysis of four smoking cessation program packages: (a) nicotine gum plus a self-help manual with an intrinsic motivational orientation; (b) nicotine gum plus a self-help manual with an extrinsic motivational orientation; (c) intrinsic self-help manual only; and (d) a brief booklet containing tips for stopping smoking (control). Their special interest was in participants' internal attribution for success in quitting smoking, which was measured 6 weeks after intake. This putative mediator, one that might be influenced by any or all of the program packages, was believed to be of particular importance in determining successful maintenance of nonsmoking status after program completion.

---

[5]Incomplete mediation also could be produced if the single-construct model were correct but the mediator of sexual responsibility were poorly measured. Poor measurement may stem from unreliability, poor content validity (lack of adequate coverage of the construct), or a combination of both.

The researchers measured each participant's smoking status at regular intervals up to 1 year after intake. The results of the mediational analysis met the three conditions of mediation specified by Judd and Kenny (1981a); internal attributions for success partially mediated successful maintenance of nonsmoking status.[6]

Mediational Analysis in Multicomponent Programs With Multiple Mediators

The further extension of mediational analysis to multicomponent intervention programs that target multiple mediators raises new issues, particularly ones associated with the simultaneous investigation of the specific effects of each of several different program components on individual mediators. The small theory of the intervention typically becomes considerably more complex. Exactly how to apportion variance among competing mediational paths becomes less definitive. The statistical tests of the model also increase in difficulty, and the impact of problems in study design or measurement of the mediators becomes more serious.

To illustrate some of these issues, we consider data from a trial of the second generation of two programs originally developed by Reynolds, West, and Aiken (1990) to increase the incidence of screening mammography in eligible, asymptomatic women. Screening mammography is a low-dose X ray that can detect breast cancer in its early, treatable form. In this trial, Aiken, West, Woodward, Reno, and Reynolds (1994) implemented an educational (E) program based on the health belief model (HBM; Becker & Maiman, 1975). The HBM specifies four putative mediators of an individual's willingness to engage in health-protective behavior. Applied to breast cancer screening with mammography, these are a woman's perceptions of her susceptibility to breast cancer, the severity of breast cancer, the benefits of screening mammography, and barriers to screening mammography. These four mediators were expected to influence the woman's intention to get a screening mammogram. The HBM treats the four mediators as being coequal (i.e., it specifies no sequence in which they might act or any interactions among them).

A second, theoretically more intensive educational plus psychological (EP) intervention was also developed and implemented. This program included the full E program plus psychological compliance exercises. Using the constructive research strategy, eligible women ($N = 295$) were assigned to a control group (C), the E program, or the EP program. Measures of the

---

[6]Complications in this conclusion arise because of the focus of the analysis only on those participants who had successfully quit 6 weeks after intake and the nature of the outcome measures (smoker vs. nonsmoker, duration of nonsmoking status [time to failure]). The latter problem can be addressed through the use of alternative analysis strategies to test Conditions 2 and 3 (see MacKinnon & Dwyer, 1993).

2A.   Condition 1: Effect of intervention on mediators.

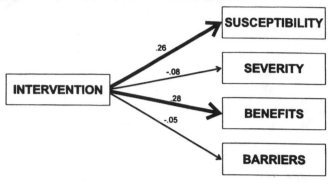

2B.   Condition 2: Effect of intervention on outcome.

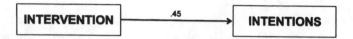

2C.   Condition 3: Complete mediational model with mediational paths through all four mediators. (Correlated errors between Benefits and Barriers are omitted from figure for clarity.)

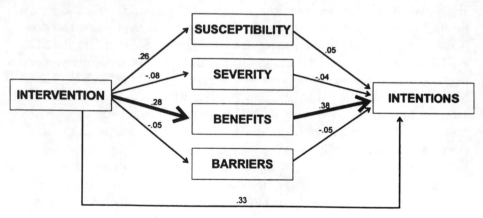

Figure 2. Analysis of mediation in a multicomponent mediational model: Mammography intervention.

four putative mediating variables and the outcome variable of intentions to get a screening mammogram were gathered immediately following program presentation.

Because the E and EP program led to equivalent results on the putative mediators and outcome variable, we collapsed them into a single intervention program for ease of presentation of the results of the mediational analyses. Tests of the three conditions of mediation (Judd & Kenny, 1981a) yielded the following results (see Figure 2).

2D. Reduced mediational model with only susceptibility as mediator.

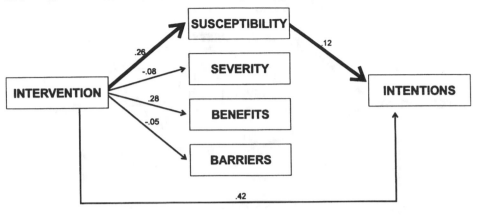

2E. Reduced mediational model with only benefits as mediator.

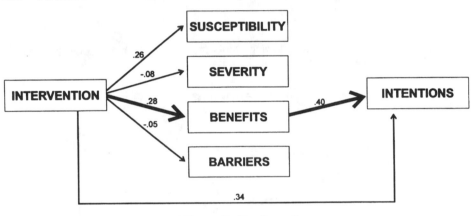

(*Figure 2.* Continued)

1. *Program to mediators.* Figure 2A shows that the intervention package led to higher perceptions of two of the putative mediators, susceptibility to breast cancer, $F(1, 285) = 20.68$, $p < .001$, $\beta = .26$, and benefits of screening mammography, $F(1, 282) = 23.15$, $p < .001$, $\beta = .28$. Neither the perceived severity of breast cancer ($\beta = -.08$) nor perceived barriers to screening mammography ($\beta = -.05$) were significantly affected by the intervention.

2. *Program to outcome.* The intervention package led to a significant increase in the outcome variable, intentions to get a screening mammogram, $F(1, 265) = 66.69$, $p < .001$, $\beta = .45$ (see Figure 2B).

Three of the putative mediators, perceived susceptibility to breast cancer, $r(264) = .23$, perceived benefits of screening mammography, $r(261) = .49$, and perceived barriers to screening mammography, $r(262) = -.19$,

2F. Respecified mediational model, following Ronis (1992), in which Susceptibility and Severity serve as precursors of Benefits.

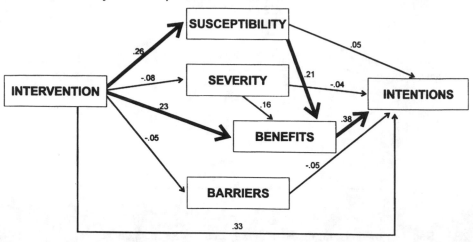

2G. Final mediational model, following Ronis (1992), in which Susceptibility and Severity serve as precursors of Benefits.

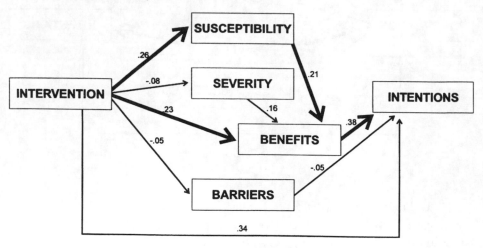

(*Figure 2.* Continued)

showed significant relations with intentions to get a screening mammogram. Perceived severity of breast cancer was not significantly related to intentions ($r = -.01$). Perceived susceptibility and benefits thus were candidates for a role as mediators of intervention effects because they both were changed by the intervention and were correlated with the outcome.

3. *Demonstration of mediation.* We tested the third condition of mediation using the structural equation model depicted in Figure 2C. Consistent with the HBM, we specified indirect paths from the intervention

through the four putative mediators to intentions. In addition, we specified a direct (unmediated) path to intentions to allow for a test of completeness of mediation. We allowed the errors of measurement between perceived benefits and barriers to correlate. The model yielded marginal fit, χ^2 (5, N = 267) = 35.30, $p < .001$, comparative fit index (CFI) = .86.[7] Only perceived benefits had a significant path to intentions ($p < .001$). The direct path from intervention to intentions remained significant ($\beta = .33$, $p < .001$), although it was reduced from its value ($\beta = .45$) when no mediators were included in the model. This analysis of mediation supported the role of benefits as a mediator of program effects, but it failed to support the role of perceived susceptibility when these two correlated mediators, $r(283) = .28$, $p < .001$, were both included in a single analysis.

We also fit a reduced model in which the paths from all four putative mediators were set to zero and only the direct path from intervention to intentions remained. This model fit extremely poorly, χ^2 (9, N = 267) = 92.08, $p < .001$, CFI = .60. There was a significant reduction in fit from the model shown in Figure 2C: The chi-square difference test (χ^2_Δ; Bentler & Bonett, 1980) comparing the model depicted in Figure 2C and this reduced model yielded χ^2_Δ (4, N = 267) = 56.78, $p < .001$. This result supported the presence of mediation.

We then explored the roles of susceptibility and benefits as putative mediators. In our first approach, we examined the difference in model fit between a model that included no mediators versus a model that contained only one of the mediators (susceptibility or benefits). Stated otherwise, we separately tested for improvement in fit with the addition of each single putative mediator.

Figure 2D shows the single mediator model for susceptibility. In this single mediator model, the intervention had its effect on intentions only through the direct path from the intervention to intentions and the single indirect path from intervention through susceptibility to intentions. In the model containing susceptibility, the path from susceptibility to intentions was significant ($\beta = .12$, $p < .05$). Adding the path from susceptibility to intentions significantly increased the fit over a model that contained no mediators, χ^2_Δ (1, N = 267) = 4.81, $p < .05$. One interpretation of this result is that perceived susceptibility also may serve as a mediator but that its role may be masked when perceived benefits are also included in the model.

Partly because of the complexities that may arise in tests of models involving multiple putative mediators, MacKinnon (1994) recommended a fourth condition for establishing mediation. He proposed that each mediated path be tested directly for statistical significance. Sobel (1982) pro-

---

[7] The sample size of 267 is the minimum sample size for the dependent variable in the model: intentions.

vided a large sample test of significance of the mediated path when there are two links (i.e., intervention to mediator and mediator to outcome). The test may be written as

$$z = \frac{b_1 b_2}{\sqrt{b_1^2 \sigma_{b_1}^2 + b_2^2 \sigma_{b_1}^2}},$$

where b_1 is the regression coefficient for the path from the intervention to the mediator, b_2 is the regression coefficient for the path from the mediator to the outcome, $\sigma_{b_1}^2$ is the square of the estimate of the standard error of b_1, and $\sigma_{b_2}^2$ is the square of the estimate of the standard error of b_2 (b_1 corresponds to a and b_2 corresponds to b′ in Figure 1A, Condition 3). In the present illustration, b_1 is the coefficient for the path from the intervention to susceptibility, and b_2 is the coefficient for the path from susceptibility to intentions. The results of simulation studies (MacKinnon & Dwyer, 1993; MacKinnon, Warsi, & Dwyer, 1995) suggest that Sobel's test is accurate even given sample sizes as small as 50. MacKinnon and Tein (1996) extended this test to models involving three or more mediational links.

The test of the indirect effect is implemented in a slightly modified fashion in EQS (Bentler, 1995, p. 73): as a z test for the significance of the total indirect effect of a variable (here, intervention) on an outcome (here, intentions) through one or more mediators. If there is only one mediator in the model, then the test is of the significance of the single mediational path and is identical to the test described in the above equation. With several mediators, the test provided in EQS is of the total mediation provided by the set of mediators considered simultaneously. In our single mediator model of susceptibility, consistent with the chi-square difference test, the test of the mediated path from intervention through susceptibility to intention was likewise significant ($z = 1.97$, $p < .05$).

The chi-square difference test and Sobel's (1982) test were repeated in a second model in which perceived benefits was the sole mediator (see Figure 2E). In the test of change in model fit by the addition of benefits as the sole mediator, the path from benefits to intentions was large and significant ($\beta = .40$, $p < .01$). Adding perceived benefits to a model containing only the direct path from intervention to intentions substantially improved the fit, $\chi_\Delta^2 (1, N = 267) = 55.38$, $p < .001$. The comparable EQS z test of the indirect effect was significant ($z = 4.01$, $p < .001$). This model, which included the indirect path through benefits to intentions (see Figure 2E), provided only a marginal fit to the data, $\chi^2 (8, N = 267) = 37.42$, $p < .001$, CFI = 86. The path from the intervention to intentions to get a mammogram remained significant ($\beta = .34$, $p < .001$), which is consistent with an interpretation of only partial mediation by perceived benefits.

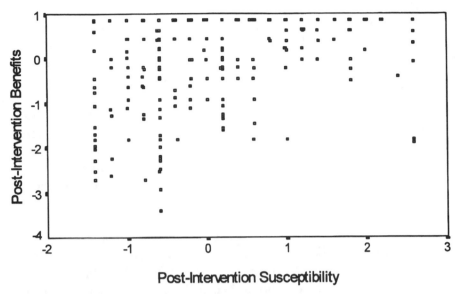

Figure 3. Scatterplot of post-intervention benefits against post-intervention susceptibility.

Interaction Between Mediators

Thus far, all of the mediational models we have considered have examined the effects of single mediational paths or the additive effects of multiple mediational paths. Such models do not allow for the possibility of an interaction between the putative mediators. We probed this possibility in a regression analysis predicting intentions from posttest susceptibility, benefits, and their interaction; there was no evidence of an interaction, $t(259) = -.05$. However, even with what most psychologists would consider a substantial sample size and the negative results for the interaction, we cannot confidently conclude that there was no interaction in the population. The test of the interaction was weakened because posttest susceptibility and benefits were correlated ($R = .28$). Figure 3 highlights the difficulty of detecting the interaction. Both before and after intervention, there were almost no women who reported that they perceived their susceptibility to be high but the benefits of mammography to be low. As we discuss later (see also Pitts & West, 1997), such off-diagonal cases are required for an adequate test of interactions.

An Alternative Model of Mediation

The two individual mediational models of susceptibility and severity left us with the ambiguous outcome that each putative mediator taken separately appeared to have a mediational role, whereas taken together, only perceived benefits exhibited significant evidence of mediation. This is precisely the problem researchers face in multiple regression analysis when two predictors, each correlated with the criterion but also well correlated with one another, are included in the same regression analysis. Although Becker and Maiman's (1975) original characterization of the HBM treated the four model constructs of severity, susceptibility, benefits, and barriers as coequal predictors of behavioral outcomes, Ronis (1992) postulated that perceived susceptibility and severity should be considered causally prior to perceived benefits, as in the model of Figure 2F. In this model, the intervention is hypothesized to cause changes in perceived susceptibility and severity, which in turn lead to changes in perceived benefits. Finally, perceived benefits predict intentions to obtain screening. Ronis argued that a woman would not likely perceive the personal benefits of a health action unless she perceived herself to be highly susceptible to a severe health threat. When we estimated Ronis's model, it provided an excellent fit to the data, $\chi^2(3, N = 267) = 9.11$, $p < .05$, CFI $= .97$. The path from perceived susceptibility to benefits was significant ($\beta = .21$, $p < .01$), completing a mediational path from intervention through susceptibility to benefits and then to intentions. This path is in addition to the mediational path from intervention through benefits to intentions.

The model in Figure 2C with paths through all four mediators to intentions is nested under Ronis's (1992) model in Figure 2F, in that the model in Figure 2C lacks only the paths from susceptibility and severity to benefits. The fit of Ronis's model was significantly better than the model of Figure 2C, $\chi^2_\Delta(2, N = 267) = 26.18$, $p < .001$.

The total effect of a mediator on the outcome can be estimated as the sum of the direct effects of the variable (for susceptibility, its direct path to intentions) plus the indirect effect (for susceptibility, its indirect path through benefits to intentions). In Becker and Maiman's (1975) original HBM model, shown in Figure 2C, the total effect of susceptibility on intentions (.046) was identical to its direct effect because no indirect effects through other variables were specified in the model. In Ronis's (1992) model, shown in Figure 2F, the total effect of susceptibility on intentions was .126. The gain in the total effect reflected the strong indirect impact of susceptibility on intentions mediated by benefits.

In a final model, Figure 2F was modified to eliminate the direct paths from perceived susceptibility and severity to intentions, as shown in Figure 2G. This yielded a test of whether the effect of susceptibility (and severity, if any) could be characterized as being completely mediated through perceived benefits. This model again fit well, $\chi^2(5, N = 267) = 10.35$, ns, CFI $= .95$, and yielded no decrease in fit from the model shown in Figure 2F, $\chi^2_\Delta(2, N = 267) = 1.24$, ns. We concluded that perceived susceptibility had a strong mediational role, suggesting that it made an important contribution to the perception of the benefits of screening, as Ronis (1992) had hypothesized. Unfortunately, we do not have the definitive test of this minitheory: Implementation of an additional intervention condition in which perceived benefits is not preceded by a discussion of susceptibility to breast cancer.

The previous example illustrates the extension of mediational analysis to the probing of multiple potential mediators between the intervention and the outcome variables. It also illustrates the extension of mediational analysis to tests of small theories that propose longer causal chains between the intervention and the outcome variable. Judd and Kenny (1981b) outlined a mediational analysis of the Stanford Heart Disease Prevention Project (Maccoby & Farquhar, 1975), in which mass media and personal interventions were expected to increase knowledge about diet and heart disease. This increased knowledge, in turn, was expected to change participants' dietary behavior, which in the long run was expected to lead to lowered physiological indicators of risk for heart disease (e.g., blood cholesterol and triglyceride levels). Bryan et al. (1996) provided yet another demonstration of longer mediational chains in their study of condom use intentions. They confirmed the presence of mediational paths from their intervention to both sexual responsibility and control of the sexual encounter, discussed earlier. In turn, responsibility and control predicted condom use self-efficacy, which predicted intentions to use condoms.

LIMITATIONS OF MEDIATIONAL ANALYSIS

Mediational analysis provides a useful and economical method for examining the contributions of individual components and the processes through which they operate to produce the outcome. Successful mediational analyses have now been accomplished for a number of preventive intervention trials (Aiken, West, Woodward, Reno, & Reynolds, 1994; Bryan et al., 1996; Donaldson, Graham, & Hansen, 1994; MacKinnon et al., 1991, Wolchik et al., 1993). Nevertheless, there are important limitations of mediational analysis that must be clearly recognized.

Two Layers of Theory in Mediational Analysis

Mediational analysis involves two layers of theory, both of which must be adequately developed for mediational analysis to lead to valid conclusions. The first is the basic psychosocial theory that specifies risk and protective factors and the processes through which they affect the development of the desirable or undesirable behavior. Such theory is ideally based on longitudinal investigations that study the natural course of development. However, basic psychosocial theory is mute as to how these processes can be changed through intervention. Consequently, researchers need to articulate a second layer of theory, program theory, that specifies precise operational methods of changing these processes. Program theory specifies the link from each component of the program to one or more constructs in the psychosocial theory. Only if researchers can precisely specify the construct that is targeted by each program component can mediational analysis achieve its full potential. We consider these two layers of theory in detail below.

Model of the Precursors of the Behavior

The first layer consists of the basic psychosocial theory that forms the basis of the model of the precursors of the undesirable or desirable behavior. Although this theory may be simplified relative to a complete model of the development of the behavior, it is far more than a list of coequal precursors or risk and protective factors. It must include specification of the relationships among the precursors themselves and their links to the ultimate outcome of interest. For example, Becker and Maiman's (1975) original characterization of the HBM as having four coequal predictors of health behavior—susceptibility, severity, benefits, and barriers—is one characterization of relationships among purported mediators. Ronis's (1992) conception that susceptibility and severity are necessary precursors of benefits, which, in turn, leads to behavior, is substantially different. Different models containing the same precursors but with different relationships among them and with the outcome of interest will lead to different estimates of the importance of individual mediators. Ronis's model led to much larger estimates of the role of perceived susceptibility in the instigation of health behavior than did the original HBM formulation. The mediational models tested and used to characterize how interventions have their actions depend critically on the adequacy of the model of how the mediators combine to produce the targeted behavior.

Theory of the Program

The second layer is the program theory. The program theory specifies the linkages between specific components of the intervention and the mediators. Program components do not always produce the effects that researchers expect on the mediators they expect, potentially leading researchers to fallacious conclusions about how mediators relate to behavior. A manipulation ostensibly designed to increase young women's perception of their control over their partner's behavior in sexual encounters might instead lead the young women to increase their sense of sexual freedom and consequently their number of sexual partners. One might conclude that increasing perceived sexual control per se leads to less safe sexual behavior, when it is in fact the unmeasured mediator of increased sexual freedom that is producing the undesirable behavior.

Figure 4A is an initial illustration of the two layers of theory underlying mediational analysis. We begin with a simple psychosocial model in

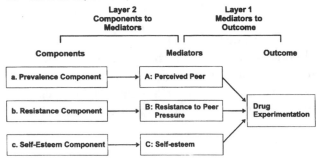

4A.   One-to-one map from components to mediators

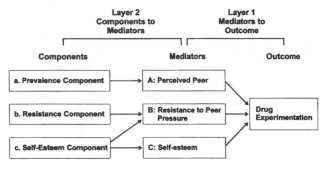

4B.   Multiple mediators affected by the same component I

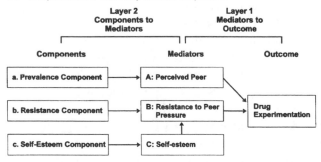

4C.   Multiple mediators affected by the same component II

Figure 4. Two layers of theory in mediational analysis.

which experimentation with illicit drugs (the outcome variable) is predicted by three coequal mediators: perceived prevalence of use by peers,
resistance to peer pressure, and self-esteem. Layer 1 of theorizing specifies
the relationships of the three purported mediators to the outcome. Layer
2 shows that the intervention consists of three distinct components, with
each targeted at a specific mediator: component a targets prevalence, component b targets resistance, and component c (self-esteem enhancement)
targets self-esteem. Thus, the program theory of the intervention is simple:
Each component is assumed to affect only one mediator. Figure 4B introduces some additional complexity on the program theory side. Here, com-

ponent c, self-esteem enhancement, is now expected to affect both corresponding mediator C, self-esteem, and mediator B, resistance to peer pressure. Figure 4C retains the original simple program theory, but it introduces additional complexity on the psychosocial theory side. Here, a change in the mediator of self-esteem has no direct impact on drug experimentation. Rather, changes in self-esteem lead to changes in resistance to peer pressure, which in turn affect drug experimentation.

Specification Errors

Specification errors are failures to correctly characterize a process being modeled. Specification errors can occur in the program theory, in the psychosocial theory, or in both layers of theory. Six potential problems are of special note. The first two relate to potential deficiencies in the program theory; the second two relate to deficiencies in both the program theory and the psychosocial theory; and the last two relate to potential deficiencies in the psychosocial theory. In this section, we consider only models in which relationships are linear and additive. In later sections, we consider models in which these relationships do not hold.

1. The intervention may contain components that are not identified by the program developers. For example, many interventions include a nonspecific component of building a therapeutic or medical relationship between participants and the intervenor (Higginbotham et al., 1988, chaps. 4 and 5). These unidentified components may add to (or subtract from) the effects of other components on the mediators, may be necessary conditions that must be in place for the specified program components to exert their influence, or may have their own direct effects on the outcome variable.

2. Each component may potentially affect more than one mediator. Such cross-influence (Jensen-Campbell, Graziano, & West, 1996) increases the difficulty of attributing changes in the mediators and the outcome to specific program components.

3. Each component may potentially influence a mediator not included in the psychosocial theory of the behavior (as in the case of sexual freedom, discussed earlier), which directly affects the outcome, actually bypassing the putative mediator.

4. Each component may potentially affect an important unmeasured third variable, which in turn causes both the mediator and the outcome.

5. The mediators and the outcome may mutually influence each other (bidirectional causality).

6. The presence of one of the mediators may contribute to the

successful operation of a second mediator (as in the case of the perceived susceptibility and benefits described earlier).

As one illustration, consider Figures 4A and 4B, which show the interpretational difficulties that can arise under Problem 2, a single program component that affects more than one mediator. The two-layer theoretical models of Figure 4A versus Figure 4B provide the same map of mediators onto the outcome but different maps of the program components onto the mediators. The test of mediation in both models involves a regression equation in which the outcome, drug experimentation, is predicted from the three mediators: A, perceived peer acceptance of drug use; B, resistance to peer pressure; and C, self-esteem. Suppose we found that mediator C added no prediction to mediators A and B. Suppose further that our program theory was that shown in Figure 4A (i.e., each component influences only one mediator). We might conclude that the self-esteem component (c) could be eliminated from the program because the self-esteem mediator C contributed no unique prediction of the outcome. However, suppose the true program theory was that shown in Figure 4B. Here, the self-esteem component of the program affects both mediators C, self-esteem, and B, resistance to peer pressure. To the extent that self-esteem is a strong common cause of both mediators B and C, B and C will be highly correlated, and mediator C will contribute little to prediction of drug experimentation over mediator B. Dropping the esteem component (c), however, can be expected to weaken the intervention substantially. Without using a dismantling design in which the full program including all components (abc) is compared with two reduced versions containing components ab and components ac, respectively, such cross-influence of component c on resistance to peer pressure will be extraordinarily difficult to detect.

Each of these six potential problems can lead to serious misconclusions of the role of the putative mediators in the model. Techniques for detecting some forms of specification errors in mediational analysis have been discussed by James and Brett (1984). Design enhancements, discussed next, can also address some of these problems.

Design, Measurement, and Analysis Issues

The same issues of design and measurement that affect researchers' ability to provide unbiased estimates of treatment effects also affect their ability to estimate the role of mediators in behavior change. In addition, special problems are created by the use of multiple mediator models.

Treatment Assignment and Program Effects on Mediators

Mediational analysis as applied in preventive trials is a hybrid between experimental and correlational (structural equation) approaches. Judd and Kenny's (1981a) Conditions 1 and 2 are experimental tests whose interpretation requires successful random assignment to the intervention groups. When quasi-experimental assignment to groups is used, an adequate model of the processes through which participants were assigned or selected themselves into intervention groups must be developed (see chap. 4 in this book for an example). Such selection models are necessary to equate groups statistically at the outset of the study to obtain relatively unbiased estimates of the treatment on both the mediators (Condition 1) and the treatment outcome (Condition 2). All of the standard requirements for obtaining unbiased estimates of treatment outcome effects (Cook & Campbell, 1979; Higginbotham et al., 1988, chap. 2; Judd & Kenny, 1981a) also apply to obtaining unbiased estimates of mediated effects.

Correlational Aspects of Mediational Analysis

The test of Condition 3 is at its heart correlational; its interpretation depends on meeting a number of assumptions associated with the use of multiple regression analysis with a mediator or set of mediators serving as predictors of treatment outcome. We have presented the mediational analysis of Aiken, West, Woodward, Reno, and Reynolds's (1994) intervention in terms of structural equation models. Embedded in these structural equation models are a series of regression equations in which the treatment outcome is predicted from one or more mediators plus the intervention variable itself. The familiar difficulties with multiple regression analysis are in full force in mediational analysis: (a) measurement error or unreliability of mediators as predictors, (b) correlated mediators, and (c) interactions among mediators.

Measurement error in any of the putative mediators can bias the results of a mediational analysis. In the single mediator case (e.g., see Figure 2), measurement error in the mediator will produce an underestimation of the importance of the mediational path. One might mistakenly conclude that an effective program component targeting an unreliably measured mediator had a weak or nil effect, not because of failure of the component to influence the mediator, but because of unreliability of measurement of the mediator the component was purported to modify. Measurement error has much more complex effects when it exists in multiple putative mediators in models such as that depicted in Figure 3. Researchers are not guaranteed that the direction of bias will be downward (underestimating mediation). When measurement error exists in even one of a set of correlated mediators, the coefficients of all of the mediators may be biased (see discussions of measurement error in Aiken & West, 1991; Duncan, 1975; Kenny, 1979). This problem can be overcome by the use of structural equation models using multiple indicators of each of the mediator constructs (Judd & Kenny, 1981b) but often at a cost of requiring a larger sample size to achieve proper estimation of the more complex model.

Correlation among mediators is inherent in designs in which several mediators are targeted by a single intervention simultaneously. Correlations among putative mediators may exist before the intervention because the mediators form a network of variables influencing a single outcome, such as a correlation of .35 between responsibility for sexuality and perceived control of the sexual encounter in Bryan et al. (1996) and of −.36 between perceived benefits of and barriers to mammography screening in Aiken, West, Woodward, and Reno (1994). Any interventions that affect multiple mediators simultaneously will typically increase the magnitude of these initial correlations. The correlations between mediators that form the basis of mediational analysis are total correlations, that is, they are correlations computed by pooling the data from all groups in the intervention design, ignoring group membership. These total correlations reflect two sources of relationship: within-class correlation and between-class correlation. The between-class correlation reflects differences between the means of the mediators across groups (e.g., intervention vs. control). The between-class correlation between two components will increase if the intervention increases the difference between the intervention and control means on both mediators simultaneously (i.e., a successful effect of the intervention on both mediators), even if there is no within-class correlation between the mediators in each group of the design. The increase in between-class correlation produced by the intervention accounts for potentially sizable total correlations among mediators after an intervention.

The test of Condition 3 of mediation requires that the mediators and the intervention serve as predictors of the outcome variable in the regression equation. With a high interpredictor correlation, there are difficulties in apportioning unique variance to the mediators and the intervention, large standard errors of the path coefficients, and low statistical power for the tests of mediation. Larger sample sizes can compensate partially for the problems with the standard errors and statistical power if the interpredictor correlations are not too high. Far better is the use of factorial or fractional factorial designs in which each intervention component is designed to target one specific mediator, thereby reducing the multicollinearity among the mediators.

Interactions of several forms can be incorporated into mediational analysis. Tests of interactions of an intervention with the participant's level on a pretest measure (e.g., initial level of symptoms) can be accomplished with straightforward extensions of the techniques described earlier (see Baron & Kenny, 1986, and James & Brett, 1984, for techniques; see Wolchik et al., 1993, for an empirical example). More problematic are two other forms of interactions that may be specified correctly by our two layers of theory but that may be difficult to test: (a) interactions between mediators as they influence behavior and (b) interactions between program components in their effects on individual mediators. These two forms of interactions often cannot be probed effectively when the prevalent treatment package strategy design is used in the randomized trial. The treatment package strategy tends to produce correlations between mediators because of the between-class component of the total correlation. This means that off-diagonal cases (i.e., high on one component, low on the other component) will be rare, particularly when the intervention produces large effects on both mediators. The existence of such off-diagonal cases is absolutely essential if stable estimates of interaction effects are to be produced (Pitts & West, 1997). Strong tests of such interactions require that additional intervention conditions containing components that target only one of the two mediators be added to the design. As we earlier illustrated in Figure 3, our mammography data were inadequate to test the interactional hypothesis because the intervention only strengthened the preexisting association between women's perceived susceptibility to breast cancer and belief in the benefits of mammography screening.

Comment

Despite these clear potential limitations, mediational analysis remains a promising, efficient method of probing the processes through which treatment components exert their effects on the outcome variable. These techniques can be applied to prevention trials involving more than two intervention conditions, multiple mediators, and extended causal chains. They also can be extended to other forms of outcome variables (e.g., dichotomous; MacKinnon & Dwyer, 1993) and even relationships between linear growth processes. Theoretically, these techniques also can be extended to cases in which curvilinear relations between variables are expected. When the assumptions are met, these techniques provide strong tests of the program theory and the basic psychosocial theory and thus have the potential to enhance the contribution of intervention trials to basic psychosocial research. Limited techniques exist for investigating the extent to which the assumptions are violated and in some cases for correcting for effects of these violations. In addition, several features may be added in the design of the intervention trial that can help minimize several of these potential problems.

IMPLICATIONS OF THE INTERPLAY AMONG COMPONENTS IN INTERVENTION DESIGNS

Throughout our discussion, we have encountered issues of the interplay among components in intervention designs. The additivity of the effects of components first arose as an issue in the context of fractional factorial designs. The designs shown in Exhibit 1 lead to the same estimates of the effects of individual components only under one strong assumption:

No interactions whatsoever exist among components. If and only if this is so will any combination of components, presented in any order whatsoever, yield the same impact of the individual components as when the components are presented alone. The fractional factorial designs provide information about specific components standing alone, or specific component combinations that have been implemented, but they do not indicate how combinations of components that have not been observed will affect outcomes.

Even complete factorial designs are limited in one particular way: They provide information on the effects of a multicomponent interventions only in the order in which the components are implemented. Researchers may learn that a 3-week intervention with one component a week is significantly more effective than any 2-week intervention consisting of two of the three components. This, of course, does not indicate whether one would attain the same effectiveness of the 3-week intervention if the components were presented in a different order.

Free-Standing Versus Context-Free Components

In the course of designing an intervention, it is useful to consider the logical relationships among components. Some components may be context dependent (i.e., their effects may depend largely on the set of components in which they are embedded and in the sequence of presentation of these components). The existence of such context-dependent components illustrates a fundamental difference between traditional basic research designs and applied intervention research. In basic research, researchers often counterbalance orders of treatment components, for example, through the use of Latin square designs (Winer, Brown, & Michels, 1991). In this context, researchers view the variation in outcomes produced by presenting materials in different sequences as nuisance variance that confounds what they wish to study. By contrast, in applied intervention research, the order of components, which may be dictated by theory or logic, is likely to be critically important. In the mammography trial (Aiken, West, Woodward, Reno, & Reynolds, 1994), the base intervention was an educational program that clarified the benefits of mammography screening, whereas the intensified program added psychological compliance exercises (e.g., role-playing asking a physician for a mammogram referral) following completion of the educational program. From the perspective of intervention design, it is difficult to imagine implementing a program in which the mammography compliance exercises came first, followed by information on why mammography was beneficial. The compliance exercises required the raison d'être provided by the information about benefits of mammography (which in turn apparently were given a raison d'être by the susceptibility manipulation). It is likely that there are components that cannot stand on their own, such as our set of compliance exercises, absent any program content to set the context for the component.

This reasoning leads to the conclusion that the complete factorial design, the sine qua non of experimental design, often may not make logical sense from an intervention design perspective. One may be driven to use fractional factorial designs because there are only some combinations of components that make logical sense.

Researchers may more rarely encounter components that are context free and that thus may be added to a variety of interventions. In the Perri et al. (1988) diet intervention, the aerobic exercise component might easily have been added to any one of the more clinical or social psychological components. Exercise components have been added to diverse interventions such as smoking cessation (e.g., Marcus, Albrecht, Niaura, Abrams, & Thompson, 1990), anxiety reduction (Pertruzzello, Landers, Hatfield, Kubitz, & Salazar, 1991), and treatment of depression (North, McCullagh, & Tran, 1990). We suspect that components such as exercise that can be adjoined to a variety of more content-oriented components are rare.

We suggest a two-question test of the status of any program component in the course of intervention design: (a) Could the component be presented alone and make logical sense? (b) In a set of components, could a specific component be presented first, or must it be preceded by other components that then render it meaningful? These questions will guide the component combinations that might be implemented in an evaluation design.

The Map of Components Onto Mediators

At the base of our presentation is a simple program theory in which individual mediators are modified by individual program components. However, such targeted effects of the components on the corresponding mediators may not be the case at all, as we illustrated in Figure 4B. In a program designed to increase social acceptance of aggressive children by their peers, a behavioral control component designed to decrease aggressive behavior may simultaneously increase a measure of social skills because children substitute more socially acceptable behavior for the aggressive behavior. The behavioral control component may be said to have cross-influence (Jensen-Campbell et al., 1996): It affects both the targeted mediator of aggressive behavior and the nontargeted mediator of social skills. Only if there is a condition in the design that contains no program component that is specifically designed to target social skills will this cross-influence be discernible. If only the behavioral control component constituted the program, a change in social skills would necessarily be attributed to this behavioral control component. By contrast, if there are components for both mediators in the program (as in the treatment package design), the mediational analysis would indicate simply that the mediators in the model changed in response to the intervention, but it would not identify the source of the change. When we manipulate multiple components simultaneously to affect multiple mediators in the treatment package design, we cannot unambiguously parse the effects of the components on individual mediators.

This limitation of multiple manipulations can occur in subtle ways. For example, a school-based drug prevention program may have components targeting perceived prevalence, resistance to peer pressure, and self-esteem. A companion home-based drug prevention program may have components targeting only resistance and self-esteem. Comparison of the school-based with a combined school-based plus home-based program would appear to offer an excellent opportunity to probe the mediational effects of self-esteem. However, the home-based program adds new home-based prevalence and resistance components to those already contained in the school-based program, thereby confounding the manipulation of self-esteem with new forms of the manipulation of perceived prevalence and resistance to peer influence. We propose that researchers ask a question to ascertain potential confounding: Is the enhanced program identical to the original program in all respects except for the addition of the critical component? Only if the answer to this question is yes can the mediational influence of the added single component be probed clearly.

Models of Mediator Relationships

Complex models of the relationships among multiple mediators have been specified by James and Brett (1984) and Baron and Kenny (1986). Mediators may serve to moderate the mediation of other mediators. If the perceived benefits of mammography screening were to relate to intentions for screening only for women high in perceived susceptibility, one would say that susceptibility moderated the effect of the mediator benefits on outcome, a case of moderated mediation (James & Brett, 1984). Such complex relationships among mediators may be difficult to capture, as we have demonstrated for the susceptibility–benefit relationship. The models that we specify (e.g., the causal chain model in Figure 2G) may be approximations of a more complex reality. Nonetheless, we believe that these approximations often provide useful information. For example, even if one does not have a completely accurate representation of the interplay between susceptibility and benefits, one does have evidence of the important role of perceived susceptibility in producing the desired behavior.

CONCLUSION

At the beginning of this chapter, we raised two questions about the results of trials of multicomponent interventions. First, does each of the components of the program contribute to the outcome? Question 1 is best addressed through the use of factorial designs or fractional factorial designs, if certain effects plausibly can be assumed to be negligible. Second, through what processes are components of the program achieving their effectiveness on the ultimate outcome of interest? Question 2 is addressed through the use of mediational analyses. Such analyses require the specification of the two layers of a program theory and a psychosocial theory so that the hypothesized paths of influence can be articulated clearly. Such a complete specification of the theory of the intervention is rarely a feature of current reports of intervention trials. However, such clear specification allows for the development of focused statistical models that make it easier to detect results that deviate from one's theoretical expectations. This feature has considerable promise for enhancing the basic science contribution of the results of intervention trials. Mediational analyses do have important potential limitations because of their correlational base, but some of these issues can be addressed through focused analyses (e.g., statistical correction for error of measurement) or design enhancements (e.g., multiple indicators of each construct) to address specific problems. Other issues can be addressed by the use of longitudinal designs, particularly ones in which each program component is introduced in sequence over time and repeated measurements of the mediators and outcome variables are taken, following the completion of each program component. Such designs help reduce ambiguities about the causal ordering of the components and their effects on the mediators and the outcome, reducing the plausibility of several of the forms of misspecification identified earlier.

Most of the techniques discussed in this chapter make strong assumptions about the nature of the effects of the components that are of interest. These assumptions stem largely from the real-world context in which prevention research takes place and the limitations this places on the number of interventions and the combinations of components that may be reasonably constructed. If these assumptions are seriously violated, the techniques discussed in this chapter will yield biased estimates of the effects of interest. This problem afflicts other complex applied research designs as well: For example, we showed how traditional psychotherapy research designs, such as the comparative and constructive designs, also make strong assumptions about the absence of interactions that have rarely been articulated by researchers. Researchers need to use the best technique to address their specific questions of interest and to state clearly the assumptions that have been made. To the extent possible, researchers also should develop designs and analyses to probe the plausibility of the specific assumptions that have been made. When other competing theoretical viewpoints exist, special attention should be given to the inclusion of design and measurement features that allow researchers to probe the predictions of those theories as well (Coie et al., 1993).

The prevention field is in the early stages of using efficient incomplete design strategies and mediational analysis to evaluate multicomponent interventions. Researchers also are in the early stages of exploring how mediational analysis can add to both intervention redesign and basic theory. Our thinking about the assumptions and limitations of certain incomplete designs and about what mediational analysis can and cannot tell us had evolved over the several years since we first characterized these approaches in the prevention setting (West, Aiken, & Todd, 1993). We continue to be cautiously optimistic about the utility of the approaches described in this chapter. They maximize the information yield for focused questions relative to other designs, particularly cross-sectional and longitudinal designs having the same number of measurement waves that do not include random assignment to intervention conditions. This information yield comes with an important caveat: These approaches require careful thinking about the two layers of theory (i.e., program theory and psychosocial theory) involved in the evaluation design. These two layers of theory drive the selection of the experimental design, the selection and timing of measurements, the specification of the statistical models, and the conclusions to be drawn from the analyses.

REFERENCES

Aiken, L. S., & West, S. G. (1991). *Multiple regression: Testing and interpreting interactions*. Newbury Park, CA: Sage.

Aiken, L. S., West, S. G., Woodward, C. K., & Reno, R. R. (1994). Health beliefs and compliance with mammography screening recommendations in asymptomatic women. *Health Psychology, 13*, 122–129.

Aiken, L. S., West, S. G., Woodward, C. K., Reno, R. R., & Reynolds, K. D. (1994). Increasing screening mammography in asymptomatic women: Evaluation of a second generation, theory-based program. *Health Psychology, 13*, 526–538.

Anderson, V. L., & McLean, R. A. (1984). *Applied factorial and fractional designs*. New York: Marcel Dekker.

Baron, R. M., & Kenny, D. A (1986). The moderator–mediator variable distinction in social psychological research: Conceptual, strategic, and statistical considerations. *Journal of Personality and Social Psychology, 51*, 1173–1182.

Becker, M. H., & Maiman, L. A. (1975). Sociobehavioral determinants of compliance with health and medical care recommendations. *Medical Care, 13*, 10–24.

Bentler, P. M. (1995). *EQS structural equations model program manual*. Encino, CA: Multivariate Software.

Bentler, P. M., & Bonett, D. G. (1980). Significance tests and goodness of fit in the analysis of covariance structures. *Psychological Bulletin, 88*, 588–606.

Box, G. E. P., Hunter, W. G., & Hunter, J. S. (1978). *Statistics for experimenters: An introduction to design, data analysis, and model building.* New York: Wiley.

Bryan, A. D., Aiken, L. S., & West, S. G. (1996). Increasing condom use: Evaluation of a theory-based intervention to prevent sexually transmitted disease in young women. *Health Psychology, 15,* 371–382.

Bryan, A. D, Aiken, L. S., & West, S. G. (in press). Young women's condom use: The influence of responsibility for sexuality, control over the sexual encounter, and perceived susceptibility to common STDs. *Health Psychology.*

Bryk, A. S, & Raudenbush, S. W. (1992). *Hierarchical linear models: Applications and data analysis methods.* Newbury Park, CA: Sage.

Caplan, R. D., Vinokur, A. D., Price, R. H., & Van Ryn, M. (1989). Job seeking, reemployment and mental health. *Journal of Applied Psychology, 74,* 759–769.

Cohen, J. (1988). *Statistical power analysis for the behavioral sciences* (2nd ed.). Hillsdale, NJ: Erlbaum.

Coie, J. D., Watt, N. F., West, S. G., Hawkins, J. D., Asarnow, J. R., Markman, H. J., Ramey, S. L., Shure, M. B., & Long, B. (1993). The science of prevention: A conceptual framework and some directions for a national research program. *American Psychologist, 48,* 1013–1022.

Cook, T. D., & Campbell, D. T. (1979). *Quasi-experimentation: Design and analysis issues for field settings.* Boston: Houghton Mifflin.

Cooper, W. H., & Richardson, A. J. (1986). Unfair comparisons. *Journal of Applied Psychology, 71,* 179–184.

Donaldson, S. I., Graham, J. W., & Hansen, W. B. (1994). Testing the generalizability of intervening mechanism theories: Understanding the effects of adolescent drug use prevention interventions. *Journal of Behavioral Medicine, 17,* 195–216.

Duncan, O. D. (1975). *Introduction to structural equation models.* New York: Academic Press.

Durlak, J. A., & Wells, A. M. (in press). Primary prevention mental health programs for children and adolescents: A meta-analytic review. *American Journal of Community Psychology.*

Fisher, J. D., & Fisher, W. A. (1992). Changing AIDS-risk behavior. *Psychological Bulletin, 111,* 455–474.

Flay, B. R. (1985). Psychosocial approaches to smoking prevention: A review of findings. *Health Psychology, 4,* 449–488.

Gersten, J. C., Beals, J., & Kallgren, C. A. (1991). Epidemiology and preventive interventions: Parental death in childhood as a case example. *American Journal of Community Psychology, 19,* 481–500.

Hansen, W. B., & Collins, L. M. (1994). Seven ways to increase power without increasing N. In L. M. Collins & L. A. Seitz (Eds.), *Advances in data analysis for prevention intervention research* (NIDA Research Monograph No. 142, pp. 184–195). Rockville, MD: National Institute on Drug Abuse.

Hansen, W. B., Johnson, C. A., Flay, B. R., Graham, J. W., & Sobel, J. (1988).

Affective and social influences approaches to the prevention of multiple substance abuse among seventh grade students: Results from Project SMART. *Preventive Medicine, 17,* 135–154.

Harackiewicz, J. M., Sansone, C., Blair, L. W., Epstein, J. A., & Manderlink, G. (1987). Attributional processes in behavior change and maintenance: Smoking cessation and continued abstinence. *Journal of Consulting and Clinical Psychology, 55,* 372–378.

Hawkins, J. D, Catalano, R. F., & Miller, J. Y. (1992). Risk and protective factors for alcohol and other drug problems in adolescence and early adulthood: Implications for substance abuse prevention. *Psychological Bulletin, 112,* 64–105.

Higginbotham, H. N., West, S. G., & Forsyth, D. R. (1988). *Psychotherapy and behavior change: Social, cultural, and methodological perspectives.* Elmsford, NY: Pergamon Press.

James, L. R., & Brett, J. M. (1984). Mediators, moderators, and tests for mediation. *Journal of Applied Psychology, 69,* 307–321.

Jensen-Campbell, L. A., Graziano, W. G., & West, S. G. (1996). Dominance, prosocial orientation, and female preferences: Do nice guys really finish last? *Journal of Personality and Social Psychology, 68,* 427–440.

Judd, C. M., & Kenny, D. A. (1981a). *Estimating the effects of social interventions.* New York: Cambridge University Press.

Judd, C. M., & Kenny, D. A. (1981b). Process analysis: Estimating mediation in treatment evaluations. *Evaluation Review, 5,* 602–619.

Kazdin, A. E. (1980). *Research design in clinical psychology.* New York: Harper & Row.

Kazdin, A. E. (1986). The evaluation of psychotherapy: Research design and methodology. In S. L. Garfield & A. E. Bergin (Eds.), *Handbook of psychotherapy and behavior change* (3rd ed., pp. 23–68). New York: Wiley.

Kenny, D. A. (1979). *Correlation and causality.* New York: Wiley.

Kreft, I. G. G. (1994). Multilevel models for hierarchically nested data: Potential applications in substance abuse prevention. In L. M. Collins & L. A. Seitz (Eds.), *Advances in data analysis for prevention intervention research* (NIH Research Monograph No. 142, pp. 140–183). Rockville, MD: National Institute on Drug Abuse.

Lipsey, M. W. (1993). Theory as method: Small theories of treatments. In L. B. Sechrest & A. G. Scott (Eds.), *New directions for program evaluation* (No. 57, pp. 5–38). San Francisco: Jossey-Bass.

Maccoby, N., & Farquhar, J. W. (1975). Communication for health: Unselling heart disease. *Journal of Communication, 25,* 114–126.

MacKinnon, D. P. (1994). Analysis of mediating variables in prevention and intervention studies. In A. Cázares & L. Beatty (Eds.), *Scientific methods for prevention intervention research* (NIDA Monograph No. 139, pp. 127–153). Rockville, MD: National Institute on Drug Abuse.

MacKinnon, D. P., & Dwyer, J. H. (1993). Estimating mediating effects in prevention studies. *Evaluation Review, 17,* 144–158.

MacKinnon, D. P., Johnson, C. A, Pentz, M. A, Dwyer, J. H., Hansen, W. B., Flay, B. R., & Wang, E. (1991). Mediating mechanisms in a school-based drug prevention program: First year effects of the Midwestern Prevention Project. *Health Psychology, 10,* 164–172.

MacKinnon, D. P., & Tein, J.-Y. (1996). *A simulation study of multiple path mediation.* Unpublished manuscript, Arizona State University, Tempe.

MacKinnon, D. P., Warsi, G., & Dwyer, J. H. (1995). A simulation study of indirect effect measures. *Multivariate Behavioral Research, 30,* 53–71.

Marcus, B. H., Albrecht, A. E., Niaura, R. S., Abrams, D. B., & Thompson, P. D. (1990). Physical exercise improves maintenance of smoking cessation in women. *Circulation, 82*(Suppl. 3), 576.

Mead, R. (1988). *The design of experiments: Statistical principles for practical application.* Cambridge, England: Cambridge University Press.

Mrazek, P. G., & Haggerty, R. J. (Eds.). (1994). *Reducing risks for mental disorders: Frontiers for preventive intervention research.* Washington, DC: National Academy Press.

North, T. C., McCullagh, P., & Tran, Z. V. (1990). Effect of exercise on depression. *Exercise and Sport Science Reviews, 18,* 379–416.

Pentz, M. A., Dwyer, J. H., MacKinnon, D. P., Flay, B. R., Hansen, W. B., Wang, E. Y. I., & Johnson, C. A. (1989). A multi-community trial for primary prevention of adolescent drug abuse: Effects on drug use prevalence. *Journal of the American Medical Association, 261,* 3259–3266.

Perri, M. G., McAllister, D. A., Gange, J. J., Jordan, R. C., McAdoo, W. G., & Nezu, A. M. (1988). Effects of four maintenance programs on the long-term management of obesity. *Journal of Consulting and Clinical Psychology, 56,* 529–534.

Petruzzello, S. J., Landers, D. M., Hatfield, B. D., Kubitz, K. A., & Salazar, W. (1991). A meta-analysis on the anxiety-reducing effects of acute and chronic exercise. *Sports Medicine, 11,* 143–182.

Pitts, S. C., & West, S. G. (1997). *Alternative sampling designs to detect interactions in multiple regression.* Manuscript submitted for publication.

Price, R. H., Cowen, E. L., Lorion, R. P., & Ramos-McKay, J. (Eds.). (1988). *Fourteen ounces of prevention: A casebook for practitioners.* Washington, DC: American Psychological Association.

Reynolds, K. D., West, S. G., & Aiken, L. S. (1990). Increasing the use of mammography: A pilot program. *Health Education Quarterly, 17,* 429–441.

Ronis, D. L. (1992). Conditional health threats: Health beliefs, decisions, and behaviors among adults. *Health Psychology, 11,* 127–134.

Sechrest, L., West, S. G., Phillips, M. A., Redner, R., & Yeaton, W. (1979). Some neglected problems in evaluation research: Strength and integrity of treatments. *Evaluation Studies Review Annual, 4,* 15–35.

Shaffer, D., Philips, I., & Enzer, N. B. (Eds.). (1989). *Prevention of mental disorders, alcohol and other drug use in children and adolescents* (DHHS Publication No.

ADM 90-1646). Rockville, MD: U.S. Department of Health and Human Services.

Sobel, M. E. (1982). Asymptotic confidence intervals for indirect effects in structural equations models. In S. Leinhart (Ed.), *Sociological methodology 1982* (pp. 290–312). San Francisco: Jossey-Bass.

Steinberg, D. M., & Hunter, W. G. (1984). Experimental design: Review and comment (with discussion). *Technometrics, 26,* 71–130.

Webster-Stratton, C., Kolpacoff, M., & Hollinsworth, T. (1988). Self-administered videotape therapy for families with conduct-problem children. *Journal of Consulting and Clinical Psychology, 56,* 558–566.

Weissberg, R. P., Caplan, M. Z., & Sivo, P. J. (1989). A new conceptual framework for establishing school-based social competence promotion programs. In L. A. Bond & B. E. Compas (Eds.), *Primary prevention and promotion in the schools* (pp. 255–296). Newbury Park, CA: Sage.

West, S. G., Aiken, L. S., & Todd, M. (1993). Probing the effects of individual components in multiple component prevention programs. *American Journal of Community Psychology, 21,* 571–605.

Winer, B. J., Brown, D. R., & Michels, K. M. (1991). *Statistical principles in experimental design* (3rd ed.). New York: McGraw-Hill.

Wolchik, S. A., West, S. G., Westover, S., Sandler, I. N., Martin, A., Lustig, J., & Tein, J.-Y. (1993). The Children of Divorce intervention project: Outcome evaluation of an empirically-based parent training program. *American Journal of Community Psychology, 21,* 293–326.

Woodward, J. A., Bonett, D. G., & Brecht, M.-L. (1990). *Introduction to linear models and experimental design.* San Diego, CA: Harcourt Brace Jovanovich.

7

TIME SERIES ANALYSIS FOR PREVENTION AND TREATMENT RESEARCH

WAYNE F. VELICER AND SUZANNE M. COLBY

Time series analysis (TSA) is a statistical procedure that is appropriate for repeated and equally spaced observations on a single subject or unit. A practical advantage of the procedure is that it is highly appropriate for the type of data available in applied settings. A theoretical strength is that the method emphasizes the nature of the change process and is appropriate for assessing the pattern of change over time. The goal of the analysis may be to determine the nature of the process that describes an observed behavior or to evaluate the effects of a treatment or intervention. This chapter is divided into six sections.

In the first section, we present an overview of TSA methods, intro-

This work was partially supported by Grants CA27821, CA63045, and CA50087 from the National Cancer Institute and Grant AA08734 from the National Institute on Alcohol Abuse and Alcoholism. Some of the material contained in this chapter was revised from material in Velicer (1994). We thank Mark Sobell, Linda Sobell, and Patricia Cleland at the Addiction Research Foundation and M. W. Bud Perrine and John S. Searles at the Vermont Alcohol Research Center for contributing data for use in this chapter.

ducing the major concepts and issues. An example is provided that emphasizes practical issues involved in the application of TSA.

In the second section, we explain model identification, a central issue in TSA. Because time series involves repeated observations on the same unit, the data are unlikely to be independent. Statistical models that account for this dependency are available. Model identification involves specifying which of several alternative autoregressive integrated moving average (ARIMA) models best describes the series and may be used to investigate basic processes. We illustrate this with an example involving selecting the model of nicotine regulation that best represents smoking.

In the third section, we describe intervention analysis, the analysis used to determine whether an intervention will result in a change in the series. This could be either a change in level or a change in the direction of the series. The analysis involves both statistically removing the dependency in the data and assessing which intervention parameters are significantly different from zero. The analysis involves a variation of the well-known general linear model. Two types of applications have potential for the prevention and treatment areas: evaluation of the effects of a treatment program on a single individual or evaluation of organizational-level changes (i.e., program evaluation).

In the fourth section, we describe pooled time series procedures, which are used to combine the data from several different individuals or units. Because TSA involves the intensive observation of a single unit or individual, generalizability requires replication rather than representative sampling. Two alternative approaches to combining data across different units are cross-sectional analysis and meta-analysis.

In the fifth section, we address specific issues related to applications for treatment and prevention data. These include design and measurement issues for substance use assessment and corrections for seasonal data. TSA requires measures that can be repeated many times. TSA also may be influenced by long-term patterns such as a weekly or monthly cycle. Alternative methods of handling seasonal data include deseasonalization, statistical control and combined models.

We conclude with a brief discussion of several other future directions that involves topic areas currently under development. These include alternative procedures for handling missing data, the selection of an appropriate computer program, and procedures for analyzing multiple observations on such occasion (multivariate TSA).

OVERVIEW OF TSA

TSA involves repeated observations on a single unit (often a single subject) over time. The observations are assumed to be an equal time unit apart. In the area of prevention and treatment, the analysis of interest is usually an *interrupted* TSA. The interruption corresponds to the occurrence of an intervention, and the goal is to evaluate its effect. Traditional between-groups statistical procedures should not be used because repeated observations on the same unit cannot be assumed to be independent. The presence of dependency may substantially bias a statistical test that does not take it into account. The direction of the bias will depend on the direction of the dependency. Crosbie (1993) illustrated this bias in a simulation study.

The most widely used methods of analysis for time series designs are based on ARIMA models (Box, Jenkins, & Reinsel, 1994; Box & Tiao, 1965). These procedures permit the effects of dependency to be removed statistically from the data (Glass, Willson, & Gottman, 1975; Gottman, 1973; Gottman & Glass, 1978).

TSA has generated widespread interest for several reasons. First, TSAs are particularly applicable to the study of problems in applied settings, in which more traditional between-subjects designs are often impossible or difficult to implement. Many prevention and treatment programs for alcohol and other substance abuse occur in school or clinical settings. Second, time series designs are particularly appropriate for dealing with questions of causality because of the temporal occurrence of both the intervention and effect of the intervention. Third, time series designs have the additional advantage of permitting the study of the pattern of intervention effects (i.e., temporary effects vs. permanent effects; changes in slope and in level; changes in cycles, variance, and pattern of serial dependency) over and above the usual question of the existence of a mean treatment effect. The study of prevention and treatment problems in the addictive behaviors provides many situations in which time series designs are the optimal choice.

The use of time series methods also suffers from several drawbacks. First, generalizability cannot be inferred from a single study, only through systematic replication. Second, traditional measures may be inappropriate for time series designs; measures are required that can be repeated many times on a single subject, usually at short intervals. Third, many equally spaced observations are required for accurate model identification. Model identification is a necessary step to remove the dependency present in the data. Advances in methods of analysis in the past decade that have provided partial solutions to the generalizability issues and the sample size issues are discussed.

To illustrate the use of TSA, we offer the following example. Although this example is a bit atypical in terms of context and analysis, we chose it to demonstrate many of the applied issues related to time series designs and analysis. In this example, the effects of assertiveness training and muscle relaxation therapy on blood pressure (hypertension) were stud-

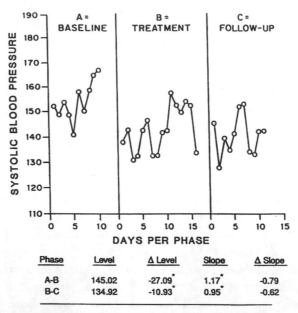

Phase	Level	Δ Level	Slope	Δ Slope
A-B	145.02	-27.09*	1.17*	-0.79
B-C	134.92	-10.93*	0.95*	-0.62

Figure 1. Example of an interrupted time series analysis. *p < .05.

ied (Printz, 1978). Figure 1 shows the results for a single participant. The baseline phase (Phase A) involved a series of regular (3 days per week) observations of the participant's blood pressure. After the 10th observation, the treatment phase (Phase B), training in assertiveness and relaxation therapy, began, and 16 more observations were taken. The follow-up phase (Phase C) signaled the end of active assertiveness and relaxation therapy training; only 11 regular measurements occurred. However, the participant was expected to continue to use assertiveness and relaxation techniques on his or her own.

The analysis estimated two parameters for each phase: level and slope. Conceptually, we fit a straight line to each series of data, with the *level* referring to the intercept of the line and the *slope* referring to the rate of increase or decrease of the series over time. A slope near zero would be presented graphically as a line parallel to the time axis. In the case of a near-zero slope, the level also can be interpreted as the mean. During Phase A, the level of the series was 145.02, and the slope was increasing. The introduction of the relaxation therapy (Phase B) resulted in a decrease of 27.09 in the level of the series (Δ level = change in level) and a decrease in the slope of the series (Δ slope = change in slope). During Phase C, there was a further decline in the level of the series and an additional (nonsignificant) decrease in the slope of the series. This indicated that the positive effects of the relaxation therapy were maintained after the end of the intervention. Both changes in (nonsignificant) level were significant and represented a positive outcome for relaxation therapy.

This example illustrates several of the strengths and weaknesses of TSA. First, it illustrates how time series can be incorporated into an applied setting. The complete study involved 8 participants (7 in addition to the 8 mentioned here); all of them had been treated by the same therapist over a 1-year period, each during a different time frame. Second, the abrupt change in the level of the series, which occurred at the same point in time when the intervention started, permits a strong causal inference about the relation between intervention and the outcome. Third, the change in slope provides additional information about the nature of the intervention effect.

The drawbacks of TSA also can be found in this example. The issue of generalizability was addressed by using multiple participants to replicate the effect. In this case, the treatment was effective for 3 participants. A potential explanation (Printz, 1978) was that the treatment was effective only when the onset of hypertension was recent in origin and less effective when the problem lasted a long time. The dependent measure used in the study was appropriate for repeated observations. The length of the series was too short to permit model identification, requiring the assumption of an ARIMA (1,0,0) model for the analysis.

The most widely used TSA procedure has been described by Glass et al. (1975; Gottman, 1973; Gottman & Glass, 1978), following Box et al. (1994; Box & Tiao, 1965). It involves a two-step process: First, the researcher identifies which of a family of underlying mathematical models is appropriate for the data. Second, the researcher uses a specific transformation determined by the identified model to transform the dependent observed variable (Z_i) into a serially independent variable (Y_i). Intervention effects then can be evaluated using a generalized least squares estimate of the model parameters. This procedure has several drawbacks, including (a) the requirement of a large number of data points for accurate model identification; (b) excessive mathematical complexity; and (c) problems with performing the model identification task accurately and reliably, even when the recommended minimum number of observations is obtained (Velicer & Harrop, 1983). Alternative procedures that avoid model identification have been proposed (Algina & Swaminathan, 1977, 1979; Simonton, 1977; Swaminathan & Algina, 1977; Velicer & McDonald, 1984, 1991).

A key concept for TSA is *dependence*. This is assessed by calculating the *autocorrelations* of various lags. A correlation coefficient estimates the relation between two variables measured at the same time. An autocorrelation estimates the relation between the same variable measured on two occasions. For example, if a researcher has a series of observations and then pairs the second observation with the first, the third observation with the second, and so on until the last observation is paired with the second from the last observation and then calculates the correlation between the paired observations, the researcher has calculated the Lag 1 autocorrelation. If a researcher pairs the third with the first and each subsequent observation with the observation two occasions behind, he or she has calculated the Lag 2 autocorrelation. The *lag* of an autocorrelation refers to how far in the past the influence exists. For simple models, autocorrelations range from 1.00 to -1.00. In the behavioral sciences, the size of the autocorrelation typically will decrease as the lag increases. The exception is seasonal, or cyclical, data, which are relatively common and are discussed in some detail later. The pattern of the autocorrelation and the related partial autocorrelations at each lag is used as the basis for identifying the specific mathematical model that underlies the data. These plots are provided in the printed output of most TSA programs. (Partial autocorrelations are mathematically complex and are not defined here; see Box et al., 1994, Glass et al., 1975, or West & Hepworth, 1991, for a detailed description.) A *white noise model* is one in which there is no dependency in the data (i.e., the autocorrelations and partial autocorrelations for all lags are zero). This data could be analyzed for slope and change in slope using a standard analysis of variance (ANOVA).

MODEL IDENTIFICATION

In an interrupted TSA, model identification often represents a first step, preliminary to the goal of the analysis, that is, the estimating and testing of the pre- and postintervention parameters (Box et al., 1994; Box & Tiao, 1965, 1975; Glass et al., 1975; McCleary & Hay, 1980; Velicer & McDonald, 1984, 1991). However, model identification can be the primary goal of a TSA. Determining the specific model of a series can identify a basic process underlying a particular behavior, thereby addressing important theoretical and etiological issues.

Unfortunately, model identification can be difficult and problematic. Although a variety of procedures has been developed to identify the model (Akaike, 1974; Beguin, Courieroux, & Monfort, 1980; Bhansali & Downham, 1977; Glass et al., 1975; Grey, Kelly, & McIntire, 1978; Hannan & Rissanen, 1982; Kashyap, 1977; McCleary & Hay, 1980; Parzen, 1974; Pukkila, 1982; Rissanen, 1978, 1986a, 1986b; Schwartz, 1978; Tsay, 1984; Tsay & Tiao, 1984), no clear consensus about which method is best has emerged. Model identification also has been problematic because of the large number of data points required for accurate identification, the complexity of the procedures, and problems with accuracy and reliability of some methods, even under ideal circumstances (Velicer & Harrop, 1983). In this section, we describe some procedures and inherent problems in model identification and illustrate the use of model identification to answer a substantive question.

Definition of Model Identification

The ARIMA (p,d,q) model represents a family of models, with the parameters designating which specific model is involved. The first parameter (p) is the order of the autoregressive parameter, and the last parameter (q) is the order of the moving average parameter. The middle parameter (d) represents the presence of a stochastic or probabilistic process, which also determines the observations in the time series in addition to the other parameters being modeled. This process is described as nonstationary because fluctuations do not occur about a fixed mean; rather, the general level about which fluctuations occur may be different at different times (see Box et al., 1994, for a complete discussion of these parameters) in the series. Each of the parameters of the model may be of order 0, 1, 2, 3, or more, although higher order models are unusual in the behavior sciences (Glass et al., 1975). A parameter equal to zero indicates the absence of that term from the model.

Model identification involves a number of aspects that can be determined with varying degrees of accuracy. Selection of the model involves determining which specific model from the ARIMA (p,d,q) family of models describes the data most parsimoniously. This is a difficult task to accomplish accurately because the different models can appear to be highly similar. Indeed, a first-order moving averages model can be represented by an infinite-order autoregressive model and vice versa.

The term *order* refers to how many preceding observations there must be to account for the dependency in the series. Accuracy is difficult because higher order autocorrelation terms are typically closer to zero than first-order terms. Therefore, the higher order terms are more likely to be included within the bounds for any error estimate. Order reflects how far into the past one must go to predict the present observation.

The term *degree of dependency* refers to how large the autocorrelations are on a scale ranging from 0.0 to 1.0. As with other dependency indicators, this can be interpreted as the strength of relationship between consecutive measurements. The accuracy of estimation is largely a function of the number of observations, with values greater than 50 providing reasonably accurate estimates (Box & Pierce, 1970; Glass et al., 1975; Ljung & Box, 1978). The degree of dependency indicates the extent to which an observation at any point in time is predictable from one or more of the preceding observations. For example, if drinking data were collected daily, then finding an Order 1 model would suggest that the previous observation $(t - 1 = 1$ day ago) was more important than the second previous observation $(t - 2 = 2$ days ago) in predicting the level of the series at time t.

The term *direction of dependency* refers to whether the autocorrelation is positive or negative. This can be determined with high accuracy when the dependency is clearly nonzero. The direction is of less interest as the degree of dependency approaches zero. The direction of dependency has clear implications. When the sign of the autocorrelation is negative, a high level for the series on one occasion predicts a low level for the series on the next occasion. When the sign is positive, a high level for the series on one occasion predicts a higher than average level on the next occasion.

Illustrations of Alternative Time Series

Figure 2 illustrates four different types of models using computer-generated data ($N_1 = N_2 = 50$) for an ARIMA (0,0,1) model (i.e., an Order 1 moving averages model). Figure 2A represents an ideal interrupted time series example with no error and no immediate change in level of 1.5 units at the time of the intervention. Figure 2B is the same model with the same change in level but with a random-error component added. The variance or the random error is 1.00. There is no autocorrelation in this model. Figure 2C is a model with the same change in level and error variance but with a large negative autocorrelation ($-.80$). Figure 2D is a model with the same change in level and error variance as in Figure 2B but with a large positive autocorrelation (.80). The impact of dependency can be observed easily. The negative dependency results in an exaggerated "sawtooth" graph with increased apparent variability. The positive dependency results in a smoother graph with decreased apparent variability. The inclusion of an intervention effect (the change in level) illustrates how difficult it is to determine whether an intervention had an effect by visual inspection alone.

Example

To illustrate the use of model identification in theory testing, we present briefly the results of a recent study (Velicer, Redding, Richmond, Greeley, & Swift, 1992) designed to determine which of three models of nicotine regulation best represented most smokers. These models seek to explain the mechanism that determines how many cigarettes are smoked in any given time period. It was posited that smoking rate would control the level of nicotine in the systems. Three measures were used in the study, but only one—number of cigarettes—is described here.

Nicotine Regulation Models

Three alternative models have been used to account for nicotine's effectiveness in maintaining smoking: the fixed-effect model, the nicotine regulation model, and the multiple regulation model. Leventhal and Cleary (1980) reviewed the literature and described each of the three models. Velicer, Redding, et al. (1992) identified each of the three models with

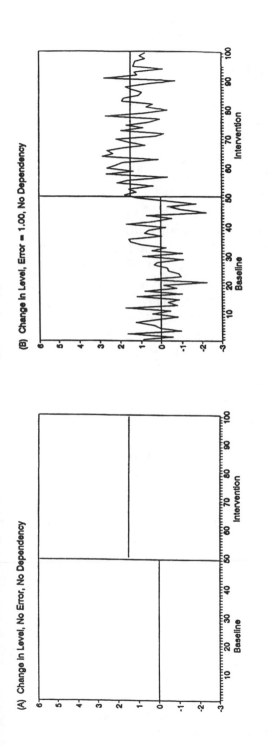

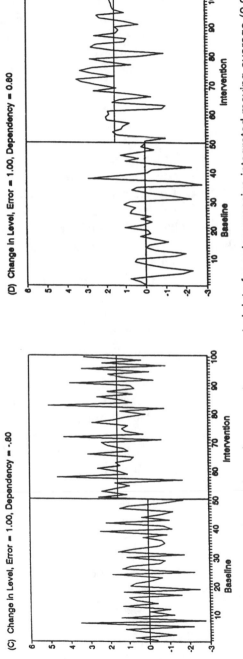

Figure 2. Illustrations of four time series using computer-generated data for autoregressive integrated moving average (0,0,1) models.

one of three broad classes of time series models: a positive dependency model, a white noise model (no dependency), and a negative dependency model.

The *nicotine fixed-effect model* assumes that smoking is reinforced because nicotine stimulates specific reward-inducing centers of the nervous system. These have been identified as either autonomic arousal or a feeling of mental alertness, relaxation, or both. According to this model, an increase on one occasion should be followed by an increase on the next occasion, or a decrease on one occasion should be followed by decreased consumption on a subsequent occasion if the same level of arousal is to be maintained. In time series model terms, this would result in a positive autocorrelation.

The *nicotine regulation model* assumes that smoking serves to regulate or titrate the smoker's level of nicotine. Departures from the optimal level (i.e., the set point) will stimulate an increase or decrease in smoking to return to this optimal nicotine level. Jarvik (1973) reviewed a large body of evidence that supports this model (also see Russell, 1977; Schachter, 1977). The model suggests that any increase or decrease in smoking caused by events in a person's environment should be temporary. The person should immediately return to his or her personal set point when the environment permits. In this model, only the set point or level is under biological control. All variations are caused by the environment. This would result in a white noise model with an autocorrelation of zero.

The *multiple regulation model* represents a more complex model designed to overcome some of the problems of the nicotine regulation model—specifically, how the nicotine set point develops and how deviations from the set point generate a craving for cigarettes. Leventhal and Cleary (1980) summarized some of the evidence that the nicotine regulation model cannot adequately account for and suggested the multiple regulation model as an alternative. This model is an elaboration of similar models by Tomkins (1966, 1968) and Solomon and Corbit (1973, 1974; also see Solomon, 1980). This model assumes that the smoker is regulating emotional states. Drops in the nicotine level stimulate craving. One way to link craving to the nicotine level is the opponent-process theory (Solomon, 1980; Solomon & Corbit, 1973, 1974), which posits that nicotine gives rise to an initial positive affect reaction, which is automatically followed by a slave opponent negative affect reaction. The opponent state becomes stronger with repeated activation and can be eliminated by reinstating the initial positive state. An external stimulus provides an alternative source for craving. The theory would predict that an increase (or decrease) in the smoking rate caused by events in a person's environment should be followed by an opposite decrease (or increase) in the smoking rate. This would result in a negative autocorrelation at Lag 1 and alternating positive and negative autocorrelations at subsequent lags.

Participants

To achieve stable autocorrelations, TSA requires a minimum of 50 data points (Box et al., 1994; Glass et al., 1975). The design of the study used 10 smokers (4 men and 6 women), from whom measures were collected twice daily for 2 months (62 days), resulting in 124 observations.

Measure of the Number of Cigarettes

Having participants monitor their own smoking behavior is one of the most commonly used measures in smoking research (McFall, 1978; Velicer, Prochaska, Rossi, & Snow, 1992; Velicer, Rossi, Prochaska, & DiClemente, 1996). This is an inexpensive and convenient means of gathering data. The accuracy and reliability of data gathered through self-monitoring are not always as high as that of data gathered through other techniques. However, the advantages of using self-monitoring typically outweigh the disadvantages.

Model Identification Procedures

Model identification involves determining whether autoregressive terms or moving average terms must be included to fully describe the data. The distribution of the autocorrelations and partial autocorrelations provides the basis for making such decisions. For an autoregressive component, the autocorrelations will decay slowly to zero for increasing lags and the partial autocorrelations will drop abruptly to zero when the appropriate lag (p) is reached. The residuals of a first-order autoregressive model, that is, an ARIMA (1,0,0) model, with a negative autocorrelation will bounce from negative to positive and back. For the moving average component, the autocorrelations will drop abruptly to zero when the appropriate lag (p) is reached, and the partial autocorrelations will drop slowly to zero. Model identification in this study was restricted to only autoregressive models, a procedure consistent with current practices (Djuric & Kay, 1992; Gottman, 1981; Velicer & McDonald, 1984, 1991). Diagnostic checks on the residuals were performed to test the appropriateness of this procedure. A third component, drift, was set equal to zero a priori for all identification problems on the basis of our preliminary evaluation of the data. Models that demonstrate no dependence are called *white noise models* and are described as ARIMA (0,0,0) models.

Five different procedures were used for model identification. First, traditional visual analysis of the autocorrelations and partial autocorrelations was performed. The visual analysis required the consensus of three raters. Four different automated methods for order identification of autoregressive models were then used: (a) predictive minimum descriptive length (Rissanen, 1986b); (b) predictive least squares (Rissanen, 1986a);

(c) predictive least absolute value (Djuric & Kay, 1992); and (d) the predictive density criterion (Djuric & Kay, 1992). Two additional methods were considered and rejected: the Akaike information criterion (Akaike, 1974) and minimum descriptive length (Rissanen, 1978; Schwartz, 1978). A recent simulation study evaluating these six criteria (Djuric & Kay, 1992) indicated that the Akaike information criterion and the minimum descriptive length tended to overestimate the order of series. In this study, these two criteria were inconsistent with either visual analysis or the other four criteria, typically finding a much higher order, so they were eliminated from consideration.

For the majority of model identifications, all five procedures converged on the same answer. When disagreement occurred, it was typically a difference of one in order, and all models were reviewed. Disagreements typically involved a low autoregressive coefficient that was approximately equal to the critical value for statistical significance. The more parsimonious fit (lower order) was used when the evidence for the higher order model was weak.

Results

Seven participants were described by a first-order autoregressive model with a moderate-to-high degree of negative dependence ($-.30$ to $-.80$). All participants reported on their smoking behavior in the morning and afternoon. The data resulted in a clear, easily identified model with a high degree of autocorrelation. This pattern is consistent with the multiple regulation model, and the study was interpreted as supporting that model.

Three participants did not show the same pattern. One of the participants worked some weeks during the day and some weeks at night. This individual also missed a number of sessions and terminated prematurely. One participant was a highly controlled smoker, smoking 15 cigarettes at predetermined intervals. All 3 participants averaged less than a pack a day. However, 2 participants who demonstrated the pattern of high negative dependence also smoked less than a pack a day.

Figure 3 shows the data for 4 participants. Two of the participants were representative of the 7 participants who were characterized by a high negative dependence. The exaggerated sawtooth shape of this type of time series is clearly observable. Two participants were representative of the 3 participants who demonstrated either a zero or low positive dependence. The time series graphs for these 2 participants are much smoother and more regular.

Findings from this study were recently partially replicated in a similar study conducted in Spain (Rosel & Elósegui, 1994). This study of 29 smokers (9 men and 20 women) examined the daily records of cigarettes smoked over a 12-week period. Virtually all of the data series (97%) were best

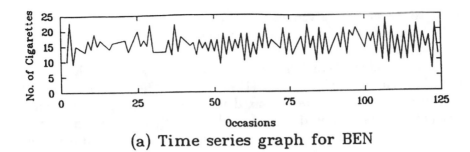

(a) Time series graph for BEN

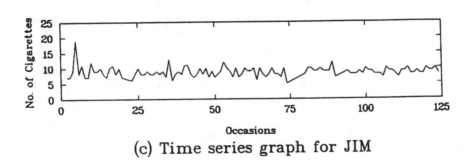

(b) Time series graph for RIC

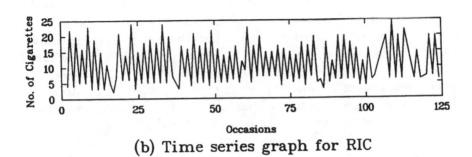

(c) Time series graph for JIM

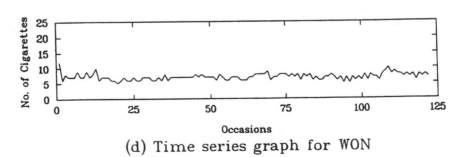

(d) Time series graph for WON

Figure 3. Illustrative time series graphs of the number of cigarettes for 4 participants.

described by autoregressive-type models, and most (75%) of these were Order 1 models; only one participant's data represented a white noise (i.e., no dependency) model.

Other findings from Rosel and Elósegui (1994) apparently conflict with the Velicer, Redding, et al. (1992) results. The data from the 29 smokers apparently supported the fixed-effect model, with 21 participants' data (73%) being described by that model (i.e., their series had positive autocorrelations); the data from 7 participants (24%) supported the nicotine regulation model (i.e., no autocorrelation detected); and only the data from 1 participant fit a multiple regulation model. However, the differences in findings were attributable to a methodological difference between the two studies. Velicer, Redding, et al. collected data twice each day, whereas Rosel and Elósegui collected data only daily. The negative autocorrelation at Lag 1 in the Velicer, Redding, et al. data would be positive at Lag 2 because $r_2 = r_1^2$ for an ARIMA (1,0,0) model. The r_2 value reported by Velicer, Redding, et al. was equivalent to the r_1 reported by Rosel and Elósegui, and both were positive. These apparently conflicting results highlight an important methodological issue: What is the "correct" interval at which to collect data? The answer to this question will depend on one's theoretical framework (e.g., the hypothesized influences on the behavior in question and the rate or cycle in which a given influence affects that behavior). In this case, the conclusion about the appropriate nicotine regulation model is clearly affected by the choice of time interval between observations. Clearly, it is critical to pay attention to the time interval when interpreting time series studies.

The other difference between the two studies was the presence of a weekly cyclic in the Spanish study. Rosel and Elósegui (1994) opined that "tobacco consumption is sustained not only because of the effect of nicotine, but also because of the effect of personal and social demand variables, which are reflected in weekly cyclical habits" (p. 1640). They found that 45% of the sample fit different 7-day lag models (i.e., weekly smoking patterns), which had not been observed in the previous research. The findings of these two studies are not necessarily at odds. Perhaps nicotine regulation processes influence smoking on a much smaller level, within broader cycles of personal and social influence. The presence or absence of a 7-day cyclic might reflect cultural differences. These two studies are an excellent illustration of the potential contribution that can be made by the time series approach to understanding the processes underlying an addictive behavior.

INTERVENTION ANALYSIS

The simplest interrupted TSA is a design that involves repeated observations on a single unit followed by an intervention, followed by additional observations of the unit. The purpose of the analysis is to determine whether the intervention had an effect. The example presented earlier and Figure 1 illustrate this approach. The analysis involves some preprocessing of the data to remove the effects of dependence. Several alternative procedures are described next. The analysis involves a general linear model analysis using a generalized least squares or Aitken estimator (Aitken, 1934; Morrison, 1983; see Equation 12). The intervention can be an experimental manipulation such as a prevention or intervention program, or it can be a naturally occurring event such as a change in policy or funding for a public program. If the intervention effect is significant, it is of prime interest to evaluate the form of the effect. One of the advantages of TSA is the ability to assess the nature of change over time. In the next section, we describe the Box–Jenkins procedure. Several variations on this procedure have been proposed to eliminate the problematic model identification step, and they are described later.

Box–Jenkins Intervention Analysis

An intervention for the prevention or treatment of substance abuse can be evaluated using a Box–Jenkins analysis. The procedure, as described by Glass et al. (1975), is a two-step process. As described earlier, the autocorrelations and partial autocorrelations are calculated for various lags. This information is the basis for identifying the specific ARIMA model (i.e., specifying the value for p, d, and q). Model identification determines the specific transformation matrix to be used. The purpose of this transformation is to remove the dependence from the data so that it meets the assumptions of the general linear model. The general linear model is the general analytical procedure that includes multiple regression, ANOVA, and analysis of covariance as special cases. Once transformed, the data are analyzed using a modified general linear model program, and the parameters are estimated and tested for significance. With the dependence in the data accounted for, the analysis follows standard estimation and testing procedures.

A typical problem would be to determine whether the level of the series has changed as a result of the intervention. The analysis is described without that transformation first. For the simplest analysis, this would involve the estimation of two parameters: L, the level of the series, and D, the change in level after intervention. A test of significance could then be performed of the hypothesis of prime interest, H_0: $D = 0$. This could be expressed in terms of the general linear model as

$$Z = Xb + a, \tag{1}$$

where Z is the $N \times 1$ vector of observed variables ($N = n_1 + n_2$), that is,

N is the total number of observations with n_1 occurring before intervention, or

$$Z = \begin{bmatrix} z_1 \\ z_2 \\ \cdot \\ \cdot \\ z_i \\ \cdot \\ \cdot \\ z_N \end{bmatrix}. \quad (2)$$

X is the $N \times p$ design matrix (see the following examples) where p is the number of parameters estimated, b is the $p \times 1$ vector of parameters, or

$$b = \begin{bmatrix} L \\ D \end{bmatrix}, \quad (3)$$

and a is the $N \times 1$ vector of residuals, or

$$a = \begin{bmatrix} a_1 \\ a_2 \\ \cdot \\ \cdot \\ a_i \\ \cdot \\ \cdot \\ a_N \end{bmatrix}. \quad (4)$$

The general linear model is an approach to data analysis that includes many familiar statistical procedures as special cases. In a multiple regression analysis, the X matrix contains the numerical observations for each of the p predictor variables for the N subjects, the Z vector contains the criteria scores for the N subjects, the b vector contains the regression weights, and a vector contains the error of prediction (i.e., the difference between the actual score on the criteria and the predicted score on the criteria). In an ANOVA, the X matrix would consist of indicator variables (i.e., the numerical values 1 or 0, which indicate group membership), and the Z vector would contain the dependent variable observations.

For this example, the vector of parameters contains two components: L and D. The design matrix is shown in the top left of Table 1.

The usual least squares solution, which minimizes the sum of the squared errors, is

$$\mathbf{b} = (\mathbf{X}'\mathbf{X})^{-1}\mathbf{X}'\mathbf{Z}, \tag{5}$$

and a test of significance for the null hypothesis, H_0: $b_i = 0$ (i.e., H_0: $D = 0$ is given by

$$t_{b_i} = b_i/s_{b_i}, \tag{6}$$

where

$$s_{b_i}^2 = s_a^2 C^{ii}, \tag{7}$$

s_a^2 is the estimate of the error variance, and C^{ii} is the ith diagonal element of $(\mathbf{X}'\mathbf{X})^{-1}$. The test statistic would have a t distribution with degrees of freedom $N - p$. This is the same test of significance that is used for testing if the regression weight for a predictor is significant in a multiple regression.

TABLE 1
Examples of Common Design Matrices for Single-Unit Analysis
($N_1 = N_2 = 6$)

Immediate and constant changes in level		Immediate and constant changes in level and slope			
1	0	1	0	1	0
1	0	1	0	2	0
1	0	1	0	3	0
1	0	1	0	4	0
1	0	1	0	5	0
1	0	1	0	6	0
1	1	1	1	7	1
1	1	1	1	8	2
1	1	1	1	9	3
1	1	1	1	10	4
1	1	1	1	11	5
1	0	1	1	12	6

Decaying change in level		Delayed change in level	
1	0	1	0
1	0	1	0
1	0	1	0
1	0	1	0
1	0	1	0
1	0	1	0
1	1	1	0
1	.5	1	0
1	.25	1	0
1	.13	1	1
1	.17	1	1
1	.03	1	1

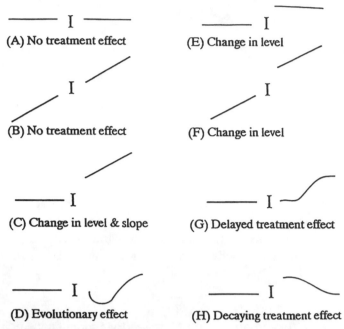

Figure 4. Eight alternative outcomes for a simple intervention design.

Figure 4 shows eight different outcomes for a simple one-intervention design. In a typical between-two-groups experimental design, only one assessment occurs after treatment. By inspecting the different patterns of change over time, one can see that selecting different points in time for the single assessment would result in much different conclusions for five of the examples (*D, E, F, G,* and *H*). The evolutionary effect (*D*) is a good example in which the intervention results in a temporary negative effect, perhaps while a response pattern is unlearned, followed by a positive effect. An early assessment would show that the treatment had a negative effect, a somewhat later assessment would indicate no treatment effect, and an even later assessment would show a positive treatment effect.

Alternative specifications of the design matrix permit the investigation of different hypotheses concerning the nature of the intervention. Table 1 contains some illustrative examples for an $N = 12$ ($n_1 = n_2 = 6$) case. The top left of Table 1 is the design matrix for an immediate and constant treatment effect. Only changes in level and slope parameters are described here. These are the most commonly examined effects in interrupted time series designs. However, time series designs provide an opportunity to examine additional change parameters that may be affected by the intervention (e.g., changes in cycles, variance, and pattern or serial dependency). Such applications are less common but can help to elucidate the nature of the effects of an intervention more fully. The top right of Table 1 is the design matrix for testing a change both in level and slope.

The bottom left of Table 1 is the design matrix for a decaying treatment effect. The bottom right of Table 1 is the design matrix for testing a delayed treatment effect.

The general linear model cannot be applied directly to TSA because of the presence of dependency in the residuals. It is necessary to perform a transformation on the observed variable, z_t, to remove dependency before the statistical analysis. A transformation matrix T must be found, yielding

$$Y = TZ \tag{8}$$

and

$$X^* = TX. \tag{9}$$

The specific form of the transformation matrix T is determined by the particular ARIMA (p,d,q) model. All transformation matrices will have a similar form, a lower triangular matrix, because the correction involves previous observations. For example, for a time series with five observations and an ARIMA $(1,0,0)$ model, the transformation matrix would be

$$T = \begin{bmatrix} 1 & 0 & 0 & 0 & 0 \\ \phi_1 & 1 & 0 & 0 & 0 \\ 0 & \phi_1 & 1 & 0 & 0 \\ 0 & 0 & \phi_1 & 1 & 0 \\ 0 & 0 & 0 & \phi_1 & 1 \end{bmatrix}, \tag{10}$$

which indicates that only the previous observation is part of the correction. For an ARIMA $(2,0,0)$ model, the transformation matrix would be

$$T = \begin{bmatrix} 1 & 0 & 0 & 0 & 0 \\ \phi_1 & 1 & 0 & 0 & 0 \\ \phi_2 & \phi_1 & 1 & 0 & 0 \\ 0 & \phi_2 & \phi_1 & 1 & 0 \\ 0 & 0 & \phi_2 & \phi_1 & 1 \end{bmatrix}, \tag{11}$$

which indicates that the previous two observations are part of the correction. Glass et al. (1975) presented an inductive derivation of the necessary transformation for these two models and other common models.

Given T, the estimate of the parameters, b, may be expressed as a generalized least squares problem:

$$b = (X'T'TX)^{-1}X'T'TZ, \tag{12}$$

and

$$b = (X^{*\prime}X^*)^{-1}X^{*\prime}Y. \qquad (13)$$

The purpose of the model identification step is to determine the appropriate transformation of Z into Y. Table 2 shows six common ARIMA models. After model identification, an estimation procedure is used to determine the specific numerical values of ϕ and θ. Appropriate tests of significance are based on asymptotic statistical theory.

The Box–Jenkins approach to intervention analysis suffers from a number of difficulties. First, the number of data points required for model identification is often prohibitive for research in applied settings. Second, even for the required number of points, correct identification is problematic (Velicer & Harrop, 1983). Third, the method is complex, making applications by the mathematically unsophisticated researcher difficult. The alternative approaches are described in the next section, all of which attempt to avoid the problematic model identification step.

Alternative Approaches

Simonton (1977) proposed a procedure that avoids the problem of model identification by using an estimate of the variance–covariance matrix based on a pooling of the observations across all subjects observed. This approach, however, requires a basic assumption. All series are assumed to be (1,0,0). Although the assumptions seem to be theoretically indefensible, empirical investigations indicate that this procedure works well in a wide variety of cases (Harrop & Velicer, 1985).

Algina and Swaminathan (1977, 1979; Swaminathan & Algina, 1977) have proposed an alternative to Simonton's (1977) statistical analysis using a profile analysis. The sample variance–covariance matrix is used as an estimator for $T'T$ in the modified least squares solution (see Equation 7). This approach, however, requires the assumption that the number of subjects is greater than the number of observations per subject. This is not a condition that is likely to be met in most applied research settings, where time series approaches are the most appropriate.

Instead of trying to determine the specific matrix, Velicer and McDonald (1984) proposed a general transformation matrix with the numerical values of the elements of T being estimated for each problem. The rationale for a general matrix is that all transformation matrices, T, have an identical form: a lower triangular matrix with equal subdiagonals. Weight vectors with five nonzero weights are accurate for most cases. A greater number of weights can be used where indicated by appropriate diagnostics (Velicer & McDonald, 1984). The accuracy of this approach has been supported by two simulation studies (Harrop & Velicer, 1985, 1990b), and it can be implemented with most existing computer programs by specifying a higher order autoregressive model such as ARIMA (5,0,0).

TABLE 2
Common Autoregressive Integrated Moving Average Models

Label	(p,d,q)	Descriptive formula	Comment
White noise	(0,0,0)	$Z_t = L + a_t$	No dependency in the data
Autoregressive Order 1	(1,0,0)	$Z_t - L = \phi_1(Z_{t-1} - L) + a_t$	Predicted from previous observations
Autoregressive Order 2	(2,0,0)	$Z_t - L = \phi_1(Z_{t-1} - L) + \phi_2(Z_{t-2} - L) + a_t$	Predicted from previous two observations
Moving averages Order 1	(0,0,1)	$Z_t - L = a_t - \theta_1 a_{t-1}$	Proportion of previous shock affects observation
Moving averages Order 2	(0,0,2)	$Z_t - L = a_t - \phi_1 a_{t-1} - \phi_2 a_{t-2}$	Proportion of two previous shocks affecting observations
Integrated moving averages	(0,1,1)	$Z_t - Z_{t-1} = a_t - \phi_1 a_{t-1}$	Stochastic drift and proportion of previous shock affect observation

POOLED TIME SERIES PROCEDURES

One of the issues involved in TSA is generalizability. How can the results from a single individual or unit be generalized to a larger population? Barlow and Hersen (1984) discussed the problem in terms of systematic replication. The example discussed previously involving the impact of relaxation therapy on blood pressure used this approach. However, this procedure involves logical inference rather than formal statistical inference. Such approaches have been described as qualitative reviews and have relied primarily on a count of the number of studies that support a hypothesis (Light & Smith, 1971). Two approaches that have been developed for statistical inference on multiple units are pooled time series designs and meta-analysis.

In the next sections, we describe an approach to pooled TSA that was proposed by Velicer and McDonald (1991). This approach is an extension of the general transformation approach described earlier. However, the same approach can be adapted with only minor alterations to implement either Box and Jenkins's (1976; cited in Glass et al., 1975) or Simonton's (1977) procedures. After that, we describe some of the recent developments in applying meta-analysis to time series data.

Pooled TSA

Velicer and McDonald's (1991) approach to TSA for multiple units represents a direct extension of the analysis for single units and requires only the use of a patterned transformation matrix. The specific choice of the design matrix x and the number of units will be dictated by the particular questions of interest. The procedure will be illustrated by a two-unit example ($K = 2$), where the design used involves only level and change in level (see the top left of Table 1).

The observations for all the units can be represented by a supervector of all the observations. A supervector is a single vector that contains a set of vectors combined in the form of a single vector rather than a matrix with multiple columns. In this case, the supervector $\mathbf{Z}$ is composed of the vector of N observations (pre- and postintervention) for each of the experimental units. For example, when there are two experimental units or individuals, with n_1 observations before intervention and n_2 observations after intervention on both Unit 1 and Unit 2, the supervector could be represented as

$$\mathbf{Z} = \begin{bmatrix} \mathbf{Z}_1 \\ \hline \mathbf{Z}_2 \end{bmatrix} = \begin{bmatrix} z_{11} \\ z_{21} \\ \cdot \\ z_{N1} \\ z_{12} \\ z_{22} \\ \cdot \\ z_{N2} \end{bmatrix}. \tag{14}$$

TABLE 3
Example of General Transformation Matrix (T) for Cross-Sectional Analysis ($k = 2$: $n_{11} = n_{12} = n_{21} = n_{22} = 4$)

1	0	0	0	0	0	0	0	0	0	0	0	0	0	0	0
W_1	1	0	0	0	0	0	0	0	0	0	0	0	0	0	0
W_2	W_1	1	0	0	0	0	0	0	0	0	0	0	0	0	0
W_3	W_2	W_1	1	0	0	0	0	0	0	0	0	0	0	0	0
W_4	W_3	W_2	W_1	1	0	0	0	0	0	0	0	0	0	0	0
W_5	W_4	W_3	W_2	W_1	1	0	0	0	0	0	0	0	0	0	0
0	W_5	W_4	W_3	W_2	W_1	1	0	0	0	0	0	0	0	0	0
0	0	W_5	W_4	W_3	W_2	W_1	1	0	0	0	0	0	0	0	0
0	0	0	0	0	0	0	0	1	0	0	0	0	0	0	0
0	0	0	0	0	0	0	0	W_1	1	0	0	0	0	0	0
0	0	0	0	0	0	0	0	W_2	W_1	1	0	0	0	0	0
0	0	0	0	0	0	0	0	W_3	W_2	W_1	1	0	0	0	0
0	0	0	0	0	0	0	0	W_4	W_3	W_2	W_1	1	0	0	0
0	0	0	0	0	0	0	0	W_5	W_4	W_3	W_2	W_1	1	0	0
0	0	0	0	0	0	0	0	0	W_5	W_4	W_3	W_2	W_1	1	0
0	0	0	0	0	0	0	0	0	0	W_5	W_4	W_3	W_2	W_1	1

Table 3 shows an example of the patterned general transformation matrix that could be used to transform the serially dependent Z_i variables to the serially independent Y_i variables. In this example, there are two experimental units, each with four observations before intervention and four observations after intervention. The w_i entries represent the values of ϕ and θ required for any ARIMA (p,d,q) model. For example, if an ARIMA (1,0,0) model was identified, the values would be $w_1 = \phi_1$ and $w_2 = w_3 = w_4 = w_5 = 0$. Alternatively, if the general transformation approach is used, only the numerical values for w_1, w_2, w_3, w_4, and w_5 are estimated with no attempt to identify them as values of ϕ or θ.

This transformation matrix will always take the form of a partitioned matrix with repeating transformation matrices on the block and null matrices elsewhere. For seven units, this could be represented as

$$T = \begin{bmatrix} T^* & 0 & 0 & 0 & 0 & 0 & 0 \\ 0 & T^* & 0 & 0 & 0 & 0 & 0 \\ 0 & 0 & T^* & 0 & 0 & 0 & 0 \\ 0 & 0 & 0 & T^* & 0 & 0 & 0 \\ 0 & 0 & 0 & 0 & T^* & 0 & 0 \\ 0 & 0 & 0 & 0 & 0 & T^* & 0 \\ 0 & 0 & 0 & 0 & 0 & 0 & T^* \end{bmatrix}, \qquad (15)$$

where each T^* is an $N \times N$ lower diagonal transformation matrix ($N = n_1 + n_2$) and 0 is an $N \times N$ null matrix. The example in Table 3 shows all the elements for a two-unit example. The occurrence in the null ma-

TABLE 4
Example of a Design Matrix (**X**) for a Cross-Sectional Problem With
Level and Change in Level Analysis

Full model				No difference in intervention effects			No difference in individual effects		No intervention effects
1	0	0	0	1	0	0	1	0	1
1	0	0	0	1	0	0	1	0	1
1	0	0	0	1	0	0	1	0	1
1	0	0	0	1	0	0	1	0	1
1	1	0	0	1	1	0	1	1	1
1	1	0	0	1	1	0	1	1	1
1	1	0	0	1	1	0	1	1	1
1	1	0	0	1	1	0	1	1	1
1	0	1	0	1	0	1	1	0	1
1	0	1	0	1	0	1	1	0	1
1	0	1	0	1	0	1	1	0	1
1	0	1	0	1	0	1	1	0	1
1	1	1	1	1	1	1	1	1	1
1	1	1	1	1	1	1	1	1	1
1	1	1	1	1	1	1	1	1	1
1	1	1	1	1	1	1	1	1	1

trices in all positions except the diagonal reflects the assumption of independence of the different units.

The use of a properly parameterized design matrix will permit comparisons between different units. Table 4 shows an example. The full model includes four parameters that reflect level and change in level for both units and the difference between the two units on preintervention and postintervention changes in level. If the last parameter (i.e., the difference between the units on the postintervention change in level) is not significant, the next design (i.e., no difference in intervention effects) would be adopted, reflecting no difference between the two units in intervention effects (a change in level). Differences between units would seem likely to be fairly common for most problems. However, if no such differences exist, the next design (i.e., no difference in individual effects) would be appropriate. The no-intervention-effects design would be appropriate if there were no intervention effects or differences between units.

The procedure can be generalized to any number of units and any choice of design matrix. Implicit is the assumption that a common transformation matrix is appropriate for all units. This assumption seems reasonable if the nature of the series is viewed as being determined by an underlying process specific to the construct under investigation. As with any of the analytical approaches, diagnostic indicators such as Ljung and

Box's (1978) test may be used to test the fit of the model. The basic form of the design matrix should be based on the analyses of the individual units, a priori knowledge when available, or both.

The approach described here has a number of advantages. First, it is a direct extension of the general transformation approach developed by Velicer and McDonald (1984). This approach avoids the problematic model identification step and has received a favorable evaluation in several simulation studies (Harrop & Velicer, 1985, 1990b).

Second, the approach described here also can be adapted to two of the alternative methods of analysis. For the Glass et al. (1975) approach, a specific transformation matrix corresponding to a particular ARIMA (p,d,q) model would replace the general transformation matrix. Following Simonton's (1977) approach, the ARIMA (1,0,0) transformation matrix would be used for all cases instead of the general transformation approach.

Third, the approach is a simple and direct extension of existing procedures. It can be implemented using a slight modification of existing computer programs. The problems of adaptation will involve problems of size and speed created by the use of supervectors rather than an increased complexity of the analysis.

Meta-Analysis

An alternative procedure to combining data from several individuals or units is meta-analysis. Procedures for performing a meta-analysis have been well developed for traditional experimental designs (Glass, McGaw, & Smith, 1981; Hedges & Olkin, 1985; Hunter & Schmidt, 1990; Tobler, 1994). However, meta-analysis procedures have not been widely applied to single-subject designs. Busk and Serlin (1992) discussed the problems of applying meta-analysis to this area. Two problems are as follows: Primary research reports often have relied on visual analysis (Parsonson & Baer, 1992) rather than on TSA, resulting in a lack of basic statistical information in the published research reports (O'Rourke & Detsky, 1989). (b) Alternative definitions of effect size must be developed that are appropriate for time series data. Allison and Gorman (1992) and Busk and Serlin (1992) reviewed some alternative effect size calculations appropriate for time series designs.

APPLICATIONS FOR TREATMENT AND PREVENTION DATA

The topics discussed in the previous sections—model identification, intervention assessment, and pooled TSA—represent the three critical analysis issues that are relevant to all areas of time series research. In the following section, we discuss several time series issues with particular emphasis on how they relate to alcohol and other substance use research.

Design Issues

A number of critical design issues must be addressed before applying TSA to alcohol research problems. First, the unit of analysis must be defined. For several examples discussed here, the unit of analysis is assumed to be a single individual. Treatment outcome studies, even if they involve many participants, can be analyzed profitably as a series of studies at the individual level. The outcome of the studies can be treated as replications and combined using cross-sectional procedures or meta-analytical procedures. If differences exist between subjects, a hypothesis can be generated and a systematic replication procedure used (Barlow & Hersen, 1984). Alternatively, the unit can be an aggregate group of people, and the interventions (e.g., policy changes) can apply only at the group level. The same methods of analysis can be applied to the group data.

Studies of this type are referred to as *evaluation studies*. A recent study of this type was conducted examining the impact of two interventions on narcotics use and property crime (Powers, Hanssens, Hser, & Anglin, 1991). Powers et al. concluded that methadone treatment has long-term benefits in reducing drug use and property crime but that legal supervision had the opposite effect of increasing both property crimes and narcotics use.

Only simple designs have been described here. More complex designs involving multiple interventions may be appropriate, and the analysis procedures generally differ only with respect to the design matrix used. A variety of textbooks discuss alternative designs and the relation of the designs to different threats to validity (Campbell & Stanley, 1963; Cook & Campbell, 1979; Glass et al., 1975). These include, but are not limited to, designs that compare the experimental time series with a nonequivalent control series, multiple group crossover designs, designs that allow for tests of interactions between two or more treatments, delayed intervention designs, and designs that incorporate a nonequivalent dependent variable series.

Measurement Issues

Appropriate measures for TSA are those that are quantitative and can be repeated for many observations across time at regular intervals (e.g., blood pressure, number of cigarettes smoked per day, number of standard drinks per day). In this section, we review several methods for collecting drinking data in time series designs and the strengths and limitations of each.

Daily Diary Methods

Self-monitoring a target behavior by recording in a daily diary is a commonly used method of data collection. Participants use a diary or calendar to record the extent to which they engage in a target behavior for specific intervals of time. Exact dates and amounts (i.e., for drinking behavior) will be more accurate using daily recording than those obtained by retrospective assessment. However, noncompliance with daily diary methods is often a significant problem. Researchers have attempted to overcome the lack of compliance by combining the use of diaries with frequent appointments at the laboratory to turn in data (e.g., every 12 hr, every day), but the utility of this approach is likely to be limited to special populations (e.g., college students). For most populations, transportation and time constraints are likely to result in a lack of compliance. Daily telephone calls to participants (or call-ins by participants) can help verify compliance with a minimal additional burden on the participants.

Ecological Momentary Assessment

To assess individuals' naturalistic behavior over extended periods of time yet still retain more experimental control than daily diaries permit, ecological momentary assessment (EMA) may be used (Shiffman et al., 1994; Stone & Shiffman, 1994). In the experience-sampling paradigm, participants are given a handheld computer that "beeps" them at random intervals, prompting time to complete an assessment at that time. Participants also may be instructed to initiate an assessment on the computer in response to the occurrence of some event (e.g., smoking a cigarette). This paradigm is a high-tech version of self-monitoring; respondents enter their data into the computer's interactive framework rather than writing in a diary or log. EMA can be used to investigate the relationships among and between various behaviors, self-reported internal triggers, and external situational factors (Litt, Cooney, Morse, Bastone, & Kadden, 1995; Shiffman et al., 1994). Behavioral data yielded from EMA would generally be appropriate for TSA to examine behavioral patterns over time. One caution, however, is that EMA can present problems for TSA depending on the extent to which the prompting beeps are spaced nonrandomly.

Advantages of EMA include experimenter-controlled sampling intervals, standard programmable questions prompting participants, and participants entering their own data into the handheld computers, which then can be uploaded to a PC for analysis. The flexibility available in programming the computers provides the experimenter with a broad array of options for choices of experimental design and assessments. (A detailed description of the EMA hardware and software is available in Shiffman, Paty, Gnys, & Kassel, 1993.)

A disadvantage of the EMA approach is that it is potentially intrusive and burdensome to participants over an extended period. Reporting compliance was high (92%) in the Shiffman et al. (1994) sample of smokers, but participants only assessed for 1 week. Moreover, only compliance with the experience-sampling paradigm can be measured. Finally, this approach requires the provision of participants with relatively expensive equipment to keep with them at all times in the natural environment. Computer damage or loss is a concern that may be particularly relevant for assessing heavy drinkers or alcoholics over time.

Interactive Voice Response System

To specify drinking patterns more precisely over time than retrospective reports and to reduce reporting burdens to participants, researchers at the Vermont Alcohol Research Center developed a telecommunication approach, the Interactive Voice Response (IVR) System (Searles, Perrine, Mundt, & Helzer, 1995). In this study, 51 participants reported their alcohol consumption for 112 days on the IVR system by entering their data daily using the touch-tone pad of their telephone. Each day, participants answered 11 questions relating to drinking and variables believed to affect consumption (e.g., stress level). Participants entered directly into an automated database. The volunteer sample consisted of both normal drinkers and individuals (almost 50% of the sample) who were not seeking treatment but who subsequently qualified for an alcohol dependence diagnosis according to the Composite International Diagnostic Interview—Substance Abuse Module. Representative IVR data from 2 participants in this study are shown in Figure 5.

The overall reporting compliance rate of 93% indicates the feasibility of collecting detailed daily reports from participants over an extended period. Moreover, compliance was equally high among alcohol-dependent individuals and normal drinkers.

The IVR system methodology has two noteworthy disadvantages: training requirements and expense. Volunteers who participated in this study completed a detailed 2-hr training session (in groups of 8 or 10) before using the IVR. Compliance was at least partially motivated by a monetary compensation system that included rewards for each daily report, plus bonuses for consistency in compliance (e.g., every day of the week). The maximum compensation for any participant was $250, excluding payments for training and in-person interviews. (For details about the compensation system, see Searles et al., 1955.) These disadvantages are offset by the efficiency of automated data entry by participants, by the reduced burden and intrusiveness for the participant, and by the long periods of time (e.g., 112 days) over which one can collect accurate and valid data. The high compliance rates also are suggestive of a more representative sample of participants (i.e., the procedure seems acceptable to a high propor-

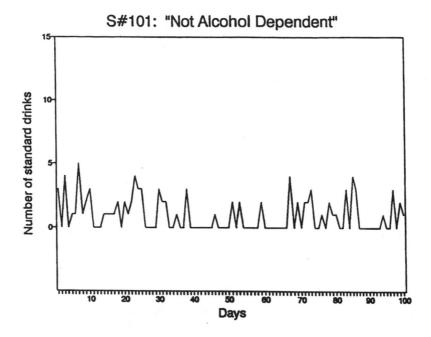

S#101: "Not Alcohol Dependent"

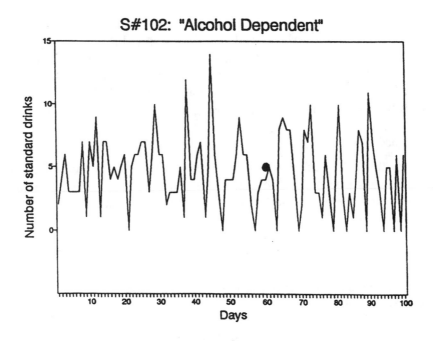

S#102: "Alcohol Dependent"

Figure 5. Illustrative time series graphs of daily drinking data obtained with the Interactive Voice Response System. S = subject number.

tion of volunteers). As telecommunication advances, some of the training and compliance issues are likely to be minimized. For example, as voice recognition replaces the touch-tone pad as an input device, training time will decrease. (Technical information on the implementation of the IVR automated system may be found in Mundt, Perrine, Searles, & Walter, 1995.)

Cyclical Data

The presence of cyclical or seasonal data is a potential confounding variable in time series data. Daily data gathered on individuals often have a weekly or monthly cycle. Three alternative procedures have been proposed to deal with cyclical data.

Deseasonalization

In some content areas, the cyclical nature of the data is well-known. For example, in the economic area, much of the data is adjusted for seasonal effects before it is reported. These seasonal adjustments, based on a priori information, remove cyclical trends from the data before any TSA is conducted.

Statistical Control

An alternative method of adjusting for seasonal effects is to find some variable that is sensitive to the same seasonal effects as the dependent measure but that cannot be affected by the intervention. This variable then could be used as a covariate. The cyclical effects would be controlled statistically. Some of the problems in using a covariate are discussed next.

Combined Models

A third alternative approach involves the use of combined models. (McCleary & Hay, 1980, discussed this approach in detail.) As an example, suppose we have a time series that is represented by a Lag 1 moving averages model, that is, a (0,0,1) model

$$Z_t - L = A_t - \Theta_1 A_{t-1}. \tag{16}$$

Furthermore, assume that a seasonal component of Lag 7 is present. This could be modeled as

$$Z_t - L = A_t - \Theta_7 A_{t-7}. \tag{17}$$

The time series therefore would be described as an ARIMA (0,0,1) (0,0,1)$_7$ model, or

$$Z_t - L = (A_t - \Theta_1 A_{t-1})(A_t - \Theta_7 A_{t-7}). \qquad (18)$$

Daily drinking data that fit this model would be interpreted as indicating that the participant's level of drinking on any given day is significantly predicted by both how much he or she drank on the previous day and how much he or she drank on the same day of the previous week. Rosel and Elósegui (1994) found that combined autoregressive models commonly describe smoking behavior. The authors provided a highly accessible description of combined models applied to addictive behavior in that article. Unlike the first two approaches, the combined-models approach presents difficulties for the extension of this procedure to either pooled procedures or multivariate time series approaches and would require longer series.

Cyclicity as the Object of Study

In the only study we could find that reported TSA of individuals' daily drinking data, six alcohol-dependent and six nondependent drinkers' patterns of drinking were compared (Mundt, Searles, Perrine, & Helzer, 1995). Participants were matched on alcohol quantity and frequency. Results indicated that the alcohol-dependent participants' drinking patterns were dominated primarily by weekly cycles, whereas nondependent drinkers' behavior appeared to occur in more prolonged cycles of several weeks or months. Mundt, Searles, et al. suggested that this distinction may have implications for the progression toward, versus prevention of, the consequences of alcohol use that constitute alcohol dependence.

FUTURE DIRECTIONS

There are several other issues of interest for time series applications that are currently under development. We discuss them briefly here.

Missing Data

Missing data are an almost unavoidable problem in TSA and present a number of unique challenges. Life events will result in missing data even for the most conscientious researchers. In the model identification study on nicotine regulation (Velicer, Redding, et al., 1992) described previously, missing data were a relatively minor problem. Four participants had no missing data (i.e., all 124 observations were available). For 4 other participants,

4 or fewer observations were missing. Only 2 participants had significant amounts of missing data (115 and 97 observations available).

Little and Rubin (1987) provided the most thorough theoretical and mathematical coverage of handling missing data in a TSA. The problem has received little attention in the applied behavioral sciences area. Rankin and Marsh (1985) assessed the impact of different amounts of missing data for 32 simulated time series, modeled after 16 real-world data examples. They concluded that with up to 20% missing data, there is little impact on model identification but that the impact is pronounced when more than 40% are missing. In an extensive simulation study, Colby and Velicer (1997) compared four different techniques of handling missing data: deletion of missing observations from the analysis, substitution of the mean of the series, substitution of the mean of the two adjacent observations, and a maximum-likelihood estimation (Jones, 1980). The mean of the series was judged to be unacceptable. The mean of the adjacent points and deletion worked well for a large number of cases, but not for all cases. The maximum-likelihood procedure was the best procedure across all conditions.

Computer Programs

Analysis of time series data requires the use of a computer program. Fortunately, several programs have become available in the past two decades. Unfortunately, the quality of the available programs is uneven. Harrop and Velicer (1990a, 1990b) evaluated five programs: BMDP (Dixon, 1985), GENTS (Velicer, Fraser, McDonald, & Harrop, 1986), ITSE (Williams & Gottman, 1982), SAS (SAS Institute, 1984), and TSX (Bower & Glass, 1974). Simulated data from 44 different ARIMA models were used to assess the accuracy of the programs (Harrop & Velicer, 1990b). Three programs produced generally satisfactory results (i.e., TSX, GENTS, and SAS). One was inaccurate across a wide range of models (i.e., ITSE), and one was occasionally inaccurate and occasionally failed to complete the analysis (i.e., BMDP). The original ITSE contained an incorrect formula, and an amended version of this program, ITSACORR, is available (Crosbie, 1993). The overall evaluation of the computation features and quality of documentation was not favorable (Harrop & Velicer, 1990a). Some of the programs evaluated by Harrop and Velicer (1990a, 1990b) have been modified substantially since inclusion in the study (e.g., BMDP, ITSE, and SAS), and TSA features have since been added to widely used statistical packages, such as SPSS Trends (SPSS, 1988) and SYSTAT (Wilkinson, 1986). A new comparative evaluation of time series programs is needed; Harrop and Velicer's (1990a, 1990b) studies provide a useful framework for evaluating current programs.

Multivariate TSA

TSA on a single dependent measure involves many of the procedures common to multivariate statistics because two vectors of unknowns must be estimated simultaneously: parameters and coefficients, which represent the dependency in the data. The term *multivariate time series* denotes the observation of more than one variable at each point in time. Multivariate time series data can be analyzed in different ways depending on the goal of the study.

If one of the variables is conceptualized as the dependent variable and any additional variables are viewed as being unable to be influenced by the intervention, the appropriate analysis has been labeled a *concomitant variable analysis* (Glass et al., 1975) and is a direct analog of the analysis of covariance. The covariate is used to statistically remove some variation from the dependent measure, thus increasing sensitivity. Two problems arise: (a) What is the proper lag between the covariate and dependent variable? (b) How should dependency in the covariate be handled? One application of this procedure is to control the effects of seasonality in the data (discussed earlier).

Alternatively, all of the observed variables could be conceptualized as dependent measures. This is a direct extension of the multivariate ANOVA. The unique problems are determining the appropriate lags for relating the dependent measures (McCleary & Hay, 1980; West & Hepworth, 1991) and the possibility that a single model may not be adequate to explain the dependency for all the variables. Alternative approaches could involve dealing with all p dependent measures simultaneously, combining the p measures into a single weighted composite, or defining a set of m new composites ($m < p$) and interpreting these composites independently. Peña and Box (1987) described one approach to this area, but we do not think that examples of applications have appeared in the behavioral science literature yet.

Instead of focusing on changes in slope or level, a multivariate time series may want to focus on the structure of the variables. This represents an extension of P-technique factor analysis (Cattell, 1963, 1988), in which a Variables × Occasions data matrix is used instead of the usual Variables × Subjects data matrix. However, P-technique factor analysis is not appropriate when there is dependency, which is highly likely in time series data, because depending can bias the estimates of the factor loadings (Wood & Brown, 1994). The recently developed dynamic factor analysis (Molenaar, 1985, 1987; Molenaar, De Goodjer, & Schmitz, 1992) permits serial dependency on the data and includes P-technique factor analysis as a special case. However, several difficulties exist in applying this model, both practical and theoretical. Wood and Brown described an implementation of the dynamic factor model using SAS macros and presented an evaluation of this approach.

CONCLUSION

TSA has a tremendous potential for applications to prevention and treatment research. During the past decade, several procedures have been developed that are designed specifically for analyzing longitudinal data. TSA can be viewed as the prototypical method for analyzing longitudinal data. All of these recently developed procedures for analyzing longitudinal data share the common characteristic of requiring a high-speed computer to perform the analysis. For TSA, the combination of computational advances and alternative statistical procedures has increased the ease of application to a wide range of potential applications. Two of the early drawbacks, the large sample size required for model identifications and problems with generalizability, have been largely overcome in the past decade. TSA can now be viewed as representing one of a number of potential methods of data analysis available to all researchers rather than as a novel and difficult procedure. Researchers are now reaching the point in the prevention and treatment research area in which the data analysis method will be matched to the research problem rather than the research problems being limited by the available methods of analysis.

REFERENCES

Aitken, A. C. (1934). On least squares and lineal combination of observations. *Proceedings of the Royal Society of Edinburgh, 55,* 42–47.

Akaike, H. (1974). A new look at the statistical model identification. *IEEE Transactions on Automatic Control, 19,* 716–723.

Algina, J., & Swaminathan, H. A. (1977). A procedure for the analysis of time series designs. *Journal of Experimental Education, 45,* 56–60.

Algina, J., & Swaminathan, H. A. (1979). Alternatives to Simonton's analysis of the interrupted and multiple-group time series designs. *Psychological Bulletin, 86,* 919–926.

Allison, A. B., & Gorman, B. S. (1992, August). *Calculating effect sizes for meta-analysis: The case of the single case.* Paper presented at the 100th Annual Convention of the American Psychological Association, Washington, DC.

Barlow, D. H., & Hersen, M. (1984). *Single case experimental designs: Strategies for studying behavior change.* (2nd ed.). Elmsford, NY: Pergamon Press.

Beguin, J. M., Courieroux, C., & Monfort, A. (1980). Identification of a mixed autoregressive-moving average process: The corner method. In O. D. Anderston (Ed.), *Time series: Proceedings of the International Conference held at Nottingham University* (pp. 423–436). Amsterdam: North-Holland.

Bhansali, R. J., & Downham, D. Y. (1977). Some properties of the order of an autoaggressive model selected by a generalization of Akaike's FPE-criterion. *Biometrika, 64,* 547–551.

Bower, C., & Glass, G. V. (1974). TSX [Computer program]. Boulder: University of Colorado.

Box, G. E. P., Jenkins, G. M., & Reinsel, G. C. (1994). *Time series analysis: Forecasting and control* (3rd ed.). Englewood Cliffs, NJ: Prentice Hall.

Box, G. E. P., & Pierce, W. A. (1970). Distribution of residual autocorrelations in autoregressive-integrated moving average time series models. *Journal of the American Statistical Association, 65,* 1509–1526.

Box, G. E. P., & Tiao, G. C. (1965). A change in level of nonstationary time series. *Biometrika, 52,* 181–192.

Box, G. E. P., & Tiao, G. C. (1975). Intervention analysis with application to economic and environmental problems. *Journal of the American Statistical Association, 70,* 70–92.

Busk, P. L., & Serlin, R. C. (1992). Meta-analysis for single-case research. In T. R. Kratochwill, & J. R. Levin (Eds.), *Single-case research designs and analysis* (pp. 187–212). Hillsdale, NJ: Erlbaum.

Campbell, D. T., & Stanley, J. C. (1963). *Experimental and quasi-experimental design for research.* Chicago: Rand McNally.

Cattell, R. B. (1963). The structure of change by P- and incremental r-technique. In. C. W. Harris (Ed.), *Problems in measuring change* (pp. 163–198). Madison: University of Wisconsin Press.

Cattell, R. B. (1988). The data box. In J. R. Nesselroade & R. B. Cattell (Eds.), *Handbook of multivariate experimental psychology* (pp. 69–130). New York: Plenum Press.

Colby, S. M., & Velicer, W. F. (1997). *A comparison of four alternative procedures for handling missing data in a time series analysis.* Manuscript submitted for publication.

Cook, T. D., & Campbell, D. T. (Eds.). (1979). *Quasi-experimentation: Design & analysis issues for field settings.* Chicago: Rand McNally.

Crosbie, J. (1993). Interrupted time-series analysis with brief single-subject data. *Journal of Consulting and Clinical Psychology, 61,* 966–974.

Dixon, W. J. (1985). *BMDP statistical software* [Computer program manual]. Berkeley: University of California Press.

Djuric, P. M., & Kay, S. M. (1992). Order selection of autoregressive models. *IEEE Transactions on Acoustics, Speech, and Signal Processing, 40,* 2829–2833.

Glass, G. V., McGaw, B., & Smith, M. L. (1981). *Meta-analysis in social research.* Beverly Hills, CA: Sage.

Glass, G. V., Willson, V. L., & Gottman, J. M. (1975). *Design and analysis of time series experiments.* Boulder: Colorado Associate University Press.

Gottman, J. M. (1973). N-of-one and N-of-two research in psychotherapy. *Psychological Bulletin, 80,* 93–105.

Gottman, J. M. (1981). *Time-series analysis.* New York: Cambridge University Press.

Gottman, J. M., & Glass, G. V. (1978). Analysis of interrupted time-series experiments. In J. Kratochwill (Ed.), *Strategies to evaluate change in single subject research* (pp. 237–285). New York: Academic Press.

Grey, H. L., Kelly, G. D., & McIntire, D. D. (1978). A new approach to ARIMA modeling. *Communications in Statistics, B7,* 1–77.

Hannan, E. J., & Rissanen, J. (1982). Recursive estimation of mixed autoregressive moving average order. *Biometrika, 69,* 81–94.

Harrop, J. W., & Velicer, W. F. (1985). A comparison of three alternative methods of time series model identification. *Multivariate Behavioral Research, 20,* 27–44.

Harrop, J. W., & Velicer, W. F. (1990a). Computer programs for interrupted time series analysis: I. A qualitative evaluation. *Multivariate Behavioral Research, 25,* 219–231.

Harrop, J. W., & Velicer, W. F. (1990b). Computer programs for interrupted time series analysis: II. A qualitative evaluation. *Multivariate Behavioral Research, 25,* 233–249.

Hedges, L. V., & Olkin, I. (1985). *Statistical methods for meta-analysis.* Orlando, FL: Academic Press.

Hunter, J. E., & Schmidt, F. L. (1990). *Methods for meta-analysis.* Newbury Park, CA: Sage.

Jarvik, M. E. (1973). Further observations on nicotine as the reinforcing agent in smoking. In W. L. Dunn, Jr. (Ed.), *Smoking behavior: Motives and incentives* (pp. 33–49). Washington, DC: V. H. Winston.

Jones, R. H. (1980). Maximum likelihood fitting of ARMA models to time series missing observations. *Technometrics, 22,* 389–396.

Kashyap, R. L. (1977). A Bayesian comparison of different classes of dynamic models using empirical data. *IEEE Transactions on Automatic Control, 22,* 715–727.

Leventhal, H., & Cleary, P. D. (1980). The smoking problem: A review of the research and theory in behavioral risk modification. *Psychological Bulletin, 88,* 370–405.

Light, R. J., & Smith, P. V. (1971). Accumulating evidence: Procedures for resolving contradictions among different research studies. *Harvard Educational Review, 41,* 429–471.

Litt, M. D., Cooney, N., Morse, P., Bastone, E., & Kadden, R. (1995, May). *Evaluating cues for craving in treated alcoholics: A field study.* Paper presented at the Seventh International Conference on the Treatment of Addictive Behaviors, Noordwijkerhout, The Netherlands.

Little, R. J. A., & Rubin, D. B. (1987). *Statistical analysis with missing data.* New York: Wiley.

Ljung, G. M., & Box, G. E. P. (1978). On a measure of lack of fit in time series models. *Biometrika*, 65, 297–303.

McCleary, R., & Hay, R. A., Jr. (1980). *Applied time series analysis for the social sciences*. Beverly Hills, CA: Sage.

McFall, R. M. (1978). Smoking cessation research. *Journal of Consulting and Clinical Psychology*, 76, 703–712.

Molenaar, P. C. M. (1985). A dynamic factor model for the analysis of multivariate time series. *Psychometrika*, 50, 181–202.

Molenaar, P. C. M. (1987). Dynamic factor analysis in the frequency domain: Causal modeling of multivariate psychophysiological time series. *Multivariate Behavioral Research*, 22, 329–353.

Molenaar, P. C. M., De Gooijer, J. G., & Schmitz, B. (1992). Dynamic factor analysis of nonstationary multivariate time series. *Psychometrika*, 57, 333–349.

Morrison, D. F. (1983). *Applied linear statistical methods*. Englewood Cliffs, NJ: Prentice Hall.

Mundt, J. C., Perrine, M. W., Searles, J. S., & Walter, D. (1995). An application of interactive voice response technology to longitudinal studies of daily behavior. *Behavior Research Methods, Instruments, and Computers*, 27, 351–357.

Mundt, J. C., Searles, J. S., Perrine, M. W., & Helzer, J. E. (1995). Cycles of alcohol dependence: Frequency-domain analyses of daily drinking logs for matched alcohol-dependent and nondependent subjects. *Journal of Studies on Alcohol*, 56, 491–499.

O'Rourke, K., & Detsky, A. S. (1989). Meta-analysis in medical research: Strong encouragement for higher quality in individual research efforts. *Journal of Clinical Epidemiology*, 42, 1021–1024.

Parsonson, B. S., & Baer, D. M. (1992). The visual analysis of data and current research into the stimuli controlling it. In T. R. Kratochwill & J. R. Levin (Eds.), *Single-case research designs and analysis* (pp. 15–40). Hillsdale, NJ: Erlbaum.

Parzen, E. (1974). Some recent advances in time series modelling. *IEEE Transactions on Automatic Control*, 19, 723–729.

Peña, D., & Box, G. E. P. (1987). Identifying a simplifying structure in time series. *Journal of the American Statistical Association*, 82, 836–843.

Powers, K., Hanssens, D. M., Hser, Y.-P., & Anglin, M. D. (1991). Measuring the long-term effects of public policy: The case of narcotic use and property crime. *Management Science*, 37, 627–644.

Printz, A. M. (1978). *Stress reduction in the treatment of essential hypertension: A clinical trial utilizing assertion and relaxation coping skills*. Unpublished doctoral dissertation, University of Rhode Island, Kingston.

Pukkila, T. M. (1982). On the identification of ARIMA (p,q) models. In O. D. Anderson (Ed.), *Time series analysis—Theory and practice: 1. Proceedings of the International Conference held at Valencia, Spain, June 1981* (pp. 81–103). Amsterdam: North-Holland.

Rankin, E. D., & Marsh, J. C. (1985). Effects of missing data on the statistical analysis of clinical time series. *Social Work Research and Abstracts, 21*, 13–16.

Rissanen, J. (1978). Modeling by shortest data description. *Automatica, 14*, 465–478.

Rissanen, J. (1986a). Order estimation by accumulated prediction errors. *Journal of Applied Probability, 12A*, 55–61.

Rissanen, J. (1986b). Stochastic complexity and modeling. *Annals of Statistics, 14*, 1080–1100.

Rosel, J., & Elósegui, E. (1994). Daily and weekly smoking habits: A Box–Jenkins analysis. *Psychological Reports, 75*, 1639–1648.

Russell, M. A. (1977). Nicotine chewing gum as a substitute for smoking. *British Medical Journal, 1*, 1060–1063.

SAS Institute. (1984). *SAS/ETS user's guide, Version 5 edition.* Cary, NC: SAS Institute.

Schachter, S. (1977). Nicotine regulation in heavy and light smokers. *Journal of Experimental Psychology: General, 106*, 5–12.

Schwartz, G. (1978). Estimating the dimension of a model. *Annals of Statistics, 6*, 461–469.

Searles, J. S., Perrine, M. W., Mundt, J. C., & Helzer, J. E. (1995). Self-report of drinking using touch-tone telephone: Extending the limits of reliable daily contact. *Journal of Studies on Alcohol, 56*, 375–382.

Shiffman, S., Fisher, L. A., Paty, J. A., Gnys, M., Hickcox, M., & Kassel, J. D. (1994). Drinking and smoking: A field study of their association. *Annals of Behavioral Medicine, 16*, 203–209.

Shiffman, S., Paty, J. A., Gnys, M., & Kassel, J. D. (1993). *A computer method for field collection of self-monitoring and base-rate data.* Unpublished manuscript, University of Pittsburgh, Pittsburgh, PA.

Simonton, D. K. (1977). Cross-sectional time-series experiments: Some suggested statistical analyses. *Psychological Bulletin, 84*, 489–502.

Solomon, R. L. (1980). The opponent-process theory of acquired motivation: The costs of pleasure and the benefits of pain. *American Psychologist, 35*, 691–712.

Solomon, R. L., & Corbit, J. D. (1973). An opponent-process theory of motivation: Cigarette addiction. *Journal of Abnormal Psychology, 81*, 158–171.

Solomon, R. L., & Corbit, J. D. (1974). An opponent-process theory of motivation: I. Temporal dynamics of affect. *Psychological Review, 81*, 119–145.

SPSS. (1988). *SPSS-X trends.* Chicago: Author.

Stone, A. A., & Shiffman, S. (1994). Ecological momentary assessment (EMA) in behavioral medicine. *Annuals of Behavioral Medicine, 16*, 199–202.

Swaminathan, H., & Algina, J. (1977). Analysis of quasi-experimental time series designs. *Multivariate Behavioral Research, 12*, 111–131.

Tobler, N. (1994). Meta-analytic issues for prevention intervention research. In L. M. Collins & L. A. Seitz (Eds.), *Advances in data analysis for prevention in-*

tervention research (NIDA Research Monograph No. 142, pp. 342–403). Rockville, MD: National Institute on Drug Abuse.

Tomkins, S. S. (1966). Psychological model for smoking behavior. *American Journal of Public Health, 68,* 250–257.

Tomkins, S. S. (1968). A modified model of smoking behavior. In. E. F. Borgatta & R. R. Evans (Eds.), *Smoking, health and behavior.* Chicago: Aldine.

Tsay, R. S. (1984). Regression models with time series errors. *Journal of the American Statistical Association, 79,* 118–124.

Tsay, R. S., & Tiao, G. C. (1984). Consistent estimates of autoregressive parameters and extended sample autocorrelation function for stationary and nonstationary ARIMA models. *Journal of the American Statistical Association, 79,* 84–90.

Velicer, W. F. (1994). Time series models of individual substance abusers. In L. M. Collins & L. A. Seitz (Eds.), *Advances in data analysis for prevention intervention research* (NIDA Research Monograph No. 142, pp. 264–301). Rockville, MD: National Institute on Drug Abuse.

Velicer, W. F., Fraser, C., McDonald, R. P., & Harrop, J. W. (1986). Computer program GENTS. Kingston: University of Rhode Island.

Velicer, W. F., & Harrop, J. W. (1983). The reliability and accuracy of time series model identification. *Evaluation Review, 7,* 551–560.

Velicer, W. F., & McDonald, R. P. (1984). Time series analysis without model identification. *Multivariate Behavioral Research, 19,* 33–47.

Velicer, W. F., & McDonald, R. P. (1991). Cross-sectional time series: A general transformation approach. *Multivariate Behavioral Research, 26,* 247–254.

Velicer, W. F., Prochaska, J. O., Rossi, J. S., & Snow, M. (1992). Assessing outcome in smoking cessation studies. *Psychological Bulletin, 111,* 23–41.

Velicer, W. F., Redding, C. A., Richmond, R., Greeley, J., & Swift, W. (1992). A time series investigation of three nicotine regulation models. *Addictive Behaviors, 17,* 325–345.

Velicer, W. F., Rossi, J. S., Prochaska, J. O., & DiClemente, C. C. (1996). A criterion measurement model for health behavior change. *Addictive Behaviors, 21,* 555–584.

West, S. G., & Hepworth, J. T. (1991). Statistical issues in the study of temporal data: Daily experiences. *Journal of Personality, 59,* 609–662.

Wilkinson, L. (1986). SYSTAT: *The system of statistics.* Evanston, IL: SYSTAT.

Williams, E. A., & Gottman, J. M. (1982). A *user's guide to the Gottman–Williams time-series analysis computer programs for social scientists.* Cambridge, England: Cambridge University Press.

Wood, P., & Brown, D. (1994). The study of intraindividual differences by means of dynamic factor models: Rationale, implementation, and interpretation. *Psychological Bulletin, 116,* 166–186.

8

THE INTERACTIVE EFFECT OF ALCOHOL PREVENTION PROGRAMS IN HIGH SCHOOL CLASSES: AN ILLUSTRATION OF ITEM HOMOGENEITY SCALING AND MULTILEVEL ANALYSIS TECHNIQUES

ITA G. G. KREFT

In this chapter, I deal with problems related to measurement scale and measurement level of variables in an analysis of school-based prevention program research, which is illustrated using a data set collected by Graham, Collins, Wugalter, Chung, and Hansen (1991). Problems of measurement scale of variables are different from problems of measurement level of variables, although there is a relationship. The scale of the variable determines the options for data analysis techniques, and analysis techniques for data collected at different levels of the hierarchy (the student and the school class in our data) assume interval scale variables.

In school-based prevention program research designs, the data have

I want to thank John Graham for allowing me to use his data.

a hierarchically nested structure, in which students are nested in school classes. The most important variables are pre- and posttest alcohol consumption, or pre- and posttest smoking, as measured before and after drug prevention programs are administered. Drinking is measured as the number of drinks of alcohol per week, per month, or per lifetime. Smoking is measured as the number of cigarettes smoked per week, per month, or per lifetime. Other variables include gender, parents' socioeconomic status (SES), the behavior of friends, and rebelliousness. All these variables are measured at the individual student level, but the program is delivered to school classes. If the appropriate unit of analysis is the student instead of the class, the problem of intraclass correlation needs to be solved because students in the same class are not independent observations. Researchers in the past have opted for class-level analysis, which avoids the problem of intraclass correlation, but it subsequently ignores individual student characteristics. Another disadvantage of an aggregated analysis is that the results are not necessarily valid at the student level. Inferences about students based on class-level analysis can be biased. This is known as *aggregation bias* (see Robinson, 1950).

Multilevel analysis incorporates both levels in the model so that no choice needs to be made between an individual-level analysis and an aggregate class-level analysis. The advantages of such a strategy for the analysis of school-based prevention research are substantial. Obviously, using the students as unit of analysis enhances the number of observations and thus the power of the analysis compared with an analysis at the school class level. The technique corrects for intraclass correlations. Intraclass correlations are assumed to be present when units in the same group share a history or environment. In school-based research, students in the same class are assumed to be more similar to each other than to students in other classes because of the shared school experience and school climate. Multilevel analysis, as proposed in this chapter, is a linear regression technique with varying (more precisely, "random") coefficients. The coefficients estimate effects of individual student characteristics on alcohol consumption and are allowed to vary randomly at the higher level, the school class. These models, called *random coefficient* (RC) *models* for the analysis of hierarchically nested data, are more general and complicated regression models than traditional regression models.

The problem with the measurement scale of variables arises after a multilevel regression technique is chosen. Variables can be used successfully in regression only if the measurement scale of these variables is at least interval. Many variables in data are of a Likert-type scale at best, and most often are not even that. In the example used in this chapter, the scale of the variables is "never" (1), "hardly ever" (2), "sometimes" (3), and "most of the time" (4). The four categories are indicated by the numbers 1, 2, 3, and 4, but the numbers 1, 4, 6, and 8 or 1, 5, 7, and 9, and so on, are equally useful because all contain the same information about ordering. When the values one assigns to categories are used for calculation (e.g., to calculate) or for executing a regression, it makes a difference which numbers are used. In particular, when responses are concentrated at one end of the scale, as is the case for some of the variables, it is debatable whether the sale of these variables is interval. One way of checking for this assumption is to execute a homogeneity analysis and compare the original category quantifications with the outcome of such an analysis.

Rescaling of categorical variables into variables with an interval or numerical scale has several advantages for an analysis because it makes the variables fit for multilevel analysis and reduces the number of potential explanatory variables in models. This scaling method also is used to summarize correlated variables that measure the same theoretical construct. In my data, three variables that measure a type of behavior labeled *rebelliousness* are scaled into one single variable. This type of data reduction is especially important for RC modeling. The freedom to allow coefficients to vary over classes in RC models means that more parameters have to be estimated. The trade-off is that seemingly simple models with only a few explanatory variables tend to become complex, so that the use of a small number of explanatory variables is advisable. To reduce the number of correlated explanatory variables, techniques such as homogeneity analysis are helpful. Before I go into more detail about homogeneity analysis and RC models, I briefly describe the data.

DATA DESCRIPTION

Throughout this chapter, I use data collected by Graham, Marks, and Hansen (1991) during the Adolescent Alcohol Prevention Trial (AAPT), a longitudinal study of students. The data are a subset of the AAPT data, with 1,400 students in 118 classes, measured at two points in time: once in seventh trade, the pretest of 1987, and once in eighth grade, the posttest of 1988. The level of alcohol consumption or the number of cigarettes smoked was measured before and after the administration of drug prevention programs in seventh and eighth grades, respectively. In all analyses, the response variable is posttest alcohol, or posttest smoking, predicted by several explanatory variables, some at the student level and some at the school class level. The student-level variables are pre- and posttest alcohol use, or pre- and posttest smoking, rebelliousness, and background variables such as gender, SES, and race. Characteristics of students are added to the analysis models as control variables. The variables of gender (1 = male, 0 = female) and race (White = 1, other = 0) are dichotomous.

The class-level explanatory variables are normative education, (NORM; coded 1 for students who receive this program and 0 for all others) and aggregated variables such as class mean for rebelliousness and class mean for alcohol use. The two means are used as proxies for class climate. A low mean for alcohol consumption creates a climate in which alcohol consumption is not a regular feature for students in that class. It is assumed that alcohol consumption, as well as smoking, are social events and stimulated by high levels of consumption in a class. Furthermore, a low mean level of rebelliousness is an indication of an orderly classroom. The hypothesis tested in this chapter is that alcohol consumption and smoking can be related to the degree of rebelliousness in seventh grade.

HOMOGENEITY ANALYSIS

Three rebelliousness variables were rescaled using the software HOM-ALS (short for homogeneity analysis by alternating least squares). The name HOMALS, like LISREL, is a technique (see Gifi, 1990; Van der Geer 1993a, 1993b) as well as a software program (Categories, 1990). The technique is known as "correspondence analysis." The concept of homogeneity can be explained as follows: By using the technique of HOMALS, one obtains perfect homogeneity in relation to the three variables if these three can be replaced by a single variable that contains the same information. If perfect homogeneity cannot be attained, the researcher should look for maximum homogeneity. The search for this single variable can be compared with the search for a principal component, as in traditional principal-components analysis (PCA). The three variables I use in my search for one single variable are all nominal, with four categories each (see Table 1). The scaling into one single summary variable is done in two steps: (a) In Step 1, the nominal and ordinal variables are transformed (see Table 1), and (b) in Step 2, a classic PCA is executed. Then, depending on the outcome of the PCA, the transformation of the variables is adjusted and a new PCA on these adjusted variables is done. The two steps are repeated until the process stabilizes.

In the first step with the rescaling of variables, different numbers are assigned to the original categories of the variables. After convergence, the new categories (see the second column in Table 1) reflect the distance of the categories as they appear after execution of the HOMALS analysis on this data set.

The categories of the original variables, for instance, Variable 3, are "hardly ever or never," "sometimes," "often," and "most of the time." These categories are indicated, respectively, by the numbers 1, 2, 3, and 4, which seems to imply that the scale of these variables is an interval one. To check for the appropriateness of this assumption, a HOMALS analysis is executed, and the original category quantifications are compared with the "optimal" HOMALS category quantifications (see Table 1). Table 1 shows

TABLE 1
Three Variables for Rebelliousness

Category	HOMALS quantification	No. observations
Rebel Variable 1: How much of what you learn in school is a waste of time?		
1. Hardly any or none	−0.90	441
2. Some of it	0.07	568
3. Most of it	0.85	329
4. All of it	1.29	62
Rebel Variable 2: Is it worth getting into trouble if you have fun?		
1. No, never	−0.78	649
2. Yes, but hardly ever	0.38	449
3. Yes, sometimes	1.09	236
4. Yes, most of the time	1.23	66
Rebel Variable 3: How often do you do things you have been told not to do?		
1. Hardly ever or never	−1.52	124
2. Sometimes	−0.51	542
3. Often	0.52	496
4. Most of the time	0.86	238

Note. Rebel = rebelliousness; HOMALS = homogeneity analysis by alternating least squares.

that the ordering of the categories is still the same but that the distance between categories is no longer constant. The distance between Category 4 "most of the time" and Category 3 "often" is smaller in Variable 3. In the same way, one finds that for Variable 2, the distance between Category 3 "sometimes" and Category 4 "most of the time" is smaller than between other categories.

Description of HOMALS as a PCA

HOMALS was described earlier as a classical PCA on optimal quantified variables. PCA is the traditional method used for data reduction of numerical multivariate data. If data contain categorical variables or have mixed measurement levels, then classical PCA is not an appropriate technique. Better techniques are HOMALS and PRINCALS (Categories, 1990), which are generalizations of PCA. These generalizations can be best described in terms of the two iterated steps: a scaling step and a PCA step.

The scaling shows that the assumption of an interval scale was too strong (see Table 1). In the next step, the three rescaled variables are summarized into one single scale for rebelliousness, which can be illustrated with a cross-break table of the first two variables of rebelliousness (note that three variables can be summarized in three bivariate tables, of which only one is shown here; see Table 2).

If one were to analyze such a table in the usual way (e.g., with a chi-square statistic), one would conclude that many students who think that schoolwork is hardly ever a waste of time (Category 1) also think that it

TABLE 2
A Cross-Break Table Between Two Variables
Measuring Rebelliousness

Rows: "Is it worth getting into trouble if you have fun?"
Columns: "How much of what you learn in school is a waste of time?"

Category	Hardly any	Some of it	Most of it	All of it	Total
Never	297	88	47	9	441
Hardly ever	250	212	80	26	568
Sometimes	91	129	90	19	329
Most of the time	11	20	19	12	62
Total	649	449	236	66	1,400

is not worth getting into trouble for fun (297 of the 441 who think so). On the other hand, of the 649 students who think that school is "hardly ever" a waste of time, 91 think that having fun is sometimes worth getting into trouble for, and 11 students think it is worth getting into trouble most of the time. Of the 329 students who think that having fun is sometimes worth getting into trouble, 90 think that school is mostly a "waste of time," and 19 even think that school is a waste "all of the time."

That the three variables do not measure exactly the same thing also is clear if the correlation between the original variables is calculated. In Table 3, one can see that these correlations, using the original category quantifications, are low. None is higher than .35.[1] The three variables correlate, respectively, .75, .70, and .70 with the new variable for rebelliousness, HOMALS. The original variable correlate .32, .25, and .35 with each other, which is much lower than with the new HOMALS variable.

Transformation of the original category identifications (from 1 to 4) to HOMALS quantifications is based on the idea of optimalization of correlations among variables. In Table 3, the correlation between the newly constructed variable (HOMALS) and the original variables is shown. These correlations are calculated in the traditional way in SPSS by using the original variables with the original category quantifications. In the output of the HOMALS program, these correlations are called *discrimination measures*. A discrimination measure is defined as the proportion variation that a variable, transformed in Step 1, has in common with the first dimension of the PCA analysis, which is executed as Step 2. The three

---

[1]This problem is equally large in the measurements for alcohol consumption. The variables have 8-point scales with categories such as 1 = none, 2 = a sip, 3 = part of a drink, 4 = 2–4 drinks, 5 = 5–10 drinks, 6 = 11–20 drinks, 7 = 21–100 drinks, and 8 = 100+ drinks. The same question is repeated for lifetime, over the last month, and over the last week with slightly different scales. Assuming equal distances over these scales is disputable. Besides, these variables are extremely skewed to nondrinkers (Category 1) and show inconsistencies over questions. Scaling these variables with HOMALS and converting them into one single variable improve the reliability of a measurement for drinking behavior considerably. The latter application of HOMALS appears in Kreft (1996, in press).

TABLE 3
Correlations Between Three Rebelliousness Variables and the HOMALS Dimension

Variable	Rebel 1	Rebel 2	Rebel 3	HOMALS
Rebel 1	—			
Rebel 2	.32	—		
Rebel 3	.25	.35	—	
HOMALS construct	.70	.75	.70	—

Note. Rebel = rebelliousness; HOMALS = homogeneity analysis by alternating least squares.

discrimination measures (read the squared correlations) are .50, .60, and .53, respectively, for the three variables. It shows that the three variables contribute equally well to the new dimension, with the second variable having a slightly higher discrimination measure. As a result of standardization, the discrimination measure of a variable is also a measure of the variance of the rescaled variable. The more variance, the more distance is present between the categories of that rescaled variable, and the more that variable contributes to the underlying dimension. In my data set, the variable with the largest variance, or the largest discrimination measure, is Variable 1, "How much of what you learn in school is a waste of time?"

HOMALS creates a weighted sum of the three variables, by way of "borrowing of strength." The first principal component (or first dimension) is the weighted sum of the three variables with maximal variance:

$$PC_1 = w_1Y_1 + w_2Y_2 + w_3Y_3. \tag{1}$$

The weights (w) in Equation 1 are the correlations of the variables with that dimension. The weights or component loadings are chosen by the technique in such a way that it maximizes the distance between different categories of the variables (e.g., between the categories of "never" and "always") and also minimizes the distance between students who answer the same for that variable. As is shown earlier, in Table 2, students who fall in the same category for one variable may not necessarily fall in the same category for the other variable. By alternating least squares, the optimalization process alternates between the best least squares solution for the scaling of the categories to the best least squares solution for the scaling of the students. Just as in other scaling techniques, a measure for similarity is expressed as distance, as shown in Figure 1.

The category quantifications of all three variables in Figure 1 show that categories are scaled far apart on both dimensions. Individual observations (called *objects* in HOMALS output) of the students are scaled in the same dimension. The same principle applies to category scaling as to

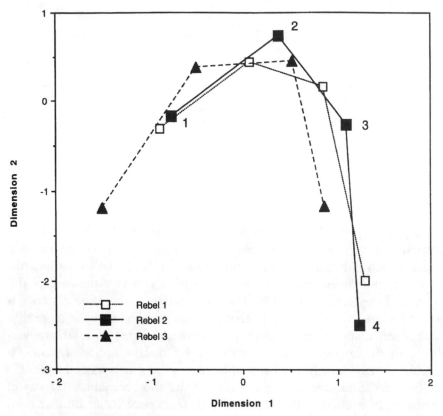

Figure 1. Category quantifications of the three rebellious variables.

object scaling. Categories that are often chosen together by respondents are scaled close together, and students with the same answering patterns are scaled close together. If one imagines the students in the figure who answer Variable 2, "yes sometimes," they would be scaled so that they are positioned in space around this category, which is Category 3, dark square.

A variable "discriminates" well between students if its discrimination measure is large. This is the same as the variable having a large variance because its categories are far apart. At the same time, the distance between a student score on the dimension and the categories to which he or she belongs needs to be as small as possible, based on the principle that the student and that category resemble each other. The solution is a compromise. A category (see again Figure 1) is the center of all students who score in that category.

Figure 1 shows that categories are defined at two dimensions, and subsequently there are two scores for each student, one score on Dimension 1 and one score on Dimension 2. The first dimension has the largest eigenvalue and the highest discrimination measures for all three variables,

TABLE 4
The Prediction of Alcohol Use by Rebelliousness in Two Ways

Variable	Regression analysis 1		Regression analysis 2	
	b	SE	b	SE
Rebel 1	.12	.03		
Rebel 2	.16	.03		
Rebel 3	.13	.03		
HOMALS construct			.24	.02

Note. Rebel = rebelliousness; HOMALS = homogeneity analysis by alternating least squares.

where an eigenvalue is defined as the average of the discrimination measures. The eigenvalue for Dimension 1 is the average of .50, .60, and .53. The object scores of students on this first dimension are used as the scores on the newly created variable of rebelliousness in subsequent analyses, where a high score indicates a high level of rebelliousness.

In Table 4, the results of two traditional regression analyses are reported. The first one shows the regression coefficients of three variables for rebelliousness predicting the alcohol posttest. The second analysis has only one regression coefficient predicting alcohol posttest, which is the effect of the new HOMALS construct for rebelliousness. The last analysis explains 6%, whereas the analysis with the three separate items (Rebels 1, 2, 3) explains 7% (R^2s = .07 and .06, respectively). The advantage of using only one variable, the HOMALS construct, is that multicollinearity is avoided while the model fit is not significantly reduced.

INTRODUCTION TO MULTILEVEL MODELING

Using All Measurements at the Student and Class Levels

When samples of existing groups, such as schools or school classes, are drawn, classes instead of individuals are assigned to treatments. Note that the concept *group* is used to refer to natural groups, such as school classes, and does not refer to the concept of treatment or treatment groups. The data have a natural nested hierarchy in school-based prevention programs, in which students are nested in classes and classes are nested in schools. As a result, researchers collect data at all levels of the hierarchy and are interested in the effect of measurements obtained at different levels. Questions are asked about the effect of student characteristics (e.g., rebelliousness) and class-level characteristics (e.g., mean rebelliousness level of a class) on the response variable (either drinking or smoking). In summary, researchers want to analyze the data collected at different levels simultaneously in a single analysis. However, analyzing this type of multi-level data has its specific problems. Problems such as intraclass correlations make traditional analysis techniques less well suited for this type of data. Multilevel data need multilevel techniques.

The Need for Multilevel Models

Observations that are close in time, space, or both are more likely to be similar than observations far apart in time, space, or both. Students in the same school are more alike than students in different schools because of shared experiences, shared environment, and so on. This sharing of context causes some dependency of the observations, also known as an *intraclass correlation* (see Barcikowski, 1981; Cochran, 1977). An intraclass correlation is the degree to which individuals share common experiences. In traditional linear models, the effect of omitted variables is summarized in the error term of the model. The assumption here is that individual errors are unrelated to each other because the omitted variables have a random instead of a structural effect. Because observations from the same group are not unrelated, and students in the same class, for instance, share at least some characteristics that are not modeled, a covariance between individual error terms will be present in regression models on the basis of such data. The omitted variables in my analyses represent structural influences of variables representing the shared school environment. For instance, in school-based prevention research, the differences among schools in school climate and peer pressure will remain largely unmeasured but are of great importance. School climate makes observations within schools more alike than observations between schools. The resulting intraclass correlation inflates the observed alpha level in traditional analyses, for instance in the F test of the analysis of variance (ANOVA; see Barcikowski, 1981). To avoid intraclass correlations, drug prevention researchers traditionally analyze the data at the group level by aggregating student characteristics to the school or class level. This practice does not really correct for intraclass correlations and leads to a loss of important student-level information.

The Analysis of Covariance as an Alternative

The object of interest in drug prevention program effectiveness research is clearly the effect of the program on the individual behavior of students. If one is willing to ignore the intraclass correlation analysis and its effect on the alpha level, an analysis of covariance (ANCOVA) is the best technique to establish program effects. An ANCOVA, however, has a disadvantage for these data. I can use it for testing whether drug prevention programs are effective, but I cannot go beyond that single conclusion.

If a program has an effect, I do not know where and when it has the optimal effect. If I find that programs have no effect (as I will find in this study), I have no means to explore what other influences are acting on the onset of drinking and smoking of teenagers. Neither can I establish whether the program has a possible effect through interaction with other characteristics present in the environment. For instance, "What is the effect of a drug prevention program in classes with a large number of rebellious students, as compared with classes with a low number of rebellious students? And what is the effect of drug prevention programs on special groups of students, such as high-risk students, and on boys as compared with girls?" These questions assume the existence of interaction effects between school class or student characteristics and drug prevention programs.

Interaction effects between characteristics of students (the lowest level in this research) and characteristics of school class, including the drug prevention intervention (the second level in this research), are called *cross-level interactions*. Cross-level indicates that interactions are between characteristics of one level, the student, and the other level, the class. Questions with cross-level interactions cannot be answered using an ANCOVA. These questions need a more sophisticated technique. Such techniques are available in different software packages for the analysis of hierarchically nested data (see the Appendix). They can handle these types of questions and can also take care of the intraclass correlation. Before introducing the RC model on which these techniques are based, however, I discuss the main distinction between single-level analysis (i.e., either at the single level of the student or at the single level of the class) and multilevel analysis. In multilevel analysis, a distinction is made between the variance within and between classes, a distinction that can be explained best by showing that variances of variables in multilevel data can be divided in two parts: within and between groups. The analogy between variances of variables and variances of coefficients can be made.

Variance Between Classes and Variance Within Classes and RCs

In hierarchically nested data with two levels of measurement (i.e., the class and the student), the variances of variables, as well as the covariance between two variables, can be divided into a between-schools class and a within-schools class matrix. The distinction of a within and a between variation in variables is not as straightforward and differs from technique to technique. Starting with the variances between (B) and within (W), I know that the total (T) variance of explanatory variable X and response variable Y in a regression can be divided into a between- and a within-groups compound, written as variance total (V) is

$$V(X_T) = V(X_B) + V(X_W) \qquad (2)$$

and

$$V(Y_T) = V(Y_B) + V(Y_W), \qquad (3)$$

where the indexes T, B, and W denote total variance, between-groups variance, and within-groups variance, respectively. The total covariance (C) between variables X and Y can be divided in the same way in a within and a between part, as follows:

$$C(X_T, Y_T) = C(X_B, Y_B) + C(X_W, Y_W), \qquad (4)$$

where C denotes covariance.

The regression coefficients for a student-level analysis, ignoring the fact that the students are clustered within classes, is denoted by the regression coefficient over the total sample, b_T. Moreover, in an aggregated regression, with classes as the unit of analysis, the coefficient b would be defined as a between-groups coefficient, b_B. A regression coefficient for within groups, as in the pooled within regression coefficient in ANCOVA, would be defined as b_W. These three coefficients will not yield necessarily the same values, as is clear from the following definitions (see also Robinson, 1950):

$$b_T = C(X_T, Y_T)/V(X_T)$$

$$b_B = C(X_B, Y_B)/V(X_B)$$

$$b_W = C(X_W, Y_W)/V(X_W). \qquad (5)$$

The different definitions of regression coefficients also can be explained by using the correlation ratio. The correlation ratio is the percentage group variance of a variable:

$$\eta^2(X) = V(X_B)/V(X_T)$$

$$\eta^2(Y) = V(Y_B)/V(Y_T). \qquad (6)$$

Equation 6 shows group variation in the response variable Y as the percentage of the total variance in Y declared between groups, which is the definition of the intraclass correlation. If groups are equal in their means for the response variable, $\eta^2(Y)$ is zero and so is the intraclass correlation. If groups are heterogeneous and much different from each other, $\eta^2(Y)$ is large, and the intraclass correlation is large.

The coefficients in regression are related to this correlation ratio in the following way. The best estimate of b for the regression over the total sample, irrespective of group membership, is b_T. In most school-based research in which the variables are measured at different levels, b_T has a value that is a weighted composite of b_B and b_W, with weights $\eta^2(X)$ and $1 - \eta^2(X)$, as shown in the following equation (see Boyd & Iversen, 1979; Burstein, 1980; Duncan, Curzort, & Duncan, 1966):

$$b_T = \eta^2(X)b_B + [1 - \eta^2(X)]b_W. \tag{7}$$

Equation 7 shows that b_T is only a valid estimate for the student-level slope (b_W) if grouping is unrelated to the outcome of the research or if there is no context effect and $\eta^2(X) = 0$. In a regression model over the total sample, b_T does not separate context effects from individual effects, which makes the total model not a good model for the data. On the other hand, an aggregated class-level model does not estimate individual student effects, and such a model is equally inappropriate for the data.

If a researcher is interested in both effects, the student level (the within effect) and the class level (the between effect), the conclusion is that a total analysis only gives reliable estimates if $b_T = b_W$ and $b_B = 0$, which means that there is no school class-level effect; all variation is within students. The same is valid for aggregated analysis, which only gives reliable estimates of b_B when $b_T = b_B$, where $b_W = 0$ (i.e., when there is no student effect and all variation in the important variables is at the class level). For school-based prevention program research, the expectation is that some of the variation in drinking and smoking is at the individual student level, and some is at the class level, the level at which the drug prevention treatment takes place. One could get a valid picture of both b_B and b_W by doing both analyses, but this would not provide an opportunity to incorporate cross-level effects.

The idea of fixed and random coefficients applies equally to a distinction of variation within and between contexts. In ordinary regression models, the parameter estimates, the coefficients that specifying the regression line, are the intercept and slopes. Traditionally, these coefficients are assumed to be fixed, whereas in RC models, the coefficients have values that are assumed to vary randomly over contexts or varying over school classes in the data. A random coefficient for the slope parameter has a mean slope, estimated over all students and all classes, plus a variance over school classes. This variance is a measure of deviation of school classes from the overall estimated value for the slope. The same is true for the intercept. The overall intercept is estimated as one single value over all students, and its variance is a measure for the deviation of school classes from this overall intercept.

RC Models for Multilevel Analysis

The next section includes a technical discussion of RC models. For readers seeking an overview, the parts that can be easily skipped. For technical details, also see the Suggested Reading list.

I start with the following basic equation:

$$\underline{Y}_{ij} = \underline{a}_j + \underline{b}_j X_{ij} + \underline{e}_{ij}. \tag{8}$$

Equation 8 shows a simple regression equation with one explanatory variable, the alcohol pretest (X) predicting the alcohol posttest (Y). The equation looks like the usual regression equation, except that the coefficients are underlined. This convention is introduced (following De Leeuw & Kreft, 1986) to distinguish random coefficients from fixed coefficients by way of underlining. In all equations, the index i is used for students, and index j is used to distinguish school classes. A traditional regression equation has only one random term: the student-level error term (e_{ij}). Equation 8 represents an RC model instead of a traditional regression model. The underlining and the subscript j for intercept and slope indicate that more random terms are present than the one for the student level only. The class-level errors for intercept and slope are in Equations 9 and 10, in which each coefficient has its own error term.

$$\underline{a}_j = \gamma_{00} + \underline{\delta}_{0j} \tag{9}$$

$$\underline{b}_j = \gamma_{10} + \underline{\delta}_{1j}. \tag{10}$$

Equation 9 shows that the intercept $(\underline{a}_j)$ is underlined and has a subscript j, which means that it is allowed to vary randomly from school class to school class, as indicated by the error term, $(\underline{\delta}_{0j})$. Equation 10 shows the same, but here the regression coefficient $(\underline{b})_j$ for individual pretest alcohol consumption (X_{ij}) on individual posttest alcohol consumption $(\underline{Y}_{ij})$ is allowed to vary. The subscript j is an indication that the coefficients vary over the j contexts.

For each error term, a variance is estimated, in which a large error variance is a sign of large variation among school classes for that particular coefficient. A large variation in a coefficient among school classes also indicates that a traditional regression analysis with fixed coefficients would not fit the data well because a significant variance means that classes differ from the fixed regression coefficient. The opposite also is true: If the error variances of the intercept, slope, or both are small, the traditional (fixed) regression line fits well. In the latter case, the line would represent all school classes well because individual classes do not differ from the overall solution. A fixed slope is comparable to the ANCOVA, in which the pooled within slope is estimated. In RC models, hypotheses are tested that school classes differ in their overall means (see Equation 9), as well as in their slope, here the relationship between pre- and posttest (see Equation 10), or both.

Description of Notation in Equations 9 and 10

Variable a_j is the random intercept, b_j is the random slope, and e_{ij} is the microlevel error term. It is assumed that e_{ij}s have zero expectation, are independent, and are normally and identically distributed. The variance of e_{ij} is equal to s^2. The simple model described in Equations 9 and 10 contains no variables measured at class level. The only indication of the presence of class effects is the subscript j. The equations express the properties of the random slope and intercept in terms of overall population values plus error. Equations 9 and 10 could be expanded easily by including class-level explanatory variables. What follows next is valid for both cases, with or without a class-level variable.

The subscripts in Equations 9 and 10 are defined as follows: The first index is the number of the variable at the microlevel, and the second represents the number of the variable at the macrolevel. Hence, γ_{st} is the effect of the macrolevel t on the regression coefficient of microvariable s. Zero signifies the intercept (i.e., the variable with all values equal to 1, either at the micro- or at the macrolevel). For instance, γ_{00} is the effect of the macrolevel intercept on the microlevel coefficient of the intercept. The macrolevel errors (or variances) δ_{0j} and δ_{1j} in Equations 9 and 10, respectively, indicate that both the intercept a_j and b_j are allowed to vary over contexts. The estimate for the intercept in Equation 9 is γ_{00}, whereas δ_{0j} (the macroerror term) measures the deviation of each context from the overall or mean intercept. The same happens in Equation 10, where the slope estimate across all contexts is γ_{10}, and δ_{1j} represents the deviation of each context from this overall or mean slope. Substituting Equations 9 and 10 in Equation 8 shows in Equations 11a and 11b that an RC model resembles a regression model, with only a complicated error term (in parentheses in Equation 11b):

$$Y_{ij} = (\gamma_{00} + \delta_{0j}) + (\gamma_{10} + \delta_{1j})X_{ij} + e_{ij}. \qquad (11a)$$

Expanding and rearranging terms in Equations 11a and 11b:

$$Y_{ij} = \gamma_{00} + \gamma_{10}X_{ij} + (\delta_{0j} + \delta_{1j}X_{ij} + e_{ij}). \qquad (11b)$$

Equations 9 and 10 show that the parameters of RC models with two levels include *regression parameter estimates* and *variance components*. The fixed parts of the regression coefficients are represented by γ_{00} and γ_{10}, the first terms of the macrolevel Equations 9 and 10. The random parts of the regression coefficients are $\underline{\delta}_{0j}$ and $\underline{\delta}_{1j}$ with variances w_{00} and w_{11} and covariance w_{10}. The macrolevel disturbance is $(\underline{\delta}_{0j} + \underline{\delta}_{1j}X_{ij})$, whereas the microlevel disturbance $\underline{e}_{ij}$ is assumed to be unrelated to these macrolevel disturbances.

The variances of the macro errors $\underline{\delta}_{0j}$ and $\underline{\delta}_{1j}$ and their covariance are parameters of the model and are given in the matrix Ω. The terms in Ω are referred to as *variance components* of the model. For the omegas; the subscripts all refer to macrolevel variables. This means that ω_{st} is the covariance between random regression coefficients s and t. Zero refers again to the random intercept:

$$\Omega = \begin{array}{c c c} & \underline{\delta}_{0j} & \underline{\delta}_{1j} \\ \underline{\delta}_{0j} & \omega_{00} & \omega_{01} \\ \underline{\delta}_{1j} & \omega_{10} & \omega_{11} \end{array} . \tag{12}$$

In the application of RC modeling to my data, I used the program VARCL (Longford, 1990; see the Appendix for a description of the different software for the analyses of hierarchical linear models).

RESULTS

The application of this multilevel analysis starts with the most simple model using one explanatory variable: pretest alcohol consumption, predicting the response variable, posttest alcohol consumption. The goal is to establish how much variation in intercept and slope is present in my data. If no significant variation among school classes is found in this model, I know that school classes behave in the same way. In that case, no RC model is needed to fit the data because classes show no differences and no context effects are present, including no effect of drug prevention program NORM. In Table 5, the result of this analysis is reported.

As expected, the coefficient for the pretest was significant, showing that it predicted the posttest level of alcohol consumption. More interesting, however, was that both variances for the random coefficients were significantly different from zero, indicating that both intercept and slope varied in a significant way over classes. The next logical step was to find the explanatory variables at the class level that could explain these differences among school classes. The most obvious variable was the drug prevention program NORM, coded 1 for classes that received this program and 0 for all other classes.

TABLE 5
An RC Model With Alcohol Use as the Response Variable

Variable	Estimate	SE
Fixed part variable		
Intercept	0.97	NA
Pretest	0.27	.07**
Random part Level 2 variances for		
Intercept	0.11	.04*
Pretest	0.40	.06**
Covariance	0.04	.01**
Deviance	3,632.90	

Note. The model has a random intercept and a random slope. NA = not available. VARCL output does not provide a standard error for the intercept coefficient.
*$p < .05$. **$p < .01$.

Second Analysis: Adding the Class-Level Variable NORM

A next step was to add second-level variables to the model, variables that could take away some or all of the variation in intercept, and in slope. The slope showed a large variation and differed widely across school classes, more than intercepts did, which means that variation among classes was largely in the relationship between pre- and posttest. To explain that variation in the coefficient for pretest, I introduce the variable NORM in two ways, as main effect and as moderator effect. In the first analysis in this section, I introduce NORM as interacting with the intercept and in the second analysis as interacting with the slope of the pretest, a so-called *cross-level interaction*, or moderator effect. The algebra involved in this modeling is explained next and can be easily skipped.

I begin again with the basic Equation 8:

$$\underline{Y}_{ij} = \underline{a}_j + \underline{b}_j X_{ij} + \underline{e}_{ij}.$$

In the analysis, NORM is introduced as Z_j in the equations. In the first analysis in this section, NORM is related only to the intercept, as shown in Equation 12a:

$$\underline{a}_j = \gamma_{00} + \gamma_{01} Z_j + \underline{\delta}_{0j}. \tag{12a}$$

In the second analysis of this section, NORM is again introduced, but this time in relation to the random slope for pretest, as in Equation 12b:

$$\underline{b}_j = \gamma_{10} + \gamma_{11} Z_j + \underline{\delta}_{1j}. \tag{12b}$$

This last equation resembles Equation 12a, containing the same variable Z_j. The difference between both equations becomes clear when I substitute Equations 12a and 12b in Equation 8, which yields Equation 13. In Equation 13, an interaction term is present (Z_jX_{ij}). Observe the subscripts in the last term, indicating a cross-level interaction because Z_j (NORM) has the subscript j for groups, whereas the X_{ij} (pretest) has the subscripts ij for individuals i in groups j:

$$Y_{ij} = \gamma_{00} + \gamma_{01}Z_j + \gamma_{10}X_{ij} + \gamma_{11}Z_jX_{ij} + (\underline{\delta}_{0j} + \underline{\delta}_{1j}X_{ij} + \underline{e}_{ij}). \quad (13)$$

Note that Equation 13 is not much different from Equation 11b, except for two new explanatory variables, Z_j and Z_jX_{ij}. The error term is still the same, consisting of three parts (in parentheses).

The results of the two multilevel analyses with NORM are shown in Table 6, in which Model 1 has NORM as a main effect and Model 2 has NORM as main effect and moderator effect. The most important conclusion based on the two analyses in Table 6 is that the drug prevention program NORM had no significant effect. NORM was not effective as a main effect or as an interaction effect. The interaction effect showed that NORM did not significantly affect the relationship between pre- and posttest alcohol consumption in school classes in which this program was administered, compared with school classes that did not receive this program. Interestingly, the estimates of the fixed coefficients (in the first part of Table 6) changed over the two models. The addition of an interaction effect between the two variables in the model caused both to change in magni-

TABLE 6
Two Analyses With NORM as the Second-Level Variable
and Interaction

Variable	Model 1		Model 2	
	Estimate	SE	Estimate	SE
Fixed part coefficients				
Intercept	0.99	NA	0.90	NA
Pretest	0.27	0.07*	0.36	0.09*
NORM	−0.06	0.05	0.16	0.15
NORM × Pretest			−0.21	0.14
Random part Level 2 variances for				
Intercept	0.11	0.04	0.10	0.04
Pretest	0.40	0.06	0.40	0.06
Covariance	0.04	0.01	0.04	0.01
Deviance	3,631.68		3,629.29	

Note. NA = not available; NORM = normative education.
*$p < .05$.

tude as a result of multicollinearity between the main variables and the interaction variable.

The conclusion that NORM is not effective in reducing or changing alcohol consumption can be reached in different ways on the basis of the output of this analysis. The first way is by looking at the individual coefficients and comparing them with their respective standard errors. However, looking at individual coefficients can be misleading because correlations among variables in the model can make some coefficients appear insignificant, even though they are important. Comparing the goodness of fit of the total model is a far better way to establish whether NORM is effective. I do that by comparing deviances of models.[2] The difference in deviances between the two models in Table 6 is given as follows: $3,631.68 - 3,629.29 = 2.39$. From the small differences I conclude that the addition of a crosslevel interaction does not lead to a substantial improvement of model fit. A comparison of the model in Table 5, in which no NORM is present, with Model 1 in Table 6 shows the same insignificant difference of $3,632.90 - 3,631.68 = 1.22$ in deviance. Another method is observing the second-level variances of intercept and slope. If these are reduced by adding NORM to the model, one may find some effect. If NORM is effective as a main effect, the intercept variance will decrease. If adding the cross-level interaction with NORM affects the variance of the slope, one finds some effect of NORM here. Comparing the second-level variances over the two models in Table 6 and the model in Table 5 shows that the variances have not changed in any significant way by adding NORM or as main effect on the intercept variance or as a cross-level or moderator effect on the slope variance.

More Complex Multilevel Models

In the next analysis, five student-level explanatory variables and two class-level explanatory variables were used. The student-level variables in the model were sex, race (White = 0, other = 1), SES, pretest alcohol use, and rebelliousness. The second-level variables were NORM (the prevention program; yes = 1, no = 0), mean level of alcohol use in a class, and the mean level of rebelliousness of the school class. An interaction between NORM and mean rebelliousness also was added to the model.

In Model 1 of Table 7, an analysis is reported in which the hypothesis was tested that NORM had an interaction effect with rebellious classes.

---

[2]The deviance of a model is minus 2 times the log likelihood. The log likelihood results from maximum-likelihood estimation, the method used to estimate the parameters in the model. The difference in deviances between models is distributed as a chi-square distribution. The difference can be compared in the usual way with the number of degrees of freedom gained, when a smaller, more parsimonious model is fitted. The degrees of freedom are calculated as the difference in the number of parameter estimates among models.

TABLE 7
An RC Model With Alcohol Use as the Response Variable, a Random Intercept, and Fixed Slopes

Variable	Model 1		Model 2	
	Estimate	SE	Estimate	SE
Intercept	1.00	NA	1.03	NA
Sex	−0.06	0.05		
Race	0.01	0.04		
SES	0.01	0.01		
Pretest	0.37	0.07**	0.24	0.03**
Rebelliousness	−0.23	0.06**	−0.20	0.03**
NORM	0.17	0.10	−0.06	0.05
Alcohol mean	−0.10	0.12		
Rebelliousness mean	0.00	0.12		
Interaction (NORM × Mean Rebelliousness)	−0.13	0.17		
Random part Level 2 variance for intercept	0.10	0.05*	0.10	0.05*
Deviance	3,653.69			3,667.86

Note. NORM = normative education; SES = socioeconomic status; NA = not available.
*$p < .05$.   **$p < .01$.

Rebellious classes resented the program message, making NORM ineffective, whereas it was hypothesized that NORM would be more effective in classes with low levels of rebelliousness.[3] The main effect of NORM also was included in this analysis. Although it was shown before that NORM had no significant main effect, I kept NORM in the analysis as the most important variable of this data. To test the conclusion that pretest as well as student rebelliousness significantly affected posttest alcohol consumption, I fit a new model, Model 2 in Table 7, in which all variables with nonsignificant parameters were deleted. The deviance of the latter model was 3,667.85. Comparing the two deviances of the models in Table 7 yielded a difference of 14.16, with six more parameters estimated in the first model.[4] I concluded that Table 7 shows that gender, SES, and race had no significant effect on the posttest after controlling for pretest. No support was found either for the hypothesized interaction between rebelliousness level of a school class and NORM. NORM showed no significant main effect or moderator effect.

---

[3] This hypothesis was based on personal communication with John Graham, who collected the data used in this chapter.

[4] In the remainder of this chapter, models are discussed in terms of goodness of fit instead of observing individual coefficients. Although the asterisks indicate that a coefficient was significant, my conclusions are based on the total model fit (deviance and degrees of freedom) rather than on a single test of individual coefficients.

TABLE 8
Individual Model for Alcohol Use With Two Random Slopes and the
Class-Level Drug Prevention Program NORM

Variable	Estimate	SE
Fixed part variable		
Intercept	1.07	NA
Pretest	0.20	0.07*
Rebelliousness	0.20	0.03*
NORM	−0.05	0.05
Random part second-level variances for		
Intercept	0.08	0.04
Pretest	0.41	0.06*
Rebelliousness	0.14	0.03*
Deviance	3,539.42	

Note. NORM = normative education; NA = not available.
*$p < .01$.

Model 2 in Table 7 Repeated, With Random Slopes

In the next table, the same model as in Table 7 was fitted, except for a more extensive random part. All student-level coefficients for this model are random, making it a true RC model. In Table 8, three instead of one random effects are reported: the intercept variance and the two slope variances, one for pretest and one for rebelliousness. A comparison of the deviances between this model and the previous one (in Table 7) shows a large improvement of fit for the model in Table 8. The addition of the two random slopes (and the three covariance estimates) lowered the deviance to 3,539.42, a difference of 128.43, with 5 degrees of freedom, for the five extra variances that need to be estimated. This large difference in deviance indicates that a model with random slopes fit considerably better than a model with only a random intercept. The conclusion so far is that the fit of the model improved considerably by allowing slopes for pretest and rebelliousness to be random. The same was indicated by the fact that the variances for both slopes were highly significant. In the random part of Table 8, only the variances are reported, whereas the three covariances between the second-level variances (also part of the parameter estimates of the mode) are omitted.

Adding Cross-Level Interactions

A next step was to find class-level explanatory variables that were related to the variation of the two slopes and that "explained" why school classes were different in their relations between pre- and posttest and between rebelliousness and posttest. Something in the class context had lowered the relationship between prealcohol and postalcohol use in some classes. The question is, Why did rebelliousness and pretest have different

TABLE 9
Model With Alcohol as the Response Variable, Two Random Slopes,
and Two Cross-Level Interactions

Variable	Estimate	SE
Fixed part		
Intercept	1.05	
Pretest	0.23	0.07**
Rebelliousness	0.22	0.04**
Pretest × NORM	0.04	0.05
Rebel × NORM	−0.06	0.04
Random part second-level variances for		
Intercept	0.01	0.005*
Pretest	0.17	0.02**
Rebelliousness	0.02	0.004**
Deviance	3,536.70	

Note. NORM = normative education; Rebel = rebelliousness.
*$p < .05$. **$p < .01$.

effects on posttest alcohol consumption in some classes than in others? Obviously, my first choice was the program NORM expecting to see a negative coefficient as an indication of the lowering effect of NORM on these two variables that so strongly predict alcohol use. For that reason, I added two cross-level interactions to the next model, one between student pretest and NORM and another between student's rebelliousness and NORM. The results are shown in Table 9, indicating that the interactions were not significant and, more important, that the model fit was not significantly better than the fit of a model without such interactions. The difference in deviances between the models in Table 8 and Table 9 was 2.72 with 2 degrees of freedom.

Thus far, my attempt to find effects of NORM as main effect or as moderator effect has been unsuccessful. For illustrative purposes, I repeat the same analyses with another pre- and posttest. In the same data set, measures were present for pre- and posttest smoking. In the next analyses, I used this pre- and posttest in the search for NORM effects, again either as a main effect or as a cross-level or moderator effect.

ILLUSTRATIONS OF MULTILEVEL MODELING AND SMOKING

Illustration of a Significant Interaction Effect With Smoking

I was more successful in finding NORM effects with smoking as the response variable and pretest smoking as one of the explanatory variables. In Table 10, a significant cross-level interaction effect is reported. The cross-level interaction was between the program NORM and the student-level variable of rebelliousness. The same analysis was executed as when alcohol is the response variable (see Table 9), in which the same HOMALS

TABLE 10
Random Coefficient Model for Smoking With a Cross-Level Interaction

Variable	Estimate	SE
Fixed part variable		
Intercept	0.69	
Pretest	0.46	0.14**
Rebelliousness	0.12	0.03**
Rebel × NORM	−0.08	0.04*
Random part second-level variance		
Intercept	0.06	0.04
Pretest	0.64	0.12**
Rebelliousness	0.05	0.04

Note. NORM = normative education.
*$p < .05$. **$p < .01$.

construct for rebelliousness and the same drug prevention program NORM were part of the model. The only difference was that pre- and posttest were measured in the number of cigarettes smoked per week. As before, both student-level variables, pretest, and rebelliousness had random coefficients. On the basis of the hypothesis that NORM would have a lowering effect on the relationship between rebelliousness and smoking, I added this variable to the model as interacting with rebelliousness. The model shown in Table 10 tested whether the variance among school classes in the coefficient for rebelliousness could be (partly) attributed to the drug prevention program NORM.

Table 10 shows almost the same results as in the analyses with alcohol as pre- and posttest, in which pretest and rebelliousness were significantly related to posttest smoking. The difference is in the interaction term, where, this time, a significant effect is observed. The effect of this interaction was also clear from the variance of the slope for rebelliousness, which was reduced as a result of adding the interaction with NORM to the model. The variance is no longer significant. The negative coefficient for the interaction term Rebel × NORM meant there is a suppressing effect of NORM on the (strong and significant) relation between rebelliousness and the response variable: smoking. The coefficient for rebelliousness (.12) is reduced by a value of .08 in classes in which students received the program NORM. Students who did not get NORM had a zero value for this interaction. Table 10 also shows that the variance for the slope of the pretest is still significantly random over school classes, but I have not found class-level variables that could "explain" this variation.

CONCLUSION

Research on school-based drug prevention programs has not been successful in showing strong effects of any type of drug prevention program.

Many methodological problems are present in the analysis of this type of complex data, mostly related to measurement scale of variables and the analysis method. Previous research in this field made use of aggregation of student-level variables to class level to avoid the bias introduced when intraclass correlation is present. From the literature (e.g., Robinson, 1950), it is known that an aggregated analysis over the same data, in which student-level variables are aggregated to the class level, does not necessarily produce the same results as an analysis at the student level. Aggregated correlation coefficients are known to become larger and may even show a reversal of the sign. This aggregation bias is called the "Robinson effect" after Robinson's article, which strikingly illustrates this point. For that and other reasons, multilevel analysis seems to be the best technique at this moment. The expectations for the analysis of this type of data with multilevel analysis were high, but the results were disappointing. The drug prevention program NORM did not show a main effect under any condition; however, the weak but significant interaction effect between NORM and rebelliousness seems promising for future research. This type of analysis also invites research that determines what type of students are at risk for alcohol abuse and smoking and what type of drug prevention program would be most effective for such specific groups. Studies showing interaction effects between programs and individual characteristics support the conclusion that the same treatment is not effective for all types of students, most likely creating a need for drug prevention programs with different treatments for different groups of students.

No final conclusions can be drawn about the possibility that programs have a differential effect and that different programs for different students are needed based on my analyses alone. Before such conclusions can be reached, support is needed from other sources, either empirical evidence or theory. The significant cross-level interaction of the program NORM with rebellious students was not supported by theory, nor was it predicted by researchers in the field. To the contrary, the expectation was the opposite. It was expected that rebellious students would resent the program more than nonrebellious students and that mean levels of rebelliousness in classes would interact with NORM. This last hypothesis was not supported either, as shown by the analysis reported in Table 7, where the class mean of rebelliousness shows no significant effects.

Causal statements that are based on regression analyses without a supporting theory can be misleading, especially when a more complicated regression model, such as the RC model, is used (also see Draper, 1995). The smoking analyses results indicate a possible direction for future research, whereas the alcohol analyses do not show any such promise. Homogeneity analyses, in which variables are scaled, may offer help for constructing types of students in the same way I did with the scale for rebelliousness. If special groups of students are distinguished, in the analysis, the effects of drug prevention programs can be tested in new ways than has been done in the past. It may be found that drug prevention programs are not effective with all students but only for special types of students.

REFERENCES

Barcikowski, R. (1981). Statistical power with group mean as the unit of analysis. *Journal of Educational Statistics, 6,* 267–285.

Boyd, L. H., & Iversen, G. R. (1979). *Contextual analysis: Concepts and statistical techniques.* Belmont, CA: Wadsworth.

Burstein, L. (1980). The analysis of multilevel data in educational research and evaluation. *Review of Research in Education, 8,* 158–233.

Categories. (1990). *HOMALS.* Cary, NC: SPSS.

Cochran, W. G. (1977). *Sampling techniques.* New York: Wiley.

De Leeuw, J., & Kreft, I. G. G. (1986). Random coefficient models for multilevel analysis. *Journal of Educational Statistics, 11,* 57–85.

Dempster, A. P., Rubin, D. B., & Tsutakawa, R. K. (1981). Estimation in covariance components models. *Journal of the American Statistical Association, 76,* 341–353.

Draper, D. (1995). Inference and hierarchical modeling in the social sciences. *Journal of Educational and Behavioral Statistics, 20,* 115–148.

Duncan, O. D., Curzort, R. P., & Duncan, R. P. (1966). *Statistical geography: Problems in analyzing areal data.* New York: Free Press.

Gifi, A. (1990). *Nonlinear multivariate analysis.* New York: Wiley.

Graham, J. W., Collins, L. M., Wugalter, S. E., Chung, N. K., & Hansen, W. (1991): Modeling transition in latent stage-sequential processes: A substance use prevention example. *Journal of Consulting and Clinical Psychology, 59,* 48–57.

Graham, J. W., Marks, C., & Hansen, W. B. (1991). Social influence processes affecting adolescent substance use. *Journal of Applied Psychology, 76,* 291–298.

Prosser, R., Rasbach, J., & Goldstein, H. (1991). *ML3 Software for two-level analysis: Users guide.* London: Institute of Education.

Robinson, W. S. (1950). Ecological correlations and the behavior of individuals. *Sociological Review, 15,* 351–357.

Van der Geer, J. P. (1993a). *Multivariate analysis of categorical data—Applications: Advanced quantitative techniques.* Newbury Park, CA: Sage.

Van der Geer, J. P. (1993b). *Multivariate analysis of categorical data—Theory: Advanced quantitative techniques.* Newbury Park, CA: Sage.

SUGGESTED READINGS

Sources Providing an Overview of Multilevel Modeling

Aitkin, M. A., & Longford, N. (1986). Statistical modelling in school effectiveness studies. *Journal of the Royal Statistical Society, 149A*, 1–43.

Bryk, A. S., & Raudenbush, S. W. (1987). Applying the hierarchical linear model to measurements of change problems. *Psychological Bulletin, 101*, 147–158.

Bryk, A. S., & Raudenbush, S. W. (1992). *Hierarchical linear models: Applications and data analysis methods.* Newbury Park, CA: Sage.

Bryk, A. S., Raudenbush, S. W., & Congdon, R. T. (1996). *HLM, hierarchical linear and nonlinear modeling with HLM/2L and HLM/3L programs.* Chicago, IL: Scientific Software International.

Kreft, I. G. G. (1994). Multilevel analysis methods: Introduction to special issue on multilevel analysis. *Sociological Methods and Research, 22*, 283–300.

Kreft, I. G. G., & de Leeuw, J. (1994). The gender gap in earnings: A two way nested multiple regression analysis with random effects. *Sociological Methods and Research, 22*, 319–342.

Kreft, I. G. G., de Leeuw, J., & Aiken, L. S. (1995). The effect of different forms of centering in hierarchical linear models. *Multivariate Behavioral Research, 30*, 1–21.

Kreft, I. G. G. (1995). Hierarchical linear models: Problems and prospects. *Journal of Educational and Behavioral Statistics, 20*, 109–115.

Kreft, I. G. G., de Leeuw, J., & van der Leeden, R. (1994). Review of five multilevel analysis programs: BMDP-5V, GENMOD, HLM, ML3, VARCL. *The American Statistician, 48*, 324–335.

Longford, N. T. (1990). *VARCL: Software for variance component analysis of data with nested random effects (maximum likelihood).* Princeton, NJ: Educational Testing Service.

Longford, N. T. (1994). *Random coefficient models.* Oxford, England: Oxford University Press.

Mason, W. M., Wong, G. Y., & Entwissle, B. (1984). Contextual analysis through the multilevel linear model. *Sociological Methodology*, 72–103.

Searle, S. R., Casella, G., & McCulloch, C. E. (1992). *Variance components.* New York: Wiley.

Sources Providing Empirical Applications of Multilevel Modeling

Bock, R.D. (Ed.). (1988). *Multilevel analysis of educational data.* San Diego, CA: Academic Press.

Hox, J. J., Kreft, I. G. G., & Hermkes, P. L. J. (1991). Multilevel models for factorial surveys. *Sociological Methods and Research, 19*, 493–511.

Kreft, I. G. G., & de Leeuw, J. (1991). Model based ranking of schools. *International Journal of Educational Research, 15*, 45–61.

Kreft, I. G. G., & de Leeuw, E. D. (1988). The seesaw effect: A multilevel problem? *Quality and Quantity, 22*, 127–137.

Kreft, I. G. G., & Aschbacher, P. R. (1994). Measurement and evaluation issues in education: The value of multivariate techniques in evaluating an innovative high school reform program [Special issue]. *International Journal for Educational Research*, 21, 181–195.

Kreft, I. G. G. (1994). Multilevel models for hierarchically nested data: Potential applications in substance abuse prevention research. In L. M. Collins & L. A. Seitz (Eds.), *Advances in data analysis for prevention intervention research* (NIDA Research Monograph No. 142, pp. 140–184). Rockville, MD: U.S. Department of Health and Human Services.

Kreft, I. G. G. (1996). The evaulation of the effect of drug prevention programs on alcohol consumption of high school students with homogeneity and multilevel analysis (NIDA Report No. 1). PERC-Publication No. 2, California State University, Los Angeles.

Kreft, I. G. G. (in press). An illustration of item homogeneity scaling and multilevel analysis techniques in the evaluation of drug prevention programs. *Evaluation Review*.

Raudenbush, S. W., & Bryk, A. S. (1986). A hierarchical model for studying school effects. *Sociology of Education*, 59, 1–17.

Raudenbush, S. W., & Willms, J. D. (Eds.). *Review of schools, classrooms and pupils, international studies of schooling from a multilevel perspective*. San Diego, CA: Academic Press.

APPENDIX
ANALYSIS PACKAGES FOR ANALYZING MULTILEVEL DATA USING HIERARCHICAL LINEAR MODELS

Multilevel modeling software has now become readily available, although under different names. One package clearly uses the already existing random-effects model from the experimental research tradition (see Dempster, Rubin, & Tsutakawa, 1981) by naming the software package VARCL (variance component analysis). Other developers (Bryk, Raudenbush, & Congdon, 1996) had a class of substantive problems out of the observation research tradition in mind and named the package hierarchical linear models. Prosser, Rasbach, and Goldstein (1991) highlighted the way the data are collected at three levels of the hierarchy (ML3, where the name MultiLevel is combined with the number 3, the number of hierarchies the package is able to handle). ML3 and VARCL allow for three levels of nesting, whereas the other two packages allow for two levels of nesting.

HLM, Version 2.20 was written by Bryk, Raudenbush, and Congdon. The manual was written by the same authors and Seltzer. The program is available from Scientific Software, Inc., 1525 East 53rd Street, Suite 906, Chicago, IL 60615. Further information can be found at http://www.gamma.rug.nl/iechome.html.

MIXOR and MIXREG were written by Don Hedeker. MIXOR does multilevel analysis with an ordinal outcome variable, and MIXREG does multilevel analysis with autocorrelated errors. Binaries for the PC and Macintosh formats and the manuals can be obtained from ftp://ftp.stat.ucla.edu/pub/apps/msdog/hedeker.

MLn, Version 2.2, is software for two or more levels of analysis and was written by Rasbach. The manual was written by Prosser, Rasbach, and Goldstein. The program is based on theoretical work done by Goldstein. It is available from the Multilevel Models Project, Institute of Education, 20 Bedford Way, London WC1H OAL England. For more information, see http://www.ioe.ac.uk/hgoldstn/software.html.

PROC MIXED is the mixed-model analysis component of the SAS statistics system. It is comparable in options and possibilities to BMDP5V. Further information can be found at http://www.sas.com/.

TERRACE was written in XLISP-STAT by James Hilden-Minton for his dissertation. It differs from the other programs mentioned here because it concentrates on diagnosis. It analyzes only two-level models but is completely open and thus relatively easy to extend. It can be obtained, with source code and documentation, from http://www.stat.ucla.edu/consult/nels/papers/index.html.

VARCL was initiated by Aitkin and Longford and is written and maintained by Longford. More information can be obtained at http://www.gamma.rug.nl/iechome.html.

III

IMPROVING
METHODOLOGICAL
QUALITY

9

EXPLORING THE MEASUREMENT INVARIANCE OF PSYCHOLOGICAL INSTRUMENTS: APPLICATIONS IN THE SUBSTANCE USE DOMAIN

KEITH F. WIDAMAN AND STEVEN P. REISE

Much research and debate has been motivated by the following question: How can researchers establish that a test measures the same trait dimension, in the same way, when administered to two or more qualitatively distinct groups (e.g., men and women)? Alternatively, we may ask, Are test scores for individuals who belong to different examinee populations comparable on the same measurement scale? Furthermore, if scores across groups are on the same measurement scale, do the groups differ in interpretable ways on the constructs represented? These general questions fall under the rubric of "invariance" testing, that is, investigating the invariance across groups of relations among psychological measures. In this chapter, we discuss several forms of invariance that may be distinguished

This work was supported in part by intramural grants from the Academic Senate, University of California, Riverside, by Grants HD-21056 and HD-22953 from the National Institute of Child Health and Human Development, and by Grants G0085300208 and H023C80072 from the U.S. Office of Education. The most helpful comments by Peter Flannery on a previous version of this chapter are gratefully acknowledged.

and tested, review confirmatory factor analysis (CFA) approaches to addressing questions of this sort, present analyses of empirical data to demonstrate how to perform and interpret such analyses, and outline several knotty problems that must be confronted in future research to provide a complete consideration of the invariance of psychological instruments.

Reise, Widaman, and Pugh (1993) wrote an article on the use of CFA and item response theory (IRT) procedures for evaluating the measurement equivalence of psychological tests. Since that time, interest in this topic has continued to grow, and new developments and issues have arisen (see Byrne, 1994; Meredith, 1993; Millsap, 1995). In what follows, we describe several concepts and advances contained within recent contributions to the measurement invariance literature. We then describe the data set to be used in our study and the types of analyses we conducted, including how the results of these analyses should be interpreted.

MEASUREMENT INVARIANCE

To compare groups of individuals on their level on a trait or to investigate whether trait-level scores have differential correlates across groups, one must assume that the numerical values under consideration are on the same measurement scale (Drasgow, 1984, 1987). That is, one must assume that the test has "measurement invariance" across groups. If trait scores are not comparable (i.e., scores are not on the same measurement scale) across groups, then differences between groups in mean levels or in the pattern of correlations of the test with external variables are potentially artifactual and may be substantively misleading (Drasgow, 1984, 1987; Meredith, 1993).

Because establishing measurement invariance of a test across distinct groups is critical to progress in many domains of psychology, much discussion has been devoted to this topic (e.g., Byrne & Shavelson, 1987; Drasgow & Kanfer, 1985; Frederiksen, 1987; Hui & Triandis, 1985; Linn & Harnisch, 1981). One central principle, evident throughout this literature, is that psychological measurements are on the same scale (i.e., comparable) when the empirical relations between the trait indicators (e.g., test items) and the trait of interest are invariant across groups. That is, for test scores to be comparable across ostensibly distinct examinee populations, the observed test items, or indicators, must have identical, or invariant, quantitative relationships with the latent variable for each population of interest (cf. Meredith, 1993). When tests meet this criterion, they are said to display measurement invariance. For a variety of reasons, which include the recent, increased accessibility of sophisticated computer programs, researchers have become more concerned with the issues surrounding the assessment of measurement invariance.

As Windle, Iwawaki, and Lerner (1988) explained, the primary way of assessing measurement invariance has been through the use of factor analytic techniques and "involves the study of similarities and differences in the covariation patterns of item-factor relations" (p. 551). Before the 1970s, various heuristic strategies for evaluating the invariance between two or more factor structures were proposed (e.g., Reynolds & Harding, 1983). Although discussions of these techniques still appear in the psychometric literature, interest in them has declined substantially with the advent of more sophisticated methods for confirmatory modeling of item–latent variable relations using CFA (Jöreskog, 1971) and item response theory (Lord, 1980) models.

However, the definition of measurement invariance—that the relations of latent variables with their indicators must be identical across groups—is a broad one. Factor analysis, item response theory, and other approaches also may be subsumed under this definition (cf. Meredith, 1993; Reise et al., 1993). The primary point is the importance of establishing the invariance across groups of the relationship of a latent variable to each of its indicators.

THE LINEAR CFA MODEL

Factor analytic models have been the most commonly invoked when discussing issues related to measurement invariance. When representing measurement invariance within a factor model, we turn to what may be termed *factorial invariance* to distinguish invariance within factor analytic models as a special case of the more general notion of measurement invariance. Within factor analytic approaches, we distinguish various forms of factorial invariance, including configural invariance as well as weak, strong, and strict factorial invariance. First, however, we offer a basic orientation to the common factor model to provide a context for distinguishing among the different types of factorial invariance.

Applications of CFA for testing measurement invariance were first presented in the early 1970s (Jöreskog, 1971; McGaw & Jöreskog, 1971). In the typical CFA model, each measured variable is identified as y_{ji}, where j refers to the jth measured variable ($j = 1, \ldots, p$) and i denotes the ith individual ($i = 1, \ldots, N$). Note that each y_{ji} score is represented as the deviation of the raw score for person i from the mean of variable j, or $y_{ji} = (Y_{ji} - \bar{Y}_j)$. Each measured variable is represented as a linear function of one or more latent variables, η_k ($k = 1, \ldots, m$), and a stochastic error term, ε_{ji}. For now, we assume that each y and η score is represented as the deviation of the score from its respective mean, although we introduce mean terms in a later section. Given the deviation score form for the y

and η scores, the relationship of a measured variable to the latent variables may be represented as a linear model, or regression model, as

$$y_{ji} = \lambda_{j1}\eta_{1i} + \lambda_{j2}\eta_{2i} + \cdots + \lambda_{jm}\eta_{mi} + \varepsilon_{ji}, \tag{1}$$

where λ_{jk} is the regression coefficient representing the regression of y_j on η_k (or the regression weight for predicting y_j from η_k) and other terms are as defined earlier.

If an equation such as Equation 1 is written for each of the p observed variables and these are concatenated into matrices, we have the following matrix equation:

$$\mathbf{y} = \mathbf{\Lambda}\boldsymbol{\eta} + \boldsymbol{\varepsilon}, \tag{2}$$

where $\mathbf{y}$ is a $(p \times 1)$ column vector of scores on the p measured variables for individual i, $\mathbf{\Lambda}$ is a $(p \times m)$ matrix of the loadings of the p measured variables on the m latent variables, $\boldsymbol{\eta}$ is an $(m \times 1)$ column vector of scores on the m latent variables for the ith individual, and $\boldsymbol{\varepsilon}$ is a column vector of error terms, or measurement residuals for the ith individual.

To provide a more concrete representation of Equation 2, assume that we have six measured variables (so $p = 6$) and two latent variables (so $m = 2$). Also assume that the first three measured variables load only on Latent Variable 1 (or Factor 1) and the second set of three variables load on Factor 2. Under this specification, the linear model for individual i embodied by Equation 2 would look like the following:

$$\begin{bmatrix} y_{1i} \\ y_{2i} \\ y_{3i} \\ y_{4i} \\ y_{5i} \\ y_{6i} \end{bmatrix} = \begin{bmatrix} \lambda_{11} & 0 \\ \lambda_{21} & 0 \\ \lambda_{31} & 0 \\ 0 & \lambda_{42} \\ 0 & \lambda_{52} \\ 0 & \lambda_{62} \end{bmatrix} \begin{bmatrix} \eta_{1i} \\ \eta_{2i} \end{bmatrix} + \begin{bmatrix} \varepsilon_{1i} \\ \varepsilon_{2i} \\ \varepsilon_{3i} \\ \varepsilon_{4i} \\ \varepsilon_{5i} \\ \varepsilon_{6i} \end{bmatrix}, \tag{2a}$$

where all terms are as defined earlier. At this point, the $\mathbf{\Lambda}$ matrix in Equations 2 and 2a is the only model matrix with parameters (the λ_{jk}s); the remaining two matrices in the model, $\boldsymbol{\eta}$ and $\boldsymbol{\varepsilon}$, contain theoretical scores for individual i on the common factors and unique factors, respectively. The compact form of Equation 2 and its expanded, mathematically identical counterpart Equation 2a provide a summary of the linear models for the six measured variables. Thus, from Equation 2a, one can see that the equation for the first measured variable, which loads only on the first factor, is

$$y_{1i} = \lambda_{11}\eta_{1i} + 0\eta_{2i} + \varepsilon_{1i} = \lambda_{11}\eta_{1i} + \varepsilon_{1i},$$

and the model for the fourth measured variable, which loads only on the second factor, is

$$y_{4i} = 0\eta_{1i} + \lambda_{42}\eta_{2i} + \varepsilon_{4i} = \lambda_{42}\eta_{2i} + \varepsilon_{4i}.$$

If we obtain a sample of N participants with scores on the six measured variables, the only changes to Equation 2 would be a redefinition of the order, or size, of three of the matrices. Specifically, $\mathbf{y}$ would become a $(p \times N)$ matrix of scores of the N participants on the p measured variables, $\boldsymbol{\eta}$ would become an $(m \times N)$ matrix of the scores of the N participants on the m common factors, and $\boldsymbol{\varepsilon}$ would become a $(p \times N)$ matrix of scores of the N participants on the p measurement residuals (or, equivalently, the p unique factors). Note that this "redefinition" of the three matrices simply expands the three matrices $\mathbf{y}$, $\boldsymbol{\eta}$, and $\boldsymbol{\varepsilon}$ along the participant mode i, so that each individual has a column vector in each of these matrices. Given this specification (i.e., with scores of N participants on the p measured variables) of Equation 2, one may postmultiply each side of Equation 2 by its transpose, divide each side of the equation by $(N - 1)$, and the result is

$$\boldsymbol{\Sigma} = \boldsymbol{\Lambda}\boldsymbol{\Psi}\boldsymbol{\Lambda}' + \boldsymbol{\Theta}_\varepsilon, \tag{3}$$

where $\boldsymbol{\Sigma}$ is a $(p \times p)$ matrix of covariances among the p measured variables, $\boldsymbol{\Lambda}$ is (as defined earlier) a $(p \times m)$ matrix of the loadings of the p measured variables on the m latent variables, $\boldsymbol{\Psi}$ is an $(m \times m)$ matrix of covariances among the common factor scores (i.e., among the η_{jk} scores), and $\boldsymbol{\Theta}_\varepsilon$ is a $(p \times p)$ matrix of covariances among the measurement residuals (i.e., among the ε_{ji} scores).

Equation 3 is a *covariance structure* model, so named because it is a linear model that represents the covariances among the p measured variables. Equation 3 also represents an interesting aspect of covariance structure models: Although it is difficult to estimate directly the scores on the common factors, the η_{jk}s, and the measurement residuals, the ε_{ji}s, we can estimate the covariances among these scores in the $\boldsymbol{\Psi}$ and $\boldsymbol{\Theta}_\varepsilon$ matrices, respectively. The covariances among the common factors, in the $\boldsymbol{\Psi}$ matrix, are usually freely estimated, but the $\boldsymbol{\Theta}_\varepsilon$ matrix is often constrained to be a diagonal matrix, consistent with the assumption that the measurement residuals are mutually uncorrelated. Given these conditions, we may write Equation 3 in expanded notation as

$$
\begin{bmatrix}
\sigma_{11} & \sigma_{12} & \sigma_{13} & \sigma_{14} & \sigma_{15} & \sigma_{16} \\
\sigma_{21} & \sigma_{22} & \sigma_{23} & \sigma_{24} & \sigma_{25} & \sigma_{26} \\
\sigma_{31} & \sigma_{32} & \sigma_{33} & \sigma_{34} & \sigma_{35} & \sigma_{36} \\
\sigma_{41} & \sigma_{42} & \sigma_{43} & \sigma_{44} & \sigma_{45} & \sigma_{46} \\
\sigma_{51} & \sigma_{52} & \sigma_{53} & \sigma_{54} & \sigma_{55} & \sigma_{56} \\
\sigma_{61} & \sigma_{62} & \sigma_{63} & \sigma_{64} & \sigma_{65} & \sigma_{66}
\end{bmatrix}
$$

$$
=
\begin{bmatrix}
\lambda_{11} & 0 \\
\lambda_{21} & 0 \\
\lambda_{31} & 0 \\
0 & \lambda_{42} \\
0 & \lambda_{52} \\
0 & \lambda_{62}
\end{bmatrix}
\begin{bmatrix}
\Psi_{11} & \Psi_{12} \\
\Psi_{21} & \Psi_{22}
\end{bmatrix}
\begin{bmatrix}
\lambda_{11} & \lambda_{21} & \lambda_{31} & 0 & 0 & 0 \\
0 & 0 & 0 & \lambda_{42} & \lambda_{52} & \lambda_{62}
\end{bmatrix}
$$

$$
+
\begin{bmatrix}
\theta_{\varepsilon11} & 0 & 0 & 0 & 0 & 0 \\
0 & \theta_{\varepsilon22} & 0 & 0 & 0 & 0 \\
0 & 0 & \theta_{\varepsilon33} & 0 & 0 & 0 \\
0 & 0 & 0 & \theta_{\varepsilon44} & 0 & 0 \\
0 & 0 & 0 & 0 & \theta_{\varepsilon55} & 0 \\
0 & 0 & 0 & 0 & 0 & \theta_{\varepsilon66}
\end{bmatrix},
\tag{3a}
$$

where $\sigma_{jj'}$ is the variance of variable j, if $j = j'$, or the covariance of variables j and j', if $j \neq j'$, $\Psi_{kk'}$ is the variance of factor k, if $k = k'$, or the covariance of factors k and k', if $k \neq k'$, $\theta_{\varepsilon jj'}$ is the variance of the measurement residual for variable j, if $j = j'$, or the covariance of the measurement residuals for variables j and j', if $j \neq j'$. In Equations 3 and 3a, three of the matrices are symmetrical matrices, that is, values below the diagonal are mirror images of values above the diagonal. Thus, Σ has $[p(p + 1)/2]$ unique elements on or below the diagonal, Ψ has $[m(m + 1)/2]$ unique elements on or below the diagonal, and Θ_ε has $[p(p + 1)/2]$ unique elements on or below the diagonal, although only the p elements on the diagonal of Θ_ε are typically allowed to vary from zero on an a priori basis (as shown in Equation 3a).

If we fit the model in Equations 3 and 3a to a sample covariance matrix based on a sample of N participants, we should rewrite Equation 3 in the following way:

$$
\mathbf{S} \cong \hat{\Lambda}\hat{\Psi}\hat{\Lambda}' + \hat{\Theta}_\varepsilon = \hat{\Sigma},
\tag{4}
$$

where $\mathbf{S}$ is the $(p \times p)$ observed sample covariance matrix among measured variables and the $\hat{\Lambda}$, $\hat{\Psi}$, $\hat{\Theta}_\varepsilon$, and $\hat{\Sigma}$ matrices contain sample estimates of the population parameters in the corresponding matrices in Equations 3 and 3a. As shown in Equation 4, the observed covariances among the p measured variables in S are approximated by the linear CFA solution $\hat{\Lambda}\hat{\Psi}\hat{\Lambda} + \hat{\Theta}_\varepsilon$, which in turn produces $\hat{\Sigma}$, which contains estimates of the population covariances among the measured variables, Σ, under the assumption that the stated model is a proper representation of the data and therefore holds in the population.

For multiple-group linear CFA modeling, Equation 4 may be modified to denote group membership as

$$S_g \cong \hat{\Lambda}_g \hat{\Psi}_g \hat{\Lambda}_g' + \hat{\Theta}_{\varepsilon g} = \hat{\Sigma}_g, \tag{5}$$

where all matrices are as defined earlier, except for the addition of the g subscript to denote that the matrices were derived from the gth sample.

The models in Equations 1–5 are *covariance* structure models that are meant to be applied only to covariance matrices. Among others, Cudeck (1989) discussed the ways in which the application of covariance structure models to correlation matrices, even in one-sample analyses, may lead to inaccurate results. In multiple-group modeling, additional important issues arise; as a result, analyses must be performed on within-groups covariance matrices, not on within-groups correlation matrices. Within-groups correlation matrices are inappropriate for multiple-group analyses because investigating the variance across groups of various model parameters, such as the regression weights (i.e., the $\hat{\lambda}_{jk}$ estimates) relating latent variables to measured variables, requires that the scores on the measured variables must be on the same scale across groups. Standardizing the data separately for each of the g groups (e.g., to a z-score metric, with unit variance for each measured variable within each group) would lead to different rescalings of measured variables within each group. That is, if the different within-groups standard deviations are used for calculating the z scores on a particular variable within each group, then a deviation from the mean of a given magnitude would mean different things across groups. This differential rescaling of the measured variables within each group would destroy the comparability across groups of the common scale for the measured variables and would therefore lead to an inability to compare parameter estimates meaningfully across groups. Further details on these and other more technical matters are discussed in many standard references, such as Jöreskog (1971) and Jöreskog and Sörbom (1989).

The CFA models in Equations 1–5 are useful for examining the factorial invariance of psychological measures. However, Meredith (1993) argued that only weak forms of invariance may be tested using this model. Stronger forms of invariance require the consideration of means on the measured and latent variables. To do so, we leave each Y_{ji} score in its raw score form (not as a deviation from its mean) and then rewrite Equation 1 as follows:

$$Y_{ji} = \tau_j + \lambda_{j1}(\alpha_1 + \eta_{1i}) + \lambda_{j2}(\alpha_2 + \eta_{2i}) + \cdots + \lambda_{jm}(\alpha_m + \eta_{mi}) + \varepsilon_{ji}, \quad (6)$$

where τ_j is the intercept for predicting the observed variable Y_{ji} from the latent η variables, α_k is the mean on the kth latent variable or factor, and all other terms are as defined earlier.

If we wish to write a matrix equation for the model in Equation 6, we would rewrite Equation 2 as

$$\mathbf{Y} = \boldsymbol{\tau}\boldsymbol{\mu}_\tau' + \boldsymbol{\Lambda}(\boldsymbol{\alpha}\boldsymbol{\mu}_\alpha' + \boldsymbol{\eta}) + \boldsymbol{\varepsilon}, \quad (7)$$

where $\mathbf{Y}$ is a $(p \times 1)$ vector of raw scores on the p measured variables for person i, $\boldsymbol{\tau}$ is a $(p \times 1)$ vector of intercepts for the p measured variables, $\boldsymbol{\alpha}$ is an $(m \times 1)$ vector of means on the m factors, $\boldsymbol{\mu}_\tau'$ and $\boldsymbol{\mu}_\alpha'$ are (1×1) matrices of unities (1.0s) for participant i, and all other terms are as defined earlier.

In more concrete form, the two additions to Equation 7 are as follows:

$$\boldsymbol{\tau}\boldsymbol{\mu}_\tau' = \begin{bmatrix} \tau_1 \\ \tau_2 \\ \tau_3 \\ \tau_4 \\ \tau_5 \\ \tau_6 \end{bmatrix} [1], \quad (7a)$$

$$\boldsymbol{\alpha}\boldsymbol{\mu}_\alpha' = \begin{bmatrix} \alpha_1 \\ \alpha_2 \end{bmatrix} [1], \quad (7b)$$

and all other matrices are defined as in Equations 2 and 2a.

Equation 7 was written for a given participant i. If we obtain a sample of N participants, then we have the following dimensions for the matrices in Equation 7: (a) $\mathbf{Y}$ is a $(p \times N)$ matrix of raw scores of the N persons on the p measured variables; (b) $\boldsymbol{\mu}_\tau'$ is a $(1 \times N)$ row vector of unities (or 1.0s) for the N participants; (c) $\boldsymbol{\mu}_\alpha'$ is a $(1 \times N)$ row vector of unities (or 1.0s) for the N participants; (d) $\boldsymbol{\eta}$ is an $(m \times N)$ matrix of scores of the N participants on the m factors; (e) $\boldsymbol{\varepsilon}$ is a $(p \times N)$ matrix of scores of the N participants on the p measurement residuals; and (f) $\boldsymbol{\tau}$, which is $(p \times 1)$, $\boldsymbol{\alpha}$, which is $(m \times 1)$, and $\boldsymbol{\Lambda}$, which is $(p \times m)$, are as defined earlier.

Postmultiplying each side of Equation 7 by its transpose and dividing by N yields

$$\mathbf{M} \cong \hat{\boldsymbol{\tau}}\hat{\boldsymbol{\tau}}' + \hat{\boldsymbol{\Lambda}}(\hat{\boldsymbol{\alpha}}\hat{\boldsymbol{\alpha}}' + \hat{\boldsymbol{\Psi}})\hat{\boldsymbol{\Lambda}}' + \hat{\boldsymbol{\Theta}}_\varepsilon = \hat{\mathbf{M}}, \quad (8)$$

where $\mathbf{M}$ is a $(p \times p)$ moment matrix (or matrix of raw sums of squares and cross-products of the measured variables), $\hat{\mathbf{M}}$ is the estimated population moment matrix assuming the model is correctly specified, and all other terms are as defined earlier. To ensure understanding at this point, we briefly compare elements of covariance and moment matrices. The typical element in a covariance matrix, $s_{jj'}$, may be written as $s_{jj'} = r_{jj'}s_j s_{j'}$, where $r_{jj'}$ is the correlation between variables j and j' and s_j and $s_{j'}$ are the standard deviations for variables j and j', respectively. By contrast, the typical element in a moment (or sums of squares and cross-products) matrix, $m_{jj'}$, may be written as $m_{jj'} = r_{jj'}s_j s_{j'} + \bar{Y}_j \bar{Y}_{j'}$, where $\bar{Y}_j$ and $\bar{Y}_{j'}$ are the means for variables j and j', respectively. Thus, the elements in moment matrices retain information about the means of the measured variables together with their covariances. That is, each element in a covariance matrix is an index of the correlation between two variables weighted by (or, more specifically, multiplied by) their standard deviations, or $s_{jj'} = r_{jj'}s_j s_{j'}$. Each element in a moment matrix simply adds information about the means of the two variables to the covariance, using the formula $m_{jj'} = r_{jj'}s_j s_{j'} + \bar{Y}_j \bar{Y}_{j'}$.

As shown in Equation 8, the observed sums of squares and cross-products among the p measured variables in $\mathbf{M}$ are approximated by the linear CFA solution $\hat{\tau}\hat{\tau}' + \hat{\Lambda}(\hat{\alpha}\hat{\alpha}' + \hat{\Psi})\hat{\Lambda}' + \hat{\Theta}_\varepsilon$, which in turn produces $\hat{\mathbf{M}}$, which contains estimates of the population sums of squares and cross-products among the measured variables, $\mathbf{M}$, under the assumption that the stated model is a proper representation of the data and holds in the population.

If the general model in Equation 8 is extended to a multiple-group context, we have

$$\mathbf{M}_g \cong \hat{\tau}_g \hat{\tau}_g' + \hat{\Lambda}_g(\hat{\alpha}_g \hat{\alpha}_g' + \hat{\Psi}_g)\hat{\Lambda}_g' + \hat{\Theta}_{\varepsilon g} = \hat{\mathbf{M}}_g, \tag{9}$$

where all matrices are as defined earlier, except for the addition of the g subscript to denote that the matrices were derived from the gth sample.

At least four major points should be made about the inclusion of intercept terms for measured variables in the $\hat{\tau}$ matrices and means for the latent variables in the $\hat{\alpha}$ matrix in Equations 7–9:

1. In most previous discussions of factorial invariance using multiple-group CFA, the $\hat{\tau}$ matrices have not been included in the models. This limits the presentation in a number of ways. As we will show, the distinctions drawn by Meredith (1993) among different forms of factorial invariance require specifying and testing certain hypotheses concerning the $\hat{\tau}$ matrices. Failing to include the $\hat{\tau}$ matrices enables the testing only of weak forms of factorial invariance, and researchers typically will want to test stronger forms of invariance. (These issues are discussed in greater detail later.)

2. Including the $\hat{\alpha}$ matrices in Equations 7–9 enables the representing and testing of mean differences on factors across groups. In typical approaches, CFA models have been used to test invariance across groups of the factor patterns as well as the covariances among the latent variables using a model such as that shown in Equation 5. However, including means of the measured variables, in $\hat{\tau}$, in Equations 7–9 allows the identification of elements in the $\hat{\alpha}$ matrices, enabling one to test mean differences across groups on the latent variables. Thus, including the means in these analyses allows a more complete understanding of group similarities and differences on the latent variables.

3. Furthermore, whereas structural models are usually fit to covariance matrices, incorporating the $\hat{\tau}$ and $\hat{\alpha}$ matrices into Equations 7–9 necessitates the fitting of structural models to moment matrices. As discussed earlier, moment matrices are raw-score cross-products matrices among the measured variables, and the elements of such matrices are difficult to interpret directly. Fortunately, this is not necessary. Indeed, one may fit models such as those shown in Equations 7–9 without directly considering the multiple-group moment matrices. Most structural modeling programs, such as LISREL 8, allow the researcher to list the correlations among measured variables, along with the respective standard deviations and means of these variables, as input to the program. Then, the moment matrices are implicitly calculated and evaluated. Just as a covariance structure model like the one shown in Equation 5 reproduces an estimated population covariance matrix, a moment structure model that incorporates $\hat{\tau}$ and $\hat{\alpha}$ matrices, as in Equations 7–9, yields an estimated population moment matrix. Moreover, moment structure models may be evaluated using statistical and practical criteria of fit in precisely the same way as covariance structure models.

4. Finally, we must comment on identifying structural models for moment matrices. Identification of any structural equation model involves the fixing of certain parameter values at non-zero values to allow the statistical estimation of the remaining parameters of the model. In a covariance structure model, one parameter associated with each latent variable—either a factor loading or the factor variance—must be fixed to a nonzero value to establish the scale for the latent variable. In a moment structure model, one must additionally fix all of the factor means to a particular value in one group, so that the means may be estimated in the remaining groups.

Any given structural model may be identified in any of a variety of ways. As mentioned earlier, one factor loading on each latent variable may be fixed at unity, or the variance of each latent variable may be fixed to a nonzero value, such as unity. Different ways of identifying a particular model will almost certainly lead to differences in all parameter estimates. However, all measures of fit of the model to the data remain invariant. At least as important, the key parameters reflecting group differences on latent variables, although having different numerical values, have invariant interpretations because the models involve simple rescalings of the latent variables. This is loosely analogous to performing a linear transformation of one variable, which leaves its correlations with other variables unchanged. Thus, interpretations of the strength of relations with other variables are invariant under the alternate linear transformations of the variable.

However, invariant interpretations of the structural model will hold only if appropriate invariance constraints have been imposed. For example, consider a two-group situation in which a simple one-factor model is assumed to hold in each group. In one way of identifying the model, assume that Group 1 has a mean of 0.0 and a standard deviation of 1.0 on the latent variable, whereas Group 2 has a mean of 0.50 and a standard deviation of 1.5. Under a second choice of identifying the model, Group 1 may have a mean of −0.33 and a standard deviation of 0.67, and Group 3 has a mean of 0.0 and a standard deviation of 1.00. Under both specifications, the following conditions hold: (a) Group 2 has both a higher mean and a larger standard deviation than does Group 1, (b) the Group 2 mean is 0.5 Group 1 standard deviation units above the mean of Group 1, and (c) the Group 2 standard deviation is 1.5 times as large as the Group 1 standard deviation. As a result, the essential relations among the group means are invariant under the different rescalings, and all interpretations of the results therefore remain invariant under the different rescalings. In the following sections, we refer to this essential invariance of estimates across different rescalings of the latent variables as invariance under appropriate rescaling factors, or ARF invariance.

FACTORIAL INVARIANCE

In the preceding section, in which we detailed several aspects of CFA models for multiple-group data, we set the stage for an informed discussion of factorial invariance. As we will show, the different forms of factorial invariance are attained by constraining corresponding parameters in various matrices in Equation 9 to be equal across groups. We now turn to the task of distinguishing among various forms of factorial invariance, including a consideration of the specification of these models and the interpretation of their estimates.

Before doing so, we first distinguish between nonmetric and metric invariance. In this chapter, we use the term *nonmetric invariance* to refer to specifying the same pattern of fixed and free parameters for a given matrix across all groups without imposing any additional constraints on the parameters. The parameters therefore are estimated freely within each group and may vary across groups. By contrast, *metric invariance* refers to constraining parameters to be equal, or numerically identical, across groups. Thus, under metric invariance, not only is the pattern of fixed and free parameters the same across groups, but the parameter estimates themselves are forced to be equal across groups.

Configural Invariance

The first, basic form of factorial invariance we discuss has been called *configural invariance* (Horn, McArdle, & Mason, 1983). The central requirement of configural invariance is that the same pattern of fixed and free loadings in the $\hat{\Lambda}$ matrix holds for each group. If the same pattern of zero and nonzero loadings holds across groups, the same configuration of loadings of tests on factors is observed; hence, the term *configural invariance*.

Referring back to Equation 9, configural invariance is specified by having the same pattern of fixed and free elements in the $\hat{\Lambda}_g$ matrices of each of the g groups. However, the parameters estimated in the $\hat{\Lambda}_g$ matrices are allowed to vary freely across groups. As a result, the $\hat{\Lambda}_g$ matrices are not numerically invariant across groups, so we retain the g subscript on the $\hat{\Lambda}_g$ matrices to denote the fact that different parameter estimates are obtained across groups. Indeed, none of the five matrices in Equation 9 are invariant across groups, so g subscripts are present on all matrices.

Configural invariance involves the nonmetric invariance of the factor pattern across groups. Configural invariance has some utility within a set of models reflecting invariance across groups, but the interpretation of group differences is severely compromised. The utility of the configural invariance model stems from its role as a baseline model. When moving to models that invoke metric invariance constraints (discussed in the following section), one may test the difference between the more restricted metric invariance model and the less restricted configural invariance model. If the difference in fit is large, metric invariance across groups may not be an acceptable assumption and the researcher may have to settle for mere configural invariance. Configural invariance is consistent with the presumption that similar, but not identical, latent variables are present in the g groups.

However, the problematic interpretation of the configural invariance model stems from the lack of invariance of crucial parameters across groups.

With a configural invariance model, one cannot test group differences on any parameters associated with the latent variables because invariant latent variables have not been identified in the g groups. Indeed, under configural invariance, group differences in means and variances on the latent variable as well as covariances among the latent variables are not uniquely identified. As a result, different ways of fixing the scale of measurement of the latent variables may yield different parameter estimates and, more important, different interpretations of the results. For example, fixing the first factor loading on each factor to unity will yield certain estimates of means and variances on the latent variables and covariances among the latent variables. If one instead fixes the second factor loading on each factor to unity, the solution would be identified. The factor means, variances, and covariances under the two methods of identification, however, would not provide parameter estimates that have an invariant interpretation; group differences in means, variances, or both would vary across methods of identifying the solution. In short, parameter estimates under configural invariance are not ARF invariant. To yield invariant interpretations of results, one must move to forms of metric invariance that provide ARF-invariant parameter estimates.

Metric Factorial Invariance

Meredith (1993) distinguished several forms of factorial invariance, forms that he termed *weak*, *strong*, and *strict* factorial invariance. All these are forms of metric invariance, which connotes the constraining of all elements in certain matrices to invariance, or equality, across groups. Furthermore, the three types of metric factorial invariance are hierarchically nested, with additional constraints for strong invariance imposed on the weak invariance model and additional constraints for strict invariance imposed on the strong invariance model. As will become apparent as we proceed, ever stronger statements about cross-group differences on measured and latent variables are possible as additional constraints are placed on parameter estimates.

Weak Factorial Invariance

Weak factorial invariance is the first and most basic form of metric invariance. Basically, weak factorial invariance holds if the only invariance constraints invoked involve the relations of the latent variables to their indicators. The estimates are contained in the $\hat{\Lambda}_g$; if the $\hat{\Lambda}_g$ matrices are constrained to invariance across groups, the g subscript is dropped from these matrices, leaving Equation 9 with the following appearance:

$$\mathbf{M}_g \cong \hat{\tau}_g\hat{\tau}_g' + \hat{\Lambda}(\hat{\alpha}_g\hat{\alpha}_g' + \hat{\Psi}_g)\hat{\Lambda}' + \hat{\Theta}_{\varepsilon g} = \hat{\mathbf{M}}_g, \tag{9a}$$

where all terms are as defined earlier and the lack of a subscript on the $\hat{\Lambda}$ matrix denotes the across-group invariance constraints on parameter estimates in this matrix.

If the weak factorial invariance constraints are placed on a model and the model is deemed to fit the data adequately, then group differences in latent-variable variances and covariances become identified in an ARF-invariant fashion. That is, regardless of the way in which one chooses to identify the model, leading to differences in many parameter estimates, the same rescaling of parameter estimates occurs for each sample. Therefore, the ratios of the standard deviations across groups for a given latent variable remain invariant, as discussed previously. Moreover, if one were to rescale the estimated within-group factor covariance matrices, or the $\hat{\Psi}_g$ matrices, into correlation matrices, the correlation matrices would be invariant over alternate ways of identifying the model. Because of this invariance of correlations and the relative standard deviations, any substantive interpretation of group differences in variances or covariances among latent variables will remain invariant over rescalings of the latent variables, although certain scalings might lead to more direct interpretations than will others.

Strong Factorial Invariance

Strong factorial invariance involves one set of additional constraints over and above those defining the weak factorial invariance model. Specifically, these additional constraints involve the intercepts of the measured variables, which are contained in the $\hat{\tau}_g$ matrices. If the estimates in these matrices are constrained to invariance across groups, the g subscript on the $\hat{\tau}$ matrices are dropped, and Equation 9a becomes

$$\mathbf{M}_g \cong \hat{\tau}\hat{\tau}' + \hat{\Lambda}(\hat{\alpha}_g\hat{\alpha}_g' + \hat{\Psi}_g)\hat{\Lambda}' + \hat{\Theta}_{eg} = \hat{\mathbf{M}}_g, \qquad (9b)$$

where all terms are as defined earlier and the lack of subscripts on the $\hat{\Lambda}$ and $\hat{\tau}$ matrices indicates the across-groups invariance constraints on parameter estimates in these matrices.

When invariance constraints are imposed on the elements in both the $\hat{\tau}$ and $\hat{\Lambda}$ matrices, group differences in the mean level on the latent variables become identified in the ARF-invariant fashion. Indeed, we may say that strong factorial invariance constraints must be imposed to represent and test group mean differences on the latent variables in any meaningful fashion. Group mean differences may be identifiable mathematically (i.e., estimated) with less-than-complete invariance constraints on the $\hat{\tau}$ and $\hat{\Lambda}$ matrices. However, it makes little sense substantively to do this because different ways of identifying a model will lead to substantively different conclusions about across-group differences in means, variances, or both on the factors. Once the strong factorial invariance constraints are imposed on the $\hat{\Lambda}$ and $\hat{\tau}$ matrices, any method of identifying a model will provide substantively invariant interpretations of across-group differences in factor means and variances.

When factorial invariance analyses are based on covariance matrices, the means of the measured variables are subtracted from scores in each group before calculating the covariance matrices. If the means are not "added back" in any fashion and analyses are thus based solely on covariance matrices, the $\hat{\tau}_g$ and $\hat{\alpha}_g$ matrices fall out of Equation 9, leaving the model in Equation 5. Then, one may test only what Meredith (1993) called "weak factorial invariance," but one cannot test strong factorial invariance because elements in the $\hat{\tau}$ matrices cannot be estimated or tested.

Strong factorial invariance has at least one major strength over weak factorial invariance: Strong factorial invariance reflects the hypothesis that the entire linear model representing the relationship of the latent variables to a given measured variable, both the raw-score regression weights and the intercept term, is invariant across groups. If strong factorial invariance holds, group differences in both means and variances on the latent variables, which represent the constructs in psychological theories, are reflected in group differences in means and variances on the measured variables. Moreover, strong factorial invariance is required to identify the mean differences across groups on the factors in the ARF-invariant fashion. That is, different ways of fixing the scale of each latent variable lead to different rescalings of the latent variables, but the relative group differences, and therefore the interpretations of group differences, on the latent variables remain invariant across these rescalings.

Strict Factorial Invariance

Just as strong factorial invariance results from placing additional constraints on the weak factorial model, so strict factorial invariance builds on strong factorial invariance by invoking still further across-group constraints on parameter estimates. The additional constraints that define the strict factorial invariance model involve the unique factor invariances, or measurement residuals, contained in the $\hat{\Theta}_{\varepsilon g}$ matrices. When these invariance constraints are invoked, Equation 9b becomes

$$\mathbf{M}_g \cong \hat{\tau}\hat{\tau}' + \hat{\Lambda}(\hat{\alpha}_g\hat{\alpha}_g' + \hat{\Psi}_g)\hat{\Lambda}' + \hat{\Theta}_\varepsilon = \hat{\mathbf{M}}_g, \tag{9c}$$

where all terms are as defined earlier and the lack of subscripts on the $\hat{\Theta}_\varepsilon$ matrix indicates the across-group invariance constraints on parameter estimates in this matrix.

The addition of the invariance constraints on elements in the $\hat{\Theta}_\varepsilon$ matrices yields a final model, shown in Equation 9c, that has certain conceptual advantages over Equations 9a and 9b. One obvious advantage is the absence of subscripts for the g groups on three of the five model matrices in Equation 9c, specifically the $\hat{\tau}$, $\hat{\Lambda}$, and $\hat{\Theta}_\varepsilon$ matrices. The lack of subscripts implies the invariance over groups of estimates in these matrices; any interpretation of results with this model would be simplified because of the need to consider a smaller number of estimates.

A second advantage of the strict factorial invariance model is, almost surely, far more important: If group differences in the $\hat{\tau}$, $\hat{\Lambda}$, and $\hat{\Theta}_\varepsilon$ matrices are negligible, then group differences in means and variances on the measured variables are a function only of group differences in means and variances on the common factors. That is, the common factors are entirely responsible for any group differences in means and variances on the measured variables; all group differences on the measured variables are captured by, and attributable to, group differences on the common factors.

Despite these advantages, strict factorial invariance may not hold for a variety of reasons. One of the most obvious reasons concerns the potential increase in residual variance of a measured variable as its variance caused by the latent variable increases. In developmental research, investigators often find that an age-related increase in mean level on a measured variable is accompanied by an increase in variance. If this occurs and if reliability of the measured variable remains approximately constant across age levels, error variance must increase in concert with the increase in reliable variance. If these results obtain, strict factorial invariance should not hold. This is not, however, a major failing because group differences in means and variances on the latent variables are still identifiable in an ARF-invariant fashion if strong factorial invariance holds.

Summary

As discussed earlier, the various forms of metric factorial invariance —weak, strong, and strict—are defined by hierarchical sets of constraints on the $\hat{\Lambda}$, $\hat{\tau}$, and $\hat{\Theta}_\varepsilon$ matrices. Of these, invariance constraints on the $\hat{\Lambda}$ and $\hat{\tau}$ matrices are the most important when framing substantive questions. Once across-group constraints are imposed on the $\hat{\Lambda}$ and $\hat{\tau}$ matrices, group differences in means and variances on the latent variables are identified in an ARF-invariant fashion, as are the covariances (and correlations) among the latent variables. Thus, for most substantive research questions, constraints on the $\hat{\Lambda}$ and $\hat{\tau}$ matrices—embodying strong factorial invariance —would usually be considered crucial. By comparison, additional constraints on the $\hat{\Theta}_\varepsilon$ matrices, resulting in strict factorial invariance, are nice but not necessary. In fact, there are reasonable bases for expecting that the $\hat{\Theta}_{\varepsilon g}$ matrices will vary significantly across groups under sampling from a population, even though the $\hat{\Lambda}$ and $\hat{\tau}$ matrices should show invariance across groups (cf. Meredith, 1964, 1993).

Metric Invariance of Latent-Variable Covariances and Means

To this point, we have discussed metric factorial invariance involving across-group invariance constraints on the $\hat{\Lambda}$, $\hat{\tau}$, and $\hat{\Theta}_\varepsilon$ matrices. Two matrices remain in Equation 9 on which invariance constraints may be placed: the $\hat{\alpha}_g$ and $\hat{\Psi}_g$ matrices. We discuss constraints on these two matrices in turn.

Invariance of Covariances Among Latent Variables

Across-group invariance constraints may be placed on the variance–covariance matrix among the latent variables, the $\hat{\Psi}_g$ matrices. If one constrains all elements in the $\hat{\Psi}_g$ matrices to invariance across groups and if these constraints are imposed on the model in Equation 9c, the result would be

$$\mathbf{M}_g \cong \hat{\tau}\hat{\tau}' + \hat{\Lambda}(\hat{\alpha}_g\hat{\alpha}_g' + \hat{\Psi})\hat{\Lambda}' + \hat{\Theta}_\varepsilon = \hat{\mathbf{M}}_g, \qquad (9d)$$

where all terms are as defined earlier and the lack of subscripts on the $\hat{\Psi}$ matrix indicates the across-group invariance constraints on parameter estimates in this matrix.

At least three points must be made when considering invariance constraints on the $\hat{\Psi}$ matrices:

1. Invariance constraints on the $\hat{\Psi}$ matrices are substantively interpretable only if across-group metric invariance constraints have already beem placed on the $\hat{\Lambda}$ matrices. As noted earlier, the covariances among latent variables are ARF invariant only if the $\hat{\Lambda}$ matrices are constrained to invariance across groups. If the $\hat{\Lambda}$ matrices have not been constrained to invariance across groups, any constraints on the $\hat{\Psi}$ matrices typically will have no substantive interpretation.

2. If invariance constraints are placed simultaneously on all elements in the $\hat{\Psi}$ matrices, this represents a complex constraint on factor variances and factor intercorrelations. That is, invariance constraints on all elements of the $\hat{\Psi}$ matrices may lead to a significant worsening of fit if groups differ in variances on the factors, correlations among the factors, or both. Models may be specified to allow separate tests of the variances on and correlations among the latent variables (see, e.g., McArdle & Nesselroade, 1994), but this topic is beyond the scope of this chapter.

3. Finally, many have argued that metric invariance of the $\hat{\Psi}$ matrices should not be expected (cf. Meredith, 1964, 1993). Under random sampling of individuals in a population, se-

lection of a sample may be related to variables in the factor analysis. If this occurs, the $\hat{\tau}$ and $\hat{\Lambda}$ matrices should still exhibit metric invariance across groups, but the $\hat{\Psi}$ matrices would be expected to show clear differences across groups. Still, if imposing invariance constraints on the $\hat{\Psi}$ matrices results in little worsening of fit, the resulting model—with $\hat{\Psi}$ invariant across groups—is elegant.

Invariance of Means on the Latent Variables

The final matrices on which metric invariance constraints may be placed are the $\hat{\alpha}_g$ matrices, which contain the means of the latent variables. If one constrains all elements in the $\hat{\alpha}_g$ matrices to invariance across groups and if these constraints are imposed on the model in Equation 9d, the result would be

$$\mathbf{M}_g \cong \hat{\tau}\hat{\tau}' + \hat{\Lambda}(\hat{\alpha}\hat{\alpha}' + \hat{\Psi})\hat{\Lambda}' + \hat{\Theta}_\varepsilon = \hat{\mathbf{M}}, \qquad (9e)$$

where all terms are as defined earlier and the lack of subscripts on the $\hat{\alpha}$ matrix indicates the across-groups invariance constraints on parameter estimates in this matrix.

Metric invariance constraints on elements of the $\hat{\alpha}$ matrices make sense only if metric invariance constraints already have been imposed on both the $\hat{\tau}$ and $\hat{\Lambda}$ matrices. As discussed earlier, parameters in the $\hat{\alpha}$ matrices are ARF invariant only after the $\hat{\tau}$ and $\hat{\Lambda}$ matrices are constrained to invariance across groups. If the $\hat{\tau}$ and $\hat{\Lambda}$ matrices have not been constrained to invariance across groups, any constraints on the $\hat{\alpha}$ matrices will have no direct substantive interpretation.

Summary

In this section, we have discussed across-group metric invariance constraints on the $\hat{\alpha}$ and $\hat{\Psi}$ matrices: the matrices of means on, and variances and covariances among, the latent variables, respectively. Clearly, successful invariance constraints on these matrices may be desirable because parsimonious structural models would result from across-group metric constraints on all five model matrices. However, constraints on the $\hat{\alpha}$ and $\hat{\Psi}$ matrices are not nearly as crucial for representing data as the constraints on the $\hat{\tau}$ and $\hat{\Lambda}$ matrices, discussed earlier. Constraints on the $\hat{\tau}$ and $\hat{\Lambda}$ matrices are necessary to establish that the same latent variables are identified in each group; only if such constraints are invoked does it make sense to ask about mean or variance–covariance differences across groups on the latent variables. As with constraints on the $\hat{\Theta}_\varepsilon$ matrix, invariance constraints on the $\hat{\alpha}$ and $\hat{\Psi}$ matrices are helpful but not necessary for providing an easily interpretable representation of the data.

Partial Metric Invariance

In the foregoing, we discussed various kinds of invariance within CFA models in the standard fashion. When invariance constraints are to be imposed across groups on a particular matrix, we assumed that all parameters in the given matrix would be constrained to invariance across groups. Clearly, this is not necessary. For example, one may impose what may be termed *partial metric factorial invariance* (cf. Byrne, Shavelson, & Muthén, 1989; Reise et al., 1993). Under partial metric factorial invariance, only some of the parameter estimates in the $\hat{\Lambda}$, $\hat{\tau}$, and $\hat{\Theta}_\varepsilon$ matrices may be constrained to invariance across groups, and the remaining estimates may vary freely across groups.

We mentioned the topic of partial metric invariance here for completeness, but we do not discuss it in detail. The consideration of ideas and procedures related to partial metric invariance in any depth is beyond the scope of this chapter and would necessitate a much longer presentation. However, note that the notion of partial metric invariance is open to some dispute in the technical literature, especially partial metric factorial invariance. Although partial metric factorial invariance models may be specified (Byrne et al., 1989) and group differences in means and variances on the latent variables may be identified in an invariant fashion (Reise et al., 1993), many experts on structural modeling argue that partial metric factorial invariance models are not viable models for demonstrating that true ARF-invariant latent variables are identified. This clearly is a topic that will require further attention.

AN EMPIRICAL EXAMPLE

In this research, we explored the factorial invariance, across gender groups, of several measured indicators related to one type of substance use: current attitudes and behaviors about smoking. In particular, we tested for several types of factorial invariance as described earlier, including configural, weak, strong, and strict factorial invariance. Once factorial invariance was demonstrated, we also tested for metric invariance of the means on, and covariances among, the substance use latent variables across the gender groups. We provide a step-by-step demonstration of how to conduct invariance analyses, and the discussion is meant for readers with minimal experience in the structural modeling field.

Method

We selected variables from a large data set that was collected as part of an ongoing project on the lifestyles and values of youth (Johnston,

Bachman, & O'Malley, 1995). Since 1975, Johnston et al. have conducted annual assessments of large, nationally representative samples of high school seniors to document trends in attitudes and behaviors related to a wide array of licit and illicit drugs.

Participants

The participants in the Johnston et al. (1995) study were 16,500+ high school seniors. Subsets of students responded to one of six questionnaires that contained partially overlapping sets of items. Because we chose items from Form 5 of the Johnston et al. data set, we had a total sample size of 2,805 participants. In addition, because we intended to illustrate how to perform invariance analyses rather than to test a priori theory, we restricted our attention to the 1,796 Euro-American students in the sample. Of these 1,796 participants, 835 were male and 961 were female. The invariance analyses were then performed across the two gender groups. After dropping participants with missing data on items, we were left with 661 male and 812 female students, on whom all analyses reported in this chapter were based.

Instruments

We selected items from the Johnston et al. (1995) data set to serve as indicators of four latent variables. In doing so, we followed the basic stipulation that three indicators are required to identify a latent variable well (Jöreskog & Sörbom, 1989). To see why this is the case, consider the covariances among indicators for a given latent variable. If the latent variable has three indicators, there are six unique variances and covariances among the indicators. Moreover, seven parameters are associated with the latent variable: three factor loadings, three unique variances, and one factor variance. If one of these parameters is fixed to a nonzero value to identify the latent variable, we have as many parameters to be estimated ($n = 6$) as unique variance–covariance elements ($n = 6$). In the submodel for this latent variable, the model is termed *just identified*, with as many parameters to be estimated as there are unique variance–covariance elements. If a latent variable has only two indicators, the submodel is underidentified, with more parameter estimates ($n = 4$) than unique variance–covariance elements ($n = 3$). Although a latent variable with two indicators will still be identifiable if the latent variable is correlated with other latent variables, it is safer to have three indicators per latent variable (see Rindskopf, 1984, for an interesting discussion of these issues).

The 11 items we selected from the Johnston et al. (1995) data set are shown in Table 1. For each item, we provide a short descriptor (e.g., *cool*) that will be used later in tables and text to identify each item, list

TABLE 1
Measured Variables From Johnston, Bachman, and O'Malley's (1995) Study

Short label	Variable number	Item wording
Cool	v5421(v5427)	In my opinion, when a guy (girl) my age is smoking a cigarette, it makes him (her) look cool, calm, in-control.
Insecure	v5422(v5428)	In my opinion, when a guy (girl) my age is smoking a cigarette, it makes him (her) look insecure.
Independent	v5423(v5429)	In my opinion, when a guy (girl) my age is smoking a cigarette, it makes him (her) look rugged, tough, independent.
Conforming	v5424(v5430)	In my opinion, when a guy (girl) my age is smoking a cigarette, it makes him (her) look conforming.
Mature	v5425(v5431)	In my opinion, when a guy (girl) my age is smoking a cigarette, it makes him (her) look mature, sophisticated.
Trying	v5426(v5432)	In my opinion, when a guy (girl) my age is smoking a cigarette, it makes him (her) look like he's (she's) TRYING to appear mature and sophisticated.
Enjoy	v5433	Smokers know how to enjoy life more than nonsmokers.
No harm	v5435	The harmful effects of cigarettes have been exaggerated.
Don't mind	v5437	I personally don't mind being around people who are smoking.
Ever smoked	v5101	Have you ever smoked cigarettes?
Last 30 days	v5102	How frequently have you smoked cigarettes during the past 30 days?

Note. For items *cool* through *trying*, the first variable number for each item (v5421–v5426) used the male referent (e.g., guy, him), and the second variable number (v5427–v5432) used the female referent (e.g., girl, her).

the item number using the Johnston et al. (1995) numbering scheme, and give the exact text of the item as it appeared on the survey.

First, we selected six items to represent two constructs that reflect respondents' perceptions of peers who smoke: Perceived Coolness of peer smokers and the Perceived Insecurity of peer smokers. Johnston et al. (1995) developed two sets of items with common stems that were differentiated by gender of the referent. One set of items had the common stem "In my opinion, when a guy my age is smoking a cigarette, it makes him look. . . ." Six items were then generated by completing the preceding stem with (a) "cool, calm, in-control" (cool); (b) "insecure" (insecure); (c) "rugged, tough, independent" (independent); (d) "conforming" (conforming); (e) "mature, sophisticated" (mature); and (f) "like he's TRYING to appear mature and sophisticated" (trying).

A second set of items had the common stem "In my opinion, when a girl my age is smoking a cigarette, it makes her look. . . ." Six items were again generated by completing this stem with terms identical to the ones for male respondents, except for the following changes: "independent and liberated" (independent) and "like she's TRYING to appear mature and sophisticated" (trying).

To keep our data manageable, we selected the six items that used the male referent for male respondents and the six items that used the female referent for female respondents. In this way, the six indicators in each group represented each participant's perceptions of same-sex peers who smoked. As discussed in the Results section, we hypothesized that these size variables would be indicators for two latent variables: Perceived Coolness and Perceived Insecurity of peer smokers.

The remaining five items shown in Table 1 were used as indicators of two latent variables: Attitudes Toward Smoking and Smoking Behavior. The first two items were "Smokers know how to enjoy life more than nonsmokers" (enjoy) and "The harmful effects of cigarettes have been exaggerated" (no harm). Both of these items clearly reflected cognitive attitudes or beliefs regarding smoking. The third item (don't mind) appeared to have both attitudinal (or belief) and behavioral components, reflecting a lack of concern about being around people who smoke as well as actually being around others who smoke. The final two items asked whether the respondent had ever smoked (ever smoked) and how much the respondent had smoked during the past 30 days (last 30 days). These two items were clear markers of a Smoking Behavior factor.

The first 9 items listed in Table 1, items *cool* through *don't mind*, were answered on a scale ranging from 1 (*disagree*) to 5 (*agree*). Responses to the 10th item, *ever smoked*, also were made on a scale ranging from 1 (*not at all*) to 5 (*regularly now*). The last item, *last 30 days*, was answered on a scale ranging from 1 (*not at all*) to 6 (*about one and one-half packs per day*).

Analytical Procedures

In this study, we had a total of 11 measured variables (i.e., items) in each group, and we assumed that four common factors were present in each group. Hence, for both the male and female samples, the input data consisted of three matrices of statistics on the observed variables: an 11 × 1 vector of means, an 11 × 1 vector of standard deviations, and an 11 × 11 matrix of correlations. Because these matrices were large, we did not include a table that listed all of them. However, we include an Appendix, which provides a LISREL 8 program that fits our strong factorial invariance model to the data. In the program laid out in the Appendix, a two-group model is shown. The first group contains all data and model specifications for the sample of young men, and the second contains all data for specifications for the sample of young women. Thus, interested readers may use the information provided in the Appendix to fit all models discussed in this chapter, to verify their ability to arrive at the same indexes of model fit and so on as we reported in the Results section. Indeed, we encourage readers to fit the models discussed later in this section, to gain familiarity with the types of analyses discussed in this chapter.

Our Equation 9 and its variants 9a through 9e suggest the principle by which estimated structural models can be evaluated: Latent-variable models imply particular moment matrices. The statistical acceptability of an estimated model depends on how close the estimated moment matrices $\hat{M}_g$ are to the observed moment matrices M_g.

There are two typical ways of judging the adequacy of an estimated structural model. First, certain methods of estimation (e.g., maximum likelihood) yield a likelihood ratio chi-square statistic to test whether the moment matrices reproduced from the estimated parameters, $\hat{M}_g$, differ significantly from the observed sample moment matrices, M_g. In the multiple-group modeling context, a single chi-square value assessing aggregate fit across the $\hat{M}_g$ and M_g matrices for the multiple groups is obtained. If this chi-square value is statistically significant, there is a statistical basis for rejecting the tested model in favor of an alternative model with one or more additional parameters. If the chi-square value is statistically nonsignificant, the model is an adequate representation of the data.

In addition to evaluating the chi-square value for each model, we also evaluated the difference in chi-square values for nested structural models. If one model can be obtained by placing restrictions on parameter estimates in a second model (restrictions such as fixing parameters to zero), and the first model introduces no parameter estimates not contained in the second model, then the first model is nested within the second. In such circumstances, the difference in chi-square values for the two models, or the $\Delta\chi^2$, is distributed as a chi-square variate with degrees of freedom equal to the difference in degrees of freedom for the two models, or Δdf. Using the $\Delta\chi^2$ value, one may test the statistical significance of the difference in fit of the two models. If the $\Delta\chi^2$ value is statistically significant, the less restrictive model provides a significantly better fit to the data.

The likelihood ratio chi-square statistic appears to be overly sensitive to trivial discrepancies between $\hat{M}_g$ and M_g if sample size is large (e.g., Bentler & Bonett, 1980), as in the current study. Hence, structural models are often evaluated using so-called practical indexes of fit (Bentler & Bonett, 1980; Marsh, Balla, & McDonald, 1988). Although the relative merits of practical fit indexes are much debated, two principles should be followed to enable a more complete evaluation of model fit. First, two or more indexes of practical fit should be calculated for each model to ensure that similar characterizations of model fit are obtained. Second, no structural model should be accepted or rejected on statistical grounds alone; theory, judgment, and persuasive argument should play a key role in defending the adequacy of any estimated model.

To assess practical fit of models to data, we used five practical fit indexes: (a) the ratio of the chi-square for a model to its degrees of freedom; (b) the root-mean-square error of approximation (RMSEA) proposed by Steiger and Lind (1980); (c) the corrected Akaike information criterion (CAIC); (d) the Tucker–Lewis index (TLI; Tucker & Lewis, 1973); and (e) the comparative fit index (CFI), which was derived independently by Bentler (1990) and McDonald and Marsh (1990).

We used the χ^2:df ratio in our study in a heuristic, descriptive manner. The χ^2:df ratio performed poorly in the Marsh et al. (1988) Monte Carlo study of practical fit indexes. Marsh et al. found that the χ^2:df ratio was influenced by sample size, and there is no general agreement about the optimal or adequate magnitude of the χ^2:df ratio (e.g., the χ^2:df ratio should be below 3.0 or the model should be rejected). As a result, we used the χ^2:df ratio only to assess relative fit, following these steps: First, we established the χ^2:df ratio for a baseline model, or configural invariance model, with no invariance constraints. This provided an index of the amount of misfit per degree of freedom we accepted in the baseline model. We then evaluated the $\Delta\chi^2$:Δdf ratio for the *change in fit* between models to determine whether the lack of fit associated with the additional restrictions was discrepant from the χ^2:df ratio for the baseline model. If the $\Delta\chi^2$:Δdf ratio for a given restriction or set of restrictions is large, the restrictions lead to relatively larger amounts of misfit per degree of freedom than does the baseline model. In such cases, the restrictions place too much strain on model fit and should be relaxed.

The RMSEA is an absolute-fit measure, assessing badness of fit of a model per degree of freedom in the model. The lower bound of the RMSEA is zero, a value obtained only if a model fits a set of data perfectly. Browne (1990) stated that RMSEA values of about 0.05 indicate a close fit of a model to data and that values of about 0.08 reflect a reasonable fit of a model. Browne also developed a statistical test of "close" fit, which tests whether the RMSEA is significantly larger than .05, the criterion value of the RMSEA indexing close fit of a model to data. Recent work by Browne and Cudeck (1993) showed that the RMSEA performs well as an index of practical fit.

The CAIC is a modification of the Akaike information criterion. CAIC values do not fall on any standard metric. The primary way of interpreting CAIC values is as follows: Smaller values of the CAIC indicate better fit of the model to the data.

Turning to the final two practical-fit indexes, Marsh et al. (1988) found the TLI to be among the best of the then-available indexes of practical fit; the CFI, derived to improve the small-sample performance of the

TLI, has performed somewhat better than the TLI in recent simulations in conditions with small sample sizes (Bentler, 1990). These two practical-fit statistics are relative-fit indexes (cf. Bentler, 1990; McDonald & Marsh, 1990), indicating roughly the proportion of covariation among indicators explained by the model relative to a null model of independence in the indicators. Values near 0.0 indicate poor fit, whereas values near 1.0 indicate good fit. TLI and CFI values above .90 are typically considered satisfactory, but values above .95 are preferred (cf. Tucker & Lewis, 1973).

Finally, as with the chi-square statistic, we also computed the difference in practical-fit indexes between nested models. If practical-fit indexes change greatly when restrictions are placed on a model, then the restrictions must be fully justified theoretically or they should be relaxed.

Results

Testing Factorial Invariance Across Groups

The core tests of factorial invariance across groups in CFA models involve testing whether the factor loading matrices, $\hat{\Lambda}_g$, and the measured variable intercept matrices, $\hat{\tau}_g$, in Equation 9 are invariant across groups (cf. Alwin & Jackson, 1981; Meredith, 1993; Sörbom, 1974). That is, within the context of this study, the 11 measured variables had to relate to the four latent variables in the same way for the male and female samples.

Establishing the baseline model. When investigating factorial invariance within a multiple-group CFA model, the first step is to specify a baseline model that fits the data adequately. This baseline model is essentially a model with configural invariance, meaning that values in all model matrices are freely estimated for each group, given minimal constraints to identify the model in each group. This freely estimated, baseline model then serves as a benchmark against which the fit of more restricted models is compared.

In any CFA model, an indeterminacy exists between the scale of the factor loadings (the $\hat{\lambda}_{jk}$s, relating the latent variable to the measured variables) and the variance of the latent factor, η. That is, the values of the factor loadings depend on the scale of the latent factor. To identify the scale for the item parameters, the scale for the latent variable must be specified or vice versa. Reise et al. (1993) discussed this problem in considerable detail; here, we identify the baseline in the same fashion as Reise et al. did with their Baseline 3 specification. Under this specification, we did the following: (a) The factor variances for the four latent factors were fixed at 1.0 in the male sample, (b) the corresponding parameters were estimated in the female sample, (c) the first factor loading on each latent variable was constrained to invariance across groups, (d) the factor means were fixed to zero in the male sample, and (e) the τ parameter associated with the variable that loaded first on each factor was constrained to invariance across groups. To ensure complete understanding here with regard to the third and fifth points, consider the measured variable *cool*. We constrained the factor loading for cool on the first factor to be invariant across groups, as per the third point, and we constrained the $\hat{\tau}$ parameter for cool to be invariant across groups, as per the fifth point. Such across-groups constraints on one factor loading and one intercept, or $\hat{\tau}$, parameter per latent variable were sufficient to identify all remaining parameter estimates in the second group given the fixing of the factor variances in the first group. Moreover, the factor scores were scaled as z scores in the male sample, with means of zero and standard deviations of 1.0, and this enabled us to estimate differing means and standard deviations on the latent variables in the female sample.

Our a priori hypotheses with regard to the baseline model were as follows: (a) Four variables—cool, independent, conforming, and mature—would load on the Perceived Coolness factor; (b) three variables—insecure, conforming, and trying—would load on the Perceived Insecurity factor; (c) three variables—enjoy, no harm, and don't mind—would load on the Attitudes Toward Smoking factor; (d) three variables—don't mind, ever smoked, and last 30 days—would load on the Smoking Behavior factor; (e) all unique factors would be uncorrelated; and (f) the four common factors would be freely intercorrelated in both samples.

In the foregoing, two variables were hypothesized, on an a priori basis, to load on more than one factor. The first of these items was conforming; conforming behavior may reflect actions to be emulated and admired, showing acceptance of and identification with group norms, but conforming behavior also may be perceived as an overt attempt by an unaccepted peer to curry acceptance from the peer group. Thus, conforming was expected to load on both the Perceived Coolness and Perceived Insecurity factors given the complex interpretation of the behavior. The second item, as mentioned earlier, was don't mind. Individuals who rate themselves high on this item have accepting attitudes toward people who smoke and also are likely to spend more time around people who smoke. As a result, we expected don't mind to load on both the Attitudes Toward Smoking and the Smoking Behavior factors.

A total of three alterations to these a priori specifications were made to the initial baseline model, based on modification indexes, that indicate likely improvement in fit associated with modifications in model specification. These three modifications were as follows: (a) The unique factors for enjoy and last 30 days were allowed to covary in each group, based on the large modification index for this parameter in the female sample; (b) enjoy was allowed to load on the Perceived Insecurity factor in each group, in addition to loading on the Attitudes Toward Smoking factor; and (c) a

TABLE 2
Fit Indexes for Alternative Structural Models

Model	χ^2	df	χ^2:df	RMSEA	CAIC	TLI	CFI
1. Baseline	142.10	66	2.15	.028	872	.983	.990
2. Model 1 + $\hat{\Lambda}$ invariant (weak factorial)	158.54	77	2.06	.027	797	.984	.989
3. Model 2 + $\hat{\tau}$ invariant (strong factorial)	169.24	84	2.01	.026	750	.985	.989
4. Model 3 + $\hat{\Theta}_\varepsilon$ invariant (strict factorial)	263.14	96	2.74	.034	744	.975	.978
5. Model 3 + $\hat{\Psi}$ invariant	207.18	94	2.20	.029	705	.982	.985
6. Model 3 + $\hat{\alpha}$ invariant	214.11	88	2.43	.031	762	.979	.983

Note. All chi-square values were significant at the .001 level. RMSEA = root-mean-square error of approximation; CAIC = corrected Akaike information criterion; TLI = Tucker–Lewis index; CFI = comparative fit index.

loading by independent on the Smoking Behavior factor was estimated in each sample.

Given the foregoing, the final baseline model contained a total of 15 factor loadings per group and 12 unique factor variance–covariance elements per group (due to the one unique factor covariance estimated), and the remaining matrices—$\hat{\tau}$, $\hat{\Psi}$, and $\hat{\alpha}$—remained specified in accord with our a priori expectations. With the minor modifications to the a priori model, the baseline model had an adequate level of fit, as shown in Table 2. Specifically, the baseline model, termed *Model 1*, had a χ^2:df ratio of 2.15, an RMSEA of .028, and both TLI and CFI values greater than .980. As a result, despite the statistical significance of its chi-square statistic, Model 1 was deemed to have reasonable fit to the data, especially considering the large sample sizes in both groups.

Testing for weak factorial invariance. With fit values from the baseline, or configural invariance, model established, the hypothesis of weak factorial invariance, embodied in the test that $\hat{\Lambda}_1 = \hat{\Lambda}_2$, could then be evaluated. We tested this hypothesis by modifying Model 1, invoking the additional constraint that the $\hat{\Lambda}$ matrix be invariant across the male and female samples. The resultant chi-square from this restricted model, shown in Table 2, may be compared with the respective value for the baseline model because the weak factorial invariance model is nested within the baseline model (cf. Bentler & Bonett, 1980, on nested models). The weak factorial invariance model, identified as Model 2, is nested within the baseline model because one may arrive at the weak factorial invariance model simply by applying constraints on parameters in the baseline model. As discussed earlier, the difference in chi-square values between two nested models is itself distributed as a chi-square with degrees of freedom equal to the difference in degrees of freedom for the two models. If the restricted, nested model results in a nonsignificant increase in chi-square (or $\Delta\chi^2$) over that

TABLE 3
Differences in Fit of Alternative Structural Models

Model comparison	$\Delta\chi^2$	Δdf	$\dfrac{\Delta\chi^2}{\Delta df}$	Difference			
				RMSEA	CAIC	TLI	CFI
Model 1 vs. 2: Testing invariance of $\hat{\Lambda}$	16.44	11	1.49	−.001	−75	.001	−.001
Model 2 vs. 3: Testing invariance of $\hat{\tau}$	10.70	7	1.53	−.001	−47	.001	.000
Model 3 vs. 4: Testing invariance of $\hat{\Theta}_\varepsilon$	93.90*	12	7.83	.008	−6	−.010	−.011
Model 3 vs. 5: Testing invariance of $\hat{\Psi}$	37.94*	10	3.79	.003	−45	−.003	−.004
Model 3 vs. 6: Testing invariance of $\hat{\alpha}$	44.87*	4	11.22	.005	12	−.006	−.006

Note. For all model comparisons, the second-listed model is more restricted than, and is nested within, the first-level model. For example, for the Model 1 vs. 2 comparison, Model 2 is nested within Model 1. Given the way in which differences in practical-fit indexes were computed, negative values of the RMSEA and CAIC indicate better fit for the more restricted model, whereas negative values of the TLI and CFI indicate worse fit for the more restricted model. RMSEA = root-mean-square error of approximation; CAIC = corrected Akaike information criterion; TLI = Tucker–Lewis index; CFI = comparative fit index.
*$p < .001$.

for the less restricted model, then the hypothesis of weak factorial invariance is tenable. The differences in fit indexes for alternative structural models are shown in Table 3. Note, however, that we do not report the difference in the $\chi^2:df$ ratios for Models 1 and 2 in Table 3; rather, we report the $\Delta\chi^2:\Delta df$ ratio for the difference in the chi-square measure of fit for the two models.

Because one factor loading per latent variable was constrained to invariance in the baseline model, the weak factorial invariance model was obtained by constraining the remaining 11 factor loadings to invariance across groups. This accounted for the difference of 11 *dfs* between Models 1 and 2, shown in Tables 2 and 3.

As shown in Table 3, constraining the $\hat{\Lambda}$ matrix to invariance across groups led to a statistically nonsignificant decrease in model fit, $\Delta\chi^2(11, N = 1,328) = 16.44$, *ns*. The practical indexes of fit provided a similarly positive view with regard to this restriction. The $\Delta\chi^2:\Delta df$ ratio for the change in chi-square was 1.49 (or 16.44/11), which was even smaller than the $\chi^2:df$ ratio of 2.15 for the baseline model, suggesting that the additional constraints invoked to yield Model 2 led to an even smaller lack of fit per degree of freedom as held for the baseline model. Under such circumstances, Model 2, the more restricted model, would be preferred. Moreover, the TLI and RMSEA both improved slightly, the CFI was only marginally worse, and the CAIC was improved (i.e., lower). Overall, Model 2 appears to be clearly preferable to the less restricted Model 1.

Testing for strong factorial invariance. As noted earlier, the strong factorial invariance model, identified in Table 2 as Model 3, was attained by adding across-group invariance constraints on the $\hat{\tau}$ matrices to Model 2. In Models 1 and 2, 4 of the 11 elements in the $\hat{\tau}$ matrices were constrained to invariance across groups, given the manner in which we identified the models. In Model 3, the remaining 7 elements of the $\hat{\tau}$ matrices were constrained to invariance across the male and female samples. As a result, Models 2 and 3 differed by 7 dfs.

As shown in Table 3, constraining the $\hat{\tau}$ matrices to invariance across groups led to a statistically nonsignificant decrease in model fit, $\Delta\chi^2(7, N = 1,328) = 10.70$, ns. Once again, the practical indexes of fit yielded a similar message. The $\Delta\chi^2 : \Delta df$ ratio for the change in chi-square was 1.53 (or 10.70/7), which was smaller than the $\chi^2 : df$ ratio of 2.15 for the baseline model, suggesting that the additional constraints invoked to yield Model 3 led to a small lack of fit per degree of freedom relative to the baseline model. This result suggests that constraints on the $\hat{\tau}$ matrices "cost" little in terms of model fit. Once again, the RMSEA improved slightly, as did the TLI, and the CFI was unchanged. Furthermore, the CAIC improved greatly because of the efficiency (i.e., larger number of degrees of freedom) of Model 3. Taking all fit index values into account, the strong factorial invariance model, Model 3, is clearly preferable to the less restricted, weak factorial invariance model, Model 2.

In addition to its relatively better fit when compared with Models 1 and 2, Model 3 is also preferable on another point that is of considerable theoretical importance. Specifically, under Model 3, both the means on the latent variables as well as the variances on and covariances among the latent variables are ARF invariant. This means that interpretations of differences across the male and female samples with regard to mean level, variance–covariance, or both on the latent variables are invariant across the particular manner in which the model was identified.

Testing for strict factorial invariance. The strict factorial invariance model requires across-group invariance constraints on the $\hat{\Theta}_{eg}$ matrices in addition to those defining the strong factorial invariance model. Imposing these constraints resulted in the model we termed *Model 4*. The relative fit of Model 4 is shown most clearly by considering the difference in fit between Models 3 and 4, shown in Table 3. The difference in statistical fit between Models 3 and 4 was large, $\Delta\chi^2(12, N = 1,473) = 93.90$, $p < .001$, yielding a large 7.83:1 ratio of the difference in the chi-square to its degrees of freedom. The RMSEA showed a relatively large increase (i.e., worsening) of .008, the CAIC improved only slightly (decreasing by 6 units), and both the TLI and CFI declined by .01 or more. Taking these fit index values into account, we decided that imposing across-group constraints on the $\hat{\Theta}_{eg}$ matrices resulted in too great a cost in terms of model fit. Therefore, we opted to offer the strong factorial invariance model, Model 3, as providing the optimal CFA model for our data.

Testing Invariance Across Groups of Covariances Among and Means on Factors

Having settled on the strong factorial invariance model as the best representation of the measurement model parameters, we turned to testing the invariance of the variance–covariance matrices among the latent variables as well as the factor means across the male and female samples. Tests of parameter estimates in these matrices are not crucial for investigating factorial invariance, but they are most useful for studying differences between groups on the latent variables.

Testing invariance of factor variance–covariance matrices. To test the invariance of factor variance–covariance matrices across the male and female samples, we simply constrained all elements in the $\hat{\Psi}$ matrices to invariance across groups. When across-group invariance constraints were placed on the 10 elements in the $\hat{\Psi}$ matrices, we arrived at the model identified as Model 5. The comparison between Models 3 and 5 led to a statistically significant change in fit, $\Delta\chi^2(10, N = 1,473) = 37.94, p < .001$, and the $\Delta\chi^2 : \Delta df$ ratio of 3.79 was high. The RMSEA, TLI, and CFI were only modestly poorer as a result of this respecification, and the CAIC was once again improved. At this point, given the relative unimportance of invariance of factor variance–covariance matrices for studying factorial invariance and the relatively large $\Delta\chi^2 : \Delta df$ ratio, we decided that placing invariance constraints on the $\hat{\Psi}$ matrices "cost" too much in terms of model fit to the data. Thus, we chose not to impose the invariance constraints on the $\hat{\Psi}$ matrices across the male and female samples, deciding that Model 3 was preferable to Model 5.

Testing differences in mean level on the latent variables. Testing differences between the male and female samples in their mean levels on the latent variables involved invariance constraints on the $\hat{\alpha}$ matrices. Adding these constraints to our currently best fitting model, Model 3, resulting in Model 6, whose fit indexes are shown in Table 2. As shown in Table 3, the difference in statistical fit between Models 3 and 6 was significant, $\Delta\chi^2(4, N = 1,473) = 44.87, p < .001$, and the $\Delta\chi^2 : \Delta df$ ratio of 11.22 was large. Moreover, all of the practical-fit indexes—RMSEA, CAIC, TLI, and CFI—showed poorer levels for Model 6 than for Model 3. Thus, we decided that Model 6 also "cost" too much in fit relative to Model 3, leading to our choice of Model 3 as the optimal representation of these data.

Evaluating Parameter Estimates From the Final Structural Model

As noted earlier, we decided that Model 3 was the best representation of the data. Model 3 embodies the imposition of strong factorial invariance constraints. Hence, all elements in the $\hat{\tau}$ and $\hat{\Lambda}$ matrices were invariant across the male and female samples, although elements in the $\hat{\Theta}_\varepsilon$, $\hat{\Psi}$, and $\hat{\alpha}$ matrices varied across groups.

Measured variable intercept parameters. Parameter estimates in all five model matrices are provided in Table 4. The elements in the $\hat{\tau}$ matrix, listed in the first and second columns of the top half of Table 4, ranged from 1.56 to 3.61. These estimates had small standard errors, ranging from 0.04 to 0.06. As a result, all of these measured variable intercept terms were large, falling at least 36 SEs from zero.

Factor loadings. In columns 3 through 10 of the top half of Table 4, the factor loadings from the $\hat{\Lambda}$ matrix are given. These loadings are in covariance metric, so they are somewhat difficult to interpret directly. All 13 of the loadings hypothesized on an a priori basis were large, ranging from 0.45 to 1.33, with a median loading of 0.82. Moreover, these estimates had small standard errors, ranging from 0.03 to 0.06. As a result, these 13 loadings fell from almost 9 to more than 30 SEs from zero. These statistics suggest that all of the factor loadings were fairly large. Moreover, about 67% of the loadings were consistent with commonalities above .50, which means that the indicators tended to display moderately high levels of common variance. The two loadings estimated due to empirical considerations—the loading of enjoy on Factor 2 and independent on Factor 4—were fairly small (0.29 and −0.16, respectively) but significant (with z values between 5.0 and 6.0). These loadings were numerically small and are of no major theoretical importance; they were required to allow the baseline model to fit well and did replicate across the male and female samples, but future researchers should replicate these effects before much effort is expended in their interpretation. All in all, the elements in the $\hat{\tau}$ and $\hat{\Lambda}$ matrices that were hypothesized on an a priori basis appear to be at least moderately large or larger, confirming our hypotheses regarding the structure of variables in this domain.

Measurement residual variances. The measurement residuals, or residual variances of the measured variables, from the $\hat{\Theta}_{\varepsilon g}$ matrices are shown for the male and female samples, respectively, in columns 11 and 14 of the top half of Table 4. Once again, because these estimates are in covariance metric, the estimates are difficult to interpret directly because they ranged from 0.19 to 1.48. However, given the small standard errors, which ranged from 0.02 to 0.08, the elements in the $\hat{\Theta}_{\varepsilon g}$ matrices tended to fall at least 10 SEs from zero. Therefore, although the residual variances tended to represent less than 50% of the variance of each measured variable, the small standard errors showed that none of these estimates was close to zero.

Latent-variable variances and covariances. The factor covariances, from the $\hat{\Psi}_g$ matrices, for the male and female samples are shown in the middle of Table 4. Recall that the factor variances were fixed at 1.0 in the male sample, so these are not shown in Table 4. The resulting factor covariances for the male sample are shown below the diagonal of this section of the table; these covariances are correlations (i.e., standard covariances) attributable to the fixing of the factor variances at unity in this sample. The

TABLE 4
Parameter Estimates From Structural Model 3

Variable	$\hat{\tau}$ PE	$\hat{\tau}$ SE	Factor 1 PE	1 SE	2 PE	2 SE	3 PE	3 SE	4 PE	4 SE	$\hat{\Theta}_\epsilon$ M PE	M SE	F PE	F SE
					Measurement model parameters									
Cool	1.69	0.04	0.83	0.03	0*		0*		0*		0.35	0.03	0.19	0.02
Insecure	3.28	0.05	0*		0.95	0.04	0*		0*		0.78	0.06	0.91	0.06
Independent	1.93	0.04	0.95	0.04	0*		0*		−0.16	0.03	0.41	0.03	0.48	0.03
Conforming	2.64	0.04	0.45	0.04	0.60	0.04	0*		0*		1.34	0.08	1.48	0.08
Mature	1.69	0.04	0.82	0.03	0*		0*		0*		0.28	0.02	0.19	0.02
Trying	3.61	0.05	0*		1.01	0.05	0*		0*		0.77	0.07	0.58	0.06
Enjoy	1.56	0.04	0*		0.29	0.06	0.80	0.06	0*		0.44	0.05	0.36	0.03
No harm	1.91	0.04	0*		0*		0.62	0.04	0*		1.01	0.06	0.85	0.05
Don't mind	2.72	0.05	0*		0*		0.55	0.06	0.61	0.06	1.34	0.08	1.16	0.06
Ever smoked	2.38	0.06	0*		0*		0*		1.33	0.04	0.26	0.05	0.33	0.04
Last 30 days	1.65	0.05	0*		0*		0*		1.04	0.04	0.43	0.04	0.34	0.03
					Covariances among latent variables[a]									
Factor 1			**1.12**	**0.10**	−0.42	0.06	0.74	0.07	0.69	0.06				
Factor 2			−0.30	0.05	**1.18**	**0.12**	−0.76	0.08	−0.71	0.07				
Factor 3			0.74	0.04	−0.67	0.05	**0.93**	**0.08**	0.80	0.07				
Factor 4			0.50	0.04	−0.62	0.03	0.61	0.04	**1.04**	**0.09**				
					Means on latent variables									
M			0*		0*		0*		0*					
F			−0.08	0.06	0.27	0.06	−0.30	0.06	0.02	0.06				

Note. Parameters with asterisks were fixed to reported values to identify the model. The residual covariance between *enjoy* and *last 30 days* was 0.01 ($SE = 0.02$) for the male sample ($z = 0.39$, *ns*) and 0.10 ($SE = 0.02$) for the female sample ($z = 5.28$, $p < .001$). M = male sample; F = female sample; PE = maximum-likelihood parameter estimate.

[a] Factor variances for the male sample (not shown) were fixed to 1.0 to identify the model, so the covariances among factors for the male sample, shown below the diagonal of this matrix, are correlations (or standardized covariances). The boldface values on the diagonal are the estimated factor variances for the female sample, and the values above the diagonal are the covariances among factors for the female sample.

values in boldface on the diagonal are the factor variances for the female sample, and the values above the diagonal are the covariances among factors for the female sample. At least two trends should be noted with regard to the factor variance–covariance matrices:

1. Factor variances differed little between the male and female samples, in that estimated factor variances for the female sample were highly similar to the fixed values of 1.0 for the male sample, falling within 1–1.5 SEs of the value for the male sample.

2. A highly similar pattern of covariances among the latent variables was found for the male and female samples. Factors 1 and 2, Perceived Coolness and Perceived Insecurity of peer smokers, covaried negatively and at a relatively low level. Perceived Coolness (Factor 1) covaried positively and strongly with both Attitudes Toward Smoking and Smoking Behavior, Factors 3 and 4, respectively, whereas Perceived Insecurity (Factor 2) covaried negatively and strongly with the latter two factors. Finally, Attitudes Toward Smoking and Smoking Behavior were strongly and positively related.

Given these trends, one might wonder why the test for invariance of the $\hat{\Psi}$ matrices led to a relatively large change in fit. The key differences appear to rest with two covariances that appear to differ moderately across the male and female samples. Here, we refer specifically to the covariance between Factors 1 and 4 (.50 and .69 for the male and female samples, respectively) and the covariance between Factors 3 and 4 (.61 and .80 for the male and female samples, respectively). These covariances, which were consistently higher for the female sample, imply greater consistency between perceptions and attitudes toward smoking and actual smoking behaviors for the female than the male students. Further research should determine the replicability of this result, which may be an interesting gender-related question.

Factor means. Finally, the means on the latent variables for the male and female samples are presented in the bottom of Table 4. The factor means were fixed at zero in the male sample, as shown in Table 4, which enabled estimation of the factor means in the female sample. These estimates reveal that the male and female samples differed little on Factors 1 and 4. However, female students scored about 0.25 SD above the male students on Factor 2 (0.27) and almost 0.33 SD below male students on Factor 3. The mean difference on Factor 2 suggested that female students were more aware than the male students of the "showy" aspects of smoking: Smoking is often used as a way to gain acceptance by peers, rather than representing rational, mature behavior. Furthermore, the mean difference on Factor 3 showed that female students had lower attitudes toward, or acceptance of, smoking than did male students.

Summary. The CFA model, particularly Model 3, appeared to fit the data for both male and female students well. Two of the five model matrices, $\hat{\tau}$ and $\hat{\Lambda}$, were invariant across the two samples, embodying strong factorial invariance of the four factors in the male and female samples. The third matrix, $\hat{\Theta}_\varepsilon$, had values that varied across samples; sometimes male students had larger residual variances, and other times female students had larger residual variances. The final two matrices, $\hat{\Psi}$ and $\hat{\alpha}$, showed interesting patterns of similarity and difference across samples. By inspection, it appears that 8 of the 10 elements in the $\hat{\Psi}$ matrices might be successfully constrained to invariance across samples, as could 2 of the 4 estimates in the $\hat{\alpha}$ matrices. Doing so would lead to a model with partial metric invariance of the $\hat{\Psi}$ and $\hat{\alpha}$ matrices, along with full metric invariance of the $\hat{\tau}$ and $\hat{\Lambda}$ matrices. Such a model would be still more elegant and parsimonious than our Model 3, but issues of partial invariance are beyond the scope of this chapter and must await consideration at a later date.

Cautions About Model 3

Despite the good fit of Model 3 to the data, we note several reasons to be cautious when interpreting estimates associated with Model 3. These include the following:

1. Certain aspects of the model were data driven, particularly the specification of two factor loadings and one residual variance in each group. To our credit, we estimated the post hoc parameters in both samples, so that the model specification was identical across groups. Moreover, the two nonhypothesized factor loadings replicated well across the male and female samples, lending support to the idea that these should replicate in other samples. However, structural modeling is used properly when competing a priori models are compared. If some aspects of models are based on data-driven specifications, these should be verified in other samples, essentially through cross-validation across samples, before much time and effort are expended interpreting them.

2. Model 3 is only one of a large number of models that could be specified for our data. We argued earlier that we consider Model 3 to be a better model for the data than any of the competing models, from Model 1 through Model 6. However, yet another model, with a decidedly different form than any of the models we considered, could fit the data even better than did any of our proffered models, and researchers should not remain unaware to such possibilities.

3. Finally, we note the quality of the data. All of the data for our analyses were obtained from ratings on 5- or 6-point scales. Structural models are based on stringent assumptions —such as the linearity of relations among variables—and rating scale data may provide only weak bases for such assumptions. This could account for some degree of model misfit in all of our models; stronger conclusions would be reached if the data on which analyses were based had stronger measurement properties (i.e., more continuous measurement scales).

ISSUES IN MEASUREMENT INVARIANCE

In the foregoing sections, we discussed a variety of issues related to representing, testing, and interpreting factorial invariance analyses. We now address a number of issues related to invariance research, issues that reveal additional complexities that will be the focus of our research in the future.

Latent Versus Emergent Variables

Psychologists, in their varied research pursuits, use a most interesting yet challenging mélange of theoretical constructs. For example, current journals contain articles on diverse theoretical entities such as locus of control, body image distortion, narcissism, need for cognitive closure, sexual self-schema, and agreeableness. Researchers commonly accept the premise that psychological constructs, such as the list just given, exist at different conceptual levels or have differential breadth (e.g., narrow vs. broad). They seldom realize, however, that different types of constructs may require different types of measurement models (Ozer & Reise, 1994).

All of the models we considered in this chapter may be called *latent-variable models*, the most commonly used type of structural equation model in psychology. In a latent-variable model, the latent variable presumably affects or causes variation in its indicators. In structural modeling terms, the causal arrows go from the latent variable to its indicators, and indicators are assumed to be correlated because of the common influence of the latent variable on each of its indicators.

Recently, however, several researchers (e.g., Bollen & Lennox, 1991; Cohen, Cohen, Teresi, Marchi, & Velez, 1990) have drawn attention to a second class of measurement model, termed an *emergent variable measurement model*. In an emergent variable measurement model, causal arrows go from indicators to the latent variable. An excellent example of an emergent variable is socioeconomic status (SES), in which the indicators might be "prestige of current occupation," "current salary," "level of education," and so on. Clearly, a higher score on these indicators causes higher SES; SES does not influence its indicators. Thus, losing one's job would lead to lower SES, but this lowered status would leave one's years of attained education unchanged. This pattern of results could occur easily if SES were an emergent variable, but it could not occur if SES were a latent variable because change in a latent variable is reflected in change in all of its indicators.

The distinction between latent and emergent variables is not a trivial one. Indeed, this distinction may have profound consequences for evaluating structural models, as Cohen et al. (1990) argued that treating an emergent construct as if it were a latent variable will produce erroneous parameter estimates. Unfortunately, MacCallum and Browne (1993) identified several critical problems that may be encountered when emergent variables are specified within programs devoted to latent-variable modeling. There currently is no resolution of the issues and problems surrounding emergent variables; we hope these issues will be resolved in the near future. For now, one should remember that not all constructs should be represented as latent variables, and some modifications to procedures discussed in this chapter would be needed to represent measurement or factorial invariance of emergent variables.

Who Is in a Group?

Issues related to factorial invariance arise because researchers are concerned that the respondent population is heterogeneous. That is, an investigator may be concerned that groups within the population exist for whom the indicator variables are differentially related to the latent variables. This is an important concern because, as discussed previously, a prerequisite for comparing groups of respondents on a latent variable is that the indicators of the latent variable function equivalently across groups of respondents.

The primary benefit of the methods discussed in this chapter is that these procedures provide simple and direct ways of testing crucial hypotheses related to factorial invariance. That is, provided that the data are of good quality, CFA models provide an adaptable and powerful set of tools for investigating similarities and differences across groups in measurement structures.

Although CFA models yield solutions to a number of important statistical problems, important problems still remain when conducting measurement invariance analyses. One of the most important of these problems is embodied in the question Who is in a group? The solution to this problem is to examine carefully our definition of a group. For example, consider a study of socialization practices in which respondents consist of adults living in a large metropolitan area, such as Los Angeles. A researcher might assume that the socialization practice measures should be tested for invariance across at least three of the major ethnicities: Euro-American, Latino, and African American. There are problems in such an approach, however. For example, this approach assumes implicitly that the major focus of invariance analyses should be invariance across ethnicity groups, but this may be a questionable assumption. Given the important relations of both income and parental education with socialization practices, perhaps groups differentiated on the basis of income or parental education would be a far more crucial basis for invariance analyses than groups differentiated on the basis of ethnicity.

Furthermore, the "ethnicity group" design might suffer from another type of problem related to group membership. Consider our Latino sample. This group is likely to include third-generation Mexican Americans, first-generation Mexican Americans, recent immigrants from both rural and urban Mexico, recent immigrants from South America, and individuals from Central America. Are all of these people to be seriously considered a part of a single Latino "group" in terms of the variables collected in the study? We believe that in most cases, the answer will be no. Yet, if we further fractionate the Latino sample to reflect reasonable differences among its subgroups, will we still have sample sizes large enough to evaluate invariance? Again, frequently, the answer will be no.

To avoid these problems, we recommend that tests of measurement invariance be justified on an a priori basis, buttressed by both strong theoretical argument and large sample sizes. This means that we should justify, on psychological grounds, why we are dividing respondents into groups the way we are and how we expect the samples to differ with regard to the measurement model. Moreover, if we decide that a certain "group" should be subdivided into two or more subgroups to test an important theoretical question, a larger sample size will accommodate this. These are extremely stringent requirements given the current states of psychological knowledge and federal funding for research, but nevertheless we encourage movement toward these ideals.

Moreover, even if one detects differences between groups in crucial CFA model parameters, the CFA models do not indicate why these differences occur. Many psychological, cultural, or economic factors may contribute to the group differences observed, especially if groups were formed on the basis of variables such as gender or ethnicity. The CFA models presented in this chapter therefore are not ends in themselves. Instead, the CFA models may be used to isolate the ways in which groups differ on variables, providing a concise statistical representation of group differences and thus serving as a springboard for additional research designed to identify the sources of group differences on the latent and measured variables.

Loadings Versus Thresholds

The majority of research studies that have examined invariance have been concerned, either formally or informally, only with the equivalence of factor loadings across two or more groups of individuals. Factor loadings represent regressions of observed variables on the latent variables, and the equivalence of loadings across groups means that the manifest variables are equally saturated with the latent variable, or relate in the same way to the latent variable, across the relevant groups. Yet, there is more to the relationship of an item to a latent variable than its loadings.

As Reise et al. (1993) argued, IRT models routinely recognize at least two parameters for describing the relationship between an observed variable (e.g., a test item) and a latent variable. These two parameters are the discrimination and the difficulty of the item. The discrimination parameter represents the relationship between item endorsement and the latent variable; as a result, the discrimination parameter is analogous to a factor loading in CFA models. The second IRT parameter—the item difficulty—refers to the trait level an examinee must attain to have a 50% probability of endorsing the test item. The difficulty parameter in IRT is analogous to the measured variable intercepts, or elements of the τ matrices, in CFA models.

IRT studies of measurement invariance (see Flannery, Reise, & Widaman, 1995; Reise et al., 1993) routinely examine the invariance of both the item discrimination and difficulty parameters. In fact, group differences in the item difficulty parameters are potentially substantively more interesting than identifying group differences in the item discriminations. In addition, requiring invariance of both discrimination and difficulty parameters represents a more difficult hurdle for a measurement model to surpass than requiring invariance of only one of these sets of parameters. If one's measurement theory for a set of measured variables passes a more difficult hurdle, one rightly has more confidence that the latent trait and its indicators provide a solid basis for further research.

Although long recognized in IRT modeling approaches, the importance of testing both the factor loadings and the intercept, or $\hat{\tau}$, parameters in CFA models when testing factorial invariance has been appreciated only recently (Meredith, 1993). Indeed, testing the invariance of intercepts in CFA models enables the differentiation between weak and strong factorial invariance. Furthermore, if the $\hat{\tau}$ parameters are invariant across groups, mean differences between groups on the latent variables are ARF invariant. These were the reasons why we went beyond the typical presentation of procedures for testing factorial invariance, cluttering up our models by including the $\hat{\tau}$ and $\hat{\alpha}$ matrices. We did so because these models provided stronger tests of our measurement theories. Clearly, we encourage researchers to use the CFA models we have discussed in this chapter to evaluate the factorial invariance of their measures more stringently.

How Good Is Good?

A final issue for continued research involves procedures for evaluating the goodness of fit of CFA models. The process of evaluating whether observed relationships are invariant across two or more groups using CFA models is highly statistical and technical in nature. A quick perusal of the professional literature will uncover a plethora of statistical and practical indexes for evaluating whether invariance hypotheses are tenable given the observed data. The most common index is, of course, the chi-square test of model fit. However, because this index is highly dependent on sample size, its role in evaluating models has been downplayed in recent years. In fact, most researchers recommend computing two or more practical indexes of model fit; if these are in acceptable ranges, then the model is assumed to be an adequate representation of the data.

Yet, the fact remains that the implications to be drawn from practical-fit indexes are unclear. Even if a particular invariance model looks fairly good according to several practical-fit indexes, researchers still do not know how lack of fit may affect their substantive conclusions, especially at the level of the individual participant. We have two recommendations with regard to evaluating the fit of invariance models. First, researchers should investigate ways of representing the fit of any model at the individual level. Using IRT procedures, the fit of a model at the level of the individual respondent can be represented, and fit indexes of this type yield information on the usefulness of the model for representing the data for the individual. We are investigating similar indexes of fit at the individual level for CFA models. If such measures were validated and useful, one could then test both an invariance model and a more relaxed, noninvariance model and evaluate these alternative models at the level of the individual respondent. Doing so would allow an evaluation of the effect of imposing certain invariance constraints on the validity of each respondent's data.

Second, researchers must determine the form of invariance necessary to feel comfortable comparing respondents across multiple groups. As we have described, Meredith (1993) distinguished among several forms of invariance: weak, strong, and strict factorial invariance. Questions remain, however, such as at what level of factorial invariance should the researcher be satisfied? Should different levels of factorial invariance suffice in different substantive domains? Do statistical and practical indexes yield adequate, ultimate indexes of model fit, or could a model yield a poor representation of data despite having acceptable levels of statistical and practical fit? Answers to these questions should advance the knowledge of factorial invariance in important ways; we hope that these answers will come soon.

CONCLUSION

In closing, we hope that we have conveyed issues in testing factorial invariance in ways that illustrate the interesting, intriguing questions to be asked of data as well as the vexing questions that remain to be resolved. We continue our efforts to explore invariance issues, and we hope that this chapter will provide a useful source for future musings and excursions into representing and testing the invariance of relations among psychological measures.

REFERENCES

Alwin, D. F., & Jackson, D. J. (1981). Application of simultaneous factor analysis to issues of factorial invariance. In D. J. Jackson & E. F. Borgatta (Eds.), *Factor analysis and measurement in sociological research* (pp. 249–279). Beverly Hills, CA: Sage.

Bentler, P. M. (1990). Comparative fit indices in structural models. *Psychological Bulletin, 107*, 238–246.

Bentler, P. M., & Bonett, D. G. (1980). Significance tests and goodness of fit in the analysis of covariance structures. *Psychological Bulletin, 88*, 588–606.

Bollen, K., & Lennox, R. (1991). Conventional wisdom on measurement: A structural equation perspective. *Psychological Bulletin, 110*, 305–314.

Browne, M. W. (1990). *MUTMUM PC: User's guide*. Columbus: Ohio State University, Department of Psychology.

Browne, M. W., & Cudeck, R. (1993). Alternative ways of assessing model fit. In K. A. Bollen & J. S. Long (Eds.), *Testing structural equation models* (pp. 136–162). Newbury Park, CA: Sage.

Byrne, B. M. (1994). Testing for the factorial validity, replication, and invariance of a measuring instrument: A paradigmatic application based on the Maslach Burnout Inventory. *Multivariate Behavioral Research, 29*, 289–311.

Byrne, B. M., & Shavelson, R. J. (1987). Adolescent self-concept: Testing the assumption of equivalent structure across gender. *American Educational Research Journal, 24*, 365–385.

Byrne, B. M., Shavelson, R. J., & Muthén, B. (1989). Testing for the equivalence of factor covariance and mean structures: The issue of partial measurement invariance. *Psychological Bulletin, 105*, 456–466.

Cohen, P., Cohen, J., Teresi, J., Marchi, M., & Velez, N. C. (1990). Problems in the measurement of latent variables in structural equations causal models. *Applied Psychological Measurement, 14*, 183–196.

Cudeck, R. (1989). Analysis of correlation matrices using covariance structure models. *Psychological Bulletin, 105*, 317–327.

Drasgow, F. (1984). Scrutinizing psychological tests: Measurement equivalence and equivalent relations with external variables are central issues. *Psychological Bulletin, 95,* 134–135.

Drasgow, F. (1987). Study of the measurement bias of two standardized psychological tests. *Journal of Applied Psychology, 72,* 19–29.

Drasgow, F., & Kanfer, R. (1985). Equivalence of psychological measurement in heterogeneous populations. *Journal of Applied Psychology, 70,* 662–680.

Flannery, W. P., Reise, S. P., & Widaman, K. F. (1995). An item response theory analysis of the general and academic scales of the Self-Description Questionnaire II. *Journal of Research in Personality, 29,* 168–188.

Frederiksen, N. (1987). How to tell if a test measures the same thing in different cultures. In Y. H. Poortinga (Ed.), *Basic problems in cross cultural psychology* (pp. 14–18). Amsterdam: Swets & Zeitlinger.

Horn, J. L., McArdle, J. J., & Mason, R. (1983). When is invariance not invariant: A practical scientist's look at the ethereal concept of factor invariance. *Southern Psychologist, 4,* 179–188.

Hui, C. H., & Triandis, H. C. (1985). Measurement in cross-cultural psychology. *Journal of Cross-Cultural Psychology, 16,* 131–152.

Johnston, L. D., Bachman, J. G., & O'Malley, P. M. (1995). *Monitoring the future: A continuing study of the lifestyles and values of youth, 1993.* Ann Arbor: University of Michigan, Interuniversity Consortium for Political and Social Research.

Jöreskog, K. G. (1971). Simultaneous factor analysis in several populations. *Psychometrika, 36,* 409–426.

Jöreskog, K. G., & Sörbom, D. (1989). *LISREL 7: A guide to the program and applications* (2nd ed.). Chciago: SPSS.

Linn, R. L., & Harnisch, D. L. (1981). Interactions between item content and group membership on achievement test items. *Journal of Educational Measurement, 18,* 109–118.

Lord, F. M. (1980). *Applications of item response theory to practical testing problems.* Hillsdale, NJ: Erlbaum.

MacCallum, R. C., & Browne, M. W. (1993). The use of causal indicators in covariance structure models: Some practical issues. *Psychological Bulletin, 114,* 533–541.

Marsh, H. W., Balla, J. R., & McDonald, R. P. (1988). Goodness-of-fit indices in confirmatory factor analysis: The effect of sample size. *Psychological Bulletin, 103,* 391–410.

McArdle, J. J., & Nesselroade, J. R. (1994). Using multivariate data to structure developmental change. In S. H. Cohen & H. W. Reese (Eds.), *Life-span developmental psychology: Methodological contributions* (pp. 223–267). Hillsdale, NJ: Erlbaum.

McDonald, R. P., & Marsh, H. W. (1990). Choosing a multivariate model: Noncentrality and goodness of fit. *Psychological Bulletin, 107,* 247–255.

McGaw, B., & Jöreskog, K. G. (1971). Factorial invariance of ability measures in groups differing in intelligence and socioeconomic status. *British Journal of Mathematical and Statistical Psychology, 24,* 154–168.

Meredith, W. (1964). Notes on factorial invariance. *Psychometrika, 29,* 177–185.

Meredith, W. (1993). Measurement invariance, factor analysis and factorial invariance. *Psychometrika, 58,* 525–543.

Millsap, R. E. (1995). Measurement invariance, predictive invariance, and the duality paradox. *Multivariate Behavioral Research, 30,* 577–605.

Ozer, D. J., & Reise, S. P. (1994). Personality assessment. *Annual Review of Psychology, 45,* 357–388.

Reise, S. P., Widaman, K. F., & Pugh, R. H. (1993). Confirmatory factor analysis and item response theory: Two approaches for exploring measurement invariance. *Psychological Bulletin, 114,* 552–566.

Reynolds, C. R., & Harding, R. E. (1983). Outcome in two large sample studies of factorial similarity under six methods of comparison. *Educational and Psychological Measurement, 43,* 723–728.

Rindskopf, D. (1984). Structural equation models: Empirical identification, Heywood cases, and related problems. *Sociological Methods and Research, 13,* 109–119.

Sörbom, D. (1974). A general method for studying differences in factor means and factor structure between groups. *British Journal of Mathematical and Statistical Psychology, 27,* 229–239.

Steiger, J. H., & Lind, J. (1980, May). *Statistically based tests for the number of common factors.* Paper presented at the meeting of the Psychometric Society, Iowa City, IA.

Tucker, L. R., & Lewis, C. (1973). A reliability coefficient for maximum likelihood factor analysis. *Psychometrika, 38,* 1–10.

Windle, M., Iwawaki, S., & Lerner, R. M. (1988). Cross-cultural comparability of temperament among Japanese and American preschool children. *International Journal of Psychology, 23,* 547–567.

APPENDIX

The following is a program, written in LISREL 8 syntax, to fit our Model 3.

```
Males' (N = 661) data—Model 3, Strong Factorial Invariance Model, LY&TY inv
da  ng=2  ni=11  no=661  ma=cm
la
Cool          Insecure   Indpndnt  Confrmng  Mature  Trying
Enjoy         No_harm    DontMind
EverSmok      Lst30dys
me
    1.702  3.265  1.900  2.605  1.708  3.626  1.555  1.953  2.670  2.374  1.654
sd
    1.032  1.305  1.078  1.301  0.971  1.357  0.932  1.178  1.511  1.426  1.242
km sy
  1.000
 −.233   1.000
  .668  −.137   1.000
  .221   .172   .199   1.000
  .678  −.207   .661   .227   1.000
 −.203   .571  −.086   .244  −.157   1.000
  .436  −.180   .404   .067   .511  −.231   1.000
  .293  −.230   .280  −.023   .330  −.245   .350   1.000
  .362  −.355   .302  −.030   .349  −.333   .342   .352   1.000
  .387  −.449   .273  −.034   .361  −.429   .328   .286   .545   1.000
  .340  −.385   .225  −.029   .358  −.428   .303   .275   .479   .794   1.000
select
  1 2 3 4 5 6 7 8 9 10 11  /
mo ny=11 ne=4 ly=fu,fi ps=sy,fr te=sy,fi ty=fr al=fi
pa ly
1 0 0 0
0 1 0 0
1 0 0 1
1 1 0 0
1 0 0 0
0 1 0 0
0 1 1 0
0 0 1 0
0 0 1 1
0 0 0 1
0 0 0 1
pa ps
0
1 0
1 1 0
1 1 1 0
pa te
1
0 1
0 0 1
0 0 0 1
0 0 0 0 1
0 0 0 0 0 1
0 0 0 0 0 0 1
0 0 0 0 0 0 0 1
0 0 0 0 0 0 0 0 1
0 0 0 0 0 0 0 0 0 1
0 0 0 0 0 1 0 0 0 1
st 1.0 ps 1 1 ps 2 2 ps 3 3 ps 4 4
le
SmSxCool  SmSxIns  Attitude  Behavior
ou  ndec=3
```

Females' (*N* = 812) data—Model 3, Strong Factorial Invariance Model, LY&TY inv

```
da  ng=2  ni=11  no=812  ma=cm
la
Cool        Insecure   Indpndnt  Confrmng  Mature  Trying
Enjoy       No_harm    DontMind
EverSmok    Lst30dys
me
  1.611    3.539    1.876    2.787   1.617   3.863   1.394   1.696   2.605   2.403   1.663
sd
  0.978    1.398    1.157    1.392   0.977   1.327   0.834   1.096   1.567   1.475   1.204
km sy
  1.000
 -.278    1.000
  .700   -.186    1.000
  .113    .291     .197    1.000
  .803   -.259     .724     .136   1.000
 -.284    .595    -.160     .305  -.222   1.000
  .474   -.161     .386    -.007   .467  -.229   1.000
  .328   -.228     .261    -.106   .329  -.316    .386   1.000
  .499   -.427     .379    -.113   .471  -.435    .376    .396   1.000
  .545   -.417     .377    -.148   .507  -.478    .466    .371    .648   1.000
  .520   -.377     .365    -.095   .492  -.464    .532    .390    .592    .807   1.000
select
   1 2 3 4 5 6 7 8 9 10 11  /
mo  nk=0  ny=11  ne=4  ly=in  ps=sy,fr  te=ps  ty=in  al=fr
le
SmSxCool  SmSxIns  Attitude  Behavior
ou  ndec=3
```

Note. The following acronyms were used in the LISREL 8 syntax: da = data parameters card; ng = number of groups; ni = number of input variance; no = number of observations; ma = matrix to be analyzed; cm = covariance matrix; la = labels for observed variables; Indpndnt = independent; Confrmng = confirming; DontMind = don't mind; EverSmok = ever smoked; Lst30dys = last 30 days; me = mean; sd = standard deviation; km = correlation matrix; sy = symmetric; mo = model parameters card; ny = number of observed *Y* variables; ne = number of ηs or factors; ly = Λ matrix for the observed *Y* variables; ps (as a matrix name, before an = sign) for the Ψ matrix; te = Θ_ϵ matrix; ty = τ vector; al = α vector; pa = pattern matrix of fixed and free values; fu = full; fi = fixed; fr = free; st = start values; le = labels for the ηs or latent variables; ou = output parameter card; ndec = number of decimal places to be reported on output; in = invariance of a matrix across groups; ps (as a descriptor of values in a matrix, after an = sign) = the same pattern and start values as the first group; SmSxCool = Same Sex Cool; SmSxIns = Same Sex Insecure.

10

ANALYSIS WITH MISSING DATA IN PREVENTION RESEARCH

JOHN W. GRAHAM, SCOTT M. HOFER, STEWART I. DONALDSON, DAVID P. MacKINNON, AND JOSEPH L. SCHAFER

Missing data are pervasive in alcohol and drug abuse prevention evaluation efforts: Researchers administer surveys, and some items are left unanswered. Slow readers often leave large portions incomplete at the end of the survey. Researchers administer the surveys at several points in time, and people fail to show up at one or more waves of measurement. Researchers often design their measures to include a certain amount of "missingness"; some measures are so expensive (in money or time) that researchers can afford to administer them only to some respondents.

Missing data problems have been around for years. Until recently, researchers have fumbled with partial solutions and put up only the weakest counterarguments to the admonitions of the critics of prevention and applied psychological research. Things have changed, however. Statistically sound solutions are now available for virtually every missing data problem,

This research was supported in part by National Institute on Alcoholism and Alcohol Abuse Grants R03 AA 08736 and R01 AA 06201 and National Institute on Drug Abuse Grant P50 DA 10076. Portions of this research were presented at the annual meeting of the Society of Multivariate Experimental Psychology, Blaine, Washington, October 1995.

and many of these solutions are being incorporated into the mainstream of prevention and applied psychological research. There is no longer any excuse for using archaic (and sometimes horribly wrong) procedures such as mean substitution.

In this chapter, we outlined some of the leading approaches to dealing with missing data problems. In the first section, we discuss methods for missing continuous data. For this type of data, we recommend four approaches that are based on widely available software. Although these procedures vary in ease of use, at least three of the four require no more than modest experience with statistical analysis. These three methods are illustrated using an empirical problem.

In the second section, we discuss missing categorical data. In this case, the state of the art has been somewhat slower in reaching all levels of applied research. Methods are currently under development that will soon be as widely available as the methods for missing continuous data. In this chapter, we present the beginnings of a maximum-likelihood approach to analysis with missing categorical data. Furthermore, in the context of an empirical missing data problem, we discuss the use of a multiple imputation procedure for categorical data and touch on the use of continuous-data methods for analyzing categorical data.

In the third section, we discuss what happens when the assumptions underlying our recommended approach are not met fully. New data are presented relating to the causes of missingness. Our interpretation of these data is that the vast majority of causes of missing data may be fully explainable and fully adjusted by using the methods that we recommend.

In the fourth section, we present a general sensitivity analysis for the case in which the assumptions of the recommended missing data procedures are not met fully. We conclude from this analysis that except in extreme situations, statistical conclusions that are based on the methods we recommend are virtually the same as methods that would take all sources of missingness into account.

In the final section, we discuss new approaches, currently under development, that should be widely available to prevention and applied psychological researchers over the next few years. We conclude with a few comments about the state of missing data analysis in prevention and other applied psychological research. We suggest that prevention studies in general may be relatively free from serious attrition biases (if recommended analyses are used).

ANALYSIS WITH MISSING CONTINUOUS DATA

We discuss three types of missing data problems: omissions, attrition, and planned missingness. *Omissions* occur when a respondent fails to complete an item within a survey or fails to complete a survey. We argue that this type of missingness is little more than a nuisance. In most of our prevention work, we have seen relatively few omissions in the middle of a survey. The more common problem is that respondents fail to complete the survey once they begin it. We suggest that the main reason for this latter kind of missingness is slow reading. Thus, if reading skill, or a reasonable proxy for reading skill, is included in the missing data model (using one of the methods we recommend), the overall impact of this kind of missingness is negligible.

We use the term *attrition* when a respondent fails to show up for an entire wave of measurement. For a multiwave project, some participants disappear at one wave of measurement but reappear at a subsequent wave. Others disappear and are never measured again. We argue that the former type of attrition is virtually no problem if the recommended missing data methods are used. Data obtained at early and late waves are excellent predictors of data missing at middle waves. The latter kind of attrition (i.e., the respondent leaves and never returns) is potentially a greater problem. Because the later waves of data are missing, it is possible that the scores on the missing variables are themselves the cause of missingness (e.g., heavy drinkers avoid the measurement situation). However, the data presented in the third section of this chapter help us argue that it is unlikely that this sort of attrition presents problems for statistical conclusions beyond those that are completely adjusted when the recommended missing data methods are used.

The two kinds of *planned missingness* we have encountered are (a) the use of the three-form measurement design (see Graham, Hofer, & MacKinnon, 1996) and (b) collection of special measures (e.g., biochemical measures) that are too expensive to obtain for every respondent. Because this form of missingness is under the researcher's control, the missing data in this situation can be considered to be missing completely at random (MCAR). Beyond some loss of statistical power, this type of missingness poses minimal threats to statistical conclusions.

Missing Data Mechanisms

There are three causes of missingness (i.e., three missing data mechanisms): MCAR, accessible, and inaccessible. Data are MCAR when the cause of missingness is some random event such as a coin toss or number selected from a table of random numbers. For example, if respondents are randomly selected to receive some special measure, those who do not complete the measure are MCAR. However, except for the case of planned missingness, data are seldom missing because of some truly random event.

In many situations, the missingness is systematic (i.e., caused by some variable). Fortunately, the data may be MCAR even in this situation. If the cause of missingness is some variable (e.g., mobility of parents) that is not correlated with the variable that is missing (e.g., 8th-grade alcohol use), then the missing data are still MCAR. The big advantage of data being MCAR is that the cause of missingness does not have to be part of the analysis to control for missing data biases. Although many traditional procedures (e.g., listwise deletion) yield unbiased results when the missing data are MCAR, such methods are often undesirable, even in this situation (e.g., because of low statistical power). The missing data procedures we recommend provide a convenient and unbiased way of dealing with missing data that are MCAR.

As one might imagine, however, data are not always MCAR. As we suggested earlier, data are frequently missing systematically because of another variable. If this other variable is correlated with the variable containing the missing data, the mechanism is no longer MCAR. If the cause of missingness has been measured and is available for analysis, we refer to this as an *accessible missing data mechanism*. This is good news. If the cause of missingness has been measured and is included properly in the analysis, all biases associated with the missing data are adjusted. Little and Rubin (1987) referred to this situation as "ignorable" (they also referred to it as "missing at random"). The procedures we recommend adjust for all biases that are attributable to missing data when the missing data mechanism is accessible. However, this is true only if the cause of missingness is included in the analysis.

There are situations in which the cause of missingness (a) has not been measured and (b) is correlated with the variable containing the missingness. We refer to this as an *inaccessible missing data mechanism* (Little & Rubin, 1987, referred to this as a "nonignorable mechanism"). This situation could arise when the value of the missing variable is itself the cause of missingness. For example, heavy drinkers may be more likely to avoid the measurement situation than are light drinkers. The situation also could arise in other ways. For example, rebellious adolescents may be more likely to resist measurement. Such individuals also are more likely to use and abuse drugs and alcohol. Thus, if rebelliousness is not measured, missing alcohol and drug use information could be missing because of an inaccessible mechanism.

Missing Data Methods Recommended for Continuous Data

In this section, we outline four missing data methods: (a) the expectation–maximization (EM) algorithm (with bootstrap estimates of standard errors), (b) multiple imputation, (c) multiple-group structural equation modeling (MGSEM), and (d) raw maximum-likelihood (RML) methods.

EM Algorithm

The EM algorithm (Dempster, Laird, & Rubin, 1977; Little & Rubin, 1987), as implemented in EMCOV.EXE (Graham & Hofer, 1993), is an iterative imputation method. Briefly, missing values are imputed by using all other variables as predictors in a regression model. Using real and imputed values, sums and sums of squares and cross-products (SSCPs) are calculated (the E-step). The covariance matrix and associated regression coefficients (each variable is predicted by all others) are then calculated from the SSCP matrix (the M-step). The regression coefficients are then used to make better imputations at the next E-step, and the new imputed values are used to estimate a new covariance matrix as well as new regression coefficients. The process is repeated until the changes in the estimated covariance matrix are small enough to be deemed trivial.

After the final iteration, the EMCOV.EXE program writes out the variance–covariance estimates and vector of means. Analyses then can be conducted using that matrix as input. An important part of using the EM algorithm is that standard errors are not calculated directly for the analyses of ultimate interest. (Even though such standard errors are provided by the analysis used, they are not correct; they are based on the wrong sample size, and there is no way to include the correct sample size in the analysis.) One way to obtain standard errors in this situation is to use a bootstrap procedure (Efron, 1981, 1994; Graham, Hofer, & Piccinin, 1994).

Bootstrapping is a relatively simple procedure. One begins with the original data set. Suppose the original data set has 808 participants. In Step 1, the researcher samples cases at random, with replacement, producing a new (bootstrapped) data set containing 808 cases. Some of the original cases appear two or more times in the bootstrapped data set, and some of the original cases are not included at all. In Step 2, the researcher analyzes the bootstrapped data set just as the original data set was analyzed (e.g., EMCOV followed by a regression analysis). Suppose the main analysis is a regression analysis. The parameter estimate from this analysis (the regression weight in this case) is saved. Steps 1 and 2 are repeated numerous (e.g., 25–100) times. Suppose a researcher has obtained and analyzed 50 bootstrapped data sets. In this example, the researcher has 50 regression weights. The standard deviation of the 50 regression weights is an estimate of the standard error for that regression estimate. The researcher then divides the original parameter estimate, from the original data set, by this estimate of the standard error to obtain the critical ratio (treated like a z value).

The value of the bootstrap relies on the assumption that the original sample is representative of some population (an assumption that is common to all statistical procedures) and that sampling from the original sample is similar to sampling from the population. If the original sample is large enough, this assumption may be reasonable. That is, if the sample is large enough, then the relatively rare elements of the population also are found in the original sample and may be included in the bootstrap samples with the appropriate frequency.

It is difficult to know how large a sample is "large enough." However, it is likely that samples as small as 100 are not large enough and may produce biases. It also is likely that samples as large as 1,000 are large enough. Despite the potential limitation of not knowing exactly how large a sample is large enough, the bootstrap remains a valuable tool. As Efron (1994) pointed out, the main value of the bootstrap is in obtaining an estimate of standard errors when estimates that are based on other methods are not feasible.

Multiple Imputation

An important part of the EM algorithm is restoring error variability to the imputed values during the E-step. The EM algorithm does this by adding a correction factor to certain elements of the estimated SSCP matrix for every imputed value or combinations of imputed values. The multiple imputation procedure restores the lost variability in another way.

Part of the variability in regression-based imputation is lost because each imputed value is estimated without error. Even when there are no missing data, researchers know that the regression estimate over- or underestimates the true value. The difference between the actual and predicted values is the residual. It often is reasonable to assume that the distribution of residuals for nonmissing data also describes the distribution of residuals for the missing data. Thus, one way to restore the variability in the imputed values is to draw one element (randomly with replacement) from the distribution of residuals for data that are nonmissing and add it to each imputed value.

Another part of the variability in regression-based imputation is lost because the imputed values are based on a single estimate of the covariance matrix, which is itself estimated with error. Thus, a second aspect of the multiple imputation procedure is to obtain multiple plausible covariance matrices. One way to obtain another plausible covariance matrix is to bootstrap the data set (as described earlier) and to reestimate the covariance matrix using the EM algorithm. This bootstrapping is used in the EMCOV implementation of multiple imputation. Another way to obtain alternative, plausible covariance matrices is to use the data augmentation procedure (Tanner & Wong, 1987). This approach was used by Schafer (in press) in his approach to multiple imputation.

These are the steps to follow in multiple imputation. Suppose we choose to have five imputations. First, we would obtain a plausible estimate of the covariance matrix. From this matrix, we would generate a data set including real and imputed values. To each imputed value, we would add a randomly selected residual term (as described earlier). The analysis of choice (e.g., multiple regression, repeated measures analysis of variance, or structural equation modeling [SEM]) then would be conducted using this data set. The sample size used for the analysis would be the full sample size (pretending for the moment that imputed values are real). Parameter estimates (e.g., regression weights) of interest are saved, along with the standard errors provided by the program.

This process is repeated five times. At the conclusion of the five replications, one has five estimates of the key parameter estimate and five estimated standard errors. There are two kinds of variability here: within-imputations variability (indicated by the estimated standard errors) and between-imputations variability (indicated by the sample variance of the five parameter estimates).

A reasonable point estimate of the parameter estimate of interest is the simple average of the five estimates. To obtain a reasonable estimate of the standard error, one would combine the within- and between-imputations estimates of variability using the following formula (based on Schafer, in press):

$$SE = \sqrt{\bar{U} + (1 + m^{-1})B},$$

where $\bar{U}$ is the average of the squared standard errors for the five analyses, B is the sample variance of the five parameter estimates, and m is the number of imputations (five in this example).

MGSEM

The MGSEM procedure has been described elsewhere in some detail (Allison 1987; Bentler, 1989; Donaldson, Graham, & Hansen, 1994; Duncan & Duncan, 1994; Graham et al., 1994; Jöreskog & Sörbom, 1989; McArdle & Hamagami, 1991, 1992; Muthen, Kaplan, & Hollis, 1987). Many of these sources include LISREL or an EQS code required to make use of the procedure (LISREL code—Allison, 1987; Jöreskog & Sörbom, 1989; the LISREL code for Donaldson et al., 1994, and Graham et al., 1994, also is available from John Graham at jwg4@psuvm.psu.edu; EQS code—Bentler, 1989; Duncan & Duncan, 1994). Readers interested in this procedure are encouraged to obtain additional information from one or more of these sources. Briefly, the idea is that one divides the sample into groups, so that respondents within each group have the identical missing data pattern. For example, suppose we have five variables. For one group, all respondents would have all the data (1 1 1 1 1, where 1 = data present and 0 = data missing). For a second group, the missing data pattern might be (1 0 1 1 1), that is, for all respondents in this group, data are missing for Variable 2 but present for all other variables.

The input variance–covariance matrix and input vector of means for each group are prepared so that missing covariance or mean elements are fixed at zero and missing variance elements are fixed at one. This must be done to get around the requirement that the same number of variables must be input into each group of the analysis. The model is then estimated (e.g., in LISREL) in the following way: All factor-level parameter estimates (factor variances, covariances, and regressions) are constrained to be equal across groups (i.e., across missing data patterns). For item-level parameter estimates (factor loadings, residuals, and means), elements corresponding to nonmissing data are constrained to be equal across groups. Elements corresponding to missing data are constrained to be zero (residual variance elements are constrained to be one). Conceptually, respondents who have data relating to a particular parameter estimate will contribute to that estimate. Those who have missing data relating to the parameter estimate do not contribute anything toward that estimate.

When the models are the same (e.g., estimating manifest-variable covariance matrix or manifest-variable regressions), this procedure produces results that are virtually identical to those obtained with the EM algorithm. A major advantage of this procedure is that reasonable estimates of standard errors are provided as part of the analysis. That is, one conducts a single (albeit complicated) analysis and obtains results that adjust for missing data biases and that provide reasonable estimates of standard errors. An additional advantage is that these analyses may be conducted with any of the major SEM programs capable of conducting multiple-group analyses (e.g., LISREL, Jöreskog & Sörbom, 1989; EQS, Bentler, 1989). Another advantage of this procedure is that it allows parameter estimation in models for which some covariances are inestimable for all participants.

A drawback to this procedure is that it is complicated. Even for modest-size problems, the multiple-group procedure can be tedious and difficult to do without making errors. A more serious drawback is that the procedure is fully amenable only to problems for which there are more respondents than variables for every missing data pattern. When a particular pattern has fewer respondents than variables, the covariance matrix for that group is not positive definite and cannot be included as a separate group. In this case, one must combine missing data patterns by discarding data points within one pattern to make it identical to a more sparse pattern of missingness with sufficient numbers of participants.

RML

Two SEM programs currently allow estimation of the maximum-likelihood function at the level of the individual: Mx (Neale, 1991) and Amos (Arbuckle, 1995). These programs thus allow missing data estimation of parameters without resorting to multiple-group analysis. For manifest-variable models, these programs produce results that are virtually identical to those obtained using the EM algorithm. For latent-variable models, both approaches (RML and EM) produce unbiased estimates in the presence of missing data, but the RML approach is slightly more efficient (i.e., it has slightly smaller standard errors).

The RML procedure, especially as implemented in Amos (Arbuckle, 1995), appears to be an excellent approach to solving missing data problems with continuous data. The Amos program is a Microsoft Windows-based program with a fully functioning graphical interface, making the program easy to use, even for people with modest SEM experience. In a graphics window, one draws the model of interest. In a text window, one provides a small amount of additional information (e.g., input data set, sample size, variable order, missing data indicator), and the model is estimated by clicking on the abacus icon. Perhaps the most important advantage of the Amos program, however, is that it also provides reasonable estimates of standard errors in the missing data case.

Amos currently provides the simplest and most direct approach to problems involving continuous data. With this Windows-based SEM program, one is able to tackle a huge assortment of analytical problems (e.g., problems involving the general linear model [GLM]), solve most of the missing data problems, and obtain reasonable standard errors, all in a single, uncomplicated analysis.

A Continuous-Variable Empirical Example

The data for this example come from the Adolescent Alcohol Prevention Trial (AAPT; Donaldson et al., 1994; Donaldson, Graham, Piccinin, & Hansen, 1995; Graham, Rohrbach, Hansen, Flay, & Johnson, 1989; Hansen & Graham, 1991). In the AAPT study, we examined the relative effectiveness of four alcohol abuse prevention curricula: information about consequences of use (ICU), resistance training (RT), normative education (Norm), and a combined program. It was hypothesized (Donaldson et al., 1994; Hansen & Graham, 1991; Hansen et al., 1988) that the prevention effectiveness of the RT program component (RT and combined conditions) would be mediated by improved behavioral resistance skills. It also was hypothesized that the prevention effectiveness of the Norm program component (Norm and combined conditions) would be mediated by improved (i.e., lower) perceptions of the prevalence and acceptability of adolescent alcohol (and other drug) use.

In this chapter, we present data from a cohort of students who received the AAPT curricula as 7th graders in relatively large public schools. The data making up our model included group comparison variables (RT vs. ICU, Norm vs. ICU, combined vs. ICU); covariates measured at 7th grade (alcohol use [Alc7], cigarette use [Smk7], marijuana use [Mar7], re-

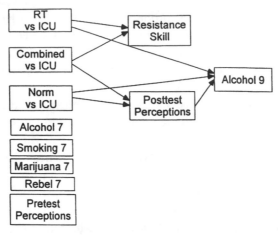

Figure 1. Mediating variable model with significant program-related paths shown. RT = resistance training; ICU = information about consequences of use; Norm = normative education; Rebel = rebelliousness; 7 = seventh grade; 9 = ninth grade.

belliousness [Rebel7], and a composite measure of perceptions of prevalence and acceptability of alcohol use among adolescent peers [Perc7]); immediate outcomes (a measure of behavioral resistance skills [Behav] and the composite measure of perceptions of prevalence and acceptability among adolescent peers [Perc7p]); and one longer term outcome variable (alcohol use at 9th grade [Alc9]).

The model tested in this example is shown in Figure 1. Only paths that proved to be significant are shown in the figure. In testing the model, all regression paths were estimated, including all paths emanating from the five covariates (i.e., Alc7, Smk7, Mar7, Rebel7, and Perc7). For this chapter, we highlight the paths relating to prevention program effects.

Three of the four missing data methods described earlier were used here: the EM algorithm, RML (Amos), and multiple imputation. For the multiple imputation method, we present results for Schafer's (in press) procedure and the EMCOV implementation (Graham & Hofer, 1995).

EM Algorithm

For the EM algorithm procedure, we used EMCOV.EXE (Graham & Hofer, 1993) to produce a maximum-likelihood covariance matrix, which then was analyzed using LISREL (Jöreskog & Sörbom, 1989). Standard errors were obtained by bootstrapping the original sample (50 bootstrapped samples were obtained). The 50 bootstrapped data sets were each analyzed with EMCOV and LISREL, and regression parameter estimates were stored. The standard deviation of each estimate (*N* = 50 data sets) was taken as an estimate of the standard error for that estimate. Table 1 shows the results for the EM–LISREL–bootstrap analyses.

RML (Amos)

The second method used was the RML method, as implemented in the SEM program Amos (Arbuckle, 1995). The results from the Amos analysis also appear in Table 1.

Schafer's Multiple Imputation

The third method used here was a multiple imputation procedure described by Schafer (in press). This procedure is currently available for Sun workstations operating within the S-Plus statistical package and should soon be available in the mainstream of prevention research.[1] As described earlier, a proper multiple imputation procedure restores variability from two sources. One should restore variability that is due to error of prediction and variability that is due to the fact that the initial covariance matrix, which is the basis for imputation, is itself only an estimate. The method used for the example shown in Table 1, which is based on Schafer (in press), controls for both kinds of variability.

A unique feature of the Schafer (in press) procedure is that the sampling of alternative plausible covariance matrices is accomplished using the data augmentation procedure (Schafer, in press; Tanner & Wong, 1987) to generate a theoretical distribution of covariance matrices. Different sample covariance matrices are drawn from this distribution to produce the imputed values for each of 10 imputations (for a more detailed discussion of data augmentation and related Markov chain Monte Carlo procedures, see Schafer, in press, chaps. 3 and 4; Spiegelhalter, Thomas, Best, & Gilks, 1995; Tanner, 1993).

Another unique feature of the Schafer (in press) procedure is that the missing data model may be for continuous data (Norm), categorical data (Cat), or mixed continuous and categorical data (Mix). The other approaches described in this section are able to handle categorical data with no missing values. However, if the data set contains categorical variables with missing values, these other approaches must treat these variables as if they were continuous. An advantage of the Schafer implementation of multiple imputation is that missing categorical data (either independent or dependent variables) are modeled explicitly as categorical data.

Before we implemented the Schafer (in press) multiple imputation procedure, the variables of the data set were transformed as follows: The three program variables (RT vs. ICU, Norm vs. ICU, and combined vs. ICU) were combined to form a single, four-level categorical variable. The pretest (Grade 7) scores for marijuana use and cigarette smoking were dichotomized into *never used* and *used* categories. The alcohol measures were

---

[1]Schafer's (in press) multiple imputation procedure for normal, continuous data (Norm) has been rewritten as a stand alone, Windows application. Please see our web site (methcenter.psu.edu) for up-to-date availability of this program.

TABLE 1
Analysis of Mediation Model With Various Missing Data Procedures

Cause Effect		RTICU[a] Behav	NormICU[a] Behav	CombICU[a] Behav	Smk7 Behav	Alc7 Behav	Mar7 Behav	Perc7 Behav	Rebel7 Behav
EM–LISREL–bootstrap	b	.365	.095	.332	−.106	.008	−.093	.028	−.104
	SE	.052	.048	.065	.053	.036	.087	.032	.045
	z	6.98****	1.99	5.10****	2.01*	0.22	1.07	0.88	2.32*
Amos	b	.365	.095	.332	−.106	.008	−.093	.028	−.104
	SE	.058	.063	.060	.053	.031	.098	.026	.041
	z	6.29****	1.52	5.49****	2.01*	0.27	0.95	1.08	2.57*
Multiple imputation (Schafer)	b	.375	.096	.330	−.111	.019	−.126	.032	−.108
	SE	.059	.055	.061	.049	.028	.074	.026	.042
	t	6.36****	1.74	5.42****	2.27*	0.67	1.69	1.26	2.56*
	df	23.3	37.1	23.9	27.1	33.3	70.0	23.2	15.3
Multiple imputation (EMCOV)	b	.349	.113	.362	−.090	.005	−.096	.016	−.086
	SE	.049	.051	.060	.060	.033	.066	.022	.038
	t	7.14****	2.23*	6.06****	1.50	0.14	1.46	0.74	2.29*
	df	44.8	54.8	25.1	17.3	19.8	298.5	37.6	18.0
Pairwise deletion	b	.369	.095	.321	−.118	.006	−.100	.038	−.070
Listwise deletion	b	.438	.199	.354	−.179	.099	−.319	.033	−.069
	SE	.096	.107	.093	.085	.051	.180	.043	.056
	z	4.56****	1.86	3.82***	2.11*	1.94	1.77	0.77	1.23
Mean replacement	b	.143	.037	.126	−.041	−.001	−.037	.014	−.027

		RTICU[a] Percpt	NormICU[a] Percpt	CombICU[a] Percpt	Smk7 Percpt	Alc7 Percpt	Mar7 Percpt	Perc7 Perc7P	Rebel7 Perc7P
EM–LISREL–	b	.004	−.117	−.270	.078	.117	.145	.366	.126
bootstrap	SE	.033	.031	.033	.029	.021	.076	.018	.027
	z	0.12	3.73***	8.13****	2.67**	5.71****	1.91	20.56****	4.70****
AMOS	b	.004	−.117	−.270	.078	.117	.145	.366	.126
	SE	.033	.035	.034	.030	.018	.055	.015	.023
	z	0.11	3.31***	7.91****	2.65**	6.67****	2.64**	25.07****	5.55****
Multiple imputation	b	.001	−.118	−.273	.085	.109	.158	.360	.110
(Schafer)	SE	.033	.037	.035	.028	.019	.078	.018	.020
	t	0.03	3.22**	7.89****	3.06**	5.85****	2.02	20.44****	5.49****
	df	414.9	207.0	288.0	1206.4	123.6	24.9	43.9	104.6
Multiple imputation	b	−.005	−.125	−.275	.084	.117	.160	.361	.131
(EMCOV)	SE	.031	.033	.032	.029	.017	.053	.015	.020
	t	0.17	3.83***	8.50****	2.93**	6.81****	3.01**	23.96****	6.52****
	df	995.2	2208.8	678.9	231.2	200.1	280.9	113.2	82.4
Pairwise deletion	b	.024	−.123	−.268	.082	.097	.117	.357	.135
Listwise deletion	b	−.024	−.191	−.209	.094	.152	.129	.489	.039
	SE	.075	.083	.072	.066	.039	.140	.033	.044
	z	0.32	2.31*	2.90**	1.43	3.85***	0.92	14.81****	0.90
Mean replacement	b	.030	−.099	−.226	.067	.096	.100	.301	.106

(Table continues on following page.)

TABLE 1 (Continued)

Method		RTICU[a] Alc9	NormICU[a] Alc9	CombICU[a] Alc9	Smk7 Alc9	Alc7 Alc9	Mar7 Alc9	Perc7 Alc9	Rebel7 Alc9	Behav[a] Alc9	Perc7P[a] Alc9
EM–LISREL– bootstrap	b	−.146	−.171	−.020	.233	.278	.270	.010	.117	−.019	.143
	SE	.059	.053	.054	.049	.036	.117	.027	.043	.038	.041
	z	2.47*	3.25**	0.37	4.73****	7.79****	2.31*	0.37	2.71**	0.50	3.50***
Amos	b	−.146	−.171	−.020	.233	.278	.270	.010	.117	−.019	.143
	SE	.052	.054	.054	.045	.027	.083	.025	.035	.039	.033
	z	2.82**	3.17**	0.37	5.20****	10.42****	3.24**	0.38	3.34***	0.48	4.35****
Multiple imputation (Schafer)	b	−.133	−.170	−.022	.198	.313	.259	.021	.102	−.021	.119
	SE	.067	.051	.048	.050	.034	.082	.024	.029	.031	.037
	t	1.99	3.35**	0.46	3.94****	9.34****	3.16**	0.85	3.52**	0.68	3.26**
	df	16.8	39.7	46.8	21.6	17.9	31.6	30.00	28.9	18.2	18.5
Multiple imputation (EMCOV)	b	−.134	−.156	−.010	.231	.282	.271	.012	.104	−.017	.143
	SE	.057	.064	.051	.038	.023	.108	.020	.032	.029	.033
	t	2.34*	2.42*	0.20	6.13****	12.22****	2.52*	0.62	3.24**	0.60	4.30***
	df	25.5	22.7	50.5	104.7	86.9	18.8	199.4	25.7	22.9	28.5
Pairwise deletion	b	−.166	−.169	−.053	.253	.234	.030	.032	.128	−.009	.120
Listwise deletion	b	.047	−.206	.169	.258	.309	.143	.047	.193	−.034	.135
	SE	.110	.121	.107	.096	.058	.203	.059	.063	.055	.071
	z	0.43	1.70	1.59	2.69**	5.30****	0.70	0.79	3.05**	0.62	1.89
Mean replacement	b	−.084	−.089	−.030	.145	.133	.019	.023	.066	−.004	.072

Note. The first row in each set contains the parameter estimates. The second row contains the estimated standard error. The third row contains the critical ratio (z or t value). The words *cause* and *effect* are used in the regression sense (i.e., predictor, predicted).
[a] All numbers in this column relate to program effects.
*$p < .05$. **$p < .01$. ***$p < .001$. ****$p < .0001$.

log transformed (log of 1 + Alc7 and log of 1 + Alc9), and the two perception variables were log transformed (log of 1.5 + Perc7 and log of 1.7 + Perc7p). The two variables Reb7 and Behav7 were reasonably symmetrically distributed and were not transformed. The multiple imputation procedure was performed using a mixed model for some categorical and some continuous variables (see Schafer, in press). After the multiple imputation procedure was performed, the log-transformed variables were reverse transformed to their original scales, and the 10 multiply imputed data sets were written out.

The 10 data sets were then analyzed using LISREL (Jöreskog & Sörbom, 1989). The results of those analyses (parameter estimates and standard errors) also appear in Table 1.

EMCOV Multiple Imputation

Also included in Table 1 are the results from the EMCOV implementation of multiple imputation. For the EMCOV analysis, the first covariance matrix was obtained using EMCOV on the original data set. The 2nd to 10th covariance matrices were obtained by bootstrapping the original data set (using the BOOTSAMP utility). Each bootstrapped data set was then analyzed using EMCOV, producing a total of 10 different but plausible covariance matrices. For each covariance matrix, a data set containing imputed values (TEMP.DAT) and a data set containing a vector of residuals for each variable (TEMP.RES) were obtained using the COV-IMP utility (Graham & Hofer, 1995). For each of these imputed data sets, residual terms were sampled (from the TEMP.RES data set) and added to each imputed value (using the ADDRES utility). For the EMCOV multiple imputation analyses, the variables of the data set were analyzed in their untransformed state. The two dichotomous variables Smk7 and Mar7 remained dichotomized. Thus, the data set analyzed was the same as that analyzed by Amos and the EM–LISREL–bootstrap procedures.

Other Procedures

For comparison purposes, parameter estimates for this data set also were obtained using pairwise deletion, listwise deletion, and mean substitution. Standard errors also were obtained using listwise deletion. Results for these procedures appear in Table 1.

Results: Comparison of Procedures

The results from Table 1 show that the parameter estimates for the EM–LISREL–bootstrap and Amos procedures were identical (to three decimal places). The estimates from the Schafer multiple imputation procedure were also highly similar, as were those based on the EMCOV multiple imputation. Figure 2 shows the findings relating to the prevention program

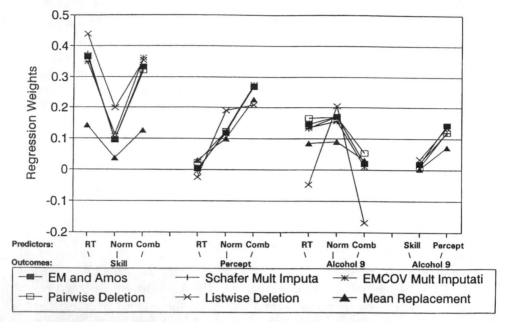

Figure 2. Regression parameter estimates (program-related effects only). RT = resistance training program vs. control; Norm = normative education program vs. control; Comb = combined (RT and Norm) program vs. control; Skill = resistance skills; Percept = perceptions of prevalence and acceptability of peer alcohol and drug use; Alcohol 9 = alcohol use at 9th grade.

effects (i.e., program effects on each of the two mediators, program effects on 9th-grade alcohol use outcome, and mediator effects on the outcome). As shown in Figure 2, parameter estimates for the four recommended analyses, as well as for pairwise deletion, were virtually the same. As expected, the estimates that were based on listwise deletion were highly variable: Some were too high, and some were two low. Estimates that were based on mean substitution consistently underestimated the values obtained by the recommended methods.

The standard errors for the four recommended procedures were also highly similar. In general, we would expect the bootstrapping procedure to provide good standard errors when the data are continuous and reasonably distributed and when the sample size is large enough. In general, we would expect the standard errors from the Amos analysis to be as accurate as standard errors in any SEM program. As with all SEM programs, these estimated standard errors will be best when the data are reasonably multivariate normally distributed. In general, we would have greater confidence in the estimated standard errors when at least two of the recommended analyses are performed and yield similar estimates.

Figure 3 shows the standard errors related to the program effects analyses. As shown in the figure, the estimates for the recommended analyses all were similar. The standard errors based on the listwise deletion analysis

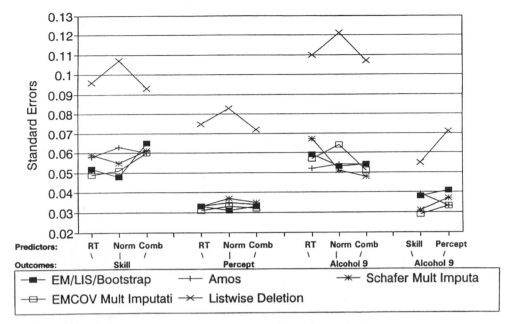

Figure 3. Standard errors (program-related effects only). RT = resistance training program vs. control; Norm = normative education program vs. control; Comb = combined (RT and Norm) program vs. control; Skill = resistance skills; Percept = perceptions of prevalence and acceptability of peer alcohol and drug use; Alcohol 9 = alcohol use at 9th grade.

were consistently high; many useful data must be discarded to perform the analyses with listwise deletion. Standard errors were not obtained for the pairwise deletion and mean substitution procedures because there is no statistical basis for choosing any particular sample size. Bootstrapping could be used to obtain standard errors for these analyses, but if one is going to do bootstrapping, one should be using the EM algorithm.

Figure 4 shows the critical ratios (i.e., parameter estimates divided by standard errors) for the analyses relating to the program effects. If we assume that these critical ratios are all interpreted as z values, the recommended analyses all yield highly similar statistical conclusions. As expected, the z values for listwise deletion analyses were substantially lower than for the recommended analyses. In fact, for listwise deletion, none of the tests involving the outcome variable (alcohol use at Grade 9) were significant.

Substantive Conclusions

Two kinds of program effects are shown in Figure 1. The first is a *direct effect* (i.e., a significant path directly from the program membership variable to the Alc9 outcome variable). The second kind of effect is an *indirect,* or mediated, *effect* (i.e., a significant path from the program mem-

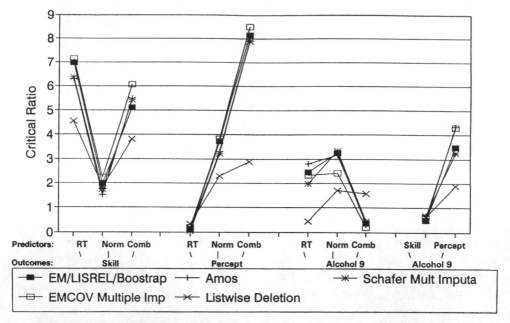

Figure 4. Critical ratios (t or z) for program-related effects only. RT = resistance training program vs. control; Norm = normative education program vs. control; Comb = combined (RT and Norm) program vs. control; Skill = resistance skills; Percept = perceptions of prevalence and acceptability of peer alcohol and drug use; Alcohol 9 = alcohol use at 9th grade.

bership variable to the hypothesized mediator and a significant path from the mediator to the Alc9 outcome variable). Mediated effects also can be thought of as "explained" effects. The mediator explains the program effect on the outcome. The direct effect, on the other hand, can be thought of as an unexplained effect. There was a significant effect, but that effect was not explained by changes in the mediating variable (MacKinnon & Dwyer, 1993).

Given this background, the substantive results shown in Figure 1 and Table 1 are promising. First, the Norm program (compared with ICU) had a significant beneficial effect on 9th-grade alcohol use. Part of the Norm effect was mediated by (explained by) perceptions measured immediately after the program. The Norm program also appeared to have a significant effect on 9th-grade alcohol use that went beyond what was explained by perceptions measured immediately after the program.

The combined program (compared with ICU) also had a significant effect on 9th-grade alcohol use. This effect was explained entirely by (mediated by) the level of perceptions measured immediately after the program.

The hypothesized mediated effect relating to the RT program did not materialize. Although the RT program (compared with ICU) had a large and significant effect on resistance skills measured immediately after the program, the resistance skills measure was not related to 9th-grade alcohol use. The most likely reason for this pattern of results was outlined recently by Donaldson et al. (1995). We assume that kids want to resist drug offers. However, if this assumption is not met, all the skills in the world will not translate into reduced drug use. As Donaldson et al. (1995) found, among students who clearly felt that adolescent alcohol use was inappropriate, the behavioral skills measure was a significant predictor of subsequent alcohol use.

Although the hypothesized mediated effect of the RT program did not materialize, we did find a significant direct, beneficial effect of the RT program on 9th-grade alcohol use. Although the effect remains unexplained, it was in contrast to the nonsignificant harmful effect of the RT program observed in this cohort for 8th-grade outcomes (Hansen & Graham, 1991).

ANALYSIS WITH MISSING DICHOTOMOUS DATA

Analysis of missing categorical data is not as well developed as analysis of missing continuous data. Nevertheless, statistically sound strategies are currently under development and will be available shortly in the mainstream of prevention research (Little & Rubin, 1987; Winship & Mare, 1990).

Analyses Specifically for Categorical Data

In this section, we describe a method to analyze categorical data when some observations or variables are missing (as outlined in Rindskopf, 1992). The model used to analyze the data is a general regression model for frequency data (Grizzle, Starmer, & Koch, 1969). Specifically, the generalized linear model with composite links described by Thompson and Baker (1981) and Rindskopf (1992) is applied. It is a generalized linear model because both categorical and continuous dependent measures are special cases of the model. *Composite links* refer to the linking of observed frequencies with frequencies that are not observed because of missing data. In this model, the frequencies (or some function of the frequency such as a proportion) in each category is the dependent measure rather than a score for each individual respondent, as in ordinary regression. Variables coding cell membership such as control or treatment group, present or absent at measurements, are the predictor variables. Weighted least squares are used to estimate the parameters of the model, in which the weights are determined by the underlying hypothesized distribution of the frequencies. In many cases, the observed frequencies are assumed to follow a Poisson distribution.

We use the same notation as Rindskopf (1992),

$$\eta = x\beta,$$

where x is the design matrix coding the group membership, interaction effects, and missingness groups for each frequency; β is a vector of regression parameters; and η is a vector that is a function of the means of the dependent variable Y. Generalized linear models include a link function $\eta = g(\mu)$ relating μ, the expected mean of Y, to η and an error from the exponential family of distributions.

Thompson and Baker (1981) described a method for extending the generalized linear to missing data as follows:

$$\mu^* = C\mu,$$

where the matrix C specifies which elements of the unobserved vector of frequencies (μ^*) are summed to result in an estimated observed frequency (μ). The use of a C matrix to correct unobserved and observed data is the key part of using generalized linear models for partially observed data. The new generalized linear model is then expressed as

$$E(Y) = \mu^* = C\mu, \quad \mu = h(n), \quad \eta = x\beta,$$

where μ^* and Y are $n \times 1$ vectors, β is a $p \times 1$ vector, x is an $m \times p$ matrix, and C is an $n \times m$ matrix (n is the number of frequencies, p is the number of effects in the models, and m is the number of elements in the complete data). Using the exponential function for $H(\cdot)$, $\mu^* = C \ EXP(x\beta)$; x is the design or model matrix where m or the observed frequencies are what is being modeled. The analysis proceeds by finding the weighted least squares solution. The matrix C allows for the representation of estimated observed frequencies as sums of cells in the fully observed and partially observed frequencies. A SAS IML/MATRIX program was written on the basis of a program described in Rindskopf (1992).[2] Standard errors can be obtained by inverting the information matrix. The correct specification of the C matrix linking observed and partially observed frequencies is the most difficult part of using this approach because the C matrix must be specified. Applications of this method in real prevention data have not led to different conclusions than analysis of only complete data.

Multiple Imputation

In the previous section on continuous data, we presented an analysis that was based on a multiple imputation procedure (Rubin, 1987; Schafer,

---

[2] The program was written by and is available from David MacKinnon at atdpm@asuvm.inre.asu.edu. The program will need to be adapted to the analysis, especially the C matrix coding unobserved frequencies.

in press). For that analysis, the imputations were performed with a mixed model for continuous and categorical data. The categorical variables in the model were smoking and marijuana use at the 7th-grade pretest (Smk7 and Mar7) and the four-level variable condition.

If the outcome variable of interest were distributed as Smk7 and Mar7 were (i.e., virtually dichotomous), a mixed model like the one Schafer (in press) used could be used for the imputation step. On the other hand, if the outcome variable of interest were distributed more or less continuously (e.g., as with the two alcohol variables in the examples presented in the previous section), then the data could reasonably be imputed using the continuous model but be analyzed as categorical. For example, if the researcher wanted to explore whether a prevention program would affect whether adolescents increased from minimal alcohol experimentation but the amount of increase was not important, he or she might prefer to analyze the dependent variable as dichotomous rather than continuous. We are not advocating that researchers should feel free to dichotomize continuous variables for analysis. However, to the extent that it is a reasonable course of action, the missing data can be handled in this fashion, especially when the sample size is large.

Using Continuous-Data Models

A third method for analyzing categorical data is to treat the dichotomous variables as if they were continuous and to use the procedures described earlier for continuous data. Although this is not a perfect solution to the problem of categorical data, it may be reasonable in many cases. For example, this approach may be reasonable when the response proportions for dichotomous variables are not too extreme. Although what is "too extreme" may depend on several factors, a 70–30 split for the two categories is probably not too extreme in this sense. However, some bias may be present in estimates when the response proportions for a dichotomous variable are as extreme as 95–5.

Empirical Data Example

We now present a brief data example for the latter two approaches. The data used in this example are the same as those used in the examples for continuous data. The program variables used in the example were the RT program versus ICU; the information-only comparison group (RTICU); the Norm program versus ICU (NormICU); and the combined program versus ICU (CombICU). As covariates, we used cigarette, alcohol, and marijuana use at Grade 7 pretest (Smk7, Alc7, and Mar7). These were all dichotomized, as described later. Two continuous covariates were rebelliousness (Rebel7) and perceptions of prevalence and acceptability of adolescent use of alcohol and other drugs (Perc7). The main dependent variable was a dichotomized version of an index of alcohol use at the Grade 9 posttest. The two hypothesized mediating variables were not included in the analysis models described later. However, they were included in each of the missing data models, so any value they had for predicting (and thereby adjusting for) missingness was retained.[3]

In the previous section on missing data analyses for continuous data, we described briefly a multiple imputation procedure. In the example presented earlier, we imputed 10 data sets based on AAPT data using a mixed model. The main dependent variable was an index of alcohol use at Grade 9 (Alc9), and one of the primary covariates was the same index taken at Grade 7 (Alc7). These two indexes were reasonably continuously distributed in the data and were imputed using a continuous-variable model. However, they could reasonably be dichotomized in the imputed data sets and analyzed using categorical data analytic procedures.

In each of the 10 imputed data sets, we dichotomized the variables Alc7 and Alc9 to correspond to two levels of alcohol use: 0 = minimal alcohol experimentation or less and 1 = more than minimal alcohol experimentation. The 10 imputed data sets were analyzed using SAS PROC CATMOD with the ML and NOGLS options. RTICU, NormICU, CombICU, Smk7, Alc7, and Mar7 each were dichotomous variables. Rebel7 and Perc7 were continuous and included in a DIRECT statement. The results of the PROC CATMOD analysis of multiply imputed data sets appear in Table 2.

We also dichotomized the Alc7 and Alc9 variables as described earlier in the original data set containing missing values. This data set was analyzed directly with Amos and with EMCOV and LISREL. Standard errors for the latter analysis were derived by obtaining 25 bootstrap samples of the original data set and analyzing each with EMCOV and LISREL. The standard errors shown in Table 2 are the standard deviations of the parameter estimates across the 25 bootstrap samples.

Comparison of Procedures

We take the Schafer (in press) multiple imputation procedure to be the gold standard here: If this procedure is available, we recommend its use.[4] As the direct approaches become more widely available (e.g., the

---

[3]For the multiple imputation procedure, the two mediating variables were included in the imputation model. For the Amos analysis, the two variables were included as additional dependent variables, and the residual variances for all dependent variables were allowed to be correlated. For the EM–LISREL–bootstrap analysis, the two mediating variables were included in the EMCOV analysis but were not included in the LISREL analysis.

[4]Schafer's (in press) multiple imputation procedures for categorical and mixed data (Cat and Mix) are currently being rewritten as stand alone, Windows applications. Please see our web site (methcenter.psu.edu) for up-to-date availability of these programs.

TABLE 2
Results of Analysis of Dichotomous Data

Method and variable	Parameter estimate	SE	Critical ratio (t or z)
Multiple imputation			
RTICU	−.084	.101	0.83
NormICU	−.200	.083	2.41
CombICU	−.023	.069	0.34
Amos			
RTICU	−.036	.029	1.24
NormICU	−.087	.032	2.75
CombICU	.010	.030	0.34
EM−LISREL−bootstrapping			
RTICU	−.036	.033	1.10
NormICU	−.087	.037	2.37
CombICU	.010	.019	0.56

method described at the outset of this section), they should also be useful in this situation. However, until these more statistically sound procedures are available, a reasonable option is to analyze dichotomous data with methods intended for continuous data. Our example using these methods was not meant to prove the value of this approach in all cases. On the contrary, we recommend that researchers use this approach only with caution. Nonetheless, as the results in Table 2 suggest, the two continuous data methods reasonably approximated the statistical conclusion obtained from the more appropriate multiple imputation procedure. The critical ratios from the Amos analysis were somewhat higher than those based on Schafer's multiple imputation. The critical ratios for the EM−LISREL−bootstrap procedure were slightly lower than those based on Schafer's multiple imputation.

CAUSES OF MISSINGNESS IN A LONGITUDINAL PREVENTION STUDY

An Empirical Study of the Causes of Attrition

As part of the final wave of the AAPT study, we collected a large amount of data on the causes of missingness as part of an attrition study. For the cohort studied in this chapter, 3,027 respondents had data for the pretest. Of these, 1,865 (62%) also had data at the final wave (Grade 11). The breakdown for participants with data for the attrition study are shown in Table 3.

The various reasons for missingness at the final wave, based on the attrition study, are summarized in Table 4. As shown in Table 4, the chief

TABLE 3
Breakdown for Respondents in the Attrition Study

n	Subtotal	Subtotal	Category
2,491			Had data for attrition study
	1,836		Had data for all cause-of-missingness questions
		837	Also had data for final wave
		999	No data for final wave
	655		Partial data from attrition study (e.g., no. attempts, dates)
		534	Also had data for final wave
		121	No data for final wave
536			No data relating to attrition study
	494		Had data for final wave
	42		No data for final wave
3,027			Total with data at pretest

Note. Pairs of values in column 3 sum to the value in column 1, one row above.

reasons for attrition were moving out of the area, being unresponsive to mailouts, and having an incorrect address. Other reasons accounting for a large number of lost data were previous parental and respondent declines, an uncooperative school district, and dropping out of school. The remaining reasons for attrition, as shown in Table 4, were relatively rare.

To understand the causes of missingness, we entered several key pretest variables and the reasons for missingness from the attrition study into

TABLE 4
Reasons for Missingness

Description	% of cases in attrition study	Were data eventually obtained? (n)	
		No	Yes
Moved away from area	44	344	458
Nonresponsive to previous mailout	35	442	207
No contact, bad address, and so on	28	391	115
Previously declined to participate	12	180	49
Uncooperative school district	12	76	136
Dropped out of school	6.9	45	82
In jail	1.3	14	9
Pregnant	1.3	6	17
Family problems	1.0	8	11
Home situation	0.9	5	12
Reported not receiving materials	0.8	4	10

Note. Percentages shown are based on the 1,836 respondents who had data on reasons for missingness. Up to five reasons were given for each respondent, so percentages do not sum to 100.

a regression model predicting missingness at Grade 11. Also included in this analysis were three variables constructed by the data collectors during the attrition study. The first ("attempts") was the number of attempts made to track and measure a respondent who did not immediately provide data. The second ("refuse") was a variable tapping the number of failures to find the respondent that could reasonably to be thought of as having to do with a respondent's characteristic (e.g., being in jail could be thought of as being due to a participant's characteristic, whereas an uncooperative school is not reasonably thought of as a participant's characteristic). The third variable ("drugs2") was a data collector's rating of whether the reason for missing data was related to drug use (1 = yes, 0 = no). The results of this analysis are shown in Table 5.

As shown in Table 5, pretest variables accounted for only 4.4% of the variance in missingness at Grade 11. However, the variables measured in the attrition study, including the three data collectors' ratings (attempts,

TABLE 5
Prediction of Missingness and Drug Use at Grade 11

Variable	Prediction of present and missing data at Grade 11			Predictiion of drug use at Grade 11		
	b	r	R^2 improvement	b	r	R^2 improvement
RTICU	−.02	−.08		.04	.02	
NormICU	−.01	−.04		−.02	−.04	
CombICU	.02	.08		−.00	.00	
Alc7	−.00	−.06		−.13****	−.26	
Smk7	−.00	−.09		.23****	.38	
Mar7	−.03	−.10		.16****	.38	
Grades7	.05**	.16	.044	.09***	.28	.225
Attempts	.08****	−.09		−.02	.04	
Drugs2	.10****	.09		.12**	.23	
Refuse	−.55****	−.45		.00	−.01	
Declines	−.22****	−.20		−.05*	−.03	
Dropout	−.02	.04		.09**	.17	
Family problems	−.01	.02		.04	.08	
Homesit	.02	.03		−.02	−.01	
Jail	−.01	−.03		.00	.09	
Moved	.03*	.05		.07**	.10	
No contact	−.43****	−.31		.05*	.10	
No Mater	.09****	.03		−.02	−.02	
Unresponsive	−.12****	−.29		−.06*	−.04	
Pregnant	.04*	.04		−.02	.01	
Uncooperative	.31****	.04	.454	−.00	−.01	.048

Note. DV1 = Does the individual have data at Grade 11? (yes = 1, no = 0); DV2 = index of drug use at Grade 11. Regression and correlation parameter estimates are based on a LISREL analysis of a correlation matrix produced with EMCOV. Significance levels are based on analysis with Amos. Overall R^2 = .498 in prediction of DV1. Overall R^2 = .273 in prediction of DV2. R^2 improvement for Grade 7 is the R^2 with just those variables in the model. R^2 improvement for uncooperative is the R^2 improvement when all those variables are added to the model.
*$p < .05$. **$p < .01$. ***$p < .001$. ****$p < .0001$.

refuse, and drugs2), accounted for an additional 45% of the variance. Overall, the variables entered in the model accounted for nearly 50% of the variance in missingness at Grade 11. It is important that for each of the variables shown in Table 5, data were eventually obtained for a substantial number of the respondents for whom that reason for missingness was relevant. Thus, in addition to being able to predict missingness for these variables, we are able to use these same variables in a regression model predicting drug use at Grade 11. Table 5 also shows that regression model.

The results for prediction of drug use at Grade 11 show almost the reverse pattern as those shown for prediction of missingness at Grade 11. The variables measured at the Grade 7 pretest accounted for nearly 23% of the variance in Grade 11 drug use (a composite index of cigarette, alcohol, and marijuana use), whereas the variables from the attrition study accounted only for an additional 5% of the variance.

As we stated previously, for missingness to be a problem, the variable causing missingness must be related to the variable containing the missing data. The results summarized in Table 5 suggest that although variables we measured indeed accounted for a substantial proportion of the missingness in Grade 11 drug use, they were largely uncorrelated with Grade 11 drug use itself. Thus, we argue that the missingness in Grade 11 drug use behaved largely as if it were MCAR. In fact, the part of the missingness that was not MCAR but was explained by these measures was adjusted completely by the analyses that we recommend.

Furthermore, only six variables were significant predictors of both missingness at Grade 11 and Grade 11 drug use (grades at 7th grade, the drugs2 rating, declines, moved, no contact, and unresponsive). However, for all but one of these variables (no contact), the sign of the regression weights was the same for prediction of missingness and drug use at Grade 11. Higher grades were associated with more data at Grade 11 and greater drug use at Grade 11.[5] Higher probability of drug involvement (the drugs2 rating) was associated both with more data at Grade 11 and greater drug use at Grade 11. More declines were associated with fewer data and less drug use. Moves were associated with more data and more drug use. Nonresponse to previous mailouts was associated with fewer data and less drug use. In each of these cases, the pattern of associations suggested that any missing data bias would, if not adjusted by the methods we suggest, suppress (not inflate) true program effects.

The fifth variable, no contact (e.g., bad addresses), was associated with fewer data and higher drug use at Grade 11. Thus, missing data bias

---

[5]The finding that higher grades were associated with higher drug use at Grade 11 could be due to the following: White students are more likely to be native English speakers and are thus likely to get better grades. White students also are known to have the highest levels of use in many adolescent samples.

TABLE 6
Program Effects Analysis Including and Excluding Attrition Study
Variables in Missing Data Model

Variable	Attrition study variables included			Attrition study variables excluded		
	β	SE	CR	β	SE	CR
RTICU	−.002	.041	−0.04	.004	.041	0.10
NormICU	−.106	.044	−2.41	−.100	.044	−2.25
CombICU	−.007	.042	−0.18	−.010	.043	−0.23
Alc7	−.070	.012	−6.04	−.076	.012	−6.57
Smk7	.199	.021	9.34	.194	.022	8.99
Mar7	.157	.023	6.85	.175	.023	7.55
Grades7	.080	.021	3.79	.073	.021	3.42

Note. Regression weights (β) were estimated using the covariance metric in Amos. Standard errors and critical ratios (CRs) were given from the Amos output. CRs may be interpreted as a *z* value.

associated with this pattern, if not adjusted by the methods we suggest, would inflate true program effects.

We argue that the combined effects of these variables was to slightly suppress true program effects. However, we also point out that the effects of these variables were minimal. Table 6 shows the program effects analysis when all variables (from Grade 7 pretest and attrition study) were included in the missing data analysis, compared with the same analysis when only the Grade 7 pretest variables were included. Note that the NormICU program effect was significant in both models but was slightly stronger when the attrition study variables were included. When the attrition study variables were included, all variables (i.e., program variables, Grade 7 covariates, attrition study variables, and Grade 11 drug use) were read into the Amos program, but the attrition study variables were all modeled as additional dependent variables. Correlations were estimated between all pairs of dependent variable residual variances. This type of model takes the effect of these variables into account for missing data purposes but does not affect the regression estimates. That is, this approach does not force the researcher to test a model that is not theoretically meaningful. When the attrition study variables were excluded, only the program variables, Grade 7 covariates, and Grade 11 drug use were read into the Amos program.

What About the Remaining Missingness?

If one collects data from a random sample of those initially missing and makes proper use of the new information (see, e.g., Graham & Donaldson, 1993), one can have the greatest confidence about whether the data that are still missing are missing because of an inaccessible missing data mechanism. However, it also may be possible to be reasonably confident about the missing data mechanism if one has other data available. We have reason to believe that the data that remain missing in this cohort do not contribute bias to the program effects analyses beyond what is already controlled fully by the analysis procedures we have used here.

First, as part of the attrition study, we included the variable (attempts) that counted the number of attempts to obtain the respondent's data and the variable (refuse) counting the number of refusal-related attempts. These variables can be thought of as proxies for the level of difficulty in obtaining the respondent's data. We can think of collecting data as having several levels of difficulty, such as "easy," "moderately difficult," "very difficult," and "extremely difficult." Assume that the respondents for whom we still have no data fit into the extremely difficult category. To the extent that the characteristics of the people in this group are related to those in the other categories in a straightforward way (e.g., linearly related), then including the difficulty variables (e.g., our proxies, attempts, and refuse) in the missing data model adjusts completely for the remaining missing data biases.

Second, Biglan et al. (1987), in extending the work of Hansen, Collins, Malotte, Johnson, and Fielding (1985), suggested examining the attrition status by pretest use interaction. They argued that if there is a significant interaction, there may be a problem caused by differential attrition. In particular, if more people are missing from the program than from the control condition, and if those who are missing have higher levels of use at the pretest, then there may be a problem in interpreting program effects attributable to attrition. Alternatively, if approximately the same proportion of respondents is missing from both program and control groups, but those who drop out of the program group have higher levels of use than those who drop out of the control group, there also can be a problem caused by differential attrition.

For this AAPT cohort, there were no significant interactions for the RTICU and NormICU comparisons and attrition at any of the grades (8, 9, 10, or 11). For the CombICU comparison, there were no significant interactions for attrition at Grades 8, 9, and 10. However, there was a significant interaction for attrition at Grade 11.

One way to think of the logic of the Biglan et al. (1987) interaction test is that drug use at the pretest is a proxy for drug use at the posttest. If there is differential attrition based on the pretest measure, there also may be differential attrition based on the posttest measure (which is missing for some people). Graham and Donaldson (1993) argued that one should not take too literally the observed patterns based on pretest data because it is the corresponding pattern on the missing variable itself that matters. The patterns observed for the pretest measure may be misleading. Still, there may be a way to extend further the logic of the Biglan et al. test if one has data from multiple waves.

TABLE 7
Zero-Order Correlations With Missingness at Grade 11

Variable	r with drugs11	r with missingness by condition				
		Overall	ICU	RT	Norm	Comb
Drugs7	.44	−.10	−.06	−.11	−.04	−.18
Drugs8	.52	−.10	−.07	−.12	−.05	−.18
Drugs9	.63	−.14	−.22	−.05	−.01	−.25
Drugs10	.80	−.19	−.19	−.11	−.13	−.31

Note. For the missingness variable, data present = 1 and data missing = 0.

If drug use at the attrition year is the cause of missingness at the attrition year, we would expect a particular pattern of correlations between drug use measured at various years and missingness at the attrition year. Specifically, the better the proxy is for drug use at the attrition year, the stronger its correlation should be with missingness at the attrition year. In general, we would expect drug use measures taken closer to the attrition to be better proxies than drug use measures taken further from the attrition year. For example, in this AAPT cohort, the correlations between drug use at Grade 11 and drug use at Grades 7, 8, 9, and 10 were .44, .52, .63, and .80, respectively. Not surprisingly, the highest correlation with Grade 11 drug use was Grade 10 drug use.

The correlations between drug use and missingness at Grade 11 (data present = 1, data missing = 0) appear in Table 7. These correlations were obtained using the EMCOV. The overall pattern of correlations is consistent with the idea that drug use at Grade 11 might have been at least a partial cause of missingness at Grade 11. There was almost a perfect relationship between the goodness of the proxy (i.e., the correlation with drug use at Grade 11) and the correlation with missingness at Grade 11.

Note, however, that this pattern was not substantially different for the different conditions. Although no formal test was performed here, it seems clear that the ICU and Norm conditions, for which the major program effects were found, had highly similar patterns.

Table 8 shows the correlations between drug use measured at various

TABLE 8
Zero-Order Correlations With Missingness at Grade 9

Variable	r with Drugs9	r with missingness by condition				
		Overall	ICU	RT	Norm	Comb
Drugs7	.54	−.09	−.10	−.11	−.01	−.13
Drugs8	.68	−.10	−.10	−.11	−.07	−.12
Drugs10	.76	−.14	−.20	−.10	−.08	−.19
Drugs11	.63	−.09	−.10	−.07	−.10	−.13

Note. For the missingness variable, data present = 1 and data missing = 0.

years with missingness at Grade 9 (the year relevant to most of the analyses performed in this chapter). Although the overall pattern was somewhat consistent with drug use at Grade 9 causing missingness at Grade 9, that pattern was not substantially different across the various conditions, especially for the ICU and Norm conditions.

For attrition at 8th and 10th grades, even the overall pattern of missingness was not consistent with drug use at the attrition year causing missingness at the attrition year. Moreover, there was no pattern of differential attrition for the ICU and Norm conditions.

USE OF RECOMMENDED METHODS WHEN MECHANISM IS INACCESSIBLE: A SENSITIVITY ANALYSIS

It is often noted that the missing data procedures outlined in this chapter assume that missingness is caused by completely random or accessible factors. Many people (erroneously) conclude from this that the methods are therefore inappropriate when the assumptions are not met. Indeed, it is true that use of the recommended missing data methods does not guarantee unbiased results to the extent that the missingness mechanism is inaccessible. There are good reasons, however, why the recommended methods should be used even under these circumstances.

First, even when the missingness mechanism is inaccessible, the recommended methods produce less biased results than other, more traditional methods (e.g., complete cases analysis or analysis with pairwise deletion). Second, even if methods were to be used that would take the inaccessible missingness into account, the first step would be to use the procedures that we recommend here.

Most important, we argue that inaccessible missingness is relatively rare and, even when it is present, generally has relatively little effect on the statistical conclusions of the study. We suggested in the previous section that the effects of inaccessible mechanisms may be minimal in the study we described, and we argued that inaccessible attrition in many prevention and applied psychological research situations may be less of a problem than often feared.

In considering the causes of missingness, it is misleading to say that the (one and only) missing data mechanism is inaccessible. Different people have different reasons for being absent from measurement, and even one individual may have several different reasons for being absent. All these things must be taken into consideration. In discussing this issue, we say that we have an inaccessible attrition mechanism when the missing dependent variable is itself the cause of its own missingness. However, even when the dependent variable is the cause of its own missingness, it may or may not be a problem.

To illustrate this point, we present a brief sensitivity analysis to demonstrate the range of effects on the interpretation of program outcomes when the dependent variable is the cause of its own missingness. In this context, many factors must combine before this situation presents a problem for interpretation of a prevention study. Table 9 shows how this sort of missingness might affect the mean in the program condition of a hypothetical evaluation study.

First, imagine that our hypothetical study has a 50% attrition rate (for this study, assume that alcohol use at 9th grade is the main dependent variable). Second, we assume (conservatively) that half the respondents who are missing are missing at least partly because of their 9th-grade alcohol use. That is, we assume that half of the attrition is due to factors that have nothing to do with the person's 9th-grade alcohol use. As shown in the cumulative effective column of Table 9, this means that the effect of attrition is reduced to 25% (50% of 50%).

Next, we theorize about the degree to which attrition is due to 9th-grade alcohol use. That is, even among those for whom 9th-grade alcohol use is a cause of attrition, it will generally not be the only cause. For example, a particular respondent may say, "I don't want to go to school today because they are doing that drug measurement study, and I don't want to have to say I use drugs." However, that same person might add, "Besides, my car has a flat tire, and I don't have my homework done, and my friend is mad at me," and so on. In other words, people generally have several reasons for being absent, only some of which are directly related to their alcohol use. In addition, even for this individual, it could be that this exact set of conditions would lead the person to stay away from school only part of the time. That is, there is a substantial random component to the person's behavior. Assume that on average, half (50%) of the reason for missingness in these cases is due to 9th-grade alcohol use. As shown in Table 9, the cumulative effect is down to 12.5% (50% of 25%).

Even if 9th-grade alcohol use were the sole cause of attrition, it may still not be a problem. It is important to examine the degree to which 9th-grade alcohol use is predicted by the other variables that have been measured. If those other variables accounted for 100% of the variance in 9th-grade alcohol use, there would essentially be no missing information (e.g., see Schafer, in press). In longitudinal studies, it is not surprising to find that variables from previous years of the study account for 50% or more of the variance of the main dependent variable. That means that even if the dependent variable is the cause of its own missingness, only 50% of the missingness is unique (i.e., only 50% is accessible). After considering this factor, the cumulative effect of 9th-grade alcohol use as the cause of missingness is down to 6.25% (50% of 12.5%).

This 6.25% can reasonably be thought of as the proportion of the cause that is inaccessible. However, even this may or may not be a problem.

TABLE 9
Sensitivity Analysis for Effects of Inaccessible Missingness on Program Outcomes

Source	Assumptions for inaccessible missingness			
	Highly conservative		Less conservative	
	Proportion	Cumulative effect	Proportion	Cumulative effect
Proportion of cases with attrition	.50	.50	.30	.30
Proportion of attrition cases for which 9th-grade alcohol use is any part of the cause	.50	.250	.25	.075
Within those, the proportion of cause that is actually due to 9th-grade alcohol use	.50	.125	.50	.0375
Proportion of 9th-grade alcohol use not accounted for by other variables	.50	.0625	.60	.0225
Proportion of differential attrition	.50	.0313	.25	.0056
Effect on scores in program group	.40	.0125	.20	.0011
Results of hypothetical evaluation study[a]				
Control group mean	4.402		4.402	
Unadjusted program group mean	3.964		3.964	
$t(998)$	2.308		2.308	
p	.0198		.0198	
Adjusted program group mean	4.026		3.970	
$t(998)$	1.982		2.277	
p	.0448		.0216	

[a] $n = 500$ per group. $SD = 3.0$ in each group.

Next, we must consider the degree of differential attrition. In particular, we should examine the extent to which more inaccessible attrition occurs in the program group than in the control group. Graham and Donaldson (1993) have shown that differential attrition is no problem when missingness is accessible and that even inaccessible attrition is no problem at all to interpretation of program outcomes if there is no differential attrition. If all the inaccessible attrition occurred in the program group, and none of it occurred in the control group, the 6.25% cumulative effect noted earlier would be appropriate.

However, it is extremely unlikely that any study would have this magnitude of differential attrition. Suppose (conservatively) that 75% of the inaccessible attrition occurred in the program group and that 25% occurred in the control group. This would mean that only half the attrition would be a problem. As shown in Table 9, incorporating this factor brings the cumulative effect to 3.13% (50% of 6.25%).

Finally, we must estimate the degree to which inaccessible attrition affects the scores themselves. Rubin (1987) suggested that one way to model inaccessible (nonignorable) missingness is to add something to the imputed values obtained. He suggested, for example, that one could add 20% to each imputed score, with the idea that the imputed score is assumed to underestimate the actual score. Although this 20% figure is arbitrary, it does not seem unreasonable (a more systematic sensitivity analysis could be undertaken by specifying a range of reasonable values). For example, suppose a person had missing data for the variable measuring recall of alcohol use in the past 30 days. Suppose that the imputed value for the person was 5, a scale score that translates into 5–10 drinks in the past 30 days. Adding 20% to this scale score would give the person a score of 6, which translates into 11–20 drinks in the past 30 days. Adding 20% to each score seems reasonable. However, to be even more conservative, we assumed that the effect on scores was not 20% over the imputed value but 50% over the imputed value (see the left columns of Table 9).

Combining all these effects means that 3.13% of the scores in the program group should be increased by 50%. That is, the overall mean in the program group would be increased by 1.57%. This represents our estimates of the effects of inaccessible attrition under conservative assumptions.

For the other half of the sensitivity analysis (the right two columns of Table 9), we examine the effects of less conservative assumptions (taken mainly from the study we described in the previous section of this chapter). The bottom line for those assumptions is that the mean in the program group would be increased by 0.11%.

We next examine the effects of these assumptions on a hypothetical program evaluation study. Suppose the control group mean is 4.402 and that the program mean is 3.964 (two means taken from our empirical study). We assume that only the program group mean is affected by the inaccessible missing data mechanism. That is, the value 3.964 is too low because of the missing data. Under the conservative assumptions, we argued that 3.13% of the scores would be affected. We assume that the mean for this group is higher by 1.00 than the mean for the other 96.87% of the program group. If the true value is 40% higher than the imputed value for the 3.13%, then the true mean for the program group, after adjustment, should be 4.026. Under less conservative assumptions, the true mean, after adjustment, should be 3.970. To perform the hypothesis tests under these assumptions, we assume further that the standard deviation is 3.0 in each group and that there are 500 participants per group.

As shown in Table 9, the statistical conclusions are highly similar in the unadjusted and adjusted case regardless of whether the conservative or less conservative assumptions are made. When the conservative assumptions are made, the estimated t value falls from 2.31 to 1.98. Under the more realistic assumptions, the t value is virtually unchanged, falling from 2.31 to only 2.28.

The extremely small effect of inaccessible missingness on the interpretation of program effects shown in this example is, of course, dependent on the assumptions made for the factors presented in Table 9. If these assumptions are substantially different in a particular study, the bottom line effect also will be affected. Although it is hard to imagine an actual situation in which inaccessible attrition is even more extreme than that depicted with the conservative assumptions shown in Table 9, it is possible.

In summary, although attrition in some studies may prove to be more of a problem than shown here, it is likely that problems that are due to inaccessible missingness in most intervention studies will be minimal. We encourage researchers to do the type of sensitivity analysis depicted in Table 9 to be more sure about what might be happening in their own study.

WHERE DO RESEARCHERS GO FROM HERE?

What Is Best? Statistical Considerations

From a statistical viewpoint, the best missing data procedures do several things. First, they allow one to take into consideration all available causes of missingness. This amounts to allowing the inclusion of all variables that are related to the missing data process, whether or not the variables are of direct interest in the analysis. It also amounts to allowing the inclusion of all relevant linear and nonlinear combinations of variables. Second, the best procedures take the distribution of the data into account. If some of the variables are continuous and some are categorical, the missing data procedure explicitly models both kinds of data. Finally, the best procedures provide reasonable estimates of standard errors.

From this statistical viewpoint, all the procedures provide a relatively easy way to take all known causes of missingness into account. Perhaps the best from this point of view is the multiple imputation procedure described by Schafer (in press). It handles continuous data, categorical data, and mixed (continuous and categorical) data. It provides reasonable estimates of standard errors. The only caution for the multiple imputation model is that one should be careful that the model used is at least as general as the model to be used to analyze the data. In one sense, this is more of a caution than a requirement. It is possible that a situation could arise in which only linear effects are related to the missingness but that nonlinear effects are of interest in the analysis. Under these conditions, using a completely linear missing data model might be appropriate.

If the analysis of interest involves the GLM (e.g., t tests, correlation, multiple regression, analysis of variance, factor analysis, path analysis, SEM) and one's data are reasonably normally distributed, an excellent choice is the Amos program (Arbuckle, 1995). In the simplest case with Amos, the missing data model is limited to the analysis model. As described in our categorical variable example, however, it is relatively easy to include other variables that affect the missingness without affecting the analysis model of interest (i.e., include them as additional dependent variables). Furthermore, standard errors are a convenient by-product of the main analysis. The main limitation of the Amos program is that it does not use a different model for continuous and dichotomous variables containing missingness. In many instances, however, this should be a minimal limitation. If the dependent variable is dichotomous and logistic regression is the analysis of choice, then this is a somewhat more important limitation.

When it is appropriate, the multiple-group SEM approach is equivalent to using Amos. However, because the multiple-group SEM procedure requires that each missing data pattern have more respondents than variables, Amos is preferable in a wide variety of situations.

A third possibility is the multiple imputation procedure as implemented in EMCOV (Graham & Hofer, 1995). This procedure is also limited by the fact that the missing data model does not take categorical data into account.

The fourth possibility is the direct analysis with EMCOV. This procedure also has the limitation of not dealing explicitly with categorical data. In addition, this procedure relies on bootstrapping for obtaining standard errors. Although many researchers have considerable faith in bootstrap-estimated standard errors, others question the value of the bootstrapping procedure as a general tool.

Practical Considerations

From a practical viewpoint, the best procedures are statistically sound but weight convenience and availability over statistical precision and efficiency (small variability around parameter estimates). If the analysis of interest involves the GLM, Amos may be the approach of choice from this perspective because it is easy to use, even for a relative novice. However, although Amos is not a particularly expensive program, some researchers may prefer to use an approach that is in the public domain. In this case, EMCOV (Graham & Hofer, 1993) and Mx (Neale, 1991) may be reasonable options. Alternatively, one may prefer the multiple-group SEM model approach (Allison, 1987; Muthen et al., 1987).

In the case of Mx, an SEM program that also has the raw maximum-likelihood feature, the hitch is that estimated standard errors may be approximate only in some situations. A way around this problem may be to use a bootstrapping procedure as a backup for estimating standard errors.

In the case of EMCOV (Graham & Hofer, 1993), the parameter estimates are identical to those obtained in the RML procedures when the models involve only the manifest variables. When the model involves latent variables, the EMCOV procedure, which operates on the manifest variables, produces parameter estimates that are unbiased but slightly less efficient (slightly larger empirical standard errors) than estimates obtained from Mx or Amos.[6] Still, estimation with EMCOV is easy, and the slight loss in efficiency is generally trivial. The other problem with analyses based on EMCOV (or other EM algorithm approaches) is that standard errors are not provided as a by-product of the analysis. The good news is that a bootstrapping procedure with as few as 25 replications may provide reasonable estimates of the standard errors. The bad news is that if the distribution of parameter estimates is not symmetrical in the bootstrap samples, then one will probably prefer to generate 2,000 bootstrap samples to obtain reasonably stable estimates of the confidence intervals (e.g., Efron, 1994). With data sets of any size, producing 2,000 bootstrap samples is, to say the least, computationally intensive.

The multiple-group SEM procedure may fail to qualify as a good approach from the practical viewpoint. It is cumbersome at best and often requires the researcher to discard large amounts of data points (whole cases almost never have to be discarded) to obtain missing data patterns with enough cases to be analyzed. However, this approach does have the desirable quality of requiring no new software because the common SEM pack-

---

[6]Models such as Amos that handle the analysis and missing data work at the same time are the most efficient (least variability around the parameter estimates) models available when the model is correct. However, when the model is not correct (this could happen with large, complex structural models), such models are likely to produce parameter estimates that are less efficient than multiple imputation.

ages can perform this analysis. This approach also is highly useful for certain specialized models (e.g., cohort-sequential designs) in which certain covariances are not available for any respondents.

Perhaps the best of the practical approaches to missing data analysis is the multiple imputation procedure. This procedure is extremely flexible and generally may be adapted to be useful with any data analysis procedure. In addition, reasonable estimates of standard errors can be obtained with relatively easy arithmetic at the conclusion of the analysis phase. Analyzing the multiply imputed data sets is a little harder than analyzing just one, but it is typically an easy matter simply to change the input data set name and run the analysis again and again.

The only real problem with the multiple imputation approach has been that it was not available widely. However, programs for performing these analyses are currently being developed by Joe Schafer (in press) at the Pennsylvania State University. These public domain programs, Norm (for continuous data), Cat (for categorical data), Mix (for mixed continuous categorical data), and Pan (for special longitudinal models and clustered data), which are fully available for Sun workstations, are currently being developed as stand alone Windows applications. Norm is available now, and Cat, Mix, and Pan will be available soon. Please see our web site (methcenter.psu.edu) for additional information.

What Is Best for Categorical Models and Non-GLM Continuous-Data Models?

EM Algorithm

The statistical answer for these models is the same as given earlier. When the data are truly dichotomous, one should use methods that make assumptions most appropriate for that kind of distribution. As mentioned earlier, EM algorithm programs for analyzing dichotomous data are currently available. However, the versions of these programs available at present are cumbersome and hard to use. On the other hand, given the number of people who analyze categorical (e.g., dichotomous) data, it will not be surprising to see in the near future a general purpose, easy-to-use EM algorithm program for analysis of dichotomous dependent variables with dichotomous and continuous independent variables. Such a program should provide unbiased parameter estimates as well as reasonable standard errors.

Multiple Imputation for Categorical and Mixed Models

Still, the best promise for analyses that involve categorical data or non-GLM continuous data is the multiple imputation procedure. As long as the model for performing the multiple imputations is at least as general as the analyses planned for the data, one does the imputation step once and then spends the remaining time analyzing the same (multiply imputed) data sets using data analysis tools that are familiar and that provide theoretically interpretable statistical conclusions. Using software already available, it is possible to generate multiply imputed data sets using a mixed model for categorical and continuous data. Interactions that may be important in the analysis phase may be incorporated into the missing data phase. As with the models for continuous data, the models for mixed continuous and categorical data allow one to estimate reasonable standard errors using a little simple arithmetic at the conclusion of each analysis. These software advances will soon be available in the mainstream of prevention and applied psychological research.

CONCLUSION

The evidence we presented in this chapter (especially in the third section) is to some extent circumstantial. We did not present data from a random sample of previously missing people and draw conclusions about those still missing based on this sample (Graham & Donaldson, 1993; Rubin, 1987). Nevertheless, we believe that the data we did present make a reasonable case for the idea that the data still missing attributable to attrition at worst introduce only minimal bias into the statistical conclusions regarding program effects. In fact, we believe that the pattern of results is such that the data still missing introduce no bias beyond what is fully adjusted by using the missing data analysis procedures we have recommended here.

Furthermore, as illustrated in the sensitivity analysis we presented, we suggest that the nature of attrition in most prevention studies may be similar in many respects to what we found in this study. The main reasons participants leave such studies may have little to do with motivations about the study or about their own alcohol or drug use. For example, as we have shown in this study, the several factors that accounted for the largest percentage of missing data at Grade 11 were relatively uncorrelated with drug use at Grade 11. In addition, the pattern of relationships for most of these factors would lead to suppression of true program effects (if left uncontrolled), not inflation.

Critics of prevention research have pointed to attrition rates and have simply dismissed such studies without any consideration about the causes of missingness. In addition, critics often point to one or two factors (e.g., differential attrition based on pretest factors), which, from our vantage point, only superficially imply attrition bias. As Graham and Donaldson (1993) pointed out, conclusions based solely on patterns of pretest variables can be misleading. We suggest that it may be time for critics to stop suggesting that just because there may be a problem, there necessarily is a problem caused by missing data. We argue that on the contrary, it is likely that there are minimal missing data biases if one makes use of the procedures we have recommended in this chapter.

In summary, we have presented evidence that people leave prevention studies for reasons that have relatively little effect on the statistical conclusions (if the data are analyzed as we suggest). We suggest that it is time for the burden of proof to fall on the critics of prevention studies. Unless they can provide hard data to back up their criticisms, they should accept the analyses we recommend as dealing with attrition problems completely.

REFERENCES

Allison, P. D. (1987). Estimation of linear models with incomplete data. In C. Clogg (Ed.), *Sociological methodology 1987* (pp. 71–103). San Francisco: Jossey-Bass.

Arbuckle, J. L. (1995). *Amos users' guide*. Chicago: SmallWaters.

Bentler, P. M. (1989). *EQS structural equations program manual*. Los Angeles: BMDP Statistical Software.

Biglan, A., Severson, H., Ary, D. V., Faller, C., Gallison, C., Thompson, R., Glasgow, R., & Lichtenstein, E. (1987). Do smoking prevention programs really work? Attrition and the internal and external validity of an evaluation of a refusal skills training program. *Journal of Behavioral Medicine, 10,* 159–171.

Dempster, A. P., Laird, N. M., & Rubin, D. B. (1977). Maximum likelihood from incomplete data via the EM algorithm (with discussion). *Journal of the Royal Statistical Society, B39,* 1–38.

Donaldson, S. I., Graham, J. W., & Hansen, W. B. (1994). Testing the generalizability of intervening mechanism theories: Understanding the effects of adolescent drug use prevention interventions. *Journal of Behavioral Medicine, 17,* 195–216.

Donaldson, S. I., Graham, J. W., Piccinin, A. M., & Hansen, W. B. (1995). Resistance skills training and alcohol use onset: Evidence for beneficial and potentially harmful effects in public and private Catholic schools. *Health Psychology, 14,* 291–300.

Duncan, S. C., & Duncan, T. E. (1994). Modeling incomplete longitudinal data using latent variable growth curve methodology. *Multivariate Behavioral Research, 29,* 313–338.

Efron, B. (1981). Nonparametric estimates of standard error: The jackknife, the bootstrap, and other resampling methods. *Biometrika, 68,* 589–599.

Efron, B. (1994). Missing data, imputation, and the bootstrap. *Journal of the American Statistical Association, 89,* 463–475.

Graham, J. W., & Donaldson, S. I. (1993). Evaluating interventions with differential attrition: The importance of nonresponse mechanisms and use of follow-up data. *Journal of Applied Psychology, 78,* 119–128.

Graham, J. W., & Hofer, S. M. (1993). *EMCOV reference manual.* Los Angeles: University of Southern California, Institute for Prevention Research.

Graham, J. W., & Hofer, S. M. (1995). *Reference manual for COVIMP, a multiple imputation procedure used in conjunction with EMCOV.* University Park: Pennsylvania State University, Department of Biobehavioral Health.

Graham, J. W., Hofer, S. M., & MacKinnon, D. P. (1996). Maximizing the usefulness of data obtained with planned missing value patterns: An application of maximum likelihood procedures. *Multivariate Behavioral Research, 31,* 197–218.

Graham, J. W., Hofer, S. M., & Piccinin, A. M. (1994). Analysis with missing data in drug prevention research. In L. M. Collins & L. Seitz (Eds.), *Advances in data analysis for prevention intervention research* (NIDA Research Monograph No. 142). Washington, DC: National Institute on Drug Abuse.

Graham, J. W., Rohrbach, L., Hansen, W. B., Flay, B. R., & Johnson, C. A. (1989). Convergent and discriminant validity for assessment of skill in resisting a role play alcohol offer. *Behavioral Assessment, 11,* 353–379.

Grizzle, J. E., Starmer, C. F., & Koch, G. G. (1969). Analysis of categorical data by linear models. *Biometrics, 25,* 489–504.

Hansen, W. B., Collins, L. M., Malotte, C. K., Johnson, C. A., & Fielding, J. E. (1985). Attrition in prevention research. *Journal of Behavioral Medicine, 8,* 261–275.

Hansen, W. B., & Graham, J. W. (1991). Preventing alcohol, marijuana, and cigarette use among adolescents: Peer pressure resistance training versus establishing conservative norms. *Preventive Medicine, 20,* 414–430.

Hansen, W. B., Graham, J. W., Wolkenstein, B. H., Lundy, B. Z., Pearson, J. L., Flay, B. R., & Johnson, C. A. (1988). Differential impact of three alcohol prevention curricula on hypothesized mediating variables. *Journal of Drug Education, 18,* 143–153.

Jöreskog, K. G., & Sörbom, D. (1989). *LISREL 7 user's reference guide.* Mooreseville, IN: Scientific Software.

Little, R. J. A., & Rubin, D. B. (1987). *Statistical analysis with missing data.* New York: Wiley.

MacKinnon, D. P., & Dwyer, J. H. (1993). Estimating mediated effects in prevention studies. *Evaluation Review, 17,* 144–158.

McArdle, J. J., & Hamagami, F. (1991). Modeling incomplete longitudinal and cross-sectional data using latent growth structural models. In L. M. Collins & J. L. Horn (Eds.), *Best methods for analysis of change: Recent advances, unanswered questions* (pp. 276–304). Washington, DC: American Psychological Association.

McArdle, J. J., & Hamagami, F. (1992). Modeling incomplete longitudinal and cross-sectional data using latent growth structural models. *Experimental Aging Research, 18,* 145–166.

Muthen, B., Kaplan, D., & Hollis, M. (1987). On structural equation modeling with data that are not missing completely at random. *Psychometrika, 52,* 431–462.

Neale, M. C. (1991). *Mx: Statistical modeling.* [Available from M. C. Neale, Box 3, Department of Human Genetics, Medical College of Virginia, Richmond, VA.]

Rindskopf, D. (1992). A general approach to categorical data analysis with missing data, using generalized linear models with composite links. *Psychometrika, 57,* 29–42.

Rubin, D. B. (1987). *Multiple imputation for nonresponse in surveys.* New York: Wiley.

Schafer, J. L. (in press). *Analysis of incomplete multivariate data.* New York: Chapman & Hall.

Spiegelhalter, D. J., Thomas, A., Best, N., & Gilks, W. (1995). *Bayesian inference using Gibbs sampling (version 0.50).* Cambridge, England: MRC Biostatistics Unit, Institute of Public Health.

Tanner, M. A. (1993). *Tools for statistical inference: Methods for the exploration of posterior distributions and likelihood functions* (2nd ed.). New York: Springer-Verlag.

Tanner, M. A., & Wong, W. H. (1987). The calculation of posterior distributions by data augmentation (with discussion). *Journal of the American Statistical Association, 82,* 528–550.

Thompson, R., & Baker, R. J. (1981). Composite link functions in generalized linear models. *Applied Statistics, 30,* 125–131.

Winship, C., & Mare, R. D. (1990). Loglinear models with missing data: A latent class approach. *Sociological Methodology, 20,* 331–367.

APPENDIX
OBTAINING SOFTWARE

EMCOV (John Graham and Scott Hofer)

Researchers may download the EMCOV software free of charge from the Pennsylvania State University FTP server. Send E-mail to John Graham (jwg4@psu.edu) for further information and to obtain instructions for downloading the program and associated utilities.

Norm, Cat, Mix, Pan (Joe Schafer)

Additional information may be obtained about these programs by writing to Joseph L. Schafer, Department of Statistics, Pennsylvania State University, University Park, PA 16802. Also see our web page http://methcenter.psu.edu.

Amos (Jim Arbuckle)

Amos is commercial software available from SmallWaters in Chicago. E-mail info@smallwaters.com for additional information. Researchers may also download a free demonstration version of the program from the following Web site: http://www.smallwaters.com.

11

PRACTICAL POWER ANALYSIS FOR SUBSTANCE ABUSE HEALTH SERVICES RESEARCH

MICHAEL L. DENNIS, RICHARD D. LENNOX, AND MARK A. FOSS

SIGNIFICANCE AND OVERVIEW

Statistical power is the probability of successfully producing reliable findings, or "statistical significance," if a researcher's hypothesis is true. Essentially, it is the probability of finding what a researcher is looking for given that it is there. Although this would seem like an essential step in planning a research study or evaluating findings from others, most researchers have had little training in its constructive use. For some, instruction consisted of no more than a single lecture in a graduate statistics course that focused primarily on the role of the number of participants. Failure to consider statistical power probably has been one of the biggest shortcom-

This work was based on more than two decades of our collective experience doing power analysis for both basic and applied research efforts. In this sense, we need to thank all our colleagues for the opportunity to work with them and their willingness for us to share this work with the field. We also would like to thank Michael Windle, Len Thomas, Michael Prendergast, and Jeremy Bray for technical comments and Joan Unsicker for helping us produce this chapter. Actual production of this chapter was supported by Grant P50-DA06990 from the National Institute on Drug Abuse.

ings of community-based intervention research, including prevention, treatment, and health services delivery (hereafter referred to as *field studies*).

Although power, or "sensitivity," analysis has been well received by methodologists (Cohen, 1990), there are several important reasons why it has yet to be transferred to general practice. It requires calculation of statistics that are still relatively unfamiliar to most community-based researchers (e.g., effect sizes, design effects), and it is not set up well for research that is more exploratory, involves numerous questions, or has a complicated design. Another barrier has been the incorrect impression of many researchers that the only way to increase power is to increase the sample size, which is often fixed by logistical constraints in many community-based studies.

The goals of this chapter are as follows: (a) to review the need for power analysis to be used more in prevention and other community-based research with specific interventions; (b) to provide a basic overview of the history, evolution, and meaning of power analysis; (c) to present a practical approach to incorporating power analysis into new research planning; and (d) to identify several issues and techniques that affect the power of data already collected and published. The chapter is meant to be a primer and key to other materials. Throughout this chapter, we cite more detailed resource materials in each area. We also provide numerous detailed summary tables that typically have been sufficient for most of our own planning needs. (A more detailed methods bibliography, tables, and glossary are available through our Web site: http://www.chestnut.org.)

THE STATE OF PRACTICE

Although power analysis has long been recognized as necessary by most methodologists and required in National Institutes of Health proposals, only a few researchers are sufficiently trained to implement it. Furthermore, a basic effort needs to be made to familiarize researchers with the available work and make it accessible to them (Institute of Medicine, 1980, 1987, 1989, 1990). Before getting into the technical aspects of power analysis, we begin by reviewing the current state of practice to help readers understand why power analysis is so important.

Statistical Power in Practice

Methodologists repeatedly have demonstrated that the published academic literature is grossly "underpowered" statistically and routinely analyzed in ways that make it almost useless for prevention and treatment practitioners (Cohen, 1962; Dennis, 1994; Dennis, Huebner, & McLellan, 1996; Detksy, 1989; Lamas et al., 1992; Lipsey, 1988, 1990). Consider, for example, Lipsey's (1990) analysis of 1,859 statistical tests compiled from 39 meta-analyses of prevention and services research from several fields, including alcohol use, drug use, psychology, health, criminal justice, and education. He found an average Type II error (i.e., falsely saying something did not work when meta-analysis showed that it did) rate of 55%. This means that if an intervention works, it would be more accurate to flip a coin to decide whether a result was significant than to use a statistical test as commonly (mis)used. The primary problem was that although the effect size in the meta-analyses was .45, the average study only had about 40 people per condition, which would require a much larger effect size of .74 to be detected with 90% power. (Note that effect sizes, discussed later, are standardized measures of difference or change and are typically calculated as the difference in means divided by the pooled or control group standard deviation.)

Other Methodological Problems

The power problem can be addressed by increasing the number of participants, improving the design, or improving the analysis model (each of which is discussed later). Unfortunately, a methodological meta-analysis of 168 intervention studies (Lipsey, Crosse, Dunkle, Pollard, & Stobart, 1985) indicated the following: (a) Less than 30% of the researchers even considered the sensitivity of their outcome measures, and only a handful took the basic steps to improve what they had. (b) Less than 30% of the researchers mentioned, let alone measured or used data on, treatment protocol implementation or "dosage." (c) Despite the complexity of their interventions, only 31% of the researchers had any theory, "logic model," or even hypotheses about why they might work (most focused on labels, components, process outcomes, or strategies for gaining participation). (d) Although 77% of the studies involved multidimensional and multiple-exposure interventions, more than 84% of the researchers analyzed only the independent variable as a categorical dichotomy or black box (e.g., using a chi-square or analysis of variance [ANOVA]).

Note that although many people use randomization as a surrogate for study quality, it does not address power or any of the aforementioned problems. It is not surprising, then, that the mere presence of randomization has turned out to be a weak predictor of being able to find an effect in recent meta-analyses (i.e., there are bad experiments and good quasi-experiments; Heinsman & Shadish, 1996). Furthermore, many of the preceding limitations have been compounded in recent literature reviews relying on counts of how many studies reach statistical significance or randomization as the primary measure of study quality (e.g., Edwards & Steinglass, 1995; Luborsky & Singer, 1975; Miller et al., 1995; Saxe, Dougherty, Esty, & Fine, 1983; Saxe & Goodman, 1988).

TABLE 1
Analysis of Mean Effect Size, Type II Error, and Sample Sizes From a Meta-Analysis of Family Based Alcohol Interventions

Type and number of comparisons[a]	Mean effect size[b]	% of finding Type II errors[c]	Minimum[d] sample size for 80% power ($\alpha = .05$)	Actual sample size per group	
				Mean n per group	Low n per group[e]
Initiating change (5)	1.75	40	10+	15.6	3 of 8
Family systems (8)	0.53	67	64+	25.3	8 of 9
Primary rehabilitation (18)	1.04	72	17+	21.7	16 of 24
Relapse prevention (3)	1.00	67	18+	24.2	0 of 3
Total	1.02	67	18+	21.4	27 of 34

Note. Table adapted from Dennis, Huebner, and McLellan's (1996) methodological reanalysis of Edwards and Steinglass (1995).
[a]Thirty-one comparisons made between 34 groups in 21 studies.
[b]Unweighted mean of effect sizes.
[c]Number of nonsignificant comparisons divided by number of comparison assuming that all should have been significant given that all average effect sizes exceeded 0.25.
[d]Based on Dennis (1994).
[e]Number of groups with a sample size less than that required for 80% power ($\alpha < .05$) out of the total number of groups.

In a reanalysis of Edwards and Steinglass (1995), for instance, Dennis, Huebner, and McLellan (1996) found large-to-medium effects of interventions both overall ($\bar{d}$ = 1.02) and in terms of several specific types of interventions: getting people to initiate treatment ($\bar{d}$ = 1.75), family systems interventions ($\bar{d}$ = 0.53), primary rehabilitation ($\bar{d}$ = 1.04), and relapse prevention ($\bar{d}$ = 1.00). However, 67% of the tests evaluated in the individual studies showed no significant difference (Type II error). Of the 34 groups used in the 31 statistical comparisons, 27 had an insufficient number of participants per group to achieve 80% power relative to the average effect sizes that were eventually found. These data are summarized in Table 1 by type of interventions and overall.

As with Lipsey's (1990) earlier general findings, sample size was just one of the problems. Of the 31 original comparisons evaluated by Edwards and Steinglass (1995), 21 used binary outcomes such as "any use" versus "abstinence" (requiring a 50-percentage-point difference to reach statistical significance with 80% power). Even those that used interval counts (e.g., days of drinking) did little or nothing to correct for the large right skew caused by the real zero in such counts. It also is interesting that studies with larger sample sizes or longer follow-up periods tended to actually have smaller effects. This is important because all but five of the larger studies involved randomization. Although randomization is often useful, these findings help to illustrate that other aspects of power, sample heterogeneity, design, implementation, and analysis also are extremely important for producing meaningful and valid results in this area.

Heterogeneity in Community-Based Research

A less recognized but even greater problem in community-based research is the increasing heterogeneity of the individuals being studied, the problems they are presenting with, the amount of interventions they receive, and the number of outcomes needing evaluation (Dennis, Wechsberg, Rasch, & Campbell, 1995; Hansen & Collins, 1994; Kazdin, 1992; Rapkin & Luke, 1993; Uebersax, 1995). Under such circumstances, one cannot assume that the average effect of the average intervention is meaningful because it may be little more than an artifact of the sites, case mix, or degree of implementation (Dennis, Godley, et al., 1996). Indeed, the "average effect" may actually be an artifact of the sites and client case mix chosen for the study. To illustrate the paradox of this "ecological fallacy," consider a hypothetical study randomly assigning employees to a pregnancy prevention program being evaluated on the basis of the number of employees getting pregnant. Simply changing from companies with 90% women in the workforce to 50% to 10% would dramatically reduce the possibility of pregnancy, the average effect, and the power to detect any relative effect of the pregnancy prevention program. Although this example is relatively obvious, consider whether an intervention's effect or appropriateness varies with the composition of the sample (e.g., in school grades covered, socioeconomic status, reading level). Although these problems could be addressed using representative sampling, stratification, or blocking, few researchers have tapped into the increased power by doing so (Dennis et al., 1996).

In a longitudinal study of HIV prevention, for instance, Dennis, Wechsberg, et al. (1995) found that simply grouping people on the basis of their gender and types of sexual partners in the past 30 days (i.e., celibate, male heterosexual, male bisexual, homosexual, female heterosexual, female bisexual, lesbian) allowed us to predict 12%–20% of the variance in sexual behaviors 6 months later. Similarly, dividing this group into three target populations (i.e., needle users, crack users, or both) helped predict 21%–38% of the variance in drug use behaviors 6 months later. Unfortunately, neither of these sample typologies predicted much variance in the other's outcomes. To do this, it was necessary to combine them in an empirical cluster analysis. The eight risk groups resulting from this cluster analysis did the same or better than any one simple typology, explaining at follow-up 13%–20% of sexual behaviors, 31%–36% or better of the drug use variables, and 63% of the variance in their joint distribution (vs. 33% and 43% of the joint distribution for the two simpler typologies).

The resulting risk group can be used as a highly effective covariate or blocking variable to either increase the observed effect size by 40% or decrease the sample size for a given level of power (80%) and Type I error (.05). Using it as a covariate or as blocking variable would reduce the sample size required to detect a given effect size of (a) .01 from 1,569 to 199 people, (b) .35 from 274 to 35 people, and (c) .50 from 68 to 10 people. Thus, ignoring subgroups makes us risk misinterpretation and using them dramatically increases our statistical power or cuts our costs. (Kraemer, 1981, provided a more extensive discussion of how power analysis is related to other aspects of research design and their costs.)

EVOLUTION AND THEORY OF POWER ANALYSIS

Origins of Power Analysis

Modern interest in statistical power (and what became meta-analysis) stems from Cohen's (1962) critique of the 1960 *Journal of Abnormal and Social Psychology*, in which he demonstrated that the average rate of power was only 18% for correlations of .2, 48% for correlations of .4, and 83% for correlations of .6 and that on average it was less than 50%. The idea of power, however, was first proposed by Neyman and Pearson (1928, 1933) as an extension of hypothesis testing developed by Fisher (1925). Neyman and Pearson proposed a model of statistical inference in which power is used as a criterion for developing and selecting statistical tests. If two tests of the same hypothesis are proposed, the test with the greater power under identical conditions is preferred. The goal is to identify the uniformly most powerful test (i.e., under all conditions). Standard parametric tests are uniformly the most powerful when the parametric assumptions are met. Widespread use of power analyses was initially hampered by the lack of power charts and tables of the noncentral F distribution and because it was vehemently denounced by Fisher (1966; Gigerenzer, 1987; Pearson & Hartley, 1954; Sedlmeier & Gigerenzer, 1989). The first comprehensive set of tables by Lehmer were not published by the National Bureau of Standards until 1960 (Scheffé, 1959). The blending of hypothesis testing and power analyses and the use of power analyses for meta-analysis, however, was not fully realized until Cohen (1962). Subsequently, literally dozens of studies in dozens of fields have replicated the initial findings, and Cohen's (1977, 1988) book *Statistical Power Analysis for the Behavioral Sciences* is widely recognized as the definitive source.

The development of power analysis gave researchers a tool to measure the various decisions that are made in designing a study (e.g., sample size, measurement instruments, analytic procedures) have on the sensitivity of the research to detect differences (e.g., treatment effect vs. no treatment). However, having been born out of the statistical decision model proposed by Fisher (1925, 1935) and refined into a dichotomous decision model (null vs. alternative hypothesis) by Neyman and Pearson (1933), power analysis generally has been applied only within this context. This focus on hypotheses testing has been widely criticized by many methodologists, particularly those conducting meta-analyses, who realize how often such decision rules misinform both the investigator and the field (Bangert-Drowns, 1986; Cohen, 1988; Dennis et al., 1996; Lipsey, 1990; Sedlmeier & Gigerenzer, 1989).

Although power is linked directly to a specification of an alternative hypothesis, the results of a power analysis directly address the issue of point estimation (e.g., a population mean, the difference between two population means). It was Neyman (1935a, 1935b) who, using the principles underlying the concept of power, proposed the idea of *confidence intervals*. The width of the confidence interval around the sample statistic (e.g., sample mean, difference between two sample means) is an index of precision of estimation. The smaller the interval, the more precise is the estimate and the more powerful is the corresponding statistical test. In this way, power and precision of estimation are two sides of the same coin. The advantage of using confidence intervals is that they give a more comprehensive representation of research finds than a simple statement rejecting or accepting a null hypothesis. Methods for constructing confidence intervals for sample statistics can be found in most modern statistical textbooks. Although rarely reported, because effect size indexes are linear functions of the sample statistics, one also can form confidence intervals for the effect size estimates.

Evolution of Power Analysis in Practice

Cohen's (1977, 1988) core work, *Statistical Power Analysis for the Behavioral Sciences*, focused on two particular themes: (a) estimating the power of various sample sizes for small, medium, and large effects (which he defined as .2, .4, and .8 for ANOVA designs on the basis of several meta-analyses of the literature) and alphas of .10, .05, and .01 and (b) the power of various statistical designs and outcomes translated into effect sizes (using reported significance levels and sample sizes). His books show literally hundreds of alternative ways of calculating power for different types of measures, designs, and available information. Mathematically, it is the definitive source and contains many detailed examples and tables. These virtues, however, often make it an intimidating text for many readers.

Kraemer and Thiemann's (1987) book, *How Many Subjects? Statistical power analysis in research*, refocuses and combines Cohen's (1977, 1988) themes to provide a more readily accessible method for estimating sample size requirements as a function of expected effect size, research design, and alpha. They introduced a new parameter—delta (Δ)—to reflect the design-adjusted effect size. This is a particularly important innovation because it makes it easier to directly compare the power (in terms of sample size requirements) of multiple designs.

Lipsey's (1990) book, *Design Sensitivity*, adds two important dimensions to this discussion. First, through several methodological meta-analyses, he demonstrated the problems with current practice research, specifically in terms of power analysis and more broadly in terms of overall measurement and analysis. Starting with some of the basic design differences discussed by Cohen (1977, 1988) and Kraemer and Thiemann (1987), Lipsey further explored how other design features affect power, including considerations such as types of measures, use of covariates, use of blocking variables, and the use of repeated measures.

Later in this chapter, we present a practical approach for designing studies and prioritizing what is often a laundry list of questions in large community-based studies. This approach assumes that (a) the number of participants is largely fixed because of logistical constraints, (b) the level of power must be 80% or more to meet reviewer requirements, and (c) only minimal a priori data exist for making detailed power estimates. In this context, power analysis is used to identify the minimal detectable effect size (with 80% power and an alpha less than .05 in a two-tailed test) and compare them across multiple questions and design variations.

FUNDAMENTALS OF CALCULATING POWER

Logic

Both hypothesis testing and power analysis are involved in the calculation of conditional probabilities based on an assumed distribution. Figure 1 illustrates this by showing two distributions that are actually different. Hypothesis testing is conditional on the assumed distribution of the standard or comparison group under the null hypothesis, shown in the figure as the solid line curve going from Points A to E. Power analysis is conditional on the assumed distribution of the enhanced or experimental group under the alternative hypothesis, shown in the figure as the dashed curve going from Points B to F. Both are dependent on the questions, variables, designs, effect sizes, and distributions that are assumed and often have to be estimated using normal (as in this figure) or other standard distributions. They are normally evaluated using the conditional probabilities of three sources of error: (a) Type I—the probability of saying there is a statistically reliable difference between the two groups when there is not, (b) Type II —the probability of saying there is not a statistically reliable difference when there is, and (c) Type III—the probability of saying there is a statistically reliable difference in one direction when there actually is one in the opposite direction.

Type I error is often referred to as alpha (α) and somewhat misleadingly as "statistical significance." In Figure 1, it is the area with horizontal lines under the standard curve between Points A and C plus the area between Points D and E. Type II error is often referred to as beta (β) and is the inverse of power (i.e., power is equal to $1 - \beta$). The probability of beta is the gray area under the experimental curve between Points C to D, and the power is the remaining area under the experimental curve

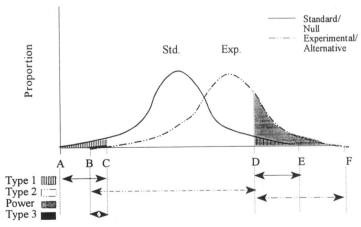

Figure 1. Comparison of distributions, types of error, and power.

between Points B and C plus D and F. Type III error is relevant only when doing a one-tailed test of a directional hypothesis. This is the black area under the experimental curve between Points B and C.

Although the probability of Type III error approaches zero in this illustration, it is a particularly important concept in power analysis. Most researchers primarily use two-tailed tests and hypotheses, but because they have inadequate sample sizes, many try to inflate their power estimates in proposals and articles by calculating power for a one-tailed test. They then further exaggerate their estimates by ignoring attrition in follow-up, substantial measurement error, or insensitive designs. Under these unrealistic assumptions, they often accept only a moderate level of power (e.g., 70%) to justify grossly inadequate sample sizes to find what they are looking for. Failure to discuss these issues in a such a power analysis will often lead to criticism by a reviewer who understands that actual power for the real tests in such a case will probably fall well below 50%.

Basic Components

Although the formulas vary depending on distribution and design, all power analyses have six basic parameters:

- the sample size (n);
- an effect size (d);
- the probability of a Type II error, or beta (β);
- the probability of a Type I error, or alpha (α);
- the type of distribution;
- whether this is for a one- or two-tailed test.

Once any five parameters are specified, the sixth parameter can be estimated. Most power analyses assume an alpha of .05 or less, a normal distribution, and a two-tailed test; they then focus on estimating either the sample size, effect size, or probability of a Type II error (to calculate the power as $1 - \beta$). Calculations are typically done with a set of graphs or tables such as those presented in this chapter or in other texts (e.g., Cohen, 1988; Kraemer & Thiemann, 1987; Lipsey, 1990) using spreadsheets to help with calculations (the spreadsheets for our tables can be downloaded from http//www.chestnut.org) or speciality software (e.g., GPower, Nquerry, PASS/NCSS). It should be noted that the use of .05 as a cutoff for Type I error is a social norm—one that many statisticians oppose.

Hypothesis testing, power analysis, and virtually all inferential statistics compare some term that quantifies the effect attributable to the hypothesized cause with another term that quantifies the effect attributable to error. This is best thought of as a problem of signal detection, in which the challenge is to determine whether the evidence in support of the hypothesis is large enough given the surrounding field of error to allow confidence in the observed effect or determine that it is simply a result of random fluctuation in the data. Although early textbooks focused on increasing power through larger sample sizes, more recent work has concentrated on reducing the background noise to magnify the observed effect size (which is a ratio of "true" effect size signal to noise).

Effect Size

An effect size can be a difference between two means, variance estimates, distributions, percentages, pretest to posttest change scores, regression coefficients, production functions, discriminant functions, or structural equations. In can be calculated regardless of power and used to assess the sensitivity or power of a given design. Conversely, one can estimate the minimum detectable effect size on the basis of assumptions about the sample size, design, and desired level of power.

There are detailed formulas for calculating effect sizes (ESs) for different types of measures, tests, and design (see Cohen, 1977; Kraemer & Thiemann, 1987; Lipsey, 1990). The most common five equations are shown in Equations 1–5.

$$ES = (M_{Exp.} - M_{Std.})/SD_{pooled}. \tag{1}$$

$$ES = (M_{Exp.} - M_{Std.})/SD_{Std. only}. \tag{2}$$

$$ES = 2R/SQRT(1 - R^2). \tag{3}$$

$$ES = SQRT\{4(\chi^2)/[n - (\chi^2)]\}. \tag{4}$$

$$ES = 2*arcsin(P_{Exp.}) - 2*arcsin(P_{Std.}). \tag{5}$$

Equations 1 and 2 are similar to a t test except that they use the standard deviation instead of the standard error. Although the first is the most widely used in meta-analyses, it assumes homogeneity of variance between the groups. In community-based experiments in which there are often variance effects attributable to varying degrees of implementation, participant willingness to use the services, or Client × Treatment interactions, we recommend that the latter be used to increase power (Dennis, 1994; Dennis & Boruch, 1994; discussed later). Equations 3 and 4 are common shortcuts used to calculate effect sizes from a published multiple correlation, multiple correlation squared, or chi-square statistic. Equation 5 is Cohen's (1977) arcsine transformation for calculating an effect size from a difference in two proportions (e.g., percentage relapsing). As we demonstrate in the next sections of this chapter, the observed effect sizes also can be increased (or decreased) depending on the design and amount of measurement error.

When Lipsey (1990) studied the distribution of effect sizes in 168 meta-analyses, he found that the lower 33% ranged from 0.00 to 0.32 (midpoint = 0.15), the middle 34% ranged from 0.33 to 0.55 (midpoint = 0.45), and the top 33% ranged from 0.56 to 1.2 (midpoint = 0.90). Note that such effect sizes are measures of practical significance and vary in what is considered important by field. An effect size of 0.01 (change of less than 1%) would be considered trivial in most psychology studies but could represent an important effect in the spread of a deadly virus. For meta-analytic reviews of the range of effect sizes in multiple fields, see Lipsey (1990) or Sedlmeier and Gigerenzer (1989). For more on other empirical approaches to measuring clinical significance, see Jacobson and Truax (1991).

Evolution of Power Software

As power analysis has become increasingly more common, so, too, have the spreadsheets and simple programs to help do them. Freeware for calculating the power of simple t tests and F ratios is readily downloaded for noncommercial use. One of the most common of these is part of the U.S. Centers for Disease Control's EpiInfo statistical software (which can be downloaded from ftp://ftp.cdc.gov/pub/epi/epiinfo). Another is Erdfelder, Faul, and Buchner's (1996) and Buchner, Faul, and Erdfelder's (1992) stand-alone GPOWER (which can be downloaded from ftp.ini-trier.de or http://www.psychologie.uni-bonn.de/allgm/mitarbei/privat/dilger_s/gpower_e.htm). Researchers who need help using FTP sites or who have a more complicated design requiring commercial software should see Len Thomas and Charles Krebs's (1997) review and Web site at the Centre for Applied Conservation Biology, University of British Columbia (http://www.interchg.ubc.ca/cacb/power/). Established in May 1996, it contains hyperlinks and contact information on more than 50 other noncommercial and commercial software vendors. If one is already using a general commercial package (e.g., SAS, SPSS, or Excel), this Web site also contains information on macros that have already been written for them. Several of these general statistical packages also have added "power" commands that retrospectively calculate the power of a specific analysis done on real data (i.e., in addition to the probability of alpha, they also report the power for the observed difference, design, and sample size).

For the most part, these programs take over the sometimes tricky job of calculating the power and provide additional insight into ways to improve the design. For example, some programs accept estimates of variance reduction built into the design as additional parameters that may affect the power of a study. A few of the more advanced programs allow the researcher to specify the reduction in error variance (i.e., noise) achieved through the use of covariates and improved measurement (i.e., increasing the number of items in a scale or modeling and removing the effects method artifacts in a structural equation model). Most, however, are simply making post hoc adjustments following the procedures outlined later in this chapter.

Although useful in planning designs and analysis, these computer programs still rely heavily on the user to provide reliable estimates of inputs with which to make the calculation. Poor estimates of reliability and covariation in the design phase will, of course, distort the calculation, just as would a poor estimate of effect size or clustering effects. Still, the reduced time needed to make a calculation may increase the awareness of the need for power analysis and result in an increase in its use.

Although the last major review of power software that we could find is dated (Goldstein, 1989), it does offer some critical things to look for when evaluating computer software: (a) whether it is a specialized package or integrated into a larger statistical package; (b) which specific analysis tests it calculates power for; (c) what kinds of distributions it uses; (d) whether covariance or measurement reduction terms can be entered; (e) the ease with which it can be learned or used; (f) its ability to output tables or graphs that can be used in word processing (e.g., for proposals); and (g) accuracy. In Goldstein's original comparison of 11 commercial power software packages, the estimates of power for even just simple t tests ranged from as little as 0.5% to as much as 10%, with most of the packages varying from one another by less than 1%. The reason for these variations is that even statistical packages involve some level of approximation that is based on their author's assumptions.

PRACTICAL POWER ANALYSIS FOR PLANNING

Approach

A number of students and researchers may be trying to do a power analysis or simply trying to understand how to better work with a statistical consultant. In general, we subscribe to Bob Stout's recommendation that the principal investigator should learn how to do at least basic power analysis and do it "early and often" throughout the design and conduct of their study. In this section, we explain a practical step-by-step approach for doing this kind of practical power analysis. This is an approach that we have developed over the years working with researchers conducting studies related to alcohol, drug abuse, mental health, and physical health. Although power analysis was often required for proposals, sample sizes typically were specified or at least severely constrained by the budget or other logistical considerations. Moreover, the proposals were typically being reviewed by committees containing at least one person who would not accept unrealistic assumptions (i.e., much less than 80% power). Thus, we place less emphasis on "how many participants" or "how much power" and more emphasis on "prioritizing" analyses and improving study design.

Where to Start

Power analysis works only when the user is trying to estimate something specific. If there are multiple questions or outcomes, in theory the user could do a different power analysis on each. In practice, it is better to focus on the central questions. Although the questions will obviously vary by study, most fall into one or more of the following forms: Who is being served? To what extent are the neediest being served more? What services were provided? To what extent is one of two or more ways more effective? To what extent is one of two or more ways more cost-effective or benefit–cost effective (Bloom, 1995; Boruch & Cordray, 1980; Dennis, Fetterman, & Sechrest, 1994)?

To start a power analysis, the researcher will need to identify (a) the core questions and hypotheses; (b) the core dependent and independent variables; (c) any constraints on the questions, design, or sample size; and (d) preliminary data on the distributions of these variables and their relationships. Most researchers can determine the first three by brainstorming with colleagues. When the researcher is conducting his or her first study, getting preliminary estimates of effect sizes for the fourth issue often is the most difficult because of gaps in the community-based literature and how the data were reported. Furthermore, what the researcher does find will often concern different populations and interventions than he or she has proposed. For this reason, our approach focuses more on the minimum detectable effect size for a given level of Type I (.05) and Type II (.20 or 80% power) error for a two-tailed test. Rather than make a specific estimate from available data, we determine the minimum detectable effect and then determine whether it is consistent with the other available data.

When reviewing the questions, the researcher must next decide which of the three core methods of power analysis he or she wants to do: (a) estimating precision of the prevalence of a problem or service, (b) comparing two groups to see whether they are different at a given point in time, and (c) estimating the change over time. In any study, the researcher might actually have multiple questions and will need multiple types of power analysis. When estimating power for multiple variables, the researcher may need to do separate calculations for each and summarize them in a table. Each of these methods is discussed in turn.

Precision of a Prevalence Measure

This type of power analysis is designed to answer questions such as the following: Who is being served? Who is being missed? What services are being received? What are the problems? What are the costs? The most common types of estimates that might be made include percentages, population, dimensional measures, and ratio estimates. In more advanced research (typically in which there is prior data or research that is directly related), researchers also may be estimating the prevalence of a case mix derived from something like a cluster analysis or a dimensional measure from a simple scale, regression, factor, or structural equation. Here, the critical measure of precision is the *relative standard error*. This is simply the standard deviation of a statistic divided by its mean. In a range of 6%–94%, the relative standard error ideally would be below 30%. Below 5%, above 95%, and in general, relative standard error should never be more than 50% because at 1.96 times the standard error, the 95% confidence intervals of the estimate will include zero (i.e., not significantly different from zero). Note that dichotomous variables such as these actually have Bernoulli distribution; consequently, the approximations above do not work as well when the sample size or prevalence gets smaller.

If researchers have data, they can directly estimate the standard error (which already incorporates the sample size) and mean, to determine whether they meet these criteria. If not, Table 2 shows the standard errors for percentage estimates from 1% to 99%, and Table 3 shows them as relative standard errors (with those below the preceding criteria indicated with a dash). If researchers have a sample size of 300 people, they could detect prevalence rates from 5% to 95% with relative standard errors of 25% or less. The following is an example of how this would be stated in a report or proposal: With a sample size of 300 people, one can detect characteristics as rare as 5% with a relative standard error of 25% or less. For 5%, the 95% confidence intervals would be 5% ± 2.47%. The latter (2.47%) was calculated as 1.96 times the standard error (1.26) to generate a 95% confidence interval.

If researchers are using or have used a complicated sampling scheme or just cluster sampling (e.g., taking a sample of schools and kids within them, a sample of employers and people within a site), this may produce a "design effect" that reduces the effective sample size or level of precision for a given sample size. (For more discussion of design effects, see Donner & Donald, 1987; Graubard & Korn, 1994; Katz & Zeger, 1994; Kish, 1965; LaVange, Keyes, Koch, & Margolis, 1994.) If researchers have such a design, they need to be familiar with the calculation of design effects or use a statistical consultant because they can vary from no effect (1.0) to cutting the effective sample size in half (2.0), by a third (3.0), or, in the worst case we have seen, by one sixteenth (16.0). The prevention study in this last example had a sample size of 11,000, it was drawn from three large and different high schools in California, and it only produced an effective sample size of 687.5 (11,000 ÷ 16). Tables 2 and 3 therefore also show

TABLE 2
Standard Errors for Various Prevalence Rates and Sample Sizes

Design effect from clustered variance					Effective	Prevalence estimate (%)						
3.00	2.50	2.00	1.50	1.00	n	p: 1 / q: 99 / p*q: 1	5 / 95 / 5	10 / 90 / 9	20 / 80 / 16	30 / 70 / 21	40 / 60 / 24	50 / 50 / 25
60,000	50,000	40,000	30,000	20,000	20,000	0.07	0.15	0.21	0.28	0.32	0.35	0.35
45,000	37,500	30,000	22,500	15,000	15,000	0.08	0.18	0.24	0.33	0.37	0.40	0.41
30,000	25,000	20,000	15,000	10,000	10,000	0.10	0.22	0.30	0.40	0.46	0.49	0.50
15,000	12,500	10,000	7,500	5,000	5,000	0.14	0.31	0.42	0.57	0.65	0.69	0.71
12,000	10,000	8,000	6,000	4,000	4,000	0.16	0.34	0.47	0.63	0.72	0.77	0.79
9,000	7,500	6,000	4,500	3,000	3,000	0.18	0.40	0.55	0.73	0.84	0.89	0.91
6,000	5,000	4,000	3,000	2,000	2,000	0.22	0.49	0.67	0.89	1.02	1.10	1.12
4,500	3,750	3,000	2,250	1,500	1,500	0.26	0.56	0.77	1.03	1.18	1.26	1.29
3,000	2,500	2,000	1,500	1,000	1,000	0.31	0.69	0.95	1.26	1.45	1.55	1.58
1,500	1,250	1,000	750	500	500	0.45	0.97	1.34	1.79	2.05	2.19	2.24
1,350	1,125	900	675	450	450	0.47	1.03	1.41	1.89	2.16	2.31	2.36
1,200	1,000	800	600	400	400	0.50	1.09	1.50	2.00	2.29	2.45	2.50
1,050	875	700	525	350	350	—	1.17	1.60	2.14	2.45	2.62	2.67
900	750	600	450	300	300	—	1.26	1.73	2.31	2.65	2.83	2.89
750	625	500	375	250	250	—	1.38	1.90	2.53	2.90	3.10	3.16
600	500	400	300	200	200	—	1.54	2.12	2.83	3.24	3.46	3.54
450	375	300	225	150	150	—	1.78	2.45	3.27	3.74	4.00	4.08
300	250	200	150	100	100	—	2.18	3.00	4.00	4.58	4.90	5.00
150	125	100	75	50	50	—	—	—	5.66	6.48	6.93	7.07

Note. $SE = \{SQRT[(p*q)/n]\}/p$. 95% confidence interval is $(p - 1.95*SE)$ to $(p + 1.95 * SE)$. Dashes indicate a relative standard error greater than 50% for 1% to 5%, greater than 30% for 6% to 94%, and 50% for 95% to 99%.

TABLE 3
Relative Standard Errors (RSEs) for Various Prevalence Rates and Sample Sizes

Design effect from clustered variance					Effective	Prevalence (%)						
3.00	2.50	2.00	1.50	1.00	n	p = 1	5	10	20	30	40	50
						q = 99	95	90	80	70	60	50
						p*q = 1	5	9	16	21	24	25
60,000	50,000	40,000	30,000	20,000	20,000	7.04	3.08	2.12	1.41	1.08	0.87	0.71
45,000	37,500	30,000	22,500	15,000	15,000	8.12	3.56	2.45	1.63	1.25	1.00	0.82
30,000	25,000	20,000	15,000	10,000	10,000	9.95	4.36	3.00	2.00	1.53	1.22	1.00
15,000	12,500	10,000	7,500	5,000	5,000	14.07	6.16	4.24	2.83	2.16	1.73	1.41
12,000	10,000	8,000	6,000	4,000	4,000	15.73	6.89	4.74	3.16	2.42	1.94	1.58
9,000	7,500	6,000	4,500	3,000	3,000	18.17	7.96	5.48	3.65	2.79	2.24	1.83
6,000	5,000	4,000	3,000	2,000	2,000	22.25	9.75	6.71	4.47	3.42	2.74	2.24
4,500	3,750	3,000	2,250	1,500	1,500	25.69	11.25	7.75	5.16	3.94	3.16	2.58
3,000	2,500	2,000	1,500	1,000	1,000	31.46	13.78	9.49	6.32	4.83	3.87	3.16
1,500	1,250	1,000	750	500	500	44.50	19.49	13.42	8.94	6.83	5.48	4.47
1,350	1,125	900	675	450	450	46.90	20.55	14.14	9.43	7.20	5.77	4.71
1,200	1,000	800	600	400	400	49.75	21.79	15.00	10.00	7.64	6.12	5.00
1,050	875	700	525	350	350	—	23.30	16.04	10.69	8.17	6.55	5.35
900	750	600	450	300	300	—	25.17	17.32	11.55	8.82	7.07	5.77
750	625	500	375	250	250	—	27.57	18.97	12.65	9.66	7.75	6.32
600	500	400	300	200	200	—	30.82	21.21	14.14	10.80	8.66	7.07
450	375	300	225	150	150	—	35.59	24.49	16.33	12.47	10.00	8.17
300	250	200	150	100	100	—	43.59	30.00	20.00	15.28	12.25	10.00
150	125	100	75	50	50	—	—	—	28.28	21.60	17.32	14.14

Note. RSE = {SQRT[(p*q)/n]}/p. Dashes indicate an RSE greater than 50% for 1% to 5%, greater than 30% for 6% to 94%, and 50% for 95% to 99%.

the increased sample size required to achieve the same effective sample size (*n*) of a simple random sample or census.

Comparing Two Groups at a Single Point in Time

This type of power analysis is designed to answer questions such as the following: How do these groups differ in behaviors, needs, services, or outcomes? To what extent are services being delivered to the most needy, appropriate, or targeted group? To what extent are some approaches more effective in reaching and keeping the target population involved? Which of two interventions is relatively more effective or cost-effective? The most common types of estimates that might be made include effect sizes, *t* scores, percentage point differences, correlation coefficients (simple or multiple correlation), or the percentage of variance explained (R^2). Note that in several multistage designs, quasi-experiments, and nonparametric research, one will need to transform or estimate one of these parameters using other methods that are beyond the scope of this chapter. (For special issues related to estimating power when randomly assigning clusters other than the unit of analysis, see Donner, Birkett, & Buck, 1981; for use with regression discontinuity and cut of trials, see Cappelleri, Darlington, & Trochim, 1994; for use with logistic regression, see Knoke & Burke, 1980.) Here, we focus on the effect size as estimated (*d*) or as known or hypothesized (δ).

Table 4 shows the smallest detectable effect size and its equivalent *t* score, percentage point change, correlation, and squared correlation by various sample sizes per group (for pairwise comparisons) or within-group degrees of freedom (for regression). For the latter, the researcher would need to add another person for each variable in the equation to calculate the total sample size required. To calculate the smallest detectable effect for a given number of observations, we have specified that we want to have statistical power of at least 80% power in a two-tailed test with a Type I error rate of .05 or less. The effect size of a percentage point change is based on the arcsine transformation presented earlier assuming initial rates ranging from 20% to 80%. For instance, if one has a sample size of 135 per group, one would be able to detect a medium effect size of 0.36 or more. If one has a sample size in between two rows in the table, one can use the lower number or interpolate between the rows. If the proposed sample sizes per group are unequal, one will need to use their harmonic mean in using Table 4 (e.g., $N_{harmonic} = 2*N_{Exp}*N_{Std}/N_{Exp} + N_{Std}$). Unequal allocation to groups has only a small effect on the total sample size for a 70–30 split, but it can more than double the required total sample size when the split is 90–10.

Also notice that as the sample size goes down, the smallest detectable effect goes up. As the effect size goes up, notice that the *t* test goes up slightly (it already takes sample size and distributions into account), the

TABLE 4
Smallest Detectable Effect Size, Percentage Point Change, Correlation, and Percentage of Variance Explained for Various Sample Sizes Assuming Two Groups, 80% Power, 5% Type I Error Rate, and a Two-Tailed Test

Sample size		Smallest detectable outcomes with 80% power				
n per group[a]	Within-groups dfs (γ)[b]	Effect size $(\|d\|, \|\delta\|)$	t score $(\|t\|)$	% point differ-ences $(\|P_2 - P_1\|)$	Correlation coefficient $(\|\rho\|, \|R\|, \|r\|)$	% of variance ex-plained (PVE, r^2)
39,243	78,485	0.02	2.8	1–5	.01	0.0
9,810	19,618	0.04	2.8	1–5	.02	0.0
4,359	8,717	0.06	2.8	1–5	.03	0.1
2,452	4,902	0.08	2.8	1–5	.04	0.1
1,569	3,136	0.10	2.8	5	.05	0.2
1,089	2,177	0.12	2.8	5–10	.06	0.4
800	1,598	0.14	2.8	5–10	.07	0.5
612	1,223	0.16	2.8	5–10	.08	0.6
484	965	0.18	2.8	10	.09	0.8
392	781	0.21	2.9	10–15	.10	1.0
324	645	0.23	2.9	10–15	.11	1.2
272	541	0.25	2.9	10–15	.12	1.4
232	461	0.27	2.9	10–15	.13	1.7
200	397	0.29	2.9	15	.14	2.0
174	345	0.31	2.9	15–20	.15	2.2
152	301	0.33	2.9	15–20	.16	2.6
135	268	0.36	2.9	15–20	.18	3.2
120	238	0.38	2.9	15–20	.19	3.6
108	214	0.40	2.9	20	.20	4.0
97	192	0.42	2.9	20–25	.21	4.4
80	158	0.47	3.0	20–25	.23	5.3
68	133	0.51	3.0	25	.25	6.2
57	112	0.56	3.0	25–30	.27	7.3
49	96	0.60	3.0	30	.29	8.4
42	83	0.65	3.0	30–35	.31	9.6
38	73	0.69	3.0	35	.33	10.9
33	64	0.74	3.0	35–40	.35	12.2
30	57	0.79	3.1	40	.37	13.7
26	51	0.84	3.1	40–45	.39	15.2
24	45	0.89	3.1	45	.41	16.8
18	35	1.01	3.1	50	.45	20.2
14	27	1.13	3.1	>50	.49	24.0
12	22	1.26	3.1	>50	.53	28.1
10	18	1.39	3.1	>50	.57	32.5

[a]The number of people per group represents the minimum to detect a given set of outcomes with 80% power and a 5% probability of Type I error with a two-tailed test.
[b]When other techniques are used, the number of blocking, other covariate variables, and intervention variables (random assignment) need to be subtracted from the total and the remaining number (within groups) used here.

TABLE 5
Estimated Effect Size for

P2	θ	0.01 / 0.20	0.05 / 0.45	0.1 / 0.64	0.15 / 0.80	0.2 / 0.93	0.25 / 1.05	0.3 / 1.16	0.35 / 1.27	0.4 / 1.37
0.01	0.20	0.00	−0.25	−0.44	−0.60	−0.73	−0.85	−0.96	−1.07	−1.17
0.05	0.45	0.25	0.00	−0.19	−0.34	−0.48	−0.60	−0.71	−0.82	−0.92
0.10	0.64	0.44	0.19	0.00	−0.15	−0.28	−0.40	−0.52	−0.62	−0.73
0.15	0.80	0.60	0.34	0.15	0.00	−0.13	−0.25	−0.36	−0.47	−0.57
0.20	0.93	0.73	0.48	0.28	0.13	0.00	−0.12	−0.23	−0.34	−0.44
0.25	1.05	0.85	0.60	0.40	0.25	0.12	0.00	−0.11	−0.22	−0.32
0.30	1.16	0.96	0.71	0.52	0.36	0.23	0.11	0.00	−0.11	−0.21
0.35	1.27	1.07	0.82	0.62	0.47	0.34	0.22	0.11	0.00	−0.10
0.40	1.37	1.17	0.92	0.73	0.57	0.44	0.32	0.21	0.10	0.00
0.45	1.47	1.27	1.02	0.83	0.68	0.54	0.42	0.31	0.20	0.10
0.50	1.57	1.37	1.12	0.93	0.78	0.64	0.52	0.41	0.30	0.20
0.55	1.67	1.47	1.22	1.03	0.88	0.74	0.62	0.51	0.40	0.30
0.60	1.77	1.57	1.32	1.13	0.98	0.84	0.72	0.61	0.51	0.40
0.65	1.88	1.68	1.42	1.23	1.08	0.95	0.83	0.72	0.61	0.51
0.70	1.98	1.78	1.53	1.34	1.19	1.06	0.94	0.82	0.72	0.61
0.75	2.09	1.89	1.64	1.45	1.30	1.17	1.05	0.94	0.83	0.72
0.80	2.21	2.01	1.76	1.57	1.42	1.29	1.17	1.06	0.95	0.84
0.85	2.35	2.15	1.90	1.70	1.55	1.42	1.30	1.19	1.08	0.98
0.90	2.50	2.30	2.05	1.85	1.70	1.57	1.45	1.34	1.23	1.13
0.95	2.69	2.49	2.24	2.05	1.90	1.76	1.64	1.53	1.42	1.32
0.99	2.94	2.74	2.49	2.30	2.15	2.01	1.89	1.78	1.68	1.57

Note. $\theta = 2*\text{arcsine}(\text{SQRT } P)$. Effect size = $2*\text{arcsine}[\text{SQRT}(P2)] - 2*\text{arcsine}[\text{SQRT}(P1)]$.

two correlational statistics go up more (they take into account distributions), and the required amount of percentage point changes goes up dramatically. One would therefore need to either pick one measure or summarize this analysis as follows: With a sample size of 135 per group after the expected attrition, we should be able to detect an effect size of 0.36 or more with 80% power in a two-tailed test with alpha of .05 or less. This is the equivalent of reliably explaining 3.2% or more of the variance via regression or observing a 15- to 20-percentage-point change in abstinence from alcohol.

If a researcher is proposing any subgroup analyses (e.g., effects on women, minorities, or program completers), he or she would repeat the process using the expected sample sizes from the subgroup. Also note that these sizes would be the final sample sizes per group (or subgroup) for the core analysis. To the extent that attrition or nonresponse is expected, they would need to be further inflated by dividing them by the expected completion rate ([desired n]/[1 − attrition rate]). Thus, if a sample of 272 is desired and an attrition rate of 15% is expected, the evaluator would need to start with the following: 272/(.85) = 320 individuals per group.

Differences in Proportions ($P2 - P1$)

P1 and θ											
0.45	0.5	0.55	0.6	0.65	0.7	0.75	0.8	0.85	0.9	0.95	0.99
1.47	1.57	1.67	1.77	1.88	1.98	2.09	2.21	2.35	2.50	2.69	2.94
−1.27	−1.37	−1.47	−1.57	−1.68	−1.78	−1.89	−2.01	−2.15	−2.30	−2.49	−2.74
−1.02	−1.12	−1.22	−1.32	−1.42	−1.53	−1.64	−1.76	−1.90	−2.05	−2.24	−2.49
−0.83	−0.93	−1.03	−1.13	−1.23	−1.34	−1.45	−1.57	−1.70	−1.85	−2.05	−2.30
−0.68	−0.78	−0.88	−0.98	−1.08	−1.19	−1.30	−1.42	−1.55	−1.70	−1.90	−2.15
−0.54	−0.64	−0.74	−0.84	−0.95	−1.06	−1.17	−1.29	−1.42	−1.57	−1.76	−2.01
−0.42	−0.52	−0.62	−0.72	−0.83	−0.94	−1.05	−1.17	−1.30	−1.45	−1.64	−1.89
−0.31	−0.41	−0.51	−0.61	−0.72	−0.82	−0.94	−1.06	−1.19	−1.34	−1.53	−1.78
−0.20	−0.30	−0.40	−0.51	−0.61	−0.72	−0.83	−0.95	−1.08	−1.23	−1.42	−1.68
−0.10	−0.20	−0.30	−0.40	−0.51	−0.61	−0.72	−0.84	−0.98	−1.13	−1.32	−1.57
0.00	−0.10	−0.20	−0.30	−0.40	−0.51	−0.62	−0.74	−0.88	−1.03	−1.22	−1.47
0.10	0.00	−0.10	−0.20	−0.30	−0.41	−0.52	−0.64	−0.78	−0.93	−1.12	−1.37
0.20	0.10	0.00	−0.10	−0.20	−0.31	−0.42	−0.54	−0.68	−0.83	−1.02	−1.27
0.30	0.20	0.10	0.00	−0.10	−0.21	−0.32	−0.44	−0.57	−0.73	−0.92	−1.17
0.40	0.30	0.20	0.10	0.00	−0.11	−0.22	−0.34	−0.47	−0.62	−0.82	−1.07
0.51	0.41	0.31	0.21	0.11	0.00	−0.11	−0.23	−0.36	−0.52	−0.71	−0.96
0.62	0.52	0.42	0.32	0.22	0.11	0.00	−0.12	−0.25	−0.40	−0.60	−0.85
0.74	0.64	0.54	0.44	0.34	0.23	0.12	0.00	−0.13	−0.28	−0.48	−0.73
0.88	0.78	0.68	0.57	0.47	0.36	0.25	0.13	0.00	−0.15	−0.34	−0.60
1.03	0.93	0.83	0.73	0.62	0.52	0.40	0.28	0.15	0.00	−0.19	−0.44
1.22	1.12	1.02	0.92	0.82	0.71	0.60	0.48	0.34	0.19	0.00	−0.25
1.47	1.37	1.27	1.17	1.07	0.96	0.85	0.73	0.60	0.44	0.25	0.00

If a researcher has data, the observed differences between two percentages should be converted into an effect size using a table (e.g., Lipsey, 1990), calculated directly using arcsin transformation in Equation 5 (presented earlier), or approximated using Table 5. This is important because two major problems occur in prevention research as the initial proportion gets smaller. First, the same amount of percentage point changes requires a much larger effect size. Second, there is often a floor effect attributable to zero (e.g., one cannot reduce a rate of 10% use by 20 percentage points).

If one has already completed an analysis, one also can work backward through this table looking up the effect size or correlation to see what sample size would have been required to have 80% power. This is important because if the researcher has done a small sample size study that produces a medium or large effect size but does not reach "statistical significance," the researcher should not treat it as "no effect." What the researcher should do is treat it as an underpowered preliminary study and estimate the effect sizes observed (albeit potentially unreliably) and the sample size that would be required to confirm it with 80% power. Then, in a discussion section of an article or preliminary studies section of a grant, use this information to call for "further research to try and replicate these promising findings with a more appropriate sample size and design." Ideally, one should identify a range of effect sizes from a meta-analysis or at least the uncertainty (i.e., confidence intervals) of the estimated effect sizes (see Thomas, 1997).

Evaluating Change Over Time

These types of power analyses are designed to answer questions such as the following: Are things getting better or worse or remaining about the same? Which of two interventions produces the greatest change? Do the effects last? Do two or more functions have the same shape or survival curve? Do the interventions produce the same type or direction of change across clinical subgroups? Here, with between-groups comparisons, the most common types of estimates include effect sizes, t scores, percentage point differences, correlation coefficients (simple or multiple correlation), or the percentage of variance explained (R^2). Many researchers also will directly create a change score (i.e., score at Time 2 minus score at Time 1) and use it as a dependent variable. In addition to the expected effect size (d), here we also focus on Kraemer and Thiemann's (1987) design-adjusted effect size delta (Δ).

Table 6 shows a comparison of the required sample sizes per group of the two group comparisons discussed previously with that required for a pre–post within-groups and a pre–post between-groups comparison. Sample sizes are calculated to detect the design-adjusted effect size (Δ) with 80% power, given a Type I error (α) of .05 or less and a two-tailed test of significance. The minimum sample size requirements are given for five possible unadjusted effect sizes ($ds = 0.10, 0.25, 0.50, 0.75,$ and 1.00) by five possible correlations between repeated outcome measures ($rs = .01, .25, .50, .75,$ and $.90$) by the three types of analysis. Although the within-groups pre- and posttest comparisons are statistically more efficient than the between-groups comparisons, the latter are used in randomized field experiments and are presumed to produce better causal evidence (Cook & Campbell, 1979; Dennis, 1994; Fisher, 1960).

Although there is a diminishing rate of return, repeated observations can reduce the required sample size by fivefold or more (Hayes, 1981). For normally distributed data, a pretest measure that is correlated .50 or more with later outcome measures will improve statistical power (e.g., pre- and postmeasures of drug use or employment). If it is correlated less than .50, however, using the pretest measure as a covariate or to calculate a change will actually decrease design sensitivity. This is particularly likely if a dependent variable is used as an inclusion or exclusion criteria (e.g., drug use, in treatment). Because everyone starts at one place, there will be no correlation between Time 1 and Time 2. This kind of fanspread effect also may occur to a lesser extent if there is any kind of regression to the mean.

TABLE 6
Critical Effect Sizes (Δ) and Sample Size Requirements for Between-Groups, Within-Groups Change, and Between-Groups Change at Posttest and Change Designs ($\alpha = .05$, $\beta = .20$, Two-Tailed)

Expected		Between-groups comparison		Within-groups change		Between-groups change	
($|d|$, $|\delta|$)	($|r|$, $|\rho|$)	Δ_1	n_1/group	Δ_2	n_2/group	Δ_3	n_3/group
0.10	.10	0.05	1,569	0.07	800	0.04	2,452
0.10	.25	0.05	1,569	0.08	612	0.04	2,452
0.10	.50	0.05	1,569	0.10	391	0.05	1,569
0.10	.75	0.05	1,569	0.14	199	0.07	800
0.10	.90	0.05	1,569	0.22	80	0.11	323
0.25	.10	0.12	272	0.18	120	0.09	483
0.25	.25	0.12	272	0.20	97	0.10	391
0.25	.50	0.12	272	0.24	67	0.12	271
0.25	.75	0.12	272	0.33	35	0.17	135
0.25	.90	0.12	272	0.49	15	0.27	53
0.50	.10	0.24	68	0.35	31	0.18	120
0.50	.25	0.24	68	0.38	26	0.20	97
0.50	.50	0.24	68	0.45	18	0.24	67
0.50	.75	0.24	68	0.58	10	0.33	35
0.50	.90	0.24	68	0.75	6	0.49	15
0.75	.10	0.35	31	0.49	15	0.27	53
0.75	.25	0.35	31	0.52	13	0.29	45
0.75	.50	0.35	31	0.60	10	0.35	31
0.75	.75	0.35	31	0.73	6	0.47	16
0.75	.90	0.35	31	0.86	6	0.64	8
1.00	.10	0.45	19	0.60	10	0.35	31
1.00	.25	0.45	19	0.63	9	0.38	26
1.00	.50	0.45	19	0.71	6	0.45	18
1.00	.75	0.45	19	0.82	6	0.58	10
1.00	.90	0.45	19	0.91	6	0.75	6

Note. Critical effect sizes (Δ) and number of people per group are calculated for a two-tailed test of $\alpha = .05$ (or one-tailed test of $\alpha = .025$) for pairwise comparisons of two conditions with 80% power ($\beta = .20$). They are based on Kraemer and Thiemann (1987, pp. 46–47, 109–110) and calculated as

$$\Delta_1 = \{\delta/[2(1-\rho)]\}/\{\delta/[2(1-\rho)]\}^{1/2} + 1]^{1/2}, \text{ and } n_1/\text{group} = (\nu + 1)/2;$$

$$\Delta_2 = \{\delta\}/\{\delta + 4\}^{1/2}, \text{ and } n_2/\text{group} = (\nu + 2)/2; \text{ and}$$

$$\Delta_3 = \{\delta/[2(1-\rho)]^{1/2}\}/\{\delta/[2(1-\rho)]^{1/2} + 4\}^{1/2}, \text{ and } n_3/\text{group} = (\nu + 1)/2,$$

where δ is Glass's effect size, ρ is the correlation between repeated measures, and ν is the total degrees of freedom from the book's master table.

(Random assignment does not eliminate this problem; it simply allocates it approximately equally between the subgroups.) Thus, although they are intuitively appealing, change scores can often decrease reliability and sensitivity and will generally be less statistically desirable than analysis of covariance.

For more information on other models for evaluating change, see Collins and Horn (1991). For special issues in power analysis with regression discontinuity and cutoff-based randomized clinical trials, see Cappelleri et al. (1994). For special issues that arise in evaluating change in crossover studies, see Jones and Kenward (1989). For special issues in single-subject designs, see Barlow and Hersen (1984).

OTHER SPECIAL ISSUES

Stratification and Blocking

Recall from our earlier discussions that power analysis is analogous to signal detection. Parametric analyses typically involve a ratio of the variance explained by the group difference (e.g., males vs. females, standard vs. experimental) divided by the remaining unexplained variance. Although it has a cost in degrees of freedom, an analysis of covariance can be used to partial out additional variance from the denominator. This is analogous to improving signal detection by reducing background noise. Two special cases—stratification and blocking—are particularly important because they do not pose some of the potential threats to validity of post hoc modeling. Stratification is dividing people or units into subgroups before sampling, and blocking is dividing people or units into subgroups before randomization. Even simple blocking variables (e.g., gender; whether someone is using alcohol, drugs, or both; whether someone is under court supervision) can often reduce sample size requirements and increase power. Equations 6 and 7 show the effect of stratification and blocking on an F statistic: V_B is the variance explained by dividing the sample into b groups before randomization, V_I is the variance explained by the interventions and comparison groups, and V_U is the remaining unexplained variance. Similarly, i is the between-groups degrees of freedom (number of groups minus 1), b is the degrees of freedom for the blocking variable (number of blocks minus 1), and u is the remaining or within-groups degrees of freedom (N minus I minus b minus 1):

$$F_{(i, u+b)} = \frac{V_I}{(V_U + V_B)}. \tag{6}$$

$$F_{(i,u)} = \frac{V_I}{(V_U)}. \tag{7}$$

Generally, when a blocking variable is correlated .3 or more with the dependent variable, it increases the sensitivity (i.e., it reduces background noise and brings the "observed" effect size up closer to the "true" effect size). When it is correlated less than .3, it can actually decrease sensitivity because of reduced degrees of freedom. When multiple blocks are used, it is necessary to consider the marginal change in the multiple correlation to decide whether to add further blocking dimensions. Generally, there is a diminishing return to adding additional blocks. One of the most promising methods of block (if the existing data allow it) is to block on clinical subgroups that have been identified through practice or statistical procedures such as cluster analysis (e.g., Babor, Dolinsky, et al., 1992; Babor, Hofmann, et al., 1992; Dennis & Wechsberg, 1996; Rapkin & Luke, 1993; Uebersax, 1995).

Dennis and Wechsberg (1996) were able to decrease the sample size requirements by four- to eightfold using effective blocking. Conversely, for a given effect size, blocking can be used to adjust the observed effect size. This multiplier can be calculated as the square root of 1 minus the percentage of variance explained (r^2) by the blocking variable, as shown in Equation 8:

$$\text{SQRT}(1 - R_{\text{blocking}}^2). \tag{8}$$

Thus, if the stratification or blocking variable explains 10% of the variance, it will increase the observed effect size by a factor of 1.04; if it explains 30%, it will increase the observed effect size by a factor of 1.2; if it explains 50%, it will increase the observed effect size by a factor of 1.41; and if it explains 75%, it will increase the effect size by a factor of 2.0. Table 7 shows the effect of the percentage of variance explained by covariates or blocking on the observed effect size.

Checking for Homogeneity of Variance

One of the most unnecessary and easily remedied power problems is to verify the appropriateness of a given test. It is standard practice in statistical textbooks (e.g., Hayes, 1981; Kraemer, 1992; Pedhauzer, 1982) to spell out the assumptions of each test and discuss the robustness of the test to violations. Yet, the defaults used by most statistical software (and consequently by most researchers) assume that there are no violations. Unfortunately, this is often a false assumption in community-based research, and ignoring violations may reduce statistical power by 40% or more. One of the most common violations is that of the homogeneity of variance between groups. It occurs for several reasons, including when one is collapsing data across different subgroups or having different degrees of implementa-

TABLE 7
Impact of Blocking and Covariates on "Observed" Effect Size and the Minimum Sample Size (per Group) to Detect an Effect (for 80% Power, $\alpha < .05$)

% of variance explained by blocking	Effect size adjustment	Initially observed effect size					
		Small effect $(d = .20)$		Medium effect $(d = .40)$		Large effect $(d = .80)$	
		d'	n	d'	n	d'	n
0	1.00	0.20	453	0.40	108	0.80	29
5	1.03	0.21	392	0.41	103	0.82	28
10	1.05	0.21	392	0.42	97	0.84	26
20	1.12	0.22	358	0.45	89	0.90	23
30	1.20	0.24	298	0.48	82	0.96	21
40	1.29	0.26	252	0.52	70	1.03	17
50	1.41	0.28	216	0.56	57	1.13	14
60	1.58	0.32	163	0.63	45	1.26	12
70	1.83	0.37	128	0.73	34	1.46	10
80	2.24	0.45	89	0.90	23	1.79	10[a]
90	3.16	0.63	45	1.26	12	2.53	10[a]
95	4.47	0.89	24	1.79	10	3.58	10[a]

Note. Effect size adjusted = (ES initial)/$\sqrt{(1 - \text{PVE})}$. d' = Observed effect size calculated as initial effect size times adjustment for removing noise from the error term. PVE = percentage of variance explained.
[a] $n \geq 10$.

tion between groups and in experimental protocols in which not all clients receive the same amount or respond the same way.

On the positive side, this can be tested easily using statistical software. In most cases, it is done simply by dividing the variance estimate of one group by the other to obtain an F statistic (with $n_{exp} - 1$, $n_{Std} - 1$ dfs). It is important to realize that knowing the mean effect indicates nothing about the variance effect or vice versa, although each can be combined into a distribution effect by dividing by only the standard group variance. Using real data from a study to increase retention in treatment (Dennis, 1994), for instance, the F statistics for these three different effects were as follows: (a) a mean effect (mean differences divided by pooled variance) of $F(1, 87) = 1.89$, ns; (b) a variance effect (variance of experimental divided by variance of control) of $F(46, 43) = 2.65$, $p < .0001$; and (c) a distribution effect (mean differences divided by control group variance) of $F(1, 45) = 2.19$, $p < .05$. Thus, in this case, there was not enough power to detect the main effect on retention using the mean test, but there are clearly effects on the variance and distribution (more people were retained).

Unfortunately, few software packages are set up to do a distribution effect test or calculate effects as shown in Equation 2. In several packages, the final (but simple) calculations have to be done by hand. It also is important that this distribution test not be confused with a statistical adjustment for independent samples that is included in most statistical packages. The most common of these adjustments (Snedecor & Cochran, 1989) is to take the square root of the sum of the two variance estimates (each divided by its sample size). This is appropriate for collapsing across subgroups or strata (e.g., gender, class grade, work site), but it is not appropriate for an experimental analysis because it produces something between a mean effect (which uses the pooled variance) and a distribution effect (which uses only the control group variance). Furthermore, little is known about the distribution of variances "constructed" this way, making power analysis difficult (i.e., one would need to estimate or assume some noncentral distribution).

To compare these formulas empirically, consider an actual example we presented earlier from an experiment in which we encouraged counselors to engage their clients more actively about vocational issues (Dennis & Boruch, 1994). Equation 9 shows the calculation of an effect using the pooled variance term with the mean effect formula presented earlier in Equation 1. Equation 10 shows the calculation of an effect using the standard group variance term using the distribution effect formula presented earlier in Equation 2. The control group variance in this case is small (everyone receives no sessions or one session), whereas the enhanced group varies considerably and the pooled variance is between the two:

$$\text{ES} = (M_{\text{Exp.}} - M_{\text{Std.}})/SD_{\text{pooled}}$$

$$= (3.63 - 2.54)/4.19 = 1.09/4.19 = .26. \tag{9}$$

$$\text{ES} = (M_{\text{Exp.}} - M_{\text{Std.}})/SD_{\text{std. only}}$$

$$= (3.63 - 2.54)/3.41 = 1.09/3.41 = .40. \tag{10}$$

By switching from the pooled to the standard-group-only standard deviation, the observed effect size was increased from .26 to .46 (54%). Note that this was done, not by changing the difference, or true effect, but by removing noise from the variance, or error term. Another way of understanding the importance of this is to look at its effect on sample size (and consequently costs). For the sample level of power (80%), the required sample size was decreased from 252 to 108 (67%).

Measurement Error

One of the hidden drains on statistical power is measurement error. As previously noted, less than 30% of the published studies in Lipsey's (1990) meta-analysis even mentioned reliability or validity. Among those that did, most viewed item- or scale-level reliabilities of .7 or higher as acceptable. However, even these levels of measurement error reduce the expected value of an observed correlation ($Rx'y'$), which is the product of the true correlation (Rxy) times the square root of the two reliabilities ($Rxx * Ryy$), as shown in Equation 11:

$$\text{expected } Rx'y'(\text{observed}) = Rxy(\text{true}) * \text{SQRT}(Rxx * Ryy). \tag{11}$$

Thus, the observable correlation will be proportionately reduced by measurement error unless both items are measured perfectly. For example, if both the dependent and independent variables had measurement reliabilities of .7, the expected/observed correlations would be reduced by a factor of .7. Table 8 shows the reduction from the true correlation to the observed correlation for different levels of measurement error in the independent (Rxx) and dependent (Ryy) variables as well as their effect on the effect size and required sample sizes. Therefore, an effect size of .20 would be .14, .40 would be .28, and .80 would be .54. Because smaller observed effect sizes are harder to detect, these reductions either are lost or have to be made up by increasing the corresponding sample sizes.

It therefore is wise to consult several sources to identify and select potential measures that are (a) statistically sound (items with a test–retest reliability of .6+, scales with internal consistencies of .7+, items or scales that appear reliable because they are correlated with the targeted outcome behaviors at .7+) and (b) developed, validated, and normed on a similar

TABLE 8
Impact of Measurement Error on $\bar{d}$, R and N to Detect Effect (for 80% Power, $\alpha < .05$)

Max Sqrt($Rxx*Ryy$)	Small effect (=.20)			Medium effect (=.40)			Large effect (=.80)		
	$\bar{d}$ obs	Robs	Min n	$\bar{d}$ obs	Robs	Min n	$\bar{d}$ obs	Robs	Min n
Error Free	0.20	0.10	358	0.40	0.20	108	0.80	0.37	29
1.0	0.20	0.10	358	0.40	0.20	108	0.80	0.37	29
0.9	0.18	0.09	484	0.36	0.18	135	0.71	0.33	37
0.8	0.16	0.08	612	0.32	0.16	163	0.62	0.30	46
0.7	0.14	0.07	800	0.28	0.14	216	0.54	0.26	61
0.6	0.12	0.06	1,089	0.24	0.12	75	0.46	0.22	83
0.5	0.10	0.05	1,569	0.20	0.10	358	0.38	0.19	120
0.4	0.08	0.04	2,452	0.16	0.08	612	0.30	0.15	187
0.3	0.06	0.03	4,359	0.12	0.06	1,089	0.22	0.11	358
0.2	0.04	0.02	9,810	0.08	0.04	2,452	0.15	0.07	706
0.1	0.02	0.01	39,243	0.04	0.02	9,810	0.07	0.04	3,406

Note. Robs = SQRT($Rxx*Ryy$)*R true; $\bar{d}$ obs = 2*Robs/SQRT(1 − Robs²); where Rxx and Ryy are the reliability of measures x and y, Robs is their observed correlation, $\bar{d}$ obs is the mean observed effect size of their difference, and Min n is the required sample size per group to detect this effect size with α = .05 in a two tailed test.

population. Note that after a 15-year focus on test–retest reliability, the pendulum in methodological circles is now shifting back to internal consistency and tests of validity (Lennox & Dennis, 1994; Nunnally & Bernstein, 1994) because reliability can be increased artificially simply by adding irrelevant but stable questions (e.g., shoe size) or using broader time periods (e.g., lifetime vs. past month). Increasing test–retest reliability often can make them less valid (to the construct being measured) and less sensitive to change (e.g., lifetime reports cannot go down). The latter happens because, as the time between test and retest goes up, reliability (i.e., correlation of a question with the same question asked again) shifts from measuring precision to stability. On the other hand, items that are internally valid (i.e., correlated with each other) or externally validated (i.e., correlated with another type of question) are by definition at least as reliable (precise) as the observed alpha or correlation.

Simply switching from the analysis of individual items to sets of related items (which reduces measurement error) often can increase statistical power by 10%–50%. Furthermore, such "construct" scales are often more relevant. For example, many more people will respond that they have "traded sex for drugs" rather than responding that they "have been a prostitute." Similarly, more men will report having "sex with other men" than will identify themselves as "homosexuals." Furthermore, each of the forms of these constructs conveys unique information about a person that is not represented in the other. Rather than picking one as the definition, it is more important to put them together in a simple scale or index.

Although there are literally hundreds of standardized measures available, finding one that has been used with a particular population to evaluate changes in a particular behavior can be like searching for a needle in a haystack. To make matters worse, many resource books include copies of various instruments but do not give their original references or summarize their psychometric or substantive properties. For some useful published resources, see those summarized in works by the Addiction Research Foundation (1994), Allen and Columbus (1995), Bausell (1991), Fischer and Corcoran (1994a, 1994b), Friedman, Granick, Sowder, and Soucy (1994), Jenkinson (1994), McDowell and Newell (1987), and Rounsaville, Horton, and Tims (1993). For those familiar with the World Wide Web, other places to see include directories of substance and dependence sites at the Web site operated by the American Psychological Association's Science Directorate (http://www.apa.org/science/test.html), the National Institute on Alcoholism and Alcohol Abuse (http://www.niaaa.nih.gov/), the National Institute on Drug Abuse (http://www.nida.nih.gov/otherresources. html), their subcontractor AI Research (http://min.com/air/sprtweb.htm), and the Society for Prevention Research (http://yates.coph.usf. edu/research/psmg/index.html).

If a researcher needs to develop and evaluate (or replicate) the reliability of an item or scale, he or she cannot simply use the multiple correlation of reliability for calculating power because it is too liberal (i.e., anything better than zero). Instead, the researcher needs to calculate whether it is reliably better than a given level of reliability. Table 9 shows effect sizes for testing various levels of reliability against a minimum value of .5, .6, .7, .8, or .9.

Estimating the Power in Structural Equation Models

These types of power analyses are designed to answer questions such as the following: What is the causal process underlying the observed pattern of data? Is matching associated with better outcomes (e.g., a Participant × Intervention interaction)? Does one path or structural model better fit the data than another? The most common types of estimates that might be made include a t test or z score for individual parameters or chi-square for goodness of fit. However, as we demonstrate shortly, the issues involved here are much different, and much less guidance is available.

Some of the statistical procedures that use a deviation strategy to evaluate goodness of fit, such as a log-likelihood ratio, produce a particular sort of dilemma for determining the statistical power of the test. Structural equation models with latent variables and techniques implemented in statistical software such as LISREL, EQS, and AMOS are designed to estimate the structure of a covariance matrix in terms of several parameters. For example, confirmatory factor analysis estimates the covariance matrix among multiple indicators of the single variable in terms of (a) a factor loading that quantifies the relationship between each of the indicators and the common factor (which is composed of the variance shared among all indicators in the set); (b) a variance term for the latent variable; and (c) an error term that quantifies the unique variance in each indicator.

In the case in which the indicators are thought to measure only the same construct, there is hypothesized to be only one factor underlying the covariance among the indicators. The factor equation is

$$Yi = \lambda_{i1}\eta_1 + \varepsilon_i, \tag{12}$$

where Yi is the ith indicator, λ_{i1} is the factor loading connecting the indicator to the common factor η_1, and ε_i is the unique variance in the ith indicator. The goodness-of-fit test is a chi-square to the difference between the covariance matrix estimated from Equation 12 and the observed covariance matrix. The error in the model is the basis for the statistical test of the model that implies that a significant fit of the covariance yields a nonsignificant difference between the modeled covariance matrix and the observed matrix. Thus, support for the alternative hypothesis comes in the form of a nonsignificant chi-square rather than the usual significant chi-

TABLE 9
Required Sample Size for a One-Tailed Test With P2 Greater Than P1 for Various Levels of Statistical Power

Correlation			Level of statistical power ($P2 > P1$, $\alpha = .05$)					
Criterion (P1)	Actual (P2)	Delta[a]	99%	95%	90%	80%	70%	60%
.50	.60	.14	798	548	435	315	240	185
.50	.65	.22	319	220	175	127	98	76
.50	.70	.31	158	109	87	64	50	38
.50	.75	.40	91	64	51	38	30	23
.50	.80	.50	56	39	32	24	19	15
.50	.85	.61	35	25	21	16	13	12
.50	.90	.73	22	16	12	12	12	12
.50	.95	.86	14	12	12	12	12	12
.60	.70	.17	539	371	294	213	163	126
.60	.75	.27	194	134	107	78	60	47
.60	.80	.38	102	71	57	42	33	26
.60	.85	.51	55	38	31	23	18	15
.60	.90	.65	30	21	18	14	12	12
.60	.95	.81	17	12	12	12	12	12
.70	.80	.23	293	202	160	117	90	70
.70	.85	.37	76	61	44	35	28	21
.70	.90	.54	46	33	27	20	17	13
.70	.95	.75	20	15	12	12	12	12
.80	.90	.36	115	80	64	47	37	29
.80	.95	.63	34	24	20	15	13	12

Note. Sample size was calculated as "$v + 2$" from delta using Kraemer and Thiemann's (1990) formula for testing the difference between two product–moment coefficients assuming bivariate normal distributions and unequal variance. If variances are assumed to be equal, then the interclass correlation coefficient can be used and the sample size requirements are reduced by 1.

[a] Delta = $(P2 - P1)/(1 - P2*P1)$.

square. It is at this point where the power dilemma occurs: An insufficient sample increases the likelihood of producing an undersized chi-square and concluding that the model fits the covariance matrix when it does not. Alternately, an especially large sample size increases the likelihood that the difference between the modeled and observed covariance matrix will be considered significant when the difference is substantively inconsequential.

To complicate matters further, the determination of the significance of the individual parameters in the model is usually tested with a t test or z score, both of which rely on the traditional hypothesis-testing paradigm when small samples usually create false-negative results. Conversely, with even a moderately large sample, it is extremely difficult to find a statistical fit using the chi-square test. There have been many attempts to devise statistical fits that are not inflated by the sample size, but none has yet gained widespread acceptance. A detailed discussion of these statistics is beyond the scope of this chapter, but for more information, see Kaplan (1995), Kaplan and Wenger (1993), and Saris and Satorra (1993). There are several current books on the market dealing with the problem of statistical power in much more detail.

CONCLUSION

Power analysis has several flaws in current practice and has already proved useful as a planning tool. In this chapter, we have reviewed the need for power analysis in community-based research, provided an overview of its history and basic components, presented a practical approach we use for power analysis, and discussed other key issues that affect power in practice. We also have tried to help direct interested readers to both published and electronic resources related to statistical power and other issues important in community-based research. This said, there is still much work do to related to power analysis. Meta-analytic studies are just beginning to be done in community-based prevention and treatment research. Methods for structural equations and multiple group comparisons still need to be worked out, and software needs to be further developed to help with power analysis. We hope that this chapter will encourage at least some colleagues to join in these efforts.

REFERENCES

Addiction Research Foundation. (1994). *Directory of client outcome measures for addictions treatment programs.* Toronto, Ontario, Canada: Author.

Allen, J. P., & Columbus, M. (Eds.). (1995). *Assessing alcohol problems* (Treatment

Handbook Series 4). Bethesda, MD: National Institute on Alcohol Abuse and Alcoholism.

Babor, T. F., Dolinsky, Z. S., Meyer, R. E., Hesselbrock, M., Hofmann, M., & Tennen, H. (1992). Types of alcoholics: Concurrent and predictive validity of some common classification schemes. *British Journal of Addictions, 87,* 1415–1431.

Babor, T. F., Hofmann, M., DelBoca, F. K., Hesselbrock, V., Meyer, R. E., Dolinsky, Z. S., & Rounsaville, B. (1992). Types of alcoholics: I. Evidence for an empirically derived typology based on indicators of vulnerability and severity. *Archives of General Psychiatry, 49,* 599–608.

Bangert-Drowns, R. L. (1986). Review of developments in meta-analytic method. *Psychological Bulletin, 99,* 388–399.

Barlow, D. H., & Hersen, M. (1984). *Single case experimental designs: Strategies for studying behavior change* (2nd ed., Pergamon General Psychology Series No. 56). Elmsford, NY: Pergamon Press.

Bausell, R. B. (1991). *Advanced research methodology: A guide to resources.* Metuchen, NJ: Scarecrow Press.

Bloom, H. S. (1995). Minimum detectable effects. *Evaluation Review, 19,* 547–556.

Boruch, R. F., & Cordray, D. S. (1980). *An appraisal of educational program evaluations: Federal, state, and local agencies.* Evanston, IL: Northwestern University.

Buchner, A., Faul, F., & Erdfelder, E. (1992). GPOWER: A priori-, post hoc-, compromise power analysis for the Macintosh [Computer program]. Bonn, Germany: University of Bonn, Psychological Institute.

Cappelleri, J. C., Darlington, R. B., & Trochim, W. M. K. (1994). Power analysis of cutoff-based randomized clinical trials. *Evaluation Review, 18,* 141–152.

Cohen, J. (1962). The statistical power of abnormal–social psychological research: A review. *Journal of Abnormal and Social Psychology, 65,* 145–153.

Cohen, J. (1977). *Statistical power analysis for the behavioral sciences.* New York: Academic Press.

Cohen, J. (1988). *Statistical power analysis for the behavioral sciences.* Hillsdale, NJ: Erlbaum.

Cohen, J. (1990). What I have learned (so far). *American Psychologist, 45,* 1304–1312.

Collins, L. M., & Horn, J. L. (Eds.). (1991). *Best methods for the analysis of change: Recent advances, unanswered questions, future directions.* Washington, DC: American Psychological Association.

Cook, T. D., & Campbell, D. (1979). *Quasi-experimentation: Design and analysis issues for field settings.* Boston: Houghton Mifflin.

Dennis, M. L. (1994). Ethical and practical randomized field experiments. In J. S. Wholey, H. P. Hatry, & K. E. Newcomer (Eds.), *Handbook of practical program evaluation* (pp. 155–197). San Francisco: Jossey-Bass.

Dennis, M. L., & Boruch, R. F. (1994). Improving the quality of randomized field experiments: Tricks of the trade. In K. J. Conrad (Ed.), *Critically evaluating the role of experiments in program evaluation* (New Directions in Program Evaluation No. 63). San Francisco: Jossey-Bass.

Dennis, M. L., Fetterman, D., & Sechrest, L. (1994). Integrating qualitative and quantitative evaluation methods in substance abuse research. *Evaluation and Program Planning, 17,* 419–427.

Dennis, M. L., Godley, S. H., Godley, M. D., White, W. L., Scott, C. K., Foss, M. A., Senay, E. C., Hagen, R. J., & Bokos, P. J. (1996). Drug Outcome Monitoring System (DOMS): Developing a new paradigm for health services research. *Journal of Mental Health Administration.*

Dennis, M. L., Huebner, R. B., & McLellan, A. T. (1996). *Methodological issues in treatment services research.* Rockville, MD: National Institute on Alcoholism and Alcohol Abuse.

Dennis, M. L., & Wechsberg, W. M. (1996, August). *Methodological lessons from the NIDA AIDS Outreach Program.* Paper presented at the 104th Annual Convention of the American Psychological Association, Toronto, Ontario, Canada.

Dennis, M., Wechsberg, W., Rasch, R., & Campbell, R. (1995). *Methodological lessons from the NIDA AIDS Outreach Program: Improving measurement, power and analytic models in cross-site analysis.* Paper presented at the annual meeting of the American Evaluation Association, Vancouver, British Columbia, Canada.

Detksy, A. S. (1989). Are clinical trials a cost-effective investment? *Journal of the American Medical Association, 262,* 1795–1800.

Donner, A., Birkett, N., & Buck, C. (1981). Randomization by cluster. *American Journal of Epidemiology, 114,* 906–914.

Donner, A., & Donald, A. (1987). The analysis of data arising from a stratified design with cluster as unit of randomization. *Statistics in Medicine, 6,* 43–52.

Edwards, M. E., & Steinglass, P. (1995). Family therapy treatment outcomes for alcoholism. *Journal of Marital and Family Therapy, 21,* 475–509.

Erdfelder, E., Faul, F., & Buchner, A. (1996). GPOWER: A general power analysis program. *Behavior Research Methods, Instruments, and Computers, 28,* 1–11.

Fischer, J., & Corcoran, K. (1994a). *Measures for clinical practices—A source book: Vol. 1. Couples, families and children* (2nd ed.). New York: Free Press.

Fischer, J., & Corcoran, K. (1994b). *Measures for clinical practices—A source book: Vol. 2. Adults* (2nd ed.). New York: Free Press.

Fisher, R. A. (1925). *The design of experiments* (1st ed.). Edinburgh, Scotland: Oliver & Boyd.

Fisher, R. A. (1925). *Statistical methods for research workers* (1st ed.). Edinburgh, Scotland: Oliver & Boyd.

Fisher, R. A. (1960). *The design of experiments* (5th ed.). New York: Hafner.

Friedman, A. S., Granick, S., Sowder, B. J., & Soucy, G. P. (1994). *Assessing drug abuse among adolescents and adults: Standardized instruments* (NIH Publication No. 94-3757) Rockville, MD: National Institute on Drug Abuse.

Gigerenzer, G. (1987). Probabilistic thinking and the fight against subjectivity. In L. Kruger, G. Gigerenzer, & M. Morgan (Eds.), *The probabilistic revolution: Vol. 2. Ideas in the sciences.* Cambridge, MA: MIT Press.

Goldstein, R. (1989). Power and sample size via MS/PC-DOIS computers. *The American Statistician, 43,* 253–260.

Graubard, B. I., & Korn, E. L. (1994). Regression analysis with clustered data. *Statistics in Medicine, 13,* 509–522.

Hansen, W. B., & Collins, L. M. (1994). *Seven ways to increase power without increasing N* (NIDA Research Monograph No. 142). Rockville, MD: National Institute on Drug Abuse.

Hayes, W. L. (1981). *Statistics* (3rd ed.). New York: Holt, Rinehart & Winston.

Heinsman, D. T., & Shadish, W. R. (1996). Assignment methods in experimentation: When do nonrandomized experiments approximate answers from randomized experiments? *Psychological Methods, 1,* 154–169.

Hunter, J. E., & Schmidt, F. L. (1990). *Methods of meta-analysis: Correcting error and bias in research findings.* Newbury Park, CA: Sage.

Institute of Medicine. (1980). *Alcoholism, alcohol abuse, and related problems: Opportunities for research.* Washington, DC: National Academy Press.

Institute of Medicine. (1987). *Causes and consequences of alcohol problems: An agenda for research.* Washington, DC: National Academy Press.

Institute of Medicine. (1989). *Prevention and treatment of alcohol problems: Research opportunities.* Washington, DC: National Academy Press.

Institute of Medicine. (1990). *Broadening the base of treatment for alcohol problems.* Washington, DC: National Academy Press.

Jacobson, N. S., & Truax, P. (1991). Clinical significance: A statistical approach to defining meaningful change in psychotherapy research. *Journal of Consulting and Clinical Psychology, 59,* 12–19.

Jenkinson, C. (1994). *Measuring health and medical outcomes.* Lynn, England: UCL Press.

Jones, B., & Kenward, M. G. (1989). *Design and analysis of crossover trials* (Monograph No. 34). London: Chapman & Hall.

Kaplan, D. (1995). Statistical power in structural equation modeling. In R. H. Hoyle (Ed.), *Structural equation modeling* (pp. 100–137). Thousand Oaks, CA: Sage.

Kaplan, D., & Wenger, R. (1993). Asymptotic independence and separability in covariance structure models: Implications for specification error, power, and model modification. *Multivariate Behavioral Research, 28,* 483–498.

Katz, J., & Zeger, S. L. (1994). Estimation of design effects in cluster surveys. *Annals of Epidemiology, 4,* 295–301.

Kazdin, A. E. (Ed.). (1992). *Methodological issues and strategies in clinical research.* Washington, DC: American Psychological Association.

Kish, L. (1965). *Survey sampling.* New York: Wiley.

Knoke, D., & Burke, P. J. (1980). *Log-linear models* (Quantitative Applications in the Social Sciences Series No. 07-020). Newbury Park, CA: Sage.

Kraemer, H. C. (1981). Extension of Feldt's approach to testing homogeneity of coefficients of reliability. *Psychometrika, 46,* 41–45.

Kraemer, H. C. (Ed.). (1992). *Evaluating medical tests.* Newbury Park, CA: Sage.

Kraemer, H. C., & Thiemann, S. (1987). *How many subjects? Statistical power analysis in research.* Beverly Hills, CA: Sage.

Lamas, G. A., Pfeiffer, M. A., Hamm, P., Wertheimer, J., Rouleau, J. L., & Braunwald, E. (1992). Do the results of randomized clinical trials of cardiovascular drugs influence medical practice? *New England Journal of Medicine, 327,* 241–247.

LaVange, L. M., Keyes, L. L., Koch, G. G., & Margolis, P. A. (1994). Application of sample survey methods for modeling ratios to incidence densities. *Statistics in Medicine, 13,* 343–355.

Lennox, R. D., & Dennis, M. L. (1994). Measurement error issues in substance abuse services research: Lessons from structural equation modeling and psychometric theory. *Evaluation and Program Planning, 17,* 399–407.

Lipsey, M. W. (1988). Practice and malpractice in evaluation research. *Evaluation Practice, 9,* 5–24.

Lipsey, M. W. (1990). *Design sensitivity.* Newbury Park, CA: Sage.

Lipsey, M. W., Crosse, S., Dunkle, J., Pollard, J., & Stobart, G. (1985). Evaluation: The state of the art and the sorry state of the science. *New Directions for Program Evaluation, 27,* 7–28.

Luborsky, L., & Singer, B. (1975). Comparative studies of psychotherapies: Is it true that "everyone has won and all must have prizes?" *Archives of General Psychiatry, 32,* 995–1008.

McDowell, I., & Newell, C. (1987). *Measuring health: A guide to rating scales and questionnaires.* New York: Oxford University Press.

Miller, W. R., Brown, J. M., Simpson, T. L., Handmaker, N. S., Bien, T. H., Luckie, L. F., Montgomery, H. A., Hester, R. K., & Tonigan, J. S. (1995). What works? A methodological analysis of the alcohol treatment outcome literature. In W. R. Miller & R. K. Hester (Eds.), *Handbook of alcoholism treatment approaches: Effective alternatives* (2nd ed., pp. 12–44). Boston: Allyn & Bacon.

Neyman, J. (1935a). On the problem of confidence intervals. *Annals of Mathematical Statistics, 6,* 111–116.

Neyman, J., with K. Iwaszkiewica & St. Kolodziejczyk. (1935b). Statistical problems in agricultural experimentation. *Journal of the Royal Statistical Society B, 2*(Suppl.), 107–180.

Neyman, J., & Pearson, E. S. (1928). On the use and interpretation of certain criteria for purposes of statistic inference. *Biometrika, 20A,* 175–240, 263–294.

Neyman, J., & Pearson, E. S. (1933). On the problem of the most efficient tests of statistical hypotheses. *Philosophical Transactions of the Royal Society of London Series A, 231,* 289–337.

Nunnally, J. C., & Bernstein, I. H. (1994). *Psychometric theory* (3rd ed.). New York: McGraw-Hill.

Pearson, E. S., & Hartley, H. O. (1954). *Biometrika tables for statisticians* (Vol. 1). Cambridge, England: Cambridge University Press.

Pedhauzer, E. J. (1982). *Multiple regression in behavioral research: Explanation and prediction* (2nd ed.). Chicago: Holt, Rinehart & Winston.

Rapkin, B. D., & Luke, D. A. (1993). Cluster analysis in community research: Epistemology and practice. *American Journal of Community Psychology, 21,* 247–277.

Rounsaville, B. J., Horton, A. M., & Tims, F. M. (Eds.). (1993). *NIDA diagnostic source book.* Rockville, MD: National Institute on Drug Abuse.

Saris, W. E., & Satorra, A. (1993). Power evaluations in structural equation models. In K. Bollen & J. S. Long (Eds.), *Testing structural equation models* (pp. 181–204). Newbury Park, CA: Sage.

Saxe, L., Dougherty, D., Esty, K., & Fine, M. (1983). *The effectiveness and costs of alcoholism treatment* (Health Technology Case Study 22). Washington, DC: Office of Technology Assessment.

Saxe, L., & Goodman, L. (1988). *The effectiveness of outpatient vs. inpatient treatment: Updating the OTA report* (Health Technology Case Study 22 Update). Washington, DC: Office of Technology Assessment.

Scheffé, H. (1959). *The analysis of variance.* New York: Wiley.

Sedlmeier, P., & Gigerenzer, G. (1989). Do studies of statistical power have an effect on the power of studies? *Psychological Bulletin, 105,* 309–316.

Snedecor, G. W., & Cochran, W. G. (1989). *Statistical methods* (8th ed.). Ames, IA: Iowa State University Press.

Thomas, L. (1997). Retrospective power analysis. *Conservation Biology, 11.*

Thomas, L., & Krebs, C. (1997). A review of statistical power analysis software. *Bulletin of the Ecological Society of America, 78.*

Uebersax, J. S. (1995). Latent class analysis of substance abuse patterns. In L. Collins & L. Seitz (Eds.), *Advances in data analysis for prevention intervention research* (NIAAA Research Monograph No. 142). Bethesda, MD: National Institute on Alcohol Abuse and Alcoholism.

12

ASSESSING THE METHODOLOGICAL QUALITY OF RESEARCH IN NARRATIVE REVIEWS AND META-ANALYSES

ROBERT L. BANGERT-DROWNS, ELISABETH WELLS-PARKER, AND
ISABEL CHEVILLARD

A perennially vexing problem in interpreting evaluative and research results in any domain is variation in study quality. The quality of individual studies constrains any effort to induce generalizations from a body of research. When evidence is drawn from studies of dubious integrity, a reviewer's conclusions are at best less convincing than they otherwise might have been. Worse, results drawn from studies of varying quality may show greater variation than if they had come from consistently "good" studies. In the worst case, "poor" studies might be systematically biased, confounding accurate identification of interactions among constructs.

Narrative and meta-analytic reviewers have devised systematic schemes for assessing the quality of primary research. Invariably, reviewers have had to contend with three questions: Who defines the notion of

Preparation of this article was supported partly by a grant from the National Institute on Alcohol Abuse and Alcoholism (5R01AA07796).

quality? Should ratings of quality be global or refer to specific study elements? How can judgments of quality be made reliably? In this chapter, we present typical strategies for evaluating study quality, define characteristic strengths and weaknesses of these strategies, illustrate a new approach for using expert judgments of quality, and discuss some standards for future attention to this issue.

AN EMPIRICAL VIEW OF STUDY QUALITY

When Glass (1976) first articulated meta-analysis, which is the application of statistically sensitive procedures to a literature review, he argued that one of its advantages would be a more systematic treatment of the problem of study quality. According to Glass, narrative reviewers often skirt the issue by carefully culling suspect studies and relying on research that meets presumed consensual standards of acceptability. Unfortunately, these standards are rarely stated explicitly (Jackson, 1980).

In Glass's (1976; Glass, McGaw, & Smith, 1981) view, selective strategies of narrative reviewers have two drawbacks. First, they can introduce considerable personal bias into the review process. Judgments of research quality may correspond strongly with a reviewer's familiarity with particular schools of research or the degree to which research conforms to a reviewer's assumptions about a field. Second, even if reviewers could make valid and consistent judgments of study quality, they typically fail to examine relations between differences in quality and study findings. If differences in study quality are related to study findings, reviewers might be justified in rejecting large amounts of data derived from more poorly controlled studies, or perhaps reviewers could adjust their findings somehow to account for differences in quality.

Glass's (1976) solution to the problem of methodological quality was an empirical one. Using meta-analysis, all studies relevant to a given question would be located; each study would be coded on any number of study features, including methodological quality; study outcomes would be translated to a standardized difference between treatment groups, the effect size; and conventional statistics would be used to explore relations between study features, including methodological quality, and study outcomes. For example, in a meta-analysis of psychotherapy effects, Smith and Glass (1977) used a three-level variable to indicate the internal validity of studies. This variable was entered into regression analyses with other variables to examine its relations with study outcomes measured in effect sizes. According to Glass, if study quality proves to be independent of study outcome, research articles can be integrated regardless of methodological adequacy without fear of misinterpreting findings. If different degrees of quality are related to study outcomes, appropriate strategies (e.g., elimination of poor studies, differential weighting of findings, or differential interpretation of findings) can be implemented.

This simple empirical solution to the problem of study quality has a number of difficulties, however. First, this solution fails to resolve a fundamental question: How does one define quality? Even though meta-analysts may check statistically whether their determinations of quality are related to study findings, they can disagree as much as narrative reviewers about the criteria for determining quality.

Second, determining whether quality is related to study findings is a complex task. Comparing mean effect sizes associated with categories of study quality is insufficient to determine whether poor-quality studies should be combined with good studies in a review. Differences in methodological quality may not bias an average treatment effect but increase its variance. Poorer quality studies, even though their results average the same as good-quality studies, may contribute spurious outliers to a review. These outliers can have especially powerful influences on the mean effects of smaller subgroups of studies being compared on other features.

Study quality can interact with other study features. Imagine that among 40 studies of differential spatial ability in male and female participants, 20 are judged to be of "good" methodological quality and 20 "poor." Imagine further that half of the poor-quality studies used computer-displayed spatial ability tasks and the other half used paper-and-pencil tasks and that the same is true of the good-quality studies. Looking only at quality, averaged effect sizes of good and bad studies might not differ, and looking only at type of task, computer-displayed and paper-and-pencil tasks might not differ in average findings. An interaction could be obscured by looking only at the main effects: Female participants might do better on computer-displayed tasks in well-controlled studies, and male participants might do better on computer-displayed tasks in uncontrolled studies. If reviewers had assumed that study quality made no difference on the basis of overall mean and variance, this interaction might never be detected.

Several scholars have voiced disagreement with Glass's (1976) empirical approach. Certainly, combining studies with "weak" and "strong" designs, even if there is evidence that quality distinctions are unrelated to research findings, seems contrary to the considerable efforts researchers make to design studies that are as precise, valid, and convincing as possible. Eysenck (1978), an early critic of this approach, railed against Glass's strategy as "garbage in, garbage out."

This criticism has been echoed more recently, although perhaps not so baldly. Rather than consider quality an issue of study coding, some meta-analysts argue that methodological quality is an issue of study selection. Slavin (1984) reviewed eight meta-analyses and concluded that they inadequately attended to issues of methodological quality. He proposed a literature review procedure called "best evidence synthesis" (Slavin, 1986).

Among other things, best evidence synthesis attempts to rest its conclusions on only those studies considered to meet the highest standards of research integrity in a given area. Another adaptation of meta-analysis, study effect meta-analysis (Bangert-Drowns, 1986), although less selective than best evidence synthesis, typically screens studies with "fatal" methodological flaws, such as substantial differential attrition rates or large, uncorrectable pretreatment differences between groups.[1]

How has meta-analysis fared in practice? Has quantification enabled reviewers to become more systematic, explicit, and precise in their treatment of the study quality problem? In the broadest sense, this question is hard to answer. When a meta-analyst codes and analyzes a particular methodological feature, it is not always clear whether the effort is to determine study quality. For example, a reviewer who examines the relation between publication date and study outcome might be said to be checking some aspect of external validity (in this case, the temporal generalizability of a given finding). However, how does one interpret a strong relation between publication date and study result? One cannot arbitrarily decide that either more recent or older studies are more valid. Most reviewers likely would explore the possibility of some substantive explanation; perhaps research methods have changed over time and differentially influenced study effects, or a particular treatment has been refined and made more powerful over time, or cultural changes have increased the potency of treatment. Discovery of this relation adds a valuable nuance to the interpretation of meta-analytic findings, but it does not lead one necessarily to judge particular studies untrustworthy. Many meta-analysts code for methodological and contextual study features, but they may not conceive of these features as being related to study quality.

Do meta-analysts explicitly and systematically investigate the relation between study quality and study findings? In her doctoral research, Barley (1989) examined 56 meta-analyses of educational research conducted between 1983 and 1986. One third of these meta-analyses (19 reviews) made no mention at all of study quality, and 6 meta-analyses excluded studies on the basis of quality criteria given only general discussion and justification. Just slightly more than half of the meta-analyses examined methodological issues, and nearly 10% used a single variable to designate methodological quality.

In a more extensive survey of meta-analyses in the human sciences,

---

[1]In a subtle way, the issue of study quality in research synthesis not only appears in study selection and coding but sometimes in an analytic strategy as well. For example, some approaches to data analysis, such as homogeneity testing, weight study effects by sample size as they are cumulated. This implies that studies with larger samples are superior to other studies by virtue of this one feature, sample size. Their findings are "magnified" in integration regardless of other aspects of methodological design, the integrity of research or treatment implementation, or the degree to which the treatment exemplifies the variables under consideration.

Lipsey and Wilson (1993) examined 302 meta-analyses on psychological, educational, and behavioral treatments. Less than 10% of these meta-analyses (27 reviews) categorized studies according to methodological quality, as Smith and Glass (1977) had done in their meta-analysis of psychotherapy effects.

In short, meta-analysis faces some of the same theoretical and practical difficulties as does the narrative review in the treatment of study quality. Meta-analysis can improve the sensitivity and precision of pattern detection across studies that investigate the same underlying constructs with roughly the same method yet yield inconsistent findings. Narrative review is the method of choice when reviewing studies that are not replicative or quantitative but can be conceptually synthesized. In either type of synthesis, reviewers often neglect to qualify their conclusions in response to variations in study quality. Presumably, this does not reflect a naive belief among reviewers that all colleagues' work is equally valid. More likely, it reflects an ignorance of the degree and the ways in which study quality might obscure the conclusions of review, a pessimism about making judgments of study quality more valid than personal opinion, or an effort to achieve editorial brevity by dropping discussion of confounding quality issues for the sake of emphasis on substantive conclusions.

CRITERIA FOR ASSESSING METHODOLOGICAL QUALITY

What might characterize ideal strategies for research reviewers to address variation in methodological quality? Probably no single strategy could be applied universally; indeed, optimal strategies should be tailored to particular characteristics of the literature being reviewed. However, a few criteria may characterize ideal strategies regardless of the reviewed domain.

1. Criteria for judgments of study quality should be explicit. Explicit criteria for quality are available for public scrutiny and permit readers of a literature review to evaluate the review's scope of consideration and adequacy of treatment. Explicit criteria increase the possibility that procedures for determining quality will be reliable and replicable.
2. Criteria for judgment of study quality should be valid. Reviewers can justify the validity of criteria in many ways, from simple appeals to face validity to more sophisticated calibrations of the defined criteria with consensual opinions of a given research community. Ideally, a reviewer should provide a clear justification for how and why particular criteria for quality were selected, and these criteria should address standards of quality possessed by researchers in the domain being reviewed.

3. Procedures for determining quality should be systematic and reliable. Even if criteria for judgments of study quality are carefully crafted and justified, their application to research studies can be done haphazardly. Procedures for applying quality criteria should be explicit and replicable and checks installed to promote or evaluate their consistent execution.

STRATEGIES FOR ASSESSING METHODOLOGICAL QUALITY

Wortman (1994) borrowed Cook and Campbell's (1979) validity framework to explicate evaluative efforts in the literature review. According to Wortman, a reviewer must evaluate primary research in two ways: The reviewer first must determine the relevance of a study and then its acceptability. Deciding the relevance of a study corresponds roughly to evaluating what Cook and Campbell called "construct validity" and "external validity." This is chiefly done during the study selection process. The reviewer decides whether the operations investigated in a study reflect constructs of interest to the reviewer and situations to which the reviewer wishes to generalize conclusions. Deciding the acceptability of a study largely involves evaluating what Cook and Campbell called "internal validity" and "statistical conclusion validity." Acceptable studies are relatively free of bias; the research design and analytical procedures permit accurate assessment of causal (and correlational) relations among observed variables. The work of the reviewer thus passes through three phases: (a) study selection (evaluating the construct and external validity of studies), (b) assessing the degree of bias in studies (evaluating studies' internal and statistical conclusion validity), and (c) adjusting for bias among acceptable studies whenever possible.

For Wortman (1994), internal validity took priority in the assessment of study quality: "The designs with the fewest threats to internal validity should be considered of highest quality" (p. 106). It is primarily those variables associated with internal validity that define the degree to which bias operates in conclusions about relations observed in studies. Still, Wortman recommended coding studies for some features related to all four types of validity. He offered, for example, variables having to do with a study's publication history (e.g., source, date of publication, and type of editorial review) and participant and setting characteristics as a way of obtaining some information about the generalizability (external validity) of a study's findings. Other variables, such as random assignment to treatment groups and participant attrition rates, could capture aspects of internal validity.

Cooper (1989) distinguished between two types of coding for aspects of methodological quality. A reviewer could code each study for the presence or absence of particular threats to validity. A reviewer thus would determine whether a study was controlled for historical effects, maturation of participants, or experimenter biases, for example. Cooper regarded the coding of threats to validity as an improvement over simply distinguishing between "good" and "bad" studies because of increased precision of description. Determinations of threats to validity, however, are not always straightforward and may require integrating information from various parts of a study and making inferences about exactly what a researcher did. Cooper preferred a second strategy, the same that Wortman (1994) suggested: coding specific features of studies that might be related to threats to validity. Cooper believed that coding specific methodological features would require less inference and judgment on the reviewer's part than coding the presence of more general validity threats. However, Cooper argued that an integrated approach, coding both threats to validity and methodological features, was an optimal strategy because specific methodological features may not always represent adequately general threats to validity and vice versa.

Literature reviewers have used a variety of strategies to rate methodological quality. We group the strategies into three categories: univariate, multivariate, and summative strategies. These approaches are not necessarily exclusive, and some reviewers use more than one in a review.

Univariate Ratings of Methodological Quality

In the early meta-analysis of psychotherapy effects, Smith, Glass, and Miller (1980) used a single variable to categorize studies into three levels of internal validity. "High" internal validity studies randomly assigned participants to treatment and indicated low mortality rates (less than 15%) that were equivalent across treatment and control groups. Studies with "low" internal validity neither randomly assigned participants nor used effective matching strategies, or they reported severely disproportionate attrition rates. "Medium" quality studies failed either to assign participants randomly or to mitigate attrition, but not both. Smith et al. found virtually no relation between the rated internal validity of studies and study outcomes ($r = .03$). Interrater agreement for the internal validity variable was not reported.

Many meta-analysts followed these pioneers and attempted to rate the quality of studies using a single variable. Single-variable quality ratings typically rest on notions of internal validity but vary in degree of explicitness of definition and rationale. Single-variable depictions of study quality also differ in their complexity; some capture only a single feature the reviewers deemed important, and others attempt to depict quality more holistically.

Examples of single-variable ratings of study quality illustrate the range of ways in which this approach is implemented. In a meta-analysis of the effects of new curricular programs on student achievement, Kyle (1982) used exactly the same procedures as described by Smith and Glass (1977), a rating of internal validity that addressed two methodological dimensions: participant assignment procedures and participant mortality. Glass and Smith (1979), reviewing the effects of class size on student achievement, distinguished between "well-controlled" and "poorly controlled" studies solely on the basis of participant assignment. Researchers who used random assignment reported greater effects for small class sizes than did those who used intact classrooms. The authors favored the findings of the well-controlled studies (i.e., those using random assignment or matching strategies) as being more indicative of the true impact of class size. Lyons and Woods (1991) used a three-component rating of internal validity (subject assignment, subject mortality, and reactivity of outcome measure) to rate studies of rational-emotive therapy. They found that studies with higher ratings also reported higher effect sizes, suggesting that the "average" study probably underestimates the effect of rational-emotive therapy because of methodological weaknesses.

In a meta-analysis of the Frostig program for developing visual perception in children with learning problems, Kavale (1984) grouped effect sizes into low, medium, and high internal validity "based on criteria adapted from Campbell and Stanley (1963)" (p. 138). Similarly, Shaver, Curtis, Jesunathadas, and Strong (1989), investigating modification of attitudes toward people with disabilities, used an overall rating of internal validity that was based on unspecified criteria. In both reviews, single-variable ratings of internal validity attempted to describe the general integrity of individual studies. However, specific evaluative criteria and the process by which criteria were applied were not described and may have been "intuitively" and subjectively constituted. Kavale found the average effect of the Frostig program to be significantly weaker among studies in the low category of internal validity than the medium and high categories, although the correlation between internal validity and study outcome was low ($r = .12$). Outcomes in Shaver et al. also showed only a small correlation with internal validity, although only 2% of the studies in this review were coded as having "high" internal validity.

These examples demonstrate some of the strengths and weaknesses of the univariate approach to assessing study quality. On the positive side, a single quality variable is easy to conceptualize and analyze. Unfortunately, a single quality variable may be too simplistic (as in using participant assignment as the only indicator of quality) or too global or subjective.

Although univariate methods of quantifying differences in study quality have some face validity, it is never easy to show that a reviewer's criteria or procedures for judging differences in quality are anything other than personal preference. Critics might argue that emphasis solely on internal validity, for example, is misplaced, that external validity, construct validity, and statistical conclusion validity are just as or even more important. Others might emphasize internal validity equally but disagree with particular operationalizations of ratings of quality.

Denham and Almeida (1987) made a noteworthy attempt to root their univariate judgments of quality in standards of a larger community of researchers. In a meta-analysis of interventions to improve children's social problem solving, the authors used a survey of American Psychological Association members (Koulack & Keselman, 1975) to rate the quality of publication sources. Studies were rated "good" if they appeared in the top 60% of journals rated by American Psychological Association members for importance. Such a variable takes advantage of professionals' opinions of the quality of journals as well as the editorial standards and peer-review processes that constitute the system of scholarly publication.

Denham and Almeida (1987) also used a second variable to rate studies as good or fair depending on how they addressed three issues: participant assignment to treatment, the "blindness" of raters of social adjustment, and the presence of an appropriate control group. (The exact way in which these three criteria generated a single rating was unreported.) Both methods of rating quality showed that studies given lower ratings reported higher average effects on some outcomes.

Multivariate Ratings of Methodological Features

Cooper (1989) argued that univariate judgments of study quality were too imprecise. He advocated a "mixed approach" to coding study quality, one that identifies specific methodological features as well as general threats to validity. This is a multivariate approach to determining study quality.

Variables that code for specific methodological features can be used to capture explicitly different facets of methodological quality. In the Smith et al. (1980) meta-analysis of psychotherapy outcomes, several variables that related to quality of research design (e.g., blinding of the experimenter to treatment assignment of research participants, method by which clients were solicited for research, and reactivity of outcome measure) were coded in addition to the categorization of internal validity. Indeed, the reactivity of the outcome measure, which is the degree to which a measure is influenceable by the researcher or participant or is more congruent with a treatment than a control, proved to be more strongly related to study findings than the measure of internal validity.

Amato and Keith (1991), acknowledging the significant variation in methodological sophistication of research relating parental divorce and well-being of children, selected four variables to differentiate the quality of studies: the source of the sample of participants, the sample size, the use of single- versus multiple-item measures of outcomes, and the use of statistical controls or matching of participants. These four variables displayed different patterns of relations with seven different types of outcomes.

Similarly, Eagly and Johnson (1990) used four variables to capture differences in methodological sophistication in research on relations between gender and leadership style: whether the independent variable was confounded with other variables, the basis of selection of people to be rated, the identity of the raters, and the type of rating instrument. The authors reported difficulty in analyzing relations between these methodological features and study outcomes because of uneven distributions across different categories of the features and because of confounding among features. However, they observed that the identity of raters was related to rated gender differences in leadership style.

Kulik, Kulik, and Bangert-Drowns (1990) reviewed research on the effectiveness of mastery learning programs. Seven variables differentiated methodological features of studies that might confound interpretation of treatment effects: method of participant assignment, whether treatments were taught by the same teacher, whether treatments were delivered during the same semester, whether treatments differed in the frequency of testing, whether treatments differed in the amount of instructional feedback provided, whether outcome measures were locally constructed or standardized, and whether outcome measures were objectively or subjectively scored. Only one of these variables was found to be significantly related to measured treatment effects; studies that used standardized outcome measures yielded treatment effects that were consistently lower than those from studies with locally constructed tests.

Obviously, reviewers differ in specificity and comprehensiveness in their coding of aspects of methodological quality. Univariate strategies tend to be the most global. (Some single variables, such as the presence or absence of random assignment of participants to treatment, are highly specific, but they are used to represent the global quality of the study.) Multivariate approaches tend to be more specific. The coding of threats to validity represents an intermediate level of generality; coding methodological features is most specific and concrete.

Perhaps the greatest advantage of the multivariate over the univariate strategy is the precision of interpretation it permits. Although a single variable can provide gross distinctions among different degrees of quality, multiple variables can determine specifically which aspects of research method are related to study outcome and the degree of that relation. Because of the specificity of multiple variables, it also is possible that they could be more reliably coded than more global constructs. It is more likely, for example, that two raters will agree on whether participants were randomly assigned to treatments or whether treatments and controls were implemented simultaneously than the degree to which a study is "internally valid."

However, the multiple-variable strategy has some disadvantages. First, there is the possibility of "capitalizing on chance." The more methodological variables a reviewer investigates, the more likely one will demonstrate a relation with study outcome by chance alone. Second, the specific investigated threats to validity constitute the reviewer's definition of methodological quality, but the rationale for selecting these variables is often intuitive, unsystematic, or unreported. "There is no systematic and logical procedure for [making these selections]," said Glass and Smith (1979, p. 5) of their independent variables in the class size meta-analysis. "One simply reads a few studies from the literature of interest, talks with experts, and then makes a best guess" (Glass & Smith, 1979, p. 5).

Finally, for all its precision, the multiple-variable approach to investigating research quality may obscure important study differences because different aspects of quality may be interrelated in important ways. A study that randomly assigns participants to treatments is not necessarily superior to other studies that use naturally occurring groups. For example, participants in a study using random assignment might know the desired outcome of the experiment and can benefit personally from performing that outcome. A second study might use nonrandom assignment but show evidence of group equivalence and control for participants' knowledge of experimental purpose and the likelihood of personal benefit. A general measure of quality is more likely to catch such a distinction than coding separately for method of participant assignment, knowledge of outcome, and potential for personal gain.

Summative Scores for Methodological Quality

A third strategy for assessing methodological quality in a literature review is to create a summative score by summing across ratings for multiple methodological features. This combines some of the advantages of the single-variable rating (e.g., less likely to capitalize on chance, more "holistic" rating) and of the multiple-variable strategy (e.g., more likely to yield reliable ratings, more likely to be defined explicitly).

Sackett and Haynes (1976), in an extensive narrative review of compliance with therapeutic regimes, developed a scheme for scoring methodological quality of studies. Their rating protocols emerged out of practice, "through a process of repeated refinement and assessment for multiple observer agreement" (Sackett & Haynes, 1976, p. 194). The review team assigned points for different levels of six study features: study design, selection and specification of study sample, specification of the illness or condition, description of the therapeutic regimen, definition of compliance, and compliance measures. Features differed according to the number of levels and thereby contained an implied weighting. For example, study design had four levels and therefore could receive up to 4 points; definition of compliance had three levels ranging from 0 to 2 points. Special "bonus points" were awarded for unusually careful procedures. Points for all features were added together to create an overall score for each study that could range from 0 to 23.

Brown (1992) applied the protocol devised by Sackett and Haynes (1976) in her meta-analysis of diabetes patient education research. High- and low-quality studies were distinguished at the median score of 12. Differentiations of high and low quality consistently were related to different mean effect sizes, but the magnitude of the mean effect sizes depended on the type of outcome being examined.

In a narrative review of 11 studies of primary prevention for child abuse and neglect, MacMillan, MacMillan, Offord, Griffith, and MacMillan (1994) used a summative approach to analyze study quality. Nine dimensions were allocated differential point values. Quality of client follow-up, for example, could receive 0–5 points, whereas the reliability of outcome measurement could receive 0–2 points. Points simply were summed across features, for a maximum of 25 possible points. The 11 studies ranged in quality scores from 8 to 23, averaging 16. The authors used these scores to give special weight to conclusions from superior studies and discount the findings of the weak studies.

In a meta-analysis of the effects of examiner familiarity on test performance (Fuchs & Fuchs, 1989), two raters coded 13 studies on 9 design-related features. Features included, for example, method of assignment of examinees to treatment, the number of examiners in the study, and the fidelity of treatment. Each feature was given a score of 1 or 0 as acceptable or unacceptable, respectively. The authors reported that interrater agreement on methodological features (i.e., the percentage of perfect agreement between raters obtained on six randomly selected studies) ranged from 67% to 100%, averaging 89%. Each feature also was given a weight (1 or 2) according to its presumed importance. A study's rating for methodological quality therefore was the sum of the products of feature scores and weights divided by the number of applicable study characteristics. No relation was reported between methodological quality and study outcomes.

Stock et al. (1982) tested two strategies for rating quality of research on life satisfaction. A univariate approach yielded an average interrater reliability (measured in terms of the correlation coefficient [r]) of only .52. Using a summative strategy that summed across nine variables, average interrater reliability increased to .66. More experienced coders using a summative strategy demonstrated higher reliability (r = .85), however, and the authors underscored the importance of training procedures for coders as an important determinant of reliability.

Some reviewers have proposed standardized forms or processes for generating summative ratings of methodological quality. Barley (1989), for example, constructed the Methodological Quality Assessment Tool, a rating protocol of 23 recommended items derived from an examination of the meta-analytic literature and consultation with several meta-analysts. The items are grouped into four sections: evidence of a well-planned study, control of threats to internal validity, control of threats to external validity, and adequacy of measurement and analysis. Each item is to be scored on a 4-point scale: superior, adequate, omitted, and inadequate. The average item rating is considered the methodological quality rating. Such a scoring scheme assumes that each criterion is equally important to study quality, although it is possible to weight the items differentially. Each item also is given a "certainty" score: 1 if the rating can be made with certainty or 0 if uncertain. The average of these certainty scores constitutes a reporting clarity score.

The Quality of Study Rating Form (Gibbs, 1989), with 14 criteria, was "based on features of studies often described in research methods texts" (p. 57). Raters give each criterion either a rating of 0 or a predetermined number of points. Gibbs assigned points to criteria so that perfect scores would sum to 100. Although a reviewer could change these point values, Gibbs assigned, for example, 20 points to random assignment, 16 points for outcome measures with face validity, and 10 points for outcome measures that are checked for reliability.

Chalmers et al. (1981) created three forms to determine an index of randomized control trial quality. These forms assess the study design (15 features), the statistical analysis of the trial (11 features), and the presentation of trial results (5 features). Each feature is assigned a total possible number of points; for example, masking participant group assignment from the investigator was assigned a maximum score of 10 points, and the use of appropriate statistical analysis was assigned 4 points. Study design variables accounted for 60% of the overall index, statistical analysis for 30%, and presentation of results for 10%. An overall index is obtained by summing item points and dividing by the total possible score from all applicable items.

Although these applications of summative strategies for assessing methodological quality are systematic, they also demonstrate some deficiencies of this approach. Often, no rationale is given for the particular study features reviewers choose to code. Furthermore, rationale often is missing for the magnitude or distribution of weights applied to methodological features. Fuchs and Fuchs's (1989) review suggests an additional problem: When coders rate each feature's "acceptability" rather than just its absence or presence, coding reliability may be diminished.

Shirk and Russell (1992), in a meta-analysis of 29 studies of child and adolescent therapy, determined an empirical basis for the weighting system that generated their summative quality scores. Eight methodological problems "commonly mentioned in outcome studies as important validity threats" (Shirk & Russell, 1992, p. 704) were identified. Five "expert methodologists" indicated their perception of the importance of each of these problems on a 6-point scale, and the average score for each variable across the five raters was considered to be the weight for that problem. Two independent judges coded for the presence or absence of problems in each study. Shirk and Russell reported that the percentage of agreement between raters averaged 84%, ranging from 69% to 96.6%; kappas averaged .63, ranging from .33 to .92. For each study, the sum of weights for all absent problems constituted the rating of methodological quality. The correlation between quality and effect size was .23; lower quality studies reported psychotherapy effects half as low as higher quality studies.

Anchored Scales for Rating Methodological Quality

Each strategy for rating study quality has particular advantages and weaknesses. The multivariate strategy can permit more reliable coding and analysis of specific aspects of quality but loses the advantages of more holistic quality ratings and the simplicity of working with one or few quality-related variables. The summative rating approach can combine the advantages of multiple- and single-variable strategies; however, few reviewers provide justification for the particular variables that constitute the composite and for the ways in which these variables are weighted and summed.

In a recent meta-analysis of remedial programs for intoxicated drivers, Wells-Parker, Bangert-Drowns, McMillen, and Williams (1995) experimented with the use of anchored rating scales as a means of producing explicit, reliable, and justifiable criteria for the ranking of quality. In devising a method for rating quality, we kept three goals in mind (Wells-Parker & Bangert-Drowns, 1990):

1. Several studies significantly influenced policy formation and program development in this area. Such studies could not be ignored, even if methodological quality was poor. Our coding scheme had to differentiate an enormous variation in type and quality of research design on a common scale in a way that was convincing and relevant to policymakers and program developers.
2. A comprehensive meta-analysis should provide guidelines for future research. We wanted to create a coding scheme that would define strong design features and could be used to identify research features that were ignored in the area or were most likely to yield useful findings.
3. We sought to base judgments of quality not on our own assessments, but on the consensual judgments of a larger group of experts in this field. A consensus of experts, such as primary researchers and policy and program designers, could in-

crease the acceptability of the final results of the meta-analysis to the very groups most likely to use the findings.

We settled on a four-phase strategy for creating scales for judging the quality of research:

Phase 1: Defining dimensions of quality. Five prominent experts in the area of remediation for intoxicated driving generated a set of dimensions that would describe important aspects of study quality. These dimensions were comprehensive, incorporating internal validity, qualities of outcome measurement, and issues of external validity and integrity of the interventions. Project staff examined the generated dimensions for conceptual commonalities, simplifying and integrating terms whenever possible. The experts were consulted again to determine whether the integrated list reflected their concerns, especially if any of their concerns had been neglected inadvertently. Ultimately, these experts identified six dimensions of research quality: method of participant assignment to comparison groups, participant attrition, initial comparability of groups, equivalence of outcome measurement among groups, adequacy of outcome as a measure of intervention goal, and integrity of intervention implementation. Detailed descriptions of each dimension were composed. (Note that these dimensions were created specifically with the driving-under-the-influence [DUI] remediation literature in mind. Experts in other fields would be expected to create different criteria that are more closely tied to characteristics of research in those fields.)

Phase 2: Operationalizing dimensions of quality. On the basis of detailed descriptions, a second group of five experts generated brief operational examples of poor, mediocre, good, and excellent implementations of each dimension. For example, excellent to poor examples of random assignment procedures as well as nonrandom, matched sample procedures were developed for the dimension relating to equivalence between compared groups. As the examples were generated, considerable overlap among the first three dimensions (participant assignment, participant attrition, and initial comparability) became obvious. These three dimensions were combined into a single "grouping strategies" dimension. Literally hundreds of examples were generated for all four methodological dimensions.

Phase 3: Confirming operationalizations. To confirm correspondence between the examples and the dimensions they were designed to reflect, an independent reader was given a randomized set of examples and the list of dimensions and was asked to sort the operational descriptions into the dimensions they were meant to represent. This method confirmed the independence of dimensions and identified a few ambiguous anchors for revision or elimination.

Phase 4: Creating rating scales. A final panel of five experts were asked to rate every example on a scale ranging from 1 (*excellent design*) to

7 (*invalid design*). Means and standard deviations of ratings for each item were determined. Operational examples whose ratings showed the greatest agreement among raters (i.e., the lowest standard deviations), who demonstrated the range of methodologies encountered within that dimension, and whose mean values covered the range of quality (scores ranging from 1 to 7) were selected to constitute a rating scale.

This four-phase process allowed primary researchers and policymakers to participate in determining the definitions and operational criteria for judging quality of research in their area of expertise. The product of this process was a set of detailed, specific descriptions of different possible implementations corresponding to four dimensions of research quality. Each description had a corresponding average rating determined by a panel of research experts in the domain of review that could be used as an anchor point for rating each dimension.

To assist raters in using the anchors, we constructed two forms. A scoring protocol described each of the four dimensions. The protocol grouped anchors for each dimension into ranges (e.g., 1–1.5, 1.5–2.5). General characteristics of anchor examples within each range were summarized, followed by each specific descriptive example listed with the average rating given by the expert panels in the order of their rating. A rating form also was constructed. This form asked a series of methodological questions to obtain the information necessary to complete the ratings. After recording this descriptive information, raters had to assign a rating for each dimension and give a reason for the assignment. Finally, raters were asked to give a univariate quality score (without specific anchors) with a rating rationale.

Every study in the meta-analysis was rated on four dimensions of quality:

1. *Grouping strategies.* These addressed most threats to internal validity, indicating the method of group assignment, the extent to which the groups were equivalent except for treatment, and the presence of confounding biases such as extensive or differential attrition. In this meta-analysis, control groups were defined as those participants who received no remediation intervention but might have received standard sanctions such as jail, fines, or actions against one's driver's license. Studies in which all groups received some remediation were judged to be lacking a control group, even if a study's authors designated some minimal remediation as a control comparison.

2. *Measurement equivalence.* Raters indicated whether outcome measurement processes were the same for the compared groups.

3. *Measurement adequacy.* This dimension reflected the reliability, validity, and goal appropriateness of the study's outcome measures.

4. *Intervention integrity.* Raters indicated the degree to which each comparison group received the intended treatment. Treatments that retained a large contingent of noncompleters, indicated high absenteeism, or showed evidence that treatments were not delivered as designed received lower ratings.

To check the reliability of the anchored rating scales, we asked two independent raters to rate 40 studies on the four quality dimensions and the univariate rating of quality. The grouping strategies dimension received the highest interrater reliability ($r = .95$), and the univariate quality rating also was high ($r = .83$).[2] Of all the quality dimensions, grouping strategies had the largest correlation with the univariate quality rating, about .90. This suggested that raters' univariate ratings of quality were based largely on grouping strategies.

Interrater reliability on the remaining three quality dimensions (i.e., measurement equivalence, measurement adequacy, and intervention integrity) proved low, with correlations ranging from .38 to .52. These low interrater correlations do not reflect necessarily low interrater agreement for these dimensions, however; they were more indicative of restricted ranges and missing values on these variables. Many studies, for example, provided no information regarding intervention integrity, and ratings for measurement adequacy ranged from about 2.7 to 5.5 (rather than the full

[2]Numerous measures have been proposed to indicate "interrater reliability," although some are more commonly recommended than others (e.g., Goodwin, Sands, & Kozleski, 1991; Whitehurst, 1984). The percentage of ratings about which raters agree is the simplest and most easily interpreted measure. However, the simple percentage can be said to overestimate true interrater agreement in that one would expect some agreement among raters simply by chance; the kappa statistic (Berry & Mielke, 1988; Cohen, 1960) is the ratio of observed agreements beyond those expected by chance to the total number of observations minus agreements expected by chance. The intraclass correlation provides the ratio of variance attributable to the rated phenomena to the variance attributable to the phenomena and error (e.g., rater disagreements, interactions between raters and phenomena, and random error; Shrout & Fleiss, 1979; Whitehurst, 1984). When the ratings are on an interval or ratio scale, Pearson product–moment correlations can be obtained between raters.

Each measure of interrater reliability provides different information about the correspondence among raters' evaluations. In retrospect, we might have done well to make multiple measures of interrater reliability, but our primary goal at the time was not to determine whether there was absolute agreement among raters but proportional agreement. That is, we wanted to know to what degree our two raters agreed on the relative value of studies rather than to what degree they precisely agreed on the numerical estimate assigned to the quality of those studies. If Raters A and B both gave their highest and lowest scores to the same studies respectively, this would be reflected in higher Pearson product–moment correlations, and we would be reassured about our scale's interrater reliability even if one of the raters tended to give generally higher or lower ratings to studies than the other rater. The most serious drawback to using the Pearson product–moment correlation in this context proved to be restriction of range caused by missing data or the preponderance of scores falling in some circumscribed range.

range of 1–7) because of the frequent use of relatively unreliable traffic-related outcome measures, such as DUI recidivism.

The measurement equivalence quality dimension was found to correlate with the grouping strategies dimension (inter- and intrarater correlations ranged from .57 to .80). In factor analysis, a strong factor with loadings from grouping strategies, measurement equivalence, and univariate quality scores was found and confirmed in a secondary follow-up. This hinted at the existence of a more global group equivalence dimension for these raters that incorporated grouping strategies (e.g., random assignment, pretreatment equivalence, low attrition) and measurement equivalence between groups, and this factor was strongly related to these raters' judgments of overall quality.

Ratings of grouping strategies were the most reliable measure of methodological quality and were found to be highly related to these raters' determinations of overall quality. Because the other quality dimensions did not have these attractive features, grouping strategies was considered the best measure of study quality in the meta-analysis. Of 191 studies of DUI remediation, only 2 received virtually perfect scores between 1 and 1.5, 7 received ratings between 1.4 and 2.4, and 6 received ratings between 2.5 and 3.5. These 15 studies met the highest standards of random assignment, closely monitoring random assignment to ensure adherence to less than 10% deviation and providing evidence of pretreatment equivalence. Studies rated between 3.5 and 5.0 used random assignment but either did not provide information about adherence to assignment and group pretreatment equivalence or reported increasingly serious but nonbiasing or correctable deviations from random assignment. Ratings above 5.0 on the grouping strategies dimension reflected increasingly serious weaknesses in grouping strategies: random assignment with evidence of nonadherence, nonrandom assignment with evidence of pretreatment differences, self-selected groups, and groups with large attrition rates (>50%). Studies scored above 6.0 showed obvious and uncorrected biases likely to favor one treatment over another or they used pre–post single-group designs. Seventeen percent of the sample of studies were rated from 6.0 to 6.5; 33% of the sample received ratings between 6.5 and 7.0.

Did the anchored ratings of methodological quality contribute to the analysis of DUI remediation outcomes? A number of regressions were conducted to test for relations between DUI recidivism and methodological features. These regressions included all four methodological quality dimensions as variables as well as variables coding for the way in which effect sizes were calculated, for sample sizes associated with the effect sizes, and for the degree of statistical significance associated with the effect sizes. The grouping strategies quality dimension was the only methodological variable that was found to be related significantly and meaningfully to recidivism effect size.

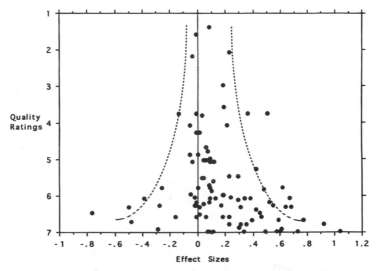

Figure 1. Scatter plot of the relation between recidivism effect sizes and ratings of methodological quality for studies of remedial programs for intoxicated drivers.

The correlation between methodological quality (as indicated by the grouping strategies quality dimension) and effect sizes for DUI recidivism was .18; it was slightly more likely that better controlled studies would show higher recidivism rates among treated DUI offenders. However, a scatter plot revealed that this modest linear relationship was not as noteworthy as the relation between methodological quality and the variance of recidivism effect sizes (see Figure 1). Studies whose grouping procedures were most tightly controlled and least problematic (receiving the numerically smaller score) converged more closely around an average effect size of 0.10; less well-controlled studies diverged more markedly from this mean.[3]

Because of the added variation in effect sizes attributable to variation in methodological quality, we sought to conduct subsequent analyses on subsets of the DUI remediation studies reflecting higher methodological quality. We tested cutoff points on the grouping strategies dimension at 6.0, 5.5, and 5.0. For each cutoff score, methods variables were regressed on the recidivism effect sizes. When only studies reaching a quality rating of 5.5 or better were included (thus excluding studies with lower ratings), no methodological variable was related significantly to effect size. Further reducing the cutoff point to 5.0 substantially reduced the number of studies

---

[3]Sample sizes in studies included in this meta-analysis ranged from 60 to 153,128, with a median sample size of 1,145. If effect sizes had been weighted by sample size with this literature, the outcomes of studies with enormous numbers of participants would have been treated as being much more precise than outcomes of smaller studies and thus implicitly treated as if they were of superior quality. In fact, the linear correlation between sample size and methodological quality as measured by anchored scales was small ($r = .09$).

in the review with no benefit in reducing the amount of variance explained by methodological variables. The 5.5 cutoff point on the grouping strategies dimension therefore was considered optimal.

Ironically, this sophisticated multiphase procedure to develop anchored ratings of methodological quality generated a construct not unlike the informally invented internal validity scale used by Smith et al. (1980) in their investigation of psychotherapy effects. Like Smith et al., experts in the area of DUI rehabilitation emphasized issues of group equivalence as being primary to ratings of methodological quality, although the DUI experts also identified quality of outcome measurement and intervention integrity as being important. This need not always be the case. Experts in other research domains may emphasize other dimensions as being paramount to study quality. Researchers of general deterrent strategies such as legislative and policy changes or advertising campaigns, for example, might value time series designs over the quasi-experimental designs valued by the experts in DUI rehabilitation. In addition, quality dimensions in other domains may not be constrained by a lack of information in reports or restriction of range. The final form of anchored scales is dependent on the literature being reviewed, the determinations of experts in the area, and the reliability of the scales when used. Furthermore, the anchored scale coding scheme was more explicitly defined than that of Smith et al. and emerged from experts in the field being reviewed and from empirical application of those standards to studies in the domain. Methodological assessments that are based on anchored scales thus may be more acceptable to the review's audience. Given these benefits, procedures for developing anchored scales for assessing methodological quality seem to be promising.

CONCLUSION

Narrative and meta-analytic literature reviews provide ample evidence that methodological quality can be related to study outcomes and thus confound the interpretations one can draw from a body of research. However, the relation between quality and outcome is not consistent among different research domains, and accounting for variation in study quality is a thorny problem. Meta-analysis has extended but not ended the conversation about appropriate methods of analysis for methodological quality. In domains in which it is appropriate, meta-analysis provides an opportunity to investigate quantitatively the relations between dimensions of methodological quality and study findings, but many meta-analysts do not pursue these investigations. Narrative and meta-analytic reviewers who have examined quality have faced three chief problems:

1. How is quality defined? Perhaps most important, who provides the definition? Judgments of quality can be as implicit

and subjective in meta-analysis as they traditionally have been in narrative review. More explicit definitions can have face validity, appealing to standards of quality typified in textbooks of research design. Better definitions of quality would rely on consensual judgments of experts in the domain, if such are available. Several approaches to determining such consensual judgments are possible. Koulack and Keselman (1975), for example, relied on the publication source as a way of indirectly accessing colleagues' assessment of research quality. Shirk and Russell (1992) and Wells-Parker et al. (1995) directly involved area experts in judgments of quality. Definitions of quality derived from area experts can be tailored to the specific domains being reviewed and can be most relevant and convincing to the intended audience of the review. Exception might be made, however, in cases in which a reviewer suspects that a methodological bias pervades an entire area. In this case, judgments of quality independent of those made by experts in the area are necessary.

2. Should ratings of study quality be global or specific? Rating specific aspects of quality (as in multivariate strategies) makes more detailed analysis possible and improves the likelihood of reliable ratings, but this procedure also fragments the judgment of quality and increases the likelihood of identifying a spurious relation between quality and study outcome by chance. The decision need not be of an "either–or" nature. Reviewers have both used an overall rating of quality and rated more specific quality-related features (e.g., Smith & Glass, 1977). Use of a summative score of methodological quality can take advantage of the strengths of both the multiple- and single-variable rating strategies as long as sufficient rationale is found for the particular features coded and their relative contributions to the overall score. Shirk and Russell (1992), for example, used expert ratings to determine the relative weights of the elements of the summative quality score. Wells-Parker et al. (1995) used expert-defined anchor scales for more holistic assessments of study quality as well as a multivariate strategy to code for specific study features.

3. How can judgments of quality be made reliably? Many scholars are skeptical, some with empirical justification (McGuire et al., 1985), that reliable judgments can be made of study quality. However, a number of the reviewers cited here found reasonable rates of interrater agreement in their judgments. It makes sense to believe that the more specific and less complex the rating, the more likely it can be made reliably. Cod-

ing the presence or absence of a study feature, for example, should be more reliable than determining subjective, general scores for internal validity. Use of anchored scales also should improve the reliability of quality ratings.

The literature, however, suggests this is not always the case. Stock et al. (1982) found that changing from a univariate to a summative strategy increased interrater reliability (measured correlationally) only by a small amount. In Wells-Parker et al. (1995), there was greater interrater reliability for an overall quality rating than for several carefully constructed anchored scales. Raters in Shirk and Russell (1992) had about as much agreement in judging the presence or absence of features as the raters in Fuchs and Fuchs (1989) did judging the acceptability of features. Reliability of coding may have much to do with the training of raters, the clarity and thoroughness of available reports, or design complexities that may differ from one research domain to another. Reviewers should monitor and maintain high coding reliability and be willing to abandon certain conceptualizations or operationalizations of quality if they prove unmanageable.

In general, when narrative or meta-analytic reviewers have attended to issues of methodological quality, more sophisticated approaches to the problem seem to be evolving. Narrative reviewers are less likely to present only their subjective judgments of quality but tend to be more explicit and systematic in their evaluations. Narrative reviewers who are concerned about methodological quality more frequently resort to quantitative coding. In the world of meta-analysis, earlier reviews were more likely to rely on single-variable strategies for examining quality; summative scores, which originally were rare, are now more common. Single-variable ratings, multiple-variable ratings, and summative scores do not exhaust the possibilities for rating methodological quality. New approaches, such as the use of anchored scales, are bound to be tried. Reviewers, of course, should adapt their strategies to the special demands of different domains and to the constraints of available resources. The adequacy of these strategies always will be judged, however, by the same standards: the validity and utility of the definition of quality and the reliability of the rating procedures.

REFERENCES

Amato, P. R., & Keith, B. (1991). Parental divorce and the well-being of children: A meta-analysis. *Psychological Bulletin, 110,* 26–46.

Bangert-Drowns, R. L. (1986). A review of developments in meta-analytic method. *Psychological Bulletin, 99,* 388–399.

Barley, Z. A. (1989). Assessment of quality of studies for inclusion in meta-analyses (Doctoral dissertation, University of Colorado, 1989). *Dissertation Abstracts International, 50A,* 575.

Berry, K. J., & Mielke, P. W., Jr. (1988). A generalization of Cohen's kappa agreement measure to interval measurement and multiple raters. *Educational and Psychological Measurement, 48,* 921–933.

Brown, S. (1992). Meta-analysis of diabetes patient education research: Variations in intervention effects across studies. *Research in Nursing and Health, 15,* 409–419.

Campbell, D., & Stanley, J. (1963). *Experimental and quasi-experimental designs for research.* Chicago: Rand McNally.

Chalmers, T. C., Smith, H., Jr., Blackburn, B., Silverman, B., Schroeder, B., Reitman, D., & Ambroz, A. (1981). A method for assessing the quality of a randomized control trial. *Controlled Clinical Trials, 2,* 31–49.

Cohen, J. (1960). A coefficient of agreement for nominal scales. *Educational and Psychological Measurement, 20,* 37–46.

Cook, T. D., & Campbell, D. T. (1979). *Quasi-experimentation: Design and analysis issues for field settings.* Boston: Houghton Mifflin.

Cooper, H. (1989). *Integrating research: A guide for literature reviews.* Newbury Park, CA: Sage.

Denham, S. A., & Almeida, M. C. (1987). Children's social problem-solving skills, behavioral adjustment, and interventions: A meta-analysis evaluating theory and practice. *Journal of Applied Developmental Psychology, 8,* 391–409.

Eagly, A. H., & Johnson, B. T. (1990). Gender and leadership style: A meta-analysis. *Psychological Bulletin, 108,* 233–256.

Eysenck, H. J. (1978). An exercise in mega-silliness. *American Psychologist, 33,* 517.

Fuchs, D., & Fuchs, L. S. (1989). Effects of examiner familiarity on Black, Caucasian, and Hispanic children: A meta-analysis. *Exceptional Children, 55,* 303–308.

Gibbs, L. (1989). Quality of Study Rating Form: An instrument for synthesizing evaluation studies. *Journal of Social Work Education, 25,* 55–67.

Glass, G. V. (1976). Primary, secondary, and meta-analysis of research. *Educational Researcher, 5*(10), 3–8,

Glass, G. V., McGaw, B., & Smith, M. L. (1981). *Meta-analysis in social research.* Beverly Hills, CA: Sage.

Glass, G. V., & Smith, M. L. (1979). Meta-analysis of research on class size and achievement. *Educational Evaluation and Policy Analysis, 1,* 2–16.

Goodwin, L. D., Sands, D. J., & Kozleski, E. B. (1991). Estimating interinterviewer reliability for interview schedules used in special education research. *Journal of Special Education, 25,* 73–89.

Jackson, G. (1980). Methods for integrative reviews. *Review of Educational Research, 50,* 438–460.

Kavale, K. A. (1984). A meta-analytic evaluation of the Frostig test and training program. *Exceptional Child, 31,* 134–141.

Koulack, D., & Keselman, H. (1975). Ratings of psychology journals by members of the APA. *American Psychologist, 30,* 1049–1053.

Kulik, C.-L., Kulik, J. A., & Bangert-Drowns, R. L. (1990). Effectiveness of mastery learning programs: A meta-analysis. *Review of Educational Research, 60,* 265–299.

Kyle, W. C. (1982). A meta-analysis of the effects on student performance of new curricular programs developed in science education since 1955. *Dissertation Abstracts International, 43,* 1104A. (University Microfilms No. 82-22249)

Lipsey, M. W., & Wilson, D. B. (1993). The efficacy of psychological, educational, and behavioral treatment: Confirmation from meta-analysis. *American Psychologist, 48,* 1181–1209.

Lyons, L. C., & Woods, P. J. (1991). The efficacy of rational-emotive therapy: A quantitative review of the outcome research. *Clinical Psychology Review, 11,* 357–369.

MacMillan, H. L., MacMillan, J. H., Offord, D. R., Griffith, L., & MacMillan, A. (1994). Primary prevention of child physical abuse and neglect: A critical review. *Journal of Child Psychology and Psychiatry and Allied Disciplines, 35,* 835–856.

McGuire, J., Bates, G. W., Dretzke, B. J., McGivern, J. E., Rembold, K. L., Seabold, D. R., Turpin, B. M., & Levin, J. R. (1985). Methodological quality as a component of meta-analysis. *Educational Psychologist, 20,* 1–5.

Sackett, D. L., & Haynes, R. B. (Eds.). (1976). *Compliance with therapeutic regimes.* Baltimore: Johns Hopkins University Press.

Shaver, J. P., Curtis, C. K., Jesunathadas, J., & Strong, C. J. (1989). The modification of attitudes toward persons with disabilities: Is there a best way? *International Journal of Special Education, 4*(4), 33–57.

Shirk, S., & Russell, R. (1992). A reevaluation of estimates of child therapy effectiveness. *Journal of the American Academy of Child and Adolescent Psychiatry, 31,* 703–709.

Shrout, P. E., & Fleiss, L. L. (1979). Intraclass correlations: Uses in assessing rater reliability. *Psychological Bulletin, 86,* 420–428.

Slavin, R. E. (1984). Meta-analysis in education: How has it been used? *Educational Researcher, 13*(8), 6–15.

Slavin, R. E. (1986). Best-evidence synthesis: An alternative to meta-analytic and traditional reviews. *Educational Researcher, 15*(9), 5–11.

Smith, M. L., & Glass, G. V. (1977). Meta-analysis of psychotherapy outcome studies. *American Psychologist, 32,* 752–760.

Smith, M. L., Glass, G. V., & Miller, T. I. (1980). *Benefits of psychotherapy.* Baltimore: John Hopkins University Press.

Stock, W. A., Okun, M. A., Haring, M. J., Miller, W., Kinney, C., & Ceurvorst, R. W. (1982). Rigor in data synthesis: A case study of reliability in meta-analysis. *Educational Researcher, 11*(6), 10–20.

Wells-Parker, E., & Bangert-Drowns, R. L. (1990). Meta-analysis of research on DUI remedial interventions. *Alcohol, Drugs and Driving, 6,* 147–160.

Wells-Parker, E., Bangert-Drowns, R. L., McMillen, R., & Williams, M. (1995). Final results from a meta-analysis of remedial interventions with drink/drive offenders. *Addiction, 90,* 907–926.

Whitehurst, G. J. (1984). Interrater agreement for journal manuscript reviews. *American Psychologist, 39,* 22–28.

Wortman, P. M. (1994). Judging research quality. In H. Cooper & L. V. Hedges (Eds.), *The handbook of research synthesis* (pp. 97–109). New York: Russell Sage Foundation.

AUTHOR INDEX

Numbers in italics refer to listings in the reference sections.

Handmaker, N. S., 403
Hannan, E. J., 216, 246
Hannan, M. T., 44, 77
Hansen, W., 77, 275
Hansen, W. B., 79, 81, 82, 86, 97, 98,
    156, 173, 180, 193, 206, 208,
    253, 275, 331, 333, 343, 352,
    363, 364, 371, 402
Hanssens, D. M., 236, 247
Harackiewicz, J. M., 184, 207
Harding, R. E., 283, 322
Haring, M. J., 428
Harnisch, D. L., 282, 321
Harris, C. W., 44, 75
Harrop, J. W., 215, 216, 230, 235, 242,
    246, 249
Hartley, H. O., 373, 404
Hatfield, B. D., 202, 208
Hawkins, J. D., xxxi, 167, 206, 207
Hay, J. W., 112, 118
Hay, R. A., Jr., 216, 240, 243, 247
Hayes, W. L., 388, 392, 402
Haynes, R. B., 415, 416, 428
Hays, R. D., 10, 38, 39
Heath, A. C., 66, 75, 124, 125, 126, 127,
    128, 129, 130, 131, 132, 134,
    135, 137, 138, 139, 140, 141,
    146, 147, 149, 153, 155, 156,
    157, 158, 159, 161, 162
Heckman, J., 112, 118
Hedeker, D., 38, 45, 75
Hedges, L. V., 235, 246
Heinsman, D. R., 369, 402
Helzer, J. E., 32, 39, 128, 159, 238, 241,
    247, 248
Hepworth, J. T., 216, 243, 249
Hermansen, L., 124, 157
Hersen, M., 232, 236, 244, 390, 400
Hesselbrock, M., 400
Hesselbrock, V., 37, 400
Hesselbrock, V. M., 155
Hester, R. K., 403
Heston, L. L., 161
Hewitt, J. K., 123, 139, 152, 157, 158,
    159, 162
Heywood, E., 124, 155
Hickcox, M., 248
Higginbotham, H. N., 169, 180, 196,
    198, 207
Higuchi, S., 133, 159
Hilbert, P., 133, 159
Hill, L., 38

Hill, S. Y., 127, 154, 159
Hilton, M. E., 46, 75
Hinde, R. A., 47, 75
Hofer, S. M., 327, 329, 334, 339, 359,
    360, 363, 364
Hofmann, M., 37, 155, 392, 400
Holder, H. D., 43, 75
Hollinsworth, T., 175, 209
Hollis, M., 331, 364
Hops, H., 46, 74, 152, 156
Horn, J. L., 16, 39, 44, 74, 292, 321,
    390, 400
Horton, A. M., 396, 404
Howard, J. M., 43, 75
Howard, R. A., 65, 75
Hox, J., 65, 75
Hrubec, Z., 124, 141, 142, 146, 147, 148,
    159
Hser, Y.-P., 236, 247
Hu, L. T., 53, 75
Huba, G. J., 10, 38, 80, 98
Huebner, R. B., 368, 370, 371, 372, 373,
    401
Huffmeister, H., 44, 75
Hughes, M., 160
Hui, C. H., 282, 321
Huizinga, D., 47, 75
Hulick, F., 46, 76
Hunt, W. A., 19, 38
Hunter, J. E., 235, 246
Hunter, J. S., 175, 206
Hunter, W. G., 175, 206, 209
Hurd, M., 113, 118

Imber, S. D, 38
Institute of Medicine, 368, 402
Irwin, M., 162
Iversen, G. R., 263, 275
Iwawaki, S., 283, 322

Jackson, D. J., 305, 320
Jackson, G., 406, 427
Jacobson, N. S., 378, 402
Jahnke, W., 80, 98
James, L. R., 197, 199, 203, 207
Jardin, R., 66, 75
Jardine, R., 140, 158
Jarvik, M. E., 220, 246
Jellinek, E. M., 5, 38, 134, 159
Jenkins, G. M., 213, 221, 245
Jenkinson, C., 396, 402
Jennrich, R. I., 45, 76

Lennox, R., 315, 320
Lennox, R. D., 396, 403
Lepold, L., 163
Lerner, R. M., 283, 322
Lessler, J. T., 11, 40
Leung, S. F., 101, 118
Leventhal, H., 218, 220, 246
Levin, J. R., 428
Levy, D. L., 156
Lewis, C., 304, 305, 322
Li, T. K., 133, 160
Liang, K.-Y., 31, 38
Lichtenstein, E., 363
Light, R. J., 232, 246
Lin, N., 162
Lind, J., 304, 322
Lindpaintner, K., 159
Linn, R. L., 282, 321
Lippert, P., 44, 75
Lipsey, M. W., xix, xxxii, 181, 207, 368,
        369, 371, 373, 374, 376, 377,
        378, 387, 394, 403, 409, 428
Litt, M. D., 237, 246
Litten, R. Z., 11, 37
Little, R. J. A., 137, 151, 153, 160, 161,
        242, 246, 328, 329, 343, 364
Ljung, G. M., 217, 234, 247
Loehlin, J. C., 128, 160
Loehlin, J. L., 130, 161
Logan, J. A., 80, 98
Long, B., xxxi, 206
Long, J., 79, 81, 82, 97, 138, 157
Long, J. L., 90, 97
Longford, N. T., 266, 276
Longshore, D., 80, 99
Lonnqvist, J., 124, 160
Lord, F. M., 283, 321
Lorion, R. P., 168, 208
Luborsky, L., 369, 403
Luckie, L. F., 403
Luke, D. A., 371, 392, 404
Lumio, M., 117
Lundy, B. Z., 98, 364
Lustig, J., xxxii, 209
Lykken, D. T., 161
Lyons, L. C., 412, 428
Lyons, M. S., 162

McAdoo, W. G., 208
McAllister, D. A., 208
McArdle, J. J., 16, 25, 30, 39, 39, 46, 55,

56, 60, 76, 292, 297, 321, 331,
        364
MacCallum, R. C., 316, 321
McCleary, R., 216, 240, 243, 247
Maccoby, N., 193, 207
McCord, J., 151, 160
McCord, W., 151, 160
McCullagh, P., 102–4, 119, 202, 208
McCutcheon, A. L., 135, 160
McDonald, R. P., 17, 39, 215, 216, 221,
        230, 232, 235, 242, 249, 303,
        304, 305, 321
McDowell, I., 396, 403
McEvoy, L., 32, 39
McFall, R. M., 221, 247
McGaw, B., 235, 245, 283, 321, 406, 427
McGinnis, R. E., 133, 162
McGivern, J. E., 428
McGonalge, K. A., 160
McGroder, S. M., 80, 98
McGue, M., 124, 129, 139, 141, 142,
        148, 149, 150, 160, 161
McGuire, J., 425, 428
McIntire, D. D., 216, 246
MacKinnon, D. P., 182, 185–6, 189,
        190, 193, 200, 207, 208, 327,
        342, 364
McLaughlin, J. K., 151, 163
McLean, R. A., 179, 205
McLellan, A. T., 368, 370, 371, 372,
        373, 401
MacMillan, A., 416, 428
MacMillan, H. L., 416, 428
MacMillan, J. H., 416, 428
McMillen, R., 418, 428
MacMurray, J., 156
Macready, G. B., 36, 38, 39
Maddala, G. S., 110, 111, 118
Madden, P. A. F., 124, 125, 126, 147,
        149, 156, 158, 159, 162
Maffei, M., 163
Magnusson, D., 47, 76
Maiman, L. A., 185, 192, 194, 205
Maisto, S. A., 40
Majcen, A. M., 61, 77
Makela, K., 117
Malotte, C. K., 352, 364
Mandel, J. S., 151, 163
Manderlink, G., 184, 207
Manning, W. G., 102–2, 105, 105–7,
        111, 112, 113, 115, 117, 118,
        120

SUBJECT INDEX

F statistic effect, 390
sample size and effect size impact,
390–392
Blood pressure changes analysis, 213–215
BMDP program, 242
Bootstrapping, 329–330
empirical example, 334, 336–342
familial data, 153
missing data, EM algorithm, 329–330,
334, 336–347
practical considerations, 360
procedure, 329–330
and sample size, 330
"Bounce back" models, 26
Box–Cox power transformation
alcohol demand, 103–104
analysis of covariance comparison,
107–109
Box–Jenkins analysis, 225–230
Breast cancer screening, 185–192, 199–
200
"Broad-band" diagnosis, 32–33

Caffeine use, 79–97
latent transition analysis, 79–97
low- versus high-risk groups, 92–96
and substance use onset, 79–97
"Carry-over" effects, 27–28
Cat program, 361, 366
Categorical variables. See also Latent class
analysis
alcohol use patterns, 46–48, 65–73,
135–137
versus continuous variable measures,
46–48
homogeneity analysis, scaling, 254–
259
latent class analysis, 23–36, 135–137
latent transition analysis, 86
Markov chain models, 65–73
missing data analysis, 343–347, 359
multiple imputation procedure, 359,
361–362
Censoring, two-part modeling, 104–107
Centre for Applied Conservation Biology,
378
Change processes
growth curve model, 55–60
latent variable models, 12–37, 43–74,
79–97
Markov chain models, 65–73
mediational analysis, 181–184

and power analysis, 388–390
sequential stages, latent transition
analysis, 79–97
time series analysis, 211–244
Change score, 388–390
Chi-square values
empirical example, factor invariance,
307–310
sample size dependence, 319
structured model evaluation, 303–304,
307–310, 319
and statistical power, 398–399
Children of alcoholics
escapist reasons for drinking, 13–14
prospective study, 12–37
Clinic-derived samples, 148–150
alcoholism risk studies, 148–150
nonrandom sampling problem, 149–
150
prevalence assumptions in, 149
Cluster-analytic methods, 48
Cluster sampling, 381
Clustered data, bias correction, 172
Cognitive measures, alcohol abuse, 6–7
Cohort-sequential sampling
alcoholism development, 151–152
two-stage sampling combination, 152
Comparative fit index, 304–305
empirical application, 307–310
in structural model evaluation, 304–
305
Comparative treatment strategy
multicomponent program evaluation,
173–174
strengths and weaknesses, 176–178
Condom use, mediational analysis, 182–
184, 193
Conduct disorder, alcoholism risk, 128
Confidence intervals
alcoholism heritability, 147–148
calculation, 381
concept, 373–374
in hypothesis testing, 373
Configural invariance, 292–293, 304
problematic interpretation, 292–293
utility of, 292
Confirmatory factor analysis, 283–315
empirical example, 305–315
goodness of fit indexes, 303–305, 319
and group differences, 316–318
intercept testing in, 318–319

Drinking friends, and alcohol use, 58–60
Drug prevention programs. *See also*
    Alcohol prevention programs
    measurement scaling, 251–259
    multilevel analysis, 251–278
Dynamic factor analysis, 243–244
Dynamic latent variables, 82–83, 90

"Ecological fallacy," 371
Ecological momentary assessment, 237–238
Econometric models, 101–117
Effect size, 377–378
    blocking impact on, 390–392
    formulas for, 377
    and homogeneity of variance, 392–394
    measurement error impact, 394–398
    in meta-analysis, 378, 422–423
    and methodological quality ratings,
        422–423
    multicomponent prevention programs,
        171–172, 180
    power analysis parameter, 376
    and sample heterogeneity, 371–372
    sample size relationship, 384–386
    stratification impact on, 390–392
EM algorithm. *See* Expectation-
        maximization algorithm
EMCOV program
    EM algorithm implementation, 328,
        334
        empirical example, 334–342
    multiple imputation implementation,
        336–342
    practical considerations, 359–360
    software availability, 366
Emergent variables
    versus latent variables, 315–316
    measurement model, 315–316
Environmental risk factors
    behavior genetics, alcoholism, 130–
        132, 138–154
    and clinic-derived samples, twins,
        148–150
    genotype interactions, alcoholism,
        130–131, 138–150
    quantification issues, alcoholism, 141–
        152
Epidemiological Catchment Area Study,
    149
EpiInfo statistical software, 378

Equality constraints, 52
EQS program, 60, 331–332, 398
Error variance. *See* Measurement error
"Escapist" motivation
    cross-path analysis, 18, 22
    prospective study methods, 12–37
    questionnaire assessment, 13
Ethnic factors
    and genetic studies, 133
    group design problems, 317
Evaluation studies, 236
Event history analysis, 137–138
Evolutionary effect, 228
Expectation-maximization algorithm
    and bootstrapping, 329–330, 334,
        336–342
    empirical example, 334, 336–342
    missing data analysis, 329–330, 336–
        347
    practical considerations, 360
Expert consensus, 418–419
Exploratory data analysis, 51
Exposure history, alcoholism, 140–141

Factor analysis
    cluster-analytic methods comparison,
        48
    latent transition analysis analogies, 85–
        86
    measurement invariance issues, 283
Factorial designs
    implementation difficulties, 170–171
    multicomponent prevention programs,
        170–171, 175–178, 200–201
    psychotherapy research, 175
    strengths and weaknesses, 176–178,
        200–201
Factorial invariance, 283–320
    basic concepts, 283–291
    emergent variables in, 315–316
    empirical example, 299–315
    forms of, 291–299
    goodness of fit of models, 319
    group membership issue, 316–317
    intercept parameter testing, 318–319
    latent variables, 283–315
    practical fit indexes, 303–305, 307–
        310, 319
    and reporting intervals, longitudinal
        studies, 15–16

Lifetime approach
  versus event history analysis, alcoholism, 137–138
  as outcome measure, limitations, 137–138
Lifetime diagnosis, 32
Light drinkers, and price elasticity, 114–116
Linear regression models, 48
LISREL
  in missing data analysis, 331–332, 334
  in multiple-group analysis, 146
  and power analysis, 398
Literature reviews. See Narrative reviews
Logit models, 105–107
Longitudinal research. See Prospective research

Mammography screening, 185–192, 199–202
MANOVA, 45
Marital discord, and alcoholism, twins, 131
Markov chain models
  adolescent alcohol involvement, 65–73
  categorical variables identification, 48, 65–73
  measurement error assumptions, 68–69
Matched-pairs design
  alcoholism risk studies, 132–133
  susceptibility locus research, 132–133
Matching strategies, meta-analysis standard, 412
Maximum likelihood estimation, 303
Mean effects, power analysis, 377, 393–394
Measurement error
  autoregressive model specification, 14–15
  factorial model, 15–16
  Markov chain models, 68
  in mediational analysis, 198
  and model specification, 14–17
  power analysis impact of, 394–398
Measurement invariance, 281–324
  assessment of, 281–324
  confirmatory factor analysis model, 283–291
  emergent versus latent variables, 315–316
  empirical example, 299–315
  group membership issue, 316–317

in meta-analysis assessment, 420–424
Measurement residuals. See Residual variance
Mediational analysis
  alternative to coequal predictor assumption, 192
  correlational aspects, 198–200
  cross-program component confounds in, 202–203
  experimental approaches, 197–199
  limitations, 193–200, 202–203
  measurement error in, 198
  and mediator interactions, 191, 198–199
  multicomponent prevention programs, 169–170, 181–205, 341–343
  multiple regression analysis problem, 191–192, 198–200
  program theory in, 193–197
  psychosocial theory in, 193–197
  "small theory" in, 181–193
  specification errors in, 196–197
  statistical tests, 187–193
Meta-analysis, 405–426
  anchored ratings scale approach, 418–426
  criticisms of, 407
  methodological quality assessment in, 405–426
  multivariate rating strategy in, 413–415
  pooled time series analysis, 235
  summative scores method, 415–418
  univariate rating strategy in, 411–413
"Method variance," 15
Methodological Quality Assessment Tool, 416–417
Metric invariance
  matrix constraints, 293–299
  nonmetric invariance comparison, 292
Minimum descriptive length model, 222
Missing completely at random, 327–328
Missing data, 325–366
  AMOS program, 333, 335–342
  attrition as cause, 327, 347–354
  categorical data, 343–347
  continuous data, 326–343
  drug use correlation, 350–354
  empirical examples, 333–343, 345–347
  expectation-maximization algorithm, 329–330, 336–338

generalized linear model, 343–344
inaccessible mechanism, 328, 354–358
  modeling of, 357
  in longitudinal studies, causes, 347–
    354
  mechanisms, 327–328
  MGSEM procedure, 331–332
  multiple imputation procedure, 330–
    331, 335–342, 344–347, 359
  practical considerations, 359–361
  raw maximum likelihood method,
    332–333, 335–338
  sensitivity analysis, 354–358
  statistical considerations, evaluation,
    358–359
  in time series analysis, 241–242
  types of, 326–327
Mix program, 361, 366
Mixed Markov model, 68
Moderate drinking, and price elasticity,
  114–116
Moment structure models
  advantages, panel data, 46
  covariance matrix comparison, 289–
    291
  estimation of, 293–298, 303
Monozygotic twins. See Twin studies
Moving average parameter, 217–219, 231
Multicomponent prevention programs,
  167–205
  basic research/applied science tension,
    168–169, 201–202
  comparative evaluation design, 173–
    174, 176–178
  constructive research strategy, 174–175
  design and analysis, 167–205
  dismantling evaluation design, 174,
    176–178
  factorial design issues, 170–171, 175–
    178, 200–202
  focused comparisons, 179
  free-standing versus context-free com-
    ponents, 201–202
  full factorial designs, 170, 176–178,
    201–202
  individual components analysis, 169
  mammography intervention applica-
    tion, 185–192
  mediational analysis, 169–170, 181–
    205
  outcome mediators, 169–170

psychosocial theory in, 193–197
  specification errors in analysis of, 196–
    197
  theoretical component, 193–197
  treatment package research design,
    173, 176–178
Multilevel analysis. See Hierarchical procedures
Multiple-group SEM procedure
  advantages and drawbacks, 332
  AMOS comparison, 359
  missing data analysis, 331–332, 359–
    360
  practical considerations, 360
Multiple imputation procedure
  categorical and mixed models, 344,
    359, 361–362
  EMCOV implementation, 336–342
  empirical example, 335–342, 345–347
  missing data analysis, 330–332, 335–
    342, 344–347, 359–362
  practical considerations, 361
  recommendations for use, 359, 361–
    362
  steps in, 330–331
  unique features, 335, 359
Multiple regression analysis
  fractional factor designs advantage, 199
  and interrupted time series analysis,
    226
  in mediational analysis, 191–192,
    198–200
  limitations, 198–200
Multiple-threshold model
  alcoholism risk, 143–147
  assumptions, 143–144
Multivariate analysis of variance, 45
Multivariate time series analysis, 243–
  244
Mx program, 360

Narrative reviews, 405–426
  anchored ratings scale approach, 418–
    424
  methodological quality assessment in,
    405–426
  multivariate rating system, 413–415
  summative scores ratings, 415–418
  univariate rating system, 411–413
"Narrow-band" diagnosis, 32–33

Sample size (*continued*)
  effect size relationship, 384–386
  and measurement error, 397–398
  in meta-analyses, 423
  in power analysis, 376, 381–388
    prevention programs, 171–172, 180
  practical issues, 171–172
  and repeated observations, 388, 390
  and sample typologies, 372
  and standard error estimation, 381–383
  stratification impact on, 390–392
Sample heterogeneity, 371–372
Sampling strategies, risk studies, 150–154
SAS program, 242
Scaling techniques. *See* Psychological instruments/tests
School-based prevention research, 251–278
  intraclass correlations problem, 260
  measurement scaling, 251–259
  multilevel analysis, 251–278
Screening mammography, 185–192, 199–200
Seasonal/cyclical data
  alcohol drinking behavior, 241
  time series analysis, 240–241
Selective placement, and adoption, 131, 147
Self-exposure history, alcohol, 140–141
Sensitivity analysis. *See* Power analysis
Sex differences
  alcohol consumption, children of alcoholics, 14, 23
  alcoholism genotype-environment interactions, 138–141
  alcoholism liability, nonrandom samples, 148–149
  multivariate model threat, 23
  and oversampling, alcoholism studies, 154
Sexual abuse, and alcoholism, 132
Sexual responsibility program, 182–184, 193
Shared environment
  alcoholism risk, 146–148
  point estimates limitations, 147–148
Sibling pairs, 134
Signal detection, 376–377, 390
Single-subject designs. *See* Time-series analysis
Skewed distributions

alcohol demand, 101–102, 105, 116–117
  and two-part models, 105, 116–117
Slope parameter
  and intervention effects, 228–229, 266–272
  in latent growth curve model, 56–57
  multilevel analysis, 263–272
  random coefficients, 263–265
  in time series analysis, 214–215, 228–229
"Small theory," 181–193
Specification errors
  detection of, 197–200
  in mediational analysis, 196–197
Split-sample validation, 107–109
Stability of diagnosis
  alcohol use/abuse, 31–36, 49–55
  autoregressive model application, 49–55
  continuous variable measures, 44–46, 49–55
  Markov chain modeling, 65–73
  and reporting inconsistencies, 32
Stage-sequential development
  latent transition analysis, 79–97
  substance abuse onset, 80–83
Standard error, estimation, 381–382
Stanford Heart Disease Prevention Project, 193
State–trait models
  adolescent alcohol involvement, 60–65
  autoregressive model alternative, 24–30, 61
  behavior dynamics measure, 60–65
  prospective studies, alcohol use, 24–30, 60–65
Statistical power. *See* Power analysis
Stratification, 390–392
  definition, 390
  F statistic effect, 390
  sample size and effect size impact, 390–392
Strict factorial invariance
  constraints, 295–296
  testing for, empirical example, 309
Strong factorial invariance
  confirmatory factor analysis, 287–289
  constraints, 294–295
  testing for, empirical example, 308–309

weak factorial invariance comparison, 295

Structural equation models
  emergent versus latent variables, 315–316
  evaluation of, 303–304
  genotype–environment interactions, alcoholism, 139
  invariance testing, 281–324
  latent transition analysis analogies, 85–86
  latent variables, 17–30, 49–55
  and measurement error, 14–16
  in mediational analysis, 197–200
  moment matrices application, 289–291
  power analysis, 398–399
  "practical fit" indexes, 303–305
  specification of, 16–17
  stability of alcohol involvement, 49–55

Student Alcohol Questionnaire, 9–10
Subgroups, and power analysis, 371–372, 386
Supervector, 232
Survival models, *xxix*
Susceptibility locus
  alcoholism risk, 132–133
  ethnic background controls, 133

"Tau-equivalent" assumption, 27
Tax decisions, alcohol, 114
Temporal reporting intervals. *See* Reporting intervals
Test–retest reliability, 394, 396. *See also* Rank-order stability
Therapeutic relationship, 196
Threshold models
  alcoholism liability, 143–147
  assumptions, 143
Time intervals. *See* Reporting intervals
Time series analysis
  alcohol drinking, 236–241
  applications, 235–241
  ARIMA models, 213, 217
  autocorrelations, 215–224
  computer programs, 242
  cyclical/seasonal data, 241–242
  daily diary methods, 237
  dependency of measures in, 213, 215–224
  design issues, 236

direction of dependency in, 217–218
ecological momentary assessment, 237–238
group data, 236
hypertension intervention application, 213–215
interactive voice response system, 238–240
intervention analysis in, 224–231
level and slope in, 214–215
missing data, 241–242
model identification, 214, 216–224
multivariate approach, 243–244
and nicotine regulation, 218–224
overview, 212–216
pooled procedures, 232–235
strengths and weaknesses, 213–215
time interval decision in, 224

Tobit models
  alcohol consumption, 109–114
  estimation, 111
  two-part models comparison, 112–114

Trait models. *See* Quantitative trait loci; State–trait models

Transformed models
  alcohol demand, 103–104, 107–109
  analysis of covariance comparison, 107–109
  interrupted time series analysis, 225–230
  pooled procedure, 232–234
  and interval scaling, 254–259

Treatment package design
  in multicomponent program evaluation, 173, 176–178
  strengths and weaknesses, 176–178

TSX program, 242

Tucker–Lewis index, 304–305
  empirical application, 307–310
  in structural model evaluation, 304–305

Twin registers, 152

Twin studies
  alcoholism, 124–125, 129–132, 140–152
  birth-record derived samples, 141–148
  clinic-derived samples, 148–150
  cohort-sequential designs, 152
  cross-sectional designs, alcoholism risk, 129
  genotype–environment factors, 130–132, 140–150

ABOUT THE EDITORS

Kendall J. Bryant, PhD, is currently a health scientist and the coordinator for the HIV/AIDS behavioral research program at the National Institute on Alcohol Abuse and Alcoholism (NIAAA). Before moving to NIAAA in 1992 Dr. Bryant was a research scientist at Yale University's School of Medicine in the Department of Psychiatry, where he conducted research on the diagnosis and treatment of substance abuse. Prior to that, Dr. Bryant was a research psychologist, designing and implementing psychological selection and screening programs for the Department of Defense at the Naval Submarine Medical Research Laboratory. He received his graduate education in personality assessment and quantitative psychology at the University of California, Berkeley, in 1983 and Wesleyan University (BA, MA) in 1976, and he carried out postdoctoral research in environmental and developmental psychology through the Institute of Human Development and the Institute of Personality Assessment and Research at the University of California, Berkeley.

Michael Windle, PhD, is currently a senior research scientist at the New York State Research Institute on Addictions and a research associate professor at the State University of New York at Buffalo. Dr. Windle completed his doctoral studies in human development and family studies at the Pennsylvania State University in 1984. He is an associate editor of *Alcoholism: Clinical and Experimental Research* and serves on the editorial boards of *Developmental Psychology* and the *Journal of Studies on Alcohol*. His research interests include high-risk behaviors related to the expression of alcohol problems and other forms of psychopathology among children and adolescents. Dr. Windle coedited *Children of Alcoholics: Critical Perspectives* (1990).

Stephen G. West, PhD, is currently professor of psychology and co-principal investigator of the Preventive Intervention Research Center at Arizona State University, funded by the National Institute of Mental Health. Dr. West received his doctoral degree in social psychology, with a minor in quantitative psychology, from the University of Texas at Austin in 1973. He was previously associate professor of psychology at Florida State University and has held visiting faculty appointments in psychology at the University of Wisconsin; University of Texas; Duke University; University of California, Los Angeles; and the University of Kiel and the University of Heidelberg in the Federal Republic of Germany. He has co-authored and co-edited several books. His most recent publications include *Multiple Regression: Testing and Interpreting Interactions* (1991), *Viewpoints on Personality: Consensus, Self–Other Agreement, and Accuracy in Judgments of Personality* (1993), and *Applied Multiple Regression/Correlation Analysis for the Behavioral Sciences* (3rd ed.). He is past editor of the *Journal of Personality* and currently serves on the editorial boards of *Psychological Methods*, the *American Journal of Community Psychology*, and the *Journal of Research in Personality*. Dr. West's primary research interests are in the design and statistical analysis of field research and the development and evaluation of theory-based preventive interventions.